"Adrian Swain has provided the public with a valuable insight into the real world of a federal narcotic agent overseas. His descriptions of the conflict in Southeast Asia between drug traffickers, national police agencies, U.S. federal narcotic agents and the intelligence community is not academic, it is based on fact and personal experiences. Adrian Swain has earned the respect of his peers and his perspective on this problem is invaluable as we continue to confront the crisis of drugs in America."

—*Peter B. Bensinger*
Administrator of the U.S. Drug
Enforcement Administration (DEA)
1976-81

"The Time of My Life is the second best thing in the last 50 years of my life (Swoosie and her genius is the number 1) . . . a sweet and wonderful story."

—*Colonel Frank Kurtz, USAF Retired*
Commander 463rd Bomb Group,
15th Air Force, Italy

". . . as a member of the *Hell on Wings* crew, I came to admire Adrian both as a pilot and as a person and was deeply interested in learning about his life. *The Time of My Life* gave me an opportunity to read a wonderful narrative of that period in our history which was the time of my life too."

—*Tylor Burton, Jr.*
Hell on Wings crew member, WW II

"An historically accurate account of service to country in war and peace; influenced by enduring family support and values. A book for all ages."

—*Senator Charles H. Smelser, Maryland*
8th Air Force B-17 pilot, England

". . . not only is the book instructive and enjoyable, but it will be invaluable to historians in the future."

—*Congressman John J. Rhodes*
Washington, D.C.

THE TIME OF MY LIFE

Adrian Swain

To Steven ~~Roberts~~

Thanks for being
my good neighbor.
Enjoy ~ Dec 2009

Adrian Swain

Published by Axelrod Publishing of Tampa Bay, Inc.
1304 DeSoto Avenue, Tampa, Florida 33606
Cover design by Drawing Board Studios, Inc.
Edited by Karen L. Jacob and Marsha P. Raymond
Typeset by New Images
Printed in the United States of America

Publisher's Cataloging in Publication
(Prepared by Quality Books Inc.)

Adrian Swain.
   The time of my life: memoirs of a government agent / Adrian Swain.
   p. cm.
   Includes bibliographical references and index.
   LCCN: 91-077659.
   ISBN 0-936417-41-2

   1. Swain, Adrian. 2. Narcotic enforcement agents—United States—Biography. 3. Air Pilots, Military—United States—Biography. 4. World War, 1939-1945—Aerial operations, American. 5. United States. Air Force—Biography. 6. United States. Central Intelligence Agency—Biography. I. Title.

HV7911.S93S93 1994   363.4'5'092
                                 QB194-567

This book is dedicated with love and affection to my father and mother and to all those friends and dear companions who so generously shared with me their hopes and fears, their joys and sorrows, and their strengths and weaknesses, which made my life complete. Special thanks to Myrtle, who started it all, my brother and sisters, Phyllis and our children—Cyndy, Tom, Bill, and Ken—and my dear wife Anno.

* * *

The author is grateful for research resources that were helpful in this work, including *The Fighting 463rd* book narrated by Harold Rubin and the Drug Enforcement Administration's publications *DEA World, Drug Enforcement,* and *The Connection,* which were valuable for verifying drug trafficking trends and related data. I purposely omitted the names of people whose identities should be protected for security reasons. Although certain intelligence operations are mentioned, classified information has been protected.

Special thanks to the following for their personal narratives that appear in the text: Richard E. Barnes, Bristol, Connecticut; Ralph M. Barnes, Perrysburg, Ohio; M. Tylor Burton, Jr., Gibson Island, Maryland; Pierre Laurent, Valence, France; and my family members Phyllis and Tom Swain. Particular thanks to my wife, Anno, without whose ongoing support and encouragement this story would not have been told. I also wish to thank Axelrod Publishing of Tampa Bay for invaluable assistance and guidance and Karen L. Jacob and Marsha P. Raymond for their skilled editing.

PREFACE

The publication of this edition of *The Time of My Life* was almost accidental. I had written an account of my life for family and friends, who persuaded me that a condensed version would be worthwhile.

Some of my classmates who graduated with me as second lieutenants in December 1943 reported that they enjoyed reading of my experiences as a B-17 pilot in the 463rd Bomb Group with the 15th Air Force in Italy. Other friends from the 8th Air Force in England thought that the story of our B-17 being shot down and our rescue by the Free French underground was exciting, which it certainly was. Those friends who went to college under the GI bill enjoyed my recountal of life at Pennsylvania State University, where I graduated with a degree in journalism before being recalled to active duty flying B-29 missions over North Korea.

My work as an FBI agent in towns along the Blue Ridge Parkway in North Carolina was interesting, but not as exciting as the years that followed when I moved to Sarasota, Florida, and married the beautiful Phyllis, a former Ford Agency model. When the war in South Vietnam escalated, my wife and our four young children lived in the Phillipines, while I worked as an operations officer with the CIA in South Vietnam. We later lived in Laos, "the land of a thousand elephants," and in Thailand, "the land of smiles."

Former USAID, CIA, military, and State Department employees who were in Southeast Asia during the Vietnam War will appreciate personal accounts about Vietcong Tet offensives, traffic along the Ho Chi Minh Trail, and Pathet Lao rocket attacks in Laos. When the war in South Vietnam finally ended, another flared up in neighboring Thailand—the war on drugs. I joined the DEA in their efforts to help the Thai police halt caravans of opiates from clandestine laboratories in the Golden Triangle, that infamous area where Thailand, Burma, and Laos are joined.

The Time of My Life is a true story of how those turbulent events that shaped America affected one man and his family. The experiences recounted here taught us that there is good and bad in every situation. The tricky part is to profit from the good and learn from the bad.

My story is not necessarily about heroic or dramatic feats, but rather what happens to many young men who dream of the future, read Horatio Alger adventure stories, and are not afraid to grab for the brass ring of opportunity when it comes around. I enjoyed participating in and contributing to the evolving panorama of our American way of life and hope that you enjoy reading this accounting.

A.S.

CONTENTS

INTRODUCTION

I was named after Pope Adrian VI, a Dutchman who reigned over the Catholic Church from Vatican City in 1522 until his death in 1523, a mere 400 years before my birth. Although my parents felt they had adorned me with an illustrious name, little did they realize how difficult and confusing this would be to all my young friends, who had more typical sounding names. This bothered me considerably during my youth, but with adulthood I rather liked the distinction of an unusual name. I later would name my sons Thomas, William, and Kenneth, all thoroughly sturdy and masculine names, and give them middle names as well (to compensate for my lack of one).

My parents, Charles Francis and Myrtle Ellen Swain, were off-spring of Scotch, Irish, Dutch, and German ancestors, and had three other children: Joan Loretta, Francis Charles (Chuck), and Nancy Anne. Joan was the artist in our family and could have achieved professional status had she been determined. Nancy was the darling of the family and still is today; a bright sunny disposition matched her generous nature and outgoing personality.

Chuck was the poet and dreamer of our family. He and his wife, Agnes, bought the 200-year-old historic Peacock Inn in Princeton, New Jersey, in 1966. Chuck later wrote and published a slim volume of poetry entitled *Poems from the Peacock Inn*. The inn was an important part of their life, wherein they provided students, local residents, and visitors with fine food and comfortable lodging for many years. One of the verses that Chuck wrote speaks to the regrets that many of us have in this life:

> "I cry for the poems never written,
>   For the novel never quite done:
> The Goliaths I could have smitten,
>   And the races I failed to run."

With his thoughts in mind, I am encouraged to write this chronicle of my lifetime and perhaps afterwards, God willing, will work on the "novel never quite done."

Adrian Swain

* * *

During my early years, we lived on a small apple farm about three miles from Baden. Father was a country school teacher and drove a Model T Ford. He later worked in one of the many steel mills that line the Ohio River from Pittsburgh to West ("by Gawd") Virginia. Mom stayed home raising the family and watching the apples grow.

Dad was an orphan. I do not know who his father was, and not much is known about his mother, although I think her name was Rachel Drane. He was adopted from the Catholic orphanage by Frank and Ella Swain, farmers who lived near the small town of Conway with its sprawling, smoke-covered railroad yard.

My Mother was the seventh and youngest child born to John and Nancy Stickel, who farmed land east of Freedom in an area that has since been converted to a major residential and business community named Wexford. The old farms have been swallowed up by houses and highways. Quiet cow pastures now move heavy traffic between Pittsburgh 25 miles to the south and dozens of towns and communities along the way.

Three Frank Swains lived in the countryside during those years. I learned later that local folks distinguished between them by the names Apple Frank, Horse-killing Frank, and Ugly Frank. For obvious reasons, I prefer to think that Apple Frank was Dad's adoptive father.

I recall few details about my Father. He wrote some terse entries in a diary when serving in the army during World War I, before he and my Mother were married. He was a private in a railroad engineering battalion in France and took some courses at Notre Dame in Paris during the occupation. He also wrote song lyrics, including verses set to music in a song entitled *Grandfather's Clock*. A copy of this song was around the house for years but unfortunately no longer exists. A man of studious habit, my Father taught in the country school until forced to leave because the school board did not support his spanking of a provocative student. Some issues never change.

As well as a teacher, an apple farmer, a mill worker, a salesman for the Hoover vacuum company, and a staunch Catholic, he was a good husband and father. Mother once told me, "it was heaven to be with him." She also mentioned that he had calluses on his knees from going to church so often. He even got into a fight at the steel mill over his faith. In those days, many Catholics were derisively known as mackerel snappers (fish eaters) and taunted by their bigoted and less tolerant coworkers. The Catholic Church had taken Dad in as an orphan and raised him until he was adopted into a good home. He was justified in defending his faith, as I would have in similar circumstances.

* * *

I did not get to know my Father very well before he died. We were living in Pittsburgh where he had a sales job with the Hoover vacuum company. I was five years old when he caught pneumonia from sitting on the cold, damp ground at a family picnic in early spring. He died in the hospital May 28, 1928, with my Mother at his bedside. Ironically that year, Alexander Fleming discovered the wonder drug penicillin that could have saved my Father's life if it had been available.

We lived in a neighborhood not far from downtown Pittsburgh known as the Hill District. To reach our home from the roadway below, we mounted a wooden stairway that seemed to stretch upward almost endlessly. There were eight or ten tiers of stairs with landings so you could catch your breath before tackling the next flight. Leafy sumac trees bending and bowing in the breeze grew profusely on the slope, crowding against the walkway and between the openings in the railings.

Our house was near the crest and very close to the edge of the hill. The view downward from our back porch was frightening. An ornate fireplace in the living room was framed with bright, green-bluish tiles and a mantel of dark wood polished and aged softly. To this day, I admire fireplaces and consider the modern ones of this age as only pale substitutes compared with the rich splendor of the one at our house on the hill. The workmanship and style of the 1900 era cannot be duplicated easily today.

I remember days filled with sunlight, green trees, and caterpillars on the leaves of shrubs growing along the shaded walkway to our front door. I also remember being awakened one night by a persistent whirring noise in the dining room and finding my mother busy peddling the foot treadle of her Singer sewing machine. She was piecing together rectangles of cloth from a tailor's sample book. The blanket that she made was wondrous in color and from predominantly brown and striped blue material that was scratchy to the skin yet warm enough to keep off the chill. Years later, I would realize that my family had not been exactly in the upper income brackets.

My Father occasionally took me on neighborhood walks along the narrow streets of Pittsburgh, some of which were formed from grey-black, shiny cobble stones obtained from the nearby Monongahela and Allegheny Rivers. These rivers join just beyond the remains of old Fort Pitt, built in 1754 and now known as Point Park, at the juncture that forms the beginning of the beautiful Ohio River. I was to live along the Ohio River and roam its hills and valleys all the days of my youth.

Gleaming yellow trucks proclaiming *Kaufmann's* in bold, black letters on the sides delivered the department store's goods through out Pittsburgh's Golden Triangle for many years; perhaps some are still in service. Today, the Pittsburgh Pirates baseball team and the mighty Pittsburgh Steelers football team both wear distinctive yellow and black *Kaufmann's* colors.

When I contracted mumps, a huge lump rose on the right side of my neck and refused to respond to treatment. I was taken to a hospital where an incision was made that allowed some trapped air to escape and left a scar about one and a half inches long. My Father came to visit and brought me a big tangerine. He sat by my bed and slowly peeled away every string and strand before he would let me eat it. I remember my Father sitting there carefully peeling that tangerine with his large fingers for me just as though it were yesterday; it reminds me how much I miss him.

There was no doubt in my mind that my Mom loved Dad. She was about thirty years old when he died. She never remarried even though she was young and pretty. Being a widow with four young children in depression times was not easy for her. My Mother was never one to talk much about adverse times and never let on if she felt sorry for herself during those lean years. All of her life, until she died in

February 1982 at 84 years of age, she never complained.

When she was a young girl, my Mother had thought about becoming a missionary. She told me that in her prayers she once said to God, "Try me, Lord." I submit that the good Lord did try her and found her to be strong yet meek, quiet yet determined, and tempered with love and compassion. Had she been born a few generations later, she would have been called a liberated woman. She had fire and spirit and more than her share of will power. So, instead of becoming a missionary in some foreign land, she left the farm and began training to become a registered nurse. It was during this time that she met my Father. They met shortly after the end of World War I and were married before she had time to finish her training. She went on to become a licensed practical nurse after my Father died and worked throughout Beaver Valley for many years. My Father was buried in the little country churchyard of the Catholic Church a few miles from the town of Baden. Every year, the Veterans of Foreign Wars visit his grave side on Memorial Day to place a small American flag by his headstone and fire three rifle shots in salute. A wild cherry tree grows near his grave providing shade. During the summer, I would visit with my Mother and other family members to fix up the grave and remember what he had been like, as I thought about my own future.

After my Father died, we lived with Aunt Cora and Uncle Gilbert Wright for about a year in their sturdy frame house, which still stands on the hillside below Uncle Gilbert's blacksmith shop. By 1930, all the state's country roads began to be paved with cement, and Model T Fords soon started to replace horses. Within a few years, Uncle Gilbert's blacksmith shop became an automobile service shop. A gasoline pump cranked by hand replaced the horse watering trough, and racks of car tires replaced the iron horseshoes and leather harness supplies. Gone too were the heat and acrid blue smoke of the blazing forge in which horseshoes were fired to a white heat before being burned and seared onto horses' hooves. I used to gawk in wonder, expecting the horses to flinch, but they never did.

Uncle Gilbert hurt his chest one day while shoeing a cranky horse and had a gnarled and distorted left thumb that he had smashed at the shop. In his last years, he had to sleep in his rocking chair, keeping his body upright because of fluid in his damaged lungs and in his legs. My Mother played cards with him for hours and spent many nights nursing him during his illness, paying him back, in part, with kindness and love for the help he gave her when our family was in need. Wright's Store became a local landmark and is still operational today, albeit more modern and larger and, of course, under different management.

* * *

Mom moved the family frequently during my early school years, probably because we were tenants and also because she wanted us to be close to good schools. I remember starting school in the usual one-room school building with my sister Joan. We moved about eight times from 1928 to 1940, all in the Beaver Valley area. My mother never explained the reason for all these moves, but the times were hard and reasonable rentals were not easy to obtain. Every move we made permitted us to walk to a good school and come home for lunch. Perhaps I learned the valuable lesson that life is full of change and it is necessary to accept and adapt to these changes, painful though they may be at times.

* * *

My Mother received only an eighth grade education while growing up in the country and wanted more for her children. She often told us that we would have to attend better schools than those provided to her if we were to reach our full potential.

We moved to the little town of Conway where the playtime activities around our house were far more memorable than our classroom achievements. A big vacant lot near our house had a steep slope that we kids spent many hours sliding down on pieces of cardboard, achieving frightening and thrilling speeds. Our hideout was a leafy cave under the branches of lilac and sumac trees that grew unattended on the edge of that lot. Here we played those childhood doctor-patient games that had to do with the differences between boys and girls. Sex had reared its intriguing head for the first time in my young life.

One of the neighborhood girls who participated in this lilac bush activity lived across the street in a house whose bedroom windows were clearly visible from our house. One bright Saturday afternoon this young lady threw back the curtain of her bedroom and struck a naked pose that was nymphlike, proud, and triumphant. Her impromptu performance was interrupted when a parental hand suddenly whisked her from sight, thus ending her riveting display. An indelible imprint still remains in my mind.

* * *

In 1929 the country was in turmoil from the disastrous stock market crash on Wall Street. Bell Laboratory was experimenting with color television, and France was beginning construction on its vaunted Maginot Line designed to repel all invaders from the east. Our family moved to a little house in Rochester just off the main street in town. The streets were paved with brick or smooth stone, and there were shiny streetcar tracks that took trolley cars as far as Pittsburgh.

Our kitchen was an all-purpose room and served as our school work study area. During rainy, cold weather days, Mom would string a clothesline across the kitchen, forcing us to duck under the wet clothes or get wet ourselves. My Mother did a lot of laundry in those days. Even with small children at home, she took in laundry and sometimes did part-time housecleaning to make ends meet. Her wages were about $3.00 to $3.50 for a load of washing and ironing, all done by hand. She worked for several families, and sometimes I helped her deliver freshly ironed clothes in a little red wagon.

* * *

I loved to read the comic strips in our evening paper, *The Pittsburgh Press*; my favorites were *Captain Easy, Wash Tubbs,* and *Freckles and His Friends.* Every Sunday there was a serialized story called *Secretary Hawkins,* who was always exploring caves or mysterious houses. Secretary Hawkins' club members wore long-billed caps with feathers to one side like Robin Hood. I too wore a cap, perhaps not as long billed, and found that a long white chicken feather was perfect.

A Texaco gas station nearby sold a brand of gasoline known as Texaco Fire Chief, which was promoted by Ed Wynn, a popular radio and screen comedian. Ed Wynn promoted red firemen's hats made from pressed paper, which were distributed at the gas station to every kid in town who asked for one.

Occasionally, I would get up the nerve to join a group of kids after school at the newspaper office where we each would be given five newspapers to hawk on the streets to late afternoon shoppers. I did not have a very loud street voice and did not always sell my quota, but those papers not sold could be returned to the office. We were paid one penny for each newspaper sold at three cents, not a bad return.

One sale that I made impressed upon me the truth of the Biblical saying, "Ask and ye shall receive." I decided to go from house to house ringing doorbells and ask if anyone wanted to buy *The Pittsburgh Press*. The usual reply was not today. Somewhat discouraged after a series of rebuffs, I climbed one more flight of stairs and rang the bell. It was opened by a tall man with glasses and a stern look. When I asked if he wanted to buy the newspaper, he stared at me, not saying anything, and then reached in his pocket and took out a coin. I handed him the newspaper, and he told me to keep the change and disappeared into his house. I looked at the coin—a quarter. I called out to thank him, feeling about ten feet tall, and then turned and fled down the stairs, flooded with the thrill of success.

In retrospect, that sale represented far more than a profit of twenty-three cents. It taught me to keep trying when times were hard; it renewed my faith in my fellow man and demonstrated that persistence, despite its highs and lows, is often well rewarded. Today, when salespeople come to my door or I am stopped on the street by deserving persons, I am a pretty easy mark.

* * *

One day when the new school year had just started, my Mother took me to *Barnett's Booterie*, my favorite shoe store. Mr. Barnett always wore a business suit, smelled wonderfully of shoes and tobacco, and wore little horn-rimmed glasses. He carefully fitted and checked the new shoes through a fluorescent box that x-rayed my feet and made them green and fleshless. It was a fascinating process that the industry subsequently abandoned when the fear of radiation swept the nation. When he asked if I wanted to wear them home, I always did.

The boots I wore home that day were magnificent and made from sturdy brown leather that reached my calves. They sported yellow, square-sided buckskin laces that fitted around metal hooks. My new boots made me feel absolutely invincible and that I could surmount any obstacle. Added power and strength seemed to come from the steel cleats that rimmed each heel and produced a most satisfactory metallic sound as I strode along the sidewalk. Best of all, just above the ankle on the outside of the right boot was a neat, snap-covered pocket that held a shiny, double-bladed clasp knife that came with the boots free of charge. I mean it when I say, "They don't make shoes like that any more!"

Other memories include my terror and worry over the neighborhood bully, Eddie Carrier, who used to chase me home now and then. He finally stopped when I fought back one afternoon from my front porch where I was cornered. I learned that even a pacifist like me has to fight back when there is no other way out; besides, I felt pretty good about myself after that.

A distinctly more positive happening was discovering that I could check out books at the public library at no cost. I thrilled to the jousting of King Arthur and his Knights of the Round Table, hated Sir Modred, and loved Lady Guinevere. Our class also was required to memorize and recite poetry. One verse in particular evokes a vivid image of that class: "Under the spreading chestnut tree, the village smithy stands. The smith, a mighty man is he, with large and sinewy hands."

Motion pictures made their first impact on me during the fourth grade. We did not have a radio in our house, and no one had television then. Mr. Winograd, the father of my classmate Leonard, owned the Majestic Theater. From Leonard we learned about the really good western movies coming to town, featuring stars such as Tom Mix, Buck Jones, Ken Maynard, and Tim Holt. Occasionally a truly frightening feature such as *Frankenstein* would appear to scare the pants off of us.

Mr. Winograd built a new theater called the Oriental Theater, a modern jewel of a building. It was like a palace inside, with dimly lit Buddhas brooding along the walls and a vaulted ceiling with little stars that twinkled. There was a huge balcony, and all the seats were comfortably padded, not like the old hardwood seats in the Majestic. Admission was ten cents for those under the age of 12 and then skyrocketed to 25 cents. Leonard could see all the movies for free, to the envy of us all.

* * *

In the summer of 1932, we moved to the northside of Rochester, almost in the country. Acres of corn higher than my head were growing in the fields near our house. I tried smoking corn silk in that field, which was a time-honored rite of passage suggested by older and therefore wiser kids in the neighborhood. My experience revealed that newspaper wrappers were not exactly the best material to use in rolling corn silk cigarettes. When lit, the smoke produced was hot and burning to my tongue. After a few abortive attempts, I abandoned corn silk in favor of dried coffee grounds, another tobacco substitute that also came highly recommended by those same older, wiser kids. This effort was a complete failure, as I could never get the darn coffee to burn. The newspaper wrapping would catch fire and flare up all around my face, while the coffee grounds dribbled down my chin.

I also learned to ride a two-wheeler, aided by the neighborhood gang, which included one kid who graciously let us ride his fine, 20-inch bike. What a thrill it was to move under your own power, wobbly at first, but finally in control.

We also tremendously enjoyed making inner tube guns. We would make the gun barrel from a piece of wood about eighteen inches long and fashion a smaller piece of wood that resembled a gunhandle. This handle was then bound tightly to the gun barrel with two stout rubber bands about one-half inch wide cut with scissors from a discarded automobile inner tube. A nail was pounded into the barrel near the handle to serve as a trigger. The gun was loaded by clipping one end of another large rubber band under the gun handle on the top side and then stretching the loose end of the rubber band very carefully over the tip of the gun barrel. The weapon fired when you pulled on the nail trigger and thus released the stretched rubber band at the target. The effective range of the average gun was 10 to 20 yards. My friends and I spent many hours making and playing with those guns, but my Mother never discovered why her scissors were so dull.

I often played card games with my brother and sisters on our shaded porch. *Hearts, Go Fish,* and *Old Maid* were our favorites. We also read books, most of which were acquired from Cousin Clarence, who had hundreds of books stored on dusty racks in his cellar. I would take 15 or 20 books at a time and then trade those in for new ones.

I discovered the Horatio Alger series this way, along with a host of detective and mystery stories. I lived vicariously the life of the heroic lad, who struggled valiantly against misfortune. Somehow, Horatio's hero always managed to turn adversity into good fortune. These stories were inspirational and influential and helped me to develop the philosophy that has guided my thinking and activity for most of my adult life: hard work is essential to the achievement of success in any venture; good works are always rewarded, often in ways you least expect; the Golden Rule does apply, that one should do unto others as you would have them do unto you; and the Good Lord helps those who help themselves.

We moved that fall to a larger, two-story frame house. This new home was very modern and had a big coal burning furnace in the basement with heating ducts to the upstairs. There was a nice bathroom, three bedrooms, and a big family style kitchen, in addition to the dining room. It was located only two blocks from Rochester General Hospital, where my Mother had trained as a nurse and my tonsils were removed. Our newest school was located about four blocks away, and there were lots of kids around with whom to spend time.

Franklin Delano Roosevelt was elected President in 1932 by an overwhelming 472 electoral college votes; the incumbent, Herbert Hoover, got 59 votes. The mood of America became more upbeat and optimistic than it had been for the past three years. With so many poor people, rampant unemployment, and the country in such a dire financial condition, the time was right for a new President and a new party to get us started again.

The new Administration moved quickly to help needy families, such as ours. Free milk for children was dispensed at our school on Saturday mornings and was so cold it made my teeth ache for a minute after drinking it down. Government surplus farm products, such as dried milk and beans, rice, corn, flour, and sugar also were made available to deserving families. Even then, our farmers were producing more than our country could readily absorb. I remember feeling like a second-class citizen standing in that federal welfare line. To receive something without working for it seemed to be wrong and caused me great embarrassment. I am sure that Mom felt the same, but she had little choice. She earned her living the best she could and even sold household products door-to-door, such as lavender scented bathroom deodorizers, kitchen scrub brushes, and scouring pads. She was on the road during the hours we were in school but usually home in time to fix supper and listen to our problems or applaud our successes. My Mother was a real go-getter.

Aunt Cora and Clarence usually brought our weekly food order on Fridays, and we never went hungry. Mom paid for it with money she made from her sales work and by helping out at Wright's store on Saturdays, cleaning house, and ironing. We kids would tag along on occasion and spend the day at Wright's store doing odd chores, like cutting the grass or helping Clarence pump gas.

My Mother also baked on Saturdays, a day I looked forward to eagerly. The ingredients for bread were mixed carefully, folded on the flour-sprinkled tabletop, and then placed in a bowl covered by a damp cloth so that the activated yeast could change the heavy dough into a puffy mound. Later in the morning when the dough was hugely swollen, Mom would let me punch it down with my fist allowing the air to escape. The yeast then would do its job all over. When the dough had been punched down two or three times, Mom would form it into little loaves and pop them into the oven. There was usually some dough left over, which was then rolled out, floured, and cut into strips about two inches wide and six inches long. These strips were lavishly buttered, topped with sugar and spicy cinnamon, and then rolled up with the ends pinched so they would not fall open. When baked, these cinnamon rolls were deliciously warm and sugary and with a hardened sweet crust on top.

Mom baked pies too, apple mostly, and sometimes cherry when they were in season. When serving the pie, she usually said, "Be careful now. The crusts will cut your throat." I thought her pie crusts were fine and told her so, but she always felt her crusts were not what they should be and never accepted the compliment.

* * *

Our neighborhood gang played games such as *Kick the Can, Statues, May I?,* and *Hopscotch,* many of which are perhaps out of date today. Fall was the time for pickup games of football, often played in our backyard. Since regular footballs were in short supply, we made our own from rolled up newspapers tied with string or a stout rubber band. These were satisfactory for passing or scrimmaging but not for punting.

Full autumn moons invited apple roasts in the cool evening atop the hill near our house overlooking the valley below. We would lounge by the fire feeling free as jaybirds, while potatoes roasted in the hot coals and Red Delicious or Winesap apples sizzled on long pointed sticks. The apples were often overdone and the potatoes somewhat raw, but a touch of salt made them perfect.

When the winter snows came and snow drifts piled up in the valley, there were snow forts to be built. Without an announced plan, all the guys would gather Saturday morning to roll up snow balls at least three feet high, big enough so they would make stout walls for the fort. Two forts were built facing each other about 30 yards apart. Snowball warfare would break out, lasting as long as there was decent snow to make snowballs or until it was time to go home and get something to eat. Rocks in the snowballs were forbidden, but it was okay to let them ice up nice and hard.

Chuck and I often took long hikes into the woods in the spring, sometimes making a fire to cook a stew made of potatoes, onions, and bacon strips thrown in for extra flavor. We would go on all-day outings, searching for fern fossils and examining mother nature's spring productions, such as the stately mayflower, purple and white violets, and the secretive jack-in-the-pulpit.

During the windy days of March after school, we flew homemade kites made from newspapers glued on salvaged sticks and held to the string around the frame with a paste of flour and water. The Buttermore brothers were our area champions and had giant kites controlled from string boxes with crank handles that let the string out or reeled it in at astonishing speeds. They would launch their kites from the edge of a grassy hill with the wind at their backs, and their kites would soar up and away across the valley until almost out of sight. Oh my, those kites were a splendid sight.

Sunday afternoons, when the spring weather was often cloudy and damp, was the best time for a game of marbles. Each player took turns shooting at the array of bright aggies lined up, one from each player, in the middle of a 10- or 12-foot ring. Any marbles you were able to knock out of the ring were yours to keep. You were permitted to keep shooting as long as your shooter stayed within the ring and you hit your target. If you missed and your shooter remained in the ring, it was fair game for the next player. If by some cruel stroke of fate he managed to knock your shooter out of the ring you were not only out of the game, you forfeited your shooting marble as well.

One game occurred in which Boots Buttermore called me a "son of a bitch." You can tell when someone is kidding and when a bad name is called in earnest; Boots was not kidding. Without thinking about it or saying a word, I walked over and popped him in the mouth with my right fist. Boots staggered back with an angry red blotch on the side of his face. He then shrugged off his jacket and rushed forward, swinging his right hand while I swung my left. We scuffled for a while, both of us jolted by the exchange of blows. He hit me sharply on the nose and I saw stars. Blood began to drip, and we both stopped fighting and resumed the game, not really wanting to do any more fighting. I tried to act as if nothing was wrong, but my nose hurt and continued to bleed until finally I had to drop out of the game and go home to tend to it. Since that scrap, I have never engaged in another fistfight.

Inspired by the onset of warm weather in the summer, someone started to build a dam across the stream that ran through the foothills where we often hiked. The stream carried cool, clear water from natural springs and the surface runoff water from coal strip mining in the surrounding hills. Gunny sacks or old grain feed bags were used to make sandbags that we piled high to dam the stream and form a pond. It was beautiful and not too deep, perhaps up to our waists at the deepest part. Ten or more of us could frolic there at the same time. We even put an old board under the top row of sandbags that formed a stubby diving board from which we jumped and leaped. One afternoon while splashing in the pond, I suddenly realized I was no longer touching bottom—I was swimming! Emboldened and elated with this discovery, I tried a few overhand strokes, made famous by Johnny Weissmuller of Tarzan movie fame. In what seemed like no time at all, I had mastered the fundamentals of the Australian crawl.

During the summer of 1934, I would drop off into slumber at the first touch of my head to the pillow. I would awaken instantly, brimming with energy for the events of the new day. There was no dreaming or tossing about waiting for sleep to come, just a total blackout. It was a special kind of careless sleep that only a happy, healthy 12-year-old lad can experience. Since then I have often wished I could find the key to that kind of slumber again.

The next school year was almost over when Mom announced that we were going to make another move, this time to a town across the Beaver River named West Bridgewater. This news was harder to take than all the others, because I would be leaving many friends behind. Classmates I had grown attached to were going to be sorely missed, but that was the way of it. On the last day of school, my sixth grade homeroom teacher offered to pay me fifty-cents for washing all the blackboards, which I did happily. Perhaps this was her good-bye present to me.

West Bridgewater was a quiet little town of some 5,000 souls and stretched for about three miles along the southern bank of the Beaver River near its juncture with the broad Ohio. This part of the Beaver River was once part of the old Erie Canal system, before its freight hauling capability was taken over by the railroads, including the Pennsylvania Railroad, the Pennsylvania and Lake Erie Railroad (P&LE), and the Baltimore and Ohio Railroad (B&O). Evidence of the old canal still remains in West Bridgewater with concrete abutments along the river banks that once served to control the rise and fall of water levels so the freight barges could pass.

Our new house had one major drawback: there was no inside bathroom. We had been spoiled by the modern conveniences of our last home but were compensated by the boating, swimming, and fishing promised by the nearby river. Although a lot different from the wide open spaces of the hills above East Rochester, this would do nicely. When the first freeze of winter came, however, I found the bathroom situation took a bit of getting used to. I will never forget those cold treks outside when the snow was falling and the winds pierced every crevice and crack in that ancient two-holer in our backyard.

* * *

In those times there was no junior high school or middle school. The elementary grades ran from one through eight and then directly into high school. Those who graduated from West Bridgewater had a choice of going to either Beaver High School or the one in Rochester. Bridgewater was too small a town to have a high school of its own. Both schools were about the same walking distance, which was a consideration since all students except those bussed in from the farm areas still had to walk home for lunch. Most of my classmates went to high school in Beaver, and I had a special reason for going there. Her name was Margaret Franz, a blue-eyed, dark-haired beauty with a dazzling smile. She was going to Beaver High School, and that was good enough for me.

Life in West Bridgewater promised to be full of new experiences. There were many neighborhood kids to meet and new places to learn about, plus the river and the woods waiting to be explored. I became friends with Bob McDade, who lived across the street.

He and I and my brother Chuck would often explore the Beaver River during warm summer days, sometimes swimming or wading in the shallows, or hunt catbirds with Bob's Daisy BB rifle in the brush or scrub trees that bordered the railroad tracks. We made slingshots and had lots of fun at some expense to the sparrow population in the area. Bob's father was the chief executive of the Beaver Valley Bus Company, and Bob and I would often get complimentary tickets to the local theaters that the bus company advertised in their buses.

This was the summer we had a radio in our house. There were some truly memorable radio programs, including the two black comedians, Amos and Andy; George Burns and his wife, Gracie Allen; Eddie Cantor; Fred Allen; Fibber McGee and Molly; and my favorite of all, Jack Benny. The Jack Benny show starred Mary, Jack's flighty wife, and was broadcast every Sunday evening, announced by jovial Don Wilson. How I would chortle when Jack visited his money vault down in the cellar, which was closely guarded by an old man inside the vault. Upon Jack's command, the rusty vault door would creak open slowly and noisily on squeaking hinges. Finally the old man would get the door open and say something like, "Oh, it's you, Mr. Benny. How have you been this year?" Jack Benny's shows were simply classics.

A family named Weidner lived about four houses from us and had three boys and three girls, just like the McDades. Their front parlor had a handsome upright player piano that played from rolls of perforated sheets inside metal cylinders. When the mechanical motor was turned on out would come marvelous music with the piano keys moving up and down in ghostly fashion, not a finger touching them; it seemed like magic. Even better than the music were parlor games like *Spin the Bottle* and *Post Office*. One young lady named Scarlet Rice, a dark-haired, slender girl who wore lots of red lipstick, sent me a message that there was a letter in the post office for me, which meant that she wanted to give me a kiss. I bashfully demurred saying I did not want to take delivery because she wore too much lipstick. She countered by saying she would take off the lipstick, and I collected my first letter, enjoying it in spite of my protestations.

That first summer I acquired a battered but serviceable brass bugle from a secondhand store for $5.00. The McDade children all played musical instruments of some kind, piano, trombone, trumpet, or drums, and I was inspired by their example. For weeks I practiced during my lunch hour on the back porch sending brassy peals of invigorating sound, some would call it blaring, across the open fields; thank goodness the neighbors never filed a complaint. Eventually, I could play taps and reveille and what I judged to be bugle charge commands. My lips were no longer sore and swollen from the pressure needed to generate good sound. I felt I was doing pretty well and was able to keep my cheeks from bulging out like the neck of a frog, one of the characteristics of all good horn men.

Unhappily, my musical career came to an abrupt and unfortunate end. A marble somehow rolled into the bugle and got stuck. I attempted to dislodge it by using the coal poker by the stove to shatter the glass. To my dismay, the marble did not shatter and became even more firmly wedged. The harder I tried to break that damn marble, the more tightly it became jammed. The soft metal of the bugle finally gave way and the marble was freed, but there was a gaping hole in my precious horn. No more would the world hear my skillful renditions floating over the fields, sharp, true, and clear. It took me days to accept this loss. I tried to remedy the damage, but repairing the hole was beyond my ken—my playing days were over.

Now that my bugle was finished, I turned my frustrated musical talents toward the harmonica and was soon able to render perfectly the first lines of the song *The Isle of Capri*. Larry Adler, the popular movie star and mouth organ virtuoso of the day, could play any kind of harmonica, large or small, and sometimes more than one at a time. He made it seem so easy, but I never progressed beyond those two lines. The bitter truth was that I would never qualify as one of Larry Adler's *Harmonicats*.

During many an idle afternoon, I would lie on the warm grass in our backyard, daydreaming and watching white clouds overhead in the hot blue sky. Dandelions had to be examined and four-leaf clovers could be found now and then, which were supposed to bring good luck. On the horizon were the double tracks of the P&LE railroad that carried freight cars as they rolled slowly, almost endlessly, across the far embankment. I would count 80 to 100 cars on the average and sometimes as many as 112, mostly laden with coal for distant mill fires. Between the P&LE tracks and our house were acres of dahlias that our neighbor planted for the commercial flower market each year. In the fall, the field burst into bloom after the first frost, becoming a riotous blend of red, white, yellow, and orange flowers waist high and waving in the breeze.

During the winter of 1936, Chuck and I experimented with the art of skiing on barrel staves. We made skis from the staves of old rain water barrels, to which we nailed leather straps to hold our boots in place. We then poured tap water over the bottoms of the staves to make them icy and were ready for action. Our ski slope was the railroad embankment with its steep pitch of about 45 degrees. We only went about half way up, but that was enough to scare the pants off of me. Chuck was much better than I and achieved terrifying speed straight ahead and downward. Suddenly his skis would depart sideways and send him flying ahead. We tried to perfect our style, but every time our skis would go off in a different direction and propel us into space. The leather straps soon gave way and our skis were rendered inoperative. That experience scared me enough that I have never again felt the urge to ski.

Ross Jack, our grade school principal, was the only male teacher in West Bridgewater. He was a good teacher and tried to prepare his eighth graders for high school, and possible college, by talking about the subjects we should be taking. He taught us some Latin and Algebra and recommended that we take college preparatory courses in high school. I remembered and followed his sound advice. If I got the chance I would go to college, so I applied the Boy Scouts' motto, "Be prepared." Mr. Jack was fond of reading quotations aloud and expecting the class to fill in the missing word. One such saying was, "A chain is as strong as its weakest .... ," to which I instantly replied, "link." My reading of Horatio Alger had paid off, for that was probably where I had read that expression. At the start of each school day we would stand by our desks, place our right hands over our hearts, and recite: "I pledge allegiance to the Flag of the United States of America, and to the Republic for which it stands; one Nation under God, indivisible, with liberty and justice for all." That wonderful Pledge of Allegiance is no longer considered appropriate for use in our public schools. I wish that some kind of pledge to our native land could be permitted now that would again promote loyalty and respect for the hard-won traditions and values of our country.

Margaret Franz was the idol of my dreams, yet it was all I could do to muster up a hoarse hello whenever we met at school or on the

street. She was as popular and outgoing as I was shy and introspec-
tive. Our teacher chose Margaret and me to play the roles of Martha
and George Washington in our eighth grade class play, which was
about what would happen if George and Martha were to be transported into today's modern world. The high point of the show came
when George inadvertently switched on the Hoover vacuum sweeper.
The loud noise of the sweeper drowned out all conversation on the
stage and startled the audience, who laughed and hooted as George
forgot how to turn off the confounded machine.

My graduating class worked to raise funds for our field trip by
selling peanut brittle at Halloween and chocolate bunnies at Easter
time. Our trip to the H.J. Heinz Company factory in Pittsburgh went
off as scheduled on a bright sunshiny Saturday. At the huge brick,
multistory plant, we saw most of the 57 varieties of pickles, relishes,
and condiments made there and were offered a nice lunch after our
tour. We boys kept together pretty much, horsing around a lot and
showing off for the girls, who ignored us completely.

School finally was out, and I felt full of knowledge and power. I
was confident that I could answer any question, solve any problem,
surmount any obstacle, or do anything asked of me. To celebrate the
event, Jim Wallace, Chuck, Bill Shulte, and I walked across the
bridge to Rochester and strolled into Isaly's Ice Cream Store, where
ice cream cones were five cents each. I usually ordered French vanilla
because it had those wonderful red maraschino cherries sprinkled in
it, but on special occasions I ordered grape. This was definitely a
grape night.

That summer on June 19, 1936, Joe Louis fought the German
heavyweight champion, Max Schmeling. Joe had a string of 26 fights
and no losses. We heard the fight on the McDade family's radio as we
lounged on the grass outside. Our hero, Joe Louis, was knocked out
in the 12th round; we could not believe it. There was a rematch the
next year at Yankee Stadium in New York, a place big enough to hold
the overflow crowd. Max Schmeling landed a punch in the first
round, but that was about all. Louis immediately hit him with a left
hook that left him almost helpless and then proceeded to batter him
all about the ring, knocking him down three times. It was all over in
two minutes and four seconds. Here was proof that no greater fighter

existed in the world than Joe Louis, the eighth son of a sharecropper family from Alabama.

Joe Louis died on April 12, 1981; his funeral was held in Las Vegas at Caesar's Palace Sports Pavilion where he was employed. He was a marvelous champion, a gentleman, with a record of 26 title fights before he retired undefeated on March 1, 1949. Because of tax problems, Joe attempted a comeback to repay Uncle Sam. In 1951, at the age of 37, he quit the ring for good. Joe Louis was buried in Arlington National Cemetery by direction of President Ronald Reagan.

* * *

My high school years in Beaver were pleasant and full of school activities. I spent all four years, from 1936 to 1940, in the same school, a pleasant change from my traveling past. I graduated in the upper two-fifths of my class of 140 students. I managed to earn a sports letter in baseball, having pitched and won a game over the Freedom Bulldogs for our Beaver Bobcats. Other accomplishments included being the sports editor for our class yearbook, the *Shingas*, which is an Indian name. Far more important, I won a $300 scholarship to Keystone Schools, Inc. a trade school for mechanical draftsmen in Pittsburgh.

During my freshman year, one of our neighbors bought a shiny new Ford sedan. The price was discussed with some awe, $800.00. New cars were a rarity then for the Great Depression was still very much with us. President Roosevelt won a second term, defeating Alfred M. Landon from Kansas and his running mate Frank Knox. Roosevelt's Vice President was John Nance Garner from Texas.

During the long winter, unusually heavy snowfalls fell in the higher elevations of the Allegheny Mountains in northwestern Pennsylvania. By mid-February, the Ohio River was a jumble of ice floes with huge shards of white jagged ice piled 20 feet high that stretched for miles. In the spring, the snows melted and the ice jam in the river began to thaw, but a new problem rose. The runoff water from the melting snows was not being absorbed by already saturated ground. The streams and tributaries that fed the Allegheny and Monongahela

Rivers soon neared flood stage as they began disgorging their over-flow into the Ohio River at Pittsburgh, 25 miles away. The ice-filled Ohio could not handle the runoff volume fast enough, and a flood threatened everyone downriver.

The night before St. Patrick's Day, March 16, 1937, the Beaver River was about ten feet above normal but still within safety limits. For dinner that night we had one of my favorites, oven baked beans. The navy beans were allowed to simmer in a heavy iron skillet in the oven set at 250 degrees for eight to ten hours. On top was a flavorful crust of brown sugar and nicely browned pieces of bacon. After serving everyone, the heavy skillet was returned to the oven because it was still hot.

That night, while we kids slept, the Beaver River was rising and water began to flow silently and snakelike through the vacant lot beside our house. Mom was keeping a watch and by 2:00 A.M. decided to wake us up and get out of the house. We moved anxiously to obey, sensing her concern, yet unwilling to leave the nice warm covers of our beds. Sleepily, we got dressed and followed her out the back door. We sloshed our way out through the backyard in single file, sometimes ankle deep in icy water, and headed for the railroad station located on high ground. We waded for one long block, which seemed like a mile, until we finally reached the road that led to the P&LE railroad embankment. We arrived at the Beaver station where we took shelter in the passenger waiting room for the rest of the night.

Early the next morning, Mom called Wright's store and relayed our predicament. She learned from Clarence that the stores in Rochester were already flooded and the water was still rising. He said he would meet us in Rochester by the train station if we could walk over the railroad bridge. Luckily, we made it over the bridge, trying not to pay attention to the swiftly moving waters just two feet below the railroad ties to each side of our walkway. We met Clarence and stayed the next two days at Wright's Store waiting for the flood to recede.

When we returned home, we found that the flood had reached the second floor and floated the mattresses off our beds. Joan's violin, which had only recently been restrung, was in soggy ruins on her bed. Slimy mud imprints were everywhere: on the rugs in the living room, in the clothes closets, on the dishes in the kitchen cupboards, and all over the wallpaper. A quarter-inch layer of mud covered the floors. The dank sour smell of decay was strong. In the kitchen, the skillet of beans had been swept from the oven. Beans were strewn all across the floor, imbedded in the film of mud. Our back porch was wrenched partially from the main house by the force of the rising flood. Our two-holer outhouse was on its side in the backyard. We were forced to move, of course, and took what could be salvaged in the way of clothing to temporary quarters that my Mother found.

Our house was never inhabited again and had to be demolished. It was a long time before Mom baked beans in that heavy iron skillet again. Within the next two years, spurred on by the magnitude of the damage wrought nationwide by this flood, the U.S. Government's Corps of Engineers began to install a series of nine dams on the Ohio River between Pittsburgh and the confluence of the Ohio and Mississippi Rivers. Thereafter, no disastrous flood such as that on St. Patrick's Day in 1937 would occur again.

We moved back to West Bridgewater to a more substantial but worn two-story frame house that rented for $15.00 per month. Happily, there was an inside bathroom, plus three bedrooms, a shaded side yard, and enough room for a small garden in the rear. Best of all, Jim Wallace, one of my favorite classmates, lived right next door. We would become close friends for many years.

In 1983, Jim Wallace retired from thirty-five years of service with the Westinghouse Electric Company in Beaver. He and his wife Theresa moved to Sarasota, Florida, where we resumed our friendship after years of separation that began with World War II. As a student, Jim set a personal record of real magnitude. He was respected by all his classmates and never missed a single day of grade school or high school. He graduated from Rochester High School with high honors for which he received a four-year scholarship to the University of Pittsburgh, graduating as a mechanical engineer.

I worked at a number of jobs during my high school years, all of which helped me to earn spending money. More important, they taught me the economics of wage earnings, of supply and demand, and of debits and credits. I learned firsthand the wisdom of my

Mother's advice that the harder you work the less you earn." She said that laborers were always easy to find at cheap wages and demonstrated by her own hard work experiences that such was the case. Clearly, trained minds and skilled labor received better pay and were in greater demand.

During my freshman and sophomore years at Beaver I was a newspaper boy for *The Pittsburgh Press*. I had 50 customers, which meant I earned 50 cents per day, one cent for each three-cent paper delivered; Sunday papers cost 10 cents, from which I got two pennies. We settled our account every week with the newspaper office, and I always managed to pay my bill. If some of my customers did not pay me, however, I would have to go into deficit spending for that week, which was not a very comfortable feeling.

Delivering newspapers was good experience and good exercise as well. We walked our routes, rain or shine, seven days a week with a load of papers hanging heavily across our stomachs and supported by a broad canvass shoulder strap. On cold days, I warmed my hands by thrusting them into the middle of the warm bundle of papers. I could triple fold and throw newspapers with speed and accuracy onto doorsteps and porches 10 yards away and never once was bitten by a dog.

One bright Sunday morning toward the end of my route, fortune smiled at me. I spied a green folded bill on the sidewalk near the corner just ahead of me. I picked it up and to my delight found it to be a five dollar bill. No one was in sight who might have just dropped it, so it could have been there all night. It must have been meant for me or perhaps was a case of good luck. I prefer to think it was a reward for being alert and observant, for being in the right place at the right time. It was a good example of the old adage about the early bird catching the worm.

During the summer one year, Chuck, Jim Wallace, and I made kayaks of canvass cloth stretched over a 10-foot-long framework of wooden stakes we obtained from the lumber yard. We painted the canvass with several coats of green outdoor paint and then fashioned double-bladed paddles. Those boats were a lot of fun and big enough to hold two people. Our small flotilla of three spent many a day on the Beaver and Ohio Rivers. Occasionally we would paddle some miles down the Ohio and spend the night sleeping under a willow tree and warmed by a driftwood fire on the shore. Sometimes we tied up to the P&LE Railroad bridge pier and caught white-bellied channel catfish that were full of fight, not like their sluggish cousins that fed off the bottom of the more placid Beaver River. Those homemade boats gave us access to the river world and were a source of real pleasure and joy. We often felt like modern day Tom Sawyers and Huck Finns, and in a way we were.

During my sophomore year, I had a job that was both depressing and a bit hard on the ego. The federal government had set up a new Aid to Students Program to help students whose family income was below a certain level. I was eligible and applied for a job after school to help our janitor sweep the high school floors, halls, and stairways. The floors were wooden and had to be sprinkled with an oiled sawdust before the accumulated dirt and refuse of the day's activity could be swept up. I worked from 4:00 P.M. to 6:00 P.M. twice a week. My earlier training in how to sweep floors was put to the test and was more than adequate, but I did not enjoy the feeling of being a janitor, honorable work though it was. I was particularly thankful that none of my classmates, especially the girls, saw me with that damn broom.

In my junior year, I found more suitable employment as a pin boy at the bowling alley. I soon learned how to set the pins and was assigned to an alley when the fall bowling season opened. There were only seven lanes, but they were the most beautifully buffed, hard maple bowling lanes in the valley. Bowling season was from early September until the end of May, when all bowling establishments had to close because none were air-conditioned.

Each game of 10 frames cost the bowler 25 cents, for which the pin boy received eight cents. I would earn between $1.50 and $2.00, not bad for those days. We pin boys deplored Tuesday night when the ladies bowled. Lady bowlers were agonizingly slow and seemed more concerned with social amenities than the bowling scores. Down there in the bowling pits, our feelings were justified as we waited for the gutter balls to dribble slowly toward us or watched the well-bowled ball heading right for the head pin but without enough force to do much damage. Our wages also were affected because it took so long for the ladies league games to be completed. We usually made up that loss on Friday night, when everyone in town seemed to want to bowl, sometimes until 1:30 or 2:00 A.M. We all learned to bowl during slack periods and to shoot pool. I managed to achieve a bowling average of about 175, not bad for a high school kid.

Orson Wells stunned all of us with his radio broadcast of H.G. Wells' *War of the Worlds* story. Many who heard the broadcast thought it was a real-life news report and were terrified that we were being invaded by aliens from outer space. Books and magazines continued to be an important part of my life. Paperback novels were in vogue and affordable at about 15 cents each. I especially watched for new monthly issues of *G-8 and His Battle Aces*. The adventure hero G-8 and his friends Nippy and Bull regularly confronted and confounded the German High Command during World War I, flying missions from their advanced aerodrome bases in France. They flew such famous allied aircraft as the *Spad* and the *French Nieuport*, but G-8 could fly any airplane, including the German *Fokker, Pfalz,* and the graceful *Albatross D-III*. I read all the books in the school library about Baron von Richthofen, the Red Baron, the most famous German fighter pilot in the history of aerial warfare. He downed 80 allied planes before he was killed on April 21, 1918, at age 25. It is comforting to know that none of his victims were American pilots.

Other star publications of that time included the magazine *Wings*, which featured aviation stories about World I heroes. The adventures of *Doc Savage* were also thrilling. His eyes contained strangely stirring flecks of gold in their depths. He possessed super intelligence and overwhelming strength and muscles that rippled beneath his golden skin. What adventures were encountered with *Lamont Cranston*, wealthy millionaire by day and by night the deadly, crime fighting *Shadow* who was armed with two murderous .45 calibre weapons that never missed their mark: "Only the Shadow knows." The works of Ernest Hemingway were important too. His story of the Spanish Civil War, *For Whom the Bells Toll*, is one of my all-time favorites. He was a superb writer of macho stories, employing sparse use of well-chosen words in a style that many others have imitated but never matched.

Sports of the season filled many of our days. One of our prized goals, discussed all winter long, was to swim in the Beaver River by

Easter Sunday. If the weather was right and Easter came late in April, we sometimes accomplished this, but not often. Spring was a special time when the sap started to rise in all young things, including me. The old baseball glove was oiled with Neetsfoot oil or Three-In-One sewing machine oil. I could throw a pretty good fastball and a big slow curve, and our high school coach decided to use me as one of his pitchers. I helped win a game over the Freedom team and thus earned a varsity letter. I also played on the Beaver Junior Legion Team until becoming ineligible on my nineteenth birthday.

This was the age of Big Band music, which was broadcast from the Glen Island Casino on Long Island and various ballrooms across the country. Tommy and Jimmy Dorsey, Glenn Miller, and Artie Shaw were big favorites. Equally popular were vocalists Frank Sinatra, the Eberly Brothers, Bob and Ray, Helen O'Connell, and Helen Forrest with the Harry James Band. In 1939, the song *Three Little Fishes* was the rage, and the ballad *I'll Never Smile Again* swept the country, with Frank Sinatra causing all the gals to swoon.

In 1940, Winston Churchill replaced Neville Chamberlain as Great Britain's Prime Minister. When Churchill delivered his "blood, sweat, and tears" speech, he spoke not only to his countrymen who were enduring the terrible bombing of their cities and homeland by German aircraft but to the world. He gained the attention of a lot of young people, including me, who until then had not been too interested in the conflict raging in Europe.

Our senior prom was held in late May 1940 at the high school gymnasium. The only girl I felt brave enough to ask was Geraldine Korn, who lived down the street. Margaret Franz was out of the question, since she had a number of boyfriends and was certain to be going with one of them. As Jerry was passing by, I asked if she would go to the prom with me. She replied that she would love to go with me but already had a date and would save a dance for me. She was nice about it, but I was disappointed. I learned my lesson not to wait until the last minute to ask a girl for such an important affair. A friend of mine was in the same fix so we decided to go together. The girls were dressed beautifully in their gowns and wearing corsages, including Jerry Korn and Margaret Franz. I did not claim my dance with Jerry; there would be other times.

Graduation from Beaver was anticlimatic, as is often the case when you look forward to something for a long time. We all wore rented caps and gowns and received our diplomas from our superintendent on a warm, muggy evening in early June 1940. Happily for me, the question of what was going to happen next already had been decided. The Keystone School scholarship, for which I had applied, was awarded to me. This was great news, for my favorite subject during the last two years was mechanical drawing. I was good at detailed work and liked the precision and exactness of it. By the end of my senior year, I was quite good at producing drawings of machinery products in black India ink that were so crisp and clear they were almost a form of art. The scholarship of $300 represented tuition for one year as a full-time student at the Keystone School in Pittsburgh. Classes were to commence in mid-June, immediately following our graduation, which meant good-bye to summer vacation.

I commuted daily on the train from Rochester, enjoying glimpses of the green-blue Ohio River screened by willow trees and wild sumacs. This was my favorite time to reflect and ponder on personal as well as historical issues. The classes at Keystone were held in a two-story, ivy-covered red brick building only a mile from the *Clark Teaberry* and *Clark Candy Bar* manufacturing plant. The scent of teaberry leaves in the morning air, as I walked across the leafy park from the railroad station to class, was appetizing and refreshing.

This was a presidential election year. Wendell Wilkie, the 1940 Republican candidate for president, his voice hoarse from making speeches, toured our area in an open sedan one sunny afternoon pleading for votes. His efforts were in vain, for Franklin Roosevelt won an unprecedented third term.

I turned 18 in September and now could be employed full-time as an adult. Not one to dillydally, my Mother found me a job in the personnel office of the National Electric Company in Ambridge. I applied and was hired on the night shift (11 P.M. to 7 A.M.) as an inspector in the rubber mill. Try as I might, I could not master the knack of vulcanizing the pinholes or bare spots in rolls of neoprene-covered electric wire that we had to inspect before they could go to final processing and shipping.

Following the Peter Principle, I was promoted to the next higher level of incompetence from the wire mill into a clerical job to help keep the records and daily tallies of production. My new office was a small, six-by-eight room high above the rumble and bump of dozens of heavy mill rollers spread out in long rows. Under the yellow glare of incandescent lighting, they ground synthetic powders into a rubbery mass between two massive rollers each about eight feet long and three feet in diameter. Bare wire and the newly created synthetic rubber were then fed into a molding machine that produced finished electrical wire. This new wire then was spooled on large reels to be cured in a heated chamber that vulcanized the rubber. Telephone companies, the U.S. Navy, and other government agencies were our chief customers. War orders became so urgent that our plant was working around the clock.

I was now on the day shift and able to resume schooling in Pittsburgh. I caught the train to Pittsburgh after work to attend evening classes and managed to complete the course in September 1941. During my last week of classes, the school placement service scheduled me for an interview as a draftsman at the Philadelphia Company. I had an appointment with a Mr. Wheeler at the office of the Pittsburgh Railways Company, which was part of the Philadelphia Holding Company. Mr. Wheeler looked at my work and told me to report for duty as soon as I could. I gave two weeks notice at the National Electric Company the very next day.

Naturally, I was nervous and excited at the prospect of my first real office job. I now had to dress nicely in a suit coat and tie. My salary was $90.00 per month, which was pretty good considering that at age 19 I was replacing an older married man who had just retired. Others in the research department where I was assigned were earning less than that, and I was quite content with my wage. Commuting daily by train, I used a monthly pass that cost $12. I was able to live at home and pay Mom rent and still have money for decent clothing and entertainment. Movies cost 25 cents and cigarettes were 15 cents a pack for brands such as *Lucky Strike, Camels,* or *Pall Malls*. There would be no more roll-your-own *Bull Durham* packages of flake tobacco or *Bugler* shredded tobacco for me; I was in the big time.

My job was to prepare detailed maps showing all the routes of the Company in different colors on big maps of the city. These maps were then used in rate hearings and other official conferences involving fare changes, route jurisdictions, and the like. Mr. Wheeler, the engineer who hired me, had spent 15 years acquiring his engineering degree from the University of Carnegie Tech by going to night school. He encouraged me to continue going to school, and I enrolled in evening classes at the University of Pittsburgh that fall.

Gone now is old Forbes Field, which was only a few blocks from campus, with its splintered wooden seats that survived many blistering hot July and August stretch drives. Cousin Clarence and I saw a few ball games there before the stadium was dismantled. I still can recall looking at the vine-covered left field wall and beyond it the tall spire of the Cathedral of Learning where I attended classes. In my mind, Pie Traynor covers third base; Mace Brown, the relief pitcher known as the Fireman, comes strolling in from the bull pen to relieve Elroy Face, whose fastball no longer had its old zing; and Ralph Kiner, the king of home run hitters, lofts a long ball far over the center field wall. KDKA radio always broadcast the Pirates' home games. The announcer delighted in acknowledging the flight of a home run ball by shouting into his mike, "Open the window, Aunt Minnie, here comes one right in the old petunia patch!"

The Pittsburgh Pirates and the NFL Steelers of today play in a splendid new concrete stadium named Three Rivers, which stands on reclaimed bottom land of the Allegheny River across from Point Park in downtown Pittsburgh. Three Rivers Stadium is just below the hill from the *Clark Teaberry* and *Clark Candy Bar* plant. My wife, Anno, our brother-in-law Wally Smith, and I attended a night baseball game at Three Rivers in August 1990 and happily watched the Pirates defeat the Cincinnati Reds. I thought I smelled teaberry leaves on the evening breeze.

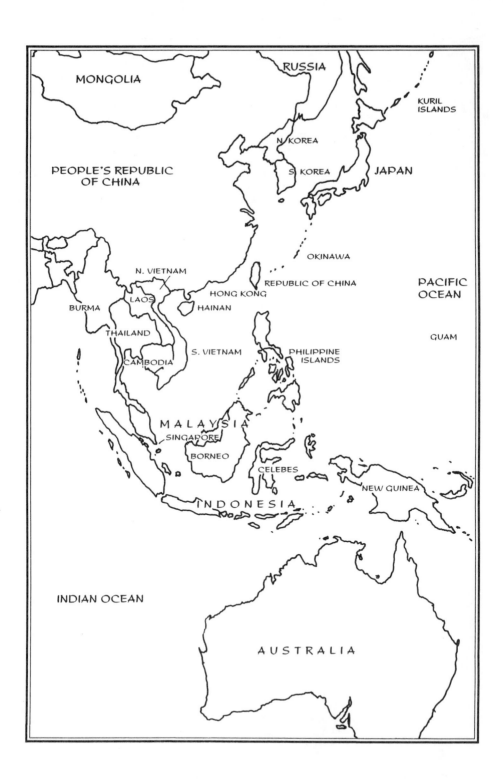

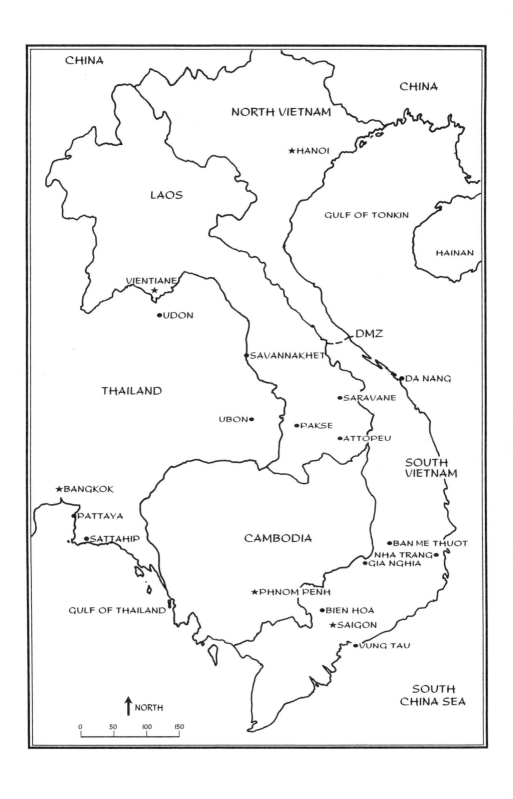

THE TIME OF MY LIFE

ONE

Into The Wild Blue

It was ten minutes past midnight on July 5, 1944, when I eased our B-17G smoothly off the runway at St. Johns, Newfoundland, and started a climb to our assigned altitude. At 9,000 feet, I cleared our flight with the tower operator and said good night. We were officially on our way. With orders assigning us to the 15th Air Force, we were bound for Italy. The hour was late and the crew settled down to sleep, wondering about the future, yet filled with awareness that we were crossing more than the Atlantic—we were crossing a threshold into the world of war.

Steve Yankura was the most important man in the crew that night. He set up his sextant in the navigation bubble, spread out his charts, and began plotting our course. We were solitary sailors in the vast ocean of space, with moonlight above and scattered clouds covering the dark sea below. The stars served as our route markers, bright and sharply defined. Steve checked them hourly throughout the night, plotting their position relative to our aircraft and keeping us on course. Bud Haenel and I took turns monitoring the engine gauges and keeping the autopilot trimmed and on the correct heading. An hour after takeoff, we were well beyond the reach of ground radio stations. Our new engines performed flawlessly, as we maintained a steady airspeed of 165 miles per hour. Our ground speed was around 200 to 225 miles per hour, allowing for favorable tailwinds and our altitude. For the rest of the night all of the crew slept except Steve, Bud and me.

With the first light of dawn and my thermos of coffee almost empty, we were about an hour from our destination. Daylight came

3

and with the brightening sky and increased visibility, I sighted a dark smudge of land against the horizon perhaps 50 to 60 miles distant; the Azores. Steve had done it; we were on course and on time, about seven and one-half hours from St. John's. By now, the crew was awake and chattering on the radio intercom, congratulating Steve on his nice work and cracking jokes. About five miles out, I eased back on the throttles and began a descent toward the runway, which was not yet visible but somewhere ahead of us between two sandy ridges. Radio contact was established, and we were cleared to land. The tower operator said, "Army 6110, you are cleared on final approach. Winds are calm."

I aimed for the valley between the ridges and swept in above the blue-green water; the air clear, our engines purring sweetly. Our ship did not want to stop flying, but I put her down after a couple of light bounces. This was a first landing for me on a pierced steel plank (PSP) runway which could be laid in short order almost anywhere once a dirt strip had been graded. The planks were about two feet wide and six feet long and hooked together to form a flexible, porous landing surface. Dust rose about us as we pulled into our hardstand and shut down our twirling propellers.

The large canvass mess tent had its side panels rolled up, allowing the Atlantic sea breezes to sweep through. The view was attractive from the little knoll where the tent was located. Assorted wooden tables with folding chairs were set on wood flooring in random fashion. This was no stateside operation, but rather a functional forward base designed to get the job done with no frills. Other aircraft were scattered about, perhaps a dozen B-17's like ours, all part of a steady buildup of bombers headed toward the Mediterranean Theater of Operations (MTO). Steve, Bud, Gary, and I wolfed down hot biscuits and ate powdered egg omelets for the first time. We had mugs of hot coffee and bacon slices cut thick, Canadian style. Our enlisted men, segregated as was the military custom, ate on the other side of the tent. Afterward, we all sat around our tables, enjoying cigarettes and coffee. Then we hit canvass cots in the sleeping quarters nearby.

The next day, refreshed and relaxed, we climbed aboard our aircraft, now dusty and looking more like the veteran she was to become.

4

We rattled over the steel planks that dipped and pulsed under our weight and took off across the remainder of the Atlantic that lay between the Azores and our next destination, Marrakech, French Morocco. This place had a look of permanency; there were numerous white stucco buildings with shuttered windows and red tile roofs near the operations flightline. Built by the French years ago, these buildings were now occupied by American GI's. There was a bustling sense of activity and purpose as uniformed personnel hustled about. Numerous aircraft were dispersed around the tarmac, mostly B-17s like ours probably in the pipeline destined for the 15th Air Force.

The weather was hot and dry, as expected. From Marrakech we flew on to Tunis, the capital of Tunisia. We soared across the northern tip of Africa, looking down on the Atlas mountain range and the yellow, dun-colored bareness of the land that stretched ahead as far as we could see. The northern boundary of this vast area was clearly defined by the brilliant waters of the Mediterranean just off our port wing. Across the narrowest part of the Mediterranean Sea, to our left and behind us now, was the hazy outline of Spain. At the large and busy airport at Tunis, we serviced the plane once more. After showering at the transient hotel, Steve, Bud, Gary, and I took a brief walk around the city. An air of desolation was present everywhere; the city we saw was sparsely populated, its buildings pockmarked by bullets and damaged by tank artillery. I felt a bit uncomfortable walking in the streets and was glad to get back to our base.

The last leg of our odyssey took us around the southern tip of Sicily and across the toe of Italy to our destination, an airstrip near Gioia, some twenty-five miles south of Bari, where headquarters for the 15th Air Force was located. I made a decent landing on another PSP runway as we arrived in Italy just in time for lunch; a good omen, perhaps. Under olive trees next to the landing strip, we enjoyed cold cuts, fresh fruit, thick slices of freshly baked Italian bread, chunks of cheese, and water from Lister bags heavily treated with chlorine. Here we parted company with our B-17, which was turned over to the maintenance crew. We climbed aboard an olive-drab truck, one with an open cargo bed and hard wooden seats along the sides, and went for a two-hour ride across the rural countryside to Celone Field, an airbase fifteen miles beyond Foggia.

Celone Field was home to the 463rd Bomb Group that was commanded by Colonel Frank Kurtz, whose daughter Swoosie Kurtz, the television actress, was born while he served in Italy. His group consisted of four squadrons and was called the Swoose Group (half-swan, half-goose), named after the Colonel's airplane, "The Swoose." It was one of five groups in the 5th Wing of the 15th Air Force, all under the command of General Nathan Twining.

Here we were on the 8th of July unpacking our gear in the Army's standard four-man tent. Our new quarters included mosquito netting on each bed with the sides of the tent rolled up to let cool air in and hot air out. It was warm but not the sticky dampness of other places we had been. A single light bulb dangled from a wire in the center of the tent. As we settled in, I thought about our Air Corps brethren in England, in decent housing with warm bathrooms and solid roofing over their heads. Those guys really had it made and I was just a touch envious. They also had English-speaking people all around them. Here, the sound of Italian voices fell strangely on my ears.

TWO

Cadet Training

December 7, 1941, Pearl Harbor day, was a date that changed many lives all over the world. Those most directly affected by the Japanese assault on our Hawaiian bases that Sunday morning were young men of military age. I was nineteen years old.

Our country went on a wartime footing. The Propeller Division of the Curtiss-Wright Aircraft Engine Company opened a new defense plant in Beaver, Pennsylvania, in the spring of 1942. An old friend was now a personnel employee at the plant. I sought him out and was accepted as a draftsman to prepare drawings for the production of hollow-bladed steel propellers for our Navy fighters in the Pacific.

The war was not going well for America in early 1942. Thus when General Jimmy Doolittle led a surprise bombing raid on Tokyo with 16 Mitchell twin-engine B-25 bombers flown off the rain-slick decks of the aircraft carrier Hornet one cloudy, cool day in April, the morale of all Americans got a tremendous boost.

On June 30, 1942, I registered for the draft, as required by the Beaver County Draft Board. In mid-August, I received a notice from the Selective Service Board to appear for induction into the U.S. Army at Fort Dix, New Jersey, on September 20. This was quite a shock, for the last thing I wanted was to be a foot soldier. My only recourse was to volunteer without delay. I wanted to become a pilot, having already learned about being an officer and a gentleman from friends who had already volunteered as aviation cadets and were now in training. That was the ticket for me.

I debated whether to become a Navy pilot, but I heard their pilot exams were the toughest of all to pass. A troubling thought also

7

occurred that I might be shot down at sea or my engine might fail over water. Perhaps my imagination was too fertile, but the consequences of a crash landing in the darkness and being all alone in a vast ocean were too much for me. I decided to try for the Army Air Corps. At least I had a chance of walking away if I had to bail out over land. The recruiting officer arranged for me to take the written examinations that very day and when I passed he told me to come back the next week for the physical exam. Even though I was young and healthy, I worried about my eyesight because I had been doing close work for the past year or so.

The eye test included reading letter charts twenty feet away, then fine print held three inches from my nose. The color blindness test involved identifying light yellow numerals that were barely discernible in a squiggle of orange, blue, and green dots. Then came the most dreaded of all: the depth perception test. Seated in a dark chamber, I was given two strings attached to white pegs set on tracks about twenty feet distant. The task was to pull the strings and line up the pegs evenly. There was no way you could fake it; if you could not align them evenly you failed the test. I was wringing wet with tension by the time all the tests were over. It had taken four hours, but I passed.

A few days later, I was notified that my application for pilot cadet training had been approved. On September 9, 1942, I was sworn in as a reserve member of the U.S. Army Air Corps and instructed to stand by at home. It would be six months before my call to active duty. The draft board unknowingly had done me a huge favor, notifying me of their intention to induct me before I was twenty years old, the legal age for the draft. I had just enough time to volunteer in the Air Corps. Other young men inducted that fall ended up with assault forces that hit the beaches at Anzio and in the Pacific.

Now that I had been accepted for flight training, it occurred to me that I should take an airplane ride. One Sunday afternoon, I took a ride in a Piper Cub for $5 at a small airport nearby. After a ten-minute flight as a passenger I was satisfied that whatever was to come would not be too difficult. In a month or so, I quit my drafting position at Curtiss-Wright, concerned that I might fail future eye tests and be sent off to the infantry. My good friends at work were understanding and perhaps a little envious. I decided to take a trip alone to prepare for being away from home. I boarded a Greyhound bus from Pittsburgh headed for Norfolk, Virginia, and spent that night and most of the next day moving steadily eastward across gray, cloud-covered land. God, this was a big country. It seemed an eternity before we arrived at Norfolk, which was crowded and rainy. I could see the ocean with its beaches patrolled by armed U.S. sailors behind coils of barbed wire. There were uniforms everywhere; my first evidence that our country was at war.

I stayed at the YMCA for three days and two nights, and the sun never came out. I asked myself why I had come to Norfolk, because I didn't know a soul there. A dance hall was nearby, and for ten cents you could dance with any of the hostesses, but I didn't have the nerve to ask. Lots of sailors were there, and I felt out of place. I kept my Air Corps Reservist card handy in case anyone asked why I was in civilian clothes; no one did. The music was good and lively, which made me feel better.

* * *

In early January 1943, I went to work as a temporary laborer for the American Bridge Company in Ambridge. I worked outside under the overhead crane that moved heavy I-beams back and forth, getting them ready for shipment. Many a cold January morning I would warm my hands and feet at the wood fire in the fifty-gallon drum while waiting for orders to be filled. It was an easy job, and I practiced focusing my eyes on distant objects and on the still visible morning stars. I worried all the time that my 20-20 vision would fall below acceptable standards. Carrots were a regular part of my diet, for it was common knowledge that all aviators ate carrots to improve their vision.

At long last, my notice to report for duty arrived. March 3, 1943, was a raw, drizzly day when a mob of raw recruits, all from the greater Pittsburgh area, boarded day coaches in the cavernous Pennsylvania Railroad Station and headed for Nashville, Tennessee. My spirits were high and while I was sorry to leave the familiar world of family behind, going off to war was the ultimate adventure. I felt footloose and fancy-free, leaving no true love behind. I believed then, and still do, that young men going off to serve their country are better off being single, hence better able to concentrate on their job. This is particularly true if that job involves a fair amount of risk, such as flying airplanes.

NASHVILLE, TENNESSEE - MARCH 1943

We arrived in Nashville late the next afternoon, tired after a restless night sitting up and talking, full of questions, getting to know our new buddies, anxious to get on with it. The reception center was a vast, sprawling encampment covered by a pall of coal smoke. Hundreds of wooden, one-story, temporary buildings stretched as far as I could see. Each barracks contained about fifty bunks, spaced closely together along each side of the long narrow room. At the foot of each bunk was an olive drab footlocker, just like the Army issue blankets on each bed. There were two potbellied coal stoves, one near each end of the room. The latrines were in separate buildings where we would line up in the mornings to catch a glimpse of our faces in the common mirror as we tried to shave.

Days passed in a blur of activities. We were issued scratchy olive drab uniforms (ODs) and a greatcoat with a high stand-up collar that helped to ward off the damp cold and sharp spring winds. Heavy Government Issue (GI) boots kept our feet warm as we marched in formation to stand in long lines at the mess hall. The Army motto, plainly posted above the food line, said, "Take all you want, but don't waste any." I recall being on kitchen police (KP) duty and washing an endless stream of pots and pans, aluminum food trays, and assorted silverware until my back ached.

We recruits also served on guard duty, four hours on and four hours off for twenty-four hours straight. Our orders were to take charge of this post and all other government property in view. I guarded my post vigilantly, billy club at the ready, since we were not yet entrusted with guns. Luckily, I never had to issue the challenge, "Halt, who goes there? Advance and be recognized."

There were formations to meet, drills to practice, and lectures to attend that dealt with military courtesy and the dangers of venereal disease (the dreaded VD). We endured a series of shots that para-

10

lyzed our arms for days, causing some luckless souls raging fevers. We were not allowed off the base for the first two weeks. There was much talk about heavy doses of saltpeter being maliciously poured into our food to reduce our sexual drive. To this day, I am not certain there is any truth in this allegation. I never actually saw any of the mysterious substance and suspect it was all a hoax.

Our first open post was delightful. Those with passes boarded buses for the "Big City." Once in town, we new soldiers thronged happily through the streets, reveling in the sight of civilian folks again and looking for an officer to salute. I never found one, for most officers knew better than to be seen on the streets of Nashville unless absolutely necessary.

Girls were the primary object of interest. While at a movie on my second night in town, I spotted a cute blonde sitting nearby. In the darkened theater, we exchanged glances from time to time. It was not by accident that we left the movie house together and started to chat in the lobby. We shared an ice cream soda at a corner drugstore, and she let me escort her home on the bus. I was delighted—my first date with a Southern belle. There was no time for a real romance, but it was nice to meet someone who seemed to appreciate what young service men were experiencing. She later introduced me to the Grand Ole Opry where Minnie Pearl shouted "Howdeeee" to a happy audience of noisy recruits.

Back at the base, we were administered a series of aptitude and coordination tests, plus some psychological and physical examinations. I passed them all and was okayed for pilot training; now I could breathe more easily. Others were less fortunate and were posted to navigation or bombardier training.

One of my buddies was John Wolff, who had studied Morse code with me twice a week in Pittsburgh at the Air Corps training center. John was quite a ladies' man, with his shock of wavy blond hair, ready smile, and sunny, outgoing personality. He made friends easily, perhaps too easily, for he contracted VD on his first open post. John knew he would not pass the urinalysis test scheduled a few days hence. A lesser soul would have panicked, but not John; he simply asked the guy at the urinal next to him for some of his specimen and John submitted it for his own. He then reported to sick bay and

11

received some penicillin that cured his problem. John was a gambler, and luck was with him.

Mail from home was very important. It was our link to the comfort, joy, and stability of a family life now fondly remembered. We clung to those links as lifelines amid the stress and strain that we homesick and bewildered young men were experiencing. Besides my immediate family, there were some girls with whom I carried on long-distance relationships. Those lovely people were helpful then, more than they will ever know.

The music of that time is indelible in my mind. We listened to such popular records as Glenn Miller's *String of Pearls, That Old Black Magic* by Frank Sinatra, Tex Beneke singing *Chattanooga Choo-Choo* with Glenn Miller's Orchestra, Artie Shaw's *Stardust*, and the classic *Getting Sentimental Over You* by Tommy Dorsey. Suddenly our time in Nashville was up. I was slated to go to pre-flight school at Maxwell Field in Montgomery, Alabama. On April 2, our troop train departed for Alabama, filled with boisterous cadets who had a full month of duty behind them.

MONTGOMERY, ALABAMA - APRIL - MAY 1943

Maxwell Field was like a movie setting, with its broad, manicured streets winding past cool, shaded stucco residences with red tile roofs where the senior officers lived. There were tall date palm trees, green grass, and a fine golf course that we viewed with admiration when panting by on our three-mile morning runs. We were introduced to the practice of hazing by our upperclassmen with a visit to the post barber where barbarians (probably derived from the word barber) sheared off our hair leaving no more than a quarter of an inch on top and almost nothing on the sides. When eating we were forbidden to look directly at our plates, our food, the table, or any of our utensils. Instead, we were to fix our eyes on the distant horizon, supposedly to improve our side and distance vision. "Who are you looking at, Mister?," was the question most often asked by our tormentors at the table. Eating was a painful process. The knife and fork were only supposed to move at right angles. "Keep your backs straight. Keep your eyes front." Improves concentration, we were told.

Penalties or demerits were awarded for minor infractions of these rules. Penalties resulted in punishment tours that were walked off on the drill ground outside the barracks on Saturdays. We learned to form quickly into military groups for everything: meals, classes, physical training (PT), and even going to the post theater. We learned how to count cadence too: "Hup, Tuup, Threep, Forp," we all joined in. We soon knew how to quick-step, double-time, and route-step, which meant do it any way you wanted. We would double-time to the exercise field every day where hundreds of cadets, row upon orderly row, sweated in the clear, hot sunlight.

President Roosevelt toured Maxwell Field in early May. We were not told of his coming until we were formed on the field at parade rest. As his open convertible slowly cruised by, I caught a glimpse of FDR smiling and waving from the back seat, his car surrounded by a convoy of other cars. That was my only sight of the President, our Commander in Chief. We were all impressed that he had taken the time to look us over. None of us knew then that FDR was a polio victim and paralyzed from the waist down.

Our barracks were white, two-story wooden buildings. Standard bunks, each with footlocker, stood along the walls, with a broad aisle down the middle. The upperclassmen occupied the second floor, while we lowerclassmen were on the first floor. At least the latrines were on each floor, rather than outside as they had been in Tennessee. It was still crowded, however, and we had to look over each others' shoulders to shave, which was required whether you had a beard or not. One upperclassman endeared himself to us as we policed, picking up bits of paper, matchsticks, or any other foreign matter. "All I want to see is a lot of asses and elbows out there," he called out.

Our thirty days of servitude passed with agonizing slowness. We spent our classes studying aircraft recognition, Morse code (which I had already mastered), military courtesy, and other classification or administrative matters, which were often enjoyable, because it was our only time away from our tormentors. Evening hours were not sacred either. Woe unto him who failed to jump to immediate and rigid attention when an upperclassman appeared in his bunk area. Extra duty meant scrubbing latrines or other menial tasks. Every

Saturday morning there was an inspection by the company commander, or his adjutant, who often wore the dreaded white glove. Demerits and penalties flowed freely if the white-gloved finger discovered dust on tops of bunk rests, light fixtures, or any woodwork within reach. Thanks to our military planners, we were so busy from dawn to 9:30 P.M. that there was little time for homesickness.

Bob Hope visited our base that spring. His steady stream of jokes and one-liners putting down the base commanders, upperclassmen, and others in the limelight had us helpless with laughter. Marilyn Maxwell, Jerry Colona, and Les Brown and his Band of Renown were some of his entourage. He was a tonic to all and furnished joyful memories that lasted far longer than the brief time he spent with us. God bless him for all his services.

Suddenly, we were the upperclassmen and free to leave the post; oh my but we were spiffy now, so tanned and fit. The Jefferson Davis Hotel in town was the rally point. Although I did not drink beer or hard liquor in those days, there were others who did. More than one cadet was helped to bed at the Jefferson.

We had plenty of money to spend, since our pay was fifty dollars per month and our living expenses almost nothing. It was nice to order ice cream sodas, sundaes, or hamburgers and french fries at Liggett's or Walgreen's drugstore and flirt with the waitresses who seemed to like cadets' attention. *Coca-Colas* cost five cents from the battered coin-operated machine at our barracks and ten cents in town. Having a choice of how and where we spent our money made a big difference.

We usually sang as we jogged in formation along the wide streets of the post, feeling athletic in our blue sweat pants with white stripe and white T-shirts. I was a platoon sergeant, having won that position because of my height and military bearing I think, as much as anything. My job was to run at the rear of our platoon counting cadence and shouting instructions like, "Keep your heads up" or "Close it up, close it up." That was fun—I enjoyed my little taste of power.

By the end of May, we received our orders for primary flight school. I was to report to the Greenville Aviation School in Ocala, Florida. I was thrilled to learn that Silver Springs was there, the very place where some of those marvelous underwater scenes in Tarzan movies had been filmed. I was ready.

OCALA, FLORIDA · JUNE · JULY 1943

Our troop train chugged past one sleepy town after another, steadily easing its way into the Deep South. By midday, the air inside our coaches was stifling. Windows were thrown open, allowing gusts of cinder-tainted air inside; grimy dust settled everywhere. We gazed out on scrub pine trees that sheltered a few cattle in the pastures. Later we began to notice tall oak trees with Spanish moss dripping from gnarled limbs, and an occasional palmetto or scrubby palm. I loved Florida at first sight.

We arrived late in the afternoon, grimy, hot, and tired. A few trucks were waiting, and some civilians lounged about—not much of a welcoming party. A man resting on a big motorcycle introduced himself as one of our instructors. He had a darkly tanned face, a wide smile, and lots of white teeth. We loaded our gear on the trucks and headed out.

The Greenville Aviation School had two barracks, long, one-story buildings of white cement block with green trim; definitely not the military construction we were used to. Sidewalks along the buildings were covered with an extra wide overhang to provide shelter from rain or brilliant sunlight. The administration building had a tall flag-pole in front and was the centerpiece of the U-shaped compound. Several smaller buildings hidden off under pine trees housed class-rooms where we would be taught about aircraft engines, principles of flight, elementary navigation, basic weather, and aerodynamics. About a half mile distant lay the broad and grassy tarmac where we would learn to fly.

Primary training was given in the Stearman Trainer, or PT-17, which was quite a workhorse for the Army and the Navy. Two open cockpits were connected by a tube through which the instructor in the rear seat could shout instructions to the student in front. The double wings of dope-covered fabric had stout guy wires to hold them together. We had to step on the lower wing very carefully near the fuselage when climbing into the front seat. The top wing contained the gas tank. The PT-17 was a sweet, rugged airplane, although its fixed landing gear was a little close together and could cause a wing tip accident if you were not careful.

There were about seventy-five cadets in the class of 43-K and about fifteen instructors. The morning after we were processed, we marched to the flight line and stood in one long line facing our instructors. They were spread out at intervals of one to every five students and introduced by the Commandant of the 57th Flight Training Detachment, Captain Alba Kloppenstein. He made quite an impression, square-jawed and properly turned out, I took an instant dislike to him for no particular reason, although he reminded me of the enemy in one of the *G-8 and His Battle Aces* stories. We then counted off to learn who our new instructor would be.

To my delight our instructor was the smiling civilian with the darkly tanned face who had met us at the train station. I almost laughed though when he said his name was Al Sapp, because I had never met a Sapp before. However, we all came to respect and admire him in the two months we were to fly with him.

Mornings were the best time for flying, with the summer sky crystal clear and the air cooled by night breezes. By noontime, cumulus clouds popped up everywhere, causing our aircraft wings to jolt and our flight instruments to shake. We learned to tighten our seatbelts when practicing figure eights beneath these innocent-looking clouds.

We wore lightweight khaki helmets with goggles and headsets so we could hear Mr. Sapp's instructions. His voice was tinny but audible over the roaring engine. The rest of our flight uniform consisted of a one-piece coverall with zipper pockets for everything on the chest, arms, and legs so nothing could fall out during inverted flights. Most of us wore moccasins with no socks so that our feet would feel every quiver of the rudder bars.

After ten hours of instruction we were expected to solo the aircraft. It took me about twelve hours because I had difficulty keeping the nose of the aircraft straight ahead on takeoff. In exasperation, Mr. Sapp shut the engine down after another abortive attempt. We were at an auxiliary field, so at least no one could see me humiliate myself. We both had a cigarette by the side of the airplane and talked it through until I finally realized that when the aircraft's nose swung too far right I had only to apply opposite rudder to straighten out. The remedy was so simple that I could not believe my stupidity.

Mr. Sapp taught us all the basic maneuvers required by the military, such as takeoffs and landings, including some emergency landing techniques. We practiced controlled spins to the right and the left and gentle climbing turns heading 180 degrees from the original heading, known as a chandelle. The split-S involved rolling the plane over on its back and pulling the stick into your gut, immediately reversing your flight path, which was a lot of fun. We also did some slow rolls and snap rolls, but I wasn't too sharp on them because Al Sapp had broken his wrist in a motorcycle accident and had trouble demonstrating acrobatics.

We all dreaded the mandatory check flight by the military pilot to verify the work of our civilian instructors. I was the first student in our group chosen for a check ride and hoped that if I did well, perhaps it would follow that all of Mr. Sapp's group were okay. I sweated it out until after the takeoff roll. Over Silver Springs at 3,500 feet, the pilot asked me to do a four-turn spin to the right. I slowly pulled the nose of the plane to thirty degrees above the horizon and then reduced power while holding the nose straight ahead. Just as the plane was poised to stall, I kicked in right rudder, pulled the stick all the way back and let the Stearman drop like a stone, its nose straight down in a tight spin to the right. Once, twice, three times, we spun. At exactly three and one-half turns, I banged in left rudder, popped the stick forward to recover airspeed and started to climb back to altitude. It was a perfect four-spin stall—right on the money.

Before I could congratulate myself further, the check pilot pulled the throttle off and the engine died. That was his way of telling me to pretend there was an engine failure; it was up to me to find an emergency landing field and to land safely if I could. At 1,500 feet, there was not much altitude or time to waste. I stuck the nose of the plane down slightly to establish a safe glide and I looked around. Smoke from a small brush fire indicated winds were calm. Ahead lay a nicely cleared pasture with no cows in sight. I would try it but had to keep an eye on the fence at the near end, watch my airspeed, and also watch for other aircraft. I fishtailed the plane to lose some airspeed

17

because I was too high and maybe a little too fast. I kept talking silently to myself as I glided down, aiming for the near end of the pasture. Just as I was easing over the split-rail fence, the check pilot pushed his throttle forward and I climbed out of there. I had passed the test.

One other flight was particularly memorable. At the end of a practice session, I headed for the landing field and was startled to see a huge black storm cloud settling over the runway. I started a descent toward the rain-swept runway and prepared to land. Just the day before, Al Sapp had given me some useful advice about landing in a cross wind. Keep the nose of the plane turned into the wind and crab the plane sideways to keep your approach parallel to the runway. When you are just about to land, kick rudder at the last second to bring the nose of the plane straight down the runway. Be sure your landing gear is headed straight down the runway, not sideways. That way you'll avoid getting a wing tip and make a decent crosswind landing.

Luckily, I did just as he said and greased that little Stearman onto the runway as slick as a whistle, tail high, and with some power on. I rolled down the runway and across the field in the rain, tapping lightly on the brakes and making "S" turns so I could see ahead. I reached the hanger to find a pleased and smiling Al Sapp and a very disgruntled parachute rigger. The rigger was upset because the parachute I had been sitting on was soaked by rain draining down my backside. I didn't care and I was just glad to be back.

* * *

Weekends in Ocala were restful and relaxing. Most of the boys spent a lot of time in the local pubs, where I often joined them because I liked their company. There were occasional USO dances in town that the local girls attended and a movie theater on the square. My most vivid memory was of visiting Silver Springs, a tourist attraction that featured Ross Allen and his Alligator Farm. Allen wrestled monstrous alligators, to our horror, and never got hurt. Swimming in the springs was a real treat, with the temperature a constant 72 degrees and the water so clear and cool it was like swimming in air. Today, the reptile farm is gone, and a modern attraction now features glass-bottomed boats that meander over the springs, showing its underwater wonders to visitors from all over the world. Major hotels have built accommodations along the roads near the springs, which is now considered one of the top family attractions in Florida.

Flight training was nearing an end at Taylor Field. My flight proficiency report said that I was "deliberate, attentive to minor details." My overall rating was "A" for flight work as well as academics and "AA" for general pilot ability. Al asked me what kind of aircraft I wanted to fly when my training was over. It was time for him to include each student's wishes with his own recommendation. Naturally, I said fighters. Then he gave me the facts of life, that cadets over six feet tall were not likely to be selected for fighters, especially since the emphasis was on turning out bomber pilots. He explained that if I were selected as a bomber pilot, I would probably get trained as the first pilot, not the copilot. I took his advice and eventually became a four-engine pilot in charge of a ten-man bomber crew. If Al Sapp had not told me about the height limitation, I probably would have asked for single engine training and been assigned as a copilot on a bomber crew. I later learned that happened to many single engine jockeys.

While at Taylor Field, I logged 65 hours of flight time and made 285 landings in the old reliable PT-17. Today, this venerable plane, with some modifications, flies low-level insecticide missions over sugarcane fields in south central Florida. I knew I would miss the simple life in Ocala, including the evening retreat ceremony when the flag was lowered while canned music blared over the loudspeaker, and the reveille that roused us in time for breakfast. We had all the fresh eggs and bacon we wanted, grits, plenty of hot toast with jam or marmalade, and milk, coffee, or orange juice. There were fresh cantaloupes and other melons in season and an apple to stick in our flight suit pocket. We had it made, and we all knew it. My next assignment was to report to Cochran Field in Macon, Georgia, for basic training.

MACON, GEORGIA - AUGUST - SEPTEMBER 1943

Cochran Field was an abrupt return to full-fledged military life. The 275 miles between the peace and quiet of pastoral Ocala and Macon might as well have been 10,000 miles. It was another world.

19

Cochran Field was located near what is now Warner-Robbins Air Base, a huge installation covering the area that used to swarm with aviation cadets being trained in the single-engine, all-metal, Basic Trainer (BT-13), known as the Vultee Vibrator. The BT-13 was produced by the Chance-Vought Aircraft Corporation and was durable, honest, and reliable.

Our routine continued essentially as before, with a weekly schedule split between ground school and flight training. We were housed in the usual wooden, two-story, white frame structures. Each two-man room contained a desk, clothes rack, and two iron-framed beds. I roomed and became close friends with a fellow from Somerset County, which lies east of Pittsburgh in beautiful rolling countryside.

My memory of those days at Cochran Field includes feeling that there was more time to look at the passing parade without the constant urge to press ahead every minute of the day. I also began making more serious entries in *Dear Diary*. One of my pal's father came to visit us one weekend and urged us to stop smoking cigarettes. No such luck; we were both inveterate smokers and smoked like chimneys. Cancer was not a threat in those days. Even our Hollywood heroes Humphrey Bogart, John Wayne, Alan Ladd, Gary Cooper, and Clark Gable all smoked. Only Walter Pidgeon smoked a pipe.

My instructor was a cocky, bantam-weight fighter pilot who was not too impressed with my size or my ability to fly acrobatics, and my end-of-training report card so stated. I did well with the flight checks, since acrobatics were not that significant for a bomber pilot. Night flight training without the benefit of landing lights was scheduled during August when the moon was down. You really needed good night vision and depth perception to find the field and then put that rascal on the ground safely. We lost one or two airplanes in that exercise, but not one of my comrades, thank God. One cadet quit the program voluntarily because he could not adapt to night flying. He was transferred to Navigator's School without delay.

Low-level, cross-country navigation flights were fun, both at night and by day. The night before a round robin flight, I would plot the course on our flight charts, compute the time, distance, and airspeeds between each point, and then calculate our estimated time of arrival. We could not do this while flying, because we were busy picking out checkpoints below that kept us on course, such as railroads, water towers, rivers, and small towns.

Ground school classes included meteorology, instruments, link training, radio procedures using Morse code, and lots of physical training. The blazing August and September sun cooked us as we jogged around the brush over gullies and dry streambeds far out in the wilds beyond the airfield. We also were introduced to the high altitude chamber to test our reactions under artificial atmospheric conditions. We took off our oxygen masks briefly, because the air was very thin and contained little oxygen. The chamber then was rapidly depressurized so we would know how it felt suddenly to be without oxygen and return to sea level in an emergency situation. All in all, the experience was interesting and our bodies adapted with minimal pain and anxiety.

Saturday mornings were reserved for the weekly parade. All squadrons paraded around the sun-baked flight line in close formation and then passed by the reviewing stand. Twice I was the color guard, which meant that I carried the flag at the head of our formation. After the review, we were allowed off the base until Monday morning, unless you had really screwed up during the week.

The Lanier Hotel downtown was our favorite rendezvous. The lobby was crowded with cadets every weekend, coming and going night and day. Macon was a hospitable town of friendly Southerners who were easy to like. There was an active USO, plus a girls school about fifteen miles away. Occasionally, the school would hold a dance and invite cadets to attend. There was never a shortage of volunteers to fill the buses provided by the base motor pool. I attended once or twice and had fun dancing, romancing, and talking with the fine young Southern maidens.

Jesse Waldrip, a cadet from Georgia, was with me on an afternoon navigation flight on my twenty-first birthday. About an hour out of Macon we became lost in the clouds. We had to descend below the cloud deck to find some kind of landmark, a railroad or a town, and reorientate ourselves. Jesse was in front flying the plane, while I was in the rear navigating. As our Vultee gently glided lower and lower across pastures and woods, nothing looked familiar. We were getting pretty low and kept easing toward the ground, but Jesse did not seem to mind. Finally, I saw that we were closing fast on some trees just ahead and figured that Jesse was trying to give me a scare. He did, so much so that I nudged the stick back just enough that we went swishing over the treetops with no room to spare. A pretty close call. When we were safe and on track again, it turned out that Jesse thought I had the stick and I thought he had it. A near miss, but no harm done, except to my nerves.

The 40-hour check flight was one I dreaded, because I was still weak on acrobatics. When the check pilot asked for a snap roll to the right, I managed to do the only good snap roll I had ever done—it was a miracle. I had passed again. My instructor advised in his report that I was "slow in retaining instruction." Not the most glowing report, but I rated well on military neatness, attention to duty, cooperation, judgment, and common sense and was given an "A," or average general pilot rating. That was acceptable to me. I was just glad it was over.

Many of my classmates were assigned with me to advanced twin-engine training at Moody Field in Valdosta, Georgia. None of us were unhappy to leave Cochran Field. The heat rash and dog days of August were behind us, and I wondered if Moody Field might be more comfortable.

VALDOSTA, GEORGIA - OCTOBER - NOVEMBER 1943

The small country town of Valdosta is about 150 miles south of Macon. It was the shortest move I had made to date. Twin-engine advanced flight training was done in the AT-10, a nice airplane to fly after you got used to working with two engines instead of one.

My instructor was a quiet, competent guy with a good sense of humor. He was also a fellow Pennsylvanian and easy to get along with. The day after I arrived at Moody, my brother Chuck was assigned to the reception center at Nashville, eight months to the day after I had made the same trip.

On October 12, 1943, Italy declared war on Germany, her former ally. Good news for our allies, of course; but I felt that Italy's action would not make much difference in the war, although it was still one

22

less enemy to fight. By mid-October, I had soloed the AT-10 and mastered the technique of working two engines. There were many more instruments on the panel, but the basic controls were the same. The best part of twin-engine training was the comfort of having another pilot working alongside me.

Our classroom studies and flight line duties were much the same as before. We mastered the theory about how our cockpit instruments functioned and studied the murderous .50 calibre machine gun. There were courses on naval recognition and naval forces, general aircraft operations, flight rules and regulations, and the requirements for passing the instrument flight examination. This exam, called the 50-3, required the student pilot to be "under the hood" and unable to see out while flying the aircraft, relying entirely on instruments. For safety's sake, the instructor sat in the copilot's seat to watch for other air traffic. The student was entirely on instruments from takeoff to landing. Included in the test were a series of precise turns, several changes of direction and altitude, a recovery from an unusual position, and finally the radio orientation. The student pilot had to descend gradually and make an approach to the runway following the radio beam that was sounding in his headset. If all went well, the instructor would say, "Okay, you can come out now," and you would look down and see the runway. It was quite a thrill and very reassuring to know the radio beam was reliable and you were good enough to fly the beam home.

We were then introduced to the intricacies of formation flying. The AT-10 tended to wobble with every throttle change when I first tried flying in close proximity to another aircraft. Much effort and concentration was required to fly close to another plane without touching. It was hard work and not much fun, but I handled myself well as a beginner.

By early November, cool fall weather broke over the Southland. We were issued dark brown leather A-2 aviator jackets, which were much admired. Measurements were taken for officers' uniforms we would wear on graduation day set for December 5, 1943. I ordered a heavy silver and black onyx class ring with our class number 43K, to be picked up after graduation.

Our base theater was relaxing and provided cheap entertainment when time permitted; admission was only 25 cents. John Wayne starred in *Guadalcanal Diary*, a morale-boosting movie that was filmed in black and white and many years later touched up in color and shown on late night television.

I also enjoyed skeet shooting. If you had played a lot of football or baseball, as I had, shooting skeet came easily, because the principle of leading the target was the same. Out of my last round of 25 possible clay targets, I broke 22. Of a total 150 shots, I scored about 70 percent; not too bad. I often thought that if I had become a fighter pilot, I probably would have been a good air-to-air marksman. I would never know as a bomber pilot.

My final report at Moody said I was "steady, but tries too hard, nervous but thorough." That sounds about right; I know I tried hard. I logged 33:20 hours of dual instruction and flew 38:50 hours of solo time. There were 12:20 hours spent in the Link trainer practicing instrument climbs, turns, and descents and 20 hours of instrument time. As usual, my academic and off flight line requirements were all "A's." I was recommended for combat pilot training in heavy bombardment.

Some of us were singled out for consideration as flight instructors. The day before graduation, we were all in the operations lounge having coffee and shooting the bull. I thought to myself that I really did not want to be an instructor. That was not what I had in mind, but if that was what they wanted, I could handle it.

There was no need to worry. When my name was called, I strolled into the CO's office and promptly forgot all my previous military training. I failed to come to attention and render the proper hand salute; I realized my error immediately. The Captain smiled at me very coldly and left me standing at parade rest. I felt silly and self-conscious, not able to go back and make my entrance again. The damage was done.

The interview was mercifully brief. The captain asked me if I would like to become an instructor pilot.

"No sir," I responded, " I would rather continue with combat training and go overseas." After a few more comments, I was allowed to escape from that awkward business, this time making a snappy salute. Had I been married with a family to consider, I would have been interested in becoming an instructor, but I had a great curiosity and desire to see the world. With the enthusiasm and energy of youth, I was anxious to get on with the adventure before it was all over.

My hopes came true, and I received orders to proceed to Hendricks Field in Sebring, Florida, for training in the Boeing B-17 (B for bomber), the famed Flying Fortress. Graduation in the base auditorium was anticlimactic. My mother could not make it because of some unavoidable work; besides, it was a long, cold trip from Pennsylvania to Georgia for her to make alone. John Peacock's dad, an Army Colonel, was there to pin on his son's wings. It was a proud moment for both Peacocks, no pun intended.

* * *

We new pilots scattered to the winds. My train left late that night; I had 10 days leave plus three days travel time. The trip home was relaxing after the stress and constant pressure of the past few months. I ate and slept and looked out the window, content to let the world go by for awhile. We chugged up the eastern seaboard by way of Atlanta, Richmond, and Washington, moving northwesterly into Pennsylvania and along the Juniata River to Altoona with its famous horseshoe curve where I watched the last car in our train from the front car window. We climbed slowly up the steep grade of the Alleghenys, and finally into Pittsburgh. I felt pretty cocky, dressed smartly in my new uniform of forest green trousers and matching shirt with those shiny silver wings just above the left breast pocket.

From the Greyhound Station, almost across the street from Penn Station where I had departed for Nashville only last March, I called a friend and made arrangements to see her later. The air was chilly and the sky overcast, which was not unusual for Pittsburgh, where the steel mills pumped smoke and ash into the sky, day and night. The wartime economy was booming, and you could almost feel the strength and energy of the dynamo that was often called the Steel City.

The next ten days passed busily, happily, and in a bitter-sweet haze. I was delighted and pleased to be home and surprised at some of the changes that had taken place. My brother Chuck was now at Maxwell

Field for preflight training. My sister Nancy was a senior at Rochester High School, dating a lot, and corresponding with at least twenty servicemen. My mother was working as a practical nurse and in great demand. Joan was still employed at Curtiss-Wright and had married Charles Carson, who was now in Italy with a Railroad Engineering Battalion and doing fine.

We spent many happy hours sitting around the green kitchen table that I had made in my shop class at Beaver. Mom cooked her usual fine meals, and the coffee pot was always simmering on the range as we caught up with each others' activities. I experienced wartime rationing for the first time. Cigarettes were no problem, for I had brought along several cartons from the post exchange; but there were some shortages and waiting lines at food stores. Ration stamps were required to buy the basic necessities of life, but there were no serious shortages. Our neighborhood and our nation was not starving. My social calendar was full, and my main concern was juggling dates with all my girlfriends and keeping them unwitting of each other.

A girlfriend and I went to see Frank Sinatra at the Stanley Theater in downtown Pittsburgh. He looked so frail and tiny, alone in a bright blue spotlight on the big stage. What a marvelous voice he had then and has now, some forty or more years later. With those high notes gone and the smooth delivery of tone a bit huskier, his voice is still a pleasure to hear. In those early days, he sang with the mellow Tommy Dorsey band, which was exceeded only by Glenn Miller's band in national popularity.

After the show, it was fun to mingle with the crowds thronging the sidewalks and enjoying the pre-Christmas atmosphere. Most of the stores were open late, their windows bright and inviting. Every now and then a soldier or sailor would pass, and we would exchange snappy salutes, proud of the uniforms we wore and recognizing each other as fellow fighting men. Gimbel's Department Store window displayed a chubby Santa Claus who was bobbing and weaving, hands waving in the air, and laughing loudly as if he knew something very funny: "Ho Ho Ho Ho Ho, Oh Ho Ho Ho...." It was contagious, and I stood laughing with that crazy Santa until my stomach hurt. It was so good to be home.

The Time of My Life

America was approaching total mobilization. The draft age had been lowered to 18 years and raised to 36 years. The railroads were busier than ever moving a constant stream of tanks, trucks, jeeps, and related war material manufactured by the Detroit auto plants, which had been converted almost overnight to wartime production. Ten minutes looking at the volume of freight in the yards and one could gauge the extent of military production. Tanks covered by tarpaulin were in trains more than 100 cars in length. As far as the eye could see, trains were loaded with military equipment and even anti-aircraft guns; all waiting to move eastward toward embarkation ports. It was a sobering yet impressive sight.

I departed for Florida on December 15, my last day of leave. Time passed easily since I had a comfortable sleeper, and the meals were superb, served on freshly starched table linen in the dining car. To my pleasure, several of my old buddies were on board and we compared notes, embellishing accounts of our amours to make a better impression.

THREE

The Flying Fortress

Hendricks Field had wide, rugged runways shaped in a triangle, a rather unusual design that adapted readily from B-17 flight training to sports car racing after the end of World War II. The annual endurance test for sports cars has been held in Sebring for the past twenty-five years or more. Only a few old-timers, like myself, remember the spit-and-polish flight line and operations buildings, the row of student officer barracks, the bustling post exchange, and the headquarters building and Officers Club. Now pickup trucks and other commercial vehicles occupy the aprons and flight line ramps once filled with B-17s. I will always remember Hendricks Field as the place where my comrades and I learned about being aircraft commanders; the place where we learned to fly the ruggedly beautiful Flying Fortress.

SEBRING, FLORIDA - DECEMBER - FEBRUARY, 1944

We were commissioned second lieutenants and were expected to know more about world conditions and to take on additional responsibilities. Soon we would be given crew assignments before going overseas to combat: perhaps to the fabled 8th Air Force in England. None of us actually gave the future much thought. We were too busy learning our trade and having fun; tomorrow would take care of itself. Today I know better, but then I was a typical young man of that age: ready, willing, able, and anxious to do my job as well as I could. "Not for us to reason why," Kipling wrote of the fabled Bengal Lancers who were about to charge into the Valley of Death in India, "Ours is but to do or die."

Adrian Swain

I remember the Army Air Corps song we sang so proudly, swinging along in formation: "Off we go, into the wild blue yonder, off with one helluva roar; We live in fame or go down in flame. Nothing can stop the Army Air Corps." None of us took seriously the part about going down in flame. My goal was simply to learn how to fly an aircraft; I never once thought about dropping bombs. Not until I was actually overseas did I realize what all the long, hard training was meant to accomplish.

The B-17 aircraft was quite a change from the tidy, twin-engined AT-10. Four of everything were in the cockpit, including four propeller pitch controls and throttles, cowl flaps, wing flaps, and landing gear toggles. These all became familiar through daily use, so familiar I could find them blindfolded. My new instructor was Lt. Bill Miller, memorable for his gentlemanly way, his slight nervousness, and constant cigar smoking. He liked me because I was one of his best instrument pilots. On nights when the clouds were thick and fog covered the dark waters of Lake Okeechobee, he would put me on the controls and assign extra observers at both side windows to reduce the risk of a midair collision or flying into the ground. Miller was especially alert because one night just after Christmas, we lost a plane in the fog and five men perished. From then on, all training flights were canceled whenever fog moved into the area. I discovered later that Lt. Miller was a rookie instructor, and we were his first group of students.

I learned to love the B-17. It was very solid and stable, and I felt quite secure and confident looking out at those four Wright-Cyclone radial engines, each with 1,200 horsepower. The B-17 could fly on any two of her four engines and could limp home on one engine if there was enough altitude to glide most of the way. I could see through the navigation bubble into the forward compartment where the navigator and bombardier did their work; the engineer was behind me in the upper machinegun turret. He could see everything fore and aft, easily come down to talk with me, handle fuel transfer valves, or manually crank down our main landing gear should the hydraulic system fail. We pilots had it made: lots of well-trained help, good companions, and a neat little office.

Physical training kept pace with the increasing work load on the flight line, but even that was fun. Our time was less structured, and we frequently played touch football to keep in good shape. Our student pilots could have fielded a championship team if time permitted.

Some of the movies we saw at the base theater included *Kings Row* starring Ronald Reagan and Ann Sheridan. Reagan played the role of a young man whose leg was amputated at the knee by a sadistic doctor. It was a moving scene when our President-to-be clutched at the empty space below his knee and screamed, "Where's the rest of me?" Spencer Tracy, Irene Dunne, and Van Johnson starred in *A Guy Named Joe*, a beautiful story about Air Force pilots going up a cloudy stairway to heaven when they died. It was a very timely flick for wartime, as well as a touching story.

* * *

During altitude flights up to 20,000 feet, we used our turbo-supercharged engines to ascend to that cold, clean air where sunlight seemed white hot as it streamed in through the windows. We used our oxygen masks and carried bright yellow bottles about the size of small watermelons that were filled with enough oxygen to keep you alive for about 16 minutes. These bottles were useful when you had to leave your regular position and walk through the bomb bays to visit the rear gunners and the radio operator.

Occasionally we had long-distance training flights. Three student pilots were selected to accompany Major Bierney on a flight to Kelly Field in San Antonio, Texas. We did all the piloting, alternating with stints on the navigation and map table, while Major Bierney took notes on our performance. It was a routine weekend administrative flight. Monday morning we discovered that our crew chief had accidentally nudged our plane against a B-24 during the preflight warmup. It would take a few days to repair some minor damage to our B-17's wing tip. We could not believe our good fortune. For the next five days, we stayed at the Gunter Hotel in downtown San Antonio, which had great room service, fresh sheets, and excellent food. There also were a lot of pretty women in the area. It was delightful; we had one continuous but discreet party, our suite serving as headquarters. Major Bierney had friends in town, so we never saw him until it was time to depart.

Aside from our nightlife filled with movies, dining, and dancing, we saw the first snowfall in four years in San Antonio. We toured the famed Alamo where Davy Crockett and Jim Bowie fought and died in 1836 defending it against Santa Anna and his Mexican army during the Texas Revolution. We saw the shallow, muddy Alamo River as it meandered through the city, which you could jump over if you had a good running start. All too soon, it was time to return to reality and Hendricks Field.

Not all my training flights were so enjoyable. One afternoon while returning to base, visibility began to diminish and high clouds started to build up. We dodged clouds, flying in and out at an altitude of 2,500 feet, until I spotted the familiar triangular outlines of our field about ten miles away. I radioed for landing instructions and upon clearance landed nicely in a light rain and taxied to the parking area. We were met by a crew chief who asked me where we were from. We were the first B-17 ever to land at Punta Gorda, a little town north of Fort Myers. How embarrassing; I hurriedly filed a corrected flight plan with base operations and departed for home on the correct heading.

On February 16, 1944, most of our group received orders to report to Plant Park in Tampa for crew processing and further assignments. My flight book showed I had logged 105 hours, which included 20 hours of instrument time and 210 landings. A few married officers were assigned to Boca Raton on the east coast of Florida. I think being married had something to do with their assignment to that rather posh location.

TAMPA, FLORIDA - FEBRUARY - APRIL 1944

Plant Park was a sprawling mass of canvass tents crowded into the baseball field used by the Cincinnati Redlegs for spring training. I was assigned to a four-man tent with three bombardiers, all waiting for assignments. On rainy days, there was considerable mud in the outfield. We had to move carefully on duckboards to and from the latrines located under the grandstands.

The winter sun was hot as blazes. Hundreds of aircrew members milled around in winter uniforms, hot, sweaty, and getting more sunburned every day. It was a relief when we finally got orders to change to summer khakis.

In early March, the newspaper headlines were filled with news of daylight bombing raids on Berlin by U.S. aircraft from bases in England. We lost 68 bombers in one disastrous raid. A frightful number of men were downed—680. The news caused a rather fatalistic reaction among those of us who might well be doing the same thing in the near future. With the confidence of youth, however, we believed that such a fate could only happen to some other poor soul, not to any of us.

We attended courses on how to camouflage buildings and bulky objects, such as tanks, trucks, or a parked aircraft, using netting and variegated painting. For entertainment in the evening, we visited a dog track nearby. I never really got interested in betting on the dogs, who would frantically chase a mechanical rabbit at the end of a moving wand. The dogs never once caught the rabbit. I wondered whether they were really stupid or just liked to run. Rumor had it that leaves were being granted. Just for the heck of it, I put in for ten days and got it! I bought a ticket out of Tampa and was on my way by nightfall.

Spring was pleasant in the Valley. I walked by the Beaver River, breathing in that cold, crisp air that I remembered from just a year ago when I departed for Nashville; it seemed so much longer than one year ago. My sister Joan was ever the matchmaker, introducing me to a number of her girlfriends. For a guy without a car, I managed to get around pretty well by bus and train and with friends who had transportation. Ironically, I did not have a driver's license yet at the ripe old age of twenty-two, but I could fly a B-17. When my leave ran out, I left Pittsburgh on the midnight train as it began to drizzle. I was back in Tampa on the first official day of spring, glad to be in the warm sunshine with my buddies.

* * *

The battle for Cassino was raging in Italy. Our heavy guns and bombers had pounded the monastery on Mt. Cassino to rubble. The fortress-like monastery dominated the heights some seventy miles

33

southeast of Rome and was savagely defended by the Germans, who were successfully delaying the advance of the Fifth Army. It took months of yard-by-yard ground fighting and heavy casualties on both sides before Cassino fell, the final assault being led by Polish infantry.

Orders were posted assigning me to MacDill Field, almost within walking distance of Plant Park. Old Hendricks Field pals Charlie Smelser, from Maryland, and Bud Souther, from Florida, were also assigned to MacDill Field. My brother Chuck was at Douglas Field in Georgia in primary flight training.

On our last night at Plant Park, Smelser, Souther and I journeyed across the Gandy Bridge to the Coliseum in St. Petersburg, where we enjoyed the sight and sound of Ina Ray Hutton's all-girl orchestra. Ina Ray and her girls were terrific, playing fine danceable music, with Ina making an extremely attractive leader in her clinging gown under the bright spotlight. The ballroom could easily accommodate more than a thousand people either on the dance floor or seated in tables around the perimeter. The spacious hall was very comfortable, and the music beautifully amplified; a fitting occasion to end our stint in Plant Park.

GI trucks rumbled across town and deposited us at MacDill Field. Our temporary, one-story wooden barracks, now called BOQ's for Bachelor Officer Quarters, were poorly ventilated and unairconditioned but still better than the tents at Plant Park. The heat and humidity smothered us, as mosquitoes threatened to carry us off at night. We slept under netting, sprayed our rooms with bug repellant, kept all the doors and windows open, and sweated it out.

Soon after our arrival, a meeting was called to meet the base commander and other staff personnel and also to announce crew assignments. We had been looking forward to this day for a long time. Of the fifty-five 10-man crews assembled that morning, I only clearly recall those assigned to Crew 246 listed under my name on the Special Orders distributed. It read as follows:

2nd Lt. Swain, Adrian (NMI)	Pilot
2nd Lt. Haenel, Roy J.	Copilot
2nd Lt. Yankura, Stephen	Navigator
2nd Lt. Garrett, Bernard N. Jr.	Bombardier

Cpl. Coots, Robert E. Jr.	Engineer
Cpl. Swan, Richard R.	Radio Operator
Cpl. Vincent, Russell A.	Ball Turret Gunner
Pfc. Burton, Murdock T. Jr.	Waist Gunner
Pfc. Barnes, Richard E.	Tail Gunner
Pfc. Barnes, Ralph M. Jr.	Waist Gunner

Roy (Bud) Haenel, the copilot, came from Avalon, a small town near Pittsburgh on the Ohio River; we were practically neighbors. Our high school teams were in the same Class B football and basketball leagues. We got along fine, right from the start. Steve (Yank) Yankura, the navigator, was a smiling, happy-go-lucky guy with dark good looks, wavy hair, and a wide, white smile. Yank was also a fellow Pennsylvanian from New Castle, not far from Beaver Falls, and we became close friends.

Bernard (Gary) Garrett, the bombardier, was a skilled machinist from Detroit. He was married, and his wife visited at Easter and later delivered a baby boy while we were overseas. Gary had a wild streak and hit the bottle pretty hard sometimes, but he did his job and was fun to be around most of the time.

Dick Swan, the radio operator from Bristol, Connecticut, was very likeable and inspired trust and confidence. A natural leader, he had blue eyes, curly blond hair, and a calmness I admired. He started calling me Skipper. Dick married his girl in Savannah, Georgia, just before we shipped overseas in July. He asked for permission to get married, which was a nice courtesy. I gave him some time off to make the wedding arrangements and have a little honeymoon. All the crew gave him a noisy reception at the DeSoto Hotel downtown.

Ralph Barnes was a mild-mannered farmboy from Perrysburg, Ohio, who had perfect teeth. Probably the water in Ohio, with all those minerals and fluorides, kept him from getting cavities. Ralph was big and husky and had a sunny disposition. He smiled a lot, did a good job, and survived an extra-long tour of duty. Richard Barnes from Bristol, Connecticut, was a slender, brash young man full of pep and impishness, willing and eager, and very likeable. He started out as a waist gunner and ended up in the tail gun position.

Richard was dependable and showed a quick awareness of how the world operated.

Robert Coots was the senior noncommissioned officer on the crew. Married and from Alabama, Bob was short and stocky, strong, and quiet. He knew engines and the B-17 very well. He saved me from several stupid moves, and backed up Bud Haenel and me as we molded our green crew into a team. One time, we were flying a six-ship practice formation. Our B-17 had been cleared to fly, but the landing gear was not to be retracted. The dangling gear caused such a drag that our engines were gulping fuel at a horrendous rate as we used higher power settings to stay with the other planes.

I was so busy trying to keep up that I did not pay attention to the fuel gauges. Coots was watching and kept tapping me on the shoulder to tell me how low our fuel was getting until I finally realized we were in a real predicament. I radioed the flight leader about our problem, cut back on the power, and started a long, slow glide toward our runway 75 miles distant. Anxiously, we eased toward MacDill, keeping a safe altitude while gently descending in and out of clouds, our propellers at low pitch, and engines just above idle. As we neared the field, I asked the tower operator for a direct, straight-in approach. There would be no second chance if we missed and had to go around. Minutes later we drifted over the runway and touched down to the relief of all on board. While taxiing to the parking ramp, two of our engines sputtered and died, out of gas, dry as my mouth. That was a close one.

Murdock (Ty) Burton was a waist gunner and assistant radio operator. Ty was intelligent, perceptive, and a steadying influence on the crew. He was slender, yet tough and wiry, and reminded me of my brother Chuck. Russell (Vince) Vincent was a quiet, romantic-looking Latino from the Tampa Bay area. He went overseas with us but took with him an air-sickness problem that did not go away. Vince was supposed to be our ball turret gunner but eventually was grounded by the flight surgeon and finished his overseas assignment as a member of the ground crew. That is the original crew. We were a stalwart bunch, but no better or worse than hundreds of others like us. Each had a story to tell, as I am trying to tell mine.

Our Replacement Training Unit (RTU) activities started off with three days of inoculation shots. We were being prepared for a foreign climate somewhere in Europe, but no one knew where. We then were introduced to the ten-day workweek; a schedule where crews trained for seven days and then had a three day weekend. Each day started with a 4:30 A.M. wake-up call to which I never totally adjusted. One morning our whole crew slept in and missed roll call; we were punished by having to report an hour earlier all the next week.

"A plane a day in Tampa Bay," was a slogan often heard around the base. MacDill Field was at the end of a man-made thumb of land that jutted into Tampa Bay. If you missed the runway you were likely to end up in the bay, which occasionally happened. A phosphate plant to the east, with its tall smokestack, served as a landmark to identify the airbase from a distance. Its flashing lights were a welcome beacon to help locate the field at night. To the north lay the City of Tampa; to the south was the open bay with its deep water channel into the Gulf of Mexico. St. Petersburg sprawled to the west, a sunbaked, Old South city with wide, brick-paved streets, and hundreds of green benches on the downtown sidewalks. St. Pete was the last stop on the railroad that brought shivering tourists and the New York Yankees south to the sunshine and spring training at Al Lang Field. The *St. Petersburg Times* advertised free newspapers any day the sun did not shine. I wonder if they still do that?

St. Pete was our escape valve from the pressure cooker at MacDill Field. Many of us joined the St. Petersburg Yacht Club, since guest memberships were available to all officer trainees from MacDill. Many pleasant weekend afternoons were spent aboard small sailing boats we borrowed or rented from the Club. There were lots of young ladies, related to family members of the Club with whom we socialized. The occasional social affairs we attended, such as Sunday afternoon tea dances, were well chaperoned. Those were pleasant times in an old-fashioned place among properly mannered people who were doing their best to adjust to wartime conditions. I was grateful and appreciated all they did.

During our days in the air, we practiced dropping nonexplosive bombs filled with flour over the bombing range at Avon Park; made nighttime raids on the town of Venice to practice our bomb run timing; and fired our heavy .50 calibre machine guns at targets in the

Gulf of Mexico. This training was jammed into eight weeks, and each crew member worked hard honing his skills as we began shaping into a coordinated team. When the Allies invaded Normandy, we all felt great satisfaction and some disappointment too. I wanted to be part of it and felt that history was passing me by.

* * *

The buildup of late afternoon thunderstorms always seemed to accompany the summer heat. One afternoon, all our crews were attending a briefing, which was fairly long and drawn out, simulating combat briefings to come. After the weather officer spoke, other experts talked about armaments, radio procedures, navigation pointers, and crew and plane assignments. It began to get increasingly gloomy and humid in the darkened briefing room. Suddenly, I was startled out of my lethargy when someone a few rows ahead bolted from his seat shouting "Let me out of here" and ran out the door.

He was an engineer from another crew, a tall redheaded chap whom everyone liked and admired. He simply snapped from the gloomy tension and pressure in the room. I knew just how he felt, for I was uncomfortable too; but he never returned to his crew.

We constantly practiced takeoffs and landings with three engines, how to feather an engine in the air, and all the emergency drills until responses were automatic. We practiced ditching an aircraft in water after we made a normal landing and parked in our hardstand. Life jackets always had to be worn under the parachute harness. We knew how to crank down the landing gear if the hydraulic pressure fell too low. The radio operator learned never to leave his trailing antenna extended; that fifty feet of wire hanging below the plane would be ripped off instantly if not retracted in time.

By mid-June our training at MacDill was over. I had flown 370 hours in the B-17, which when added to the 208 hours logged at Hendricks, totaled 578 hours. We were ready for assignment somewhere as a replacement combat crew; the 8th Air Force looked like a good bet to me. New orders assigned us to Hunter Field in Savannah, Georgia.

HUNTER FIELD - PROCESSING FOR OVERSEAS

It was hot and muggy when we departed Tampa on the evening train. We were a bit sobered by what lay ahead, realizing that now we were leaving the practice field for the real contest. Our train moved quietly across the state and up the coast toward Savannah. By dawn, we could feel cool morning air, dryer and more invigorating. Our appetites were more than ready when the dining car opened for business; bacon, eggs, toast, grits, and hot coffee never tasted better.

Hunter Field was not far from town. Its runways were busy with aircraft activity, and its hardstands or parking revetments were crammed with shiny, unpainted B-17s, their aluminum alloy wings and fuselages glinting in the bright sunlight. We spent eleven days at Hunter Field being processed to go overseas. We completed wills and powers of attorney and were issued new summer flying clothes including gloves and khaki baseball caps with long bills. We were now members of the 3rd Air Force Staging Wing. Most importantly we took command of a brand new B-17G Flying Fortress and were ordered to proceed to Dow Field in Bangor, Maine, for further dispatch to an undisclosed overseas destination.

Somewhere in all of this, Dick Swan managed to get married the weekend before our departure. The tavern at the DeSoto Hotel was the scene of the reception. We all toasted the new bride and groom and were particularly polite to the military police who patrolled the area. Some of the crew got carried away with the excitement and had headaches to prove it the next morning.

I was delighted that the adventure into the unknown was about to begin but disappointed that I would not have a chance to visit the Valley. I realized that the prospects for the future were definitely brighter; to look ahead is usually much better than to look behind. How often, after all, does a young guy from West Bridgewater get a chance to fly a brand new B-17, worth about a quarter of a million dollars, across the Atlantic?

We tested the aircraft and swung the compass on the ground to verify we were reading the same headings in the air. We also checked the Norden bombsight for in-flight accuracy. Everything was in A-1 condition, and we were all very proud of our ship. Dick Swan and the boys named her *Hell on Wings,* and before long the name was on the nose of our B-17. We were then instructed to pack our personal gear. One B-4 bag and one duffel bag per man could go with us on the ship, with one extra duffel bag per man to follow by boat. It took almost six months for my extra duffel to arrive, but by then I had forgotten what was in it.

On June 30th, we fastened our seatbelts and powered up those big new engines. Surging off the runway, light as a thistle, I curved her around to a northerly course. We cruised easily at 11,000 feet, enjoying the ride and comfortably cool air at that altitude. Speeding over Manhattan, we looked down on ant-like bathers at Jones Beach and glimpsed the Statue of Liberty. It was a glorious day, the sky blue, clean, and bright. We soon started a gradual descent over New Hampshire preparatory to landing. The Grenier tower operator cleared us to land at Dow Field and bid us good day.

Once on the ground with engines shut down, we went into the operations office. Steve Yankura appeared flushed and uncomfortable and said he felt feverish. We checked him into the base hospital where his temperature was found to be 102 degrees. He was put to bed in the observation ward immediately; what a way to spend your last weekend in the States. Steve was stuck there with the flu for the next three days, while the rest of us were restricted to the base for security reasons.

The next day after Steve was released from the hospital, we flew from Dow Field to St. Johns's, Newfoundland. It was so far north that there were eighteen hours of daylight every day. Our barracks were primitive but solid, their gray painted exteriors scoured and streaked by the harsh winds that blew most of the year. The bleakness of the area was depressing, especially after the green lushness of Florida.

The 4th of July, however, was a brilliantly sunny day. Several of us took a hike outside the base and discovered a fine lake called Dead Man's Pond. Its waters were created from melting snow from the past winter. Tall pines encircled the lake, creating a very private setting. There were other hikers too, some fishing and others just sunbathing. Sparked by the warmth and brightness of the day, I impulsively took off my clothes and dove in.

I felt as though I had instantly turned blue. I bravely tried to swim a few strokes, willing my icy body to respond; but it was too cold. I fairly jetted out of that ice water, to the amusement of sunbathers more cautious than me. My last swim in the States was not soon forgotten.

After supper, we were briefed for a midnight departure that would take us across the Atlantic Ocean to the Azores. The winds aloft were favorable at midnight for the 1,700 miles that lay between St. John's and those small Portuguese islands off the coast of North Africa. Our final destination was still a military secret contained in our sealed orders that were not to be opened until we were in the air.

FOUR

The Swoose Group

Upon opening our orders, we learned that we were headed to Celone Field in Italy, home of the 463rd Bomb Group. Our crew was assigned to the 774th Squadron, commanded by Major Emerson Tolle. We all met the Squadron Commanding Officer (CO) and his staff officers and had a day or so to get acquainted with other personnel. Each squadron was responsible for the care and maintenance of its personnel and aircraft. For most of us, the mess hall was the most important part of our unit. The officer's mess hall also served as our "O" Club in the evenings. It was a simple one-story rectangular building with a flat roof supported by crudely mortared tufa stone walls. Two windows provided light but almost no ventilation. It had rustic charm and was furnished with solid wooden tables and decent chairs. Our meals were served by a swarthy Italian man who spoke little English but was pleasant and willing to please. He served as short-order cook, baker, waiter, and dishwasher. He was always busy.

Our basic military menu was improved by the addition of fruits and vegetables from the local markets. All vegetables were washed in chlorinated water to prevent infections. We were served powdered eggs and reconstituted milk, which had a definitely chalky taste. Usually we did not complain about the food, but some of us found the daily ration of a giant Atabrine tablet literally hard to swallow. Atabrine tended to turn your skin yellow but was taken to suppress malaria, which was prevalent in this area.

Our bathing facility was a stone and mortar building with a flat roof about eight by ten feet in size. A couple of shower nozzles were gravity fed from a hot water tank on the roof. Hot water was scarce and available on a first come, first serve basis. In the fall and winter, the cold weather and limited supply would make this facility obsolete. Within a month, most of us opted for the ten-mile truck trip to Foggia every weekend to use public shower facilities where for a few lira you could get all the hot water you wanted.

Our latrine was a separate but equally spartan facility, a "two-holer" that was drafty on windy days and located on a side path near our sleeping area. It was not a place where you were prone to linger. Shaving was best accomplished by using our steel helmet filled with water heated over the flame from a can of Sterno. Small, Army-issue stainless steel mirrors were fine to see by. All in all, keeping clean-shaven without a bathroom was done easily right in the privacy of our own tent.

The single runway at Celone was about 6,000 feet long and oriented northwest and southeast to take advantage of the prevailing winds that blew from the Adriatic Sea. Line mechanics performed their maintenance right there on the hardstands off the taxiways, rain or shine. Our control tower and operations building also served as storage facilities. On mission days we would check out parachutes, survival kits, navigation charts, and boxes of rations for in-flight lunches.

The day after our arrival, I was taken for an orientation flight and checked out in formation flying. By the 13th of July, I was scheduled for my first combat mission as copilot. It was standard procedure for new pilots to fly five missions as copilot with an experienced pilot and crew before flying their own missions. Our mission was the German marshalling yard at Verona, Italy.

The squadron formed into its group pattern and headed for Verona in northern Italy. At approximately 22,000 feet, we lined up for our bombing run, which required straight and level flight for a minimum of two minutes, enough time for the bombardier to track and lock his bombsight on the marshalling yards below. We were most vulnerable to fighter and antiaircraft attack during this period. When we were about four minutes out, the pilot motioned for me to put on my steel helmet, which was stashed under my seat. I had never worn one before and clumsily put it on over my regular cloth helmet and oxygen mask. I saw some scattered bursts of gray-black smoke smudge the sky ahead. The aircraft in front of us began to open their bomb bay doors, and we did too. Just as we steadied on our bomb run, my steel pot slipped off my head and tumbled into the bombardier/navigator tunnel below, hopelessly out of my reach. Feeling naked and chagrined, I endured this baptism of fire and tried to ignore the threatening shellfire bursting about us.

I witnessed the abrupt appearance of "ack-ack" puffs and could see a dull redness in the center of some of the bursts and almost see the hot shards of steel that came ripping out of the center. For the most part, the sound of exploding shells was muffled by our roaring engines; occasionally a burst was close enough to hear a distinct "whump" like a truck backfiring. The airbursts were pretty in a way, but vicious and malignant in their intent to knock us out of the sky. Suddenly, our aircraft lifted slightly in the air as our bomb bays emptied their heavy load. Then came the steep turn away, all of us following the leader, diving slightly to gain airspeed, eager to get the hell out of there.

After it was all over, I thought it was not too bad; only forty-nine more missions to go. Every combat crew member was required to fly fifty missions, but some missions counted double because the targets were more difficult. The Verona sortie counted as a single mission because it was not too lengthy and there was no enemy fighter opposition. My first mission was a milk run compared to others. Most of them were deep into Germany against heavily defended targets more than 500 miles from home; these sorties counted as doubles.

Taking advantage of fine summertime weather, our crew flew every day. By the end of July, we had completed twenty missions. By mid-August, the stage was set for an invasion of southern France. Its purpose was to relieve pressure on Allied troops surging eastward from the beachheads of Normandy, where the invasion of June 6th had first stunned the enemy. Now the Germans were digging in and resisting stubbornly. Prime Minister Churchill (Winnie) and Generalissimo Joseph Stalin (Uncle Joe) both wanted a second front. Winnie wanted to attack the soft underbelly of the Nazi empire from Italy, and Uncle Joe wanted a second front anywhere that would relieve his troops fighting the Nazis on the western front of Russia.

For the past two days our group had been targeting enemy shore batteries along the coast of southern France. At our next briefing, the senior operations officers scheduled themselves to go on the mission, a sure sign that something special was in the offing. The 463rd BG was briefed to support the invasion of southern France by knocking out bridges over the Rhone River. This was to deny German troops with their equipment use of these bridges to retreat toward the Fatherland. Our specific target was the bridge at Valence. We were instructed to fly at 15,000 feet (a fairly low level for our B-17s) and drop 500-pound demolition bombs. We were to fly a squadrons-in-trail formation whereby each squadron of six ships was to drop their bombs together. Each squadron would follow the lead squadron, one after another, over the target so that at least one of the four squadrons should hit the bridge and knock it out. No fighter opposition or antiaircraft opposition were expected in the area; it would be a piece of cake. Our bombardier, Garrett, was happy. This was his big chance; his bombs might score the big hit. I was happy as well, because this would be my 32nd mission, more than halfway through.

All of our crew were ready, except Bud Haenel, whose place was being taken by Nyles Jones, a new pilot flying his first mission. Yankura, Garrett, and Ralph Barnes were in the front of the aircraft with us; while Swan, Dick Barnes, Coots, Ty Burton, and Morris Vincent manned the rear stations. As we stowed our personal gear, I noticed Coots and Garrett carefully cache two ripe cantaloupes in the bomb bay. Coots said they planned to eat the melons on their way home from France. A smart idea, as our regular lunch of dry crackers and cheese from the K-rations left something to be desired.

Five minutes before engine start-up we climbed aboard. I walked carefully past the two waist gun positions, around the ball turret gun, through the radio room, and across the narrow catwalk between the two bomb bay doors. There were 12 500-pound bombs hanging there, yellow bands around the nose, ugly, and deadly. The bombardier was to arm these weapons by pulling the firing pins after we were airborne, usually over the Adriatic when gunners test-fired their .50 calibre machine guns.

Jones was in the right seat, adjusting his harness and flak suit, which was like a baseball umpire's chest protector. We could either sit on it to protect the family jewels or wear it over our chest to protect the heart and lungs; I wore mine over my chest. There was a half-inch thick armor plate on the back of my seat, and the ground crew had padded the seat bottom with a spare piece of flak suit material, so I was in good shape for this trip.

I slid open the pilot's side window to allow fresh air to circulate. As the other aircraft started up, we busied ourselves with the ritual of engine priming, starting, and ignition. One after another, our Wright cyclones fired up, sending smoke swirling rearward in the slipstream. The triple-blades of our propellers blurred with speed, and our plane began to quiver with power, ready to roll. We got the green flare from the tower and completed our radio checks. Each plane slowly moved after the other for takeoff. The wheat fields in the valley fifteen miles or so north of Foggia trembled with the force of B-17 Flying Fortresses taking off from Celone. Each aircraft climbed out slowly and carefully, heavy with fuel and a full bomb load, and circled until the usual pattern of six ships in two V's of three was complete. (Sometimes we flew seven planes, if our maintenance boys could get them all in commission; the seventh ship was known as Tail-end Charlie.) Our squadron continued to circle and climb until all four squadrons were in a compact, diamond-shaped formation.

I was piloting the number two plane on the right wing of our squadron leader as we flew a northwesterly course across Italy, skirted Switzerland to the south, turned west into France crossing Mount Blanc, and looked down on the Rhone Valley stretching away to the south toward the French Riviera. The sun was bright and pure as we began making a lazy 180-degree curve that would allow us to parallel the bridge at Valence. The cockpit was warm at 15,000 feet. We were used to being at 22,000 or 25,000 feet where the outside temperature was often 15 to 25 degrees below zero; even though on oxygen, the temperatures were comfortable. I unzipped my flight jacket a bit and left my .45 automatic hanging by its holster on my hip, instead of stowing it under my arm as I normally did. Our squadrons were now flying in-trail formation; the plane ahead of us was opening its bomb bay doors.

German 88 millimeter antiaircraft guns can be fearfully effective at high altitudes if their range finders are not confused by chaff (bundles of aluminum foil dropped to simulate other aircraft formations). At our relatively low altitude of 15,000 feet, we were easy to estimate. The first ominous black burst appeared dead ahead about 100 yards away, dangerously close. A second burst quickly followed, about 50 yards away—right on our track. I remember thinking that they were going to get us. The third burst whumped into our nose section from below. Our ship reared up and then veered toward the other planes in the formation. Smoke, blasts of air, and flame poured back around our pilot seats, obscuring our view. Another horrible thought was that we could blow up if fire reached a gas tank. Stunned and speechless, I reached for the alarm bell and flipped it on.

I looked at Jones, stiffened in his seat and gave him the thumbs out signal. The intercom was silent, probably because my radio connection was broken. I righted the aircraft, tried to steady her, and slapped on the automatic pilot switch, hoping it would take hold. Our bomb bay doors were open, our bombs still hanging on their shackles about 10 feet behind me. I was filled with panic as I dropped into the narrow space between our seats, searching for the exit door. The door was missing—someone had already bailed out. I looked around and could not see anyone. Steve and Garrett were probably blown away at their stations, or maybe they had gotten out. I could not see whether the engineer had gotten out yet. The urge to escape, to survive, to live, was overwhelming. I had to get out of there.

Crouched on my knees, I thrust my head and shoulders into the roaring lash of air outside the escape hatch. I suddenly realized I had forgotten my chest pack and had to find it. I pulled back and reached for my chest parachute stowed under the pilot's seat. I snapped one parachute ring to the chest harness ring, tucked the chute under my left arm like a football, jammed myself headfirst into the void, and was sucked into space. The roaring blast of air, rushing by at more than 150 miles per hour, stopped. I opened my eyes. I was spinning earthward like a tumbleweed out of control, cartwheeling head over heels. Reflexively, I extended my legs and arms and felt the spinning stop. Now I was spread-eagled on my back, looking straight up into a cloudless blue sky, softly cushioned on air. There was no sense of falling whatever. Thank God, I made it; I was flooded with a feeling of relief. Quickly, I reached for the D-ring (release) on my chest pack. It was gone—not there. I looked around for the chute and told myself not to panic. There it was, high above, twisting and turning. It dangled at the end of the extended left riser, which had been pulled loose from the chest harness by the force of the wind. Carefully I grabbed the chute, not letting it slip off the harness and gently pulled hand over hand, until I had it. I snapped the remaining ring of the parachute onto the vacant ring on the chest harness.

Still on my back and free-falling at more than 100 miles per hour, I pulled the D-ring and tossed the chute pack skyward. The 24-foot white canopy snapped open with a stiff jolt. I bounced from the shock like a yo-yo on a string and then hung there suspended in the harness, safe but afraid to move lest I fall out. Everything seemed to be holding together, so I relaxed, content just to drift silently downward. I looked down and around, listening. There was no rumble of aircraft, no sound of gunfire or bombs exploding, no sign of other parachutes. Below in the countryside, trees and meadows were becoming distinct. There were orderly farm fields, some thickly wooded areas, and vineyards here and there. There was no sign of the Rhone River or the town of Valence. The only sign of modern man was the railroad track. Standing stationary on the track were a dozen or more freight cars with no engine. First I wondered if the train might be filled with German troops, but that was not likely because there was no engine. Trees that first looked like bushes now were getting to be large as life. I suddenly realized that I was heading right for those freight cars.

Twisting gingerly on the chute risers, I managed to sideslip my chute just enough to miss the last car on the train. I crunched down onto the rock ballast alongside the track; no damage done, thank God. I quickly gathered my collapsed parachute, anxious to hide the evidence. There was no time to dig a hole. A freight car door was open. I looked in; it was empty and smelled of hot dusty wood and melting tar. I hastily piled the soft mass of silk into a dark corner and got out of there.

Bordering the railroad track was a vineyard, beautiful green acres of grapevines, three feet tall, in perfect well-tended rows. I dropped on my stomach and crawled on the warm sandy ground between the rows, away from the train as fast as I could. The only sound was that of my own breathing. At least I was moving, doing something. I crawled far into the vineyard, stopping now and then to listen, but only heard the sound of insects and birds. Was it possible that nobody saw me drop from the sky? I crawled and listened, then crawled and listened some more. Maybe I would wait until darkness; but there were hours of daylight left. At the far end of the row, I stopped and took inventory. My .45 Colt automatic was missing, blown away in the wind. I cursed myself for being so careless, for wearing it on my hip like a John Wayne character. I still had my sheath knife, though, laced inside my trousers to my left leg just above the boot.

Someone was coming; I could hear voices in the distance. I peeked out from the grapevines but saw nothing in the country lane that ran alongside the field. The sounds were coming from where the lane curved into a wooded area. Still as a deer in the brush, I listened. One of the voices was soft and melodious, a girl or woman. Then two people appeared, both in civilian dress, a woman and a younger man strolling along as if out for a walk in the park. I stepped out into the lane, waiting until they saw me. They stopped and stared, frightened, tense. I extended my arms, hands open, and started to walk slowly toward them, calling out, "I am an American, American."

The young lad, about fourteen years old, understood me. We shook hands and stood in the lane trying to talk to each other, with me telling him all about being shot down and landing in the parachute, knowing no French. He told me his name was Pierre, while talking excitedly all the while in French with Germaine, his aunt, who did not speak English. Pierre clearly understood that I needed help and said we must hurry. I noticed that he was wiry and of medium height, with a tanned face, dark hair, and alert brown eyes. His aunt was taller and slender, with light brown hair tied back. She wore a simple summer frock and walked along quietly as Pierre chattered on, saying we would go to their farmhouse, which was less than a quarter mile away. Their two-story farmhouse stood off the lane and on a long driveway shaded by trees. Pierre's mother and younger brother Michel met us, and there was more urgent talk among them. While his mother gathered some food, Pierre explained that he would take me to a cave in the hills nearby for safekeeping. German patrols were active in the area and would kill everyone in the house if I were found there. Pierre's father was still at work at his lumber mill in town and would come to see me later.

Pierre led the way, carrying a bag of food that contained a loaf of home-baked bread, several white cheeses, some rosy peaches, and a bottle of red wine. We took a trail into the woods behind the house and ducked off the trail down a bushy slope into a hillside clearing. There was a small cave on the side of the limestone hillside, half-hidden by bushes, yet open to sunlight and fresh air. There was room enough for two or three people. The curved opening was about ten feet wide at its base and eight feet high at the center. Its roof sloped backward and down to the rear of the cave about ten feet away; the floor was sandy dirt. Pierre left me there, promising to return tomorrow. For a recognition signal he would whistle the melody ". . .it's a long way to Tipperary, it's a long way to go." He asked me if I knew the song and I said of course I did; but he whistled it for me to make sure. We then shook hands, and he disappeared into the bush.

It was quiet and time to take stock of the situation. My .45 was gone, but I still had the K-bar sheath knife; a lot of good that would do if a German showed up with a rifle. I had a slight flesh wound on my left shoulder where my jacket was ripped by some sharp piece of metal. My right ankle was a little sore from landing on the rock ballast by the freight cars, and my teeth ached from sinus pressure changes caused by free-falling from three miles up. I estimated I had opened my chute about 2,500 feet above ground, because it was not very long after it opened before I hit ground. My cap was gone, as well as my sunglasses.

I was wearing summer khaki pants and a long-sleeved shirt with 2nd Lieutenant bars on the collar and silver pilot wings just above the left breast pocket. Inside my flight jacket I found a treasure: two packs of four cigarettes each wrapped in cellophane, but very old and musty. My regular pack of cigarettes went down with the plane. Best of all, I found my escape kit. It was a watertight, plastic packet containing a map of Europe printed on oiled silk about two feet square. It was fairly detailed, but nowhere could I locate Valence; Lyon was the nearest town I could identify. The kit also contained iodine, bandages, a morphine Syrette™, water purification tablets, and matches in a waterproof container.

It was late afternoon by now, a long time since I had eaten breakfast in that other world so safe and far away. As I ate bread with slabs of tasty goat cheese, cut with my sheath knife, I wondered how the invasion was going. Even more, I wondered how the rest of my crew were doing and whether they survived. My soul was flooded with guilt that I had not done a better job of getting them out of that mess. I had been too trusting of the briefing officer, who said there were no antiaircraft guns in the area. I had allowed my guard to drop and had not prepared the new pilot properly; he might be dead now. I knew now that we had flown the mission at a dangerously low altitude—we were sitting ducks. I later learned that one other plane had been shot down. Twenty men were out of action, death and destruction had been brought to innocent civilians, and for all I knew, the bridge at Valence was still in use.

The first night in the cave on the cold ground was not very restful, but I finally slept, exhausted by the trauma of the day. I thought of home, of my Mom and family, and longed to be safe with them, not here in this fearful place. I said the Lord's Prayer and remembered the words of Ralph Waldo Emerson, which my Mom had sent me in a letter:

> *So nigh is grandeur to our dust,*
> *So near is God to man,*
> *When duty whispers low, "Thou must,"*
> *The youth replies, "I can."*

* * *

I remained in the cave area for three days, waiting for the immediate threat of Germans to pass. I felt sure that American forces had landed successfully and would soon be in the area. Besides, the Free French Forces Interior (FFI) were in the countryside and would help if they could.

Pierre's father, Jean Laurent, came late in the afternoon of the second day. He was a short, plump, balding man and owned a lumber business in town. Mr. Laurent had been an aviator in the Lafayette Escadrille during World War I. It was hard to believe that this middle-aged businessman had been a fighter pilot. We discussed escape plans. I would have to discard my military clothing, of course.

The first plan was for me to ride on the back of Mr. Laurent's bicycle across the Valence Bridge past a German checkpoint. Pedestrians and bicycles could use the bridge, but no heavy traffic was allowed. Once across, I would be delivered to the FFI, which was fine. However, getting past the checkpoint on the bridge worried me. Pierre said that I could pretend to be a mute if the guard stopped me. I thought to myself, what would the guard say when he saw my size twelve army boots; that would be a dead (pardon the pun) giveaway. I told Pierre that this plan was not a good idea. We would all be killed this way. I could not picture myself on the back of a bike peddled by a rather short Frenchman, being stopped on the bridge, and then me standing beside him. I am over six feet tall, and we just did not look like a father and son. I think Pierre's father was happy when I turned down the scheme.

A much better plan evolved the third day. Clothes were found for me to wear: black civilian pants that were six inches too short, an old, white long-sleeved shirt, and a dark beret; I would keep my army boots. In exchange, I gave my flight jacket to Pierre, my collar insignia bars and the contents of my escape kit to father Laurent, and my pilot wings to Aunt Germaine. I kept only my sheath knife and dog tags on a chain around my neck. The new plan called for an FFI escort to drive me to their headquarters somewhere near Grenoble, taking a route that avoided checkpoints.

Around mid-day, I followed Pierre from the woods to their farm-house where three rough, rather sinister-looking men were waiting by an ancient, black, chrome-trimmed Citroen. The four-door sedan had a cylindrical, boiler-like tank strapped on the front fender, part of a charcoal-burning device that made fuel that powered many civilian vehicles in petrol-starved France during the war. High speed was not possible; but who cared, it worked.

The three Maquis, or FFI men, were polite yet taciturn, direct in speech, hard-eyed, and suspicious. One of them seemed to be in charge. He asked about my .45 automatic and was quite disappointed when I told him it had been lost. To make up for the loss of the weapon he had hoped to gain, I unstrapped my sheath knife and presented it to him. He tested the blade with his thumb, grinned at me, and said it was okay. Goodbyes were brief. I gave Pierre my squadron mailing address and purposely did not write down his name or address; he said he would write. Then it was time to go. A driver and one guard sat in front, the short leader and I in the rear. The small vehicle was crowded but was comfortable enough.

We puttered along country lanes and quiet secondary roads. Traffic was as sparse as our conversation; only a few bikers and an occasional pedestrian were visible. Traffic picked up when we reached a town called Romans. There were homes, commercial buildings, and more people walking or on bicycles. We slowed down and turned into what appeared to be the town square, where I saw gray-clad troops strolling around. I slid back in the seat as we drove across the square, hoping no one was looking. The leader was unconcerned, so I decided not to worry. He turned and asked with gestures whether I would like a drink.

Surprised, but agreeable to anything he wanted, I nodded. The driver abruptly turned into a narrow, cobblestoned street off the square and parked. We entered the side door of a small tavern that faced the open square. I could see civilians walking about and beyond them barricades made of wooden triangular posts strung with triple strands of barbed wire. A dozen or more German soldiers were lolling about behind the barricades, some airing their bedding, others smoking cigarettes, at ease in the afternoon sun and completely oblivious to our presence.

Inside the bistro, a few middle-aged men were at the dark wooden bar. After greetings were exchanged with one and all, for this place obviously was their regular hangout, we bellied up to the bar for a round of anisette. The sweet, licorice-flavored drink was cool, milky-white, and quite delicious. The FFI men chatted with the aproned bartender, motioning toward me as they related what was happening. Their disrespect for the German garrison was evident. It seemed as though they wanted to be challenged. I was apprehensive but tried not to show it; after all, they were the hosts.

A short time later, we boarded our Citroen and drove out of town into the hills. We circled and climbed for several miles until we reached a high, stonewalled fence. The armed guard at the gate recognized our vehicle and motioned us in. We entered the courtyard of a secluded, stately manor house, which now served as headquarters for the Maquis. There were perhaps twenty or more people coming and going in the courtyard and on the open grounds nearby; and there was something familiar about one of them. To my great delight, it was Steve Yankura talking to another slightly familiar guy, Bernie Garrett. By the time I had greeted them, along came copilot Jones and Morris Vincent. They did not recognize me at first; we were all pretty well disguised in our civilian clothes, scruffy beards, and berets. We could have passed for Frenchies. Our reunion was happy, all talking at once and comparing notes. I discovered that everyone in our crew had bailed out safely, but Ralph Barnes had been wounded by shrapnel and captured by the Germans. Bob Coots was also wounded and probably taken captive. The others were all safe at another Maquis camp nearby. Another ship from the 463rd BG had gone down from antiaircraft gunfire at the bridge at Valence. More than likely, the guns were on freight train flatbeds sitting on a railway siding when we headed for the bridge; bad timing for us.

Our reunion was joyous indeed and made even more so by news that the 7th Army was rapidly moving northward up the Rhone Valley from the Riviera. Our FFI friends were eager to join the fray and wanted to honor their American guests by having us lead a raid on the German garrison at Romans. Their plan would have us acting as their advance scouts waving the flag of liberation, or something equally risky. The role of the liberator, although meant to be complimentary, did not strike me as wholesome or necessary. I wondered whether these Frenchmen were all as bold and crazy as they seemed and whether they really thought I would be stupid enough to accept. There was no way I was going to volunteer to be a ground soldier.

I pleaded my case, saying I was trained to fly airplanes and knew nothing about fighting war on the ground. I told them I appreciated the honor but did not feel qualified to lead valiant Maquis liberation forces into battle. That seemed to get me off the hook. One of the Maquis fighters was nicknamed Tarzan. He was tall and broad shouldered, had a dark mane of hair and fierce eyes, wore a sharp knife at his side, and walked with a swagger.

There was a swimming pool in the garden off the patio where I swam one cool morning before a breakfast of roasted chicory coffee and hot bread. A young Frenchman was there, and we enjoyed a brief respite that fine, bright morning.

Upstairs in the bathroom, I washed my face in cold water and looked in the medicine chest. There was a safety razor and one much-used, slightly rusty, double-edged blade. My beard was scratchy and bothersome; a shave was definitely in order. Long minutes later, my beard was gone, with only slight cuts and scrapes on the face beneath. I can not remember a more delightful, if excruciating shave.

At dinner one night with a dozen or more Maquis companions, I was seated next to an English-speaking French officer. When he learned I was a downed bomber pilot, he asked if I knew how much damage our bombs had caused the townsfolk at Valence. I said I had no idea and was distressed by the implication of personal responsibility his question held. He said that many civilians had been killed in the raid, that much property had been destroyed, and that the bridge was still there. It was an uncomfortable dinner hour for me. I did not dare ask where the planes had fallen for fear of being told that our plane had fallen on the town with bombs still aboard.

The next day, the FFI leaders had another plan. They would take me to another FFI unit, which was working with an advance U.S. reconnaissance team who would arrange for the return of our crew. I was to travel with an FFI courier who had room only for me; the others would follow later.

This plan was much better but was soon overtaken by fast-moving events. The courier delivered me to a three-man Army team in the hills about 50 miles away. The U.S. Captain was able to file a report to his commander using his portable radio, while we took turns cranking the generator. The 7th Army Headquarters then relayed information about our crew to the 15th Air Force in Italy, who in turn advised our 463rd Bomb Group and squadron.

I bivouacked with the team in a barn, awaiting the advancing troops of the 7th Army. The reconnaissance team continued to scout the area and check leads provided by their FFI counterparts. Their job was to radio reports on any German troop movement. It was a quiet time for me, occasionally interrupted by the sight of a lone German fighter plane flying low, hedgehopping behind the rugged hills to the south, probably on a courier mission. There was a small FFI field hospital nearby occupied by a dozen or more convalescing FFI fighters and staffed by one doctor and a nurse.

One Sunday, we Americans were invited to lunch alfresco under the trees near the FFI farmhouse. We sat around a wooden picnic table on the grassy slope of the meadow overlooking the valley and mountains. The food consisted mostly of Army rations and was supplemented by small servings of boiled potatoes, marvelously tasty French bread, hard goat's cheese, ripe peaches, and red wine. We ate one course at a time, sipped wine or water, and talked. I listened mostly, hungry as a bear, relaxing and enjoying the simple festive occasion, happy because now I was safe and secure.

Within a few days, 7th Army troops caught up to our advance post and I was delivered into the hands of the Red Ball Express. This was the Army's trucking system now engaged in restocking fast-moving 7th Army units with food, ammo, medicine, cigarettes, clothing, toothpaste, and other necessities. It did not take me long to outfit myself.

The Red Ball drivers were a rough and ready bunch and very willing to give me a lift back down the pipeline to the beach. I hopped aboard a truck driven by a corporal who really knew how to move along. Each driver was on his own and had orders to deliver his load and then beat it back to the supply dumps. Their day began before dawn and ended at nightfall. They would grab a hot meal from any Army field mess along the way and sleep under their truck if they had to.

The first day, our route followed a network of dusty roads that wound through the mountains well off the beaten track. Near the town of Crest about lunchtime, we pulled off the road where three other truckers had stopped. Lunch was cold C-rations; but when you are hungry, pork and beans, cheese, some crackers and jam, and water from a canteen is just fine. I was busy chowing down when a shrill whistling sound froze my blood. The sharp blast that followed sent us snaking on our bellies under the truck as fast as we could move. There was another blast close by, then another, and then nothing. Silence rang in my ears, while we waited for a few moments. Then almost of one accord, we scrambled out from under the trucks, leaped aboard, and zoomed out of there before German gunners took another shot at us.

My driver said he thought the shells came from an isolated gun battery up the hill, probably manned by German gunners pulling back from the beachhead. They must have thought our little group of four trucks was pretty decent target. Even so, the experience was extremely frightening. I was more used to being fired upon while inside an airplane where the noise of exploding shells was snatched away by the wind and muted by the rumble of engines. Being shelled while lying under a truck where you hear every bit of the explosion and even smell the smoke is something much different. I was never more certain that I was correct in my earlier decision to avoid becoming a foot soldier. Needless to say, I kept a wary eye on the hills for the next half hour, but all remained quiet. The weapon that fired on us was probably the all-purpose 88 millimeter gun originally designed as an antitank weapon. Highly mobile and with a gun muzzle that could be elevated from a horizontal position to almost straight overhead, the German gun was very versatile and ideal for use against tanks, trucks, troops, and aircraft, as I knew all too well.

Within two days I was back in civilization, close to the hustle and bustle of military activity around St. Tropez where the 7th Army Headquarters was now established. Before checking into headquarters, I did a little sightseeing in San Rafael where our invasion forces had come ashore on August 15. Many supply ships were now waiting in the crowded harbor to be unloaded. I bummed a ride out to one of the ships aboard an Army DUKW, an amphibious vehicle with an inboard motor that powered a propeller when operating on water. On land, it could be shifted into rearwheel drive and become a cargo-carrying truck. We can thank our Detroit GMC automotive geniuses for producing this one. I enjoyed the ride into the deep blue waters of the Mediterranean. At the Army finance office, I obtained a cash advance after showing my dog tags as identification. Now I would not have to beg for food at field mess halls. I borrowed pen and paper too and wrote to my family. My mother saved the letter, which follows:

The Time of My Life

August 26, 1944

Dear Mom, Jo & Nan -

There is no way of telling just when this letter may reach you, but I just wanted you to know a true Swain is hard to knock off. There is much to tell about what has happened since the 15th of August when I and my buddies had our little accident, but for the most part, it must go unwritten. Later perhaps you can find out in greater detail.

The French people have helped us out considerably. Knowing no French made it hard but always there was some person who knew enough English to make some sort of a conversation. It is surprising—some of the quaintest characters know perfect English. I met one old gentleman who had been at Cambridge and held a position on a New York newspaper.

I have become separated from my crew members. After three days of hiding out in the hills, I was taken to the Free French hideout and there met Yankura, Garrett, Jones (a new copilot), and our ball turret operator. Haenel did not fly with us that day and perhaps he has written you. I imagine he felt pretty bad about not being with his crew, but I was breaking in a new pilot.

I left my buddies then to go to another headquarters to see about getting us out. They were to follow, but as yet I haven't seen hide nor hair of them. "C'est la guerre," so on I went. I've met a lot of swell boys on my way back. Picked up some clothing and have been eating and sleeping fine. I started to grow a beard—had quite a nice one at that, but I couldn't stand it after 3 or 4 days.

You would love to see this country Mom. Truly, it is more beautiful than anything I have ever seen. There are quite high hills and mountains, with long rolling valleys and plains, dotted with villages and farmhouses. The acres of grass are rich and green, and the sun always seems to shine. Sort of like I imagine Scotland and Ireland to be like. The people themselves are clean and healthy. The smaller children are rosy with health. The Germans have burned a lot of homes, but they seem to have plenty to eat. No fat people though—all of them nice and slim. Most of the girls are quite beautiful, with fine features and slim figures. Nothing at all like the unhappy Italians. These French are very neat and clean, more polite and courteous than many Americans. Naturally they are enthusiastic, I've never shaken so many hands in my life.

I plan to stay awhile and enjoy this while I can, so don't worry too much. I can handle myself. Take care of thee. All my love, Adie.

* * *

Tactical headquarters of the 12th Air Force, which flew light and medium bombardment aircraft (B-26 marauders and B-25 Mitchell bombers) plus troop carrier and supply ships (C-46s and C-47s), was located in Toulon, east of the big port city of Marseille. I finally was able to rejoin the other members of our crew at Toulon, except Barnes and Coots. They claimed they were just waiting around for me for a couple of days; so much for FFI plan number two.

We managed to get a flight to Italy and spent the night at a military airfield outside Rome; a better description would be quarantined. The next day we were delivered to the 15th Air Force Headquarters in Bari for repatriation; here we were sanitized and examined by medics. All our clothing was removed and burned for fear of disease; fortunately, none of us had lice. My little black beret was taken and destroyed, despite my plea that it had sentimental value. Dressed in fresh uniforms, we were debriefed at length by intelligence officers for any information of possible military value. We learned that the war was going well for our side; the Germans were retreating from France and slowly being squeezed in a powerful pincers movement.

We were called evadees, a term for air crew who had evaded capture through the assistance of resistance fighters. The rumor mill said we would not be allowed to fly more missions over Germany, because if we were shot down again we might be forced to divulge names of resistance people and methods they used to help others escape. I was happy to hear that our combat days were probably over.

The next day a B-17 came to Bari to return us to Foggia. We had dinner that night in our old familiar mess hall with Bud Haenel and then sat around telling war stories and reading mail that had accumulated during our absence. By now it was the end of August; only two weeks had passed since our bailout over France, but it seemed more like two years.

* * *

An excerpt from the personal account of the Valence mission by Richard Barnes, our nineteen-year-old tail gunner, is reprinted below, with his permission. He recounts what happened to him and others in our crew after bailing out over France.

I descended the last 100 feet very fast and hit the ground hard, hurting my left knee. I pulled my chute and harness off and saw that Dick Swan had landed 50 to 60 feet away. We made our way to a ditch nearby. Dick's head was bleeding from flak fragments that had glanced off his forehead. We then saw what looked like a farmer running toward us. Dick challenged him with his .45. He was there to help us, and we followed him to a clump of bushes. Soon other French civilians gathered around, shaking our hands and kissing our faces. We were the first Americans they had seen in a long time. Burton then joined us. We undressed and exchanged clothes with the farmers—now we could be shot as spies.

After dressing, the farmers gave us two Maquis guides to take us to a safe hiding place. We started running through the fields, into the woods, and along a small brook. About 10 minutes later we heard gunfire from the area we had just left. We kept running, the two Maquis taking us through the safest places. At the sound of an airplane, we ran for cover in a clump of bushes. It was a JU-88 buzzing the area, most likely looking for the airmen who had bailed out of their crippled B-17. After running and walking, we reached a small village and were taken into a house where a woman applied first aid to Dick's head wounds. Burton and I were all right except for a few sore spots. I had already forgotten about my sore left knee with all the running and walking we did. The Germans would kill these people if they found out they helped us. They offered us cigarettes and wine. French tobacco is much stronger than ours. I sure enjoyed the smokes and the wine. After spending about an hour at this house, our two guides brought us to a farmhouse up on a hill overlooking the village. They gave us bread and wine and then we were off again. The farmer had a horse and buggy rigged up, and we felt relieved knowing we would not have to walk. We rode for about two hours and arrived at a small town where a Maquis chief lived. The FFI chief questioned us and took our names.

Dick Swan felt a bit weak, so we rested for a while. They then took us to another village where we ate and drank some more wine in a cafe. We talked to a few people who could speak some English. We met a nice elderly Frenchwoman who spoke perfect English. She wrote a greeting for me in English and signed it—I still have that piece of paper. The French people welcomed us with open arms. We were the first Americans they had seen in years. After a while, a Maquis fighter came to take us on the remainder of our journey to an FFI hideout in the hills about 125 to 150 miles from the American lines. After bidding farewell to the two guides who brought us to the hideout, we went upstairs to a room with hay strewn on the floor where we were to sleep. Even the hay on the floor felt soft after a hard day. Two FFI fighters brought us three quarts of wine that we drank while watching a night bombing attack on Valence.

We spent seven days up in the hills. Most of the time we listened to the war news and tried to learn some French. We tried to keep informed of the progress our troops were making in this new invasion. I went for supplies with a group of Maquis a few times. We were all armed and ready for the Germans. We would go through the villages picking up foodstuffs, fuel, and wine. One night, we three Americans acted as sentries guarding a truck that brought a few Maquis fighters to a new camp that was closer to the German garrisons. Next evening we went out with a party of men to await a night drop of supplies and guns. The plane that was supposed to drop these items by parachute never arrived. We waited until 4 o'clock in the morning before returning to our hideout. We had fairly good meals there. We used to lie on our backs sunning ourselves and peacefully watch German planes fly low over the hills with their Swastika's easily visible.

Early on the 7th day, we received news that the city of Romans was liberated by the FFI. We heard that some of our crew had participated in the battle. The Maquis brought six German prisoners to our camp. We found out that Swain, Yankura, Jones, Garrett, and Vincent were near Romans. Ralph Barnes was in a hospital with a severe flak wound in his arm. Bob Coots was still unaccounted for. Let's hope that he is still alive. We also found out that 10 minutes after we left the area where we landed, the Germans arrived and picked up our clothes and parachutes. It's damned good we got out of there when we did. We wanted to be reunited with our other crew members. The Maquis camp was moving also. We got permission from the Maquis chief to leave our hideout in the hills. We thanked them for all they had done for us, but how could we ever repay these wonderful and brave people.

We took off for Romans in a car that broke down in a village on the way. Trucks loaded with members of the underground movement soon arrived on their way to their new camp, and we left with them. While leaving the village, we witnessed some men shaving the head of a woman who was accused of shacking up and collaborating with the Germans. It was dark and quiet when we reached Romans. All the Germans at the garrison in Romans were either killed or taken prisoner. The truck driver brought us to a cafe where a party was being held for the brave FFI fighters who fought so gallantly that day to liberate Romans. After we ate and drank with these men, one of the Maquis chiefs told us they would help us find our crew in the morning.

When we woke up in the morning to board trucks, I knew something screwy was happening. There must have been over 500 Maquis boarding vehicles of all types. We found out that we were to attack a German garrison on the outskirts of Valence. Hell! We wanted to find our crew members, not fight Germans. Besides, the three of us were unarmed. We rode for about an hour and then stopped near a farmhouse where all the men got out of the vehicles. Swan, Burton, and I were told to take cover and found shelter behind a three-foot-high brick wall. All of a sudden, machine-gun fire opened on us, and chips of the brick wall started splattering us. The Germans had ambushed us. The Maquis fighters spread out trying to guard themselves from the gunfire. Steady machine-gun fire went on for about 10 minutes, and then there was sporadic gunfire.

Some of the Frenchmen were making a break for it back toward Romans, so we did the same thing. We would run for a while and then fall flat on our faces when we heard gunfire. The Germans were now putting up light artillery not too far behind us. After a while, we came to a wooded section and rested. The machine-gun fire could be heard but was no danger to us, although some artillery bursts were still coming uncomfortably close. We kept running until we came to a road. In the past few hours, the three of us had come damned close to getting our asses shot off. I think it is a hell of a lot safer in our flying machine (SOMETIMES). I don't think I would like to be in the infantry. I guess we were just lucky again today.

While walking along the road, we saw a Frenchman and asked him how far we were from Romans. Burton had to talk to him in French to try and prove we were Americans. We walked for a while when a man and his daughter came riding along on bicycles. This Frenchman could speak English and said he would take us to the French leader of the Maquis in Romans. On our way, we stopped at his house to wash up and get some wine and brown bread. We then went on to Romans, hoping to find our crew members. We soon arrived at the Maquis chief's headquarters and learned where some of our crew members were. The chief took us to a cafe and ordered beer for us, when who should walk up to us but Lt. Garrett, our bombardier. He was dressed in French civilian clothes and really looked like a fine Frenchman. We finished our beer, and Garrett took us to what looked like the grounds of a college, which the Germans had taken over and used as their garrison. Out in the courtyard were Yankura, Jones, and Maurice Vincent. They told us that our skipper Lt. Swain was staying at a farm on the outskirts of town. We now had seven of our crew together, and it sure felt good. They told us that Ralph Barnes was picked up in a French hospital by the Germans, one of his arms shot up pretty bad, and Bob Coots, our engineer, was still unaccounted for.

The next day we tried to figure a way to get to the southern coast of France. The northern end of Romans was being shelled by the Germans still in Valence. Yankura, Swan, Burton, and I were waiting at the hotel where we were to have supper with the other three crew members. We then saw the American troops and truckloads of FFI moving out of Romans and going south. We ate supper and went back to the garrison to discover that Jones, Garrett, and Vincent had left on trucks with the French. We found out the Americans and the Maquis were massing together at a village just north of Valence. A FFI fighter said he would take us to the village in the morning.

When we got there, the streets were crowded with FFI and Americans from the 45th waiting for some Americans tanks to lead us into Valence. I prayed that the tanks would never come, as I did not want to play fighting soldier again. I figured our luck could hold out just so long. My prayers were answered. The tanks never arrived, so they forgot about the assault on Valence and we made our way back to Romans. When our crew got back to the garrison, we made plans to get the hell out of this area and make our way back to the southern coast of France. That night the Maquis had a little party in our honor. Before going to bed, we planned the safest route so we would not meet up with any more Germans.

Early the next morning, we began the 50-mile trip to Grenoble where there was supposed to be a division of Americans from the 7th Army. We started out walking but before long were picked up by a French Maquis truck. On our way we were buzzed by an ME-109 and parked under a tree in case the German made another pass. We were also stopped by some FFI and had to identify ourselves with our dog tags. They thought we were Germans dressed in civilian clothes. After

65

questioning us for a few minutes they allowed us to go on. We arrived in Grenoble in the afternoon and contacted an American liaison officer who helped American airmen who had been shot down and were MIA (missing in action). A train was heading south the next morning, so the American put us up in a classy hotel for the night. We all took a bath and tidied up before having a nice meal at the hotel.

We boarded an old-fashioned European train the next morning and were given rations to eat on the way. We arrived at a supply depot after a slow, four-hour ride, meeting some more American airmen who were also trying to get back to their bomb groups in Italy. We boarded a truck that brought us to the 7th Army Headquarters where we were interrogated by an officer and then fed, after which we boarded another army truck bound for the coast. We entered St. Tropez in the early evening and were brought to headquarters where shipping orders were prepared for us to go back to Italy by boat.

The next morning we were going to breakfast when who do we meet but Skipper Swain. It was neat to see him again. We told him about the boat trip back to Italy. He told us there was an airfield about 20-30 miles away and that maybe we could hitch a ride on a C-47 or something. We left at noon and arrived at the airfield a few hours later . Being very lucky again, the eight MIAs in our crew boarded a flight to Italy. After landing at Bari, we spent a few days in a hospital getting checked over and defumigated. We were informed that it would be up to our flight surgeon whether we flew missions again or were sent back to the States. The hospital also forwarded word to the War Department that the eight MIAs in our crew had returned so that they could inform our families.

We were taken to the Bari airfield the next morning where a B-17 from our group flew us back to Celone Airfield and the 463rd Bomb Group. The flight surgeon there decided that we should not go back to the States because the short amount of time that we were MIA did not warrant it. He said that we did not act very war-weary and that after a little rest we would resume flying missions. After hearing that we would have to fly again, I wished the hell we had stayed in France or made our way to Switzerland where we could have been interned in a neutral country. At least we had most of our crew left, although Ralph Barnes is a POW and Bob Coots is still unaccounted for. We all hope and pray that they are still alive and safe. Two weeks passed before our crew was put on a Battle Order. We picked up a new engineer, a few replacement gunners, and new flying clothes and were ready to fly again. I hope to hell our luck holds out and that we will all complete our tour of duty.

* * *

The following letter dated September 10, 1944, arrived from Pierre Laurent with news from the south of France:

Sergeant Adrian Swain
774 Sqdn. 463rd B.G.
APO 520 c/o P.M.
Italy Air Station Foggia

Dear Adrian

I hope you are quite well since your departure. I have been told by Mr. Lemaine, the FFI man who led you to Romans, that you had started for the south of France with other airmen shot down with you on the 15th of August. I think that you could have rejoined your bombing squadron in Foggia.

Perhaps you are now at an airfield in the south of France and perhaps also near Valence. If so, I should be very happy to hear from you and to see you.

This is my address in Valence:

Pierre Laurent
31 Avenue de la Republique
Granges-les-Valence Ardèche

I live not in Valence but in Granges-les-Valence, which is facing

Valence on the other side of the Rhone. The bridge is broken but boats go through the Rhone (River) very easily. If you alight on the Valence airfield or if you have a leave, come to my address. We all should be very happy to see you again and perhaps keep you some days.

For the time being, we are in our country house. We will certainly remain here for September, but my parents are at Granges-les-Valence. Our country house address, if you remember is:

Maison Blanche
par Chatéau-euf-l'Isere Drome

If you come yourself to this address, you must follow the road leading to Romans. You stop at St. Marcel five miles from Valence and ask the way to Maison Blanche. If you come, come to the place that is more easy for you.

On Thursday, August 31st, we have seen the first Americans in their little "jeeps" and also with a great number of tanks. They have taken Valence in the morning with FFI and they rushed on to Romans and after that to Lyon.

All the country was in the greatest joy to see Americans chasing Germans whom we have borne for five years. It was much too beautiful to be believed. It was the first day of our relief.

Now Germans have gone away, but before they departed they did many ravages in Valence. They blew up the railway station with a train loaded with nitroglycerine. The explosion was dreadful, 800 houses were destroyed and 200 people wounded. We even had some damage in the country from the Germans. They blew up the railway station at Aliscan within 500 yards of our house with a train load of torpedoes, which perhaps were the famous flying bombs which the Germans launch on London. But bomb splinters hit our house, but there was no serious damage.

I have climbed up to your grotto. Many people have slept there when Germans were in the countryside. Awaiting to hear from you and I hope to see you. I shake lovingly your hand.

Your French friend
Pierre Laurent

* * *

Lt. Bernard Garrett, Jr., wrote to his wife and family about his harrowing escapades in France in a letter dated September 11, 1944. The following excerpt from his letter was published by the Detroit war plant where his father was employed:

I'll start from the first—we were hit right in the nose of the airplane. Steven and I were knocked back about 20 feet, and the plane was blazing like hell. We scrambled like mad and dived out. Most of my clothing was burned off, and I thought for awhile I didn't have any parachute on because it was only hooked on one side and my harness was burned, but I managed to open it and came down in one piece. Landed a little hard but OK. French peasants were waiting for me when I came down, and we had to hurry because German scouting planes were already in the air looking for us and I landed only a half-mile from a German garrison. I threw my parachute in an irrigation ditch and hurried into the house with the peasants. They gave me clothing and shoes, and I was out the back door and into the woods in two minutes. Later on I heard machine guns. That's when they got our engineer. Guess the Germans are so hard pressed now they don't want any prisoners.

Sat in the woods about two hours, then they came and took me to a farmhouse about three miles away where our navigator, the copilot, and one of the gunners were waiting. They didn't seem to worry about German patrols much and so we all ate, drank, and vive le France and vive la American-que. Then we went to bed because we were really quite shaken up. Just as we dozed off, they took us way back in the fields because German patrols searched the house. They were very

69

courageous people, because if we had been caught there or any trace of us they would have shot everybody in the place and burned the farm.

Just after we got to bed, the British came over and bombed a dam on the Rhone very close to us. Three bombs fell on the barn and killed some cows, also knocking us out of bed and showering dirt all over us. That bombing was horrible. It was the worst night I spent in France. We survived all right though, and the next morning they took us to the mountains to the French guerilla fighters—the Maquis army as they called themselves.

We stayed with them about 10 days until they decided to attack Romans with 400 Germans in a garrison. They had given us rifles and hand grenades. We attacked the town about 10:00 in the morning, and by 3:00 in the afternoon it was ours. About 60 Germans were killed and the rest were taken prisoner. We moved into the German major's villa—those heinies really lived like kings. Two Frenchies and I took the first two prisoners, although we started out with four. Before we had marched them two blocks, the French killed two of them. They really hate the Hun. We stayed there about three days, and then started to the coastal City of Toulon, because we heard the Americans had captured it. Then to Italy. You should have seen me all dressed in French clothes, a beret, guns slung across my back, bayonet in my belt, and two weeks' beard.

I think I'll be home in about a month, so that's a little good news. I was on my 24th mission when we were shot down.

* * *

Ralph Barnes, flying in the top turret, was hit by shrapnel and wounded in the right arm, leg, and buttocks. In later years, he also wrote of his ordeal:

I got down out of the turret and began hooking my parachute to my chest harness. My right hand was pretty useless, but I managed to kick aside or release three bombs still in their racks so I could bail out. The plane was in a dive. After I bailed out I looked up and saw the plane explode. The next thing I knew I was on the ground. Later that day a French priest took me into Valence in a horse cart borrowed from the farmer who was trying to hide me. I was turned over to the German garrison for medical attention. Luckily their doctor had been trained in New York. I persuaded him not to amputate my arm but to operate on it, which he did, without benefit of morphine or any anesthetics. He saved my arm. At Toulon, the first of six prison camps I attended over the next 11 months, I got some clothing from a young Hindu who had learned English in a missionary school taught by Rolland Scott, a cousin of mine from Toledo, Ohio. The last prison was Luckenvalde, Germany, near Berlin. We were often bombed by our own planes until our camp was liberated on April 22, 1945, by a female Russian tank commander. I weighed 205 pounds when shot down and 135 when released.

Ralph was flown to Paris for treatment and then evacuated to Crile General Hospital near Cleveland, Ohio, for a series of corrective operations on his arm before being discharged in January 1946. He returned to Perrysburg, Ohio, and got married in August 1947.

* * *

By September 3, 1944, the sprawling Ploesti oil refinery north of Bucharest, Romania, fell into the hands of the Russians. No more oil for German trucks, tanks, aircraft, submarines, or ships. One of the most heavily defended targets in Europe was no more. Our crew had been there three times, one of hundreds of B-17s and B-24s that streamed over the target in a 15-mile circuit. On our approach, still miles from the smoking target, we could see little black flies dropping from the black roil of flak bursts exploding over Ploesti. These were bombers going down, from which tiny white parachutes would occasionally appear before the anxious eyes of those still to enter the furnace. Now and then I saw the startling white and then red-black burst of a direct hit on a bomber's fuel tank. Only once did this horrid flash appear in our squadron, to a ship a few hundred feet away. Miraculously, a few parachutes blossomed from that holocaust. All during my days of flying missions my private fear was of taking a direct hit in a gas tank, but none of us talked about this unwelcome subject.

What was nice for all of us in bombers was to look way up from our plodding, disciplined flight path and see our escort fighters: the twin-boomed P-38 Lightning and the smaller, more compact P-51 Mustang. They would make lazy, looping patterns, leaving white condensation trails in the clean, cold sky five miles above earth. One of the P-51 groups had red-tailed P-51s flown by black pilots. They had an outstanding record during the war and were a godsend to those they escorted. Another group had checker-tailed P-51s, one of which was flown by Zeke Gardner, an old classmate of mine from Rochester, Pennsylvania. Now that we had regular support from P-38s and P-51s, the German Luftwaffe (meaning air weapon) was not too eager to intercept us; but their 88 millimeter antiaircraft defense made up the difference, especially around Ploesti.

The day after Ploesti fell, three bomber crews from the 774th were returned to Foggia from POW camps in Romania. These three crews had been shot down and captured during the past six months. From the twenty bomber squadrons in our wing, we lost an estimated 60 bombers over Ploesti alone. Ten men in 60 bombers means 600 men went down, although many survived as POWs. It was a steep price to pay, but the end result proved the merit of U.S. Air Corps strategy: interdict enemy oil production vital to their mechanized weaponry and thereby shorten the war.

For two weeks after our adventure in France, our crew rested and relaxed. Steve and I often went to the Red Cross canteen in town, which had ping-pong, doughnuts, coffee, a half-decent library, and an occasional movie. One night we went to a local theater called the Flagella. It was early fall now, and the evenings were getting cool. As we walked along, the smell of freshly roasting chestnuts was in the air. The night's attraction was *The Barretts of Wimpole Street*, starring Brian Ahern and Katherine Cornell. I expected a motion picture but was pleased to find it was a live presentation. After the performance, some of us went backstage to see and touch the stars. Brian Ahern was tall, handsome, and very well mannered with proper British reserve; he was mobbed by fans. Miss Cornell, on the other hand, did not appear. Understandably, the attention of hundreds of young male admirers perhaps would be overwhelming.

On September 17, I saw my name posted for the next day's operations and was sure I could not do it. After climbing into the pilot's seat the next morning, however, my hands went about their task of switching ignitions and moving throttles. Soon we were moving down the runway and into the air with a new copilot by my side (Bud Haenel now had a crew of his own). Our target was a marshalling yard in Budapest, Hungary. I was shaky on the bomb run, but luckily the flak was light and we dropped our bombs without incident. We landed okay and enjoyed some fresh doughnuts and hot coffee from the Red Cross van on the flight line. The squadron flight surgeon allowed shots of whiskey for those who requested them at the end of a mission. I never indulged all the time I was overseas, neither whiskey nor beer. I even gave my monthly ration of two cans to the guys in my tent.

* * *

September 18, 1944, was a bright, sunny Sunday and my twenty-second birthday. Our target was the bridge at Nova Sad, Yugoslavia. We loaded our bomb bays with two 1,000-pound and two 2,000-pound bombs. We had been briefed to fly at 22,000 feet and knock out a bridge defended by twelve guns. I had bad feelings about bridge targets, and when my new copilot asked if I wanted him to fly the bomb run, I gratefully nodded yes. Soon I wished I had not agreed, for now I had time to watch the black bursts of flak appearing in the distance. The ugly blossoms were right there at eye level, just like at Valence. I broke into a cold sweat, certain we were going to get hit again. In near panic, I reached out my hand ready to flip the red alarm switch on the instrument panel before me. As we turned onto the bomb run, I extended my arm, almost touching the alarm bell, ducked my head, and waited. On and on we droned, straight and level, as the flak bursts outside got louder—"whump, whump, whump"—shaking our ship with near misses. The sun may have been shining warmly in the cockpit, but I was cold with fear and screamed out, "Come on and get me, you bastards, come on and get me!"

Mercifully, I felt the lift of the plane as our bombs dropped and we curved away. The terror passed; it became relatively quiet. The other pilot looked over and said to me on the intercom, "You've got to get

73

hold of yourself." I could only nod to him, too embarrassed to speak. He was right of course, and I never came that close to cracking up again; nor did I ever let another pilot take the controls on the bomb run.

After we landed, I happened to glance behind the control column and noticed a shiny silver dollar tucked away in the canvass cover at the base of the stick. I picked it up and saw that it was minted in 1922, my birth year. Surely this was a good luck omen. Some other pilot's lucky coin was now mine. There was more good news: our crew was on orders for a week of R and R on the isle of Capri, leaving in two days. I also learned I had been recommended for promotion to First Lieutenant and put in for the Purple Heart. Today's mission was number 34, only 16 more to go.

A B-17 packed full of R and R crews flew from Foggia to Naples, about 100 miles away as the crow flies. From Naples, we were trucked to the harbor where we boarded a ferry for the 20-mile ride to the isle of Capri. Capri was all I had hoped it would be: clean and quaint, lots of tiny shops, cobbled streets, and ancient churches, a town filled with pleasant civilians and no signs of war. Even though there were some overcast days with rain, we ate good food at our hotel and got out of bed when we wanted. When the sun was out, we strolled down the hill to the shore and perhaps took a skiff out for a row. We visited the famous Blue Grotto and even tried to catch fish, without success though. Dick Swan and I had fun talking with young children who were everywhere on the town square. We would buy tasty oranges and hazelnuts on the street and browse in the shops, buying cheap cameo jewelry and brass charms to send home. I bought some postcards that were too beautiful to send to anyone and kept them as reminders of lovely Capri.

By late September, weather was becoming a disruptive influence. Low clouds and drizzling rains made our airstrip squishy under the PSP planks. If a plane taxied off the strip, its wheels easily became mired and had to be blasted out using almost full power on the two outboard engines.

We were often briefed at 0430 hours only to have the mission scrubbed before we could start engines. On one occasion, we were recalled before being given the order to remove bomb safety pins. We would be returning with our 500-pound bombs still aboard. I had never landed with a full bomb load. Our final approach had to be flown slowly and with just a little power on all engines until the moment of contact with the runway. It was essential that a good landing be made so none of the bombs could jar loose. We landed smoothly, happily for all concerned.

Once earlier, we were half way to our target and climbing around 15,000 feet somewhere over the Alps when we noticed a fuel leak. Nothing to do but cut off the fuel, feather the bad engine, apply more power to the three good engines, and try to keep up with the rest of the squadron. We managed to do so for about ten minutes but were slowly dropping back. We then decided to drop all of our bombs on the slopes of the Alps, except for one bomb we would drop on our target and thus get credit for the mission—no luck. We were still falling behind the group, so I radioed our predicament and aborted. Steve Yankura gave us a return heading, while I got the crew on alert for German fighters who might be coming up from their airfield just to the west of our position. Thankfully, no aircraft rose to try and pick us off. A pretty accurate antiaircraft battery at Split, Yugoslavia, rocked us with near misses as we sped homeward over the Adriatic, but we gathered speed in a dive that got us out of range quickly.

With increasingly cold and damp weather, we kept warm in our tents by installing oil stoves. These stoves were gravity fed kerosene or diesel fuel from 50-gallon fuel tanks outside. They worked pretty well and you could heat hot water on the stove top for shaving. Sometimes the air inside smelled like an oil refinery, and the burning fuel outside created a layer of black soot that settled everywhere, similar to downtown Pittsburgh's smog. We slept in down-filled, zippered sleeping bags cushioned by inflatable rubber mattresses on army cots. GI blankets were used for extra warmth. Our summer khakis were replaced by warmer woolen garments, olive-drab shirts and pants worn with Eisenhower jackets.

One Saturday morning our compound was rocked by a loud explosion that sounded like an incoming artillery shell. Steve and I dashed around a couple of neighboring tents to find four flight crew officers stretched out on the ground being tended by friends. A welding torch lay by a twisted fuel tank from a fighter aircraft.

Apparently, the guys had been welding a fuel line to the empty gas tank and had failed to allow for gas fumes inside. It had gone off like a bomb. Luckily, no one was seriously injured, and the four officers were soon back at work, their welding project abandoned.

As our aircraft crews and equipment sat mired in the muddy plains of Foggia, Russian troops were only 100 miles from Budapest and rapidly advancing westward. The Germans were being squeezed by the Russians from the east and by the Allies from the south and west. The 15th Air Force found the weather increasingly frustrating. When the skies were clear south of the Alps, clouds usually covered our targets to the north. Winter clouds were dense, smooth, and gray, layer upon layer of them, forcing our bombers to fly higher and higher. Now our missions were flown at 25,000 to 30,000 feet in very cold air, with temperatures as low as 40 to 50 degrees below zero Fahrenheit. Most crew members wore fur-lined flying suits with warm boots and gloves. I opted to don long underwear and extra pants, two pairs of heavy socks, and a sweater under my flight jacket. I also decided to wear my regular high-topped combat shoes without boots so I could walk out if we were downed again by flak. I wondered if survival was possible from a bailout at such frigid heights. Our bailout at 15,000 feet in mid-August was a piece of cake compared to what we now faced. To improve the odds and make me feel more prepared, I carried a little bailout kit in my jacket that contained a razor, cigarettes, some hard candy, and a toothbrush.

Because of prevailing cloud conditions, we were now using path-finder (PFF), a highly secret radar-assist to our bombsight and the latest scientific improvement to our bombing procedures. Only a few PFF "black boxes" were available, but they were effective. Using the PFF, the group's lead ship could identify certain terrain features near the target, such as river junctions near a city or unique bridge locations, and from these landmarks provide heading, time, and distance to the target. By inserting PFF data into the Norden bombsight, our radar navigator/bombardiers could now drop bombs through solid cloud cover with 50-percent or more accuracy.

Flak resistance was still encountered, but the cloud-blinded gun crews on the ground were often off target. On rare occasions, ME-109s would flash through our groups and spit 20-millimeter cannon shells at us. Even more rarely, a jet engine ME-262 would zip across the sky, giving us the once-over and going so fast we could not believe our eyes. If the German air force had been fully equipped with ME-262s, the battle for aerial supremacy could have gone their way. Our crew flew 12 missions during October, including two sorties that were recalled for which we received no credit. Our main targets were synthetic oil refineries near Vienna, Bleckhammer, Brus, and Lenz and one mission against some troop concentrations at Bologna. Steve caught a piece of flak in his chest parachute over Bleckhammer and kept it as a souvenir.

General Douglas MacArthur made good on his promise to return to the Philippines. He had been with his troops on the island of Corregidor in 1942 but was ordered to escape to Australia. He was evacuated by submarine, leaving his deputy, General "Skinny" Wainwright, behind to surrender. Now "Bugout Doug," as his detractors called him, was back in Manila, which was certainly good news.

By October 29, the Russians captured Nova-Sad, Yugoslavia, and by November 4, had captured Budapest, Hungary. In the skies over what was left of Germany, 8th Air Force fighters downed 208 German aircraft in just one day of great, swirling air battles. These record numbers indicated the growing might of U.S. aircraft and the skill of our aggressive fighter pilots.

On Sunday, November 5, I flew my last mission, the big 5-0, a long double to Vienna, Austria, to strike another oil refinery hidden by clouds. We bombed from 30,000 feet in bitterly cold air amid scattered flak bursts. Our ball turret gunner, a temporary crew member, reported that his fingers and toes were frostbitten. We landed at Foggia so he could get immediate medical attention at the military hospital and then returned to Celone. Bud Haenel finished his 50th on the same mission as I did, and Dick Barnes had only one more mission to go. Ty Burton had been in the hospital with pneumonia and fallen behind, while Steve still needed seven. Garrett was also behind and would have a much slower time finishing now that the group was averaging only three or four sorties a month. Old Adriano was *FINITO*—what a glorious relief.

* * *

The following outlines some of the events that occurred to members of the old *Hell on Wings* crew after the war ended. By no means complete, it may be of interest to those who wonder what happened to the ten young crew members who met at MacDill Field in April 1944 and went to fight the air war from Foggia, Italy.

Steve Yankura stayed in the service and was last contacted in 1949 at Westover Field, where he was a flight navigator for General Olds flying C-54s to Europe for the Military Air Transport Service (MATS). Still single, handsome, and debonair as ever, Steve was keeping company with a beautiful redhead and enjoying life. Copilot Bud Haenel was still in the service in 1945 flying for MATS out of Detroit. Bernard Garrett returned to civilian life with his family in the Detroit, Michigan area.

Ty Burton returned to civilian life, finishing his undergraduate work at Harvard and completing his master's degree in finance and business. Ty married, raised three sons and a daughter, and is now a semi-retired business consultant in Maryland. Morris Vincent finished his tour and, according to Ralph Barnes, is dead now; no further details were available. He was a fine airman who did his fair share to win the war.

Dick Swan returned to civilian life and graduated from Colorado State University with a degree in forestry. He moved to Medford, Oregon, where he raised two children and was employed for many years as the timber department manager for a lumber company. Quiet, courageous, and dependable in the air, Dick Swan was the kind of man anyone would be proud to have in the family, or as a neighbor. He was a member of the Congregational Church of Medford, where he was memorialized upon his untimely death at age 52 after suffering from bone cancer. Dick Swan had written the following in a letter to his fellow Connecticut Yankee, Dick Barnes:

"You know, France was a tremendous experience and we went thru it all—fat, dumb, and happy! It amazes me now to think back and wonder how the hell we ever survived it without getting our asses shot off! My experiences with you and the crew along with that little tour in France is something that I would not trade in for all the Crown Jewels in the world. In a way I feel sorry for the young guys today

who look upon a tour in the services as the ultimate evil—something detested far more than a jail sentence. They will never know the full meaning of the kind of comradeship that we knew."

Ralph Barnes is retired now after a long and successful career in the office supply and printing business and with the public library in Perrysburg, Ohio. The Barnes have a son, a daughter, and three grandchildren. During the winter months, they enjoy travelling in their mobile home to Florida, Tennessee, and the Carolinas. In February 1992, Ralph and Betty Barnes visited me in Sarasota, where we had a joyful reunion and rehashed our times together.

Robert Coots had been captured by German troops and taken prisoner the day we were shot down. At first we feared that Bob had been executed, but he survived the next nine months in various prisons until he was released in May 1945. He returned to his wife and family in Alabama.

Dick Barnes and I began corresponding with each other in 1985 when we discovered each other's address in the 463rd Bomb Group flyer. His accurate recollections of those days with the FFI in France have added greatly to my own account. Dick returned to civilian life in Bristol, Connecticut, got married, and settled down as a mail carrier for the U.S. postal service. After a heart attack complicated by diabetes in 1981, Dick took a disability retirement and now is one of the senior brigade who enjoys life, and walking three mile stints in the local shopping mall. His main regret is that his doctor advised against his dream of retiring to Hawaii because the heat and humidity would not be good for his heart condition.

* * *

In 1990, my wife Anno and I visited the south of France and toured Valence, Romans, and Grenoble. While in Valence, we found Pierre Laurent's name and address in the local telephone book and located his office downtown. Pierre was not in his office and had no home residence listed. The next morning I left a letter under his office door on our way out of town and later sent him photos of our visit to his office. Pierre wrote back to say he had missed us by minutes and had tried to contact us by telephone. He sent us pictures at Christmas saying he had broken his right hand and was unable to write but he was well and doing fine.

The following are letters from Dick Barnes and Pierre Laurent. They are interesting for their sense of history and for the strong memories they evoke. They add a little flavor to the lives of those of us who survived the exciting days of World War II and the air war in Italy.

Dick Barnes
Bristol, CT
October 12, 1990

Dear Adrian and Anno:

Received your letter and pictures showing Valence and the Square at Romans. It does not look familiar as a lot of rebuilding has taken place. We were at the Hotel Europa which was located on Avenue Rue St. Nicholas. From the hotel we would walk east and go up a slight hill until we reached the building where we all stayed. There were three or four buildings which formed a courtyard. There was also a swimming pool within the courtyard where I swam one day; while resting on my back at the end of the pool, I saw a German (ME-109) fly over kind of low. I waved at him. I had to laugh at these occurrences. I guess he figured I was a Frenchie or even a German. I also remember standing guard at one end of this compound area. I had an Italian carbine and some German "Potato Masher" grenades. I guess the Maquis figured Germans would be retreating along this road. But that afternoon we heard cheering and found out an American Motorized Unit had entered Romans. That night we had a party at the Hotel Europa.

I remember assembling one of the German bicycles that was stored in the building and that night I slept in the German Colonel's bed. He was the Commandant of the garrison. That's about all I remember of Romans... maybe all that area was torn down after the war. I'm glad you found where your 15 year-old friend in 1944 lived. Too bad he was not home.

80

The Time of My Life

Today, Barbara and I went to a matinee at a local cinema. It was a movie I have been waiting for. The Memphis Belle—the B-17 in the 8th Air Force in England that completed its 25 sorties. The first of all crews flying with the 8th Air Force to do so. I enjoyed it very much and I think Barbara liked it too. I think you would enjoy it. I felt like I was back flying with the 15th Air Force's Top Gun B-17 Pilot.

> *God Bless and with Love,*
> *Barbara and Dick*

Pierre Laurent
345 Avenue de la Republique
07500 Granges-les-Valence
France

January 10, 1991

My friend Adrian,

It was marvelous to hear about you since those exciting days when I met you falling from the skys on August 15, 1944. I found your letter 10 minutes too late!!

I called you on Radio Monte-Carlo and Europe No. * and all regional stations in Provence and I waited for you until you went back to the states.

I would like to send you a long letter but a stupid accident has broken my right hand—so I could not use it.

My English is too bad to phone you so I'm terribly sorry to received your good wishes before I could write you. I will send you a long letter soon.

Today, I tell you I have never forgotten you in spite of the years and I hope, perhaps this year, to meet you in Florida.

Now, I send you some photographs of my wife, Marie-Jose, my single daughter Tina, our two Yorkshire dogs, Ullo and Andy, and my Aunt Germaine who was a young woman in 1944 and nowadays is the oldest person in our family.

I tell you again of my great joy to have news from you and your family. With my best wishes and friendly greetings for the new year, I remain always faithfully

Your friend,
Pierre Laurent

* * *

Four decades and more have passed since our return from Italy. I have thought about the moral issues of harming civilians and other innocents who happened to be in harm's way; and several times I have been asked how I felt about dropping bombs on German targets. I have always felt regret over what happens in wartime, but I have never felt any personal guilt for being a bomber pilot in the service of my country. The blame for the deaths of civilians lies with Adolph Hitler and the Nazi Fascist Party who were in power from 1933 until 1945. The German Third Reich controlled all property; and, under Hitler, sought to impose on the rest of the world the dreadful concept of racial supremacy by the Aryan race. Fortunately for the rest of the world, Hitler failed.

On the Valence mission, my responsibility was to pilot a B-17 and destroy a bridge being used by Third Reich troops and their equipment. Those who died in that mission, both civilians and military, were subject to the vagaries of war. It is hard to separate combatants and noncombatants when bombs start to drop and enemy ground batteries begin to fire.

The Time of My Life

ADRIAN SWAIN, COMBAT MISSIONS FLOWN
463rd Bomb Group, 15th AF, 774 Bomb Squadron

Celone Field, Foggia, Italy

Date Flown	Target	Sortie	Mission
07/13/44	VERONA, ITALY	1	1
07/14/44	PLOESTI, ROMANIA	2	3*
07/15/44	BUDAPEST, HUNGARY	3	4
07/16/44	VIENNA, AUSTRIA	4	5
07/18/44	MEMINGEN, GERMANY	5	7*
07/19/44	MUNICH, GERMANY (ABORTED)	0	
07/20/44	MEMINGEN, GERMANY	6	9*
07/21/44	BRUX, CZECHOSLOVAKIA	7	11*
07/22/44	PLOESTI, ROMANIA	8	13*
07/24/44	TURIN, ITALY	9	14
07/25/44	LINZ, AUSTRIA	10	15
07/26/44	WIENER-NEUDORF, AUSTRIA	11	17*
07/30/44	BROD, YUGOSLAVIA	12	19*
07/31/44	PLOESTI, ROMANIA	13	21*
08/03/44	FRIEDRICHSHAFEN, GERMANY	14	23*
08/06/44	LE POUZIN, FRANCE	15	24
08/06/44	BLECHHAMMER, GERMANY	16	26*
08/09/44	GYOR, HUNGARY	17	27
08/12/44	SAVONA, ITALY	18	28
08/13/44	SAVONA, ITALY	19	29

08/14/44	TOULON, FRANCE	20	31*
08/15/44	VALENCE, FRANCE (M.I.A.)	21	33*
09/17/44	BUDAPEST, HUNGARY	22	34
09/18/44	NOVA-SAD, YUGOSLAVIA	23	35
09/20-26/44	R & R ON THE ISLE OF CAPRI		
10/04/44	MUNICH, GERMANY	24	37*
10/05/44	VIENNA, AUSTRIA (RECALL)	0	
10/07/44	VIENNA, AUSTRIA	25	38
10/10/44	MESTRE, ITALY	26	39
10/11/44	GRAZ, AUSTRIA	27	40
10/12/44	BOLOGNA, ITALY	28	41
10/13/44	BLECHHAMMER, GERMANY	29	42
10/14/44	NOVE-ZAMKY, AUSTRIA	30	43
10/16/44	LINZ, AUSTRIA	31	44
10/17/44	BLECHHAMMER, GERMANY	32	45
10/23/44	PLAVEN, GERMANY	33	46
10/29/44	MUNICH, GERMANY (EARLY RETURN)	0	
11/04/44	REGENSBURG, GERMANY	34	48*
11/05/44	VIENNA, AUSTRIA	35	50*
	TOTAL COMBAT MISSIONS:	50	
	TOTAL COMBAT TIME FLOWN	268 HOURS	

*Denotes double mission, over 500 miles to target

FIVE

Combat to College

Former combat pilots like me were usually given routine administrative duties, such as tower watch on nonoperational days. It was rather boring, but someone had to be there in case a stray aircraft landed. We shared our landing strip with a small group of British pilots who flew night bombing missions over Europe. We saw very little of these chaps but knew they were busy by the sound of their engines revving up about dusk.

Sometimes I would pilot a B-17 loaded with crew members going on leave to Naples. Bud Haenel was asked to pilot such a flight to Bari, so Steve and I decided to go along for the ride. As Bud turned on the final approach to Bari, I could see we were skimming along at a fast clip, too fast. When we touched down, more than half the runway was behind us. The end of the runway was nearing rapidly, and it looked as though we were going to run beyond it into a gully and then the rocky wall of a stone quarry. Thinking we were going to smash up, I grabbed the handles of the machine gun for stability. Just then, Bud jammed full right rudder and stomped the right brake. The bomber ground looped and reversed direction so abruptly, that forward momentum threw us around the inside of the ship like jackstraws. I hung to the gun handles for dear life as the plane settled tail first on the edge of the gully; part of our landing gear buckled, but we were at rest. All four propellers just cleared the ground. It was eerily quiet. Steve and I scrambled out the front escape hatch and ran for safety. Luckily, Bud had thrown the master ignition switch, which killed all electricity to the engines and reduced the chances of fire. Later, we kidded Bud about having to sign an accountability form for repairs to the B-17; he felt badly. Bud told me later that he really wanted to give me a good ride, since it was my first passenger ride with him as pilot. It was simple pilot error; possibly the tower had provided wrong landing directions, or the wind had shifted. Most probably, Bud had not considered the light weight of the airplane, which made it float over the runway and take up more runway than normal.

A few days after Thanksgiving, our crew received orders for a 10-day leave in Rome. A flight was not available because of bad weather, so we all boarded a muddy but reliable truck. About twenty of us were jammed side-by-side on hard wooden seats, protected from the elements by a tarpaulin over the top but open to the rear. I had a blackened eye, caused by a touch football game the day before. One of the opposing players slipped on the grass as I tagged him, and his heavy boot flew up and clipped my right eyebrow, slicing it open. Four stitches put it right, but after eight hours of jolting on the truck, my eye was so black and swollen that it looked as if I had been in a prize fight.

It was wet and drizzling when we arrived in the gloom of late afternoon. Inside the Regina Carleton Hotel where we were billeted, the atmosphere brightened considerably. There was white linen on our dining room table, a strolling violinist in a much-worn tuxedo, and an air of civilization about us. Being in the heart of Rome was like being in paradise. Steve and I gave some serious attention to our English-Italian phrase book, realizing that we ought to get a few key sentences down pat. One such phrase was critical when going out for the night in a strange city: "Dove gabinetto?" meaning "Where is the bathroom?"

A few highlights from this wonderful taste of civilization include our tours around the city. We were escorted in a fine horse-drawn carriage to the ruins of the Roman Coliseum where so many Christians were thrown to the lions over 1,900 years ago. Only a bare outline of the foundations and part of a towering wall remain of the original stadium. We groped our way down sloping tunnels leading to ancient catacombs beneath the streets. We peered through a dim labyrinth of dank, cobwebbed aisles, narrow and musty with age, the sides of which were lined with niches stacked from floor level as high as you could reach. Bones, skulls, ribs, and dust were evidence of the price paid by early Christians for their beliefs. I have often thought about their strength and wondered if I, a Christian in the 20th century, would have the courage to endure the same treatment. I am ashamed to admit that I reached out and took an old, yellowed tooth from one of those poor remains as a souvenir, which I soon discarded somewhere on my way back.

In Vatican City, amid throngs of U.S. servicemen, we strolled about St. Peter's Cathedral admiring the rich and graceful architecture, beautiful statues, and glorious paintings. Luckily, we were in time to join a small group of servicemen who were soon to be addressed by Pope Pius XII. There he was in an open assembly area near the pulpit, a thin, ascetic looking man, dressed in the white workday robes of the Church and wearing a small skullcap on the back of his head. He had a high forehead and the classic beak of a Roman nose. He wore metal-rimmed glasses that made his light grey eyes loom round as marbles and oddly compelling as he began to greet the line of waiting servicemen.

As we approached, I noticed that some Catholic men knelt to kiss the papal ring on his extended right hand and others did not. I was in a dilemma; my father was a Catholic, yet I was a Presbyterian. I was confused, wanting to do the right thing, yet too stubborn to bend my knee to anyone. When the Pope held out his hand, I took it, bowed deeply from the waist, and almost—but not quite—kissed the ring. He spoke to me in heavily-accented English, his huge eyes and steady gaze fascinating me. He asked me where I was from, and I replied from Pittsburgh, Pennsylvania, realizing with some surprise that he spoke English. He said he knew Pittsburgh, and then he nodded his head and gave me a friendly, fatherly look before the next person came forward. It was a moment forever imprinted on my mind.

Pope Pius XII was born Eugenio Pacelli in Rome in 1876. He had indeed been in Pittsburgh when he toured the United States, South America, and Europe as Secretary to Pope Pius XI. When Pius XI died in 1939, Eugenio Pacelli was elected Pope and served until his death in 1958. Pacelli was a man distinguished by his tall, slender appearance, democratic attitude, scholarship, and broad human interests. He served humanity well during World War II, setting up a remarkable underground information service for prisoners of war, helping those who sought to evade the Germans in Italy, and promoting relief programs for other war-stricken areas. He later instituted evening masses within the Catholic church and the use of common vernacular in church services. Laymen and their children could now follow the services that heretofore were delivered in Latin, which benefited the priests more than the faithful.

After the audience with the Pope, Steve and I wandered about until we found a broad staircase of stone that led us to the bell tower. We were greeted in Italian by a friendly workman who invited us to join him on the tower platform where we could see down hundreds of feet into the huge square, and far across the rooftops of Rome. This man's job was to ring the tower bells each hour, and he asked in sign language if we wanted to help him. Of course we did! Steve and I took turns pressing the mechanical release that sent twelve booming, muffled, yet powerful bell notes pealing across the city. I have taken pride over the years telling all who would listen about our giving a "time hack" to Rome from St. Peter's Cathedral.

One night, we all went to the Royal Opera House to see *Othello*. It was cool and damp, and our greatcoats were perfect for keeping us warm in the unheated theater. The music of Giuseppe Verdi was grand, and I was fascinated when Desdemona was smothered on stage with a pillow held by her jealous husband. Othello then committed suicide, ending the unhappy, four-act play. The story outline was printed in French and English, so we neophytes knew the outcome, and I kept my program as a souvenir. The Opera House was filled mostly with military people, although citizens of Rome were present too. The multitiered balconies loomed over the stage almost close enough for some front-row audience to touch the actors. We felt very much like participants in the drama, not mere spectators. The pace was slow, compared to the action one could find at *Broadway Bill's*.

Broadway Bill's was a night club typical of others in Rome, such as *The Grotto*, *The Passion Pit*, and *Rupe Tarpca*. They all featured booze, broads, and loud music and were filled every night with young men drinking, dancing, and romancing as many women as they could. The tiny dance floor was always crowded, the air hot and dense with smoke and perfume. The ladies played one amorous young man against another, making the best deal possible for this one-night stand. This was a survival business for them, because the Italian economy was nonexistent. Many beautiful young ladies from fine Roman families thus were persuaded to share the riches and the company of wealthy, raunchy, happy-go-lucky American flyers. Curfew was at midnight, and crowds would spill out of the door seeking carriage rides to wherever they were going to spend the night, hooting and laughing, some more lucky than others. Steve, Bud, and I usually became separated during the evening but joined forces later at the hotel to compare notes.

It was a wild time, yet a welcome release for most of us; risky too, for venereal disease was common. Military clinics were quite busy curing the clap, which responded readily to the wonder drug penicillin. One of our gunners mistakenly continued to take the medicine every four hours all night long when he should have stopped taking it at bedtime. As a result, excessive salts crystallized in his urinary tract, which was extremely painful. He said it was so bad that if he had a .45 within reach, he would blow his brains out. Luckily, the salts dissolved the next day, and he was fine. Much as I wanted to, I just could not get up enough nerve for one-night stands with perfect strangers who could not even speak my language.

After Rome, being back in Foggia was a distinct letdown. I began to wish for orders back to the States, but at the same time I was not anxious to leave my safe haven in the squadron. By mid-December, occasional snowfalls melted quickly but left water on our still-frozen, poorly drained tarmac. It was impossible to use our field for multiple landings and takeoffs, so we moved our airplanes, maintenance equipment, and operations to an adjacent field. I felt sorry for the flight crews who had to truck those extra miles to complete their missions.

The Army always practiced its policy of "hurry up and wait." Experience with this taught us the virtues of patience and discipline and also not to become too excited about anything. Christmas and New Year's celebrations came and went, highlighted by cards, letters, and many boxes of candy, cookies, and sweaters from home. I found that life was not too difficult when you lived day-by-day and remembered to be optimistic; things could be a lot worse.

One afternoon, we gathered for a presentation of ribbons and awards by the Commanding General of the 5th Wing, assisted by our group commander. I received the Distinguished Flying Cross (DFC) which really was an award for having survived 50 combat missions. Each pilot had to be written up in a specific citation; mine was for flying our aircraft back from a mission over Blechhammer with one engine out because of flak damage. The citation read, in part, "above and beyond the call of duty" and "without regard for his personal safety." Any pilot in a combat situation would try his damnedest to get his plane back to base with his crew. It was because of his desire to assure his personal safety that many heroic actions took place. Still, being awarded the DFC meant a lot to me, as did the other ribbons I accumulated: a Purple Heart for the minor flesh wound when I bailed out over Valence; an Air Medal for flying my first five combat missions; and an oak leaf cluster for each succeeding ten missions flown.[1]

My transfer orders to the States finally arrived! Now that I had them, I did not want to leave; but a week later on a cold, sunlit morning, I left in a B-17. I looked back on the dull, mud-colored, barren, and snow-spotted Italian plain without regret. Our tents in the distance were easily distinguished by the pall of smoke over them from all those oil heaters.

Steve, Bud, and I spent the next five days in the U.S. Army's 7th Replacement Depot outside of Naples; Garrett and Burton still had a few more missions to fly. The depot at Naples was a huge processing station jammed with thousands of incoming replacement troops and a similar horde of homeward-bound veterans of all rank, nationality, and physical condition. Some Canadian soldiers had been overseas with British Forces for five years, which their government required before they were entitled to rotate home. I felt embarrassed to be going home with barely seven months overseas. Thank God, I had joined the Air Corps and not the infantry.

---

[1] I particularly valued these awards when the war in Europe ended and early demobilization of combat veterans began. When a veteran had accumulated 85 points, according to decorations and time served overseas, he became eligible for discharge.

The Time of My Life

On January 20, 1945, we boarded the *Santa Paula*, a luxury liner now converted to a troop carrier, with the swimming pools used as cargo bays. We were assigned twelve men to a room, each containing six two-man bunks in space that formerly was reserved for two. With this being the space assigned to officers, I wondered what the enlisted men's space was like; but I had no complaints. The room was cozy and warm, and I thoroughly enjoyed the saltwater shower more than the public bathhouse in Foggia.

During fair weather, we would hang on the rails topside watching the long, white roiling of propeller wash pointing back the way we had come and feeling chilled by the cold sea air. The low scud clouds would occasionally break, admitting a brief shaft of sunlight and a glimpse of blue skies. We practiced boat drills daily in case our vessel was struck by a torpedo. The Mediterranean Sea was not likely to be infested by German submarines, but the Atlantic Ocean ahead was another story.

The third day out, our ship blew a boiler and we docked at Oran, Algeria, for repairs. The *U.S. General Gordon*, a much larger troopship, was able to take all of our passengers aboard. My new bunk was now three decks below topside, right at the waterline, in a stack of bunks five berths high. Our large hold contained more than 200 men; now I knew what our enlisted men's accommodations were like. I heard the sound of the sea gliding and hissing along the hull, with only a half-inch of metal between me and the deep blue. I told myself to have faith and not to worry too much about torpedoes. On the plus side, our new quarters were warm, and there was lots of hot water in the showers.

Soon we were underway again in a convoy of four cargo ships escorted by six destroyers zigging and zagging around us. We were allowed on decks in the evening, but there were no ship's identification lights and no cigarette smoking allowed. Signal lamps occasionally flashed messages from ship to ship within the convoy. My Morse code skill was rusty, but I could still catch a word or two.

The morning after leaving, we gazed at the brown coast of Spain with its sun-drenched Costa del Sol. We saw the imposing Rock of Gibraltar, that famous British outpost, where most of the drinking water was collected from rooftops and stored in cisterns. Soon we were in the open Atlantic on a course that would take us 200 miles south of the Azores, where we had first landed our brand new B-17. Reports that reached us later said our plane had gone down with all her crew in the spring of 1945 over one of those flak-covered targets in Germany.

For the next ten days, typical winter weather prevailed. Huge swells with foam-crested tops lifted our ship's propeller half out of the water at times. In the hold trying to sleep, we could hear the high-pitched surge of giant blades clearing water, and then subsiding to the steady rumble of drive shaft and blades. The increased pitch and roll of the ship bothered us at first, until the up, down, and sideways movements became normal and somehow soothing. We settled into a routine of eating, sleeping, snacking on candy bars, and smoking. Each of us was allowed one carton of cigarettes per week from the ship's canteen. We studied the ship's daily newspaper, which reprinted world news from radio broadcasts. The Russians were racing toward Berlin, at 25-35 miles per day. How we rejoiced—Hitler was almost finished. The 8th Air Force dominated the skies over Europe, and the Americans were on the move, pushing rapidly toward Berlin and a linkup with the Russians on the Elbe River.

On Sunday, February 5, 1945, about 1:00 P.M., we got our first glimpse of the Statue of Liberty, grey and faint in the cold cloudy weather, but unmistakable. Soon the foredecks of the *General Gordon* were crowded with men, some perched on cargo masts and other vantage points. We were all anxious to see Lady Liberty with her arm and torch thrust high, clearly outlined against the dark mass of land and highrise buildings that was New York City. We were home.

* * *

The 463rd Bomb Group flew its first combat mission in February 1944. By the end of the war, our group had completed 222 missions and lost more than 100 crews and their planes; 190 men were taken prisoner, 227 men returned without being captured, 693 were missing in action (later to be reported dead), 303 men were wounded in action, and 81 men were killed in action.[2] Its last sortie was April 26, 1945. Our most memorable mission was the flight to Berlin on March 24, 1945. The group led the 5th Wing on a raid at the Daimler-Benz tank works, the longest escorted heavy bombardment mission in the European Theater of Operations. For this outstanding effort, the 463rd was awarded a unit citation. On May 8, 1945, the war in Europe ended. By September, the 463rd was deactivated, its personnel returned to the States, its mission completed.

* * *

After the *General Gordon* berthed, ferryboats took us across the river to the railroad station in New Jersey. It then was a short ride to Camp Kilmer, named after the poet Joyce Kilmer, who lost his life in France during World War I. His poem *Trees* is a classic that many kids like me memorized in grade school. My recollection of Camp Kilmer is sharply etched with the memory of my first stateside haircut. The post barber must have thought I was on my way overseas, rather than returning, because he gave me the shortest GI "white sidewall" clipping of my life. When I stepped outside, the cold winds of February were even more frigid. My cap, which provided some warmth, seemed a size too big as it settled over my ears. I wondered what my family would think of me.

After our leave orders were issued, Steve, Bud, and I were told to report in twenty-one days to the Miami Beach Processing Center for reassignment. I then took the evening train to Pittsburgh. I arrived the next morning in the Smoky City and made a few telephone calls before boarding a Greyhound bus for the Valley.

I did so enjoy being with my Mom and the family in Bridgewater; it was great to be fussed over by sisters Joan and Nancy. I was fed so much food I thought I would pop a button on my tightly tailored shirts, and I definitely had to let out a notch or two on my belt. I was very much the hero and loved the role I played. Dressed in my forest-green jacket with wings and ribbons, I cut a fancy figure when the occasion required.

---

[2] Source of summary material is from the *Fighting 463rd* book.

There was so much to do that time seemed to fly. I often took the train to Pittsburgh to be with Bobby Chatt, my number one girl-friend. She was a cute nursing student attending Duke University in Pittsburgh. It was becoming clear that Bobby considered me a prime candidate for matrimony; but I had some problems to deal with before I could seriously consider such a move. I thought the world of Bobby; she would make anyone a fine wife. I just felt financially and emotionally unprepared for marriage, particularly in wartime. I did not have a college degree and had no particular qualifications for providing for a family, other than flying an airplane for Uncle Sam. I also had a definite aversion to marrying into the Catholic faith, which I thought was too rigid and demanding of its faithful. I also thought that because she was only five feet two inches tall and weighed about 100 pounds, she was too tiny for me. These were all pretty lame excuses, but to tell the truth, I was too much the perfectionist, selfish, and self-centered.

My brother Chuck was now at Moody Field in Valdosta, Georgia, serving as a B-25 instructor pilot. I wired him so we could meet in Valdosta when I came through enroute to Miami Beach for reassignment duty. Then I visited friends at Curtiss-Wright in Beaver; the old gang had not changed, but I had.

Being among civilians at home was my first real experience with national rationing that had been instituted by the Office of Price Administration when war broke out. The OPA immediately imposed rent ceilings and set prices on about eight million items, including beef, butter, cigarettes, shoes, and sugar. All rationed items were acquired using coupons issued in War Ration Books, which carried a stern warning that violators of rationing regulations were subject to $10,000 fines or imprisonment. Gasoline was a major headache. Car stickers were issued according to the job each driver held; "A" and "C" coupons were most common, allowing five to ten gallons of gas per month. "X" coupons, for unrestricted usage, were issued to doctors and others whose travel was critical.

There were many abuses of privilege. A major furor arose when the press disclosed that about 200 of our national Congressmen voted themselves unrestricted usage. A mobster ring was uncovered that was selling bogus "C" coupons for fifty cents each. Rustlers even slaughtered cattle for black-market meat buyers. A postwar study showed that one of every 15 businesses engaged in OPA rule violations, which explained why there were 3,100 investigators, not counting extra assistance provided by Justice Department and Secret Service agents.

Somehow the system worked. Most people cooperated, scarce supplies were stretched, and prices and rent gouging were controlled. Rationing was still a pain in the neck for those who did the household shopping, since OPA rules and regulations were constantly changing. Some housewives cultivated the neighborhood butcher, who could always find scarce meat for his most loyal customers. The tobacco shop owner was another very important person.

Gasoline rationing did not inconvenience me at all. The Beaver Valley Transit scheduled a local bus past our corner every ten or fifteen minutes. Greyhound buses ran between towns every few hours, and the P&LE and Pennsy Railroads provided dependable and regular train service. Besides, I did not have a driver's license and would not until after my discharge.

While I loafed at home and partied at night, a monumental conference was going on in Yalta, a popular Russian resort town on the Black Sea. The "Big Three," President Roosevelt, Prime Minister Churchill, and Premier Stalin were making some momentous decisions. Plans were publicly announced in mid-February 1945 for occupying Germany, establishing a new Polish government and holding a conference in San Francisco to form the United Nations.

Other secret agreements became public knowledge much later. The Russians promised to declare war on Japan within three months of the end of the war in Europe, which they did. They also seized Manchuria and the northern half of Korea, thereby setting the stage for the Korean War. None of these reports meant much to me at the time. I was sure the war would go on for two more years and that I would be sent to the Pacific to fly more missions; so, on with the party.

* * *

One of my favorite nightspots was Greystone Gardens. Green and red neon lights that winked through scrubby sumac trees softened the hard edges of the aging structure. Inside, a big dance floor was surrounded by tables with more private booths along the walls. A Wurlitzer music box glowed with brilliant, wavy, moving lights that softly illuminated the dance floor.

The sad, sentimental songs of the time were popular, memorable, and danceable. I was especially fond of Glenn Miller's *Serenade in Blue, Moonlight Cocktail, I Know Why, At Last,* and rollicking *In the Mood* and *String of Pearls*. Even though Glenn Miller died much too young, his music remains alive. In 1942, he joined the Army at age thirty-eight and formed the Army Air Force Band. The Band played for troops in this country and then went to England in 1944.

In the winter of that year, he was ordered to France. Miller hated flying and usually sat white-knuckled during the trip. He told a friend he had "the awful feeling you guys are going to go home without me; I am going to get mine in some beat-up old plane."

On a drizzling December morning before Christmas, he decided to fly to France ahead of his band and squeezed into the cabin of a single-engine C-64 Norseman. The temperature was 34 degrees at the airport and 10 degrees colder over the English Channel. The plane lacked deicing equipment, but the pilot took off anyhow into a fog, carrying Miller and another officer. They were never heard from again. It was a sad loss to those who loved Miller's music, but his memory and music remain very much with us whenever *Moonlight Cocktail* or *Serenade in Blue* is heard or toes begin tapping to *In the Mood*.

* * *

The U.S. Marines landed on Iwo Jima, February 19, 1945, and a few days later raised our flag atop Mount Suribachi. This was one of the last major land battles in the Pacific. Next on our list was Okinawa, a key island some 350 miles south of Kyushu, the southernmost home island of the Japanese empire. From Tinian, our B-29s would drop two atomic bombs on Japan that would end the war in August 1945. In my wildest dreams, I could never have imagined that I would fly B-29s from Okinawa in the Korean War five years later.

It was time to return to the war, and I was apprehensive that I would draw combat assignment to the south Pacific. I pushed that thought to the back of my mind and said good-bye to family and friends. Bobby Chatt met me at the Pittsburgh train station to say good-bye. She and I had been seeing a lot of each other. I was very fond of her and grateful for her love and support, but at my tender age marriage was only a distant possibility. For now, just being alive and taking care of the moment was about all I could handle.

The train ride south was tedious and boring after the unconfined and exciting life of a soldier on leave. When our train finally got to Atlanta the next afternoon, I could not stand another minute on board. Impulsively, I got off to bum a ride on the highway to Valdosta, some 200 miles away. I hitchhiked on a big truck and sat with the driver all afternoon and into the early evening, moving quietly through the budding spring landscape, enjoying pastoral scenes of cows in the field, and taking pleasure in the sight of country lanes untouched by war.

My brother Chuck had rented a room at the main hotel in town and joined me later that night. We visited over the weekend and had time to get reacquainted. He was lean and handsome and quite a party man, as most of us were those days. We strolled in the warm sunlight, sat on park benches, and swung on the swings in the town square, both of us slightly hung over from drinking at the Moody Field Officers Club.

On Monday morning, I boarded the Greyhound bus for Jacksonville. There I met Bud Haenel, and together we took the Seaboard Railway *Champion* for Miami Beach reclassification and reassignment. Bud and I met Steve Yankura at our billet in the Caribbean Hotel on Collins Avenue. Hundreds of Air Corps personnel were being processed here in the most pleasant surroundings. The blue Gulf Stream waters of the Atlantic were just across the street. Our dining room overlooked sandy beaches that seemed golden in the spring sunshine.

Bud Haenel drew an assignment to flight operations with the Military Air Transport Service (MATS), but Steve and I were both pulled from processing and offered assignments to the Air Corps Convalescent Center at the Don Cesar Hotel in St. Petersburg Beach, Florida. I was happy and felt great relief at the news, but at the same time felt a strong twinge of guilt because I was shirking the job I had been trained to do. I did not know it then, but many others also were being assigned to Convalescent Centers across the country, which had been established to help rehabilitate combat crew members suffering with war-related anxieties.

I stayed at the Don Cesar until the end of May 1945. The Don was a lovely old hotel built in the 1920s, with thick stucco walls that absorbed the heat of the day. Inside were great high ceilings and spacious, brightly painted rooms. It stood nine stories tall and had its own private beach on the Gulf of Mexico, a paradise, even including the mosquitoes. There was no airconditioning, of course, but our two-man rooms were quite comfortable. A cool breeze blew from the east during the day and then the west off the Gulf in the evenings.

Our days were loosely structured, requiring only that we have our temperatures read each morning before breakfast. It seemed odd. How do you take the pulse or the blood count of the brain or memory? What pills ease memories of violent death or erase guilt? Could I have saved our ship, or kept Coots and Barnes from injury and the threat of execution? Helen, our blonde, feminine, and attractive nurse helped us through the healing process, as she dutifully recorded temperatures. Her lovely smile made us all feel good.

I signed up for classes in news analysis, journalism, and hobby shop. We all exercised in some fashion: volleyball, fishing, or golfing at the St. Petersburg Country Club, where I first learned how frustrating golf could be. One of my close friends was a handsome, husky all-American boy named Del Hawkins, a former Ohio State athlete. Captain Hawkins was a 15th Air Force bombardier, a fine golfer, and a good man to stand with at the bar in the evening. He was such an admirable golfer that he never commented on how atrociously I played. We did a lot of drinking and swimming together and became healthier and more tanned as the weeks zipped by.

Another of my buddies was Captain Mac McClaron, a Mustang fighter pilot who told how terrible it was to strafe German flak towers that were positioned on beachheads and around airfields. These towers were usually forty-fifty feet high and built much like a seashore lighthouse, with a 360 degree field of fire. From there, German gunners would pour streams of machine-gun and cannon fire at the attacking P-51 fighters. Racing at the towers at speeds over 300 mph into a stream of gunfire and tracers was a contest of timing and nerve. It was a race to see whether the fighter pilot could knock out the bunkered gunners before they sent him crashing to earth. There was no time for escape by parachute. I was glad not to be in fighters after listening to Mac's story.

The medical officer talked regularly to us all. Captain Donald Barnes, a flight doctor who had served with the 12th Tactical Air Force in Europe, scheduled me for the mandatory "Flak Juice test." This meant that sodium pentothal was intravenously fed into my arm while I was strapped on a cold metal table. When the juice began to flow, I started counting backward from one-hundred as far as I could go. I slipped into that other consciousness, and he began to ask me questions about the day and time we were blown out of the skies over France. He took me back into that past, asking me to relive those moments of fear and danger that my psyche was keeping suppressed, and by so doing sought to cure the fears and concerns that were so bothersome.

The sodium pentothal may have worked, but I do not really know because Dr. Barnes never told me the results. It was painless and lasted no more than 20-30 minutes. Thinking back on the whole experience, the best medicine probably was provided by the beach and the sun. The healing balm of Mom Nature and the help of Father Time surpassed the best prescriptions our shrinks could provide. I loved the calm, warm Gulf waters at our beach. We would stroll in the sun and then rest on the sand for hours. At night, tall Australian pine trees outside our windows would sigh and rustle as they moved warm, salt-tinged air over our cool white sheets and well-tanned bodies.

Our social lives were active, often centering around the fine old Coliseum dancehall in downtown St. Petersburg, which I had visited once or twice when at MacDill Field. The Coliseum was a cavernous building, its wooden dance floor seemed almost the size of a football field. Sparkling chandeliers hung 30 or 40 feet above, sending mirrored reflector lights of various hues on the dancers below. Like moths to a flame, we Don Cesar veterans would drift toward the Coliseum on Friday or Saturday nights bearing our brown-bagged bottles of *Four Roses* whiskey (selected more for the name than the taste), because the Coliseum did not have a liquor license. Best of all, many young ladies appeared at the dancehall, having paid their own admission.

There was always a good movie to see in town. I remember *For Whom the Bell Tolls*, the Ernest Hemingway story of civil war in Spain during 1937, starring Gary Cooper and Ingrid Bergman. It was a wonderful, action-love story. The old theater in downtown St. Petersburg has probably been leveled to make room for a new building, and the old paved brick streets of St. Pete are mostly covered with asphalt. Webb's Drug Store, which billed itself as "The World's Most Unusual Drug Store," has been taken over by one of the giant chain outlets. However, the regal old Don Cesar still stands on St. Petersburg Beach, reinstated to its original status as a first class resort hotel.

* * *

No one was prepared for the terrible loss of Franklin Delano Roosevelt, who died on April 12, 1945. Our President, the only one my generation had ever known, died suddenly of a cerebral hemorrhage at 4:35 P.M. Eastern War Time (EWT) while vacationing at his favorite spa in Warm Springs, Georgia. Roosevelt was serving an unprecedented fourth term as President and Commander in Chief of our armed forces. Our national father figure, the acknowledged leader of the free world, was dead at age sixty-three. Like President Lincoln, he died before he could see the victorious end to the struggle he led. He was buried in Hyde Park, New York, his family estate, on April 14, 1945. The reins of government passed to a little known, almost obscure Vice President named Harry S. Truman, an ex-Senator from Kansas City, Missouri. The news of his rise to Presidency came like a bolt out of the blue. He was drinking bourbon and branch water with his cronies in Room H-128 (Speaker of the House Sam Rayburn's private after-hours club) when White House switchboard operators tracked him down. Truman said he felt as though the whole world had fallen on him that warm spring afternoon when he learned that Roosevelt was dead and he was President.

During the nineteen days that followed FDR's death, two other world leaders died. Adolph Hitler killed himself by firing his Walther pistol into his mouth on April 29. He was secluded in his concrete bunker four levels beneath the streets of Berlin and died the day before the Russians entered the city. His body charred with gasoline was found burned almost beyond recognition outside the bunker's courtyard; Hitler was fifty-nine years old. He had finally married his mistress, Eva Braun, earlier that day, who also died that day by swallowing a cyanide pill.

Benito Mussolini and his mistress were caught on April 26, 1945, by Italian partisan forces as they and their entourage were trying to escape across the border from Lake Como into Switzerland. Mussolini was disguised in civilian clothes and hiding in the back of a truck that was escorted by German troops when they were stopped at a checkpoint. The partisan troops took him into a field nearby and shot him. Il Duce (the leader), as Mussolini was often called, was strung up by his heels alongside his paramour for all to see; he was sixty-two years old.

With the capture of Berlin and the death of both Hitler and Mussolini, the war in Europe was practically over. After six years of darkness, the lights came on again in London and all over the world. The Russians and the Yanks joined forces just south of Berlin; Allied 5th Army troops in Italy poured northward through the Brenner Pass in the Alps into Austria; and German troops were surrendering at the rate of a division per day.

Victory in Europe (V-E Day) was proclaimed on Tuesday, May 8, 1945, officially at 6:01 P.M. EWT. Military base commanders were advised to restrict troops to their bases except for official business. The brass obviously anticipated some rowdiness, perhaps for good reason; but for the most part, the world did not explode with joy that day. Celebrations were tempered by the knowledge that the fanatical Japanese still remained a formidable foe in the Pacific. Still, it was reassuring that now all the strength and power that had been focused against the Nazis could be concentrated against the Japs; the Japanese were probably thinking the same thing.

Del Hawkins and I celebrated the day quietly at the Don with a fine swim in the Gulf. Later at dinner, we discussed the merits of the point system for voluntary discharge of veterans and realized, to our delight, that we had enough points to get out of the service. The choices were all favorable: I could go to college under the GI Bill of Rights passed by Congress in June 1944; work for one of the airlines as a pilot, although the idea of being in charge of a plane full of passengers (all without parachutes) worried me; or stay in the service. Best of all, I knew there would be no assignment to dreadful combat missions in the Pacific; what a relief.

I again met with the Don Cesar medical board and after a routine checkup was approved for return to flight duty. The next day I went to Drew Field in Clearwater. The base had been used for B-17 training but was soon converted to civilian use, eventually becoming the Clearwater-St. Petersburg International Airport. I applied for a commercial pilot's license in case I decided to work as an airline pilot. The license was issued in several weeks by the Federal Aviation Administration (FAA) in Washington, stating that I was qualified to fly four-engine aircraft and had an instrument pilot rating.

By the end of May, I was on my way once more to the Miami Beach Reassignment Center. In keeping with the Air Corps policy of sending combat crews to the base nearest their home, I was assigned to Lockbourne Air Base at Columbus, Ohio, the home of Captain Eddie Rickenbacker. Rickenbacker was a famous racing car driver and World War I ace who was credited with downing twenty-six enemy aircraft. Rickenbacker later became President of Eastern Airlines where he served for years before his death in 1973.

Lockbourne was a delightful change from the bright summer heat and humidity of Florida. The Ohio countryside was lush and green from spring rains. The manicured farmlands and dairy pastures on the way into town from the base were soothing to the eyes, and the moist country air was fragrantly sweet. Personnel actions were courteous and less harried here, a distinct change from the bustle of Miami Beach, and my duties were light. Three-day weekend passes were easy to obtain, and Beaver Valley was only about four hours away by train and much less by plane.

Between visits to the family, I kept busy flying four hours per month, the minimum needed to draw flight pay, and practicing in the Link trainer to keep my instrument flight skills current. Like a dog with a bone, I kept worrying about the pros and cons of becoming a civilian. I was uncertain about leaving the security and companionship of my Air Corps family yet knew it was the only practical thing to do.

Another problem was learning to adjust to the old way of life in the Valley after tasting the heady style of living as a commissioned officer with all its perks and privileges. I felt uncomfortable about returning to West Bridgewater where I would have to deal with my old girlfriends, including Bobby Chatt who wanted to get married and would be graduating soon from Duke University. If I had been married while in the service, I would probably stay in uniform so I could pay the bills; but I was single and had no other responsibilities for the moment. Even though I had no desire or ambition to become a career officer, it was still appealing. Then the personnel officer asked me to take an assignment in Lubbock, Texas, as an instrument instructor pilot. I told him I would let him know tomorrow. All I could think of was wind howling over dusty plains somewhere in the panhandle of northwest Texas, a place where it was bitter cold in winter and dry and hot in summer, with tumbleweeds as far as the eye could see. This was an ill omen, not promising at all. Maybe God was sending me a message.

I carefully looked at the GI Bill, which was designed for guys like me who wanted to prepare for another career that would be comparable to the rank and status I had come to enjoy. My Mom often said that getting an education was the foundation of success, that and hard work. My mind was made up; the next day I told the personnel officer to take my name off the list for Lubbock and start processing my discharge.

The more I looked at the GI Bill, the more I realized how generous it was. It provided five-hundred dollars a year for tuition and books for full-time students, plus fifty dollars per month for subsistence (seventy-five dollars if you were married). It was not quite enough to pay all the bills, but I had saved some money and could find part-time work, if needed. In years to come, the GI Bill spurred a flood of 2.2 million World War II veterans into our nation's colleges. It also offered other benefits, such as low-interest home loans. The Bill would prove an important economic factor in the first post-war decade, with costs of higher education amounting to $5.5 billion through 1956.

Life was carefree while waiting for my discharge. One of my friends at Lockbourne was Lieutenant John Succop, a blondish, witty, and bright fellow with a happy-go-lucky spirit. We partied at all the best night-spots in Columbus and often traveled together to see our families. Even though Johnny was engaged to a girl in Pittsburgh, we enjoyed our stag evenings in town dancing with an almost endless supply of girls.

My mail brought news that my brother Chuck had transferred from Valdosta, Georgia, to Dodge City, Kansas, and then to a B-26 base at Pampa, Texas. Before Chuck could get an overseas assignment, the war wound down, and he stayed in Pampa for the next year, eventually becoming squadron commander before his discharge. My brother-in-law Chuck Carson was on his way home from Italy for discharge, and Joan planned to meet him in New York City for a reunion before they returned to the Valley. Ty Burton surfaced at Chanute Field, Illinois, where the Army, in its infinite wisdom, placed him in a choice filing clerk position; he was slightly bitter. We talked on the phone a few times, and I told him of my school plans. Apparently, he too thought the idea was sound, for the next thing I knew he was back at Harvard.

By mid-July, I departed Lockbourne for Indiantown Gap, the sprawling Army base near Harrisburg for discharge. The Gap formalities were brief and to the point. It took less than a day to get my processing completed.

My final examination was a hurried and skimpy business, understandably less demanding than my entrance exam for the flight cadet program. The Army also wanted to discharge us without unnecessary liability claims for service-connected injuries. Thankfully, I was well and physically fit. They held a Big Ben alarm clock about one foot from my ear and asked if I could hear it. Of course I could hear it, the noise was deafening! I passed the hearing test.

One minor personal tragedy occurred. As I was washing up in the latrine, I took off my silver Air Corps ring with the black onyx center and my class number engraved on it and laid it on the shelf above the wash bowl. I left the ring there for only a few moments, but it was gone when I came back to get it. Sadly, I had lost my prized class ring on my last day of active duty. Perhaps this was a symbolic end to this chapter in my life.

My discharge to civilian status was effective July 19, 1945, after spending two years, ten months, and ten days in the Army Air Corps. It seemed more like ten years and was almost like leaving home again. This time, however, I felt unsure of the future, worrying about what I should do and wondering where all this would lead.

* * *

It took some time to adjust to being back in Bridgewater after the excitement of the past several months. The war was over in Europe, and I no longer felt directly involved in the struggle. I was satisfied that our side would win in the Pacific, that I had done my share, and that for all practical purposes, the war was behind me.

I immediately began checking out college possibilities. I rejected the notion of returning to Pitt where I had been a night engineering student during 1940-41, because it had too much of a big city atmosphere. After an overnight visit to Penn State, I was sure this was the college for me. Four hours away by bus from Pittsburgh lay the little town of State College. Spread out over the spacious, tree-shaded campus were stately classroom buildings with ivy-covered, red brick walls. Main Street bordered the campus and was lined with pleasant book stores, a corner restaurant where everyone took coffee breaks between classes, a couple of movie theaters, and a musty rathskeller. Fraternity and sorority houses were active, and there were adequate rooming houses for those who did not join a Greek-letter society.

The college Admissions Office was most receptive and accepted my credits in math and chemistry from Pitt. I also received fifteen credits for having achieved an officer's commission in the Air Corps and twelve more credits toward physical education requirements. This allowed me to enter the 1945 fall semester as a sophomore, which was simply great news.

The rest of the summer, I worked on the night shift at the Keystone Bakery just around the corner from our apartment. For seventy-four cents an hour[3], my work was simple enough. I would load six hot loaves of bread at a time onto wide trays, slide the trays into six-foot tall racks, and push the racks into a cooling room. I stacked bread in those cooling racks for hours until my hands seemed burned, even through thick gloves. In time, I had callouses on my palms and fingers so thick you would have thought I laid bricks for a living. There was a thirty minute break around 10:00 P.M. when I could slip home and make a sandwich, but sometimes I did not bother for there was plenty of hot bread to eat. Occasionally, I would grasp a loaf too hard, cracking the crust so badly it could not be wrapped. That damaged loaf was okay for me to eat and was delicious. I lost a few pounds sweating over the unending stream of hot loaves, but it kept me busy and out of trouble.

My brother-in-law Charles Carson was now out of the service and taught me how to drive his big Oldsmobile. By mid-September, at twenty-three years of age, I got my driver's license. My old friend Chet helped me pick out a clean, 1940 four-door Chevrolet sedan from a used car lot for six-hundred dollars; it was a light green color and my pride and joy.

Chet had been discharged with a strange malady traced back to his previous assignment in the Panama Canal Zone. We often met to chat about old times, but I worried about how thin and jaundiced he looked. He was chipper, though, and full of pride and ambition because he and his wife had a new baby girl. Ever the entrepreneur, Chet bought a dump truck and began making his living hauling loads for builders or moving contractors. Chet was a happy, hardworking, dependable guy, who always smiled and had a fine sense of humor. His energy seemed to diminish with the weight he was losing, however; and later that fall while I was away at school, Chet died of Addison's disease. I missed him, for we were close and had so much fun together growing up as teenagers.

August 1945 was a month full of historic events. On August 6, the first atomic bomb named Little Boy was dropped on Hiroshima,

---

[3] While the hourly pay scale may seem low, inflation had not yet begun to climb in 1945, and you could still buy a decent roast beef dinner for a dollar and admission to the movies was still only fifty cents at matinees.

The Time of My Life

Japan, from the B-29 Superfortress *Enola Gay*, flown by Colonel Paul Tibbits, who named the ship for his mother. The bomb was dropped from 32,000 feet and exploded 600 feet above the city, destroying an unbelievable four square miles of homes and business buildings. Shockwaves and intense heat from the explosion caused 100,000 deaths outright; another 100,000 would die later from burns and the effects of atomic radiation.

On August 8, the Russians delivered on their promise made at Yalta and declared war on Japan. On August 9, a second atomic bomb Fat Man was dropped on Nagasaki, Japan, from a B-29 named *Bock's Car*, after pilot Fred Bock. This bomb caused 75,000 deaths immediately and another 75,000 later from the radiation effects.[4]

The two bombs dropped on the Japanese in August 1945, ended the war. A year later, President Truman signed the Atomic Energy Act, which transferred control of atomic power from military to civilian hands. The Atomic Energy Commission (AEC) gave the federal government a monopoly over all fissionable processes, production, patents, and development but also allowed for a close military liaison through civilian secretaries of the various armed forces. Three years later, the Soviets tested their first weapon, and the atomic bomb race was on.

The Japanese government sued for peace on August 10, which led to an unconditional surrender agreement signed aboard the battleship *Missouri*, Admiral Bull Halsey's Third Fleet flagship, in Tokyo Bay. Although the war in the Pacific ended on August 15, V-J Day (victory over Japan) was celebrated on September 2, 1945, when all U.S. factories and major businesses closed for the joyous occasion. Under the compassionate terms of the surrender, Emperor Hirohito

---

[4]   The atomic bomb that was to become a major source of peacetime electric power was created by scientists, not by soldiers. A group of physicists, including Albert Einstein, suspected in 1939 that Hitler was working on nuclear weapons and appealed for a grant-in-aid from President Roosevelt to start research on behalf of the United States. Roosevelt allotted $6,000 to start the project; but after the bombing of Pearl Harbor, time became critical and the undertaking accelerated. By 1942, the project was turned over to the Corps of Engineers, led by General Leslie Groves, and dubbed the Manhattan Project. The first man-made nuclear reaction was accomplished in December 1942.

of Japan was allowed to remain as head of state but without any military forces ever permitted. The U.S. army of occupation that took over the reins of government was led by Supreme Commander General Douglas MacArthur.

Halfway around the world in Southeast Asia, an event of little significance to most Americans occurred on the day the Japanese surrendered. Ho Chi Minh declared the Viet Minh government to be independent of French rule in an address to half a million people in Ba Dinh Square, Hanoi, North Vietnam. Ho read the Vietnamese Declaration of Independence and proclaimed the establishment of the Democratic Republic of Vietnam. This action set the stage for a long and bitter struggle that would see the French defeated at Dien Bien Phu in 1954 and the U.S. government slowly but surely become unsuccessfully involved in a war to suppress communism in that part of the world.

SIX

Penn State to Okinawa

The transition from Army pilot to college student took about a year to complete. Once enrolled at State, I burrowed into textbooks and began the struggle to regain the powers of concentration needed to master the seventeen-hour work load I had undertaken that first semester. I lived in a small but comfortable upstairs room in a private home owned by a fine lady who lived with her mother and teenage daughter. The only men in the house were myself and two other students who occupied the second floor; the ladies were all downstairs. We did not have kitchen privileges and only saw them when we paid the rent and passed in and out the front door.

While I was busy coping with the deadlines of daily classwork and taking examinations, U.S. labor unions were fighting for wage increases all over the country. Thousands of strikes flared up involving nearly five million workers in industries such as steel, telephone and telegraph, maritime shipping, meat packing, railroads, and coal mining; the country was almost paralyzed. A major showdown occurred when the United Auto Workers (UAW), then averaging $1.12 per hour, struck 95 General Motors (GM) plants on November 21, 1945. The strike lasted for 113 days before UAW workers gained an 18.5-cent-per-hour raise, an increase quickly matched by steel industry strikers.

My routine college life became somewhat monotonous yet provided a much-needed transition into the postwar world. I was very aware of being the first in my family who could graduate from college. Lacking a definite purpose or sense of direction, I knew I had to discover my talents and where they might lead. I decided against

109

studying engineering because my math and science skills were only average but did not know what I should study.

Without any particular reason, I began taking courses in industrial psychology. These studies involved measuring workers' progress using time and motion studies and defining and measuring the speed, dexterity, and motor skills of assembly-line employees. I soon began to doubt seriously that this was what I wanted to do with my life.

I happened to be reading *The Man in the Grey Flannel Suit*, Sloan Wilson's book about a man in the advertising business. I remember that the hero wore a very expensive necktie described as "being very sincere." The book sparked the idea that the field of advertising might be suitable for an aspiring young buck like me.

I called on Donald E. Davis, a professor in the school of journalism and a counselor in the advertising department. Professor Davis was a tall, affable man with a round chubby face. He usually dressed in tweed jackets and often wore bow ties. We got along well right from the start, and he took me under his wing. He thought I would do well in the advertising department and saw to it that most of my credits were transferred to the school of journalism. I was soon taking courses in newspaper, radio, and magazine advertising techniques. My earlier training as a draftsman helped in ad layouts and in organizing visual presentations. My interest in writing helped in composing sales copy to go with product display ads. I did solid B-plus work in my new field right on through my junior and senior years.

Another highlight of my college career was being initiated into the Phi Kappa Psi fraternity in the spring of 1946. All the fraternity houses were beginning to fill up with returning service personnel. Our supper meetings were enjoyable and allowed new pledge candidates to meet the chapter brothers on neutral ground, so to speak. Mild hazing of candidates was permitted at these functions. One Sunday evening, for example, all pledges were asked to stand and recite a poem. When it was my turn, I was struck dumb, embarrassed, unable to think of anything. I stood up though, wishing the floor would open up and swallow me, and found myself blurting, "Little Jack Horner sat in the corner, eating a pumpkin pie. He stuck in his thumb, pulled out a plum, and said, Oh, what a brave boy am I." I sat down, the ordeal over and realized it was not so bad after all. This sort of hazing was helpful, a fine confidence builder for young reticent people like me.

Living at the Phi Psi house was fine, but room and board cost fifty-nine dollars a month, nine dollars more than the monthly GI allotment. I earned an additional twenty-five dollars a month waiting on tables in our dining room and later became the salaried Phi Psi treasurer. In the winter months, I took turns stoking the furnace fires morning, noon, and at bedtime to keep the house warm. There were many ways of making extra money so that my savings would last longer.

Most college students sent their laundry home once a week in a strapped laundry box at special low postal rates. There were no laundry facilities in town that I could afford, so dear Mom did it all for me. I was grateful for her support and never could have made it through those school years without her.

Our house was an ivy-covered, red-brick, two-story building with a slate roof steeply pitched so the snow would slide down easily. The main living area had a massive, stone fireplace at the far end of the spacious, wood-panelled room. On the mantel were various trophies won by Phi Psi athletes. All around the room were comfortable, overstuffed leather chairs and couches. The effect was of a rugged, male-dominated private club where the better things in life were enjoyed and respected. It was all very handsome in my eyes.

Our dining room was set off from the living area by folding glass doors and contained six sturdy, eight-man oak tables with wooden chairs to match. Each table head, assigned by the chapter president according to seniority, would say grace at dinner or ask another brother. It was a nice custom and good training. I was a table head during my senior year and recall being honored the night of our formal Christmas dinner dance when our president tapped a spoon on his water glass and asked me to say grace. The hush that fell over our dining room was the start of a special evening for me and for most of the guests.

After dinner, there was dancing to the sprightly music of Phi Psi brother Dick Berge's group of five musicians. Christmas holly wreaths bedecked the windows, and mistletoe hung over every archway. Eggnog and calorie-rich cakes, candies, and cookies covered side tables. Hard liquor and beer were available in the basement meeting room for those who wanted something heartier. Our monthly chapter meetings in this room were conducted under *Robert's Rules of Order*, which was good training for those of us who conducted meetings later in life.

Two required courses I shall never forget were both difficult and extremely worthwhile. English Composition II was a creative writing course taught by Professor Christy, a slender, youthful-looking man who wore wire-rimmed glasses and spoke softly yet with such authority that his competency and knowledge were never doubted. For the first time in a classroom, I felt flattered and encouraged by his critiques of my compositions about flying bombers over Germany. Because of Christy's influence, I wanted to learn more and to master the techniques of good writing, which I am still pursuing forty years later.

The second course was a basic public speaking requirement. Each student had to prepare and deliver oral presentations that would amuse or persuade or to serve as a discussion leader. This was most trying and agonizing for me, being nervous when I was the center of attention. Those five-minute talks were as nerve racking as flying bombers through heavy flak. I memorized all my speeches, used index cards as prompters, and pressed my hands firmly on the lectern to quiet their trembling. The instructor said I had a monotone voice but gave me good marks on preparation and speech content. Later in life, giving speeches became somewhat easier, never easy, but never as hard as those presentations at Penn State.

Spring was coming, and I was inspired to try out for the school baseball team as a pitcher. In early March, before training began, we would-be pitchers and catchers began workouts in the gymnasium, because snow and ice still covered the ball diamond. More than three years of layoff seemed too much to overcome at first. My left-hand palm puffed up from the force of the catcher's throws; my right-hand fingers were raw and tender from trying to regain ball control and throwing speed. Muscles ached in my arm and shoulder, but after a week or so it got easier. Workouts took about two hours a day from my study time, plus the time it took to walk the mile and a half between the field house and fraternity house.

Coach Bedink, a stocky, business-like man, was quiet and firm. I toiled hard to get his attention but realized as a walk-on player, he did not owe me anything; still, he did not discourage me. When spring weather arrived, the full squad went outside to practice wearing rubber-lined undershirts for warmth: fifty pitchers, catchers, outfielders, and infielders taking turns in intersquad games, getting ready for the season opener on April 15. He seemed to know what he was doing and what he was looking for in his players. I noticed he spent a lot of time with a tall, sandy-haired pitcher who wore glasses and threw a nice assortment of pitches, including a fastball, a slider, a good curve, and a change of pace. Clearly, this guy was going to be the starting pitcher. I guessed he was a holdover from last year's team, possibly a scholarship player. Yet I had hope; my fastball was not too bad, and I had a fair curve ball. The coach put me in a few practice innings and showed me how to control the ball by bringing my arm higher overhead. This tip helped, and I was able to get out most of my opposing batters. Only one or two other pitchers were as good as me, but with a 20-game schedule, the main pitcher would probably get all the work. I would have to wait a year or two before there would be room on the roster for me.

The primary reason I was at State was to get a degree, not to play ball. My courses demanded more time than I was devoting, and with a pang of regret, I turned in my uniform and locker key to become a spectator, not a player. I have never forgotten the importance of regular physical conditioning as well as mental preparation for winning in baseball or any other contest. It takes commitment, desire, hard work, and sacrifice to succeed as a ball player or as a father, businessman, politician, or writer.

After dinner on Fridays, many of us headed for the rathskellar to review the events of the week, listen to the juke box, and drink pitchers of beer. We talked of sports, girls, and grades. Movies were another chief diversion, since television was not commonplace; there was none at State College. In more metropolitan towns, beer taverns were installing TV sets featuring Friday night boxing, which was becoming very popular.

Social life at Penn State, snidely referred to as the "country club," centered around the sororities and fraternities. Members in Greek-letter societies far outnumbered "townies" (residents of State College) and students who lived in boarding houses. Our Phi Psi chapter had a social alliance with a sister sorority, the Phi Delta Gammas. Every year we cosponsored a Sunday afternoon open house and tea dance, usually in October when the leaves were red and gold. Crowds of young students joined with returning graduate students to celebrate Homecoming Week, the highlight of which was the football game played Saturday afternoon at Beaver Stadium, followed by much beer consumption at various watering holes in town. Every available bed in State College was occupied: fraternity houses, hotels, guest houses, and any rental space in town.

During the summer of 1947 after my junior year, I apprenticed in *The Daily Times* advertising department in Beaver and was paid twenty-five dollars a week. My pay was raised to fifty dollars so at least I did not quite starve. Scattered reports of flying saucers appeared around the country that summer and were all thoroughly investigated by the U.S. Air Force's Office of Special Investigations. These UFO reports were all highly classified because of national security. Hundreds of sightings were reported, checked out, and determined to be hoaxes or otherwise explainable.

My interest in creative writing had been encouraged by Professor Christy, who suggested I enter a short story contest for college students offered by the *New Republic* magazine. My submission did not win, and my disappointment was enormous. Through this exercise, I discovered I did not handle rejection very well. Later in life I learned to deal with rejection a little more gracefully, but it has never been easy to accept. I also learned that writing was very demanding work and not for the faint of heart, nor for those unwilling to practice the trade and pay the dues.

My twenty-fifth birthday was on September 18, 1947, a birthday shared by the U. S. Air Force. President Harry Truman signed the National Security Act of 1947, which made the Air Force an equal service with the Army and Navy. The Air Force started to function from a temporary base at Lowry Field in Denver, Colorado. Its first student class was composed of twenty-five percent of West Point and

Navy cadets who were scheduled to graduate in 1949. Congress and the Air Force haggled for years before Congress approved a separate Air Force Academy. Many of the academy's first buildings were built from five-dollar-contributions solicited from former Air Corps members like myself. The first class of Air Force officers graduated from the new academy at Colorado Springs, Colorado, in 1959.

The year 1947 was also significant for the development of the Marshall Plan, named for its author, Secretary of State George C. Marshall, who had been our military Chief of Staff during World War II. He drafted a plan that would provide substantial economic and social aid to European countries devastated by the war. Congress approved the plan, known as the European Recovery Plan (ERP), which poured billions of dollars into Europe over the next four years for everything from chickens to hand tools. The Soviet Union was invited to join but refused, fearing the impact the United States could have on the Soviet economy. By 1952, the ERP was completed and largely successful, judging by Western Europe's fifteen-percent increased output from before the war. The French and Italian governments had managed to expel their Communists. For the most part, however, Europeans largely ignored Marshall's additional urging for one broad economic family in Europe with free trade among its members. Today this vision is coming true as Europe moves closer to Marshall's ideal. Essentially, the plan achieved the goal of halting the spread of Communism in Europe while keeping America strong.

By early January 1948, I had completed all the required courses in the journalism curriculum. Almost before I knew it, it was time to receive my bachelor of arts degree. In rented caps and gowns, my graduation group assembled in the Beaver Auditorium on a sunny Saturday morning in early February, to receive our diplomas and have our pictures taken. I almost decided against attending because it was so anticlimactic. None of my family could come, because it was difficult to travel in the winter months. Now that my college days were over, I had to decide what to do next.

I returned to my old job at *The Daily Times*. Even though the pay was still fifty-dollars a week before taxes, I had hopes for advancement. Feeling affluent, I took out a loan for $1,000 from the local bank and bought a rather sleek-looking, green, 1946 two-door Mercury coupe for nine-hundred dollars. Now I could move around more easily, particularly when going to the Greater Pittsburgh Airport for weekend training in the Air Force Reserve Unit. I checked out in the reliable Texas AT-6, which was used extensively in single-engine pilot training during the war. It was a thrill to fly over Beaver Valley, looking down on my old swimming holes and fishing spots in the Ohio and Beaver Rivers. Occasionally I did a steep roll or dived straight down, imagining I was the ace pilot I dreamed of as a teenager reading *G-8 and His Battle Aces*. Actually, it was kind of lonely; I missed the comradeship of a copilot and crew.

One of my advertising accounts at the newspaper was a men's clothing store in Rochester owned by Irving Goodman. Once a week, we discussed whatever specials he wanted to run on men's clothing. I would then lay out the ad, selecting and inserting appropriate display art work along with advertising copy that I wrote to help sell the goods. The printers in back of the plant would cast the ad in hot lead and set it up in the page layout using the pyramid style to balance the ads and news columns for that page. In those days, huge metal presses printed the newspaper after the typesetters had finished casting. By 3:00 P.M., the presses began to roll clamorously, noisily, deafeningly loud. This procedure was slowly being replaced by photo-offset presses, a cleaner, quieter, and more efficient technique of printing newspapers that was just coming into popularity in the late 1940s.

Irving Goodman was a short, garrulous Jewish man who was pleasant and gentlemanly to deal with, very scholarly, and hardworking. Over time, we became pretty good friends. He knew about my former Air Force days and one day asked me if I would like to fly airplanes to help the Zionists in Palestine. I didn't know what to say.

I knew that Jewish refugees were trying to create an independent state of Israel and that the Palestine Arabs were bitterly resisting because they would have to give up some of their land. I also knew that the British were against the movement. Thousands of Jewish refugees who had escaped Hitler's death camps in Europe desperately needed a place of their own and were determined to establish a free Israel. Many American Jews were contributing their cash and support to the effort.

Goodman said that the Zionist movement would pay well for pilots who would fight for the cause. In short, he was asking me if I was willing to become a mercenary. I gave it some thought, flattered by the notion that I might qualify for such duty, but had to tell him I was not interested in becoming a soldier of fortune. Realistically, I knew the United States would not help me if I got shot down over Palestine; more than likely, I would become chopped meat for an Arab stew. I did not even ask what such work would pay, but I bet the money was good. Eventually, the Zionist movement was successful, although the bitter struggle between Arabs and Jews still goes on, more than 40 years since it began at the end of World War II.

The talks with Goodman were provocative, setting my mind to spinning with adventurous thoughts and reminding me of the comradeship and sense of family I had experienced in the Air Corps. Right now, however, more pressing matters demanded my attention. I needed to start making more money. It was time to ask the boss for a raise. The general manager said he could not afford to give me a raise but could give me a clothing allowance at some of the business accounts in Beaver Falls. My jaw dropped about two inches. I had never heard of paying employees in clothing. Looking back, I realize that was probably a pretty good perk, but at the time it did not strike me as a good idea. Clearly, the handwriting was on the wall. The pay at this job would never amount to much. It was discouraging news, something they had not taught me at college. The more I thought about it the more I knew there had to be a better way to make a living.

By early fall of 1948, the Berlin airlift was flying basic foodstuffs such as flour, milk, coal, sugar, and oils to West Berliners whose highway supply lines were blockaded by the Russians who were deliberately trying to increase tension between East and West Berlin. The U. S. Air Force decided to expand its airlift capability because the winter months ahead would bring increased demand for fuel and food. Four-engine pilots soon would be in short supply. Reserve units around the nation were told that any pilot interested in recall to active duty would be considered. It did not take me long to act. I qualified with over eight-hundred hours of four-engine pilot time and was in a reserve slot. The application was filled out and popped into the mail. My Air Force paycheck would almost triple that of the

Times. Salary for a 1st Lieutenant on active duty was about three hundred dollars per month. In addition there would be one hundred and twenty-five for flight pay (hazardous duty), a housing and living allowance of about one hundred and twenty-five, and free medical, dental, and travel expenses; not bad at all. Besides, I could see that the quality of my life in Beaver Valley would not amount to much.

Within thirty days, I was accepted and ordered to report to McGuire Air Force Base at Fort Dix, New Jersey, on October 10, 1948, to begin a three-year tour of duty. Without regret, I gave notice at the *Times*, dusted off my old uniforms (which still fit), packed two B-4 bags into the trunk of my freshly tuned-up Mercury, and headed east. The Pennsylvania Turnpike was spectacularly arrayed in its gold and red autumn foliage, and the coffee at the Howard Johnson Coffee Shops along the route never tasted better.

The trip took about six hours, and soon I was checking into the BOQ at McGuire Field, named after Thomas McGuire, a Pacific fighter pilot who was killed in action in World War II. McGuire Field was one of the newly formed Strategic Air Command (SAC) bases commanded by General Curtis LeMay, famed for directing the 21st Bomber Command's B-29 raids over Tokyo from the Mariana Islands in 1945.

I met the Base Commander, Colonel Frank Dunn, a regular officer with a bluff, courteous manner[1]. The Colonel explained that the need for pilots to fly the Berlin airlift was no longer critical, but I could be a copilot on a B-29 photo reconnaissance crew, which was okay with me. I had learned a long time ago that every plan was subject to change in the military. "Exigencies of the service" was the expression the brass liked to use. Getting the job done was most important to the military mind; accomplishing the mission came before all else. Once this philosophy was understood, life was not too complicated in uniform, it was a philosophy that suited me very well, most of the time. I saluted the Colonel and left the office, happy to be back on duty. I was not pleased to be moving back into a BOQ and knew my housing allowance would cover the expense of an apartment.

---

[1] Colonel Dunn was to surface later in my life as the officer in charge of Air America's civilian pilots in Vientiane, Laos, during the Vietnam War.

I immediately placed an ad in the *Trenton Times* for a furnished apartment and soon signed a year's lease on a spacious, freshly redecorated two-bedroom apartment in Trenton. It had beautiful gleaming oak floors, a sunny living room, a glassed-in sun porch, a fully equipped kitchen, and decent furnishings throughout. I asked my Mother to stay with me for a while to get her out of the Valley for a change of pace and to help me establish my new home in Trenton. She did not need to work now and agreed to come a few weeks later; within a month or so, Nancy decided to join us.

Meanwhile, I was busy in the base Information and Education Office (I&E) where my college training helped in my work in "Operation Bootstrap." This program was designed to provide self-study courses to those who wanted to obtain high school equivalent credits on their off-duty time. This was my additional duty assignment. My primary duty was learning to fly the B-29. Captain Virgil Stevens was the pilot of the crew to which I was assigned. Steve was a tall, rangy Texan who resembled John Wayne. He was about six feet four inches tall, had big shoulders and hands, weighed approximately two-hundred and twenty pounds, and could have been a model for Marlboro cigarette commercials. Steve was married with two children and had returned to active duty to support his family and pay the mortgage on his house in Texas.

For the next six months, we did a lot of aerial photography for the U.S. Coast and Geodetic Survey. We also had several extended, temporary duty flights, the most memorable being the month-long trip to Forbes Field in Topeka, Kansas. At very specific altitudes (usually 20,000 feet) and on specific headings, we would fly straight and level so our K-20 aerial camera operators could shoot precise overlapping strips acceptable for map production. The tolerances were very close, and we often had to fly the same map coverage over again. It was very tedious work.

When no flying was scheduled, I was often strapped in the Link Trainer for instrument flight training in a machine that simulated flight. In case of an accident, the Link never crashed, since its cockpit was anchored to the floor. The instructor was just outside monitoring the gauges; inside it was almost like being in the air. Such training was invaluable in helping to regain rusty instrument flying skills.

One sunny Saturday afternoon, Steve and I checked out shotguns from the Base Recreation Office to hunt dove in the wheat fields that surrounded the military reservation. The dove would come whirring up from the stubble left from wheat thrashed weeks before, and we would bang away, missing most, getting some. Steve made a deal with the cook at our club to pan-fry those delicacies. He took a share for his work, and we had the rest. They were delicious, crisp, and a little gamey, but fine when washed down with cold beer. I have never hunted dove since, and probably never will; but my-oh-my were they ever good.

Steve and I, along with about five other pilots, received orders to report to Kadena Air Base on Okinawa by mid-August. Overseas selections were based on the number of months each officer had already served overseas; those with the lowest number were chosen first. I had only served seven months during World War II and therefore had no complaints. I decided it would make quite an interesting assignment, especially since there was no shooting going on. Steve, on the other hand, had a wife and children and had not foreseen another tour overseas. He appealed his assignment and somehow wrangled a reprieve.

I had a few loose ends to clear up before departure. The apartment lease was no problem, because Nancy and my Mother were planning to stay for the next year or so. They were both working now and liked Trenton very much. In fact, Nancy was working as a nurse at Fort Dix, adjacent to McGuire Field, where she met the man she would marry within the year, Thomas Stansbury, Captain, U.S. Army, who was serving his obligatory time following graduation from medical school.

To keep fit and work off excess energy, I went to the base gym regularly to run laps, do calisthenics, and occasionally put on the heavy boxing gloves. Exercise was also helpful in thwarting the gnawing pangs of what was later diagnosed as an ulcer. At the time, I had no idea that my drive to do well and to succeed was punishing my insides; that, plus smoking a pack of cigarettes or more a day and drinking too much coffee.

Since shipment of personal vehicles was allowed for travel abroad in peacetime, I decided to drive the Mercury from Trenton to San

Francisco. The Government would pay six cents a mile for driving expenses, plus seven dollars a day for food and lodging enroute. I would have to average 600 miles per day to drive the 3,000-mile trip in the five days I was allowed. I would drive at night to avoid overheating the car engine and avoid heavy daytime traffic. To keep the engine from overheating, I planned to cruise at fifty miles per hour which meant I would be behind tł wheel twelve hours a day for five days.

It was an exciting prospect, my first opportunity to see America up close. I had seen a lot of the country from the air and had viewed city alleys and the backyards of homes from many troop trains, but driving alone across the whole United States was a unique opportunity.

The first night of travel was familiar, and by early morning I reached Chicago. I found a guest home that was clean and comfortable. I had no reservations, just my Rand McNally maps, but the roads were all major highways, and it was easy to find a place to stay. Before resting, I stopped at a service station nearby and arranged for the car to be serviced and ready to pick up by late afternoon.

The way west from Chicago opened up new worlds. The land seemed more open and inviting with car windows down and cool, clover-scented night air blowing in, I passed into Iowa glimpsing fields full of corn or pasture grasses. This was rich, abundant land. I crossed the big Missouri River into Nebraska, my first impression being one of disbelief and wonder. How poor the land looked, compared with the lushness of Iowa. The roads were full of potholes and the nearby fields were arid looking, somehow forbidding and depressing. There was no sign of welcome to visitors. Images of the poor sharecroppers in *Grapes of Wrath* flashed through my mind.

I stopped dawdling and stepped on the gas, following the old Mormon Trail that wound along the silent and ghostly north banks of the shallow Platte River. Daylight came, and I stopped for breakfast at a highway diner near Grand Island. Tall grain elevators were clustered along the railroad tracks, since this was a major grain collection and shipping point. The food tasted so good at those roadside diners in the Midwest. Used to hearty farmhand appetites, the waitresses dished up full platters of bacon and eggs, pan-fried potatoes, big mugs of steaming coffee, piles of toast, or biscuits with gravy. Plenty of high-energy, high-calorie food to keep me perking right along.

I had the car serviced and ready for the third leg of the journey. By now, I was dreaming of car headlights coming at me. Because of all the night driving and the age of my car, I had to replace the headlight dimmer switch, a simple foot-pedal arrangement, that had worn out. Otherwise, the old Merc was running cool and sweet. I veered south toward the town of Ogallala and beyond that Cheyenne and Laramie, Wyoming. (I love the sound of these old Indian names.) Off in the distant Southwest rose the great tumbling range of the Rocky Mountains. I could sense the elevations beginning to ascend, even though the road lay close to the winding river beds and valleys.

That night, motoring along the deserted mountain road, my car engine began to gasp and choke. I would ease up on the throttle, which helped smooth out the strangling noises. After a few minutes, I realized I had not thought to have the carburetor cleaned and adjusted for the oxygen-thin air of these altitudes. There was no place to fix it now, so I just poked along until the worst of it passed. The road soon leveled out, and the engine began to sound better.

There was real beauty in the night scenery and activity in this part of the country. To keep awake after midnight, I would lean out the car window for fresh air. Sometimes I would take my flashlight and transfix giant jackrabbits standing on their hind legs and peering at the intruding car; some of them were twenty inches tall. They would hop about, playfully cavorting in the moonlight, half hidden by sagebrush and range grasses in the gently rolling hollows along the roadway. Most of the time I had my radio for company, unless the distance from the broadcast studio was too great. I usually listened to country music, what else? I particularly remember Patti Page's hit tune that summer, *The Tennessee Waltz*.

Crossing the Continental Divide high up in the Wind River Range between Rawlings and Rock Springs, Wyoming, I felt alone in the moonlight, atop the world. There was a grandeur in that vast space that could not be ignored. The Continental Divide is an interesting geographical landmark; a watershed demarcation from whence rainfall either drains westward to the Pacific Ocean or eastward into the Gulf of Mexico and the Atlantic Ocean.

By the light of dawn, I was on the downhill slope and only a few hours from Salt Lake City. I found a hotel in town and rested until late that afternoon, enjoying the quietness of a room above the noise of the streets. I worried about the last two days of my journey. Temperatures on the Great Salt Lake in mid-August were 100-110 degrees during the daytime. The air was dry and humidity was not a factor. Nights were much cooler and thus better for my trusty car engine—so far, so good.

The garage mechanic near the hotel changed the oil and lubricated all necessary parts. Soon after 6:00 P.M., I embarked across the vast, seemingly endless table of salt. Dry, sun-baked, and white as snow, the salt flats began to cool as soon as the sun went down, continuing to cool until it was quite chilly by midnight. I thought I could smell salt in the air, and I could see for miles. There was nothing but the dark asphalt and gravel road that stretched ahead until it vanished. Along the way, I passed Bonneville Flats used by racing car daredevils to test their nerves and machines at speeds exceeding three hundred miles per hour. I chuckled to myself; here I was puttering along at fifty miles an hour, but at least I felt pretty sure I would make it.

By 9:00 A.M. Sunday morning, I had reached the outskirts of Reno, Nevada, famous for gambling and quick divorces. The streets were quiet, and I had no difficulty parking in front of Harrah's Casino. Inside, I found a few die-hard gamblers still hard at work, men and women alike, concentrating intently as their slot machines whirred and clanked and occasionally showered a handful of silver dollars into the catch basin of the machine. I had ten dollars to gamble and with these huge silver pieces in hand stopped at one of the card tables to play twenty-one. The dealer was a morose man in a dark suit with a white shirt and string tie. He had a poker face and was not very talkative. It was obvious he was here strictly for business.

It took me about twenty minutes to lose my ten dollars, but I was not surprised and certainly not disappointed. After all, now I could say I had gambled at one of the most famous establishments in the world. I kept a few silver dollars as souvenirs for years afterward. The rest of the day was spent resting on the outskirts of town. By early evening, I was on my way into the Sierra Nevada along the Kit Carson trail. This was fascinating country, full of historical interest to an

Easterner who had never been this way before. Skirting Carson City toward Lake Tahoe, the road climbed and wound upward. The scent of pine was everywhere, and I could glimpse blue water through the trees. At the crest of the long climb, I pulled over at a scenic overlook.

The famous Donner Pass lay to the north, named for George Donner, who led a pioneer party that was seeking a shortcut to California through the Pass when the early snows of 1846 trapped them. Only forty-seven of the eighty-seven people in the party survived, some of whom lived by resorting to cannibalism. Today, a four-lane concrete and blacktop highway has replaced the old pioneer trail. It is hard to imagine the courage, patience, and determination those early pioneers possessed. They certainly should be respected for their stamina and bravery.

Downhill again, I passed Placerville, where James W. Marshall, an employee of Captain John Sutter, found specks of gold while inspecting a millrace on the South Fork of the American River. News of this discovery spread like wildfire, setting off the great 1849 California gold rush. A rich vein of gold then was found on the western slopes of the Sierra Nevada, and thousands of prospectors flooded into the state. The unearthing of a mammoth, 195-pound gold nugget near Carson Hill was the highlight of that time, raising gold fever to a high pitch. The town of Sacramento became a boom city, and then the state capital in 1854. By 1963, Sacramento was a major seaport, after the completion of a deep water channel that flowed southward via the Sacramento River seventy-five miles to San Francisco Bay.

The final one hundred miles to Hamilton Air Force Base, located about fifteen miles north of San Francisco's Golden Gate Bridge, went pleasantly. I checked in at the main gate on August 15, 1949, exactly five years from the day I was shot down over the Rhone Valley in southern France. At Hamilton Field, I met Reginald Brunson who was just reporting in from McGuire Air Base. We kept each other company while we did all our administrative and preshipping chores and explored San Francisco.

Our ship-out date was August 24, 1949. The day before, I delivered my faithful old Mercury to the Oakland Army Port from where it would be shipped on the first available cargo vessel bound for

Okinawa. Brunson and I had stored all the removable parts of the car in a box and then locked and placed it in the trunk of the car. We greased the chrome and coated the body paint with thick wax to help ward off salt spray and moisture.

A military bus took us to the port bright and early the morning of our departure. It was a cool and sunny morning as we moved imperceptibly away from the San Francisco pier. I felt snug and secure aboard the *General Simon B. Buckner* and was amused by the idea of Air Force people being transported on the high seas in an Army ship. I thought the Navy was supposed to be in the forefront of the military sailing business.

A letter written at sea on August 28 reveals the mood of that day...

Sunday at Sea/28 August 49

Dear Mom and Nan:

Tomorrow at 9:00 A.M. we lay over at Honolulu for a day and a night. So, I'm writing a few letters to get them in the post office there. There are scheduled tours of the Island. I think I'll go on one and try to do a little souvenir shopping. This peacetime traveling is really first class. And, it's free. No charge even for our meals, which incidentally are full-course affairs served by white-jacketed Filipino boys. They are forced to serve the meals in shifts, but the schedule isn't bad. If you get hungry, there are morning bouillon hours and evening snacks at 9:30 P.M. We have four men to a stateroom with adequate locker space, bed lights on each double-deck bunk, and a washstand. Showers are down the hall. It's much like a hotel because there are boys to clean the rooms and make beds. Movies, bingo, and a sundeck are available. Mostly, I spend my time reading books from the library. The chaplains have services daily, and there is a recreation period for the children. There are roughly 2,000 passengers aboard, and many are military dependents. There are about 10 civilian women workers and school teachers, one or two of whom are going back for a second tour. So Okinawa is not such a bad place as you may be imagining. When I get settled, my car will arrive and that should make social life good. My plan is to rent the car for a nominal fee to my friends, always got an eye open for a fast buck. Went to both the Catholic and Protestant services this morning; both were short, so I didn't put in too much time. Love to you

More later, Adie

* * *

A couple of significant events occurred that would affect the United States and those of us in the Armed Forces. In June 1949, U.S. occupation troops were ordered out of Korea by President Truman, signaling to the Communists in North Korea that the Americans were no longer interested in their part of the world. They were mistaken in that judgment, because within the next year the United States and North Korea would be at war. The other event occurred on August 24, 1949, when the North Atlantic Treaty Organization (NATO) was established. The United States, Canada, Great Britain, and about ten other Western European countries agreed that an armed attack against one or more members of NATO would be considered an attack against all.

* * *

While laying over for the day in Honolulu, several of us took a four-hour bus tour. We toured the recently opened National Military Cemetery, called the Punch Bowl because it lies within a sunken depression atop an extinct volcano. Here was buried Ernie Pyle, the famous World War II correspondent noted for his superb reporting of GIs in the foxholes of World War II. We also toured the Dole pineapple processing plant where our Hawaiian guide told us his people eat very little pineapple, because it is bad for the health; I had to laugh at that. The native Hawaiian women impressed me. They were so small and dainty, and healthy looking and had fine features. Even in 1949, Hawaii was an expensive place to live. The price of gas was about thirty-two cents a gallon, about fifteen cents higher than on the mainland.

Next ports of call were Guam, Manila, and then Okinawa. So far the voyage was notable for sun-filled days and moist, salt-scented breezes. Our average speed was about twenty knots per hour, and we were scheduled to arrive in Okinawa on September 15. Seven days out of San Francisco, we crossed the International Dateline, which lay to the west of Midway Island on the one hundred and eighty degree meridian. When crossed from east to west, as we did, the ship's clocks were advanced one day. Our daily newspaper, the *Buck Up*, kept everyone posted on our location. I noted that the air temperature was eighty-seven degrees and the sea water was eighty-one degrees. Even though there was no air conditioning, it was comfortable on board because there was always a breeze stirring.

We passed Wake Island on an overcast, windy afternoon the fourth of September. There was not much to see, just the tips of three coral islets about twenty-one feet above the water. Wake Island is only about four-and-one-half miles long and shaped in a triangle. There is a harbor and an important landing strip that has been controlled by the United States since 1945.

Near Guam, perhaps 300 miles out, a solitary B-17 air and sea rescue plane buzzed our ship, flying low and slow. Everyone crowded topside and lined the railings. The graceful old Fortress was quite a sight as she cruised by showing us her bright orange tail.

I went ashore in Guam and was lucky enough to hop a ride with a Navy messenger in a jeep who was making the rounds on the island. Guam is about thirty miles long and ten miles wide and lies 3,700 miles west of Hawaii; it is the largest and southernmost island of the Marianas, which we took from the Japanese in July 1944. During the war, our Construction Battalions (CBs) built a magnificent 10,000 foot-long runway named North Field at Anderson Air Base. A self-governing U.S. Territory since 1972, Guam sends one delegate to the U.S. House of Representatives.

The sightseeing was spectacular, especially the view from the ridges that overlooked the Pacific. Below us and toward the horizon spread lush green foliage, groves of coconut palms (cultivated for valuable fiber and palm oil) along the shoreline, and fishing boats out at sea. A tropical paradise in many ways, it seemed a nice place to pull a tour of duty, especially for married men. Our ship then headed for Manila, about 1,500 miles to the west. Schools of porpoises escorted us, their sleek, speedy, dark-blue bodies zipping effortlessly through the lighter blue of the sea. I had never seen one before and was delighted to see them up close.

We docked at Manila on September 12. I vividly recall strolling along the grounds of the old Manila Hotel on the bay not far from our pier. The building was massive yet refined, a wooden structure shaded by huge monkey-pod trees, with a sweeping driveway to the front door. Wide outdoor verandas were visible through doors left open to let the breezes flow. The ceilings were high, with fans overhead turning slowly and moving the faintly musky, yet cool air.

Many guests were at the bar, so I had a cold beer and chatted with people I recognized from the *Buckner*. I ordered *San Miguel* beer, the most famous of all Filipino beers because General MacArthur, former Governor of the islands before World War II, was said to have had a business interest in the brewery. Old "Mac" had his enemies, and many Americans could not stand his ego; but I always admired him for his flamboyance, his wit, and his bravery in the face of tremendous odds during World War I and World War II. He was still going strong in Tokyo, where they revered him because he had allowed Emperor Hirohito to remain as the figurehead of the defeated Japanese Empire. In 1946, MacArthur decreed that Japanese women had the right to vote for the first time.

The Filipino people were gentle and gracious and most spoke English, even though the official language was *Tagalog*. The Philippines had become a U.S. territory in 1898 as a result of the Spanish-American War. The United States granted their independence on July 4, 1946, when they officially became known as the Republic of the Philippines. There are some 7,100 islands in the archipelago with an estimated 60 million people, four-fifths of whom are Catholic, whose faith dates back to Magellan of Spain whose government founded Manila in 1571. After the Spanish ceded the Islands, the U.S. developed and leased major military bases at Clark Field in Baguio and at Subic Bay where the U.S. Navy berthed and maintained its Pacific fleet. In 1992, treaty agreements to extend use of these bases were not approved.

We were under way again, passing Taiwan (Formosa) off the coast of Red China and heading toward Okinawa in the Ryukyu Islands about 1,000 miles north of Manila. After breakfast on the morning of September 17, we anchored in Okinawa at Buckner Bay named after the same person as our transport ship. General Simon B. Buckner, Jr., was the son of a Civil War Confederate General, and both were West Point graduates. Simon B. Buckner, Jr., commanded the U.S. 10th Army that fought and won the last great Pacific land battle against the Japanese for Okinawa and was killed in action on June 18, 1945.

We disembarked and were met by a welcoming committee from the 31st Strategic Reconnaissance Squadron. These people were smiling and talking happily, with good reason. Now with their replacements arriving, they would soon be going home. We in turn were leaving our happy home aboard ship for temporary quarters in Quonset huts. Our three-week odyssey was over, and it had been a fine trip.

SEVEN

Okinawa/Korea to FBI

The 31st Strategic Reconnaissance Squadron was stationed at Kadena Air Base near the shore of the East China Sea and in the middle of the narrow, 70-mile long island. My new home was about half-way between Tokyo to the north and Manila to the south. The capital was the port city of Naha, about 25 miles south of us, which was faintly visible on clear days from our Officer's Club located on a crest of land south of Kadena. The Air Force had a number of clubs on Okinawa, all built on the most attractive pieces of real estate that could be found.

Within a couple of weeks, Brunson, Don Nestor, Jim Snow (our squadron photographic officer), and I had settled into a fine Quonset hut that had been modified to accommodate family living. These huts could withstand almost any typhoon likely to twist along during the July to August typhoon season. The former occupants had improved our place by adding a screened covered porch. There were two airy bedrooms for the four of us, plus an extra room that became our photo darkroom. Most of the space was open for living use and furnished with bamboo chairs, some tables, a grass rug, and a desk for each of us. We had electric lights, a few fluorescent lamps, a rusty refrigerator, and a small kitchen with a hot plate, so we ate most of our meals out. There was a washing machine on the back porch where our giggling house maids did the laundry. A well-shielded light bulb burned constantly in our closets to keep the mildew under control.

My housemaid, whom I inherited with our quarters, was named Teruko. She was very short and plain looking, and smiled all the time. Each of us had a housemaid, and we all got along fine. These local women were expert at washing, ironing, and especially starching. The crease on my shirts and trousers was as sharp as a razor. Each morning the four ladies would appear, laughing and giggling, carrying little metal lunch pails filled with rice and fish.

Our squadron was about one-third short of the people we needed to do our job. The first infusion of new people, which included me, totaled about thirty men; an additional 150 people were in the pipeline. All newly assigned personnel were given their assignments and then offered a choice of additional duties. My first choice was to work in intelligence, but that plum was taken by another. I then asked for and was assigned as Squadron Personnel Officer. There was plenty of work to do, and I found the assignment challenging and demanding.

Our off-duty hours were busy as well. We were part of the 20th Air Force, which only recently had been transferred to the Strategic Air Command. Every other Saturday, we had parade formations to practice. We also went to the firing range to qualify on the carbine and .45 automatic pistols and sometimes fired shotguns on the skeet range. There were at least nine ballfields in the Kadena area, filled with would-be athletes playing whatever sport was scheduled for that time of year. Senior officers expected their junior officers to participate in at least one sport, thereby setting a good example for the younger men.

For evening leisure, we attended an outdoor theater with benches on the grass. During the rainy season, it was not uncommon to sit through a movie wearing a poncho. For the more serious minded, Japanese and Russian language classes were given after supper in our headquarters building. Voice recordings were used to provide basic language instruction. I attended a few Japanese classes hoping to learn enough to bargain and ask basic questions; such skills would come in handy when I got to Tokyo.

I waited my turn to be assigned to one of the squadron's administrative flights to Tokyo. This way I would get my monthly four hours of pilot time needed to qualify for hazardous duty pay and also get to shop on the fabled Ginza, Tokyo's Fifth Avenue. I prepared a long list of things to buy, including some Noritake China, Mikimoto pearls, and a 35 millimeter camera, all about a quarter of the price we would pay in the States. My old Mercury arrived aboard a freighter, about six weeks later, covered with dust and looking neglected but in fairly good condition. Don Nestor, who was in charge of the squadron's motor pool, got the old girl in shape. It was not long before she was spick and span and ready to go.

My fondest wish came true. On the last Friday in October, I was assigned as copilot on a B-29 to Tokyo, with an eager crew all armed with shopping lists a mile long. The following letter home tells about the trip:

30 Oct 49 (Sunday eve)

Dear Mom and Nan:

Well, here I am, back in Okinawa after a brief but nice trip to Tokyo. We departed Friday morning, spent Friday evening and all day Saturday, and then departed from Yokota Airport at noon Sunday. It is only a four and half hour flight one way to Japan, and with luck I hope to get there more often. At the PX in downtown Tokyo (a five story building), I got a nice little 35 mm camera for $28.10 and also sent a set of chinaware home for you. It should arrive early in December—you can save it and open it for Christmas. For Joan and Carson, I bought a service for 6 teaset. She'll like it, I hope. Since she has enough dishes, I rather thought a neat paper-thin teaset would be pleasing. Well, you'll get to see it one of these days. There is so much to look at and such a great variety of goods. For instance, thick Oriental Rugs with sturdy backs are $320.00; size 9x12 with plain or embossed designs. Quiet but rich looking. I would like your opinion as to whether you would like one. Then there are all sorts of materials, silks, tweeds from Scotland, rayons, etc., sold by the yard at extremely low rates. Send me a sample picture or description of the dress or drapery material, or suit for that matter, that you would like and I'll get some. Jewelry, furs, and vases, are only a few of the outstanding items to be bought. The official rate of exchange is 360 yen to the script dollar, but a 90-cent carton of cigarettes is worth at least 1,000 yen. So you see that with cigarettes your money goes a long way. I bought a little alarm clock for 680 yen, but it meant only 50 cents in script because I used cigarettes, which I just happened to have along. Don't

133

tell everything you know, though, concerning how reasonable things are! Man, it was cold up north—only 900 miles—and I picked up a sniffle, but the country is quite attractive. Next trip I'll have pictures to back up my claims, and soon too I'll have pictures of Okie and my cozy cabin. The car is a great boon, makes life worth living, but I've been too busy to get around sightseeing. The mail has been held up in Japan because of bad weather or something. Expect to get a lot of mail from you tomorrow (payday!) or the day after. Hope all is well and that you are healthy and happy.

Love and kisses, Adie

* * *

With the purchase of my Konica camera, a lot of my free time was taken up with color slide photography. Our exposed Kodak film was mailed to Honolulu for development. Jim Snow, our resident photography expert, taught us neophytes the tricks of the trade, and we began entertaining ourselves with slide shows in our Quonset. I saved most of the slides, and their images are still reasonably clear despite the passage of over forty years and the ravages of heat and mildew.

November 13, 1949, was my Mom's birthday, and I decided to call her, which involved making an appointment with the Central Transoceanic Telephone Company. The operator had alerted my Mom that an overseas call was coming through. It was an interesting experience talking over a telephone line that was sealed in a cable laid on the floor of the vast Pacific Ocean. I congratulated Mom on her fifty-second birthday and assured her that I was eating well and getting fat. She told me of her work, relayed all the news of Nancy, and said that all was going well. We had a fine connection, and took turns speaking over the one-way-at-a-time line.

Reading her letters again written over forty years ago, I am struck by the thoughtfulness and constancy of her communications. She always had something cheerful and uplifting to pass along and never complained or grumbled. Momma Swain was no saint, but she was darn close to it in my eyes. God certainly loved and cared for her, and so did I.

Late in November, mother nature sent typhoon Allyn our way. Alert Condition III was posted, which meant we should batten down the hatches. Aircrew members were alerted, in case we might need to fly our planes to safer areas. Winds gusted to about 50 mph; alert pilots sat in aircraft cockpits riding the brakes and were ready to jockey the nose of the ship into the wind if it got much higher. The danger soon ended as Allyn passed about fifty miles to the northeast.

Just before the Thanksgiving holidays, our new Commanding Officer, Lt. Colonel Edward D. Edwards, arrived from California with eleven more officers and one hundred and forty-one enlisted men, which now brought our squadron up to full strength. Our new CO was a dark-haired fighter pilot who had shot down a Japanese plane in the Aleutian Islands during World War II. Edwards was flying a Bell Aerocobra aircraft, which fired a 20 millimeter cannon through the propeller spinner and had its engine mounted amidship to the rear of the pilot. It was a rather tricky plane to fly and required good piloting skills.

Colonel Edwards was hard working and took over the reins of the squadron with determination and vigor. There was a lot of administrative work involved in getting these new people sorted out and assigned to duty. Luckily for me, one of the new officers was a well-qualified personnel Lieutenant named Ted Stern, who later became my roommate. He was promptly dubbed "Sterno," in the Japanese manner of adding an "o" to each word.

In a burst of enthusiasm for the service, I submitted an application for appointment as a career Air Force officer. I was granted an interview, at which I was thanked for my interest but politely rejected. I was disappointed, of course, but soon recovered and went on doing my job. I consoled myself with the thought that things usually work out for the best and nothing ventured meant nothing gained. Had I possessed an engineering degree, I am sure things would have been different.

The Christmas holidays were on us, and I gave my housemaid Teruko a carton of Camel cigarettes and a bottle of bright red nail polish. She was very happy; with the barter rate of cigarettes, I am sure she was able to trade for other items worth far more than the ninety cents (tax free) they cost me. My mother and sisters Nan and Joan sent me a yellow bole pipe and some aromatic tobacco, two pairs of garters to keep my stockings up (they had no elastic in those days), and a copy of the *Raft Book*. The book was about navigating at sea by the stars and was meant to be used by anyone adrift on the sea. I studied it carefully, trying to identify the star charts that came with detailed instructions; the whole business was pretty complicated. For instance, I wondered how I would steer if I were adrift in a raft. I concluded that it would be much better just not to get in such a predicament. All in all, it was a nice Christmas, with appropriate pastries, good food, and lots of eggnog to drink at the Officer's Clubs.

Warm, dry days arrived in the spring of 1950, and our squadron baseball players began limbering up for opening day with daily workouts on the diamond. I had missed the games last season and wanted badly to participate this year. Housemates Brunson and Snow helped me practice at home after work, playing pitch and catch in front of our Quonset. Within a few weeks, I began to gain ball speed and control. The fast ball was coming along, and I was working on a sweeping curve that would come over the plate and then drop downward six to eight inches—it was a devastating pitch. By early April, we began competition, and I was one of three pitchers. By mid-May, I was in a groove and pitched the most memorable game of my life one afternoon, striking out fifteen batters. They could not cope with the dropping curve ball, even when they knew it was coming. I was stiff and sore after the game, but a hot shower before going to the Officer's Club to bask in the kudos of my mates made it all worthwhile. I did not know this was the last game I would ever pitch.

The next day our crew was called into operations and briefed on a special mission to Tokyo; this was no shopping trip to the Ginza. Colonel Edwards was there and complimented me on my good game before getting down to business. We had been selected for a special temporary assignment that was so restricted we would receive full details only when we got to Japan.

The next day we were briefed at the Air Force base at Chitose on

Hokkaido Island, the northernmost of the Japanese Islands and just south of the Russian-owned Kuril Islands. Intelligence reports advised that the Russians were significantly increasing their military strength at their forward air base on Sakhalin Island. Our job was to take aerial photos of the suspect airfield and not get caught. There were MIG fighter aircraft at the base, which worried us somewhat. The course we were to fly was designed to imitate a Northwest Airlines flight enroute to Alaska, a flight that might have drifted off course. Hopefully we would appear to be committing a harmless violation of their coastal waters.

Our crew was confined to base for the next three days, waiting for weather and heavy clouds to clear the area. Knowing that the cold war between the Russian Bear and the American Eagle was beginning to heat up did not make us feel too comfortable. If the Russians sent up MIG fighters, they would have every right to force us to land. We had a 50-50 chance of pulling it off unchallenged, because we would not be more than one hundred and fifty miles off the usual airliner flight path. It could be explained as a navigation error if we were caught.

Finally, the weather cleared, and we roared off the runway, Earl Myers in the left seat and me in the right. We leveled off at about 25,000 feet (normal airline altitude), sandwiched between two layers of gray stratus clouds. The weather improved as we approached the target area. Just opposite Sakhalin, still beyond the 12-mile statutory limit usually respected by international law, we applied more power, increasing our airspeed, and turned toward our target. We began a wide sweeping turn, hoping it would show on the Russian radar that we were turning back on course. At the same time, our turn permitted our K-18 and K-20 wide-angle cameras plenty of opportunity to take photos of the suspect airfield below.

As we made our camera run, the ship's intercom was filled with tense comment as two imaginary sightings of enemy aircraft were reported. The cloud cover was a problem for our camera people and a threat to us, for who knew how many MIGs might be hidden there. We were committed, however, and our cameras continued to roll. Luckily, no MIGs appeared, and for the next five minutes we sweated it out as our ship slowly turned east. Earl then put the nose down to pick up airspeed, and with our cameras off we headed toward Japan, the risk of becoming an international incident diminishing with every turn of our propellers. Six months later, I was advised by our intelligence people that nothing unusual had been discovered by the photos we took that day. All the film was destroyed and not a word was mentioned of our flight, except perhaps in this writing.

When we returned to Kadena, we were rewarded with orders to fly one of our B-29s to Tinker Field in Oklahoma City for a major overhaul. All our aircraft were veterans of World War II missions over Japan. Their aluminum alloy fuselages were so eroded by exposure to salt air and humidity that you could poke a finger through the skin between the rib supports. Our orders were to proceed to Tinker Air Base on or about 9 June 1950, via Anderson AFB at Guam, Kwajalein in the Marshall Islands, Hickam Air Base in Hawaii, and Travis Air Base in California. Of more importance to us, we were all authorized a ten-day leave before returning to Okinawa.

Our departure day was filled with intermittent rainfall, and in the evening we climbed aboard our aircraft and taxied out. Earl cleared our departure with the tower, poured the coal to those four big, four-bladed propellers, and we climbed away.

Layers of scudding clouds blanketed the Pacific Ocean below, but soon we were in the clear cruising at 20,000 feet above the mass of whiteness below. Francis Casserly, our navigator, said we would reach Anderson Field about one o'clock in the morning. I could see some stars above and noticed that Francis was working his sextant in the forward navigation bubble to check our position. One of our primary navigation aids was the direction-finding radio, called the RDF, by which we could home on selected ground broadcast stations. The directional needle on the instrument panel would point toward the selected station and reflect a bearing for steering purposes. Using this aid on several stations, one could triangulate radio direction fixes and then calculate an estimated time of arrival.

I had used the RDF many times and knew we would have no difficulty reaching Anderson Field, so I relaxed, dreaming of home. Around midnight, an hour out of Guam, I tried our RDF and noticed the needle was wandering aimlessly from side to side. I only heard static and thought we were probably too far from the station. Earl tried to reach Anderson Field but did not get a response, and Casserly was having some difficulty getting the three fixes he needed to determine our position. By 1:00 A.M., I was still unable to find the Guam radio station, Cass had no reliable star fix, and the tower had not responded to our repeated calls. Earl took us down to 1,000 feet below the clouds for a look around. We should have been able to see the lights from Anderson Field but only saw dark choppy waters and an occasional whitecap.

Our flight engineer reported that we had two more hours of fuel on board. Earl said we would make it and decided to lean the mixture way back and start a square search pattern. Earl and I then alternated on the controls, first steering west for five minutes, then north for another five minutes, then east for ten minutes, making right turns while flying a box pattern that gradually extended each leg of our flight. Meanwhile, all hands were at the windows trying to see the lights at Anderson Field or anything. An hour passed, slowly. We were getting anxious, wondering what it would be like to land at night in the Pacific. The B-29 was not known for its flotation ability.

We had to do something soon, so we climbed above the clouds again. Earl turned on the emergency frequency and began to broadcast a distress message. About twenty minutes later, a rather calm and pleasant voice called to say that they had our position and we should continue to circle until advised. A few minutes later, a B-17 Air Sea rescue pilot radioed a course for us to steer and told us to look for a yellow flare. They had us on their radar and were above us about a mile ahead. There was the flare, a distant, flickering yellow light, slowly descending, suspended by a tiny parachute, swaying gently as it passed through the clouds trailing white smoke. Then I saw the dark silhouette of a B-17 above the flare, and we swung in behind him, beginning the descent to Anderson Field.

We landed with about twenty minutes of fuel remaining. In the morning, we had to endure the embarrassment of a Board of Inquiry regarding why we were lost. Our RDF had been malfunctioning, the winds aloft had blown us about one hundred miles off course, and Casserly had not been able to pinpoint his position because of clouds. I was so relieved to be on terra firma that the inquiry seemed trivial. Our navigator had to do some sweating though.

The remainder of our flight went smoothly. We arrived at Hickam

Field in Honolulu, after a refueling stop at Kwajalein atoll, a desolate and sun-struck place if ever there was one. At Hickam, we hurriedly cleaned up and caught a cab at the Main Gate bound for *Mamma Mia's Italian Pizza Parlor* in town. We had the biggest pizza Earl Myers could find on the menu. He had been extolling the virtues of this place for the past three days, and Casserly and I were happy to join Earl as we devoured huge slabs of hot, crusty pepperoni pizza, washed down with Chianti wine.

We spent an extra day at Hickam changing an engine cylinder. The problem was not too serious, but Earl was a conniver. He persuaded the local maintenance officer to give us some hanger space in return for the labor of our crew who would perform the cylinder change. The engine ran perfectly on test runup, and we all had an extra day on the beaches of Waikiki. We were airborne again that night and heading toward San Francisco. I remember listening to Nat King Cole on the radio as he sang that lovely ballad *Mona Lisa*, a song that still reminds me of Hawaii and that long flight from Okinawa.

We delivered our tired old B-29 to Tinker Field and then scattered in all directions. I took a commercial flight to the new Greater Pittsburgh Airport, where Joan and Carson met me. My ten days with loved ones in the Valley passed quickly. I especially enjoyed visiting with my Mom. All my life she had been a constant and loyal supporter. She always wrote loving letters, full of news about the latest activities in the family.

My mother and Nan looked around Trenton, New Jersey, after I had shipped out for Okinawa, hoping to find a piece of land with space for some horses and a decent garden. I told them I was more than happy to be the financial backer of anything they found to buy, but nothing ever came of it. This was probably just as well because before long Nancy began to get serious about Captain Tom Stansbury, the medical officer she met at Ft. Dix. When Tom went to Minneapolis to begin his year of residency training in radiology, Nan went with him, and Mom returned to the Valley where her roots were so deeply planted.

* * *

My leave was almost over on June 25, 1950, when 60,000 North Korean troops swarmed southward in a surprise attack on South Korean (ROK) troops. The invading communist forces of Kim Il Sung were backed by Russia and Red China. President Truman reacted immediately and angrily, sending back to Korea the troops we had only recently withdrawn. More important, the United Nations Security Council denounced the aggression of North Korea and authorized immediate further military support to U.S. forces now on the ground. I booked a commercial flight to San Francisco, knowing full well that our squadron would be called for photo reconnaissance work.

The Korean War was called a police action, so labeled by Harry Truman, and fought on a slender peninsula somewhat smaller than the State of Florida, bounded on the west by the Yellow Sea and on the east by the Sea of Japan. To the north, just across the Yalu River, lay the inscrutable mass of communist Manchuria. Not known to most Americans at the time was our government's very real concern that the North Korean invasion was the first thrust in a worldwide communist breakout. U.S. troops went on high alert status around the world, while Washington waited for the Russians to move against Berlin and for the Red Chinese to attack Nationalist Chinese government forces in exile on Taiwan. This whole thing was beginning to look like the start of World War III. The Korean War lasted almost three years, until July 27, 1953, and caused four million casualties, including 54,246 Americans killed, more than 100,000 Americans wounded, and 8,177 Americans missing in action. It would all end in a stalemate on the 38th parallel, just where it began on June 25, 1950.

I returned to Okinawa to find my squadron moving to Johnson Air Base in Japan, northwest of Tokyo. In my absence, Ted Stern had organized all the personnel actions necessary to get the squadron ready to go. Aircraft and crews, along with mechanics and support gear, were able to move into action without delay. Flying photo reconnaissance missions against the North Koreans was much less sophisticated and life-threatening than flying bomber missions over Germany during World War II. Our missions started with breakfast in the Officer's mess, after which we would gather at the flight operations room for takeoff at 8:00 A.M. Usually our flights were unescorted single ship missions about 700 miles across the Sea of Japan.

One of our recurring targets was Pyongyang, the capital of North Korea. It was up to the aircraft commander and the navigator to decide what approach to take, which meant selecting a flight path that would keep prevailing winds at our tail, thus helping increase our ground speed. All crew members not involved with taking film strips or flying the photo run were on the alert for enemy aircraft and antiaircraft ground fire. We occasionally saw antiaircraft shell bursts, but the North Koreans were not as well equipped in the early days of this conflict as they would be a year or so later. With the coming of autumn, our complacency about enemy responses changed.

Bob Laden was one of the few married officers whose family had accompanied him overseas. Bob had been on the *General Buckner* with me the previous September, and his wife and baby girl had joined him later. Bob and his crew were flying home from a mission over Wonsan, a major port city on the Sea of Japan, when a MIG-15 jet fighter jumped his B-29 from the rear. Bob's tail gunner fired his .50 calibre tail guns and drove off the attacker, but one engine on the port side of the B-29 was damaged. We knew there was a crippled aircraft inbound, but none of us were overly concerned because Bob was a good pilot. He was coming in for a three-engine landing, a fairly routine emergency procedure that we often practiced. It should be a piece of cake, especially since the weather was good.

The runways at Johnson, built for fighter aircraft, did not have the extra length needed for heavy bombers making emergency landings. The crippled B-29 seemed to land all right but slid off the runway, its landing gear on the pilot's side crumpling into the soft dirt. The plane plowed ahead for some distance before settling in a cloud of dust. The plane did not catch on fire, nor was there much damage, except for the shot-up engine and damage to the left wing and landing gear. Bob was killed by the impact; however, everyone else on board survived. It was particularly sad to lose a good pilot this way, for there was a much longer, and hence much safer, runway at Yokota Air Base fifteen miles away. Bob could easily have landed there. A few weeks later, our squadron transferred to Yokota, a move probably spurred by this crash.

At Yokota, we lived in comfortable two-story barracks. Ted Stern and I shared a room for the rest of my tour. Ted was a bundle of energy and a fine personnel officer.

I was delighted when I was promoted to Captain in September 1950, for the move upward was totally unexpected. Sterno, on the other hand, was a bit out of sorts because now I was the senior personnel officer. We never had any serious problems over this, and in due time Ted also was promoted to Captain. I was congratulated by the guys on the flight line. I recall that Bill B. Campbell gave me a pair of his old captain's bars, since I had none of my own. He presented them with a little speech, saying every captain should have a pair like his with some wear and tear on them so no one would know he had just been promoted. The bars he gave me were so well worn that the brass was beginning to show through the silver. I liked them and wore those old captain's bars of his the rest of my time in the service.

Time passed slowly in that limbo, where we lived in luxury with meals served on linen in the Officer's Club and then flew missions high above the ugly world of death and destruction on the ground.

I flew my 41st and final mission on June 8, 1951. Ten days later, my orders to report to Travis Air Base in California were posted. Now I could use the popular term "FIIGMO" to anyone who asked me to do something. The response FIIGMO meant "Fuck it. I got my orders" and was one of the most vulgar yet explicit expressions that originated in the Korean War. Major Ray and crew, with me as copilot, were assigned to the 5th Strategic Reconnaissance Wing of SAC, which was being outfitted with the new and enormous RB-36 Reconnaissance Bomber. The B-36 had six engines with pusher propellers, plus jet-pod engines on each wing tip; it was one big airplane.

The midnight MATS flight from Tokyo was full of happy, sleepy war veterans. We refueled in the Aleutians and then went on to Anchorage, Alaska, a barren, windswept, and bleak spot that was uninspiring, even in the month of June. There was nothing green to be seen anywhere, and I wondered what it must be like in the winter.

143

The military barracks were wind-scoured and weathered, and the air was still raw, edged with the harshness of the past winter and chilled by the ice mass to the north of us. At least the mess halls were warm inside, steaming and fragrant with the odor of good food. I was grateful to be passing through and not staying in this frontier station. God forbid that I should ever be assigned to a place like this.

We departed that night on a ten-hour flight to McChord Air Base near Seattle, Washington. Once there, we boarded an overnight train southbound for sunny California. From my window seat I could see the glistening, snow-capped peak of Mt. Rainier, some 14,000 feet high far off in the Cascade Range. We soon chugged into Fairfield-Suison, California, and were quickly processed at Travis for our 30-day leave.

Changes were noticeable in the Valley. Wartime military orders were pouring into the steel mills, and the railroads were busy moving increased volumes of war material across the nation. Diesel engines were now replacing coal-fired steam locomotives, and other antipollution efforts were gradually reducing the dirty smog that for years polluted the skies over Pittsburgh. Smokestacks now released clean white steam, not the dirty blackness of burned soft coal.

My Mother was living with Joan and Carson most of the time, except when living in the home of one of her night nursing patients. Chuckie and Agnes were living in Beaver in a house they bought to fix up for resale. Chuck taught English at Geneva College while taking night classes at the University of Pittsburgh to earn his master's degree in literature.

I made the rounds of the old haunts, visiting friends like Jim Wallace, and was reminded that life goes on in the same old way in most hometowns. I guess I was looking for the Hollywood version of a happy ending, complete with heroic deeds performed by all-American boys like me. I still did not have any idea of what I wanted out of life, and I was almost 30 years old.

* * *

The cold war in Korea continued with sporadic flareups until July 1952, when a cease-fire went into effect. The two opposing forces met at a small village named Panmunjon, near the 38th parallel, where they haggled over the details of a truce for the next two years. While all this was going on, our crew was training in the B-36.

Because many of our missions exceeded twenty hours, this monstrous aircraft required the services of three pilots. Our maximum flight time without refueling was thirty hours. The B-36 was powered by six pusher engines with the propellers mounted backward so that they pushed rather than pulled the aircraft. These propellers were complemented by four wingtip jets, used primarily on takeoffs, making a total of ten engines. The airplane was so immense that a tunnel was built in the mid-fuselage area to connect the fore and aft sections. Crew members could travel back and forth through this tunnel while stretched on their backs atop a little dolly on rollers, similar to the way garage mechanics slide under an auto in the repair shop.

The huge bomber was built by Convair but was never flown in combat. A few hundred were built and served as a deterrent force in SAC for years. The B-36 was designed by strategic planners who saw the need for a long-range bomber that could fly 10,000 miles without refueling, which in plain English meant flying to Russia with an A-bomb if needed. A number of SAC crews were selected and given military targets in Russia. The Air Force was fully prepared to strike a number of targets should war come with Russia, as was expected by some Pentagon experts. All these missions were classified "Secret", so secret that with the passage of time I have managed to forget all the details of my part in it. At the time, I did not take the whole thing seriously. I never accepted the notion that I might be ordered to fly a B-36 to Russia on a one-way trip.

SAC had to be ready for any contingency. The Cold War was a deadly serious business, serious enough that for the next forty years SAC kept an aircraft aloft over Omaha, Nebraska, twenty-four hours a day with a senior officer aboard. Should the Russians decide to nuke our underground command centers, a senior Air Force officer in touch with the White House underground command center, would be capable of ordering retaliatory missile strikes against Russian targets. A rather bleak scenario, but indicative of the concern in the United States over Soviet intentions.

When not on flight duty, we sometimes had to pull four-hour guard duty shifts to prevent unauthorized persons from gaining access to our B-36s. There were lots of rumors concerning spying and sabotage, and security was tight around our bases.

There was plenty of free time in spite of this. I took frequent trips to San Francisco, often on a Sunday afternoon, to lunch at the classy old Palace Hotel and enjoy the best avocado salad in the world. The Mark Hopkins Hotel was a regular hangout for military bachelors like me, and our Officer's Club offered first-rate Saturday night dinner dances.

Hollywood stars often made appearances at Travis. MATS flights were constantly transporting Hollywood's entertainers to and from Korea and the Far East. I remember Gary Cooper spent one Saturday afternoon with us, surrounded by admirers. A very pleasant, modest man who charmed everyone with his tall, handsome appearance and self-deprecating mannerisms. He was my most favorite movie star, and I was very sad when he died of cancer in 1962.

Socially, my life was pretty decent. There were lots of eligible ladies about, including nurses and friends or relatives of married officer friends who would spark up my evening hours. I met two lovely ladies at Travis in whom I took a more than casual interest. One was the younger sister of the squadron engineering officer, a dark-haired beauty who looked like the movie actress Susan Hayward. All we bachelor officers were smitten with her and were stumbling over ourselves in line to call on her. Her favorite excuse for not going out with me was that she had to straighten out her closets. Well, I thought, this is simply not the girl for me, too neat.

The other girl was a cute blonde college student from Sacramento who lived with her mother. She was beautiful, childish, and spoiled, with ambitions to become a model or an actress. I remember inviting her to our New Year's Eve party on base for dinner and dancing. She dressed in white and was very attractive. Everyone was envious of me, but I could not find much common ground beyond physical attraction. I soon found that she did not have much to say of interest; no doubt, she felt the same about me.

* * *

In the spring of 1952, when my three-year contract with the Air Force was about to expire, I knew I would soon have a career choice to make. When Major Ray asked me if I wanted to become a B-36 aircraft commander, a promotion up from my present copilot slot, I weighed the prospects carefully. I would have to renew my contract with the Air Force and would probably transition into piloting the B-52 jet bomber that was just beginning to come on line from the Boeing factory in Seattle. It was a tough decision.

I loved the Air Force, which had become my home. I was a good pilot, but I was still single and longed for a wife and home of my own. The life of a bachelor officer sharing quarters at some SAC base held little appeal. I weighed the other consequences of remaining on active duty thoughtfully. SAC pilots were often subject to abrupt, temporary duty assignments overseas for 30 to 90 days at a time. SAC had a reputation for being rather cold and unfeeling toward its personnel, and I knew that the prospects of a transfer out of SAC were nil. Had the group or wing personnel officer called me in to discuss these options in a more personal way, I might have stayed on active duty; but I really had enough of flying the big boys. I informed Major Ray that I did not want to become a B-36 commander.

Fortunately for me, my cousin Jack Stickel was now working at the San Francisco Office of Special Investigations (OSI), occasionally doing investigative work at Travis. During one of our meetings, he said that the FBI was looking for a few more agents and I should contact them. The FBI was a very popular organization, thanks to a television program called "This is Your FBI," which stressed the work of its agents in disclosing and uprooting communism in our country. I could picture myself in such a heroic role, so I called and made an appointment with the Special Agent in Charge (SAC) of the San Francisco Field Office.

SAC Antonelli was pleasant and austere. He asked if I had come to him on my own or been recruited by someone in the FBI. The federal government had rules against the proselytizing of one agency's employees by another. Satisfied that this was not the case and that I would be discharged from active duty with the Air Force within the next 30 days, he asked me to take a comprehensive, three-hour test of my reasoning prowess. I passed this part readily enough and then passed a physical examination. Antonelli told me that I would have to wait for my background clearance but that things looked good. If all went well, I could expect a call from FBI Headquarters in Washington within 30 to 60 days.

My active duty Air Force career ended quietly, with the issuance of orders dated April 18, 1952, authorizing me to proceed to my home of record not later than 30 April, on which date I would be relieved from active duty. The orders further transferred me to the Inactive Ready Reserve. I was given my flight records to keep, wherein I noted that my total flight time was 2,041 hours and 10 minutes, of which 645 hours were spent flying combat missions during World War II and the Korean War. Approximately 31 percent of my flight time was in combat. In retrospect, I felt that the Air Force had gotten their money's worth from me, and I from them. Now it looked as if I would become a G-man, a term often used for FBI Special Agents.

The next 60 days with Joan and Carson passed quietly as I busied myself with little chores around the house and got used to loafing. At last, on July 3rd, I was notified to report to the Old Post Office Building on Pennsylvania Avenue, July 21, 1952, for Special Agent training.

Classes were held in the Old Post Office Building through most of October. It was sixteen weeks in all, including three weeks of firearms training at the Marine Corps training camp at Quantico, Virginia. I found the classroom work, which centered on law enforcement and case histories, to be thoroughly stuffy, more so because we were in the midst of a long, hot summer and confined to non-airconditioned rooms. It was muggy, steamy, and hot, and I soon learned why Washington was nicknamed Foggy Bottom. The capital was built on low-lying marsh land at the junction of the Potomac River and its tributaries, surrounded by hills on three sides. There was no place for accumulating heat and moisture to go; it simply smothered Washington in a moist blanket. Thank God there was a federal regulation decreeing that employees working in non-airconditioned buildings be sent home when both temperature and humidity reached 86. There were several days when this happened.

Along with lectures on maintaining law and order, we were shown how to improve our skills in self-defense, a welcome respite from classwork and a chance to work off some frustrations. The highlight of all our training was the three weeks spent at Quantico, where we became proficient in using the .38 calibre pistol, Thompson submachine gun, shotgun, and rifle. Several of my classmates were former pilots, but most of the others were recent college graduates who had been recruited by the FBI on various campuses around the nation.

I lived in a rambling, three-story boarding home in northwest Washington, from where I could ride a street car downtown in about twenty minutes. The fare was ten cents each way, or three tokens for a quarter. We breakfasted at a number of coffee shops, which seemed to be on every block. My favorite was the *Hot Shoppe*, operated by the Marriot family who were just getting under way with one of the most successful food and hotel operations in America.

Our neighborhood was self-sufficient. There were several airconditioned theaters, which we attended frequently to keep cool on hot evenings. Our laundry and dry cleaning was done at a reasonably priced Chinese laundry. I rarely used my automobile. I bought a few good neckties, about an inch wide, which was the fashion in those days. All FBI agents wore neckties and a hat, of course. Somewhere in my wardrobe are a number of these antiquated neckties. My kids smirk when I speak of wearing one of my FBI ties; but they are still serviceable, and I am waiting patiently for men's fashions to come full circle.

Our instructors were all seasoned professionals. I remember one of them in particular, a rather heavy, almost overweight chap named Doyle, who had wide shoulders, a pugnacious jaw, and a droll sense of humor. He enlivened his rather dull material with war stories about agents who did wrong and were reassigned. Mr. Hoover, formally known as The Director, was wont to send errant agents to Butte, Montana. There must have been something lacking in the office at Butte, for the threat of being assigned there became very real to us, an assignment to be avoided at all costs.

Another story that was more titillating, yet just as serious, dealt with an FBI agent who developed an attractive female as an informant and soon was involved with her in more than a business way. This in itself was not illegal, but it was a violation of the agent's personal conduct code, particularly when the woman advised a senior FBI agent that she was having sex with the agent because he told her she would be arrested if she did not. When Mr. Hoover learned of this behavior, the offending agent was out on the street the next day with less than an honorable discharge. The moral of this story was clear: FBI Special Agents were not to behave this way, and the consequences were drastic.

With the approach of fall, political heat replaced the heat of summer. A presidential election was in the offing. Dwight D. Eisenhower, now retired from the military, had finally permitted the Republican Party to nominate him in opposition to Adlai E. Stevenson, the popular ex-Governor from Illinois. Ike was such a revered figure that he would have won in either party. Because the Korean War was still dragging on, Ike further endeared himself to the American public by saying, "If I am elected, I shall go to Korea."

I am not sure what Ike's going to Korea had to do with winning the election, but he won easily and went to Korea, where he used his influence in world affairs to help speed a resolution to that conflict. His running mate that year was a little-known lawyer/Congressman from California, Richard M. Nixon. They made an interesting pair, faintly reminiscent of the 1988 presidential winner, George Bush, and the little-known lawyer/Senator named Dan Quayle. Vice Presidents have a way of later occupying the presidential chair. More than fifty percent of them since World War II have done so: Harry Truman (1945-53), Lyndon Johnson (1963-69), Richard Nixon (1969-74), and George Bush (1988-1992).

* * *

While I was at Quantico enjoying life on the firing range, Ernest Hemingway broke from a long unproductive period and published a novella called *The Old Man and the Sea*. The story appeared as a special feature in *Life* magazine and was made into a movie a year or so later with Spencer Tracy starring in the role of the old fisherman. I was particularly pleased because Hemingway was my favorite author and had not written anything of note for several years. He was suffering from some sort of a writer's block or, more likely, from the effects of too much liquor. In any event, he had written another classic, and I was happy to read it.

In later years, I toured the Hemingway House in Key West, where his workshop is visited daily by vacationers from all over the world. It was in the second-floor workshop that he wrote *For Whom The Bell Tolls*. He wrote this fictional work in the early 1940s, using his experiences as a war correspondent with the Spanish Loyalists during their 1936 Civil War as the basis for the story. This splendid novel was made into a movie in 1943, with the part of Roberto played by Gary Cooper. Hemingway and Cooper became close, lifelong friends.

Back in Washington, our class was approaching graduation day. Our class advisor, himself an agent, briefed us on the protocol: "You all will be expected to be properly attired in a good, dark blue suit, with white shirt and appropriate tie. Not too flashy, mind you, and for God's sake be clean shaven. There will be no mustaches or long hair." Our advisor told us how one newly trained agent had been summarily dismissed by Mr. Hoover because he did not like his looks, or his haircut; this dismissal came on graduation day. If true, this was a crazy business I was getting into, and even though I did not actually believe it could happen, it was a possibility. I resolved to be extra careful from now on.

I later learned that such acts of dismissal were perfectly possible and legal because the FBI is an excepted service agency. Only the FBI and the Central Intelligence Agency (CIA) can fire their people without the due process of law that protects employees in the civil service and the U.S. military. In the excepted service agencies, the boss had unquestioned authority and could get rid of deadwood immediately, without preamble. We all knew that J. Edgar Hoover was our boss. Now I understood how agents kept getting sudden transfers to Butte, Montana.

All the lectures and tests on rules of evidence and law were behind us. We had learned how to take plaster of Paris casts of tire tracks in the mud, how to dust for fingerprints, and how to write Reports of Investigation. All the physical training in self-defense, and the weeks of firing on the Quantico range were now coming down to a face-to-face meeting with the man himself: Mr. J. Edgar Hoover, Director of the FBI.

On the appointed day, we lined up alphabetically in the hallway outside of the Director's door, dressed soberly in dark blue suits. When my turn came, I stepped through the door onto dark red carpeting that spread far away toward the Director's desk. The line of new agents moved slowly forward. Soon it was my turn to pause in front of Mr. Hoover's desk and say, "Sir, Special Agent Swain reporting for duty, as directed."

Mr. Hoover remained seated at his desk, watching each of us approach the throne. His desk was the large, executive type always allocated to top government officials. The Director sat buddha-like behind his desk, flanked by a large U.S. flag on one side and his Chief of Training on the other to make sure we new agents were properly identified. Mr. Hoover did not rise but extended his hand while measuring each of us carefully, almost glumly. "Congratulations, Agent Swain," he said, without smile or expression. I think he never got out of his chair because he was so short. In a room full of young giants, most of whom towered over him, he probably felt more secure staying right there and portraying the busy executive at his desk with a lot on his mind.

We filed back to our classroom for final words of wisdom from our advisors and to receive our field assignments. One jarring note occurred when one of the officials wound up his speech with this succinct statement, "Remember men, when you go out there as Special Agents of the FBI, YOU ARE STILL COPS." Those words struck home dreadfully. A cop was the last thing I wanted to be. I wanted to be a Special Agent, which meant a great deal more to me than being a police officer. That speaker must have been some kind of a nut, and I decided to ignore his advice.

My new duty post was the field office in Charlotte, North Carolina. I was quite pleased and not too surprised. In keeping with FBI tradition, all new agents from the north were sent south and all southern newcomers sent north. The first year of duty was a probationary period. We were rated General Service Grade 10, or GS-10, with a base pay of $5,500 per year. This was actually a generous starting wage for federal employees, the lowest of whom start at the GS-1 level.

The Charlotte office was directed by Special Agent in Charge Bill Murphy, who assigned me to a group of 10 to 15 other agents in

Greenville, South Carolina. There I did background investigations on applicants seeking employment with the Knoxville atomic energy installation and high school graduates who applied for work in the FBI's filing section in Washington. In the 1950s, the emerging threat of communism placed an added burden on the FBI whose task was to perform background investigations on almost everyone who worked for the U.S. Government. The search for underground communists had become big business.

The work was new and therefore interesting, and I threw myself into it, working long hours pounding on doors and interviewing neighbors, employers, and former school teachers of applicants seeking jobs in sensitive areas. I then wrote the reports that were submitted through channels to FBI Headquarters for other people to read, file, or pass onward. The paper flow was steady, and the FBI filled warehouse upon warehouse with bales of reports, most of which never saw the light of day.

When not engaged in this kind of work, I was assigned to track down servicemen who were absent without leave (AWOL). These were usually homesick kids who just went home to Mama, without realizing the consequences of their actions. Because they had crossed interstate lines, their violations became federal cases. Most of them were found at home, taken into custody, and turned over to the military police. It was a sad business, and I took very little pleasure in working AWOL cases.

Stolen automobiles were in the same category. If a stolen vehicle was taken over state lines, it became a federal case. I spent a lot of time working on auto thefts and related interstate trafficking violations. My original hope was to be involved in anticommunist activities, but I soon realized that agents working on the communist threat were all senior men who had a lot of experience. It could be years before I got the work I really wanted; I told myself to be patient.

New orders sent me to Winston-Salem, about one hundred miles north of Charlotte, where I became the assistant to the Special Agent in Charge, Carman J. Stuart, who worked alone in this office. This could be a pretty nice assignment for an old country boy like me.

On the way to Winston-Salem, I thought about an FBI practice that I never quite got used to, the concept of "voluntary" overtime instituted by J. Edgar Hoover years earlier. By this practice, all agents worked an extra hour per day, plus a half-day on Saturday. Such overtime was never recorded on our pay vouchers but was documented on our daily activities log and submitted to Headquarters. This way Mr. Hoover was able to locate every agent in his employ at any time. More important, when Mr. Hoover made his annual appearance before the Congressional oversight committee, which reviewed his budget request for the next year, he could show Congress the thousands of overtime hours his agents had worked without pay the past year. This ploy was very impressive, and the committee never failed to grant the Director all the money he asked for; sometimes he was asked if he needed more! Our boss was quite a political animal and highly respected for his integrity and bulldog perseverance. He also kept files on the Congressmen on the committee, as well as other politicians in our nation's capital. Such files helped to ensure his survival.

Winston-Salem was the home of R. J. Reynolds tobacco company and smelled of tobacco. The air carried the raw tang of tobacco leaves that were rolled into hundreds of thousands of cigarettes in huge plants throughout the area. The smell was a constant reminder that I was smoking a lot, a habit I wanted to kick but was still waiting for the "right time."

Our FBI office was on the second floor of the Post Office building downtown. The Ford sedans assigned for our use were stored in a public parking garage about a block away, but I parked my Pontiac on a side street three blocks distant so I would not have to pay for parking. Bureau agents did not take business cars home with them unless there was a special reason. I liked my new job better than the previous one, even though for the first few weeks I had to live in a small room in an old boardinghouse. My room had a single 25-watt light bulb in the ceiling for light, but the rent was reasonable. Strangely, very few motels or small apartments were available in Winston-Salem. There were several hotels in town, but their room rates were beyond the per diem allowed by the Bureau. I decided to ask my Mom if she would come stay with me for awhile. When she agreed, I called on several real estate agencies and finally located a decently furnished two-bedroom apartment.

The Time of My Life

Carman Stuart was married with a wife and two fine children. He had served about ten years in the Bureau before being assigned to his office of preference in Winston-Salem. He was a tall, quietly competent man who seemed tired all the time and had dark circles under his violet eyes, the eyes of a poet, not an FBI man. Carman once said his original goal in life was to become a trial attorney and then a judge. He was frustrated in his present job because he never got to practice the law he loved. Caught by the economics of life, providing for his family, paying for the house, auto, and furniture, became more necessary than the pursuit of personal goals. Carman and I both had ulcers, and more than once he arrived at work literally dragging and collapsed on the couch. Poor Carman was caught in the middle with little hope for a change. Having invested half of his working lifetime in the FBI, he would probably stick it out rather than start all over again.

I was assigned to cover five counties in the rolling farming country that ranged a hundred miles from Winston-Salem into the Blue Ridge Mountains of North Carolina. This was beautiful country. The names of some of the towns I worked are still familiar: Mt. Airy (where the comedian and TV star Andy Griffith was raised), Pilot Mountain, and Toast, Low Gap, Galaxy, Walnut Cove, and Madison. They were all nice country towns filled with plain, ordinary folk who were friendly and a pleasure to meet.

During my one-year tour of duty in Winston-Salem, I participated in only two arrest situations where Stuart and I were prepared to use our weapons should the fugitives resist handcuffs. One was a stolen car fugitive, the other, an older AWOL sailor who was a seducer of young men and an all-around bad guy; neither one gave us any trouble. I made one court appearance, which was related to the stolen car fugitive I arrested. In addition to the hundreds of background and security checks, I helped to investigate two bank robbery cases.

All of these activities generated a steady flow of information, that we dictated into recording machine dictation belts that were mailed overnight to Charlotte. There, FBI stenographers transcribed the contents into finished reports that were sent to the growing pile of dossier material in the Seat Of Government (SOG), the FBI's jargon for Washington, D.C.

155

One of the Charlotte stenographers was Barbara Davis, a cute brunette with big brown eyes and a pageboy haircut. She came from a nice family in Raleigh and lived in an apartment building in town where many young professional people stayed. We went out to dinner a few times when I was in Charlotte catching up on my reports. Barbara was a native Carolinian, as cute and sweet as a southern sunflower. She was quite young and very pleasant to be with and invited me to dinner once or twice, which indicated she was not afraid of me.

One of the highlights in motion picture entertainment was the advent of three-dimensional (3-D) movies. Barbara and I went to one, where we were issued special dark glasses to view the movie. These glasses made objects appear to fly from the screen into your face. A chair thrown in a barroom brawl suddenly sailed right at us; an automobile speeding along abruptly careened off the roadway straight into our laps. The effect was frightening, and shrieks and screams were common. It was a fad that caught the nation's attention for a few months, and only a few 3-D films were ever produced.

For the most part, being an FBI man had its drawbacks socially. Making lady friends was not easy. Despite my efforts to be relaxed and easygoing, upon learning that I was an FBI Agent, the ladies often would become stiff and formal, sometimes ill at ease, concerned that their behavior with me should be above reproach. This was not the way I wanted it by any means! To make my social life even more difficult, Mr. Hoover had an unwritten rule that all agents were on call twenty-four hours a day. Should you be drinking and receive a call to help with a bank robbery investigation or a stakeout, you were duty-bound to report any drinking to your supervisor. None of the new agents had any desire for a transfer to Butte, Montana, so we did not do any serious drinking or partying. In short, I was leading a very sober life. I do not recall having even one drink all the time I was assigned to Winston-Salem. Perhaps I was too conscientious, but that was the way of it.

The year passed slowly, yet pleasantly. My Mom found work in a nearby mental hospital that kept her busy and happy. She was good company and I enjoyed her tasty home cooking. Often after work, I would come home and change into jogging togs to go for a good run in the park nearby before dinner. I made a few friends, including a group of regular tennis bums and an office worker who owned a black Doberman pinscher. This splendid animal would run like a streak around the park and often startled me by suddenly appearing from my rear, giving me a nudge on the leg as she went racing by at about 10 times my speed.

During the summer months, a number of relatives came to town: Joan and Carson with their daughter Nancy and Aunt Cora. We toured the cigarette factories and marveled at the mechanized skill of great rows of automated machines tended by white-gloved operators monitoring the flood of cigarettes that came tumbling down conveyor belts like a snow storm. These were whisked away and put into cartons and then huge boxes for delivery to the whole world. It was a fabulous operation and very profitable for the R.J. Reynolds family, whose business consistently ranked in the top 100 manufacturing firms in the United States.

In late 1952 and early 1953, the first of many reports condemning the use of smoking tobacco as the primary source of lung cancer were beginning to flow from the Surgeon General of the United States. These reports contained sobering news and helped me decide to make a really serious effort to kick the habit. As all smokers know, the process is never easy. Starting on a Monday morning, I simply did not light up a cigarette after breakfast, telling myself to hold off until I got to the office. When the urge came at work, I told myself I could have a cigarette in five minutes. Every time the craving came to light up, I told myself to wait just five minutes. I kept my pack of cigarettes handy as a security blanket and told myself I could have a cigarette in five more minutes if I really needed one. Somehow it worked, and I was able to get through that day; but after supper I went to bed exhausted with the effort. In the morning, I reasoned that if I could abstain for one day, I could abstain for two. Soon I had survived a third, fourth, and fifth day without smoking. By the end of the week, I felt I had a chance of making a two-week goal, and by the end of the third week was confident enough to leave my cigarettes at home.

Since then I have never had another cigarette, thank God. It took over a year before the urge to smoke ceased. Years later, I would dream of smoking cigarettes and awaken feeling guilty about breaking my nonsmoking vow. What a relief it was to find it was only a bad dream. Such dreams illustrate how powerful is the addiction to nicotine.

* * *

The end of the year was approaching, and for the past six months I had been anguishing about whether to stay with the Bureau or resign. I talked it over with Carman, who was most sympathetic. In response to my question about how to write a letter of resignation to the Director, he said he did not know but had thought about it a lot. I wrote about ten draft letters and ended up simply stating that I wanted to resign from the Bureau, that this was not the career field for me, and that I would be glad to do anything for the Bureau in the future.

John Edgar Hoover died at the age of 77 after being the Director of the FBI from 1924 until his death in 1972. He had become so prestigious that no president was prepared to replace him, even though he often came under criticism for his authoritarian administration of the FBI. I had given the FBI career a good try, but the idea of being a policeman for the rest of my life was more than I could stand. My Mom understood and had no problems about returning to Pennsylvania to live with Joan. I concentrated on completing my casework so that I would be ready to turn in my badge, .38 revolver, and Bureau material and clean out the apartment. I also traded in my 1951 Pontiac for a more spiffy, up-to-date 1953 Buick two-door sports sedan that was two-tone green and had leather upholstery and a fine radio.

It was the end of January and very cold. I called my sister Nancy, who lived in Sarasota with her husband Tom, and asked if I could visit while I sorted out what to do next. All I knew for sure was that suddenly my ulcer was feeling better and I wanted to let the old earth take a few twirls before I got on again.

EIGHT

Sand in My Shoes

Deciding to leave the FBI was not easy, for I was thirty-one years of age and should have been settling into steady employment, not leaving a good job with Uncle Sam. I turned in my badge and gun, said good-bye to office friends, loaded the Buick with all my worldly goods, and headed south. For the first time in my adult life, I was out of a job with no serious prospects in mind. Strangely enough, I did not care.

En route to Sarasota, I paused briefly to smell the orange juice being processed in Dade City and then stopped near Tampa to spend the night. The next morning, I arrived at Nan and Tom's house on Siesta Key, where I felt right at home. Luckily for me, they decided to set up Tom's radiologist practice in Sarasota, otherwise I never would have found the lovely community that was to become my hometown.

In those early years, Siesta Key was a quiet, sun-drenched village noted for its friendly, easygoing attitude. There was always time for fishing in the bay or offshore in the Gulf of Mexico. Best of all was the finest white sand beach in all the world, stretching for over two miles to Crescent Beach and Point of Rocks.

Sarasota's population would double in the summertime and then triple in November, December, and January. Droves of tourists migrated like lemmings to the sea, impelled to warmer climate by the first thin rime on their fish ponds or the faint honking of geese streaming southward. Strangers appeared everywhere, their faces pale from life in sunless, shivering towns in snowbound Michigan, farming communities in Ohio and Indiana, old New England towns, and the Canadian wildernesses. All were snowbirds who, like me, shared a common distaste for cold weather and a love for golden sunshine. Thus began my life in Sarasota, where I would meet and marry the lovely Phyllis Warren Magee, a Yankee Doodle Dandy who was born on the fourth of July 1923.

* * *

The Gulf beaches were wide, clean, and invigorating, with fine warm sand and ever present breezes. Every morning was different, exciting, and refreshing, a distinct improvement over the smell of tobacco in Winston-Salem and the rural lifestyle of nearby communities. It was hard to believe that almost 10 years had passed since I was first assigned to B-17 training at MacDill Field in Tampa; yet here I was, standing on the beach at Siesta Key, wiggling my toes in the sand and acting as carefree as a kid out of school. I soon came down with a serious case of "sand in my shoes," a malady common to many when they first visit Sarasota and from which some never recover.

It did not take me long to settle into a routine. My day started with a walk on the beach after which I would take a long look at the morning edition of the *Sarasota Herald Tribune*. Over dinner with Nan and Tom, we would talk over the events of the day and watch the NBC news with Chet Huntley and David Brinkley. Television was relatively new to this area in 1954 and certainly an innovation to me. One event that would affect my life and that of our nation was the defeat of French forces in May 1954 at Dien Bien Phu in North Vietnam.

An unforgettable television show at that time was *Victory at Sea*, a stunning series about U.S. forces in World War II filmed by military photographers. The program was marvelously narrated by Leonard Graves, with background music by Richard Rodgers, and was a vivid reminder of the colossal scope of that conflict. I realized anew how vast and terrible that war was.

It was time to think seriously about getting a job and settling down. Nancy's vigilant network of girlfriends resulted in some casual dates and outings at the beach or neighborhood cocktail parties. It was on a blind date, however, that I met Phyllis Warren Magee, a popular and active young woman who was currently modeling in a fashion show at Sarasota's Exhibition Hall and agreed to meet me after the show at the side door of the auditorium.

Feeling like a stage-door Johnny, I appeared at the appointed time and was not disappointed. Phyllis was taller than most women, about five feet eight inches, and had a model's poise and slender figure. Her softly waved, golden hair complimented beautiful blue-green eyes and a warm smile. I do not know what she thought of me, dressed in a colorful sports shirt with tails hanging out, but we hit if off pretty well.

We got into my polished Buick with the soft leather seats and headed for St. Armands Circle to hear Charley Davies perform in the Piano Bar at the Elbow Room. I ordered drinks and began to find out more about this lovely young lady. So far, she more than met my expectations, proving to be a very perceptive and sociable person with a quick wit and sense of humor. Time slipped by easily and when we left the bar, I realized she was a very special lady who had much to offer, someone I wanted to know better.

Phyllis was divorced from her ex-Air Force pilot husband, and had a daughter, Cynthia Kingsley Magee, who was six years old when we met. Phyllis had come to Sarasota because her parents had retired there a few years before. Her father was Kenneth Carleton Warren, a former World War I pilot and manager in the Bamberger Department Store in New York City. Her mother was Evelyn Kingsley Warren, a native of Buffalo, New York, whose parents were active in the publishing, investments, and social world of Buffalo and New York City. Evelyn's sister, Jean, often visited Sarasota in the winters and took painting classes with Bob Chase. One of her paintings of pepper tree berries, sea grape leaves, and a conch shell hangs in our living room. Phyllis had one older sister, Shirley, who as a child would be upset on July 4th because she thought all the fireworks were in honor of Phyllis' birthday.

Phyllis complained after our first date that I knew all about her but she knew nothing about me. As a former FBI agent, I was accustomed to seeking information without divulging anything in return. Before long, however, I relaxed and we began to confide in each other more openly.

Aside from her physical attraction, Phyllis had many other quality attributes. Her thoughts and reactions, sense of right and wrong, essential values, and responses to everyday occurrences were quite similar to mine. She accepted the imperfections and limitations in life, as I did, and believed in making the best of things. Phyllis was courageous and mature in important matters, never allowing worry to dominate her better judgment. For example, she was honest enough to shed a husband who did not share her values and whom she could no longer love or respect. She came to Florida to start over again in the land of sunshine and oranges, where you could always catch fish to grill or pick grapefruit in your backyard without fearing nuclear bombs. It is no wonder that year after year Florida has ranked third or fourth in the nation's population growth.

In those Cold War days, the threat of nuclear attack was remote but ever present. One local contractor built bomb shelters for homeowners' backyard installation. Priced at about $5,000, only a few were sold, which collected rain water and bred mosquitoes at a horrendous rate. The few wealthy people who bought the shelters eventually had them removed or covered with dirt. I always thought they were ostentatious monuments to fear that would not do much good if we ever were bombed.

Phyllis and I saw a lot of each other during the spring and summer, dancing at the Lido Casino in the spacious ballroom that overlooked the Gulf of Mexico and sometimes double-dating with friends. We stopped at the M'Toto Room in the old Ringling Hotel and explored the old Cummer Arcade on Pineapple. The place to go on Siesta Key was the Beach Club, which had six barstools, often occupied by artists or writers who loved to tell tall tales or have a drink after their daily stint at the typewriter or easel.

Phyllis worked downtown as a secretary for architects while occasionally posing for artists and commercial photographers. I studied the want ads and found pickings pretty slim. Almost in self-defense, I began to think about writing for a living. Sarasota was full of well-known authors, and Siesta Key was one of the leading artist and writers' colonies in the country. John D. MacDonald, Elia Kazan, Budd Schulberg, McKinlay Kantor, Joseph Hayes, and Richard Glendinning, were among those living in the area. Their presence encouraged me to think about trying my hand, since I had to find some way to pay for the necessities of life. My nest egg was not going to last forever, although Nan and Tom had not kicked me out and I was debt free. Something would turn up if I kept my eyes and ears open and was receptive to new ideas. I had faith in the Horatio Alger philosophy that everything works out for the best, often in unexpected ways. I also believed that hard work was always rewarded and you had to keep at it even when the future was clouded.

John Hamel was looking for a resident manager at The Jungle Lodges he owned, which included a main house and ten nicely furnished guest cottages on the gulf to bay property. Friends and associates of the Hamels from Michigan, Illinois, Ohio, New England, and other northern spots spent their winters at The Jungle Lodges. The guest cottages were former military buildings moved to Siesta Key from an old airbase that is now the Sarasota-Manatee County Airport. The old buildings were converted into charming rustic cottages tucked away in random fashion under the canopy of live oak, slash pine, and cabbage palm trees.

John Hamel and his gracious, artistic wife, Bea, offered me a deal I could not refuse. I could live in the furnished, two-bedroom apartment above The Jungle Lodges office rent-free in return for manning the office four hours a day and handling routine maintenance in the mornings. A yardman cared for the grounds and a maid did the housework in the cottages. The rest of the day was mine, allowing me time to try freelance writing. John laughed when I told him this, as though it were a big joke, but said that was fine with him. He was a pleasant, stocky man who smoked a pipe almost constantly. About fifty years old and engaged in business in the Chicago-Detroit area, John and his wife planned to retire in Sarasota in a few years.

I moved right into my new home in the tree tops, eager to get started. Shaded by long-needle pine trees, the combined living and dining area was open to breezes on three sides and separated by a counter from a small but efficient pullman kitchen. The vines of a jasmine bush that reached the second-floor window of the kitchen were so thick they blocked the view; but it produced such a lovely fragrance that I did not have the heart to cut it back. All things considered, the apartment was very private and cozy, and I slept like a baby. With windows open on all sides, I could hear the rustle of pine branches and the distant tumble of surf on the beach.

Being ten feet off the ground, I would not be an easy target for the hordes of thirsty mosquitoes lurking outside. I lavishly rubbed mosquito repellant on my hands, face, and clothing when I had to work around the property. That first summer I remember an old B-17 flying low and slow over Siesta Key and spraying a white cloud of mosquito repellant to dampen the uprising. More often, county jeeps would cruise slowly just after dusk when the winds subsided to spray ditches and dense foliage, struggling to keep the darn pests under control.

Every morning by 8:30 I began using an old, secondhand Remington typewriter to turn out short stories of 1,200 to 1,500 words. I carefully studied the style and format of stories published in magazines such as *Collier's, The Saturday Evening Post*, and *Ladies' Home Journal*. A subscription to *Writer's Digest* also helped me to learn more about the craft I had chosen. After a month or so, I began submitting my precious works quite regularly; and just as regularly, rejection slips came flowing back. Some curt, some courteous, some with little notes of encouragement, but to my growing dismay, none came with little notes of acceptance. Clearly, this business was going to take time. I resolved to give myself a year to produce saleable short stories or decide on something else.

Meanwhile, Phyllis and I were keeping steady company, enjoying the realization that we were two kindred spirits. I was a very laid-back suitor, taking my time, and careful not to push too fast. Marriage was still a distinct possibility, for she was all that I wanted in a wife; but I was not sure how she felt. One warm July evening at her home, we were having a drink of Early Times and tapwater and talking over the events of the day when Phyllis brought up the subject in her marvelously direct yet gentle way. She wanted to know if I was interested in a long-term relationship and, if so, what I had in mind.

Her query was unexpected, but my response was ready and unrehearsed. As is often the case with important decisions, the answers seem to come almost without thought. I told Phyllis that I certainly was interested and wanted to make Sarasota my home. Before I knew what I was saying, I asked if she wanted to share her life with me. She did not hesitate either and with a beautiful smile said she did not see any reason why not. We were both happy and very much in love and decided to marry in about a month.

We were married August 10, 1954, in a simple civil ceremony at the Warren's home. It was a single-ring ceremony, with Phyllis' wide band of gold engraved PSW from AS. Only close family members attended: Ken and Evelyn Warren and Aunt Helie, on Phyllis' side; Myrtle Swain and Nancy and Tom Stansbury on my side. Cyndy was our flower girl and nicely dressed in the same color as Phyllis' bridal gown, a pale, green-blue organdy; both were quite beautiful. Phyllis wore sweetheart roses in her hair and a shoulder corsage, and Cyndy's corsage was a miniature of her mother's. Nancy was Phyllis' maid of honor and Tom was my best man. Cyndy was happily involved in helping her mother get married but not quite sure what was going on. Arrangements were made for Cyndy to stay the next week with K.C. and Ebby (as the Warren grandchildren called their grandparents) while her mother and I were in the Bahamas on a honeymoon.

Although the ceremony was brief, I remember how pleased and happy I was to have found a fine person like Phyllis to love and marry. Ken Warren was very close to his drinking daughter, so called because she was always willing in the old days up north to try his homemade applejack brandy. K.C.'s only advice to me after the ceremony was to take good care of his daughter. Knowing that he approved of the marriage and was much loved by Phyllis, I told him I would and meant it, just as I did the vow made only a few moments before "to love, honor and cherish her, until death us do part." Then we all joined in a wedding toast and some picture taking before friends, neighbors, and well-wishers arrived for the gala reception.

After dodging a hail of rice, we departed for The Jungle Lodges where I managed to carry Phyl over the threshold. My sister had slipped into the apartment earlier to set a welcoming dinner table for us with a tablecloth, candle, and centerpiece of attractive red and orange hibiscus blooms; it was lovely, peaceful, and quiet. Mr. and Mrs. Adrian Swain, young, confident, very much in love, and ready for whatever the future had in store.

We had arranged to honeymoon in Nassau, the capital of the Bahamas, at the Royal Victoria Hotel, which offered one week for

Adrian Swain

$64.00 per person, breakfast and dinner included; roundtrip airfare was $40.00 per person. Romance, adventure, sightseeing, and swimming at famous Paradise Island awaited us.

In the early morning freshness we headed for Miami International Airport, driving through Venice, Fort Myers, Naples, and then the green expanse of the Everglades. At noon, a twin-engine propeller plane swept us aloft and over the blue-green waters of the Gulf Stream. Below we could see the tropical Bahamas, an extended archipelago of about 700 islands scattered throughout 70,000 square miles of sea. Only thirty of the larger islands are populated by about a quarter million English-speaking people of European and African descent.

In no time at all, we arrived at the Royal Victoria, about a block from Rawson Square with its famous Straw Market. Our room overlooking the garden was very comfortable and airy but contained the lumpiest bed I have ever known. It was a four-poster relic with a mattress that peaked at the edges and had a valley in the middle not quite as deep as the Grand Canyon.

We quickly established a routine of exploring after breakfast and then lunching wherever we happened to be. In the evening, we dined on the outdoor patio under huge, green, opulent banyan trees. The Royal Victoria service was prompt and skilled, and our full-course dinners from soup to dessert were excellent. The open-air stalls of the Straw Market were filled with native straw and shell handicrafts, such as baskets, place mats, sunshades, and purses. More formal shops offered duty-free items, such as crystal, silver, woolens, perfume, and liquor, $200 of which we could bring back to the States.

I remember exploring the slippery moss of exposed coral when the tide was out and snorkeling in the exquisite clear waters. We climbed the 65-step Queen's staircase carved out of solid rock by slave labor many years ago that lead to Fort Fincastle atop Bennett's Hill overlooking the sea. We took guided tours to all the old fortresses where we stood and gazed seaward, imagining we were on guard against marauding pirates or attacking Spaniards. The Bahamas have their share of interesting history to tell. During the Civil War years, the islands were a center for Southern blockade runners delivering cotton bound for England. Rum-runners traversed the Bahamas with booze from Cuba going to the States during Prohibition in the 1920s. Not until tourism was developed after World War II, however, did economic prosperity come to the islands.

One morning shortly after sunrise we rose early to breakfast on the terrace and then strolled down to the wharf just in time to see fishermen unloading a catch of turtles. Three or four huge turtles, each about four feet long, were lying on their backs, feet moving helplessly. Those giants from the Gulf Stream would be delivered to hotel kitchens for later appearance on dining tables as turtle soup. I felt sorry for the poor things.

Out strolling the docks again, we noticed a U.S. Navy submarine with its gangplank down and hatch open. We approached a sailor near the hatch and asked if we could come aboard. He said the boat was open to American citizens who wanted a look. We walked up the gangplank with Phyllis leading the way dressed in black and white checkered shorts and an attractive middy blouse. Without Phyllis' prettiness, I doubt the sailor would have been so quick to invite us aboard. We crawled down the open hatch into the confined, metallic space below and inched into a tiny galley where the ship's cook sat at a small table taking a break. He, too, was impressed by the beautiful Phyllis and obviously pleased by our visit. He showed us where the provisions were stored: meat lockers jammed full of frozen steaks, mounds of bagged Idaho potatoes and yellow onions, and stores of flour for making biscuits. We roamed aft into the cramped sleeping quarters, now vacated save for one sleepy sailor who blinked at us in surprise. The rest of the crew was no doubt enjoying the pleasures of Nassau. Beyond double rows of tightly-tiered bunks was the torpedo room, which was sealed off and allowed no visitors. We found the sub visit quite interesting and stimulating, yet depressing. It takes a special kind of person to adapt to such confinement without going stir-crazy and it was certainly no place for a six-footer like me. As we left, I took a few pictures of Phyl on deck; we were both glad to be in the sunlight once again.

One cloudy afternoon we decided to take in a movie and arrived just as the show was starting. We bought tickets and found two seats about halfway down in the crowded theater. When the movie ended, the house lights came on and I noticed that we were the only white people in the audience. I knew then how it felt to be in the minority. For the first time in my life I felt outnumbered and alone in a foreign land, not very well liked, and tolerated as an outsider.

At the end of the week, we were back in Sarasota where we rejoined Cyndy, who was sure glad to see her mother. It was soon school time for Cyndy to start first grade. While Phyllis resumed her secretarial duties, I went back to the lonely, frustrating, and thus far unrewarding work of freelance writing.

It was during this first year that Cyndy's father, Walter Magee, was struck and killed by a truck while he fixed a flat tire late one night coming home from a party. We decided that I would adopt Cyndy, which was a very simple, natural, and easy procedure to work out. I loved the little girl and was happy to have her as one of the Swain family. One other significant benefit of the accident was that Cyndy received $30,000 from the truck company in a trust account. The money was invested and multiplied, providing very well for Cyndy's college and other living expenses until she married Phillip Toale in 1974.

I reactivated my membership in the Air Force Reserve by joining the unit in town. Our meetings were held twice a month on Thursday nights for which I could earn one point each toward the 35 points needed annually to be eligible for retirement. It was not hard to make the meetings, and there were correspondence courses available to earn extra points. Drill periods also were offered every two years in which one point for each day of active duty could be earned plus daily pay according to your rank.

I did not ever expect to reach retirement age in the reserves but felt it was worthwhile to participate because I already had more than five years of active duty. Joining the reserves was one of the smartest moves I ever made. I eventually acquired 22 years of service, was promoted to Major, and later was eligible at age 60 for medical coverage and a retirement check from Uncle Sam.

Even though my writing was not bringing in any money, our living expenses were so low that we lived very well for the next year on Phyl's wages and my savings. I continued trying to become a successful writer and continued not succeeding. My stomach ulcer began awaking me at night with gnawing pangs. Luckily for me, Dr. Tom was now open for radiology business and scheduled an upper gastrointestinal exam. I had to swallow about a pint of cold, chalky barium liquid and then have X-rays taken. The next day Tom told me I had an duodenal ulcer that was treatable but would get worse unless I changed my ways. He prescribed a sedative that I took every four hours for the next three weeks and put me on a diet of Jell-o, soup, soft omelets, and lots of milk. I lay around the house with no energy or desire to do anything but rest. The ulcer healed and I have never had a serious relapse. I made a determined effort to change my mental attitude and avoid getting upset over things that did not really matter. I began to laugh at myself when I got too stuffy or high on my soapbox. Realizing that so much in life was beyond my control, I stopped worrying over every tiny thing and began to separate the possible from the impossible. I learned to accept partial success and not to expect to win every battle in life; what was important was giving it a good try. Whenever ulcer pangs threatened, I simply stopped what I was doing and switched to something less stressful.

Several interesting events occurred during this time. In 1955, Prince Rainier of Monaco married America's own Grace Kelly, a former bricklayer's movie star daughter who went on to live a storybook life. Phyllis used to model with her in Arizona as she did Lucille Ball, who became famous as the comedy star and producer of the *I Love Lucy* television show.

There was also the meteoric rise to popularity of the McDonald's hamburger chain, with its distinctive golden arches. In 1955, Ray Kroc began building the McDonald's Corporation from a handful of hamburger stands into the world's largest food chain. He was 52 years old and selling restaurant supplies when a small hamburger stand in San Bernardino, California, came to his attention. He called on the tiny drive-in restaurant run by the McDonald brothers, Dick and Mac, and saw customers waiting 20 deep at takeout windows to buy the 15-cent hamburgers being cranked out assembly line fashion in a spotlessly clean kitchen. Kroc realized the possibilities and bought the franchise rights for $50,000. Seven years later he bought out the entire company for $2.7 million, which was financed at such exorbitant interest rates that the total purchase price was $14 million. Over the years Kroc built the company with a passion for uniformity.

Owner-operators had to buy meat, potatoes, cooking oil and other products from common suppliers. The company stock soared when McDonald's began purchasing the real estate on which the franchises were located. Ray Kroc died in 1984 at the age of 81. He liked to say, "The world is full of educated derelicts. Persistence and determination alone are omnipotent." Another one of his favorite sayings was "Free enterprise will work if you will." Ray Kroc's story proves it is never too late and offers incentive to all Americans who have the entrepreneurial spirit and drive to strike it rich.

While resting at home, I watched the televised Senate hearings of Senator Joe McCarthy's sensational and brutal efforts to find communists in high levels of government. He seemed like a crazed man, even accusing President Eisenhower of condoning communism in government offices. McCarthy was totally irresponsible and got away with it because Congressional immunity allowed politicians to say almost anything on the Senate floor. He did not escape entirely, however, and finally was censured for unbecoming conduct by his Senate colleagues in December 1954. His popularity died shortly thereafter and so did he in 1957.

At the University of Pittsburgh School of Medicine, Dr. Jonas Salk developed a polio vaccine that proved effective in 1954. A year later, all U.S. school children began inoculations with Salk's polio vaccine. What a blessing his discovery has been to the world. Salk was awarded many honors, including the Presidential Medal of Freedom in 1977.

President Eisenhower authorized construction of the Saint Lawrence Seaway in 1954, which kicked off one of the great engineering feats of our time by opening sea traffic between the Atlantic and the western end of the Great Lakes. It took five years to complete the complex of natural waterways, which involved deepening channels and a series of locks and canals that stretched 2,342 miles. The route moved mostly grain, iron ore, and coal; boats from more than 30 nations now use the waterway to deliver or pick up cargoes.

In August 1955, I attended two weeks of reserve training in Memphis, Tennessee, with the reserve unit to which I was assigned. Our squadron flew day and night missions, logging as many training hours as possible. The summer weather was fine, and we stayed as busy as our tired, old C-46 aircraft would permit. Although it was unlikely that we would be called to active duty, I felt uncomfortable and decided against continuing with the unit after that session. Miami was too far away, and I also just about had my pants scared off while in Memphis flying night formation. Three planes were assigned to a four-hour flight one night with no moon and our only reference points being the red or green wing tip lights and a tiny blue light under the fuselage. It was very tense with that airplane hulking about 20 feet away in the dark, identified only by the small lights and a faint outline in black. I was pretty rusty, not having flown formation since 1944, and the other pilots were not much better qualified. The old skills returned though, and somehow none of us were killed. I resigned from the squadron when I collected my paycheck for those two weeks; I did not need the money that badly. It also happened to be my first wedding anniversary, and although I called Phyl and sent her roses, I was still disappointed not to be home with her.

When I returned home, we decided to take a vacation trip. Cyndy, Phyl, and I piled into the Buick and left early in the morning, driving all day until we finally stopped at a motel outside Atlanta, grateful to have a place to lay our heads. The next morning we visited Atlanta's Cyclorama, a pictorial monument to the Civil War displayed inside a circular building. Graphic scenes vividly depicted the pillage and burning of Atlanta by Union forces under General Sherman. The display was utterly fascinating and began my never-ending interest in the Civil War.

In Chattanooga, Tennessee, we climbed the bluffs to Lookout Mountain and sat on a Civil War cannon that General Bragg and his Confederates had installed on the 2,000-foot heights. The Union forces below had been surrounded by the Confederates for almost two months until President Lincoln put General Grant in charge of the Union armies between the Appalachians and the Mississippi. Grant arrived and the rebels were driven from their mountain heights by General Joe Hooker's men who scrambled up the steep slopes and took the mountain top in a dense fog. It was an almost unbelievable feat and appropriately called the Battle Above the Clouds. The next day, General Phil Sheridan's troops stormed Missionary Ridge, where the Confederate soldiers were no longer protected by their guns on Lookout Mountain. After the battle, 4,000 rebels were captured and imprisoned. Chattanooga was won and with it control of the Tennessee River and two key railroads; from here the Union would drive south into Georgia and further divide the Confederacy.

After returning to Sarasota, it had become quite evident that we were not making much progress financially. The writing business was not paying off, and it was clearly time to do something else. As often happens, events beyond our control occur to make up our minds for us. Out of the blue, Phyl told me she was expecting a baby. I was completely surprised, but quite delighted. Thomas Warren Swain was born on May 9, 1956, and weighed five pounds, ten ounces. Thomas was named after his uncle, Tom Stansbury, and his middle name was for grandfather Ken Warren.

A nice German nanny stayed with us for ten days after Phyl came home. She was a marvelous nanny, and I soon learned to change diapers, give young Tom his feedings on time, and watch over Phyllis. He was a good baby who slept well, was alert and happy, and had no allergies or complications. Tom had auburn hair, hazel eyes, and a fine appetite that soon began to put weight on his lanky frame.

To improve our cash flow and afford more living space, Phyl and I decided to get into the real estate business. We both had experience in the business world and had dealt with the public before. Ken Warren, who was working as a sales associate with a real estate broker, probably could be persuaded to open his own office with Phyllis and me as his sales force. Within six months the details were worked out and put into operation. Phyl and I studied for the Florida State real estate examinations, which we took in Tampa. Ken Warren already had activated his broker's license and leased office space in downtown Sarasota for our new business known as KC WARREN Real Estate. We opened for business in the fall of 1956 and did well almost from the day we opened the doors; the tourist season was just starting and seasonal rental inquiries were numerous.

I continued to work at The Jungle Lodges office while contributing to the sales effort in the morning hours. Phyllis pitched in full time, first setting up the office accounting procedures and then listing and selling real estate as well. We were soon very busy, and time began to fly as we met a lot of people and made many new friends in the process.

We lived at The Jungle Lodges until Tom was more than a year old and then gave John Hamel notice of our plans to leave. We had to get into larger quarters and wanted to build our first house. K.C. worked out a deal, in the best of real estate traditions, in which he put up a lot that he owned, valued at about $1,000, and we built the house financed through a loan in Ken and Evie Warren's name. Phyllis and I would make the mortgage payments in the form of rent. When it came time to sell the house, the proceeds would go to Ken and Evie as a return on their investment; everybody would win. Thank God for fathers and mothers who are willing to help their children when help is needed.

Sarasota was bursting at the seams, money was flowing, and construction and real estate offices bloomed everywhere in a rush of post-Korean War prosperity. Real estate prices at that time were considerably lower than today. For example, a decent building lot (100' x 120') with central water (but no sewer) cost $3,000 to $5,000. Waterfront lots on the Philippi Creek with a seawall and boat access to Sarasota Bay cost $6,000 to $7,500, and buyers were snapping them up.

We moved into the house in the fall of 1957. We were busy and active in the world of real estate and with our growing family, which soon expanded to accommodate the arrival of William Adrian Swain, born August 1, 1959. I was delighted with having another member of the family and could tell that he would be a strapping man, judging from his body length. In fact, Bill attained the height of six feet three inches. He was named for Phyllis' old friend, Admiral William Shawcross; his middle name was for old Dad.

Space was getting a little tight in our two-bedroom house. We put Billy's crib in the alcove in our bedroom by Phyl's desk, where it was pleasant and quiet. We did have a minor problem with our cat, Mr. Big, who did not want to share time with the baby. Mr. Big was jealous, and to get attention he would slip into our bed late at night and drape himself over my face, almost smothering me. One day Mr. Big disappeared, and we thought he had run away in a huff. We later learned that he had climbed in a parked car's open window and been taken home by the owner, a very nice lady as it turned out. From reports we heard later, she was happy to have acquired Mr. Big, who promptly took over her household. All the same, I missed him.

Meanwhile, our business grew, and we were active listing and selling land and houses all over the south side of town. A vacant lot that was zoned for professional business gave me the idea of putting up our own office building. The timing looked good, and with luck we could catch the wave of rapid growth and profit by improving our location. Phyl and I were both high on the idea and had been discussing the tax advantages of incorporating our business and changing the name to Warren-Swain, Inc. Ken Warren would be president, Phyllis would be secretary and treasurer, I would be vice president, and Evelyn would be a director.

Some notable events occurred during this time. Film star Humphrey Bogart died of lung cancer in 1957 at age 58, as did the fashion world's leading designer, Christian Dior. The movie *Bridge on the River Kwai* came out to rave reviews. Alaska became our 49th state in 1958, followed by Hawaii in 1959. The Russians launched Sputnik III while America, lagging behind, finally put Explorer I into orbit from Cape Canaveral. We also put our nuclear-powered submarine the *Nautilus* under the polar icecap at the North Pole, a superb demonstration of our navigational skill and courage. On the sporting scene, Arnold Palmer won his first Masters golf tournament at Augusta, Georgia. Ted Williams and the Boston Red Sox baseball team, who had held spring training at Sarasota's Payne Park for 25 years, abruptly departed for Scottsdale, Arizona, and in 1959 were replaced by the Chicago White Sox.

About a year earlier, Frank Thyne had just become a qualified general contractor and suggested that we join forces. Frank's idea was that he would build custom houses from a model home display and I would sell them. We soon created Thyne and Swain, Inc., with Phyllis and Gloria Thyne as members of the new corporation. Frank quickly became adept at planning, estimating, scheduling, and building, and Thyne and Swain, Inc. started to make some progress.

In the lean years ahead, I found that working for commissions was not always easy. Sometimes I wished I had taken up hammer and saw to earn regular paychecks instead of spending days and weeks working with a new buyer in town, only to have the sale go elsewhere. Many new buyers had about as much loyalty to the salesman as they did to the peanut vendor at a ball game. It was painful and frustrating after spending days and even weeks working to find just the right property, only to have the sale made by another salesman at some open house that your buyer just happened to wander into on their own.

K.C. was lukewarm to the idea of building the new Warren-Swain office. He was afflicted with the NIH virus (meaning not invented here) and hesitant to move ahead with any plan that was not his own. Ken was persuaded to buy the corner lot on Siesta Drive only after I told him that Thyne and Swain would if he did not. It was a good thing that he bought it, because two weeks later a bank executive called and offered Ken $40,000 for the lot saying the bank wanted to build on that corner. Ken may have been tempted, but he turned it down.

Again Phyllis had to persuade her father, as only she could, that now was the time to move ahead. Over lunch, they decided on a designer for the office to be built by Thyne and Swain, Inc. Before long the building was up, providing space for Warren-Swain and two small offices that we could lease. Good rent money came from our tenants to help pay the building mortgage, and K.C. was happy. We were in a fine, extremely visible location and pleased with the design of our office.

Later, Jim Knight and I bought a little house behind our office for a long-range investment, thinking that someday the whole block would be bought out, possibly by a bank. Exactly that happened 30 years later when Sun Bank tore down all the buildings in the area and built their monstrously glittering structure. Jim and I had sold out in 1979, taking our 300-percent profit on an initial investment of $12,500. The moral of this story is simple: buy well-located properties and hang onto them as long as you can afford the taxes but avoid buying vacant land that does not bring in enough rent to cover expenses. Inflation plus supply and demand will see that profits accrue over time.

* * *

In 1960, President Eisenhower admitted he had authorized flights over Russian territory when a U2 reconnaissance plane flown by

Francis Gary Powers was downed in Russia. Powers, an employee of the CIA, was convicted of espionage and sentenced to ten years in jail but exchanged in 1962 for the Russian spy Colonel Rudolf Abel, who was in an American jail. The U2 incident caused the cancellation of an economic conference that had been scheduled between Russia, the United States, England, and France, but it also demonstrated the honesty and courage of a President who did not duck his responsibility. He admitted our country's involvement instead of claiming he knew nothing about it.

Since those days, we have had officials in high office who often lacked the courage and moral character of a Dwight Eisenhower, a Harry Truman, or a Jack Kennedy. The newer breed of politician seems to disclaim personal responsibility, vowing piously they knew nothing. Richard Nixon's Watergate shambles and Ronald Reagan's shabby behavior in the Iran-Contra affair are prime examples. Nixon let his Attorney General John Mitchell, among others, go to prison; Reagan left Admiral Poindexter, Colonel Oliver North, and General Richard Secord adrift at sea without his support, forcing them to stand trial at the hands of federally funded and politically motivated prosecutors (who happily spent millions of tax-payers' dollars) trying to blame them for what was done in the name of the President. It is a disgraceful business that has made our allies shake their heads in disbelief at the way we sometimes run our country.

By 1960, America was probably the richest and most powerful nation in the world, with almost 180 million people who shared that accomplishment. The American Heart Association issued a report on the higher death rates that prevailed among middle-aged men who were heavy cigarette smokers. In November, 43-year-old John Fitzgerald Kennedy was elected the youngest President of the United States, succeeding America's oldest President, Dwight Eisenhower, who at age 70 soon was to retire happily to his farm in Gettysburg. In Sarasota, the times were good for the Swain family.

NINE

On the Sarasota Scene

The real estate business became a full-time job now that we were Warren-Swain, Incorporated. Ken Warren was president, I was vice president, and Phyllis was secretary and treasurer, the glue that held us together. Evelyn Warren was a director and a stable influence in our family business. While not particularly active, Evie had a fine business sense and sound opinions to offer. K.C. was a good public relations man and served on the Sarasota County Board of Realtors as a director and vice president. After K.C. served his time, I also was elected as a director of the Board of Realtors.

We all worked hard and were assisted by a number of sales associates. Parker C. Banzhaf was one of the most effective salesmen in our office. Parker and his wife, Greta Lee, lived on Bay Island in an old two-story colonial home that they bought in 1959 when they came to Sarasota from the Virgin Islands. Parker was tall and debonair, the penultimate preppie, well mannered, and considerate of others. He possessed a strong New England streak of conservatism, having attended Phillips Academy in Andover, Massachusetts, as did President George Bush. Parker often mentioned to the uninformed that George Bush was a classmate with whom he shared not only old school ties but also a love of politics. Given his interest in politics and public service, it was not too surprising that Parker became known as Mr. Republican in Sarasota. It was largely because of Parker and Greta Lee that Sarasota County became a Republican stronghold on the gulf coast of Florida. When George and Barbara Bush came to town, as they occasionally did over the years, the Banzhafs hosted them and in return were hosted by President Bush in Washington. Parker could always be depended on for help or advice, or for the latest snippet of gossip. PCB, as he was often called, was on intimate terms with many Sarasotans and had a sincere interest in their welfare. These were fine qualifications for a real estate professional who would later serve with distinction as president of the Sarasota Board of Realtors.

Our new office was located near the model home built by Thyne and Swain. Displayed by Warren-Swain, it was the very latest in modestly priced Florida-style homes. Called the Sunline, it featured post-and-beam construction, a flat roof with wide overhangs, and high, earth tone stucco walls surrounding the sunlit and inviting living-dining room that led to two U-shaped bedroom wings around a garden patio. Sliding glass doors allowed the palms and pyracantha in the patio to become part of each room. Tiny blue-green tiles in the mirrored bathrooms were illuminated by softly filtered sunlight from skylight bubbles. The off-white tones in the galley kitchen were also lighted from a skylight above; a stacked washer and dryer were set by the kitchen door. A gas range and double-oven cooking center were recessed from view; the kitchen cabinets opened with the touch of a finger on secret magnetic latches; and there was a central vacuum system with outlets in every hallway. It was indeed a state-of-the-art house.

Highly polished terrazzo floors were covered with area rugs to set off the dining and living spaces. The centerpiece in the living room was a square, ultramodern, wood-burning fireplace. Frank mentioned that he thought the black stove flue venting the fireplace to the outside was a phallic symbol that seemed to offend some of the visitors at our open house. I was not sure that was possible, but perhaps he was right, for we never sold that beautiful model home. We had one serious buyer who just loved it. By the time Frank added up all the money we had invested in the house, however, the price became so high that the buyer, quite rightly, was not interested. The lesson was *never to let an interested buyer get away. Make the deal or you will find you have just bought the house yourself.*

Aside from the house not selling, the venture was moderately successful in ways that we did not expect. Frank received good publicity that enhanced his reputation as a builder of fine modern homes; he signed several contracts with people who wanted something similar to our model. Nan and Tom Stansbury bought a $7,500 lot on the fairway at Sarabay Country Club and then decided they would build after seeing our model. Architect Tim Seibert, already well known for his design skills, also gained stature from the publicity and advertising that the *Sunline Model* generated in publications such as *House Beautiful* and in local advertisements.

Although our model home generated much fanfare, the house was not very practical or comfortable for year-round family living. It was definitely not the kind of house that middle-aged retirees coming to Florida from more traditional homes in the north felt comfortable with. The flat roof was not sufficiently insulated from the heat of the summer sun, and there were no gutters or downspouts to carry off rains, which sometimes fell with tropical fury. The wooden louvered windows tended to warp, allowing heat and cold to seep in or out; and there was no airconditioning or covered garage. From my practical salesman's point of view, the Sunline was hard to sell, except to young people who could not afford it.

Frank and Gloria eventually moved into the house with their two boys and lived there until 1961, when the Swains moved in. We decided to buy out Frank and Gloria's half interest in the house so we could refinance the loan and add airconditioning plus a combination office and guest room. Even with our present three bedrooms, we discovered we would need more space. Once more, I was astounded and pleased when Phyllis told me that I would be a father again.

There are some happy memories of that house. In the backyard were two grapefruit trees, one of which was dying and had to be removed. I then discovered that citrus trees made superb firewood. I trimmed the other tree, leaving a jungle gym framework to which I tied stout ropes so that Tom, Bill, and Cyndy could climb about. An old tire hanging from the strongest limb made a fine swing that the kids loved.

The winter of 1961 was especially cold as I remember. Since firewood was expensive, Cyndy and I would hop in our station wagon and drive to groves to gather dead limbs from the orange trees. Many a cold morning I would start a fire while Phyllis prepared hot cereal, Bisquick pancakes, or everyone's favorite, bacon and eggs with whole wheat toast.

Kenneth Charles Swain was born on August 22, 1962, and was a normal, healthy baby who promised to be tall like his brothers. Phyllis was just fine for a mother almost 40 years old but decided to have a tubal ligation, which was a simple operation done before she came home.

Luckily, we had a series of good day-care helpers. Bertha Mae was the lady I remember most, a big, buxom lady with a calm and cheerful demeanor. She proved to be a good surrogate mother for our youngsters and managed to have a warm dinner on the stove by the time Phyl came home. Phyl was working in real estate as well as the insurance field and really had her plate full. I sometimes wondered how she managed to get all of her jobs done without cracking up; she was simply a marvel.

It is interesting to consider how our children came along: 1948 (Cyndy), 1956 (Tom), 1959 (Bill), and 1962 (Ken). Cyndy's seven-year edge meant that the boys would never seriously question her authority when she was left in charge. Having Cyndy made me feel as if all my earlier years as a single man were not wasted, as if she were my own. She was a big help to her mother and naturally they were very close.

Our need for more space was solved by an addition off the kitchen. The marvelous new room had its own outside door, which was especially attractive to Phyllis because she could say good-bye to the kids, go out the front door as usual, and then reenter her new room by the outside entrance. In a moment, she was in her own private office with no other interruptions to deal with.

* * *

One of the institutions that developed at our house was an annual Christmas Eve party. Following the 5:00 P.M. services at St. Boniface, after the children's carols were sung and the crèche decorated, we would return home and hold an open house for all our friends who had children. These families visited during the early part of the evening so they could go home to their own Christmas activities.

After the first wave of visitors had subsided, an older group without children would appear. Some would stay until the evening was reasonably well along and others would drift in and out, all of us enjoying Christmas cheer and snacking on sliced turkey and glazed ham.

Sometime between 10:00 and 11:00 P.M. Bill and Annie Brownell would arrive. Bill was my right-hand man whose considerable engineering skills were needed to decipher the often garbled instructions that came with all the toys we bought for our kids. For years, Bill and I struggled every Christmas Eve to assemble a variety of bicycles, climbing slides, trucks, scooters, and other mechanical marvels. It became a battle of stamina, will, and courage for us to complete the work by midnight, our progress being somewhat impeded by the draughts of Christmas cheer we sipped as we labored. Invariably, there was a screw, a nut, or other key part missing from some toy. I always suspected that some disgruntled employee on the Japanese assembly line was bent on sabotaging us. Bill and I had a lot of fun, and even now, years later at Christmas time, I think about assembling those toys with the missing parts. After all the visitors had gone home, Phyl and I would spend the next hour wrapping presents and putting them under the tree. We would get to bed just in time for the children to come bounding into our room and get us up for Christmas Day. What stamina we had!

During January 1961, the United States was still having trouble with Fidel Castro and Cuba. We had severed diplomatic relations with Cuba because Castro was taking over or nationalizing many U.S. businesses there, as well as threatening our military base at Guantanamo Bay. I remember hearing Dave Garroway on NBC Television interview some expert in world affairs, who believed that Castro would be kicked out of office in less than six months. Thirty years later he is still there; so much for expert opinion.

On April 17, 1961, we suffered a political and military setback when staging a naval infiltration of Cuba at the Bay of Pigs. The abortive assault was sponsored and operationally controlled by the CIA and planned by Richard Bissell, Deputy Director for Plans. In a poorly executed and conceived operation, Cuban expatriots in

Miami were recruited to form a liberation brigade that landed at the Bay of Pigs aboard U.S. Navy ships with their numbers painted over. The liberators were supported by a few World War II twin-engine B-26s with Cuban Air Force markings flown by CIA pilots. The plan counted on spontaneous support from local anti-Castro Cubans who reportedly were ready to rise up, join forces with the liberators and overthrow Castro.

The invasion force bogged down at the Bay of Pigs, Castro's favorite fishing ground, and was crushed by Castro's superior air and ground forces. The expected anti-Castro groundswell of support did not appear. Because Kennedy was reluctant to authorize direct involvement of U.S. military forces, the invasion ended within a few days. Over 1,000 brigade members were captured and imprisoned. President Kennedy suffered a major propaganda defeat while still in his first 90 days as President. This all happened because of poor intelligence, inadequate understanding of the forces needed to accomplish the task, and poor communications between Kennedy, his staff, high-ranking Navy officers, and Richard Bissell, who was responsible for the bungled CIA plan. President Kennedy, who had initially approved the operation, had second thoughts but was too late trying to stop it. After it was all over and he had taken full responsibility for the failure, Kennedy said, "All my life I've known better than to depend on the experts. How could I have been so stupid to let them go ahead?"

By the end of 1961, Allen Dulles, then head of the CIA and brother of John Foster Dulles, Secretary of State, was replaced by John A. McCone, a tough old shipbuilder from the west coast. Richard Bissell also resigned his post as chief of all covert operations after a career that was most notable for his success in shepherding the famous Lockheed skunk works production of the U2. This spy plane was capable of flying at altitudes in excess of 80,000 feet and photographing Soviet defense installations. A top-secret project, the U2 was completed and in use within two years, instead of the usual eight years such a project would have taken the Air Force.

Luckily for our public image and a distinct plus for the Kennedy Administration, Commander Alan Shepard (one of seven Mercury astronauts) successfully rode in a Mercury capsule that rocketed from Cape Canaveral in our space program's first suborbital flight on May 5, 1961. The following February, John Glenn, the oldest of the seven astronauts, successfully made three orbital flights around the earth aboard a capsule named Friendship 7. His charred capsule is one of the prize exhibits in the Air and Space Museum at the Smithsonian in Washington, D.C. On the strength of his popularity, John Glenn was elected Senator from his home state of Ohio in 1974.

In October 1962, John A McCone ordered the U2 to survey Cuba. After repeated flights, photographs disclosed that Russian-supplied missiles were being deployed against us. When confronted by this proof and threatened by a surface embargo on the sea lanes, Russia's Premier Nikita Khrushchev backed down and took all his missiles back to Russia. This time it was the Russians who were caught with their pants down, and a possible nuclear confrontation was averted.

When President Kennedy asked John McCone why he persisted in sending U2 planes over Cuba without any hard evidence of missile activity, he said that was what he would have done if he were Nikita Khrushchev. The moral of this story is clear: sometimes a hunch or intuition is more productive than recruiting and developing a network of trained spies to gather intelligence and it sure helps if you have a U2 at your disposal.

In the fall of 1962, we endured what was billed as the 100-year rain. An enormous low pressure system dumped record amounts of rain on us during a 48-hour period. The 12 to 16 inches of water deposited on Sarasota constituted what meteorologists say happens once every 100 years.

By late afternoon on the first day of the rain, the runoff began to flood our patio. Three inches deep, the water was about to flow into our living room and bedrooms. I splashed out to the corner of the patio, and scratched around under the pebbles to find the drain covering I had installed months ago. I yanked aside the plywood cover and with a gurgle, the flood waters began to flow. It worked like a charm; within a half hour our patio was almost dry. Needless to say, I felt heroic about all of this; for once, Murphy's law had been thwarted.

* * *

Tom and Nancy Stansbury were doing well in business and decided to build on their golf course lot at Sarabay Country Club, where Tom was a member. They built a house, similar to our Sunline model home with a fancy indoor-outdoor fishpond and a fine swimming pool off the master bedroom. One day while cruising along in his Jaguar roadster on the curving back road near his new home, Tom took a turn too fast and banged broadside into a cabbage palm tree. The car was not damaged seriously, but Tom struck his head sharply, apparently suffering no serious injury. Several days later, Tom died at home one afternoon. Nan found him when she returned home from work, but it was too late, nothing could be done. Internal injuries to the head were listed as the cause of death. Tom was only about 40 years old; what a shame to die so young with so much to live for. He had made a success of his medical practice, had plenty of money in the bank, and left Nancy with a decent income from stocks, bonds, and a contract with his junior partner that provided an income over the next several years. Nancy continued to operate the Cessna aircraft dealership at Sarasota-Bradenton airport after Tom's death and then bought the dealership at Tampa International Airport. Nan suggested that I help her sell airplanes, possibly using my real estate contacts. I thought this a good idea, especially since she would provide me with an aircraft so I could renew my commercial pilot's license. It was great fun learning to fly the little single-engine Cessna 172, after a layoff of almost 10 years. Phyllis even went up with me one afternoon for a turn over the Gulf of Mexico along Siesta Key at about 3,500 feet. I was careful not to tip over the plane or do anything unusual, for I could tell by Phyl's white knuckles that she was not very comfortable in such a little plane. She told me about taking a ride with one of the Army Air Corps pilots at Luke Field when she was a model in Arizona. The pilot, trying to show off and impress the beautiful Phyllis, did a lot of stunts and loop-the-loops, which scared her to no end and put that pilot on her blacklist.

I received my commercial license and was in business again. I do not recall selling any planes for Nancy but did ferry a brand new Cessna 182 to Tampa from the Cessna factory in Wichita, which took about 5 hours not counting a refueling stop near Tallahassee. During another flight, I was approaching the Tampa airport when I glanced south toward MacDill Field. On the runway was one of the famous Blackbird aircraft, its drooping tapered wings almost touching the ground; it was the same type U2 spy plane that CIA pilot Gary Powers had flown over Russia. It looked like the Air Force was still flying reconnaissance missions over Cuba to keep the Russians honest.

The year after Tom died, Nancy had a New Year's Eve party attended by a petite newcomer to the Sarasota area, Anne Osborne Erhart. She was an attractive, blond divorcee from Connecticut, who had three little girls and was renting a cottage on Siesta Key. It was not surprising that Anne and Phyllis found they had much in common, particularly since both had been through a divorce and faced the challenge of starting life anew without a husband. It was not long before Anno, a nickname, decided to build a home on Siesta Key. It was the start of a new life for her and the beginning of a friendship between Anne and Phyllis. Our two families would travel different paths for another quarter of a century before coming together in a totally unexpected yet rewarding way.

* * *

Nancy had met David A. Davis, a country lawyer from Bushnell, Florida, about 50 miles north of Tampa. Dave flew his own airplane to Tampa to attend court cases and often moored his aircraft at Nancy's Cessna flight line. He was a Vermonter who had stayed in Florida after graduating from Stetson law school. He made a good living working on right-of-way problems related to Interstate I-75. Dave began to court Nancy and was persistent and persuasive.

In March 1963, they were married in a little church in Tampa, after which Phyllis and I flew with them to Freeport in the Bahamas for their honeymoon. It seemed strange to be going on someone else's honeymoon, but Phyllis and I were ready to get away from the real estate rat race in Sarasota. It was also a chance for me to practice my newly licensed flying skills. At midpoint in the flight, Nancy seemed a bit apprehensive since everywhere she looked there was nothing but water. I reassured her we were on course and could expect to see land in about 10 minutes. Sure enough, out of the haze and mist ahead appeared the outlines of Grand Bahama Island.

We stayed at the Grand Bahama Hotel in a different wing from the honeymooners, which made us feel less intrusive on their privacy. It was one of the newest gambling complexes in the Bahamas, and the hotel staff was young and eager to please. Obviously the owners hoped we would drop a bundle of cash at their gaming tables, which we did not. For the next several days and nights we loafed, swam, drank rum Collins at the poolside, and even played a little golf. One night we had dinner in Freeport and visited a nightclub where we watched lithe limbo dancers do their magic to torch light and pounding drums.

After we returned to Sarasota, Nan and Dave bought some land south of town and called it the DAN ranch for Dave and Nan. The ranch had a fine pasture and a grove of live oaks where Dave built a frame ranch house with a big wood-burning fireplace. They added a barn for the small herd of cattle that gave them a bunch of tax write-offs. Dave then cleared, graded, and sodded an airstrip about 1,500 feet long, just right for his Cessna 182.

Phyllis and I visited the ranch several times with the children. Bill loved the woods and fields and liked to target practice with the .22 rifle I bought over 20 years earlier when I worked for the Pittsburgh Railways Company. The aging weapon worked fine, and we would stick tin cans or paper targets on the bole of a big oak tree far from the house at which Bill and Tom blazed away.

One time Tom took his first ride on a pony, which was shaggy and kind of frisky, since it had not been ridden very much. Dave saddled the pony and off they went, Tom tall in the saddle as he started off at a smart jog and then disappeared around the far side of the barn. Next thing we heard Tom shouting at the pony as they came around the barn toward us, the pony trotting at a brisk pace and Tom parallel to the ground clutching the saddle horn, his knees clinging to the saddle, which had slipped halfway down the pony's body. This pony did not care much for this riding foolishness and was headed back to the barn, whether Tom liked it or not. We reasoned that the wise old pony had deliberately inflated its belly when the girth was being cinched and then let the air out when Tom got in the saddle. It was not a pretty sight, and I felt sorry for Tom. After that, none of the other kids wanted to try.

* * *

On Friday November 22, 1963, at 12:30 P.M., President John F. Kennedy was shot, allegedly by a 24-year-old sniper named Lee Harvey Oswald who fired from an upper window of the Texas School Book Depository building. Kennedy was riding in a motorcade with his wife, Jackie, while in Dallas for a political appearance in support of Texas Governor John Connally, who also was severely wounded by the sniper. After Kennedy's shocking death, Vice President Lyndon Baines Johnson took the oath of office. Oswald was killed two days later by Jack Ruby, a Dallas nightclub owner who shot Oswald in the basement of the Dallas police station while in police custody being escorted between chambers. Both killings were shown live on national television for the world to see; it was bizarre. The whole nation mourned Kennedy's death and many rejoiced at Oswald's demise. Those who could were glued to their televisions watching the drama unfold: the shooting of the president, the execution of Oswald by Ruby, the long funeral procession from the Capitol down Pennsylvania Avenue on a dappled, sunlit day. Television cameras focused on the slow-moving cortege with a riderless horse following a gun carriage on which lay the flag-draped casket of the slain President; Walter Cronkite reported all the events to the nation. We watched the grieving family and the final graveside burial ceremony at Arlington Cemetery. It was a moving and mournful tribute to a popular and much loved president and an occasion that provoked questions that had no answers. Kennedy who once fatalistically remarked that if someone really wanted to kill a president, it would not be that difficult; he was right. It made me feel fragile and vulnerable and aware of my own mortality; I began to question whether I was making the best use of my time.

In 1960 at age 43, John F. Kennedy was the youngest man and first Roman Catholic ever elected President. He narrowly defeated Richard M. Nixon by a margin of 118,550 votes out of 68,335,642. His administration lasted 1,047 days and was notable for his concern for foreign affairs. He campaigned on the slogan "Let's get this country moving again" and appealed strongly to youth when he initiated the Peace Corps, which turned out to be a very successful program. In his memorable inaugural address he called on Americans "to bear the burden of a long twilight struggle. . . against the common enemies of man: tyranny, poverty, disease, and war itself. . . the energy, the faith, the devotion which we bring to this endeavor will light our country and all who serve, and the glow from that fire can truly light the world. And so, my fellow Americans, ask not what your country can do for you, ask what you can do for your country." The man was an inspiring figure, and after all these years he is still revered and his loss brings sadness to the hearts of many.

* * *

In 1964, John D. MacDonald wrote the first of his Travis McGee series, *The Deep Blue Goodbye,* in which he began using a color code in each title. John and his wife Dorothy came to Sarasota in 1951, the same year as Phyllis Warren Magee. In selecting the last name for his hero, Travis McGee, I have often wondered if John selected McGee because he knew and admired Phyllis and she was a lady everyone loved. John said that he selected the name Travis from a list of Air Force bases suggested by fellow novelist and Siesta Key buddy, MacKinlay Kantor. Travis Air Base in Fairfield-Suisun, California, is where I served my last active tour in 1952. I liked both names—Travis and McGee.

John lived in a spacious, one-bedroom home perched high on stout poles. Frank Thyne told me that he and John had spent hours together making sure the pilings were deep enough and securely fastened to withstand a hurricane that could someday come roaring in from the Gulf of Mexico. Because the home had only one bedroom, John owned a condominium nearby that was turned over to visiting New York editors or publisher friends who came to town.

I first met John in the early 60's at a large cocktail party one warm summer evening on Siesta Key. I got to know him a little better when he and Warren Rice bought some property on speculation through me. Warren Rice was the active buyer, and John MacDonald joined in just for the profit of it, dashing into our office to sign the contract and put up his half of the $50,000 sale price. He was a private, shy person but charming and witty.

Years later, I wrote to him about some drug education work in which I was involved, hoping that he might have some ideas on how to publish and market the material. He was most kind and thoughtful in responding, saying that he had little experience in such matters but thought the idea of asking for a fee plus royalties from McGraw Hill Publishers would be a good way to go.

John worked just about every day of the week, pounding away on his Brothers electric typewriter from 9:00 A.M. until late afternoon. Even toward the end of a prolific writing career, which spanned nearly forty years and generated book sales exceeding $70 million, he said he worked so hard because he enjoyed it. "Writing is fun. I don't find it tedious at all. Oh sure, maybe you're just plugging along for several days in a row. But then the next day you might get three or four pages just right that say exactly what you wanted to say. And that's a real rush, let me tell you... It's very rewarding. It is like being in a gold mine sifting sand. Then all of a sudden you strike gold."

A native of Sharon, Pennsylvania, John wrote 70 books before he died on December 27, 1986, in a Milwaukee hospital of pneumonia following heart surgery that September. John was working on his 22nd Travis McGee book at the time and living in his new home on Siesta Key. John will be missed by fans of his Travis McGee series but even more so by all his friends and admirers who knew him as a thoughtful, generous, and shy man.

* * *

In 1964, I was elected president of the Sarasota County Board of Realtors, having served three years on the board of directors. The annual Realtor's dinner dance, at which the induction of new officers took place, was held in the Forest Lakes Country Club. My old friend and a former Board President, Harold Ross, served as master of ceremonies and did a smooth job. It was a gala occasion and enjoyed by everyone except me because I had to deliver an acceptance speech while the dessert and coffee were being served. I was pretty nervous and careful to have only one scotch and water before dinner; but I got through the speech, and then was able to enjoy the rest of the evening. Phyllis was having a fine time and was beautifully dressed. The music was slow and mellow and very pleasant for dancing. I had never been the president of a group before, and it felt pretty nice.

The year passed quickly, during which I presided over monthly meetings and handled routine business. Our membership was less than 400 people with a monthly meeting seldom exceeding 75 members. Today, the membership is over 2,000 people. The board has its own headquarters with a fine auditorium, assorted meeting rooms, and the latest in computer files and multiple listing services provided by a staff of competent personnel.

At the close of my term, Lucille Heintz (married to Realtor Joe Heintz) presented me with a leatherbound scrapbook filled with news clippings and photographs of various highlights during my term. On the back page was a touching tribute written by Lucille that said, "To Adrian, a quiet man, you were loyal, honest and a very fine Realtor, and you will always be remembered, like the lovely Sarasota sunset, with warm and tender feelings from your Realtor Friends. With best wishes. . . Lucille Heintz." Thank you, Lucille. Being president of our Board of Realtors was a good experience, because it not only looked good on my business resume (ever the practical one), but I also appreciated the recognition and esteem of my fellow Realtors very much.

* * *

Effective August 1, 1965, I was put on the retired reserve roster after 22 years of service with the rank of Major, United States Air Force Reserve. My retirement pay would start when I reached age 60. There were no more reserve meetings, which was cause to celebrate.

KC and Evie were masters at conducting family cookouts, with KC grilling sirloin or tenderloin steaks about an inch and a half thick. He would fire up his grill while Evie marinated and seasoned the steaks, basting them with slatherings of bright yellow mustard over a blend of soy sauce, salt, pepper, A-1 steak sauce, and Lowry's seasoning salt. With charcoal glowing, a water bottle to dampen a too ardent flame, assorted tongs, a timer, and hickory dust at the ready, KC would start sizzling the steaks. He would judiciously time the steaks, turning them and occasionally adding hickory dust for that special flavor, while sipping a drink from time to time. Phyllis' job was to keep her father supplied with liquid nourishment while he performed his critical chore in the heat of the coals, turning and timing the meat until it was just right, nicely charred but not burned on the outside and juicy and pink in the middle. KC was fond of Imperial whiskey, but on special occasions his favorite was Cutty Sark. His objective was to drink just enough whiskey so that the steaks and KC "would get done at the same time."

Cookouts were best in the fall or winter, when KC would build an oak fire in the fireplace. There was nothing better than a cookout when the steaks were done just about dusk and we would gather with our bamboo lap trays loaded with food, seat ourselves near the warmth of the fireplace, and enjoy the companionship of friends. The succulent steak was sliced into strips, immersed in Evie's marinade, and then popped into a sliced and warmed Pepperidge Farm roll. Served with a green salad, crisp coleslaw, and Evie's famous onion dish, it was a meal fit for royalty. Evie's onion dish was made of sliced sweet onions baked with onion soup in a casserole dish so that the onions were browned on top, yet sweet and tasty and with no aftereffects. It was out of this world, even for me with a touchy stomach. Hot apple or pecan pie topped with whipped cream (served happily in precholesterol days) rounded out the meal, after which Irish coffee made you feel so contented that only the young had enough energy to keep running around.

Two of the Warren's frequent guests at these cookouts were Kay and Ray Brown. Kay Brown had been married to a man named Painton, a former correspondent for *Reader's Digest* who served in World War II with famed Ernie Pyle. After Painton died, Kay married Ray Brown, a retired editor for a sports magazine. The Paintons had one son, Fred, who became a news correspondent in Paris with *US News and World Report*, before transferring to *Time* magazine. We kept in touch with Fred and his wife, Patricia, after Kay and Ray died.

In October, when the children returned to school and the tourist population was down considerably, the Swain family would rent the Levinson cottage on the beach for a couple of weeks. We would take the kids to school and then go to the office, but at the end of the day we returned to the cottage where we had cookouts, swam a lot, played in the sand, and lived in our bathing suits most of the time. It was just the idea of going over the bridge away from the mainland that made it such a treat for us.

Two things happened that made the Levinson cottage especially memorable. The first happened one rainy day when Phyllis and young Kenny were waiting at a traffic light on their way back to the cottage. When the signal turned green, Phyllis started through the intersection and was broadsided by another vehicle. Phyllis was knocked senseless and Kenny tumbled into a heap under the dashboard. Poor Phyl suffered a badly dented cheekbone, a mark she carried for the rest of her life, and little Ken took a hard rap on his head. The other driver's insurance company paid all the hospital charges and car repairs, and Phyllis filed a suit for damages.

* * *

The second event occurred October 10, 1965, a clear, sunlit Sunday morning, on the porch of the Levinson cottage. We had been to church at St. Boniface and were drinking coffee and reading the *Tampa Tribune* and *Sarasota Herald Tribune*, when I noticed an advertisement that could change the direction of our lives. The headline that caught my eye simply said, "THIS IS NOT AN EASY JOB."

I looked it over carefully and then showed it to Phyllis. The advertisement read as follows:

THIS IS NOT AN EASY JOB

Many men will not be able to qualify for these early overseas assignments. The duties may require hazardous work under severe living conditions for extended periods of time. Candidates must have excellent physical and mental qualifications (college training is desirable, but not required). You must have investigative or police background. Military or civil government experience desirable. Experience in MIS, CIC, OSI, ONI and Special Forces sought.

The employer is a major organization which offers an excellent fringe benefits program and overseas living expenses.

Write to Mr. R.G. Marshall, stating fully your personal background, education and employment history. (No telephone calls please).

Our client is an equal opportunity employer and assumes all placement fees.

GAYNOR COMPANY, INC.
Management Consultants
850 Third Avenue, New York, New York, 10023

Phyllis knew that I was looking for a way to earn a better income than we were making in real estate. We had discussed the rising costs of everything, and while it did not bother Phyl too much, I was keenly aware that our children's college expenses were going to be high. While we were doing all right now, the trend was not encouraging, considering all the things we would be needing before long. The next day I sent a brief but comprehensive resume to the Gaynor Company in New York noting my personal history and identifying all the members of my family. I mentioned that I was presently serving as president of the Sarasota County Board of Realtors, had a commercial pilot's license, was a Major in the reserves with over five years of active duty in the Air Force, had worked as an FBI agent, and had a college degree from Penn State.

I had been reading and filing reports about our government gradually building up military and nonmilitary support for the South Vietnamese government. President Lyndon B. Johnson was moving ahead with his Guns and Butter program, as it was sometimes called, which meant that taxpayers were financing growing military support for South Vietnam while continuing to fund an ambitious and costly Great Society social program. Somehow, all of this was being done without a significant tax increase. Johnson sought to finance increased expenditures through increased tax revenues that would occur through increased job opportunities. Because he opted not to ask for belt-tightening measures needed to keep inflation under control, the cost of war goods and social services soon began to compete in the market place, inflation increased, and national debt soared. Looking back with my keen 20-20 hindsight, Lyndon Johnson's program was overly ambitious, however laudable, because he failed to rally enough support from the U.S. citizens for the military effort in Vietnam, which eventually failed. I could read what was happening in news reports and saw our expanding effort to halt the spread of communism in Southeast Asia as an opportunity for a civilian job with the federal government that would lift me out of my financial doldrums as well as provide interesting and challenging work. On Monday morning, October 25, I received a call from Mr. Byron Crosman and made a breakfast appointment to meet him at the Holiday Inn by the airport in Tampa. This was the call I had been waiting for, and believe me I was excited. The following morning, I met Byron Crosman by the entrance to the dining room, and we were seated at a nice window table and ordered breakfast.

He was a few years older than me and had a slight limp. Graying and dressed in a conservative suit, he was courteous, friendly, and pleasant. He said he was a special representative from the CIA interviewing candidates for an expanded American presence in the Far East that involved sensitive security matters. I asked if he was talking about South Vietnam, and he smiled and said nothing. When he did not deny it, I knew where the job would be. I told him that I was interested if the pay and other benefits were adequate. He filled me in by saying all the right things. My family could accompany me, and all their housing and school expenses would be paid for through a regular monthly allowance. I would be working nearby and could visit regularly, about every month or six weeks. Crosman said that my salary would be around $14,000 per year, plus an overseas differential. When he asked if that was acceptable, I told him I was interested but had to discuss it with my wife and let him know. Although our meeting was brief, it went well. We got along nicely and I liked him. He said he hoped to hear from me soon and that if all went well the next step would be a background check, a personal interview in Washington, and then some training.

On the drive home, I considered the prospect of living and working for the government in the Far East. I had served there before with no problems, the salary would more than cover all our basic needs, and there was the extra housing allowance and overseas differential to consider. It would be good for the family too. I had a strong feeling that I was meant to do this; in fact, it was the answer to my prayers. Not long before reading the advertisement, I had gone home for lunch one day, rushing between appointments, and was on my way back to the office when I stopped in Phyllis' new office and paused in the quiet room, feeling an almost overwhelming urge to pray. Without thinking I knelt down, bowed my head, and tears filled my eyes. I prayed aloud, "Dear Lord, I am about worn out trying to make my way. I have done just about everything I can to make things better for Phyllis and my family, but I need help. I can't do it alone. Please help me, and give me strength to know the way. In the name of God, Amen." I felt a distinct physical feeling of relief as though a burden had been lifted from me. My strength and energy were renewed, and I went back to work refreshed. Maybe God had been listening.

* * *

I returned from Tampa and explained the details to Phyllis. Before I had even finished relating how the family could live in Manila, she surprised me by smiling happily and saying that we should do it. "That's my girl," I said, giving her a big hug. I should have known that her courage and adventurous spirit would turn this assignment into a grand adventure for all of us. I wrote Byron Crosman that Phyllis was not upset at the prospect of living overseas for two years and it was with her complete approval that I was writing this letter.

Crosman responded quickly and said that my letter was most welcome. He forwarded a stack of application papers for me to fill out and return, as well as an explanation of CIA hiring and firing procedures that employees were required to accept. The most interesting part of the preemployment application was that all employees were required to take a polygraph test. It also noted that the investigation of new applicants was a time-consuming process that included an evaluation concerning loyalty, security, competence, and physical and emotional fitness.

I signed all of the necessary agreements and completed the application form with detailed data on myself and my family. On December 10, 1965, a letter from the CIA arrived saying I had been tentatively selected for a position, pending the completion of background investigations. It asked that I keep our business confidential and tell no one of their interest other than my spouse. I also had to sign and return an enclosed secrecy agreement. By the end of December, a letter arrived saying that interviews and a medical examination to determine my physical health and emotional stability were scheduled for January 12 and 13, 1966, in the CIA headquarters building in Langley, Virginia. As before, the letter stressed that this was not an offer of employment. The CIA would pay for our transportation by rail and up to $16 per day for our hotels and meals.

Phyllis and I were elated and decided to made the trip together. We stayed downtown at the old Harrington Hotel because it was near the bus route that went to the agency. God, it was cold that January. Phyl and I dressed as warmly as we could but were not ready for the frigid temperatures that dipped into the low teens on our arrival. In the morning, bright sunlight failed to dispel the sharp cold that cut to the bone when I stuck my head out of the hotel looking for the bus to Langley. Phyl planned to stay inside until it warmed up before going shopping. We agreed to have dinner later and maybe take in a movie when my day of testing was over.

I said good-bye to Phyl, dashed through the icy air, and boarded the bus. We moved across town and then took the 14th Street Bridge into Virginia, where I could see the Potomac River below with shards of glittering ice piled up on granite rocks. We turned onto the George Washington Parkway and climbed into the rolling hills of northern Virginia. The countryside was beautiful with snow patches here and there, the grassy land along the roadway was well cared for, and the woods beyond were stark and bare in the clear sunlight. It took us about 40 minutes to get to the CIA headquarters. The grounds were surrounded by an 8-foot-tall chain fence. As we entered the front gate our bus halted and then was waved on by the guard. We drove along a winding road lined with pine trees, past acres of asphalt-covered parking space, and stopped in front of a massive building where our bus disgorged its load of clerks, typists, stenographers, analysts, scientists, and hopeful applicants like me.

When we got out, I had a good look at the imposing, eight-story, concrete building that was the CIA headquarters. Designed by Harrison and Abramovitz, architects of the United Nations building, it was a dignified and distinguished structure with enclosed courtyards that allowed light and views of grass and shrubs from most interior corridors. I noticed that all the windows were long and narrow and those on the first floor were protected by heavy screening, probably against possible terrorist efforts. The lobby was spacious, well lighted, and open. Uniformed guards were posted at turnstiles, or maybe metal detectors, through which everyone entered. Employees with ID cards were admitted readily. Off to one side I could see a security office and a large personnel and administration area where people with appointment letters were being directed.

I checked in with a pleasant secretary who placed a call to a man named Al who then met me in the waiting area where I sat in a soft leather chair glancing over the *Washington Post*. This was a first-class operation. Al put me at ease at once. He was about my age and had a precisely controlled manner of speaking as though every word was carefully considered before it was uttered. He impressed me as a man who was under a heavy caseload and probably handling a number of people like me who were being processed. He was pleasant and easy to talk with but all business, which suited me fine.

I was with the medical people all morning undergoing routine checks and questions, having blood drawn, and completing lengthy personal history forms. After having lunch in the employees' cafeteria, which I entered wearing a visitor's badge on a chain around my neck, I met with Al who told me that if all went well with the physicals and the polygraph test, we would talk about a contract for employment. The polygraph took place after the results of the blood tests were completed and approved. Al explained that all CIA employees were polygraphed at the beginning of their employment and subject to subsequent reexamination any time, particularly after an employee has been overseas for a tour of duty in a communist-dominated country.

From some basic research, I now know that the polygraph examiner was a skilled operator, and the success or failure of the person being examined was in his hands. Dr. John A. Larson, a psychiatrist, developed the forerunner of the modern-day polygraph in 1921. His instrument made the first continuous, permanent record of three phenomena: blood pressure, pulse, and respiration. Leonard Keeler, a psychologist, later developed his apparatus with an added feature that measured changes in the skin's resistance to electricity, known as galvanic skin response. Keeler's techniques are commonly used today in police work and in business and industrial security.

The Box or lie detector, as it is often called, arouses fear even in seasoned veterans. Nervousness in people often accelerates their heart rate and blood pressure and tends to trigger a lie signal even when they have told the truth. The operator can determine the truth by using control questions that act as a norm or baseline for responses. Before the exam, the polygraph operator rehearses questions that have "yes" or "no" responses with the applicant, such as name, date of birth, and marital status. The CIA's main concern was to determine whether the applicant had any connection or sympathy with communism.

I was relatively relaxed in the examination chair, with the operator unseen behind me. A cuff was placed on my arm to measure any significant blood pressure surges; other pressure belts and tubes were placed around the trunk of my body to measure and record the rate and pattern of my breathing. A third device was held in my palm and attached to one or two of my fingers to measure any changes in electrical resistance in the skin. None of these were uncomfortable. I was asked to be as still as possible and answer "yes" or "no" to the questions asked.

After I was all wired up, the operator connected me to his detector box, which contained a sensitive recording pen that would trace my reaction impulses on a recording sheet. If a question was not answered truthfully, the recording pen would jump significantly and trace a jagged peak on the recording sheet. Questions were asked about drinking, the use of drugs, police records, homosexual inclinations, and membership or knowledge of communist sympathizers or organizations. There were no surprises, and I passed the polygraph test without difficulty.

On my return the next day, I was told that the physical exam was satisfactory. We then discussed the salary and other benefits. Assuming I passed the in-depth background investigation now in progress, I would be offered a two-year contract at the GS-12, Step 4 pay scale, which carried a base salary of $12,091. Added to this would be a 25-percent overseas differential of $3,022, plus a housing allowance of $3,333.00, for a total of $18,446. I was pleased at this, and when there were no more questions to discuss, Al told me to go home and conduct business as usual without talking to anyone outside of family. If all went well, I could expect to be offered employment and contracts to sign in three or four weeks.

Phyllis and I celebrated that night with a few drinks and a nice steak dinner. After coffee, we walked around the corner to the Warner Theater, which was showing *The Great Race* with Jack Lemmon and Tony Curtis. The movie was slap-stick and not very entertaining, perhaps because what was happening to us was more exciting. We left and went back to the hotel to relax and make plans for the future. It had been an exciting two days, and I felt on top of the world. We left for Sarasota in the morning.

Just as I was beginning to get worried, a call came from Washington saying that the background investigation had been completed and everything was in order. My reporting date would be April 12. We decided to sell our house so that we would not have to worry about mortgage payments or being absentee landlords. Just before we were ready to ship overseas, we got an offer from a young doctor with a couple of kids who loved the house. KC said he would handle the closing, because by that time the Swain family would be somewhere in Manila.

Our family had a close affiliation with St. Boniface Church, where we had been faithful attendees for the past 10 years. I made an appointment with our rector, Dr. John Ellis Large, told him of our job opportunity in Manila and Saigon, and asked him if he thought we were doing the right thing. He was such an enthusiastic supporter of the idea that you would have thought he was working for the government. He smiled broadly, his blue eyes twinkling with certainty, and said that he thought it was a wonderful opportunity for us. Considering the powerful presence he represented, it was with relief and pleasure that Phyl and I shook hands with him and said goodbye, promising to keep him posted on our activities. He said we would be sorely missed at St. Boniface, but he knew we would be back, and wished us Godspeed.

TEN

Washington to Manila

There was much to do before reporting to Washington. Our family pediatrician scheduled us for all the inoculations required for living in the Philippines: typhus, cholera, tetanus, typhoid, poliomyelitis, smallpox, yellow fever, and a tine test for pneumonia. We also needed photographs for the red-covered Official Passport used by most U.S. Government employees and families abroad. State Department people were issued a black-covered Diplomatic Passport, which was a bit more prestigious because it evoked more courtesy and status; and private American citizens were issued a blue-colored document simply labeled Passport.

When I finally got ready to go to Washington, Phyllis said she could handle most of the remaining work, such as outfitting the children with proper clothing and storing our furniture. We were allowed to take an auto and bought one of the most popular cars in America that year, a silver-colored Ford Mustang, priced at about $3,500. It was just big enough for Phyllis and the kids and would be fine for getting around on the narrow roads and streets in the Philippines.

My reporting date in Washington was the Monday after Easter Sunday. The cherry blossoms were in full bloom around the Tidal Basin, tourists were out in force, and there were no hotel rooms available downtown. I wrote to John for help, whom I had met earlier in Washington. He also had been recruited for duty in South Vietnam and was now attending classes and staying in a motel apartment with another recruit named Jim. John and I were both retired Air Force officers, and he was from Tampa. John replied within a few days, saying that I could stay with him and Jim. This was good news, for now I had two new friends who could fill me in on anything important I might have missed. I was curious about John's assignment and intrigued by his comment that the work was interesting.

On Easter Sunday evening, I flew to Washington's National Airport and then took a cab to Arlington, Virginia, where I met John and Jim at the Clarendon Motel. The efficiency apartment was tiny but adequate. I was instantly popular when I donated a bottle of Imperial to the household, after which we poured a drink and sat around the kitchen table. The rent was cheap and the kitchen was neat, although we did not plan to do much cooking at home. The living area had two couches that made into beds, and there was a rollaway cot for me under the front window. Our motel was about a mile from where our classes were being held, and a bus to Langley stopped about three blocks away.

On Monday morning I caught the bus and was at CIA headquarters within 20 minutes. Al met me in the personnel office, where I was going through more processing. He had me sign contracts for a two-year tour of duty in South Vietnam, with the family to be housed in Manila. Because of the classified nature of my assignment, I would travel overseas as a civilian employee of the U. S. Air Force. I would then report to the Commander of the Services and Support Squadron in Manila for further processing and assignment.

Later in the morning, a group of about 100 people like myself attended a general briefing in the dome-shaped auditorium outside the main building. We were briefed by several experts on the U.S. Government's increasing effort to support the government of South Vietnam and again told of the need for security at all times. We were then fully briefed on the history and traditions of the agency to which we now belonged. In the name of Admiral William Raborn, the current Director of the CIA, we were welcomed to the family. It was a professional, thoughtful, and uplifting experience, a fitting introduction to a considerate and competent organization.

Arrangements had to be made concerning bank and insurance matters, travel, and shipment of our automobile, all of which was handled by some of the most helpful administrative people I have ever known. I was assigned to a fine lady in personnel named Evelyn, who was my contact for anything regarding the Swain family's processing to Manila. Evelyn was also responsible for processing my bunkmates, John and Jim. With Evelyn there would be no nameless, faceless person conducting our affairs, as had been the case in many other personnel offices in my past. I knew I could count on Evelyn because she had recently served in South Vietnam and understood the problems and pitfalls of being overseas.

Training for new Vietnam personnel was conducted in an office building we call the Blue U, about a mile from our motel. The Blue U was a modern structure with a lot of glass windows spaced between modular panels. The overall effect was contemporary Washington; glitzy and modern, it stood alone on its corner, all blue and shiny. I missed the solid red brick and stone buildings of the Washington I knew when I was an FBI agent; they had style and grace.

Our class had 50 trainees, and John, Jim, and I were already a close-knit unit. Jim planned to leave his new wife at home until I told him that my family was going to live in Manila where I would visit them every six weeks or so. John's wife wanted to stay in Tampa, where he would be authorized a 30-day visit every six months. Our group was assigned a class counselor, an older, experienced Company man named Jack, who explained that the name Company was used by insiders when referring to the CIA. We also learned not to tell anyone we were employed by the CIA. We all had cover stories and fictitious employers if we were asked about our work. All of us had military backgrounds so we were given a false Army assignment in the Pentagon. This cover identity was to be used only in an emergency, because it was a temporary or light cover identification that would not bear close scrutiny. Jack had an office nearby and could be reached easily if we had a personal problem or needed advice on some administrative matter.

The principal training site for long-term technical and paramilitary training was conducted at the Farm, the CIA's training complex in a secluded area near Williamsburg, Virginia. Short term refresher courses for contract employees like us were conducted at the Blue U. The Company's training division knew that many of the current trainees would probably serve their two-year tour and then depart. It was a matter of principle and good intelligence that the Company kept detailed knowledge of its activities, including the Farm, on a need-to-know basis. This meant that we would be told everything necessary to do our work in Vietnam, but nothing more. It also meant that what we did not know, we could not tell someone else. This all made sense to me, but we were still all curious and anxious to learn more about our new employer.

The CIA was sometimes called the Silent Service because its employees were so tight lipped. They were simply not going to talk much to anyone outside of their immediate family. I discovered more information about the Company in newspapers and magazines than I did as an employee. I was astounded at the depth of sensitive information contained in a *Time* magazine article of February 24, 1967 that read as follows:

"... A scant fraction of the Agency's 15,000-odd employees actually go out into the cold. At Langley's elaborate seventh-floor operations center, a bank of high-speed (100 words per minute) printers receive top-secret traffic from the National Security Agency, diplomatic reports from embassies overseas, information from the Pentagon's Defense Intelligence Agency, as well as data from CIA men around the world. In Helms's office, there are secure telephones with scramblers attached—on which the President often calls.

The operations room is hooked into the White House Situation Room, the Pentagon's military command post, and the State Department through a near-miraculous phalanx of teletype machines. One data page per minute can be fed in, encoded, flashed to one of the centers, then decoded the instant it arrives. Down the hall from the operations center is a room papered with huge maps. On one set, the war in Vietnam is plotted with up-to-the-hour reports of combat action and other trouble spots...

... One major purpose of all the influx and indexing is the daily compilation of a slim white 8-in. by 10½-in. document that is hand delivered to the White House in a black CIA car every evening between 6 and 7 o'clock. It bears the CIA's emblem stamped in blue, is entitled "The President's Daily Brief," and usually runs between three and six

pages of single-spaced type, and covers the key intelligence "get" of the day.

... The Agency's overseas operations are diversified almost beyond belief. CIA men may control an entire airline (such as Air America, which runs cargo and operatives in Laos, Thailand and Viet Nam)... They may pose as missionaries, businessmen, travel agents, brokers or bartenders...

The CIA can boot its errors almost as far as its successes. There was the Bay of Pigs. CIA failed to interpret properly the consistent warnings... Naturally enough, CIA's gaffes inspire derisive headlines throughout the world. Just as properly, its successes are little known and seldom disclosed. In an open society like the U.S., there will always be a degree of conflict between the public nature of policy-making and the secret, empirical processes by which decisions must be made and implemented... What is usually overlooked, when CIA is the subject of controversy, is that it is only an arm—and a well-regulated one—of the U.S. Government. It does not, and cannot, manipulate American policies. It can only serve them."

Most of our classwork in the Blue U was supervised by two experienced field agents known as Zeke and Boris. Zeke was small, suave, and a natty dresser, while Boris was tall and had a wild Russian look. One was quiet and reserved, the other loud and flamboyant; they were quite a pair. Both had served at least five years overseas, which was required for all intelligence agents.

As any reader of John le Carré's works or Ian Fleming's 007 spy novels knows, intelligence includes surveillance techniques (conducting, detecting, and evading surveillance); communications (establishing and protecting secure links between you and your informants); sources of information (motivating, handling, and paying people who work for you); informant handling (spotting, identifying, recruiting, and testing people); intelligence requirements (tasking, prioritizing, evaluating, and assessing these needs); reports (using who, what, why, where, when, and how to make sure all intelligence is written and forwarded); and security and training (for you and all your informants). Zeke and Boris discussed these intelligence techniques and related personal experiences to illustrate their points. Neither had served in Vietnam where the natives were oriental farmers and shop keepers about 5 feet 6 inches tall. When asked whether we tall, light-skinned foreigners would stand out like giraffes in a herd of cattle, Zeke replied that it would be difficult for us to take a direct hand in intelligence collection. He said that language was the first problem, and we would have to rely on Vietnamese people who had proven themselves to be on our side and were not Communist sympathizers. Such people, called Principal Agents, could be found and properly trained, but it was not an easy process.

Zeke explained that much of our intelligence collection was being done by these Principal Agents, and we had to make sure the work they did was not being compromised. This was done by the threat of random tests on the polygraph. If necessary, the BoxMan could be scheduled to test the loyalty, accuracy, and truthfulness of any agent. This was the crux of the difficulty that Americans had collecting intelligence in Vietnam. U.S. Intelligence Officers in both the military and civilian agencies were never as fully involved in the collection of intelligence as we needed and wanted to be because of language and cultural barriers. Even the influence of the polygraph was diminished somewhat because we still relied heavily on Vietnamese interpreters. The Vietcong (Vietnamese Communists) demonstrated a more comprehensive and far-flung ability to access our intelligence than we did theirs.

We were shown numerous films that dealt with intelligence techniques as well as the Far East, or French Indochina as it was called during World War II. Quite a few of these films were sponsored by the U.S. Information Agency and narrated by Walter Cronkite. They traced historical events and provided some insight on the people who had influenced the variety of political and economic changes in that part of the world since World War II.

We also saw many Hollywood productions made for military training purposes that emphasized some of the tools of the intelligence trade. William Holden narrated some of these. One was an old FBI story that contained a sequence of events demonstrating the techniques and skills needed to establish and conduct surveillance in a city. It showed that a team of three to five people (men and women) were sometimes needed to follow a suspect without being detected. The suspect in this case wore a pair of brown and white shoes, which was his mistake, because such distinctive dress made his surveillance easy to conduct. We learned from this to dress inconspicuously and blend with the crowd.

We practiced the use of recognition and danger signals; how to leave messages in concealment devices at dead drops (secret places) that would be picked up on prearranged schedules; and what to do if we suspected we were being followed. We never were to look around or establish direct eye contact with anyone. If we were being followed to a meeting with an informant, there was a signal to pass to postpone the contact to another time and place. We learned to move in random zigzag directions while going to a meeting; pause in front of store windows and use them to mirror activity behind us; and enter a building or store by one door and duck out another. We learned to adjust posture and stride, square our shoulders, and walk differently when we needed to evade a follower in a crowd.

In addition to films and briefings, we had to study unclassified material about South Vietnam prepared by State Department and CIA specialists. This background material needs to be summarized here to help set the stage for the activities I was soon to join. The Republic of Vietnam is a narrow, crescent-shaped strip of land curving along the southeastern tip of Asia on the South China Sea. Only slightly larger than the state of Florida (which I could relate to easily), the country is about 800 miles long with the widest portion measuring less than 130 miles. To the north, across the 17th parallel and directly south of China, is Communist-controlled North Vietnam, called the Democratic Republic of Vietnam (DRV). It is interesting to note how rather cleverly, even cunningly, the Communists liked to label their single-party totalitarian organizations with democratic-sounding names. Their National Liberation Front (NLF) is a good example. To the west of Vietnam are Laos and Cambodia, and west of those two countries lie Burma and Thailand.

South Vietnam has about 18 million people, 80 percent of whom live in the rice-producing areas of the Mekong River system. The Mekong flows into South Vietnam from Cambodia on its way to the

South China Sea where it merges with the Saigon River Delta on which the capital city of Saigon is located. This lower third of the country, the rice basket of the land, is flat and often marshy. North of Saigon the land rises gradually, progressing from tropical rain forests and rubber tree plantations to upland forests and the rugged terrain of the Annamite Mountain chain. This backbone of mountains dominates the rest of South Vietnam from low-lying, fertile coastal plains to broad, high plateaus.

The region has heavy rainfall (78 inches in Saigon per year) and an average temperature of 80 degrees. More than five-sixths of the land is covered with rapidly growing natural vegetation that is dense and hard to penetrate but perfect for concealing Vietcong (VC) guerrilla terrorist activities. Ethnic Vietnamese inhabitants, who constitute more than 85 percent of the population, have a recorded history of more than 2,000 years. They are a vigorous people, mainly village dwellers, rice cultivators, or fishermen, and physically related to the Chinese with many cultural similarities such as art forms, language, and a profound respect for learning, age, and ancestry. The educated elite are almost entirely Vietnamese. There are a few minorities, including the mountain-dwelling Montagnards (less than 1,000,000), Cambodians (600,000), and smaller populations of Chams, Malays, Indians, and French. Most Vietnamese practice a mixture of Buddhism, Taoism, Confucianism, and animistic practices (belief that all natural objects have souls) that revere village guardian spirits; there are also some two million Catholics.

The Japanese occupied Vietnam during World War II and were not dislodged until they surrendered to the Allies in 1945. The French reestablished themselves in the south, while Communists, under the leadership of Ho Chi Minh, took over control of the north. The French tried but failed to win the support of noncommunist nationalists. French colonial rule in Indochina finally ended when Vietminh forces under Ho Chi Minh and General Giap routed the French military at the disaster of Dien Bien Phu in 1954.

South Vietnam had been a Republic since 1955 and was governed under a constitution that provided a strong executive, a unicameral legislature, and a judicial system with safeguards for the individual.

From 1956 to 1963, the South Vietnamese government was directed by President Ngo Dinh Diem who administered a country plagued by a ruined economy and a political life fragmented by rivalries of various religious sects and other political factions. There was also the problem of coping with more than 850,000 refugees, including some VC sympathizers, who came south after the Communists took over North Vietnam.

Ho Chi Minh expected the South to collapse and fall under his control. Diem surprised everyone by eliminating the private armies of the religious sections, and with substantial U.S. military and economic aid, he began to build a national army and an administration that was making progress in reconstructing the economy. In the late 50's the Communists realized that the South Vietnamese Government was making solid headway and began to take over by force through their underground network of Communists, the Vietcong. Using hidden caches of weapons, the VC launched a campaign of assassination and kidnapping against officials and village headmen who refused to support the Communist cause. This reign of terror persisted for several years, and thousands were killed by the VC. In December 1961, President Diem asked the United States for help in dealing with increasing VC aggression, and we sent more military advisors. By the end of 1962, the number of U.S. military advisors had increased from 900 in 1960 to 11,000, and Kennedy authorized them to fight back if fired upon.

Meanwhile, popular dissatisfaction with Diem was growing. He had replaced village and provincial elected councils with Saigon-appointed administrators. Diem also angered the sizeable Buddhist population by appointing Roman Catholics, many of whom had fled from North Vietnam, to high positions in Saigon. From the U.S. point of view, Diem and his close-knit ruling family had faults, but at least he was our man. He had drifted far from reality and was out of touch with the people as evidenced by his penchant for dressing in the costume of an ancient Vietnamese Mandarin on ceremonial occasions. A proud and difficult man, he was far from the democratic leader we hoped he might become.

The war was gradually escalating, and one horrendous event followed another. President Diem and his brother Nhu were assassinated in a coup of Saigon generals led by Duong Van (Big) Minh on November 1, 1963. President Kennedy, who knew the coup was planned but did not realize murder was involved, was very distraught. Not surprisingly, a period of political instability followed throughout South Vietnam, a condition that was immediately exploited by the VC. When President Kennedy was assassinated later that same month, Diem's widow, Madame Nhu (often called the Dragon Lady), declared from exile in Paris that Kennedy's death was retribution for the death of her husband.

It was a wild and turbulent time. President Johnson was being advised by his experts to take a more direct approach and take the war to the "real enemy," North Vietnam, rather than fight in the south as the U.S. Agency for International Development (USAID), State Department, and CIA insisted. By 1964, Ho Chi Minh decided to provide more help to the VC in the guerila war and ordered regular North Vietnamese Army (NVA) troops to the south. In August, North Vietnamese patrol boats reportedly fired on the U.S. destroyer *Maddox* on patrol in the Gulf of Tonkin. Reports differ on this action, but the incident was sufficient for Johnson to order naval planes to bomb North Vietnam. Soon an aroused U.S. Congress endorsed the Gulf of Tonkin Resolution authorizing the President "to take all necessary steps to prevent further aggression."

Other governments joined the United States in providing military aid to South Vietnam: South Korea, Australia, New Zealand, the Philippines, and Thailand. The buildup of American troop strength and other expanded American aid programs began in earnest. On March 6, 1965, two battalions of U.S. Marines landed on the beaches at Da Nang to relieve that beleaguered City. By June, 50,000 more troops arrived to fight with the Army of the Republic of South Vietnam (ARVN), now headed by President Nguyen Cao Ky, Air Vice Marshall. By the end of the year, 180,000 U.S. troops were in South Vietnam, commanded by General William Westmoreland.

On the civilian side of our involvement was a program called Revolutionary Development (RD). The RD concept, in which I was to play a role, was designed to help the South Vietnamese free their country from Communist infiltrators by helping them identify and remove the VC and to help improve the local economy and living conditions in the country. The management and overall coordination of the RD program was directed by the Military Assistance Command in Vietnam (MACV) through senior Provincial Advisors in each of the 44 provinces in South Vietnam. I did not know too much about it and certainly had no clue about what my assignment would involve.

* * *

John and I were talking one evening, and I asked him what his assignment was going to be. He said, "I'll be working in the National Interrogation Center in Saigon where all training and coordination of intelligence/interrogation personnel is conducted for the area. When information comes in from the field, it has to be processed properly. Sometimes there will be prisoners or VC sympathizers to talk to and interrogate. There is a lot of work to be done as far as training, collecting and collating of intelligence is concerned, not only at the national level in Saigon but in the outlying areas. I will be involved in setting up and conducting training classes, so I think I'll be traveling around quite a bit."

"How did you ever get that kind of assignment?" I asked.

John said, "During my active duty years, I served in Europe assigned to military intelligence. My Dad was from Germany and my mother from Czechoslovakia. So I spoke the languages pretty well. One day I was picked up in Prague by the police who suspected I was an intelligence agent, but they could never prove anything. I learned a lot about intelligence collection and interrogation procedures. They put me in isolation for days and then weeks, taking me out periodically for questioning, but I never told them anything."

"To keep my sanity I would totally occupy my mind with minute details of day-long fishing trips with my Dad. In my mind, I would get up, have breakfast, get ready, and then go out and spend the whole day with Dad in Tampa Bay. I did it for days. That kept my sanity and my mind free from fear and apprehension. They kept me in the jail for almost a month before they released me."

We never talked again about his background. I could understand how such an experience would toughen you up. When we arrived in

Saigon, John went to work in the National Interrogation Center, and I did not hear from him for another year.

* * *

Occasionally on a Friday afternoon, we would pile into cars that other trainees had brought with them and rendezvous at nearby Fort Myer. This historic old Army base in Arlington was established during the Civil War. It was part of the old Arlington House Estate, from which the Arlington National Cemetery was also created. Fort Myer now houses the 3rd Infantry (the Old Guard), which performs military funerals and conducts the Honorary Guard at the Tomb of the Unknown Soldier.

Weekends were usually party nights at Fort Myer. Sometimes if there was a big party, we could join in the after-dinner dancing. We had to be careful with some of the officers' wives who were curious about our civilian dress and usually asked where we were assigned. It was good training for us. I managed to duck most of their questions by saying I was in the Air Force Reserve or on leave in the area. I learned right there that I had to have a good cover story ready, but I found it hard to lie.

One bright and windy Saturday in spring, we three walked several miles to Arlington Cemetery and spent the morning wandering among rows of military crosses that marked the graves. Each was neatly trimmed and shaded by the bright new leaves of spring. Here rested veterans of the Civil War, the Spanish American War, World War I and II and the Korean War; and now and again there was a new grave stone over freshly turned earth that said Vietnam.

The Arlington National Cemetery was established in 1864 and was part of the estate of Robert E. Lee before he left the Union to fight for the State of Virginia. We visited the grave of President John F. Kennedy, marked by its eternal flame; nearby was the grave of his slain brother Senator Robert F. Kennedy. We noted other famous names engraved in stone that read like a who's who of American history: General John J. (Black Jack) Pershing, William Jennings Bryan, Rear Admirals Robert E. Peary and Richard E. Byrd, and Generals Claire L. Chennault (leader of the famous Flying Tigers),

Hoyt S. Vandenberg, George C. Marshall, and Omar Bradley. Joe Louis would come to rest in Arlington later.

No visitor to Arlington fails to attend the changing of the honor guard at the tomb of America's Unknown Soldiers. The memorial was carved from a piece of marble, one of the largest ever quarried, from Yule, Colorado. Before carving, it weighed 50 tons. In a sarcophagus beneath the sculpted stone lies the body of an unknown American soldier from World War I brought back from France. In 1958, the remains of unknown soldiers from World War II and the Korean War were placed in marked crypts at the head of the tomb, joined later by the remains of an unknown soldier from the Vietnam War. The honor guard of specially selected soldiers from the 3rd Infantry have off-duty quarters under the tomb. The resplendently uniformed sentry, who paces slowly back and forth on a red carpet in front of the tomb, is relieved every half hour during daylight hours from spring to fall and every hour during daylight for the rest of the year; at night the guard is changed every two hours.

By mid-June our training was completed. I received orders for shipping and storing our household effects and for scheduling airline tickets for the family to fly to the Philippines. I told Phyl that I would be coming home and would also stop in Princeton to visit Chuck and Agnes and in Freedom to see my mother and the Carsons. Then I would have almost two weeks in Sarasota before the family left for Manila. The past weeks in Washington had been quite an experience, training and working with a fine group of guys, some of them a little more gung ho than others, and learning how the CIA wanted us to conduct our affairs. It was all very impressive, and I was struck by the manner in which the Agency treated us. We were not expected to take notes, pass quizzes, or take final examinations. Perhaps we had already passed our final exam by being selected for work that few others could qualify for, let alone volunteer to carry out. The experience thus far was an ego trip, a definite confidence builder. Besides being patriotically inclined, however, I knew that without the need to provide for my family I would not be in this company of men being trained to work and live in a strange world of intrigue and violence. Still, I considered myself quite fortunate and had a sense of being in the right place at the right time.

In most people's lives, opportunities arise to grab the brass ring, but not everyone is willing to reach out when the brass ring goes by. There are so many excuses for not taking action. I have found that it all comes down to simple desire and a willingness to try, daring to take the chance and risk failure, wanting strongly enough to grab the opportunity when it comes by. If you miss, it is no disgrace; you will be stronger, more experienced, and better prepared for the next time it appears. So here I was, a small-town boy from West Bridgewater, about to participate in the third major military struggle of my lifetime against another communist-dominated enemy. There was one big difference; this time I was a civilian, not one of the uniformed troops. Older and wiser now, I found my new station in life comfortable; I was more confident and certainly better prepared.

Of all the knowledge and information provided to us at the Blue U, I have never forgotten one piece of advice that Zeke gave us: "Never become contaminated by the tools of the trade. Keep your personal lives separate from the life you may have to live in intelligence activities." I have kept Zeke's advice not only because it was sound but also because it could be applied to life in general. Over the years, I noted business associates and personal friends whose lives were destroyed by lies, deceits, false promises, trickery, and immoderate use of drugs or alcohol. To me, Zeke was saying that whatever you do in the intelligence business, do not abandon your personal standards such as honor and decency, truthfulness and dependability, and respect for church and family, but maintain the self-discipline and determination needed to get the job done. I would not infect my family with the diseases of deceit.

On weekends Phyl and I would talk on the telephone about the children and how everything was progressing with the moving plans. The kids were thriving, busy and active, and getting keyed up about the upcoming adventure. Phyl often sent me humorous and heartwarming letters and notes. Sometimes they made me homesick and I did not know whether to laugh or cry, but mostly I laughed. I tucked them away in my personal file, including one from a friend of Tom's that was brief and to the point:

The Time of My Life

"Dear Mr. Swain,

Your son Tom tells Andy and I you have hand gernad and gas boms. I would like to know if I could have some for school.
Thank you,
Mark Steed"

* * *

By 1966, Tom was in the fourth grade and a budding typist and faithful correspondent. He wrote to me about Hurricane Alma, which blew in from the Gulf of Mexico on June 6 and caused evacuation alerts throughout the area. Because Phyllis kept me posted by telephone, I knew that the family was okay and our house unscathed.

My Special Orders arrived and authorized me and the family to fly to the Philippines on or about June 24, 1966. They contained all the authorizations necessary to obtain airline tickets, ship our automobile from the Port of New Orleans, ship 350 pounds of baggage per adult person via ship and carry 66 pounds of luggage per person on the airplane. There was a reminder to have all passports, visas, and immunizations up to date and on hand.

Our trip to Manila was scheduled for July 14 which gave us more time to get ready. Cyndy had just graduated from Sarasota High School four months shy of her 18th birthday; she was quite a beauty and game for the big trip to the Philippines. She was looking into going to college, perhaps in Florida, after she took some courses at the University at Manila. Tom was 10 years old, Billy was almost seven, and Kenneth nearly four. Phyl had dressed them all in smart traveling outfits. I bought a new pair of stout walking boots at a local discount store since I was told that I would be hiking in South Vietnam. The boys were given a trim with my electric clippers, which could be the last haircut I would give them for awhile. From now on they could go to the barbershop with Phyl or by themselves. I was sure that the boys would not mind having a more professional barber trim their locks.

We were scheduled to fly Delta Airlines from Tampa to Los

Angeles and then Pan American to Honolulu for a rest before heading to Guam and Manila. All of our passports, shots, and visas were in order, and everything looked fine, until Murphy's Law surfaced in the guise of a Delta Airline strike. All their domestic flights were grounded, and nothing was moving out of Tampa to the west coast; the other major airlines went out in sympathy strikes. I telephoned the Delta reservation desk in Tampa and told them we needed to make connections in Los Angeles for the Far East. Thank God, the Delta reservation people were helpful, and they asked me to bring the tickets into the office. The next day at the Delta desk in Tampa I joined the long line of unhappy people. I waited my turn until the man at the ticket counter took my tickets and looked them over, perhaps noting that they were for official government travel. He was very courteous and thanked me for being patient. He checked with his computers and then said he could route us from Tampa to Miami on a local feeder airline. From Miami we could fly Mexicana Airline to Mexico City and then to Los Angeles. It was a bit round about, but we would get to see Mexico City, which pleased me, and still make our connection with Pan American in Los Angeles.

On the morning of the 14th, KC and Evie came over to say good-bye. It was a beautiful day with a light breeze, warm sunlight, and a few white clouds in the sky. The 13 pieces of our luggage were stashed in the rear of a van and tied with some green yarn to mark it from other baggage. All six of us and the driver then squeezed into the remaining space.

Phyllis related the following account of our trip in her diary:

"We left Sarasota at 8:15 on schedule much to the amazement of all. We left a horrible mess for Ebby, Helie, and KC to attend to; however, the fact that we even had our suitcases packed was a bit of a marvel. As we passed the phosphate plant south of Tampa with all the smoke stacks, Kenny commented, 'There is the place where they make clouds.' We boarded our flight for Miami for a pleasant and uneventful trip except for a few nervous giggles from the boys who were on their first jet plane ride. When we arrived we found a five-hour wait ahead of us. Oh brother. By this time we were already tired what with two days of frantic packing, the two hour drive to Tampa in a swaying Volks bus, non-airconditioned, loaded with our 13 pieces of luggage, and the half-hour flight to Miami. Lunch was fine, then a stroll around, then we found the Pan Am lounge which was quite grand to say nothing of being a Godsend. There were couches, johns, a bar, and carpeted floors. We found a corner to take over and to spread out our gear. The boys happily played on the floor with toys from Shirlo's goodie bag."

"Soon, however, everyone was taking little trips down the private stairs to the main terminal for one thing or another. First thing we knew Ken and Bill were missing. The airport at Miami is enormous with many escalators, creepy people, stores galore, exits, entrances, you name it they got it. . . This state of frantic affairs lasted half an hour, when they miraculously reappeared, none the worse for the wear. Bill was a bit nervous about the whole deal, never actually admitting he was lost, but just ventured that 'it took a long time to find us.'

"There was much ado about passports, tourist permits and visas, before embarking for Mexico, where we didn't want to go anyway. Keeping those little guys in tow while going through the formalities was a real horror. Finally we got on the plane for Mexico City at 5 P.M., and enjoyed dinner, all okay. The grim part came when we had to stop at Merida, Mexico, Yucatan, for customs inspection. The whole plane load of passengers and baggage had to disembark. It must have been between 95 and 100 degrees in a crummy, stifling, smelly airport; 45 minutes with hot, cranky kids, to say nothing of thirst. Had to check through 13 bags, plus passports, plus health certificates, plus five pieces of hand baggage. Ghastly! We all finally staggered back to the plane which was cool, and the stewardesses were waiting to serve us cool drinks.

"Oh yes, while at Merida, Ken asked if he had to get on another airplane, and when I said yes, he allowed as how he didn't want to. Bill, in his bull voice, said in disgust, 'Well, you don't want to stay in this dirty rotten place filled with weirdos, do you?' We then proceeded to lecture Bill on the fact that Latins were excitable and if he couldn't say something nice, to say nothing. He seemed to get the point, but later events show he didn't get it too well.

"On to Mexico City, where we arrived at 8 P.M. their time, 9 P.M. ours. Finally we managed to get all our bags together, checking about seven of them at the airport, and taking the others to the hotel where we arrived about an hour later. The taxi ride was harrowing, during which Bill loudly proclaimed that 'This guy is a careless driver!' We all pretended he was just a hitch-hiker.

"Meanwhile Adie was trying to figure out the pocketful of coins and paper money he got at the airport. The amount he tipped seemed more than pleasing so he figured he had grossly over-tipped, but VIVA LA MEXICO, or 'Who knows what's with this crazy money.'"

* * *

After a good night's sleep, we breakfasted in the hotel's bustling coffee shop, from where we could see people on the sidewalks and traffic moving along through soft sunlight. This was our first day together in a foreign land, and we were all eager to begin the day's activities, full of pep, vim, and vigor. Phyllis continues with her recollections of that morning:

"Then we went for a short walk outside but the cars seemed to be continually driving on the sidewalk, so we returned to our rooms to pack up. Then we heard Bill's loud voice outside our window, saying 'Dropping Bombs.' He was on the eighth floor, leaning out the window, with a supply of balloons or paper bags filled with water. Bill was pulled in from his bombardier's position by the window, and the lecture entitled 'Latins are excitable' was repeated. Hope it sticks this time."

No alarms sounded in the corridors, but we knew it was time to leave. Who knows what revenge-minded Mexican authorities might have visited upon the gringo Swain family in retribution for their loss of Texas in 1845. We had not been able to see much of the countryside last night, but as our brightly-hued Mexicana Airliner departed, we could see the vast sprawl of the capital city. Mexico City was 7,350 feet above sea level and built on an ancient plain that had once been a lake bed. There were mountains on all sides, and the sunken plain with its silt subsoil proved to be a poor foundation for buildings, particularly since the area was subject to earthquakes. The smoky haze over the city caused by the surrounding mountains blocking air circulation resulted in a serious automobile exhaust pollution problem worse than our own Los Angeles.

Four hours later, we approached California from the Baja Peninsula, slid past San Diego, and eased nicely into Los Angeles. The stewardess passed out more immigration landing cards, this time for our authorities in Los Angeles. Phyllis continues:

"Back through Customs again. . . get out passports. . . health certificates. . . screamed at boys to be good. . . last in line as usual . . . (while screaming at boys forty-eleven people eased in ahead of us). Customs people were very nice when told why we were coming in from Mexico and gave a perfunctory check to our 13 bags. . . . Checked in with Pan Am and found we had a delay; our 5 P.M. flight was now leaving at 8 P.M. GROAN! Five hours to kill in a nice but no-lounge airport. The day was saved when my marvelous friend Mary Albert arrived on the scene and offered to take us to her apartment in Beverly Hills. We hated to saddle her with all the kids and two long drives, but also couldn't take another five hours at the airport. We piled into her air-conditioned Cadillac for a taste of the freeways, and a general idea of Los Angeles. . . We picked up hamburgers for the kids on the way and then spent a delightful few hours in her charming apartment, overlooking the mountains. The kids watched TV. . . . Adie and I drank Scotch. Mary was really great, especially as she had no children. We met her charming husband who must have been appalled to find our gang in his home, but he never

219

batted an eyelash. Then Mary took us back to the airport, arriving at 7:30 P.M. The reason for the flight delay was the plane had just come in from Tokyo and had to be serviced. With my air nerves, I wanted to go out and help them to be sure they did a good job, but restrained myself and took another phenobarbital. Adie and I had a bite to eat while the kids soaked up another coke before we boarded the flight for Honolulu at 9 P.M. HURRAH! The boys went to sleep almost immediately, while Adie, Cyndy and I had a sip of Champagne and watched an in-flight movie."

Our flight took almost five hours, but it was only 11 P.M. local time when we arrived. My literature proclaimed Honolulu to be "the crossroads for much trans-Pacific shipping and air routes... the focus of inter-island commercial and industrial services for the State of Hawaii," and I could see why. Even late in the evening, the airport was busy and the service personnel were cheerful, polite, and bustling, as if they enjoyed their work. We saddled up once more and headed toward town in a van. I thought I could smell the sweetness of pineapple in the warm, moist air. The children were glad to be on the ground and were tired and subdued as we whizzed along the highway. There were considerably more cars and quite a few more high-rise buildings than during my last visit in 1949.

Honolulu, the capital and principal port on the Island of Oahu, was a marvelous rest stop for us. Our reservations were at the Hilton Hawaiian Village on Waikiki Beach near the vast park-like acreage of Fort DeRussey, owned by the Federal Government. We could put on a bathing suit and step outside to the pool or walk a little farther to the beach. It was delightful to be in weather much like that in Sarasota, only nicer because of the constant breeze from the Pacific. We rented a car and rubbernecked our way along Kalakaua Avenue past the Royal Hawaiian Hotel, the famous Pink Palace. We cruised by Diamond Head and then stopped at Punchbowl Cemetery, the National Cemetery of the Pacific that lies in the crater of an extinct volcano. In rows of white-crossed graves were buried more than 24,000 veterans of World War II, the Korean War, and now the Vietnam War. Among them was Ernie Pyle, the most famous World War II war correspondent, who was killed by a sniper's bullet in April

1945 while traveling with troops to Ie Shima in the Ryukyu Islands.

We wanted to visit the sunken battleship *Arizona*, our war memorial at Pearl Harbor, but the traffic worried me so we returned to Waikiki, where it was more fun for the kids. We saw a little bit of the Don Ho show and visited some of the many shops. Phyl recalls the following:

"We got the troops to bed about 8 P.M. so they would get some rest before our scheduled departure at 1:30 A.M., which we found out was now delayed until 3:00 A.M. When we got everyone up, dressed, ready to go and in our car with all the bags there were only 12 bags. Somebody snitched the 13th bag at the hotel, the smallest bag with all the drugs I had stocked up on, plus I can't remember what else, mostly cosmetics. We got to the airport and found people sleeping all over the place. Some 300 of them were backed up waiting for flights to the States because of flights that were canceled by the strike. Finally we boarded and departed Honolulu around 4 A.M. all six of us filling the row on both sides of the aisle. Ken sleeping with his feet on the bag that Helie gave me for it was just about seat height and put in front of his seat gave him a place to keep his legs up."

Our Pan Am 707 climbed out high above the clouds and flew over the deep-blue Pacific waters, arriving in Guam seven hours later to refuel. Inside the breeze-swept airport, we were confined to a spacious passenger area and enjoyed stretching our legs before commencing the last leg of our journey to Manila. For the past two days, we had been flying with the sun and thus gaining time on the clock. It is no wonder we were tired and confused. Our bodies were trying to sleep while our minds were saying it was only noontime. In addition to the 10-hour time difference, we gained a whole day when we crossed the International Dateline somewhere between Honolulu and Guam. It was now yesterday, very confusing. After another breakfast in the air, we began our descent to Manila. Our pilot eased down through bumpy white clouds that played hide-and-seek with the ground. We could not see much until we approached Manila's

International Airport south of the city and close to Manila Bay. We had no idea where to go when we arrived and hoped to be met at the arrival gate.

WELCOME TO MANILA

A young man named Leo sought us out as we were looking for our baggage. He was a handsome and debonair administrative officer from our Services and Support Group and greeted us with a warm welcome. Leo shook hands all around and was very pleasant and helpful. He joked with Tom, Bill, and Ken, appreciated our beautiful Cyndy, and had the Filipino driver help load all our bags. It did not take long to clear customs and immigration since people with official passports went through the immigration process rather quickly. We soon were in a van with the airconditioning turned up high and being driven on good roads filled with jeepneys and trucks headed toward Manila and a residential suburb known as San Lorenzo, where American families who worked for the U.S. Government were housed. Phyllis' detailed account of those first few days follows:

"It was morning in Manila, but evening to our mental processes. Felt terribly tired and yet there was so much to do. We were driven to our new home at 48 Arguilla. There we found a clean and tidy home, equipped with basic furniture. There were sheets, boiled water, silverware for six, glasses and dishes for eight, and a maid.

"The kids got up at 3 A.M., in fact we all were. We were hungry and it was morning time by our mental clocks. We did manage to get in a few more minutes of sleep but it was up and down again until about 5 when we all had breakfast. Cyndy, Adie and I all went to our office in the Embassy Annex on Rojas Boulevard to check in and to sign various applications for identification cards and the like. Ken went with us, but Bill and Tom went to the Seafront pool with a couple of neighbor friends and their mother, Delores. Her husband, Paul, is a friend of Adie's.

222

"Delores has been here a week, but obviously knows a lot more than we do. They have four children, John 3, Marcus 6, Matthew 9, and Kathy 11, so they fit rather well with our family. After we finished at the office, which was practically across the street, we met the others poolside where we had a nice lunch and then went home in a cab. The roads are pretty grim part of the way, but the sights are interesting and the poverty rather appalling. Their method of driving is out of this world, and perhaps when I am not so tired I can think how to describe it. I am still a little woozy, it is like getting off a boat after a week of tossing around. I find that floors are moving and mirrors tilting, although I seem to be the only one with this affliction.

"Tom and Ken went to sleep about 4 P.M. and never did wake up for supper. Again we were all up about 4 A.M., but at least we gained an hour over yesterday. This jetlag or mental disturbance they write about really happens. The body still goes by the old time regardless of what the clock says.

"The house is just fine. There are three bedrooms up and two baths; one bedroom down and another bath, plus dining room and living room combination. There is a basement playroom, and a basement maids room, laundry room, bath and garage. The yard is completely walled with an iron gate which is closed at all times. There is a bell that rings from the street, and then the gates are opened by the housegirl. . . . Our yard is therefore quite private, and nicely planted. The plants are much the same as in Sarasota: Bougainvillea, Frangipani, Hibiscus, Crotons, orchid trees, Ixora, Caladium, Gerbera Daisies, and a lawn of Zoysia grass. I am glad I shipped tables and lamps. Our air freight will not arrive for a while.

"Wednesday, July 20th. The last few days I have been interviewing thousands of maids. Every housegirl on the block has brought over someone. Today Sarah starts and is the cook. She was recommended through the office and I like her. Let the one who was in the house to begin with go. She wanted too much money and besides thought that as I had four children I should have at least three live-in help. She was willing to be a labadero [laundry girl and upstairs maid], but thought I should also have an Amah [nurse]. So I paid Lourdes off today. I will pay Sarah 110 pesos per month for six days a week. [110 pesos equals about $27.50 American dollars.] She will cook breakfast at any given hour and be on the job until dinner is over. She sleeps in.

"Thursday, July 21. . . . Adie and I went to Sangley Point Navy Base, about one and a half hours away by car. The office sent us a station wagon and driver for the trip because the Navy commissary and Post Exchange are far superior to the limited facilities at the Seafront facility here in Manila. The Commissary at Sangley is like a big department store with everything from appliances to toys, clothing, pots and pans, a good liquor store and a fine snack bar and restaurant. Tom had a fever so he stayed home with Sarah, Bill spent the day with the Katsos family, and Ken came with Cyndy, Adie and me. Bought like crazy at Sangley, including the big item—the TV set, plus many household things like more water pitchers. We stocked up on food. We had a cooler to store it in. Cigarettes are $1.20 per carton. Booze about $2.50 per quart, including scotch. Meat prices are about the same as at home, but many food items are far less. For example, six Pentel type pens cost fifty cents, at home you get one pen for 49 cents. All Commissary and PX sales are in American dollars. Everything else is in pesos which makes for a bit of confusion. Later we had a fabulous lunch in the officers club while we watched jets landing every ten minutes on the runway right outside our window.

"Because we had a driver, it was fun to see the countryside as we rode home. Rice paddies everywhere, with Carabou working in the fields. It was all very charming."

Our new home was inside a compound surrounded by a wall of quarried stone about eight feet high with broken pieces of glass embedded in the mortar on top of the wall. I gulped at that, for it was a clear indication that there were a lot of have-nots who might try to take something from the haves in our compound. There were several streets in the community, which contained perhaps 35 to 50 houses. A uniformed guard at the main entrance raised and lowered a metal barrier to permit cars in and out. There was no guard at night, which made me wonder at the efficiency of the whole operation. Perhaps it was just for show, since the guard's main duty seemed to be keeping out vagrants and door-to-door merchants. Even if only a token effort to maintain a certain level of security, it was still appreciated.

Our airfreight goods had not arrived yet and included blankets and pillows, extra clothing, Phyl's sewing machine and typewriter, personal files, special books, children's toys, some cooking utensils, small tables and lamps, and other items that make a home liveable. Meanwhile, we made do with what we carried with us and the temporary loan of household items from our group's warehouse. The living and dining area had high ceilings, and polished terrazzo floors gleamed in the warm sun. Ceiling fans slowly stirred the hot, dry air, for we were in the midst of the dry summer season. Room airconditioners were ordered for all the bedrooms, but there would be no central air for the remainder of the house.

"Friday, July 22. . . . Hired Dancing today for 80 pesos a month. She will sleep in also. Can't understand her too well and don't think she can understand me, but I will give her a try. Maureen Reeves called on me today. She lives next door, and comes from Houston. Her husband is with Brown and Root, construction engineers, doing work for the government in Vietnam. He is an engineer who commutes like Adie will be doing. Two other gals, wives of men in our group also called on us. That is very nice. One gal reported her car arrived in five weeks, so we hope we are that lucky.

"Adie, Cyndy and I went to Seafront and had a marvelous sirloin for $1.65, and a round of drinks for another whopping 95 cents. While waiting for a cab after dinner we met two other gentlemen, whose names escape me now, but with them was a Miss Linn who lives in our village, and is head of a fashion

225

group in town. Everyone is so cordial, it is most heartwarming.

"I must mention that we went to the big Makati Shopping Center today. It is a very elegant stateside group of stores. Not quite all the stores are completed as yet, but the supermarket is marvelous. It is like a combination of Grants, Liggetts, and Publix. Most merchandise is from the US, even the food, which makes most items more expensive than at home because the duty is so high here. I don't see how the Filipinos can afford to buy anything. Anyway, the point is, we can get anything we want but may have to pay a bit more than stateside for some items.

"Saturday, July 25. . . . this is a joyful day for us for we got two air conditioners and a ceiling fan in the living room. Believe me we needed them, for even though the weather is not much different from Sarasota, when you are used to A/C you really miss it. Adie and I went to the commissary at Seafront. We walked to our gate to get a cab but were offered a ride by a gal named Mary whose husband is with the Embassy. She has been here two years and has six children from 3 to 17. The 17-year-old girl will call on Cyndy. We also saw several from our group at Seafront, and got a ride back with Leo, who has the job of taking care of us until we get properly settled. Poor Leo. The point is the people here are really friendly. Later in the afternoon we went to Makati with Tom to get some chemistry supplies. We walked in the rain with our new umbrellas. Sorry we didn't have Ebby's rain boots."

While we were busy getting settled, I received orders that read as follows:

SERVICES SUPPORT SQUADRON (PROV)
UNITED STATES AIR FORCE
APO SAN FRANCISCO 96258

SPECIAL ORDERS   *20 July 1966*
B-26

Mr. Adrian Swain, GS-12, DAFC, PASSPORT NO. Y426216, this Organization, will proceed on or about 25 July 1966 from Manila, Philippines, reporting to Combined Studies Group, MACV, HDQS, Saigon, South Vietnam, on TDY for approximately one hundred twenty (120) days for the purpose of performing official duty. Upon completion will return permanent duty station. Variations in itinerary authorized. Travel by military and commercial aircraft (including those of foreign registry when US registry not available) authorized for travel in overseas area of TDY when scheduled military aircraft is not available. . . . During the period of this TDY individual is cleared for TOP SECRET. Immunizations will be accomplished in accordance with AFR 161-13 prior to departure.

Phillip L. Donaldson
GS-14 Commanding

If I was unable to obtain scheduled airliner flights into Saigon from either Pan American or Air France, I could get military flights in or out of our Air Force Base at Clark Field near Bagiuo, about 120 miles north of Manila. I had been briefed to report to our office in Saigon where I would be processed and given my assignment. Two friends, Paul and Jim, were already in Saigon, and I was more than ready and anxious to join them.

Tom and Bill were enrolled in the American School in Makati, and Cyndy was still looking around for something to do until fall when she could enroll in the University of the Philippines. Phyl would take care of Ken and make the best of things while I was away. I felt that the family was in good shape and capable of handling anything that could come along. The day promised to be bright and sunny when I said good-bye to Tom and Bill as they boarded their school bus at the door. Not much later, I went to the airport in an office vehicle with Phyl, Cyndy, and Kenny where they dropped me off to catch the Pan Am 707 for Saigon.

ELEVEN

Saigon to Nha Trang

O ur Pan Am flight was jammed with civilians and soldiers. Most of the civilians were contractors to help build airfields, highways, and military bases, and others trained local military and civilian leaders how to win the hearts and minds of the people in South Vietnam. As we neared Saigon, the pilot asked us to double-check our seat belts. Suddenly our plane dropped a wing and curled down and around in a steep turn. We plummeted until the pilot pulled the nose up abruptly and plopped onto the runway like a fighter plane. Someone then told us that VC snipers sometimes herded water buffalo in the rice paddies at the end of the runway and got off an occasional round of AK-47 fire into planes above.

The doors opened, relinquishing our air-conditioned air and admitting the dripping humidity of Southeast Asia: welcome to Saigon, capital of South Vietnam. Waves of heat bounced into our faces from the concrete runway. The air smelled of swampland and perfume flavored with a dollop of burned jet fuel. The crush of bodies waiting to claim suitcases and trudge through immigration and customs checkpoints was like trying to get into the Philadelphia football stadium for the Army-Navy game. We were sustained when we recognized a few friendly faces and then spotted a Vietnamese driver standing by the baggage area with a sign that said *Embassy*. Our names were on his list. He helped us load our bags and soon we were in a sedan heading downtown to the USAID Annex Building.

The building was around the corner from the American Embassy and only a stone's throw from the Saigon River (Song Sai Gon), which was crowded with ships waiting to be unloaded. Wire barricades and cement guardposts surrounded the Embassy to protect Ambassador Henry Cabot Lodge and other Americans who worked there. The Presidential Palace was a few blocks away, as were a number of hotels, some of which had been converted into military billets. I checked in with our personnel staff and thus officially reported for duty. Next stop was the finance and travel office to turn in my claims for repayment of travel expenses. This office would also schedule airline reservations for our leaves to Manila, which would be approved every month to six weeks, depending on our work schedules.

We then had interviews with personnel assignment officials who worked for the Chief of Station in Vietnam. After a few welcoming remarks, he said that he noticed I had a current pilot's rating and an Air Force background and asked if I would like to work in air operations in Saigon. I told him that I expected to be assigned wherever it seemed best and if air operations was where my help was needed then that was fine with me. He nodded in agreement and then said that the work would be in the Air Branch next door. I would work with several other people helping schedule and route aircraft carrying men, supplies, and equipment to and from our various bases. He made an appointment for me to meet the next day with Moe, the chief of Air Operations.

All newcomers were assigned billets in the Duc Hotel, a multistory building leased by our Agency about a mile from the Embassy. There was a coffee shop and a small dining room where we could get breakfast or snacks. All rooms were air-conditioned and housed two men. I was delighted to discover that my roommate was Jim, who left Manila the day I arrived. Jim and his wife, Tess, had an apartment near the Embassy in downtown Manila. I hoped we would be going back and forth on leave at the same time.

Stan, whom I met on the flight from Manila, was also billeted in the Duc Hotel. He was a nice guy with a booming laugh, a career intelligence officer who recently served in Europe. Stan and his wife, Jan, lived in our San Lorenzo Village with two adopted children, a little Greek girl with black hair and big brown eyes and a blond, blue-eyed German lad. They were comfortable to be with and became good friends of ours. Stan had been assigned to Can Tho, capital of Phong Dinh Province, in the delta south of Saigon in IV Corps.

I wrote Phyllis and the family the day after reporting to duty:

"I arrived safely and am happily billeted in fine air-conditioned quarters in downtown Saigon. The plane was four hours late, but the flight time only two hours. . . . Only a bare start has been made as to what I'll be doing, but there is a good possibility I can stay here in Saigon and work in Air Operations as an inside desk man.

"The currency exchange setup is a bit confusing. The piaster or 'P' as it is called is used everywhere. MPC, or Military Payment Script, is used in our American facilities, the Commissary and Post Exchange. Chit books, which we buy with piasters, are used at the Officers' Mess facilities in the Rex Hotel. The Rex is run by the military and the whole hotel is one big military officers' billet. . . . Anyway, my wallet is filled with paper. . . . I bought a bottle of 8-year-old *Old Forester* for $2.05. . . . Laundry is done here in our hotel and our rent is free; two men per room, with A/C, good big beds (but hard!) with a small balcony overlooking the tree-shaded street. . . . Jim and I are in room 310, which has a tub with a shower nozzle curiously designed (by the French) with a flexible metal hose and a spray nozzle with a hook that you have to place in a slot on the wall in order to direct the angle of water spraying out. Interesting idea, I've never seen anything like it.

"I suggest you would enjoy subscribing to the *Stars and Stripes*. It covers all the area, and the comics are good. . . . I've *got* to report that the weather here is delightful, cool at night with daily sprinkles or showers. The people are pleasant, much like Manila, and the city architecture resembles Paris or Rome, very stately with wide tree-lined streets. The traffic is heavy, and the hotels and restaurants are crowded with Americans of all sizes and shapes, all ages and uniforms, including quite a few civilian types and older men like me."

Adrian Swain

* * *

I was studying a *Newsweek* report of January 31, 1966 that helped me better understand what was going on around here:

". . . Saigon, most gracious of Asian cities, has become a raucous boomtown as the nerve center of the war in Vietnam. And the very boom itself underlies a curious and little-noticed fact: never before have U.S. businessmen followed their troops to war on such a scale. . . . More than 2,000 U.S. civilians have poured into South Vietnam— building plants and roads and airstrips, selling the troops everything from machetes to mutual funds, propping up the tiny nation's war-torn economy.

. . . Around the beleaguered country, military men have decreed the construction of roads, huge airbases and vast seaports. But the $500 million job isn't being done entirely by the Seabees, those "can do" magicians of World War II; instead, a consortium of construction companies—called RMK-BRJ for Raymond International of New York, Morrison-Knudsen of Boise, Brown and Root of Houston and the J.A. Jones Co. of Charlotte—have a total of 1,500 American and 22,000 Vietnamese workers toiling at 29 separate construction sites. Before the mammoth job is finished, the payroll will rise to 65,000 men, one and a half times the total of all industrial employment in the country. . . . similarly, some 225 other Americans have gone to Saigon as sutlers followed the armies of old, peddling their wares to the soldiers as long as the soldiers are there: auto salesmen, mutual fund salesmen, dealers in Florida real estate. A curvaceous blond entrepreneur books acts into enlisted men's clubs around Saigon. . . . Pan American World Airways runs fifteen scheduled flights a week through the Saigon airport, plus as many as 22 military charters.

. . . The Vietnamese economy needs all the help it can get, for Viet Cong guerrillas have shattered the agricultural base of the economy. Once the rice bowl of Asia, with rice exports worth $27 million as recently as 1960, Vietnam will have to import at least 175,000 tons of rice to keep its own people fed for the first six months of 1966."

A *Business Week* report of February 5, 1966, took a look at airbase construction.

"Airfields now consume the largest share of the construction dollars. To supplement Saigon's Tan Son Nhut, the joint venture is working simultaneously on four other bases that rival many U.S. municipal airports in size. Work on a fifth will begin soon.

"At Danang, where a 10,000 foot strip already is in full use, a parallel runway is being constructed. Dual runways of comparable length are being started soon at Tuyhoa. On top of this, there is a strong possibility that the 10,000 foot runway at Bienhoa, already in full use, will be duplicated."

During World War II and the Korean War, military runways were often made of pierced steel planks; not so today. *Business Week* explains:

"The aluminum mat is the principal new construction material of the war. The blocks, which have honey-combed interiors, are light enough to be transported by air and can be laid quickly. The 10,000-ft. strip constructed by Vietnam Builders at Camranh was ready for use in 70 days.

"The Seabees laid a similar strip at Chulai and the Army Engineers are putting one down at Phanrang. These, however, are considered interim airfields because after prolonged heavy use the aluminum begins to wear and the base beneath it shifts."

Deepwater seaports are getting their share of expansion improvements as well. *Business Week:*

"More facilities for deep-draft vessels are in the works. New piers are to be built at Camranh, Danang, and Saigon, and a new port will be developed at Vungtau, a town on the ocean not far from Saigon."

* * *

Now that I had a better grasp of the need for expanding airlift facilities in South Vietnam, I readily understood why I was being

233

asked to work in the Air Branch. I met Moe the next day and liked him immediately. The Chief of Air Branch was an old China Hand, which meant that he had served with Clair Chennault or his successors in World War II flying cargo planes over the Hump (Himalayas) from Burma into China. Moe confirmed that if I wanted to work in air operations he would like to have me. We talked over my Air Force background; I showed him my current pilot's rating and told him I would like to work for him.

Moe introduced me to his two chief assistants. Willy was a former Air Force fighter jock with the rank of Major and was from St. Petersburg, Florida. He seemed full of repressed energy, had a quick wit, and seemed shy. I later learned that he shot down a Russian Mig during the Korean War. Now he did the accounting and billing for the Air Branch, a formidable task that I did not envy. Chuck Abbot, the other assistant, was a Major on active duty with the Air Force. Tall, imposing, and a glib talker, he had the suaveness and smoothness of a practiced politician. He was assigned to the Air Branch as the liaison officer with officials at MACV, with whom the Air Branch worked closely. Moe, Willy, and Chuck shared a house not far from the Duc Hotel.

There were four other active duty airmen on loan from the Air Force. These men came to work in civilian's clothes, as did everyone else, and were Jim Brand, George Frazier, Jerry Nelson, and Roger Kaiser. I was assigned to work with them in the outer operations room next to Moe's office and I went to work feeling as if I had just caught another brass ring. This was a fine assignment; the people were nice, and all I had to do was learn how to schedule the Air America aircraft and how to communicate with everyone.

Besides the antiquated telephone service between our annex and the airport facilities, we depended on our side band radio housed in a hefty, two-foot square box with an office loudspeaker, which was capable of transmitting and receiving coded messages to and from province field stations all over Vietnam. Because the enemy could hear everything, we used coded call signs for everything and everybody to confuse all eavesdroppers, both friend and foe.

Because I wore reading glasses, Moe christened me Ben since Ben Franklin invented reading glasses. It did not take me long to feel right at home with these people, but it would take a little longer to learn everything that was going on in Air Branch. I started by acquainting myself with Air America, a proprietary corporation controlled and directed by the CIA. For years, Air America held government contracts to provide aircraft and flight crews in support of USAID programs in Southeast Asia.

Air America's main operations office was in Ton Son Nhut (TSN), where maintenance, flight line, and operations were centralized. The radio call sign for Air America was WHISKEY 1; appropriately, they called us WHISKEY 2. Air America's civilian pilots flew a mixed fleet of aircraft, including the versatile single-engine Pilatus Porter, which looked like a rubber band aircraft and could land or take off in 500 feet or less. There were also twin-engine C-45's, C-46's, C-47's, and C-123's; the Canadian-manufactured Caribou; and the VTB-18, a speedy turbojet version of the C-45. These aircraft flew cargo and personnel throughout Vietnam in response to USAID program demands.

As these programs expanded, so did our air operations work. Until now, all aircraft scheduling had been handled out of Saigon, but there was too much going on for one office to handle. Separate offices soon would be needed in Danang (I Corps) and Nha Trang (II Corps). The main office in Saigon could handle III Corps (around the capital) and probably all of IV Corps to the south around Can Tho. Whatever happened, I was flexible and learning quickly, enjoying myself both on the job and off duty.

One of our first free Sundays in Saigon, I noted there was a cargo aircraft with some vacant seats going to Vung Tau, the "French Riviera of Vietnam" on the South China Sea, about a half hour flight from Saigon. The flight was leaving at 10:30 A.M. and returning at 4:30 P.M. Jim said he would go with me, so we boarded the C-47 with some secretaries from the Embassy and headed out. We changed clothes at a public bathhouse in Vung Tau and spent the day lounging, sunning ourselves, and drinking cold local beer called Bamuiba. All the local GI's swore that Bamuiba contained formaldehyde, but it sure tasted good to me. We bought fresh pineapple from a vendor's stand which was sweet and juicy, and were not concerned, as we probably should have been, about getting diarrhea.

235

Jim said that John, our old roommate from the Clarendon Motel, was pretty busy at the National Interrogation Center in Saigon. Jim seemed a bit down at the mouth about things, perhaps a bit uncertain about what he was doing here. He told me a little about his work with the Saigon police force, called the White Mice because of their uniforms. Jim talked of dinner parties where he and other American advisors were treated royally and offered the best of wine, women, and entertainment. Jim hinted at the disturbing ways in which the Vietnamese police conducted their business, both officially and unofficially. They had a disregard for women and in the style of our own Mafiosi were prone to provide the favors of young girls to American advisors who were interested. I did not know what to tell Jim about how to handle his business; he was the police expert, not me. I remembered what Zeke had said about being corrupted by the tools of the trade but did not say anything and was a bit worried about Jim.

* * *

All in all, the day at Vung Tau was a real treat. Vung Tau was located in a very secure area, and there was little danger of the VC raiding the camp from the sea. Although they would occasionally harass vehicles on the road between Vung Tau and Saigon, we were safe as long as we had air transport. We even had a chance to look around the area where the Revolutionary Development (RD) Program was being conducted. Secretary of Agriculture Orville Freeman had just completed a tour of RD training here in Cap Saint-Jacques, as the French called Vung Tau. He saw the 59-man teams of young Vietnamese cadre dressed in black pajamas being given weapons training, intensive political indoctrination, and a variety of courses, including security, propaganda and medical aid. The 14-week program was an intensive effort to train new cadre how to root out and destroy VC influence, improve and restore public safety, establish sound political structures in the villages, and stimulate self-help.

By mid-1966, the first cadre teams were being assigned to work in these areas from where they had been recruited. Secretary Freeman wondered if the VC would kill the pacification workers as they had many village and district chiefs in past years. If the program worked, the villagers would protect the cadre. Although a pretty fatalistic approach, in the end it worked out in favor of the young village cadre. USAID supported this effort by supplying teams of skilled advisers and materials needed for self-help programs, such as new classrooms, open-air markets, community wells, roads, small bridges, and clinics. Almost all of this material was supplied by Air America aircraft, and the flow of material was just beginning.

* * *

My first home leave was a rousing success. Pan Am's flight out of steamy Saigon was on time and delightfully airconditioned. When we got off the plane and walked toward the terminal, I could see all of my gang waving from the upper deck of the observation platform. We hugged and kissed and greeted each other with delight, and then chatted away happily on the way home to San Lorenzo for a family reunion.

Sarah and Dancing had the house sparkling, and there was plenty of excitement as we celebrated Kenny's birthday that afternoon. Some of the smaller children in the neighborhood came for cake and ice cream, and then the boys opened the presents I had for them. The family looked just great and was happy and thriving in their new environment. It had been a long month of separation, yet time had passed so quickly.

Only the upstairs bedrooms were airconditioned, and by early evening it turned hot and humid, so we all retired early. I stopped by the kids' bedroom and visited with them before they turned in for the night. Phyl and I went to our bedroom as soon as we could for a private reunion. Phyllis fixed a tray of snacks and some cold drinks so that we would not have to venture out to the hot kitchen. It was so good to hold her in my arms, and I can still recall the reluctance I felt about having to go to sleep. It had been a long, exciting day, and making love with beautiful Phyllis was not only delightfully sweet but also totally relaxing.

Our Mustang remained somewhere on the high seas, so we took cabs wherever we wanted to go: Seafront for swimming and sun-bathing, the Makati shopping center to browse, bowling with the children, or out for a family dinner. Late in the week, Phyl and I went out with Stan and Jan to a rather ritzy Spanish restaurant called the Madrid. Their car had not arrived either, so we all took a cab for a 15-minute, hair-raising ride along dark, half-built highways. One tiny miscue on the pavement and we would be in the ditch. As we zipped along, I closed my eyes until we reached the restaurant. Once safely inside, my fears and anxieties vanished. It was so different from the world outside; here was privacy in a candlelit atmosphere. The steaks were tender and served with delicate sauces and a wide range of table wines. Later, there was good music for listening or dancing. Of all the places I have been, the Madrid Restaurant rates just about tops.

This first home leave established a pattern for other leaves to follow. Phyl would plan outings that included shopping, sightseeing, and dining out. We even tried a few cookouts. While the boys were in school, the rest of us would go to Sangley Point or shopping downtown on Rojas Boulevard. The boys were enjoying school and had settled into a routine. They were assigned a fair amount of homework, which was good. Tom particularly liked his science classes, and it was not long before our budding chemist built a laboratory on a workbench in our garage.

I was back in Saigon all too soon. I was becoming familiar with most of our people in the provinces by their radio call-sign names. True names were never used on the air for obvious security reasons. Moe, for example, was known as LEGIONAIRE. Dick Secord, an Air Force Major, was known as SNAGGLETOOTH. He did not like this name, which was not very macho for a guy who had previously worked as a liaison officer with the Shah of Iran. These names changed periodically, and I recall that one of my names was COLOSSUS. Willy was BUFFALO, Chuck was MANCHESTER, Jerry was SPEEDBOAT, Jim Brand was SUBWAY, and others were BUMBLE BEE, WHISTLESTOP, MILKY WAY, BEAGLE, and SICKBED. In the interests of security, new call-sign rosters were posted at random. We never knew when a copy of the roster might fall into the wrong hands.

I was surprised to find that my roommate Jim had checked himself into the medical office just before I returned from my first home leave. He was now taking phenobarbital that a doctor had given him to calm down. He did not say much to me about what was going on, but the word was out that he would not be continuing in the program. He seemed to have developed a mild paranoia, and at the very least he was overly anxious.

I wrote to Phyllis:

"I think maybe his wife has a lot to do with his problem, but of course I don't know for sure. It is all rather sudden and shows that you never know what is going to happen. At least you can be sure that I know what the score is and am in good health mentally and physically. How could I help it with such a lovely wife and beautiful, handsome children? Also you know that all we have in this earth is temporary; the really important things are intangible such as love, honor, charity, integrity, faithfulness—the list is much longer, but you know what I mean."

Jim moved out of the Duc Hotel, and his place was taken by Dick Secord. We talked about moving into a more permanent place, perhaps the building where several other air operations personnel were staying. We would have an extra vehicle and could all chip in for the costs of our live-in cook and maids. It seemed like a good idea.

* * *

Just after I left Manila, Phyl was notified that our Mustang had arrived from New Orleans. Her letter to KC and Evie describes the event:

"Oh Joy! Cheers! Mabuhay! and all that jazz. Ye-Ye the MUSTANG arrived today. I am liberated. I am overjoyed. I even drove it in the most ghastly traffic which I can't even describe. It is every man for himself over here and he who hesitates is lost. . . . But let me back up a bit.

"After Adie took off for Saigon last Monday, things began to simmer down as the excitement of his visit wore off. I felt rotten and spent the day in bed, and don't think that all my meals weren't served on an elegant tray. Felt a little better this morning and was contemplating going back to bed for a little more of the same treatment when one of the gals, just return-ing from the office, brought me the news of the car's arrival. I immediately felt much better and decided I had a case of no-car sickness, which believe me can be very serious.

"Cyndy and I dressed for town real fast, got a cab and made tracks for the insurance agent as our stateside deal was lagging and I didn't want to drive one foot without coverage. Took care of that detail and headed for the docks. Had a real stupid driver and as I really didn't know where we were going, things got slightly out of hand. Seems no one in the dock area ever heard of the US Army Depot and the ticker kept racking up the pesos and my nerves racked up right along with it. Of course we managed to finally arrive at the right spot and it was very simple to get the car in my hands.

"After a few thousand papers but no Customs hassle, some very charming service—when I could get the attention of those in power away from Cyndy, and except for a few minor scratches and lots of dirt, we drove away in air-conditioned comfort and splendor to face the cowboys of Manila. Which we did very handily, paying them nooo mind, as we say in Noo York, and arrived home safely to find the boys had opened the gate all the way and had the garage open. It was quite exciting for all as we put on our bathing suits and went to work with our towels and sponges. All the yard boys and maids in the neighborhood were fascinated to see us working so hard, to say nothing of the bathing suit routine. We finished up in a blaze of glory as the clouds opened up with a magnificent downpour, which we didn't need at all. However, I simply drove the auto into the garage and thumbed my nose at the rain.

"Now the only thing we have to wait for is our sea shipment and that isn't too critical except for the children's bikes. I can't even

240

remember what else is coming except my typing table which I could well use.

"It will be so delightful to get dressed and hop into the car and arrive in reasonable condition instead of getting blown apart in a cab, to say nothing of being gassed. I think they have some device to pump fumes into the cabs to annoy the passengers so that it takes their minds off the crazy driving.

"Really, though, what a joy to be independent in the transportation department. It is a happy day."

* * *

It was not all work and no play for us at Air Branch. China Air Lines (CAL), whose Chinese pilots flew cargo flights for Air America, mailed invitations to a number of Air Branch personnel announcing a dinner party on Thursday, 15 September 1966. My invitation was addressed to Major Swain and requested in the name of the President of China Air Lines, General Ben Y.C. Chow. I telephoned in my R.S.V.P, noting that the dress code was described as "Sport."

We all gathered for drinks and dinner at the CAL house where pilots lived. Dinner was served in the dining room at round tables seating about 10 people each. A lazy Susan in the center of each table was filled with assorted condiments and turned so that you could reach anything you wanted. I had never seen a lazy Susan before and thought it was very efficient and practical; trust the Chinese.

There were numerous ceremonial toasts before and during dinner. A toast was made each time a new dish was brought to the table, following the Chinese custom of eating one course at a time. This involved the ritual pouring of a potent, dry, white rice wine into tiny shot glasses that held a half ounce. Everyone would hold their glass high and shout "Gombai," the equivalent of "Cheers," "Good luck," and "To your good health." By the time dinner was over, there was hardly a sober person in the room. At least eight courses were served; no one was counting, so there could have been more. Socially the dinner was enjoyable, and the food was quite good. All twenty of the

CAL pilots were pretty sharp guys who spoke English very well and held their drinks better than I did.

The CAL pilots lived in a roomy house that had ten bedrooms with two men assigned per room. The house was run like a small hotel with a deskman downstairs. There was a nice reading area and an airy dining room where the pilots and crew were served their meals. Their main office provided a finance man who would cash checks for us. We Air Branch people could drop in anytime to write personal checks and receive more piasters than we could at our own finance office. Naturally, we kept this information close to our vests.

A curfew on the general population in Saigon was in effect since early September from the midafternoon break at 2 P.M. until 4 A.M. the next morning. The curfew was in preparation for the upcoming national election that would decide whether a national constitution should be drafted. The Communists were busily urging boycotts as well as threatening violence and bullying the electors. Despite VC agitation, about 80 percent of those who had registered voted for the new constitution. The Constituent Assembly convened in Saigon on September 27 to begin drafting a constitution, which was approved six months later and took effect on April 1, 1967.

I wrote to Phyllis:

"You know the VN election news by now. I am very pleased, and might add that it was *very very* quiet in the City. The curfew restrictions were quite effective. The weather was good and apparently the people really turned out—far above expectations. I'm not sure what world reaction will be, but certainly it will be a tremendous propaganda victory for anti-communist forces everywhere."

On my birthday (September 18), I was scheduled for the required two-year physical checkup needed to keep my flight certification current. I passed without difficulty and was declared physically fit. The EKG exam for heart and circulation was not too successful, however. The technician taking the readings said there were too many generators and other pieces of electrical equipment nearby for the EKG machine to perform well. Close enough for government work, I thought and tucked in my shirt. Now I was good for two more years.

Phyllis sent some cards and letters from the boys and Cyndy and included a note saying that she and the children had acquired a miniature poodle. They named it after her birth month, July, which was pronounced *Julie* by the Filipinos. Phyllis had promised the kids a puppy when we got to Manila. Half in jest and half seriously, Phyl said that Julie was part of my birthday present and the other part was a toaster. I wondered if this was retaliation for my forgetting our wedding anniversary on August 10. I had goofed up rather badly and apologized profusely for the oversight. Besides Julie, we had two cats that came with the house, so there were enough pets for all. I would not get to see my birthday present until my next leave on October 4.

Moe sent a wire from Manila saying that he had come down with a Saigon bug and an ear infection. He eventually went to Clark Field for treatment and did not return to Air Branch for many weeks. Willy and Chuck took over running operations, which continued as usual. In fact it was better, for I was cleared for an orientation flight with an Air America pilot named Daddio who piloted a twin-engine C-45, a six-passenger aircraft, on a courier and cargo run to Dalat, Ban Me Thuot, and Pleiku.

Dalat was a one-hour flight north of Saigon and was used as a resort spot by both VC and South Vietnamese troops. The VC and ARVN had a unspoken agreement not to shoot at each other while in Dalat, and I could see why. It was simply beautiful in the cool, sweet-smelling mountains. We were met by a jeep and taken for a drive around town and a quick look at lovely tree-lined, winding streets and wide boulevards. There were plenty of parks, fountains, and lakes with fishing and swimming spas. The homes and official buildings in this French-built city were carefully manicured in the style of the French nobility. At an altitude of about 5,000 feet and wearing only a sport shirt, I felt quite chilly even in the bright sunlight.

We dropped off a rather interesting passenger from Saigon, Sister Amee, a gracious French nun of middle years dressed in a long, black robe with a wide white collar and broad-brimmed dark hat. She wore no makeup and was very interested in what was going on; her gentleness and alert, keen hazel eyes reminded me of Momma.

243

We spent only half an hour in Dalat before we took off. Languid groups of ARVN soldiers, who seemed barely big enough to shoulder a rifle, watched us depart from their log and sandbagged pill boxes located at strategic points around the strip. We headed toward the Cambodian border and flew another 20 minutes to Ban Me Thuot in the plateau region, a countryside inhabited by mountain tribesmen known as Montagnards, who closely resembled our early American Indians.[1] The principal tribes around Ban Me Thuot are Rhade and Jarai. We let off some passengers and cargo but did not go into town because the clouds were low and the air was damp and cold. Only one major road led in and out of Ban Me Thuot, and without air capability it would be difficult to make much progress developing the area.

In another half hour we were enroute to Pleiku, a sprawling military base near the 14th parallel and about 15 miles south of Kontum. The Pleiku runway was 8,000 feet long and as fine as Sarasota's best runway. It looked as if a whole hill had been bulldozed to make room for it. The surrounding hills rolled gently, all brown, smooth, and rounded. It reminded me of the hills north of San Francisco during the rainy season. There were many tent encampments and vehicle parks, most of them near the runway. This appeared to be an Air Force site, but there were a number of Army helicopters parked on the line. A three-star general arrived in an army chopper while we were waiting to refuel and was accompanied by a two-star general who, in turn, was accompanied by a full colonel. They were greeted by four MP's and escorted aboard an army Apache aircraft that quickly fired up its twin engines and disappeared into the overcast. The Army sure took care of its ranking officers, at least as far as transportation was concerned.

We departed from Pleiku with some GI hitchhikers who wanted to go to Saigon. A certain grimness hung about this place that did not appeal to me at all. I was glad to be a feather merchant, as career military people often referred to civilians serving in wartime conditions. It was cold at 10,000 feet even though we were on top of clouds

---

[1] The Montagnards, French for highlander, are members of the hill-dwelling peoples of Indochina. In Vietnam they include speakers of Mon-Khmer, Bahnar, Loven, Mnong, and Sedang; and speakers of Austronesian (Malay-Polynesian) languages such as Jarai, Raglai, and Rhade.

in bright sunlight. I thoroughly enjoyed being in the copilot's seat again even though I did not do much flying except to keep our C-45 straight and level on a south heading and at the proper altitude. Daddio landed at Saigon an hour and a half later in time for a cold Coke and a ham sandwich at the lunch counter. I was warm for the first time all day.

Sundays were usually restful, and I attended chapel services at the Rex Hotel. I would sunbathe for about a half hour on the roof of the Duc Hotel, take a nap, and finish up with an afternoon stroll about the shops and market stalls. I managed to stay busy but often wished I were in Manila.

Home leave in early October meant another joyful reunion with the family. Highlights of that visit included my first ride in our shiny Mustang through the crowded streets of Manila with Phyllis at the wheel daring the cowboys of Manila to touch her. As we drove to Seafront one morning, I told Phyl that I could feel a touch of fall in the air. It seemed a bit drier, and the trees and grass were a shade more yellow than green. Phyl laughed and laughed, tickled at the notion of fall being in the air. To her, it was still darn hot and tropical. I persisted in my view and continued to be teased for it.

Our new wonder dog, Julie, was frisky regardless of the weather. She was playful, lovable, intelligent, and slowly becoming house-broken. Cyndy and the boys were in fine shape and settled into the new way of life in San Lorenzo. There were routine chores such as install-ing a television antenna on the roof, which was eventually done by a couple of Filipinos, and getting a telephone. Phyl had been patiently going next door to Maureen Reeves' to use her telephone, but we needed one for ourselves. Telephones were not easy to obtain, and we were on the waiting list but needed a much higher priority than we had. When I returned to Saigon, I checked with our technical support guys and hit it lucky. In a letter to Phyl, I reported,

"This morning I packaged up a telephone for you. . . . We have just finished installing a new phone system here in the office. I took one of the new phone cartons and put one of the old Japanese instruments inside. I put a $10.00 customs value on the Customs label, marked it "gift", and paid 39 cents for surface shipment and mailed it to you. The postal clerk said mail to Manila, packages included, usually went by air so you might get it by the time you get this letter. Now, if you can get the phone man to use the existing jack connection, you will be in business.

"All of us were out to another Chinese dinner, at a restaurant in the Chinese section of Saigon known as Cholon.... celebrating the arrival of a new Air Force man. We had a gay time. The dinner was excellent, featuring a roast suckling pig, small but delectably laid out on the plate, and a most attractive gold-bronze color. There were other fine dishes, served on separate small plates, which included squab, octopus, abalone, corn and crab meat, and delectable sweet and sour pork served over either steamed rice or fried rice. . . . I am beginning to have slightly slanted eyes.

"Last night I went to a local cinema, next door to the Rex Hotel, which was featuring a Jack Lemmon movie in French with English subtitles. It was okay but the French speech was too fast for me. The theater was crowded. Tickets were sold as if at a ball park, seats by reservation only. This leads to some confusion when trying to find your seat in the dark but the people were courteous and reasonable. There were many family outings with women and children, plus quite a few Americans. Saigon is like it used to be in our country before television. Movies are a big part of entertainment. Tickets cost 40 to 100 piasters. The best seat costs about 85 cents, tops.

"I have already confirmed my reservations for the next two trips home—on November 11 and December 23. Because of the holidays I thought it wise to book early and be sure of a seat. Of course Moe has to approve but no problem there.

"*Mac the Knife* [as Robert S. McNamara, Secretary for Defense, was commonly known] made another flying visit here the day I got back. His visit did not stir up too much activity hereabouts, except I had to dodge a few cavalcades as Mac and his entourage went roaring back and forth to the airport. By accounts in the local paper he had a good review and seemed pleased with local conditions."

McNamara, one of the original whiz kids on a popular radio show and a former vice president in charge of number crunching at Ford Motors, was full of ideas, some good and some bad. He had one idea to sow the ground along the DMZ (demilitarized zone along the 17th parallel) between North and South Vietnam with electronic sensors monitored by our aircraft. These sensors would alert our aircraft should errant North Vietnamese troops attempt to move southward across the DMZ. A 600-yard-wide swath of land was bulldozed along the 17th parallel across miles of countryside and strewn with little sensors. The plan seemed to work at first. Electronic signals were picked up by our aircraft, and military forces were promptly dispatched only to discover that the culprits were night-prowling animals. Mac and his planners had forgotten about animals, and electronic beeps went off every time a rabbit or a deer moved. Technology worked well in the laboratory, but it certainly had its limitations along the DMZ.

* * *

Air operations work continued steadily and without any problems. Moe was due to return to Saigon after being away almost six weeks. As often as possible, I scheduled myself on flights to different areas and in different planes. In writing to my Mother and the Carsons in Freedom, I described one recent trip:

"Today, I rode out west of Saigon in a chopper. The rice paddies are badly flooded now and many roads in this region are flooded as well. Other roads are impassable—the VC blow up parts of the road from time to time. Many Districts can be reached only by helicopter and then only in daytime. The Province officer I was with made several stops to check the local situations; we visited a Special Forces camp near the Cambodian border for an intelligence briefing and then overflew several military installations which had numerous helicopters in readiness along the landing strip.

"It's interesting about the airfields out here. Some have regular blacktop all-weather surfaces and are fine, but a majority are made out of red gumbo clay, like our Georgia clay, in which are imbedded bits and chunks of granite-like stone. This mixture of stone and clay is packed down until it is hard and smooth. When it bakes under the hot sun it forms into a hard durable surface called laterite. Of course, it gets dusty when it is dry. The aircraft propellers and chopper rotor blades really can stir up a cloud of heavy red dust in a hurry. It is either muddy or dusty here. It seems to be much like Florida to me.

"Another landing strip material used here in the boondocks is an old holdover from World War II, pierced steel planking which lets the water through when it rains and is strong enough to uphold the weight of the aircraft when it gets muddy and soggy. Now there is a new kind of planking made out of aluminum, but it doesn't hold up as well because the lighter aluminum metal edges curl a bit with usage, enough to rough up tires, sometimes causing blowouts. Also at bases where jet aircraft are used, it gets really slippery with the rains; the high speed boys have been known to just slide off the end of the runway. That is not too much fun.

"It is nice that Chuck is doing so well in his new restaurant business. I have a suggestion for him. Out here when you go to dinner you are served with a rolled up hot towel, all steamy with heat and slightly mentholated. You use this to freshen your face and hands. What a treat. At the end of the meal another small towel is usually offered. The Orientals have so many nice ideas and practices, this is one of their finest. Maybe Chuck would like to try it.

"I am not so sure about eating with chopsticks, which is an art in itself. I am still learning. My problem is I tend to get muscle fatigue in my index and middle fingers which are in constant use. On the plus side, one never gets fat because you can't pick up large pieces of food with just two pointed little sticks."

It took a little while to get used to dining in an authentic Chinese restaurant. The sight of chopsticks going at high speed at a crowded table from mouth to community serving dish was certainly unusual to me. It was not unsanitary, however, for the chopsticks are used only to place food in the mouth and not chewed or licked in any way. My limited experience quickly taught me to use plain wood or bamboo chopsticks. You never would get enough to eat using more decorative ivory or plastic chopsticks, which were too slippery except for the very expert.

Dick Secord was transferred to another operation for reasons known only to the Joint Liaison Detachment to which he was assigned. Manuel, a big, bluff retired Air Force pilot with an investigative background, was his replacement. Manny spoke Spanish fluently and had five children and a new home in the suburban hills of Virginia. He was with the Company on a two-year contract and would readily fit in with our plan to move into bigger quarters away from the transient lashup at the Duc Hotel.

In a letter to Phyl on November 5, I typed out some news:

"I have been selected to go upcountry to Nha Trang, a very nice location, on the coast about 200 miles north. There is a need for an Air Ops man there, and the move may be temporary or permanent. I am looking forward to the move, for I have friends there. . . . will have adequate quarters, and get $5.00 per day extra for living expenses. As far as the house here is concerned, it will be a place to stay overnight when I come into town to catch the plane to Manila.

"Our new place at 60 Tu Duc has four bedrooms and a bath upstairs, plus a den and a bath downstairs, a nice living area and kitchen. There is a two-car garage plus a separate two bedroom and shower bath near the kitchen where the live-in help can stay. We have a guard on duty day and night plus the usual high wall with barbed wire and broken glass set in the top ready to cut off the fingers of any fool who tries to climb over. Our driveway has a high metal gate which opens inward, and that is a good thing in this crowded neighborhood of ours. We are on a rather narrow and noisy street with people all around. Right next door is a five or six story hotel building. . . . We have a phone and a radio hookup to the airport, so we are in touch with the world.

"Our combination cook-maid started yesterday. She is a recent widow about forty years old with five children. Her husband was killed in an accident on the loading docks on the Saigon River. Something dropped on him. She is dirt poor, with no income, no medical coverage, and no death benefits from her husband's death. Her teeth are betal stained, and her straight black hair, parted in the middle, is pulled back so tightly her ears stick out. She is no raving beauty in her baggy black pajamas and floppy rubber sandals; she only weighs about 90 pounds, but she is alert, fast afoot, and very energetic. Her dark brown eyes have a spark in them that seems to say she is not feeling sorry for herself and is going to make the best of it without complaining. Her children seem to be well mannered and attractive, from her eldest, a 15-year-old boy, to the youngest, a five-year-old girl. She has another daughter who is about Kenny's size, very cute and alert and actually 11 years old. My but these people are small boned and slender. Of course Manny and I felt like helping out as much as we could. We agreed to pay Nguyen, pronounced Gwynn, 3,500 piasters a month to start. We will buy most of the food at our commissary, and give her money to buy bread, eggs and fresh vegetables at the market. Split three ways this is between $60 and $70 for each of us. When I go upcountry someone else will take my place, but I'll always have a place to stay when in town for the night."

My next visit to Manila started off badly but worked out in the end. All was going well at the crowded airport as I shuffled along with other passengers at the Pan Am counter to get my passport stamped, shot record reviewed, and seat number assigned. A Vietnamese clerk at the inoculation window took my shot record and motioned me to the next window where I presented my passport. My passport was duly stamped but my shot record had disappeared. Somehow it had been swallowed up in three feet of space behind the Pan Am counter. There was much shuffling of papers and looking around on the floor behind the countertop while I watched in disbelief. The guilty clerk claimed that he knew nothing about the missing shot record. The passport clerk was polite and sympathetic and shrugged his shoulders, indicating this was surely the work of evil spirits. I was sure this was the work of a VC infiltrator whose purpose was to harass an American any way he could. I then had to go to the Pan American office nearby where an official listened to my story and typed out a letter stating that my shot record had somehow disappeared at the airport. The letter sufficed to get me on board the flight, but I would have to get a new shot record in Manila before returning to Saigon.

TRANSFER TO NHA TRANG

There was not much to do to get ready for my transfer to Nha Trang. Moe was back now and Air Branch was at full strength. As I had thought, the need for a full-time air operations man up there was due to increased logistics activity and a need to be more responsive to the requirements of the field. Moe and Willy briefed me on what to expect, saying that I would be working for Ernie, Chief of Base in Nha Trang. Moe urged me to keep in touch and let him know if I needed anything; in essence, he was saying I would be on my own. A sizeable Air America operations office was managed by a man named Ray Beatty, with whom I would be working. His office was on the flight line within thirty yards of the Company's warehouse and supply building where I would be located. From the map, I knew that Nha Trang was strung out along the shore of the South China Sea. The airstrip was approximately 7,000 feet long, running east to west from the coastline toward the hills that towered in the distance.

Before leaving Saigon, I wrote to Phyl:

"The return flight was uneventful. . . . had no difficulty with the immigration people over the shot record. . . . Right now

251

I'm at our new house typing on my Royal typewriter, which I checked out of supply along with a Pentax camera, a raincoat, one large briefcase, a medical kit filled with all sorts of basic supplies—including some multicolored cold capsules that you take every 12 hours. I also checked out a small Sony battery-powered radio, a 9 mm pistol and a light M-1 carbine in the event I ever go into the boondocks. I think my condition can be described as being *field ready*.

"I'll be leaving here next Tuesday via a cargo plane to Nha Trang. I am really looking forward to the change. Maybe the possibility of a good swim has a lot to do with my interest. Of course, the idea of being my own boss, more or less, has a lot to offer. I am told there will be a new Bronco Jeep assigned to me and that I'll be sharing a house with the communications man and the Company medic. They should prove good company and, if nothing else, can teach me a bit about their specialties. "Manny is upstairs resting while I type on the dining room table. Our cook is in the kitchen putting away the lunch things, helped by one or two of her children, who are very pleasant and good company. I do not get too familiar with any of them because then they tend to take over. Gwynn is a good cook and tries hard to please. We communicate in basic sign language. I get lots of sugar in my black coffee. . . . Manny and I find a cup of hot coffee served at bedside at 6:30 A.M. This is a great starter upper if you are slow in getting underway. This black-pajamaed wraith swoops in silently on bare feet, deposits the coffee and is gone. By 7:00 we breakfast on fresh hot French rolls, or a loaf of French bread, with butter, jam, juice and coffee. This morning, by special arrangement worked out the night before, Gwynn produced fried eggs with bacon in sort of an omelet. Clearly Gwynn is not in the same league as your Sarah, who is a real jewel. Please tell her how much I enjoy her good work in the kitchen and with our children.

"As for you and the children, I am very pleased with the development shown since last July. Just outstanding. Keep up the good work, and tell Kenny I am sorry I forgot to say good-bye to his nice green worm in the glass bottle. . . . I hope Tom gets a good blast off with his latest rocket launch when the new launching wire is in place. Billy, keep at your math; Cyndy, please don't forget to use the horn when you drive, it's the key to survival. . . . Love you all, until next time. . . . Love, Dad"

Just before Thanksgiving I arrived in Nha Trang, having flown there in a C-123 cargo ship with all my belongings. I even had managed to do a little shopping on Tu Do, a rather fancy street in Saigon, for some of the lovely pastel-colored silken material used to make the Au Dai, a dress that all the fashionable Vietnamese ladies wore. Phyl wanted to try her hand at making the attractive, flowing, ankle-length skirt that is slit on both sides to the thigh and worn over white or black clinging trousers. I bought material that was white and pale green and some light yellow according to measurements that Phyl had sent me. I also bought some lightweight camouflage material to have uniforms made for the boys.

"Dear Phyllis: 23 November 1966

Arrived here at Nha Trang early Tuesday and now at the end of the second day I can report I've been busy. All is well. I checked in with the Boss who was glad to see me and introduced me to most of the guys who work at the station called MAJESTY on the side-band radio. And my new house is just fine. House mates Fred the Medic and Jim the Communications man seem pleasant and nice company, what little I see of them. Our house is located a half block from the South China Sea where I went for a short swim. Couldn't stay long for the waves were too big. They must have been 8 to 10 feet high. The reason the waves were so high is that monsoon winds blow steadily from the east-north-east across the China Sea south of the Gulf of Tonkin. These rollers are really powerful. No one goes out over their head because of the undertow. But, oh what fun it was trying to body surf. The sand is yellow-red and very coarse, like our Atlantic Ocean sand. The sun was hot and my bald head got just a touch.

253

"Here the wind and air are quite different from Saigon. It is cooler and of course damper, being so close to the shore. Right now, a storm called *Nancy* is 200 miles off the coast and not moving much. So we have clouds, very low and with spats of rain now and then.

"Plane traffic is steady and so is my work, but that is good. The new office is quite small; one room with a big desk, two windows, a few extra chairs for people to sit at if they are waiting for a plane ride, and a sizeable side-band radio to keep me company. I handle calls from our II Corps province officers who call in asking about a shipment of goods or requesting a ride to headquarters. I also monitor radio chatter between AA aircraft pilots as they take off and land according to schedules I've prepared for them. Being on the flight line where the aircraft are parked means there is some noise to contend with. From my window I can see the AA operations building and some of the aircraft. Sometimes when one of the Porters outside revs up its Garrett engine, blasts of shrill noise and diesel-tainted air comes through openings in the prefabricated joints of our logistics building and around the doors and windows.

"Being away from Saigon is okay. I'm comfortable but have a lot of getting acquainted to do. There is a good field hospital near the flight line within a mile of us, and a lot of USAF people live across the runway from us, plus there is much RMK construction going on. They are improving our runway for one thing. Then there is the MACV and USAID compound, where our boss, Ernie, has his office on the Beach Road, about a half mile from the flight line.

"I guess the rainy season is on now, it is supposed to last until January or February, so let it rain. . . . My new Sony radio is great. I use it here in the office to pick up the Saigon broadcasts on the U.S. Armed Forces Radio which has music and news from America. The disc jockey on the morning programs introduces his show by shouting "Gooooood Morning, Vietnam", that way he gets a lot of attention. The programs have to be repeated or boosted from Saigon to Dalat and then to Nha Trang and other points farther away, because of the high hills between. [Next year, evening television programs would be shown from Saigon, using transmitters in an orbiting aircraft 3,000 feet over the city. Programs such as *Gunsmoke*, *The Man from Uncle*, and other macho shows were on the bill of fare. We Americans did not fight this war without the latest and most modern technological advances.]

With love to all, Dad. . . ."

* * *

Ernie asked me to establish a twice-weekly courier flight throughout II Corps to expedite secure delivery of our classified mail pouch and personal mail between base headquarters and field units. I set up a northbound run on Tuesdays that departed in the morning from Nha Trang, about midpoint in the region. The flight went to Tuy Hoa, Qui Nhon, and Kontum; then south to Cheo Reo, Ban Me Thuot, Gia Nghia, Bao Loc, Phan Rang, and Dalat; and back to Nha Trang by midafternoon. On Thursdays, the route was reversed so that traveling province officers would have a choice of flying the shortest route to and from their home office.

The courier route worked out pretty well and usually was flown in a twin-engine C-45 that carried six people plus two pilots. I took the courier run once to get better acquainted with the lay of the land and visit briefly with each of the province officers. My first trip was to Tuy Hoa, a 20-minute ride north, where my Blue U classmate Paul was stationed. He was glad to see me and as happy and sprightly as ever, his freckled face wearing its usual grin. Paul pointed out that Tuy Hoa was much like Nha Trang but much smaller. There was a sizeable military presence in the area, including a USAF fighter squadron operating from a new 10,000-foot runway. I felt that Paul had plenty of protection should the VC try to overrun his post.

Qui Nhon, farther to the north, was another seaside town of fair size. I picked up some sealed intelligence reports there to take to

Ernie and was told that they were "pure gold," meaning that the staff had obtained good information about the intentions and capabilities of the enemy in the area. This information came from captured Vietnamese documents, diaries, letters, and prisoner interrogation reports that were translated into English by a staff of English-speaking Vietnamese employees, who were usually Catholic and loyal to the Republic of Vietnam. The new information would be assessed and evaluated by Ernie and his staff and then disseminated to Washington. Company communications experts, like my housemate Jim, cabled the intelligence over secure lines directly to Langley. In a short time, the finished product would be in the hands of the proper agencies.

It was common knowledge that President Johnson held a tight rein on all military and political activities in South Vietnam and was briefed constantly on minute details in the field. Sometimes bits and pieces of reports from Nha Trang would be included in the President's Daily Briefing. Both military and civilian organizations were so-called customers of intelligence products prepared by Company officers in the field. Perishable intelligence (whose value was limited or exploitable only if acted upon immediately) was flashed to Saigon and Washington without delay. The White House was kept posted regularly, the Pentagon received reports about military matters, and Embassies, Civilian Operations Revolutionary Development Staff (CORDS), and USAID civilian offices received intelligence affecting civilian affairs; there was enough information for everyone.

Even though I visited all II Corps province offices via the courier and went on an occasional cargo or helicopter run, I really got to know the area best through the side band radio. I had to schedule the choppers and Porter aircraft assigned to us according to requests received over the side band. Cargo and people had to be moved in and around their districts using short laterite runways that required the Porter; we used the helicopter when there were no landing fields.

There were 44 provinces in South Vietnam, 12 of them in II Corps. About 25 to 30 field officers responded to Ernie and his staff in Nha Trang. Ernie was a former military officer who still wore his hair in a crew cut. He had a reputation for being a firm but fair manager, and we got along just fine. He told me what he wanted and I did it. I began delivering a copy of the next day's flight schedules to Ernie's house on my way home so that he knew where and how his airplanes were being used and could see the volume of air time being used in each office and which were his busiest provinces.

Province officers were divided into two categories, O for operations and I for intelligence. O officers were former military men skilled in training and instructing their people how to protect their camps and villages and prepare and maintain better defenses. They also were adept in establishing good public relations within their communities and conducted intelligence collection efforts. They sent out patrols, interrogated prisoners, and conducted liaison work with the province and district chiefs.

The I officers primarily were responsible for helping and training their cadre to seek out and develop networks and sources of information and teaching them how to obtain information needed to win the struggle for their community and province. VC locations and strengths and identification of key personnel and their plans and intentions were of primary consideration. The I officers worked the basic intelligence cycle over and over: develop sources of information, task them with needs, collect the raw data, translate and collate it, forward the product to higher headquarters, and then start the cycle over again.

In a letter to Phyllis on December 1, 1966, I wrote:

"Dearest Boo Boo:

The work here is not hard, and it is not boring, and best of all, I am on the outside. Today, for example, I had a sunbath on the beach during our extended lunch hour. . . . The waves were still too high and the sea rough. But, after that I had a chance to go on a helicopter to Cam Rahn Bay, which is the new and expansive deep-water port now under construction. The pilot had some business with some people on board one of the ships at anchor, so we swooped in and landed on the big X painted within a white circle on the deck of the *Corpus Christie*. I was amazed at what was going on below deck, for the whole inside was a depot for major repair work on Army helicopters. The entire cargo bay, perhaps half the length of a football field, was filled with men and machines, working under florescent lights with complicated electronic equipment. Men were tearing down and refitting rotor blades and engines. Chopper parts were everywhere as were a variety of machine shops. Rotary blades were being tested and replaced and engine maintenance done by a workforce of 300 army technicians and over 125 civilian technical representatives. It was hard to believe this was taking place in the middle of Cam Rahn Bay, surrounded by perhaps 30 other vessels that also may have been floating repair depots. More likely they were supply ships waiting to off-load.

"We didn't stay long. Too bad my camera was out of film. But it was an impressive sight, a testimony to American ingenuity.... Then we strapped in and our chopper lifted straight up and then dropped nose and dipped away to Nha Trang.

"Most evenings it is 6:15 and almost dark by the time I get home. After a shower and a drink it is dinner time. Our Mama-san, called Ba, runs a tight ship and is a fine cook. Dinner is promptly at 7 P.M. and well worth attendance.

"Would you believe I still haven't been to downtown Nha Trang? I really don't know where it is. However, I've found three Post Exchanges, three or four officers clubs, plus our own Company compound and bar, which offers free movies. It's quite dull here compared with the wildness of Saigon.... Wow! That is a bad place to be right now. There is much more VC harassment going on than when I was there. We all take reasonable precautions, and I am being careful.

"Last night I was awakened at 3:30 A.M. by the guard who thought I was the communications man. Jim was needed at the base communications center for some business. First thing in the morning, Fred and I put our names on our bedroom doors to avoid such rudeness. We need our beauty sleep.

"Tonight's movie was that ghastly Elvis Presley thing called *Hawaiian Paradise* we saw at the Makati Theatre in Manila. I simply could not see it again. Now there is a tropical depression off the coast causing all kinds of bad weather with constant winds and low clouds. This creates delays in aircraft schedules, and interferes with our side band radio and telephone transmissions. Even the electric power at our house is erratic; we use candles more than ever. . . . It is very interesting that you have met Ambassador and Mrs. Blair and have been invited to dinner on December 10th. I hope you will go. I'm sure there will be an extra man to be your dinner companion. . . . please let me know how it turns out.

"I miss the whole bunch of you, and am looking forward to the Christmas Holidays. Haven't been to church since I got here which is disappointing. Just too much detail on the job. Hope to get a helper soon. . . . am promised one who speaks English and French. Maybe I'll get some practice in French.

"Anyway, my love to one and all. Nite-Nite Dad"

* * *

The morning hours on the flight line were often hectic as aircraft were being boarded by province officers checking in for their return trip. Every bit of extra space on the aircraft was used to carry cargo. Boxes of uniforms, office supplies, radio gear, spare parts and tools, batteries, and the like were stashed aboard by Filipino warehouse workers, who are employees of Joe, our logistics chief, known as SMOKEY on the side band.

In spite of precautions, accidents did happen. One morning before I got to the flight line, an unusually tall and pretty Vietnamese Air America employee was delivering coffee to pilots and crew members on the flight line. While looking back over her shoulder and walking around the wing tip of a nearby aircraft, she never saw the blur of the spinning propeller just ahead of her. It hit a glancing blow of almost surgical precision, amputating her left arm at the shoulder and

259

slicing off her left ear. She was rushed to the nearby field hospital where surgeons were able to stop the loss of blood and minimize the dreadful damage. Miraculously, she was back on duty within six months, this time inside the office. God knows she was lucky to be alive.

Paul stopped on his way to Tuy Hoa from Manila and reported that Moe was still having medical problems and resting at home in Manila. We speculated that he might have to leave Saigon if the doctors did not cure him soon. Paul was a good guy and our families were now close friends. Paul even made arrangements with a Vietnamese seamstress in Tuy Hoa to make uniforms for our boys from the camouflage material I bought in Saigon. To cover my upcoming absence during Christmas, Willy sent Jim Brand from Saigon to substitute for me.

In Nha Trang, the monsoon weather continued. New Year's Eve at our little compound club was reasonably sane and safe. I remember drinking beer and avoiding the punch bowl filled with champagne and cognac. I wrote the following to Phyl:

". . . . the rains set in yesterday, part of that typhoon in the Manila area. . . . The Christmas visit with you and the kids was just fine and a real cap to a very exciting year. Will 1967 be the same? What will happen next? I can hardly wait, for we have had a great year. And thank you for all you've done for me and for our wee ones. You do make it all worth while and I'm quite proud of you. Give my love to Cyndy, Tom, Bill, Ken and to Sarah, Connie and. . . . Julie."

Enclosed in my letter to Phyl was a nice note from John D. MacDonald in response to my earlier letter saying that I had seen an old copy of his novel, *The Brass Cupcake*, in Saigon. He wrote from his place in Higgens Bay Rural Station, Mount Pleasant, New York, on January 12, 1967:

"Dear Adrian,

I am glad that a barracks-worn copy of that oldie put us in

touch. I heard you were Uncled, but did not realize you had gotten close enough to Charlie to make it imperative to remember where the nearest hole might be.

Your letter caught up to me yesterday. We've been hiding out up here, in snow up to our hocks, while I get some deadline work done—like a LOOK feature on the tribulations of one Dr. Coppolino, Sarasotan, under indictment in two states for two different murders, and now acquitted of the one in New Jersey.

Soon we wend southward for the Feb 13th trial in Sarasota: Frank Schaub prosecuting and Lynn Silvertooth presiding. [Coppolino was found guilty of murder in April 1967.]

Dorothy joins me in sending best and warmest to you and to Phyllis.

Cordially, John"

Our little compound club and bar at Ba Da Loc helped start the new year right when we became eligible to receive movies. All we had to do was maintain an audience level of 30 spectators, which we did by inviting our interpreters, translators, and cooks to join our regular and transient province officers.

On the flight line, business was steady and improving. Ernie talked of getting me an assistant, which was good news. The job still required attention seven days a week, and I was getting tired. I traveled to Qui Nhon on a courier run to see Mike and to escort a VIP from home, a new man in charge of the Vietnam Desk, who had encouraging things to say about the future of us contract people but mentioned that most assignments were made through recommendations by former associates and friends.

Rumor had it that USAID, our people, and the military were considering a shuffling of top management. The idea of restructuring made me wonder whether I might be better off as a province officer, the job for which I had been hired. I loved my work, but the office had been running smoothly and the challenge was gone. The grass looked much greener on the other side of the fence. I had begun to envy the province officers' work as being more responsible and tougher to handle than mine. There also might be more opportunities for another assignment after my two-year contract expired if I had more than one arrow in my quiver. Right now my experience was of value only to the air operations people. The province intelligence position offered broader horizons, if I could land a slot and prove myself there.

After much deliberation, I finally sent a memorandum to Ernie expressing my desire to get into the field, pointing out my qualifications for the job, and requesting a province assignment. Ernie called me into his office and agreed that air operations was running smoothly and I should be assigned to the field. He said it might take a while to work it out, but I could begin attending the regular meetings and briefings for the province people when they came in. It was months before anything changed, but I worked steadily and patiently hoping that I had not stuck my neck out too far. I wrote to Phyllis:

"15 Jan 67   Dear Phyl. . . . It's Sunday evening and just after dinner. Am having black coffee with just a spot of Ballentine's Scotch in it, and after this letter, it's off to the club to see the movie *The Oscar* whatever that is.

"I wanted to tell you I went to Saigon late Friday evening for a special dinner for all the Air Ops people, 16 in all, at the house Manny Gomez and I shared. Manny cooked a magnificent Mexican dinner. The party wasn't over until 1 A.M. and then reluctantly. On Saturday, I had more Mexican food for lunch and caught the 2 P.M. flight back to Nha Trang because there was no one minding the store. . . . I had a brief business conference with Moe and the others. Moe is well but works on a reduced schedule. He sends his very best to you and the family. He is a nice guy and thinks you are the nicest person, and so do I. . . . Our friend, Van Dam, is supposed to be heading up a three-man survey team from D.C., having to do with a possible combining of our present Air Ops with USAID. Whatever the outcome, Van Dam is supposed to stay on out here and head up the whole thing. This last information is supposed to be kept close to your vest, by this I mean no talking with Jan about it at least for a while, huh?.... I've taken a few more color shots around here, trying to finish off the roll with the pictures of Clark Field.... Can't wait until I get back on the 31st, which isn't too far away. My love to the children and a big hug and a kiss to each of my troops. Love, Adie"

By late January, the Vietnamese celebration of the Lunar New Year, Tet, had continued far beyond the official four-day period. Our Vietnamese staff fled with the winds to be with family during the holiday and join in the ritual of ancestral worship. Employees customarily received a month's wage in a red envelope, red symbolizing good luck, which was promptly spent on fireworks and gifts. Customary too was the daily, noisy barrage of fireworks intended to scare away lurking evil spirits who may attempt to disturb the souls of ancestors being visited. Our venerable cook went to Dalat, our maid went to Phan Thiet, and neither one returned for two weeks; somehow we survived the military mess halls.

In a letter to Phyllis on February 21, I mentioned a flight in a twin-engine Beechcraft with an Air America pilot.

"We landed at a red-clay laterite strip called English Field, near a town called Bong Son. I took pictures of the construction under way at the air strip, which was being used as a staging area for a helicopter-supported military operation. I noted with interest the use of huge round rubber bags or bladders, six to eight feet high, which were gasoline containers. These were the portable refueling tanks for all thirsty aircraft using the strip. A bladder could be hooked to a cable and slung under a helicopter, easily transported to and from a tanker ship at sea off Qui Nhon to the base. Quite ingenious, these Americans.

"I returned refreshed and ready for more routine business at Nha Trang. But tonight there was a good old Cary Grant picture called *North by Northwest*, shown after a steak dinner— courtesy of the Special Forces. They donated fifty pounds of

Adrian Swain

good beef to our Compound in exchange for our airlifting some of their supplies back to Saigon. A lot of this sort of bartering goes on.

".... the dry season seems to be here, because we have our air conditioners on a lot. It gets very hot by midday, but the humidity is gone, and salt water swimming is good if slightly chilly. . . . Keep up with your positive thinking on quitting smoking.... It is worth all the effort you can give it, to save your health, your teeth, and maybe guarantee you a few more years on the tail end of life to enjoy the fruits of our labors. I'm such an analytical person, I know, but that is exactly the way I see it .... Anyway, I love you and hope you can pull it off. My love to you and all the kids. My tan is getting big.... and that is not all. Love, Adriano."

I also relayed to Phyllis a brief comment in a letter to me from our friend Evelyn, who had worked in the Headquarters office of personnel. She said that her "experiences in Laos were pretty good." I mention this because Laos was another area where contract employees were being placed and a possibility for us to consider. Evelyn had served in the Far East for a number of years and knew what the score was out here. She had also served in Vientiane and knew a lot about Bangkok and many other small countries in the area.

I wrote to Phyl and included a poem by Rudyard Kipling that had been circulating around the office. It seemed most appropriate for our time and place. Kipling wrote:

"It is not too good for the Christian's health
to try to hustle the Asian brown,
The Christian riles while the Asian smiles
and he wears the Christian down.
The end of the fight is a tombstone white
with the name of the late deceased,
And the epitaph drear: "A fool lies here
who tried to hustle the East."
The Naulahka, Chapter 5

"Had a fine swim today, and yesterday got some flying in checking out a shortened courier route with one of the AA pilots. The trip was uneventful, in clear weather but with some smoky haze. Out here a primitive "slash and burn" kind of agriculture is common. The villagers axe down all trees and shrubs in acre-sized plots; they let the fallen trees dry out to be burned next spring. The ashes from the burnt trees provide potash and other fertilizers which make the land productive for three or four years. When the land is used up the "slash and burn" process is started all over again. There is lots of land, and it is cheap, so the hill farmer goes anywhere he wants. Whole tribes of people live this way. It is akin to the way our early American timber companies decimated our forests, but at least we gained something in the timber harvested. Here, nothing is saved.

"Saw a great movie, called *Born Free* all about a young lioness who grew up from a cub in Africa, then went back to the wild. A British film, made in Kenya and Nairobi. . . . Hope you get a chance to see it. . . . I am so pleased you have gone ahead and made reservations for a visit to Baguio that should be fun for all. . . . Until later, all my love, Adie."

On the way back from my last courier run, we stopped at Cheo Rio in the province of Phu Bon to see our officer in charge, a French-born American named Lou. He was currently serving at Phu Bon as penance for his part in the famous "flower pot" affair at the Duc Hotel. A few of the boys were partying on the rooftop terrace of the Duc Hotel when someone caused a huge flower pot to plummet to the street below. No one was injured, but the incident was reported through channels to Ernie in II Corps. Ernie took corrective action by reassigning Lou to Cheo Rio in Phu Bon, which soon became known as Phu Elba, after the famous island where Emperor Napoleon Bonaparte was exiled.

On May 5, I wrote to Phyl:

"I'm definitely getting relieved from the Air Ops job. Ernie says he is going to turn me loose in the field, but it will take some time to find a replacement and get him trained. The new man from Saigon, Dave Overby, has a radio name that is somehow appropriate—MOUNTAIN DEW. Dave is a big rugged guy from Kentucky with a slow easy way of moving. He seems reliable and won't take too long to get broken in."

I spoke too soon, for Dave was snatched away from me a few days later and reassigned to I Corps, where there was a more pressing need. I told Phyl:

"We are experiencing personnel shortages even though a lot of the guys are extending until the crisis is over, until September. It may well be 60 to 90 days before I get into the field, but at least the boss has agreed to send me sometime.... These things always work out for the best.

"Am fully recovered from the bad cold of a few weeks ago, and from a recent siege of weakness and miseries. The trouble was due to lack of salt, primarily. I had no pep, no appetite, sleep did not help; I had all sorts of odd feelings, but no fever. Sort of like having the flu without the flu bug. Finally the medics gave me pills for diarrhea and told me to take salt tablets. All OK now. I guess going in and out of air-conditioned rooms, and running around so much in the open jeep got to me. Several others had the same problem. Now there are salt machines to dispense tablets at all the drinking fountains.

"Got my Field Reassignment Questionnaire today. I requested Bangkok for my next assignment, so we shall see. Both Ernie and Moe have expressed the view that I should put in for Air Ops and would probably get it.

"I was thinking of Jack Humason today, remembering how nice it was when we visited Lawrenceville. Such a nice guy, and such a nice school. Maybe Tom will be interested in going to prep school there? It would be good for him, if he would not get lonely so far away from family, or vice versa. . . . Looking forward to seeing you all next Friday. . . . Love from Daddio."

* * *

In May, our whole family took a vacation at Camp John Hay in the hills north of Clark Field, where many Americans vacationed away from the muggy heat around Manila Bay. Phyl wrote to her folks:

"Adie came home May 19th and we left the next morning at 5:30 for Baguio. We traded our Mustang for Pete and Lucy's station wagon for we surely needed it. We were loaded with suitcases, golf clubs, tennis rackets, to say nothing of the six of us, plus our number one, Sarah.

"Baguio is 155 miles north of Manila in the Cordillera mountain range of northern Luzon, at an altitude of 5,000 feet. In the days before air-conditioning most government offices moved there from Manila for the summer. Seems like a simple little trip, but in this country you don't measure by miles, but by hours, and the trip took five hours. . . . The roads were really pretty good, but only two lanes all the way, and it is the only north-south route in Luzon, so the traffic is heavy with buses, trucks, jeepneys, pedicabs, calesas, bicycles, and occasionally pigs, cows, and carabao. The farther you get from Manila Bay, the more prevalent the small, slow vehicle. In some of the little towns the roads were so congested with calesas and pedicabs that one just crawls along, and they make no effort to make room for autos.

"We skirted all around the mountains, through the flat lands until the last hour which was straight up. Pretty hairy on some of the turns, but beautiful. The mountains were lush with tropical greenery and pine trees, waterfalls and streams.

"We stayed at Camp John Hay, an American base that dates back to 1903, when the base was built to serve as a military rest

267

and recreation center and named after John Hay who served as Secretary of State during McKinley's administration. We had two 2-bedroom apartments, each with living room, fireplace and well-equipped kitchen. We used the fireplaces at night and in the morning. After the 95 degree Manila heat which we have had for the past month, it was marvy. Not really cold, but fresh cool air, warm in the sun and in the middle 50's to 60 in the evening.

"The golf course is beautiful but rugged, up and down and around. Adie played the course once with Cyndy and Tom with him.

"We played a lot of tennis, Tom shows much promise, and we went bowling—the whole family, including Sarah. There is a small 18 hole putting course for the children, a putter and ball rent for ten cents, as do roller skates, and archery equipment.

"There are three restaurants on the base, a Commissary and PX, and a movie so we had plenty to keep us amused and busy. We also went shopping at one of the wood carving places; the Easter School Weaving Room, where Igorot and Ifugao Indian women make fantastic things. We visited the St. Louis Trade School which is famous for handcrafted silver, particularly the filigree work.

"We returned on Wednesday the 24th, stopping at Clark Field for lunch. Adie was to leave Thursday morning at 9:30 but due to a mixup in reservations he was on standby status. We waited until the plane was loaded before getting the word "no soap." Tired as we were from the drive on Wednesday, we headed for Clark Field again, about two hours distant, in hopes Adie could get a military flight back to Vietnam since there would be no commercial flight for two more days. We had lunch at the Officers club and then Cyndy and I left him at 5:30 so we could get back to Manila, which we did by 7:30, in spite of the fact it was dark. . . . I usually try to avoid driving at night particularly since the countryside north of Manila is reputed to be Huk [Communist] controlled country.

"It is raining today, the first lengthy rain we have had since January, and the coolness is great. Guess the hot season is over and the rainy season about to begin. . . .

"Yes, even though the newness has worn off, it is still fun and worthwhile. I can begin to see the effect for the good in the children. They will all be much more interesting people for this experience. Adie has the roughest road, but seems to be surviving well. . . . and I am very happy. There is plenty of company when I want it. I am able to spend much time with the children and enjoy it for I have no pressure of things left undone to spoil my time with them. . . . It's really quite fun living in San Lorenzo. In light of our circumstances it is rather like a large sorority. All our kids know each other and are welcomed at any home. It is a kind of neighborliness that we had in Port Washington, a situation my children have never before known, and one I remember with such fondness.

"Did I tell you that dem bums at the top have decreed that all the guys must remain on station this time for 8 weeks, due to personnel shortages. Adie won't be back until July 22, when he will get eight days, but it stinks.

"However, I will be dashed busy getting Cyndy squared away [to enter college at the University of South Florida at Tampa] so the time will pass quickly, I hope.

With much love, Phyl et al."

* * *

I returned to Saigon on a cargo flight in time to catch the courier to Nha Trang, which was as busy as ever. Ernie was just going on a 30-day leave to the States to visit his family, and Moe was already in

269

the States for another physical checkup. It would be August before I would hear anything about my new province assignment.

The Arab-Israeli Six Day War in June 1967 astonished the world with the swiftness of the Israeli victory. The war was triggered by Egypt's Nasser, who closed the Strait of Tiran to Israeli shipping and called for the immediate withdrawal of the UN Emergency Force from the Israeli-Egyptian border. Nasser signed a mutual defense pact with King Hussein of Jordan, having already pledged his support to Syria should the Israeli's invade. Feeling surrounded on all sides and blockaded by Arab enemies and further isolated by the withdrawal of UN troops, the Israelis took action. Accordingly, they struck the Egyptian Air Force on the ground, crippling the Arab world's most potent military air force, while simultaneously destroying Egyptian troops on the ground in Sinai. In a few days Israel seized the West Bank from Jordan, and the Syrians lost the Golan Heights from where they had been firing down on Israeli settlements. By the time the UN affected a cease fire on June 11, the Arab states had lost vast territory, most of their productive capacity, and much of their revenues. Psychologically and politically, the Arab defeat set the tone for many years to come and gave impetus to the rise of the Palestine guerrilla movement. I was very pleased with the lightning speed of the Israeli success and wrote to Phyl:

> "The outcome of the Israeli war is the best thing that has happened since we came over here. I am so glad we backed a winner for a change. This Vietnam deal gets progressively drawn out and costly. Joe said the other day, just think of the people who would be out of a job, if it weren't for this war. I can't argue because it is true."

This was the summer of Phyllis' venture into the world of art. Local Filipino artists were quite good and displayed their work in shops on Rojas Boulevard. The more aggressive and enterprising ones went to the homes of wealthy patrons in outlying communities. With the permission of our gate guards, they rang doorbells in the evening and were often invited in to show their paintings. Phyllis made a half dozen fine purchases that now hang in our home. Notable among them were Cesar Buonaventure's paintings of a calesa (carriage) and street scene and the fisherman's banca in Manila Bay. She bought a still life by J. Carreon and several Sariomento's, including a carabao working in a rice field during a spring rain against the backdrop of misty mountains, a fleet of junks in the harbor at Hong Kong, and an old church on a dusty street. Two bright yellow and orange paintings of straw-hatted women scything rice in a paddy also were added. Phyl's purchases cost about $8 each. They were all oils on canvass and nicely framed and distinctly improved our household decor.

Phyl's letter to her folks on July 13 noted the following:

"Golly, this is a year anniversary of the day we left Sarasota. Seems to have gone by awfully fast. Anyway, life is very pleasant in Manila, and I have no complaints. Wouldn't have missed the experience for anything.

"I am feeling fine. Also, am free as a bird in the mornings because all the kids are in school; first time in 11 years we haven't had a baby in the house, and I am not too sad. Ken has taken to school very well. The first day Connie stayed with him, but he has gone alone since then, no sweat. This morning I said, "Can you go to your room alone?" I have been delivering him to the door. He said, "Oh sure, let me give you a kiss" and off he went. Marvy. He feels so grown up.

"Tom and Bill seem quite happy about school too. There was no reluctance about going back. I think they were getting a bit bored and missed the busy routine of the bus and all the rest. I like being free to come and go without explaining where I am going.... This morning I am going to Sangley with Jan. Connie will get Ken from school at 12. It is a bit of a walk but not too tough.

"We all miss Cyndy, and hope she had a marvelous trip home to you. Hope she won't be too much trouble. And don't worry about her. She is a pretty grownup young lady. . . . Looking forward to seeing you in November. We'll do some sightseeing when you get here. Love to you both, Phyl".

271

Cyndy returned to Tampa to attend the University of South Florida and was planning to stay with KC and Evie until she found a place on campus. More important, she was going to pick up a new Mustang she ordered through the Embassy at a discount. Phyl now had no female companion to keep her company around the house.

Phyl and I experimented with sending voice recordings to each other by mail and by our friends going on leave to Manila. The tapes worked well most of the time, except when power fluctuations made our voices rise and fall, and were a fine addition to our regular letters. I usually wrote to Phyl every other day and in one mid-August letter belatedly recognized our anniversary:

"I have been replaying some of the earlier tapes and they are so much fun, I usually put one on when I have lunch at noon, and they make me feel right at home, especially Billy's whistling and Kenny's singing. Sorry I missed Billy's eighth birthday, but I know you all had a big birthday cake and all the young friends were there to help eat it.

"Happy Anniversary, darling. Seems like I missed last year too. I'm sorry. Could it be because you are not on hand to remind me? I think so. When here I don't think of such things much, and the days have a way of moving by quickly. For example, Cyndy's tape said she had been home for over two weeks, doesn't time simply vanish?"

Ernie told me in late August that he thought a replacement for me would be coming in a couple of weeks. He seemed serious and told me to resume attending the regional officer meetings. I wrote to Phyllis:

"I think I'll be assigned one of the Intelligence jobs, which has to do with liaison with provincial police rather than in paramilitary matters. If I had my druthers, I would rather do special investigative work so that when new assignments are made I would have a broader background of experience."

* * *

One Sunday, a boatload of us went to the island of Hon-Tre for an all-day outing. It was glorious and one of the nicest days I could recall. The sun was out, the boat worked fine, and we had beer and grilled steaks for lunch under the shade of a big banyan tree. While swimming, I noticed little specks in my eyes when I opened them under water. At my annual physical the next week in Saigon, the doctor told me not to worry and that these floaters were harmless and to be expected with advancing age. At 44 years of age, I did not feel all that old, but he had a point.

ASSIGNED TO QUANG DUC

My replacement turned out to be Charley from Dalat, who arrived a few days before my leave to Manila. Ernie was making quite a few personnel shuffles. Although I did not yet know it, he was sending me to Quang Duc to replace Dave and Jim, who would be transferred elsewhere.

I wrote to Phyl on August 25:

"Dearest Boo Boo Phyllis: I am feeling on top of the world these days. Am quite excited about getting out on my own to Quang Duc Province in the Highlands, just north and west of Dalat. It is cool there and not too populated. There is little VC activity and all-in-all not a critical province which means a lot of visiting firemen will not be coming my way, and yet there is room for a lot of improvement, so that any good work on my part will not go unnoticed.... I certainly love the kids on tape. I feel they are very close, and I hope they feel the same way about having Dad away but close by on tape. Anyway, I love you all, see you soon. Adie."

I caught a Pan Am flight to Manila and had a wonderful leave with the family, although my luggage remained on the plane. Luckily, I had enough clothing at the house. My bag went all the way to Honolulu and was returned on the same plane I took back to Vietnam.

273

Again, I suspected the fine hand of a VC sympathizer at work in the baggage room.

One of the more memorable events of that leave was a visit to Ah Wan, the Chinese tailor Phyl discovered. He fitted me for a blue seersucker suit with material Phyl had purchased at Clark Field. Ah Wan was a wizened, alert, middle-aged gnome who had about six men in his shop, stitching away on their foot-powered sewing machines. The suit was finished in a few days and cost 70 pesos (about $18) to make. It fit beautifully, and I wore it on the return flight to Saigon.

TWELVE

Tales from Quang Duc

The courier flight was nearing Gia Nghia, capital of Quang Duc Province, on September 17, 1967, the day before my birthday. All the way from Nha Trang I had been thinking about Quang Duc, having been to these remote highlands only briefly twice before and never dreaming it would become my home. From the side window, I noticed the reddish, laterite clay runway stretching about 3,500 feet from north to south on a green hill whose top had been sheared off and that had steep drop-offs of raw earth at each end.

Miles of green, triple-canopied forests reached west toward Cambodia, and the town of Ban Me Thuot lay to the north. Eastward was the lovely town of Dalat, where Charley had been assigned, and behind us was the quiet provincial capital of Bao Loc. Forests, streams, and an occasional Montagnard village appeared in between. Our field offices in these provincial capitals were linked to each other and to our Nha Trang headquarters by side band radios and semiweekly courier flights. It was perilous to drive here without an armed convoy because VC and NVA troops constantly patrolled the countryside bordering the Ho Chi Minh Trail. This Communist supply line ran through Quang Duc Province from north to south following the Cambodian-Vietnamese border and served as the artery through which the NVA poured their troops, tanks, and supply convoys into South Vietnam. The NVA seemed to disdain and abuse the Montagnards in the highlands, perhaps because they considered them ignorant savages hardly worth their military or political indoctrination efforts. They were more concerned with ARVN military outposts, village RD cadres, Special Forces camps, and MACV provincial compounds, which represented the U.S. Government's effort to help Saigon's leaders maintain control over the countryside.

Quang Duc province was sparsely populated and had a core of educated Vietnamese merchants who conducted most of the business in Gia Nghia and outlying district villages. Hill tribes, the slash-and-burn tillers of the soil, comprised the remainder of the population. Tribal affairs were managed by village head men and a council of elders. All national and provincial affairs were controlled from Saigon under newly elected President Nguyen Van Thieu. President Thieu appointed people loyal to him to be governors of all provinces in South Vietnam. Quang Duc's governor was a slender, 35-year-old Army Colonel named Nguyen Huu Man, whom I would call on later.

It was early afternoon when we landed and then taxied to the wooden, one-room operations building. Jim and Dave, both dressed in khaki trousers and colorful short-sleeved sport shirts, were waiting in a dusty Ford Bronco. They made a good team and were sharp, energetic, well-qualified people. I discovered that Jim's hobby was guns and other weapons; he ran a trading operation from our living room where he made trades with other officers who dropped by occasionally. They came once to swap a grenade launcher for a 9 millimeter handgun, a rare, nonmilitary weapon that was standard issue to Company field officers.

Dave had a forceful, positive attitude. He was also gentlemanly, intelligent, sensitive, and a trained piano player. His good looks and charisma generated a lot of interest from the ladies. Jim and Dave were in their early 30's; Jim was unmarried, and Dave divorced. We chatted briefly with the pilot before heading toward the compound that would be home for the next seven or eight months.

We followed a winding dirt road through a grassy valley, crossed a bridge over a stream, and then drove into a clearing with a few wooden stores that constituted the village square. It was quiet now with hardly a soul in sight since it was siesta time. We drove past a cluster of MACV structures on top of a gentle slope of high ground. Another quarter mile and a few more turns brought us to a white stucco building that housed the police station.

Jim turned our Bronco into a driveway and stopped in front of two tin roof, plywood-paneled buildings protected by a rising slope to the north. Between the two buildings were green nylon sand bags stacked knee-high to protect an underground bunker behind barbed wire. A dozen or more Claymore mines in the wire faced outward and were ready to explode if anyone attempted to infiltrate the compound. Dave said that the Nung guards were all on leave in Saigon. Nungs were Chinese professional fighters touted as the toughest, most-feared warriors in all South Vietnam. They must have gotten homesick for Saigon because they never returned. I later replaced them with stolid Montagnard soldiers who lived nearby and showed up for duty on time.

I dumped my bags in one of the vacant rooms and looked around the office. There were two good-sized bedrooms and two baths at the rear of the rectangular structure. Two smaller rooms were used as an office and a radio room. The front of the building served as a combined living room/dining room and had a small efficiency kitchen. All of the wall panels and flooring were wood, and the building had been assembled by a Company contractor using local laborers. The wind blew red dust through cracks around the windows and panel joints, which masking tape only partially sealed.

The building across the parking lot had offices and living quarters for our translators, interpreters, and maintenance personnel who had been recruited and trained in Saigon. This staff processed and prepared reports in English from a variety of Vietnamese documents that our police contacts or local offices provided.

September 19, 1967, I wrote to Phyllis:

"I have been here for about two days now, and as in any new situation all is confusion and strange. But, I like it. Being away from the rat race of Air Ops is great. This new place is in the foothills about 2,200 feet elevation and the air is clean; it is quite cool at night, but it is often cloudy, almost like it was in Baguio. We will be out of the rainy season in early October, so I have had good luck with the timing of this move.

"I will be here with one other American named Jim. His partner is being transferred to Phan Rang, to the south of us on the Coast.

"There is bedroom space for four, plenty of room for company should we have a guest. The place is furnished well in early American Sears and Roebuck maple; chairs, a large dining table, two living room couches and office equipment. Our beds are pretty hard, but not as bad as the Duc Hotel. Our drinking water is taken from the stream nearby, and is boiled and then filtered in one of those French, double-layered ceramic filtering coolers that we keep on the kitchen counter. Bath and toilet water is stored on top of our roof in six inter-connected 50 gallon drums, which we refill from the stream over by the airfield. We also have our own generator and a maintenance man who keeps it going to provide electric power for our lights, side band radio, A/C units and kitchen appliances.

". . . . our new home looks and feels somewhat like Nan and Dave's ranch house in Bushnell. There is no fireplace, but there is a lot of wood inside. . . . The furnishings are pretty decent, but there is mud and red dust everywhere. It is kind of messy for the guys here are quite careless; there are all sorts of implements on the tables and chairs, and a few half-finished projects left undone. . . . We have four vehicles, three jeeps and a big red truck for hauling supplies. There are gas drums stored outside near the generator, some tool sheds, and two heavy metal lockers I've yet to explore. There is so much red laterite clay around here it is like living in a barn in Georgia.

"There are so many new things to do, people to meet, and a whole new kind of business to learn; clearly this is going to take some time. More later, with love, Adie"

Three days after arriving in Gia Nghia, I was called back to Nha Trang for more conferences and learned that Dave was being reassigned to Phan Rang and Jim was going to Quin Nhon. I now would be handling both the Rural Development program and the intelligence efforts in Quang Duc province.

About a dozen officers were assigned to the USAID compound that I occasionally visited, which was commanded by Robert Hamblin. All military and civilian operations involved in Rural Development efforts were now members of the new Civil Operations Revolutionary Development Support (CORDS). The senior military commander in the field, General Westmoreland, was the chief, and the deputy was Robert Komer, a civilian with the rank of ambassador. CORDS was authorized to centralize and direct projects that received AID funding, such as refugee relief; the Chieu Hoi program, designed to encourage and reward VC defectors; all public safety police support; and the cadre program. CORDS also coordinated the efforts of medical aid teams and educators, agricultural specialists, and other American administrators and engineers operating in the provinces. CORDS was a huge, far-flung activity.

Dave departed for his new job, leaving Jim and me to attend staff meetings at MACV's office where we coordinated our affairs and shared military intelligence. Perhaps CORDS would be more effective with one person (Komer) in charge and end the petty bickering wherein each group competed against the others for recognition.

* * *

My first night in Gia Nghia had been interrupted by the startling blast and whistling of field artillery within 50 yards of our door. I jumped up and looked around anxiously. Jim remained seated at our dining room table laughing and told me not to worry and that I would get used to it. He said it was just random firing from the ARVN battery over the hill to keep the VC from getting too sure of themselves. Jim explained that ARVN gunners periodically fired 105 millimeter howitzer rounds at reported supply routes or trails used by VC troops. I was reassured somewhat but never did get used to it.

In the morning, Jim and I took a helicopter ride around the province, visiting our three districts; Duc Lap (where John Wayne and crew filmed the movie, *The Green Beret*), Khiem Duc, and Kien Duc. We had Revolutionary Development cadre teams in all places save Duc Lap and once a month made the rounds to pay the cadre, meet our district officials, and see our people at work. Each man was

279

dressed in a black pajama uniform and earned the equivalent of $10 U.S. per month paid in piasters. It was not much by our standards but was better than the average wage and bought a lot of food for many struggling families. Should a cadre be killed in the line of duty, his family was entitled to a death benefit payment of 10,000 piasters, which was less than $1,000 U.S. but a princely sum to a native in the province.

I only had to disburse one death benefit, which went to the mother of a young man slain by a VC sniper. It was sad to meet the poor, toil-worn and wizened woman. Between our interpreter, the bereft mother and other family members, and the Montagnard officer who brought them, we managed to conduct the doleful business. There was little I could do but express praise for the young cadre and my sorrow for the loss of her son. The solemn-faced mother had to acknowledge receipt for the money by signing her mark on an official form, which she did carefully and with quiet dignity. Somehow, it did not seem that we were doing enough in exchange for her son's life. Maybe this reminded me of my Mother, who was still receiving a monthly payment from our government as the widow of my Father, a World War I veteran. This Vietnamese lady was receiving less than a year's wages as total compensation for the loss of her son. I did not make the rules and hoped that I would not have to go through this business often.

Paying our cadre teams was one of my main tasks and involved transporting piasters and payroll forms from Nha Trang to Tien, our paymaster in Quang Duc who would journey out to the districts on payday. None of the young cadre could read or write English and would sign for their pay by pressing their right thumbs on an ink pad and then imprinting them on the roster opposite their names. Tien returned all money not disbursed within three days, whereupon I would balance the expenditures with remaining cash and turn in my accounting to Nha Trang.

Tien spoke French, pretty decent English, Vietnamese, and some M'Nong dialect and had been an RD staff employee since the program started a year ago. Tien was always prompt and never lost a piaster, but there were times when I sensed he was not paying everyone. It was possible that a sharp guy like Tien might insert some phony thumbprints on the payroll roster and pocket the wages. Graft was integral to life here, and I had to be practical since I needed Tien to make the payroll disbursements and handle the money for me. Several months later, however, when MACV detailed a big U.S. Army sergeant to help me with my liaison duties, I dispatched him to go on the rounds and to keep Tien honest.

The night before one of my inspection trips to the Kien Duc District, a VC assassination team tried to slip a grenade into the bed of the District Chief as he slept in his thatched hut. When the grenade dropped through the thatching, the Chief awakened, picked it up, and threw it right back before it exploded. The next morning the VC's stiffened body was displayed publicly on the grass in the village square. A gun is a great equalizer, however, and our RD cadre and ARVN troops were now equipped with the AR-15, which fires .22 caliber ammo. The AR-15 and M-16 rapid-fire rifles compared favorably but were not as reliable as the widely acclaimed AK-47 Russian-built assault rifle used by the VC and a host of other Russian-backed insurgents around the world.

* * *

I was awakened one night by the ominous thump of exploding mortar rounds and immediately started to dress. Jim called out my name and asked if I was awake. "You bet your ass I am," I said, strapping on my webbed canvas belt with its holster and 9 millimeter pistol. Snatching up my M-1 carbine, I jumped into the jeep with Jim, who drove quickly without lights to the MACV compound. The VC rounds were coming from sites hidden in the dark valley below our perimeter. Our mortars began to fire flares, and soon the grassy slopes and scrubby bushes of the countryside were lit by flickering yellow flares drifting slowly downwind, swaying gently, suspended by tiny parachutes. We all expected a VC assault but none came; they seemed content to fire random, harassing rounds. An hour before dawn the incoming rounds stopped, perhaps discouraged by our mortar and howitzer shells, but more likely because the VC wanted to get back to their bases along the Cambodian border before daylight.

Jim and I returned to our quarters and had breakfast before calling in a side band message of the VC attack and writing up the detailed "VC Incident Report" required by headquarters. This was the first time I had been under direct fire in South Vietnam; I did not enjoy it one bit but now felt more like a veteran of this war. I also did not relay any account of this shelling to Phyllis.

A few days later, Jim packed his bags and jumped on the courier for Qui Nhon, leaving me alone. He said he would be there on temporary duty and could come back if needed and also took one of the two translators with him. Now I would begin to earn my pay.

I wrote to Phyl on October 2 at the end of a rather long day:

"Dear Phyllis.... It seems like quite a few days since I last wrote but you have been much on my mind. I've been quite busy and not able to free enough time to put together a decent letter. Today was no exception. Went out in the chopper to visit the hamlets with a bunch of my people. After arriving at the first stop we went about our business of meeting new cadre, paying old ones, and talking to police officials, as well as having lunch with the Province Chief, the District Chief, the senior American military advisor and a lot of his staff people. Our chopper was supposed to come back at 1 P.M., but did not show up until 5 P.M. The whole afternoon was pretty well wasted.

"What I am saying is that here in the rustic provinces, things never are done as you plan. Hope to have better luck tomorrow.

"Today, when I came home there was no water in the pipes, I called for help and got that solved. I had to drive the big red truck down to the stream where our guys pumped our water drums full, and then hauled them back to fill our roof-top reservoir. I cleaned up and was about to go to the military club for dinner, but the keys to my jeep were out with someone. I had to cook my own supper, which I managed with the help of some good whiskey.

"I am being patient as I learn, but even the little things are not

282

to be taken for granted here. I am SO GLAD I have had a year
in preparation for this assignment, or I would be discouraged.
As it is, I am really not too upset. I am my own boss, and that
helps.

"The Zenith radio works well, but I miss US-style radio music.
This VN music is for the birds, too atonal for me. I had
planned on playing some tapes on the big tape recorder here,
but the night before Jim left, the motor broke. An ill omen?
This is just a minor problem. This morning I ran out of diesel
fuel for the generators. Luckily, I managed to borrow two
drums of fuel from MACV.

"This job is like a marriage. There are many adjustments to
make. The first month or so will be hard, then I hope to make it
easily enough until spring. Speaking of marriage, I am so happy
that ours has been so fruitful and close. I really love you and the
kids more each day. I miss you more now that I am living an
uncertain day-to-day existence, for I long for the days of stability. . . but would not change things a bit. I think this whole
experience has been good and I can bear up if you can.

"Give the boys a big hug and a kiss from old Dad. Be seeing you
in a week or so. Keep up the good work. Love you and think you
are an "OK" wife and mother. Adie."

My early October leave to Manila got off to a shaky start. Once
more the VC sympathizer at the airport struck, this time in the guise
of a visa problem. I was in the Pan Am line with Stan to get my
documents examined. The shot record was okay, but the Vietnamese
official examining my passport looked at it as if it were poisoned and
gave it back to me saying that my visa had expired. I stared from him
to my passport, speechless. My heart sank as I realized this meant that
I could not get to Manila. There was a strange, cramping numbness
in my solar plexus and my head started to spin. As the blood drained
from my head, I felt myself slipping down and for the first time in my
life fainted and sagged unconscious on the floor. When I awakened a

few moments later, Stan was helping me up. I was not hurt, just slightly woozy and confused, and was taken to a private waiting room nearby where a Vietnamese medical officer made me stretch out on a couch. He watched me carefully and took my pulse before releasing me. Stan, of course, left on the Pan Am flight.

Distressed and extremely unhappy about this turn of events, and vaguely ashamed at having fainted, I decided to go to Saigon to see if my friends at the Air Branch could help. Immediately my spirits improved, and I hastened to the nearby MACV motorpool and found a ride into the city. At Air Branch, Willy checked into visa renewal possibilities and found they were not too promising. It might be possible, but several days of my precious leave would be wasted. He suggested that I go back to the airport and take the next military flight to Clark Field. Willy called the airport and found there was a Southern Air Transport (SAT) flight at 4 P.M. to Clark Field. Before I left, he told me to contact Colonel Hal Sommers at Clark should I need help getting transportation into Manila. By 6 P.M., I was at Clark Field showing my passport to the military clerk at Immigration. He dutifully stamped me into the Philippines, but I could tell that he was puzzled by seeing a civilian on a military flight. I quickly telephoned Colonel Sommers, who listened to my story and then told me to wait in the VIP lounge while he arranged for a car and driver.

A worried-looking noncommissioned officer from the Immigration desk walked by once or twice not knowing how to deal with the strange civilian with the red official passport in the VIP lounge. He finally came over and asked to see my passport again. Noting the lack of a Vietnamese visa, he politely asked me to renew my visa when I got to Manila. Within a half hour, Colonel Sommers' driver appeared. This tough-looking Filipino driver had an extra jerry can of fuel, some water, extra rations, and sidearms and looked as if he were going on a safari in Africa. In all fairness, we were going through Huk-dominated territory, and he would be alone in the dark coming back; I could not blame him for being careful.

The ride home was anti-climactic and uneventful. I thanked the driver and gave him $20.00 U.S., which was pretty fair wages for the trip. Phyl arrived just after the driver departed and met me with a big

The Time of My Life

hug and a cry of joy. Stan had told her the story of the expired visa and of leaving me behind. Naturally, she never expected to see me so quickly. The SAT flight was the best of several military flights I would take in the months to come.

Right after returning to Quang Duc, I was called to Nha Trang for a three-day conference. I stayed at the Ba Da Loc compound and enjoyed good food and film fare before returning to Quang Duc with my bag full of money to pay the troops. I also had the latest instructions and a multitude of new forms required for the rapidly ballooning superstructure that had been created by CORDS.

In October, I wrote a newsletter to friends and family that I had not written to very often. It went to my old bunkie Jim, now in Kansas working for a bank, Bridgewater pal Jim Wallace, brother Chuck (and Agnes) in Princeton, Parker Banzhaf, and Dr. Large at St. Boniface on Siesta Key.

26 October, 1967. . . .

"I am sure that carbon copies of letters are nothing new so here is one from your Far East representative, who also represents the New Frontier, now known as LBJ Country, and Sarasota County, FL, USA. . . . From the wilderness of South Vietnam where people like me are known as the ADVISOR. I advise on matters of almost everything, but what it really means is that the American ADVISOR has connections with the big bag of money and if one plays his cards right one will receive monetary rewards with little or no strings attached. I am not kidding. . . .

"At the moment, my present location is in the remote stronghold of Quang Duc Province, in the highlands of SVN. I have just finished a fine repast, cooked by my own hands, that would rival the fare at Whispering Sands.

". . . . I am listening to the Voice of Australia, and can flip around the dial to BBC, VOA, America in DC, VOA in Manila, all on my fine Zenith shortwave radio. . . . For some reason, the American Armed Forces broadcasts from Saigon, Nha Trang and Pleiku do not reach through the hills and valleys of this hilly area. Even though we are at 2,000′ altitude, we are in behind a screen of hills which range upwards of 5,000′ and block some of the signals.

".... Anyway, to wind up a brief note, Phyllis and I and the boys plan to depart Manila on May 1, and will return by way of Hong Kong, Japan, and Honolulu, where we will get on a jet plane for Sarasota. So, until I see you, take care and have an extra toddy over the Thanksgiving and Christmas Holidays for the Swains. Thinking of you, and with all best wishes. Adrian."

I wrote to Phyl several days later:

30 Oct 67, Quang Duc

"Dear Phyllis.... It's a sunny Monday afternoon and I'm sitting in my Bronco at the top of the hill on the windswept airstrip waiting for the 3 P.M. courier due in ten minutes. . . .

"This past week has been uneventful, but the weather has been cool and fine. Lots of sunshine and cool air. The local towns-people are relaxing more than usual in preparation for the November 1st and 2nd national election holidays. All Vietnamese welcome a chance to goof off. It's kind of like our 4th of July. . . . There will be parades, contests and speeches, led by Colonel Man, the Province Chief. I've been invited to attend and will do as much as I can but the paper work keeps flooding in. So far, I've been able to cope. . . .

"There will be many out-of-town visitors during the holidays and there will be a buffalo ceremony which always attracts a huge crowd.

"I have ordered some Montagnard artifacts which I'll bring home, such as a hunting bow and quiver of arrows, a long-handled bamboo axe with metal blade, baby baskets with shoulder straps that *momasans* use to carry children or other goods on their backs. The ladies also weave a cloth that is most colorful, usually black trimmed in red. I will trade for these items using my extra shirts. Cold weather is coming and clothing is more valuable here than money. . . . Tien, my translator and interpreter, will do the bargaining for me. That way the price will be fair.

"Hope you are fine and the same for the kids. I think of you a lot and am looking forward to our next visit, especially now that KC and Evie are coming to visit over the Thanksgiving holidays. I have my leave request in, but have not heard any words of approval as yet from Nha Trang. . . . Here comes my Porter, right on time. Love to all. Adie"

* * *

According to a *National Geographic* article in January 1965, life for the mountain people was dominated by an endless number of spirits that rule the fate of men and animals, control the elements, and govern the harvest. These spirits were to be cultivated and placated through sacrifices. The sorcerer (village high priest) possesses high status and great influence and deals directly with the spirits. To appease them, the Montagnards may progressively offer a chicken, a pig, and then a buffalo. Sometimes these sacrifices deplete the entire livestock in a village. The ceremony includes drinking copious draughts of rice beer, a potent concoction.

A most welcome response to my newsletter was a note from Don Large dated November 6, 1967:

"Dear Adrian:

The passage of time has not served even remotely to dim our memories of you and of Phyllis. We still miss you desperately and the place just doesn't seem quite fulfilled without the presence of the Swains.

"I do get occasional news about you from Phyllis' mother whenever she and Mr. Warren are guests of Sixty Vulte, whose cabana is directly next door to ours at Sanderling, but those shreds of information are all too skimpy for our hungry hearts; so it was good of you to write both your personal note and your mimeographed report. Please continue to keep us posted whenever you can and be assured, meanwhile, you both remain as strongly as ever upon our hearts and in our prayers.

Faithfully yours, Don"

* * *

General Westmoreland's headquarters in Saigon were now in the Pentagon East, a huge, two-story prefabricated complex near Tan Son Nhut airport that could house 4,000 officers and enlisted staff. It was here that newsmen received regular and elaborate handouts and briefings as prescribed by President Johnson, who had a keen interest in news releases that portrayed him as an infallible commander in chief. This was not an easy task, since public opinion for the war was adversely affected by daily television reports shown during the dinner hour that often disputed press releases from Pentagon East. U.S. marines and soldiers were seen fighting and dying on ridges and battle fields, being ambushed in dense rain forests, or striding through the burning ruins of thatched huts surrounded by wailing peasant women and children in black pajamas. Our troops were shown as fighting and dying hopelessly, making little progress. There was no end to the suffering in sight. Public opinion polls showed that by late October 1967, the number of voters wanting to pull out of Vietnam had risen from 15 to 30 percent despite briefings to the contrary.

LBJ was aware of how quickly the public mood had turned against the Korean War and knew that the mood was turning against him in this war. The minority who opposed the war on moral grounds were becoming more vocal. On October 21, 1976, 50,000 demonstrators marched on the Pentagon chanting "Hey, Hey, LBJ, how many kids did you kill today?" The President's council advised that one way to slow the erosion of support was to emphasize the "light at the end of the tunnel" instead of battles, deaths, and danger.

The Time of My Life

Ken and Evie Warren were planning a month-long trip to the Far East that would include a week with us in Manila over the Thanksgiving holiday. Part of K.C.'s report of their visit in Manila follows:

"Monday, Nov 13. . . . We arrived at Manila on our flight from Tokyo about 9:30 A.M. Phyllis and the three boys were up on the observation deck waving at us as we came off the plane. We processed through immigration and health departments and then met the troops. Were we glad to see them! All of us piled into the Mustang and we were off to 48 Arguilla Street. Bill Tucker was in town on business (CEO of Cal-Tex Oil and an old friend of Phyl's from NY days), and he came in about 11:30 so we all had a drink. Then Ev and I decided to take a short nap. She slept four hours, but I got in six hours. Got up for dinner and then sat around catching up on Sarasota and Manila till about midnight. A long tiring day, but very enjoyable. We lost Sunday to the time change, so it was Monday in Manila.

"Tuesday, Nov 14. . . . Slept fairly late despite Monday's naps. Went down to the City and visited Seafront, the U.S.E.A. Club. The traffic is unbelievable. I wouldn't dare drive a car any more than a mile from the house. The streets are full of Jeepneys—which are 8 to 10 passenger buses. All gaily colored, with streamers and bells, and they shoot in and out of traffic like water bugs on a pond. I can see why Phyl said not to worry about Cyndy's driving. If she could drive in Manila she could drive anywhere! Had lunch at Seafront, home for a nap, and then Phyl drove us to the American Cemetery. It is most impressive. There are mosaic murals of all the battles in the Pacific. In addition to the thousands of dead buried here, the names of other men lost or missing, and buried God knows where, are engraved on huge tablets which connect the buildings housing the mosaic murals. The thousands of names led to the very sobering thought—Why?

"Wednesday, Nov 15. . . . Downtown after a leisurely breakfast to do a bit of shopping. The traffic still floors me but Phyl takes it in her stride. Phyl took us to her Chinese tailor, Ah Wan, and I got measured for a suit. Phyl had the material, a very nice thin striped cord. It will cost 70 pesos, around $17.50 U.S. Then we had lunch at the new Sheraton Hotel on the bayfront. Very plush. Found Jane Swanson [Phyl's cousin] at home. [Her husband works for Mobil Oil Overseas.] We had a nice long family visit. To the Jeffers for cocktails later, then home to dinner and the hay.

"Thursday, Nov 16. . . . Off to town again to visit a number of wood shops. Some of their things are wonderful. Ev had quite a time and I was very patient. Ev finally got rid of 160 pesos and we went to the Seafront for lunch. My bar bill for three Manhattans was 90 cents.

"Friday, Nov 17. . . . Again a leisurely breakfast. Sat around til 11:00, then took off for Clark Field to pick up Adie. The road up there is called the MacArthur Highway, no Grand Central parkway, but a fair road. We got our first look at the back country, with water buffalo working in the rice fields. Passed through several native villages or *barrios* and the houses they live in, you wouldn't believe. They have no windows, just holes; crowds of people in the narrow streets, pigs and water buffalo in the yards. It took two hours to get to Clark Field, but what a place when you get there. It is enormous, with clean winding streets. We had lunch at the Officer's club and Phyl did a little shopping. Adie got in at 4:30. He looks fine, a little thin, but trim and healthy. It took another two hours to get back to Manila, and by that time there was twice the earlier traffic. After dinner we sat around chewing the rag. Adie had brought some souvenirs from his village, principal was a Montagnard cross bow and a quiver of bamboo arrows.

"Saturday, Nov 18. . . . Adie and I went to Makati's shopping center to have some films processed and what a place that is.

Teeming with people and the supermarket we were visiting had hardware, liquor, bakery and many other shops, at least twice the size of the South Gate Publix. Came home, packed up the family and went to the Seafront. We got a table by the pool and watched the kids diving. Lunched there. Sandwiches for six, drinks for four, and the bill was four bucks. Home for a short nap. Phyl had gotten a big steak, and we had a cookout to celebrate Ev's and Adie's birthdays. It was a nice family party complete with a big birthday cake. Our Phyl had a miserable cold and sore throat, but she is carrying on but really feels mean.

"Sunday, Nov 19. . . . Nice bright, sunny day. Phyl stayed in bed for she really feels lousy. Adie took the small fry out to Seafront and later in the day Phyl and Ev and I got ready for a cocktail party Phyl was throwing for her friends to come and meet the old folks. There were about 20 guests, most of them government people, and they were a darn good looking bunch. Intelligent, vocal, pleasant, and we were very happy to meet them.

"Monday through Saturday at 48 Arguilla. Tuesday we got a ten-passenger Volkswagen bus and driver to take us on a tour of Manila, which the Swain family had not done. We saw the old cathedral, built in the old days by the Spaniards. Very interesting with a lot of very old paintings of saints inside. Billy Swain said, 'It was a nice place but they ought to get some new pictures, the ones here are old and very dirty.' We toured old Fort Santiago Diego on the Pasig River, with its dungeons where many Americans were imprisoned by the Japanese during the war only to be drowned by the rising tides of the river, because some of the dungeon cell ceilings were below the water level. We drove through a very ornate Chinese cemetery with gaudy mausoleums, probably better homes than the occupants ever lived in on this earth. Wednesday we drove to Sangley Naval Base across the Bay, where Phyl shopped at the Navy PX. We had lunch at the Officer's club. The road there is long and winding through five or six native villages and lots of rice paddies and salt beds. Back home to a delicious, sumptuous

Thanksgiving dinner, as Adie had to leave early Thursday A.M. to Clark and return to Saigon. Tommy went along to be company for Phyl on the return trip. Friday we went to town to mail some packages and to pick up my suit at Ah Wan's. It is a good looking suit and while I may have to diet some more to wear the pants comfortably, there's plenty of room for letting out. . . ."

The remainder of the Warren chronicle tells of their travels to Hong Kong for a rather pampered visit at the Peninsula Hotel, the oldest and most reputable hotel on the Kowloon Peninsula and then to Tokyo for a few days at the beautiful and long since demolished Imperial Hotel designed by Frank Lloyd Wright. After shopping the Ginza and visiting the sights in the cold and dampness of Japan, they flew to Seattle to visit Maggi and Buell Kingsley (Evie's brother Charles' son) before returning to Sarasota.

Meanwhile, I returned to Quang Duc without incident, the trip by now becoming rather routine. It had been nice to see the Warrens, and as I mentioned to Phyl, the only grim note was their horrible smoker's hack. I congratulated Phyl on her valiant efforts to quit smoking and urged her to hang on and not give in to the urge to smoke, knowing she was doing the best she could.

* * *

29 November 67, Quang Duc

"Dear Phyllis. . . . One bright spot on my recent stop in Nha Trang is the prospect of getting another man assigned with me. No matter who he happens to be, I will, of course, be delighted. . . . will let you know as soon as possible on this.

"There has been a rash of VC incidents in Nha Trang. Two of our people were injured by mortar or plastic bomb fragments while they were out on the town Saturday night. The point is, they were out. Here where I am, even though there was some enemy action last month, I am prudent as are all of us in these outlying areas. It is probably much safer here than in Nha

Trang, or in Saigon, at least for the present. I stay at home nights, am surrounded by guards and other members of the staff, all-in-all about 25 people. I say this to reassure you that all is under control and I will not take unnecessary chances. Bye for now. Love. Adie"

By early December, my new assistant arrived, a 29-year-old Special Forces senior sergeant named Nicholas Combitchie, who immediately began to make my life easier. Nick's parents operated a restaurant, so of course he knew about cooking and our cuisine improved immediately. As promised, I wrote Phyl the good news:

"Dec 9, 1967.... Dear Phyllis.... It's Saturday noon, and I am at the airstrip waiting to see if they can clear the wreckage of a C-123 which landed too hard on the runway. The hard landing caused the wheels to fold up into the fuselage. No serious damage done to crew or cargo, but the plane won't fly for a few days.

"All goes well now that I have a new man with me. He is an old hand in the Province, having been here for a year with the Special Forces, and he is good. A great help in the office, very neat and tidy, and pleasant. His name is Nicholas Combitchie, and he has many relatives in the Athens area where he has invited me to visit some day. He is engaged to a beautiful Vietnamese girl he met in Dalat. Nick will be with me until next March when his tour is up, then he expects he will go to Europe. So, I am set for awhile.

"With the extra hand on board, there are improvements to be made around here.... The weather is getting nicer and nicer. Clear and cool, and in the mornings I have to wear a heavy hunting jacket, spotted like a leopard....

"My love to you and the kids. Have they any problems I should know about? I get all sorts of problems here, but never hear of any from you and the boys. I think this is because you are such a good manager, and I love you for it.... Adie"

Nick and I began inspecting and retraining our guard force and improving our security. Nick had the troops spruce up their bunker area and ensure that the claymore mines worked. He then rewired and restrung our shortwave radio antenna, which improved our reception considerably. He decided that our 12-inch television set also needed a better antenna and took some of our Montagnard troops to find some bamboo from which he selected a sturdy, 30-foot piece that he affixed to our rooftop. The flickering black-and-white image of Matt Dillon in *Gunsmoke* was considerably brighter that evening. Next, he decided to fix the half-finished bomb shelter that Jim and Dave had started months ago. Nick first thought of logs, but trees were scarce. Ever the scrounger, he remembered something he had seen earlier. We drove out to the airstrip where Nick had noticed two metal pallets left behind by some cargo aircraft that would make a perfect roof. We spirited both pallets that very afternoon and by sundown our bomb shelter had a new roof. The troops then covered it with a double layer of sandbags, leaving ventilation and gun sight openings on all four corners. Inspired by this success, Nick and his sturdy workers stacked a layer of sandbags against the outside walls of our bedrooms to deter stray bullets zinging our way at night. As I reported to Phyl, with Nick on board I caught up on my paperwork and was not as rushed as before.

Nick was full of energy and took over doing most of our cooking. I once tried to make spaghetti the way I had learned from Phyl when Nick advised me I was not doing it correctly. Determined to prepare the one dish I felt I could handle, I took umbrage at this and politely insisted on doing it the way I had been taught. Nick grudgingly agreed, perhaps recognizing that he ought to let the boss do something around here. Later, I had to laugh, wondering why I insisted on cooking spaghetti when I had a professional in the house. Even though we both ate generous servings that night, I never again insisted on cooking. Hereafter, I set the table, cleaned up, and helped elsewhere. Nick ran the kitchen, and we dined well from then on. I will always remember how delectable were his oil and vinegar salads.

Just before I went home on Christmas leave, Nick brought his Vietnamese fiance, Danielle, from Dalat to spend the holidays with him. I was happy to meet her and happy for Nick. She was a lovely, modest, and refined young lady from a Catholic family that had fled south from Hanoi. Danielle spoke French, some English, and her native Vietnamese, and Nick was teaching her Greek.

Nick and I visited the three Special Forces camps in the province and were briefed on the latest VC activities in their areas. From all indications, the VC were becoming more active along the Cambodian-Vietnam border, with signs of a buildup possibly directed against Saigon and President Thieu's government in III Corp to the south of us.

My Christmas leave finally was approved, and again I slipped into Clark Field on a SAT 727 and was met by Phyl and Tom. Stan and a guy named Dick were also on board and managed to shoehorn into Phyl's little Mustang for the two-hour ride to Manila.

Our second Christmas in Manila was gay and fun. Phyllis invited our friends to a pre-Christmas party that was a huge success. We attended Christmas carol services at St. Timothy's Episcopal and had a quiet Christmas day at home. The boys were all pleased with their gifts, army camouflage uniforms made by Paul's seamstress in Tuy Hoa. Tom was especially pleased with a chess set from K.C. and Evie, who sent Phyl and me a Bronzewear cream and sugar service to which Phyl added salt and pepper shakers. We gave checks to Connie and Sarah, our house help, along with photographs of them with the Warrens taken during their visit. This was our first Christmas without Cyndy, now at the University of South Florida. Phyllis and I managed to get in a few games of tennis, and I was impressed with how well she and Tom both were playing. Our boys were on vacation from school, so I got to spend much more time with them than on my previous trips. By December 29, I was on my way back to Saigon, feeling quite fortunate to have spent both the Thanksgiving and Christmas holidays with my family.

During the first week in January, I was assigned another assistant, a young 24-year-old Army Lieutenant named Ronald DeCosta who arrived out of the blue. I was happy with the extra hand but thought that we now had more manpower than was needed. First, we had to teach Ron how to drive. Just out of college, Ron was a city boy from Massachusetts and had never driven a vehicle. I explained to Ron that he was a liability if he could not drive. We could be in trouble if we got in a jam and he could not drive us out of there. I decided he would be my personal driver, so we went to our parking lot and started basic Jeep training. Next we ventured out on the road by our house, and soon he was able to get me to the daily 8 A.M. MACV meeting without snapping my head too hard when he shifted gears. Actually, it was kind of fun and got the adrenaline flowing early.

We also caught up on filing, and I began to revise and review old material to make our office a bit more efficient.

January 9, 1968, Quang Duc

"Dear Phyllis:.... Now I am finding extra time for some reading for fun. Just finished a book called *The Liberation of L.B. Jones*, about life in the south, but it's not worth your time.

"We are really isolated up here. I have been talking to Charley, begging for some cargo shipments that are long overdue. All I get are promises. We all have problems. Charley's time is so short so what does he care? He is almost finished, but his replacement is not on hand. . . . I love the guy, but he is not the Air Ops man I used to be. . . . But, the sun does shine everyday, and I am not complaining too loudly.

". . . . Things are going to get worse for the next few months, but I am not too worried. . . . just thought I would mention it, for all along the Cambodian border the VC are acting up. . . . I am sure that if I keep my nose close to home, all will be OK, so that is what I plan to do. I promise to take care of the family jewels.

"Our dinner tonight was superb. One of our secretaries brought us a gift chicken along with five eggs. Tonight we had the bird for din din. Nick and Danielle baked it and it was super. Salad, French bread with coffee spiced with Cointreau for dessert. . . . Soon I will retire to my room for the night.

"The 105's are firing overhead again, even though the moon is bright and this is not supposed to be the kind of evening one expects the VC to be acting up.

"I know you really don't mind how sloppy my typing is, for it really is this evening. But I do love you and the guys, am just kind of tired and maybe will feel like finishing this a little bit better in the A.M. . . . I hope your new tennis racket is good for your game. You really don't need too much help. Ta Ta Adie"

*　*　*

General Westmoreland's 1968 campaign plan was based on the assumption that the VC and NVA were no longer capable of sustained attacks within the interior of South Vietnam. By next July, all central provinces in the interior of III Corps around Saigon would be turned over to ARVN troops. The 1968 campaign began with a spectacular parachute drop into the wilds of northeastern Phuoc Long Province, 110 miles northwest of Saigon on the Cambodian border and just south of me in Quang Duc. Other border operations placed almost 43 U.S. infantry and armored battalions along the Cambodian border in III Corps.

The plan falsely assumed that the VC were a weakened and crippled enemy. Despite high casualties and desertion rates, facts later proved that the Communists sustained relatively high combat strength. The Communists also greatly enhanced the firepower of all VC battalions, not just the regulars. During the summer and fall of 1967, 29 VC regional or provincial battalions in III Corps marched westward to sanctuaries in Cambodia where weapons shipped in Chinese freighters through Sihanoukville had been cached. There they turned in their semiautomatic M-1 Garand (World War II) rifles and other captured American arms and were reequipped and trained in the use of fully automatic AK-47 assault rifles, B-40 rocket-propelled grenade launchers, and the rest of the Soviet-designed infantry arsenal used by the North Vietnamese.

General Fred Weyland, who commanded III Corps troops, worried that while he was under orders to patrol the Cambodian border, the enemy was apparently moving into the interior of South Vietnam and shifting their forces from near or across the Cambodian border toward the populated provinces closer to Saigon. Weyland was fearful that as soon as he stripped the interior of troops to patrol the border area, the NVA and VC would team up with their local battalions and guerrillas to lay waste the RD cadre teams working in the hamlets, as well as all the other pacification projects in which he had invested so much time and effort.

Weyland went to Saigon and talked to Westmoreland about his concerns. Weyland believed that an attack was coming and asked Westmoreland for a postponement to which he agreed. Besides, Westmoreland had a more important concern at the moment; the VC seemed to be attempting a second Dien Bien Phu at Khe Sanh in northern I Corps. Dien Bien Phu was the battle in which the Vietnamese surrounded and destroyed the entrenched French forces in 1954, forcing the French to surrender and leave the country.

Hanoi was moving two infantry divisions of roughly 20,000 men with a regiment of artillery into the ridges around the airstrip and the hills above it that were hidden by the scud clouds, fog, and rains of the northeast monsoon. A real threat was building up, but it was a diversionary move by the Communists to bait General Westmoreland into moving his main forces from the south into the Khe Sanh area. It worked, and Westmoreland moved to counter with his infantry, artillery, and air power. By the end of January, he had about 40 percent of all infantry and armor battalions in South Vietnam in the Khe Sanh area, plus the marines already in place.

Early in the afternoon on January 20, an NVA lieutenant appeared outside the Khe Sanh airstrip carrying an AK-47 in one hand and a white flag in the other. He wanted to defect because he had been passed over for promotion. He cooperated with marine interrogators and described an elaborate plan to seize the base that night by capturing two key hill outposts. The main assault was to come during Tet when the U.S. and Saigon had scheduled a 36-hour cease-fire and the Communists had proclaimed seven days of no shooting during the holiday period.

The cease-fire began at 6 P.M. on January 29, Tet eve, except in the two northernmost provinces involved in the struggle for Khe Sanh. A party was held that night at a house behind the new U.S. Embassy in Saigon. The rectangular, six-story fortress was set well back from the street and encased on all sides by a concrete shield against bomb blast, rockets, and shell fire.

Ambassador Ellsworth Bunker was in charge, having replaced Ambassador Lodge in April 1967. Bunker was a 73-year-old Vermonter and a thrifty millionaire who had worked over 30 years in his family's sugar refinery business. The Vietnamese called him Mr. Refrigerator because of his natural reserve and aloofness. He was a shrewd Yankee and somewhat set in his ways but witty and entertaining when among friends. Because of his age and background, he was not one to question the credentials or judgment of generals like Westmoreland who were engaged in a war of attrition.

There were 492,900 American servicemen in South Vietnam in the "green machine," as the troops called their army, and more were coming, with a total of 536,000 by May 1968 and a peak of 543,000 in April 1969. Most officials in Saigon and at the highest levels in Washington were sure that Westmoreland had the war in hand and that the VC and NVA forces were gradually being ground up and decimated by our forces. They were in for a surprise.

During the predawn hours of January 30, U.S. and South Vietnamese installations at Da Nang, Qui Nhon, Nha Trang, Ban Me Thuot, Kontum, Pleiku, and Saigon were hit by VC assaults. In Quang Duc, our side band radio began squawking about 9 P.M. with a stream of cryptic messages between our guys in Pleiku and Kontum and from Ban Me Thuot and headquarters in Nha Trang, all reporting VC activity. Kontum was having trouble reaching Nha Trang due to atmospheric conditions. I broke in and offered to relay messages back and forth to Nha Trang, which I did for the next several hours. Kontum relayed that they were burning their classified files as a precaution against their being captured. These papers were burned in 50-gallon drums provided for that purpose, which contained some sort of incendiary material.

Nick and Ron had strapped on their side arms and were watching for anything unusual happening around Quang Duc. Our office staff was already in Saigon to celebrate Tet, but our guards were on alert. We listened to our side band radio all night. Clearly a multiplicity of VC raids were in progress against RD cadre camps and outposts, as well as radio stations and MACV compounds throughout South Vietnam. Although there had been a rash of earlier reports indicating a buildup of VC around Gia Ngia, Quang Duc was spared.

Subsequent reports from across South Vietnam showed that tens of thousands of Communist troops had violated the Tet truce with a panorama of attacks. The bulk of an NVA division stormed into Hue, north of us in I Corps, and occupied nearly the whole city and the imperial citadel for almost a month. Other VC targets included military camps and command posts, police stations, administrative headquarters, prisons, and radio stations in more than half of the 44 provincial capitals and all of the major cities. Scores of district centers and ARVN bases as well as Tan Son Nhut, Bien Hoa, and a number of other air bases were attacked on the ground or shelled to prevent them from providing air support or helicopter reinforcement to other endangered garrisons.

Around 2:45 A.M. in Saigon, a platoon of sappers in a battered taxi-cab and a small Peugeot truck leaped out and blew a hole through the wall of the new U.S. Embassy compound. Although they had plenty of B-40 rockets and explosives, they did not seize the Embassy building. Apparently, they became confused after their leaders were killed in the opening exchange of gunfire with U.S. Marine guards. They simply occupied the interior of the compound and shot it out for nearly six and a half hours until they all were killed or wounded.

Marine guards awakened Ambassador Bunker just after 3 A.M. in the second-floor bedroom of his residence to tell him about the assault on the Embassy four blocks away. Secret documents in Bunker's ground-floor office were burned in case the building was overrun. Dressed in his bathrobe and pajamas, the Ambassador was escorted in an armored vehicle to the quarters of the Embassy Security Officer. The VC also attempted unsuccessfully to seize Independence Palace, where President Thieu lived. Except for the U.S. Embassy, clearly a target of grandstand propaganda value, the VC concentrated their attacks on Saigonese enemies with the goal of collapsing the Saigon regime. They hoped to incite a revolt patterned on the August revolution of 1945 and moved 15 VC battalions, approximately 6,000 men, into Saigon and its suburbs. The sounds of their assault were muffled by the explosions of firecrackers being set off around the town by Tet celebrants.

Thanks to General Weyland, TSN airport was kept safe with tanks and armored personnel carriers, and helicopter gunships dropped flares and attacked VC troops who attempted to block Route 1 into and out of Saigon.

* * *

4 February 1968, Quang Duc

"Dear Phyllis.... Just a note in case I don't get the 6 Feb Pan Am flight, all is well here. All leaves have been canceled because of the bad situation in Saigon and at Ton Son Nhut airport. The VC have suffered a very bad defeat, with great losses to their armies, over 17,000 dead. In Saigon, eye witnesses report a lot of NVA soldiers were involved, including very young teen-agers, some only 14 years old. They got into the cities and were depending on the local VC to help and guide them. When the local VC did not appear the strangers from out of town were shot up, trapped, and pretty well wiped out.

"I'll see you just as soon as the situation clears.... If I don't get a flight I'll send a cable to Gordon Logan at Seafront.... My love to you and the boys, keep smiling. Adie."

Sunday, 11 Feb 68, Quang Duc

"Dear Phyllis.... Aside from the frustration of not being able to see you, it has not been a bad week. The whole country is restricted to quarters after 7 P.M.... Two of our four translators returned from Tet leave, and travel is very difficult in Saigon. By now I guess that all the visiting wives are out. I bet they don't get to visit again for a long time. Am glad you were not caught out here in the mess.... Many snipers are reported to be still in the streets.... but essential travel has been restored in most areas.

"In some way I am not unhappy that the Saigon population got hit as hard as it did, for now maybe some of them will wake up, perhaps maybe even get involved in their own struggle and start going after the VC in their midst, the ones who are directing

301

and helping the guerrilla activity. I know one thing, here in Quang Duc they are all pulling together and the people know which side is trying to protect and help them, and it's not the VC.... Life in Quang Duc is not too primitive these days. Our American Embassy Compound is becoming the FAT CITY OF II CORPS. Our motto is "SURVIVE IN STYLE".... My two bunkies are both good cooks and treat me well. I may get fat. With both TV and radio, we have progressed far since my arrival. See you soon I hope. Adie"

* * *

In a general letter to the family, Phyllis wrote:

29 February 1968, Manila

"Adie and four other guys came in on the 18th, via Air France, the first flight Air France made out of Saigon since the shooting started. They were to go back on the 24th, but AF decided to overfly Saigon, so they all had to return to Manila. This happened again the next week with both Pan Am and Air France deciding to overfly Saigon. But they got out of Clark Field on a military flight that arrived in Saigon around noon, which is much better than the regular flights which get in around 6:30, pretty close to the 7:00 evening curfew.

"While Adie was in Manila, his village was mortared by the VC, and in the ensuing activity his province chief [Colonel Nguyen Huu Man], the senior CORDS Official [Robert Hamblin], and the senior MACV officer [Colonel Etteridge] were killed in a helicopter apparently shot down by sniper fire. Adie showed me the newspaper report in the Manila morning paper. He said it was good that he was not there because he might have been asked on the chopper with them."

* * *

While Saigon had been saved, the war was lost; although it would continue for another seven years. The financial burden (over $30 billion annually) and the cost in human lives (20,000 Americans dead and more than 50,000 wounded up to the Tet offensive) was so high that when the 1968 Tet offensive exposed Westmoreland's war of attrition as a fiasco, the inevitable result was a psychological collapse and a domestic political crisis of historic proportions. It mattered little that VC sappers did not actually break into the Embassy, that the VC were beaten back at Saigon and at Hue, and that overall the VC and NVA had suffered a military defeat. What did matter was that the nearly defeated enemy (so described in Westmoreland's regular Pentagon East briefings, which were filled with body counts, defections, and desertion statistics) could still attack anywhere and more fiercely than ever before.

Don Oberdorfer, an American journalist who was there summed it up:

"The irony of the Tet Offensive is that the North Vietnamese and the Viet Cong suffered a battlefield setback in the war zone, but still won the political victory in the United States."

* * *

Little had been achieved by the outpouring of lives and treasure and the rending of American society. The assurances that the public had been given appeared to be false. The spectacle of Americans fighting and dying, Vietnamese peasants being burned and bombed out of their huts, and the widespread havoc being wrought in cities and towns continued to be televised to Mr. and Mrs. America during their dinner hour.

By the end of March, the effect of the Tet offensive was very apparent in the United States. Senator Eugene McCarthy almost beat the incumbent president (within 300 votes) in the New Hampshire primary. Bobby Kennedy immediately jumped in and announced his candidacy. Westmoreland returned to the United States to become Chief of Staff of the Army and was in effect kicked upstairs. Deputy General Creighton W. Abrams, a tough World War II tank commander who served with General George Patton, replaced him. McNamara had been fired earlier for displaying pessimism about the

303

war and replaced by "Old Hawk" Clark Clifford. Secretary of State Dean Rusk began to weaken and was now circulating proposals (for which McNamara had been fired) to suspend bombing North Vietnam as a step toward reopening peace negotiations.

In his memoirs, *Counsel to the President*, Clark Clifford wrote:

".... the war was not lost at home.... It was lost where it was fought, in the jungles and rice paddies of Southeast Asia, and in the offices of a corrupt and incompetent ally." As counsel to Presidents Truman and Kennedy and then as Secretary of Defense for Johnson, Clifford was to change his hawkish views and see the war "as unwinnable at any reasonable level of American participation." He saw the United States as having "underestimated our adversary" and in thinking that "the American presence on the battlefield would be sufficient to change the situation in our favor. We were wrong." He argued, "it was the hawks, not the doves, who weakened America by pursuing the war for so long.... putting our national prestige on the line at the point where our ability to control events was at its weakest. . . . We should not draw the wrong lessons from Vietnam.... we did everything we could reasonably do to help the South Vietnamese."

Clearly, the North Vietnamese were winning the battle of political and national will. President Johnson and his staff were now forced to consider the unthinkable, negotiating with the North Vietnamese. On March 31, Lyndon Johnson announced that he would restrict the bombing of the North Vietnamese and would not run for another term as president in order to hold the country together in the time he had left. Three days later, Radio Hanoi announced that they would negotiate with the Americans.

Other changes were in the making. Bob Komer, who would stay on until November 1968 as the director of CORDS activity, had asked LBJ to assign William Colby as his deputy. Reporting these events in his book, *Honorable Men, My Life in the CIA*, Colby was the Far East Division Chief in the CIA and preparing to take over the Russian Division in Europe when notified of his draft by Komer. Not one to argue with the President or Richard Helms, Director of the CIA, Colby dutifully took leave without pay from the Agency. This way he could officially and legally accept the position of Assistant Chief of Staff for CORDS. The move was to take effect at the end of January, just in time for the Tet offensive. He attended briefings on AID programs in Washington and then reported to Saigon, where he had served as First Secretary to the U.S. Embassy in 1959-62 and as Special Assistant to two ambassadors.

By the time Colby arrived, the disruptive effects of the recent Tet offensive were still very evident. Huge areas of towns and cities had been burned, bombed, and ravaged. Hundreds of thousands of refugees were homeless and in need of housing; public services were in disarray and in need of revitalizing. It fell upon CORDS to rebuild the towns, feed and house the homeless, and rebuild a capability within the South Vietnamese population to better defend themselves.

Operation Recovery got under way with the welcome assistance of American military engineers, CORDS employees, and other volunteer relief agencies. William Colby was in the thick of it but also concerned with the larger issue of security. He needed to ensure that the government of South Vietnam could maintain control of the areas being recovered. It would serve no purpose to repair the ravages of the past Tet Offensive if the VC continued to dominate the countryside.

OPERATION PHOENIX

The solution to Colby's concerns was Operation Phoenix, "Phung Hoang" in Vietnamese, meaning a mythical bird that could fly anywhere. Phoenix was designed to collect intelligence on the VC apparatus, identify its ring leaders, and root them out. The idea originated with Bob Komer in mid-1967 and was first formed with MACV, ARVN, and CORDS personnel and called ICEX (Intelligence Coordination and Exploitation). After the Tet offensive, the Phoenix Program became a CORDS-only program closely identified with Bill Colby.

Colby visited all 44 provinces and many of the larger districts, talking to his old Agency contacts, meeting newer ones like myself, and looking at the prospects for Phoenix. Colby visited Quang Duc one bright and windy afternoon and wanted to see me. We introduced ourselves and then stood by the airplane talking for about 15 minutes. I was favorably impressed with this calm, unassuming man who was full of questions and quite knowledgeable about the area. I dare say he knew more about Quang Duc than I did. He got right to the point when he asked me if I thought the Phoenix program would work. I tried to be supportive and helpful but was noncommittal, saying that I thought it all depended on how reliable and diligent our Vietnamese counterparts and their informants were in seeking out and reporting the right kind of information on who, what, and how the VCI membership operated in Quang Duc. After all, Quang Duc was not a hot military objective as far as the VC was concerned, judging by the fact that we had been by-passed in the Tet offensive.

Privately, I could not really see how it was going to work. I had reservations about the practicality of obtaining such sensitive and critical information. Assuming we did get valid data, it would be difficult to check the facts, and we could be getting a lot of false information. At the very least, some of it could be fabricated for the sake of making required reports. Maybe I was being too pessimistic. At any rate, I said that I thought the effort was worth trying and my people and I would do all we could. I never saw Bill Colby again, except in the news media following his subsequent appointment as director of the CIA in September 1973.

Colby wrote about the Phoenix program in *Honorable Men: My Life in the CIA*. An important step in Phoenix was to set up standards and procedures to ensure that the intelligence gathered on the VCI was accurate. CORDS assigned Phoenix advisers to help formulate the program's doctrine and procedures and to help the local authorities prepare files and dossiers on VCI suspects.

Forms were generated so that the reliability of the information could be examined conveniently. The general rule was that three sources had to report a suspect before he was included on the rolls. The districts were able to improve their records on the local VCI and give political briefings to match those about the main and local military forces and guerillas.

Although the objective was to contribute to the fight against the VCI, Phoenix had no forces and thus never conducted any operations against it. Phoenix was able to assemble and analyze information and then give it to the military, police, amnesty program, and local administration, which did have the forces and authority to take action against the suspects. The results of any actions were reported to the local Phoenix center and then to Saigon.

The other side of the coin and words that describe the reluctance I felt toward the program come from Neil Sheehan's book, *A Bright Shining Lie*:

"Saigon officialdom saw the glitter of extortionist gold in the Phoenix program, blackmailing innocents and taking bribes not to arrest those they should have arrested. In the rush to fill quotas they posthumously elevated lowly guerrillas killed in skirmishes to the status of VC hamlet and village chiefs. The Phoenix bird was a predator none the less. After all of these years the identity of many hamlet, village, and district cadre was common knowledge in their neighborhoods. Thousands died or vanished into Saigon's prisons. [Colby was to state in 1971 that 28,000 VCI had been captured in the whole of South Vietnam under the program, 20,000 killed and another 17,000 had defected.] The Viet Cong did not disappear, of course, nor did the fighting cease, but the guerrillas were forced into a period of relative quiescence. . . . retaining strongholds in the Cau Mau Peninsula (at the southern tip of Vietnam). . . . and along the Cambodian border."

* * *

It remained quiet in Quang Duc, and all of our programs continued as if nothing had happened. Nick would be completing his tour soon and going home to Erie, PA, where Danielle, his lovely fiance, would join him. Word from the head shed in Washington was that my departure date would be April 26, 1968, which would give me five days with Phyllis and the boys in Manila before boarding the *President Wilson* on May 1. Phyl had done all of the legwork for the journey and was worried about selling the Mustang too soon and having to ride cabs again.

The death of Colonel Man in the tragic chopper crash the month before left the province without a leader. We heard that a senior provincial officer from Ban Me Thuot had been selected and was due next week. I wrote to Phyllis on March 17, St. Patrick's Day:

"Attending ceremonies is one thing we do well here. For example, today at 10 A.M. the new province chief flanked by full military guard, visiting dignitaries, and representatives of all the people were drawn up in ranks around the Sector Headquarters Square, where he officially and formally accepted the responsibility and title of Province Chief. Flags were dipped, handed over, saluted, while we in the honorary viewing stand, where all Co Vans [Advisors] were grouped, popped up and down dutifully whenever a new speech was made. While the ceremonies were in progress, loudspeakers boomed out the sing-song tones of martial Vietnamese music, which none of us in the reviewing stand understood too well. It was a good ceremony though. The new chief seems to be a quiet, watch and wait type, who has not tried to overly impress anyone, and naturally he has the personal blessing of President Thieu who makes all such appointments. It was kind of humorous to receive round red tags, each with a red ribbon, which identified the person and job title. I had three tags, for my three job titles, so I just stacked them progressively with my name on top and then the name of the job showed below: RD [Revolutionary Development], TS [Truong Son or Montagnard], and PA [Police Advisor].

"After the ceremony, we attended a tea nearby at the Province Chief's house, actually outside on the terrace, where long tables and an outdoor bar had been set up. La Rue beer was served, as was SEGI [an Orange soft drink], with crackers and fluffy shrimp pastry cakes that look like big scalloped mushrooms that had been deep-fat fried. They were delicious. The new colonel in charge of the province had a quick chat with all the visitors and then the party broke up. There were visiting officers from the 23rd Infantry Division from Pleiku, to the north, which is the immediate superior military headquarters for Quang Duc Province. More later, love to all, Adie"

The Montagnards were burning their fields, and a sweet, blue smoke tinged the crisp, dry air. Inspired by such beauty one quiet Sunday afternoon, I stripped to my shorts and stretched out on an army blanket to catch some rays. I gazed out over our bunkers and claymore mines into the distant tree line and wondered if any VC were looking at me. The sun was so fierce that I could not take more than 15 minutes. I got so dizzy from the heat that I returned to the coolness of our house and wrote to Phyllis, my favorite pastime.

I told her about Ernie, our chief in Nha Trang, who had returned from home leave earlier this month. He had been walking the halls in Langley when someone grabbed him and asked if he wanted to go to Tokyo for his next assignment, which he accepted. Ernie had always treated me fair and urged me to take the air operations slot that personnel had offered last August. I sent back my acceptance because the job promised a year of training in Washington and then an overseas tour, hopefully accompanied by my family.

7 March 68, Quang Duc

"Dear Phyllis:

All quiet here at home in Quang Duc. We had a nice spaghetti dinner after which Nick and Ron departed for MACV to see another show. I am staying in for I may have a business meeting with Captain Chan, my neighboring police chief."

During the next regular conference in Nha Trang in mid-March, I was called into the boss' office for some rather sobering news. Ernie's replacement, a man named Dean, produced a lengthy communication from Washington about a Congressional mandate calling for a 10-percent reduction in personnel overseas. Dean said the air operations position promised me was no longer available but thought there was still room for me somewhere. He would send a cable back speaking on my behalf, if I wanted him to.

When the shock wore off, and in the weeks to follow, I began looking elsewhere for more promising work. I wrote to Congressman Jim Haley, who resided in Sarasota, asking for help. I sent another letter to the Civil Service Commission in Washington asking them to enter my name on the Civil Service Register. I suggested that Phyllis ask her Mother how to contact her brother, Uncle Charles, Vice President at Grumman Aircraft, about job opportunities there. I talked about my dilemma with Bill Searcy, my AID friend who lived in Manila. He was very confident that I would be welcomed at the Washington office of Public Safety whose director and deputy director were both former Company employees. With my air operations background and FBI experience, he thought I would be snapped up and also said there were many openings overseas, including South America. Bill's encouragement was timely and made me feel much better. I would check into this possibility when I got to Washington.

I wrote to Phyllis on March 20, 1968:

"Dear Phyllis. . . . I am on the wagon for a test period. Have had but one Scotch and Soda since last Saturday night, this being Wednesday, that is quite a dry spell. I really got tired of just belting down 2 or 3 stiff drinks before dinner, and maybe 1 or 2 after. Causes me no real pain, and I know it is a great waste of time, for you can't do any real serious thinking or reading or writing in that condition, so now I'm not drinking. . . . Maybe I'll get into a whole new frame of living for I want to be able to spend more time with the kids, enjoying them and not too impatient with them, as I often am when drinking. Also, since I'm in a confessional mood, perhaps the nervous strain I sometimes feel will lessen and I'll feel more energetic. . . .

"I hope you are not depressed about recent job developments. . . .

I find myself no longer disappointed, but am somewhat challenged by the many possibilities that lie ahead. One thing I don't see in our future is a return to life as it was at W-S, Inc. I really could not hack a return to that routine in our immediate future. . . . I am determined to get a Federal job, perhaps state, especially if we can get a good overseas post. . . . so we can get a civil service retirement arranged. Despite the recent 10% reduction and budgetary problems, I think by June we'll have something to count on. . . . See you soon, love, Adie."

While in Saigon on a personnel recruitment trip to find two new translators, I met John, my old bunkie from the Clarendon Motel. He was returning to the States on May 6 and had a job offer in Europe, which he was very skeptical about. He was not too concerned, however, since he had a job opening with an in-law in Miami. That he was a good intelligence officer I had no doubt; he kept his mouth closed and knew his trade. Years later we would meet again in Washington, where I learned he had taken the job in Europe handling agents doing cross-border operations on a contract basis.

* * *

Now that Johnson was not going to run for office again, the political fires were fueled anew in Washington. I wrote to Phyllis that I thought Nelson Rockefeller would win the nomination if he ran for office. Rocky had proven to be a good administrative man but had a big problem on the domestic scene because of his womanizing ways. I said, "Nixon is strong, but suffers the same credibility gap as LBJ. He may just win."

Phyllis wrote to her parents on April 5, concerning the move:

"Dear Mother and Dad. . . . Time is getting short and I seem to be doing nothing, just looking around at the mess, but I think I know what I plan to do with everything. . . . Have signed an agreement to sell the car for $3,140 US so that is finished and I am pleased with the price. Have $1000 in pesos on deposit which the guy will forfeit if he doesn't complete the deal. It took four trips to the Embassy and Treasury Department to get my check converted to US dollars. Four trips for everything. Nothing ever gets done right the first time. The tailor not ready, dressmaker not ready, Pan Am changes schedules and now I have to change all that anyway.

".... Boys out of school next week. Oh joy, the Seafront pool is closed for repairs.... Have completed all our shots and will pack out on April 25th.... Have decided to proceed directly to DC, in fact have made reservations at a place called Presidential Gardens in the Arlington area, not far from Langley, and a place where a lot of people like us stay while visiting headquarters.

"I have been at this typewriter all day and am pooped, trying to get my desk cleared.... Have written to Joe Steinmetz and to Bill Shawcross [Admiral commanding the USN aircraft carrier *Coral Sea* operating out of Subic Bay]. Jan and Stan have gone home and now have a $40 thou house in Fairfax, so I'll send you that address in case you need to reach us in Washington.... Am going to Sangley Point tomorrow, and to Clark Field next Wednesday with Rosemarie who has a chronic kidney problem; doesn't sound too neat, but I guess she can learn to live with it.

"That's all I can think of now. I'm so excited I can hardly do anything. So, Good Night. Happy Easter Egg—Good heavens, I don't have any egg coloring. Forgot all about Easter. Love to you both. I really adore you. Phyl"

In her spare time, Phyllis was avidly shopping in downtown Manila, especially for wooden artifacts such as bowls, plates, serving utensils, and decorative birds and animals. Most of these were made from monkeypod, a beautiful mahogany colored, two-tone wood, and were lightweight, distinctive, and perfect for Christmas presents. Some were amusing too, particularly the naked figure known as the wooden man in a barrel, who apparently had lost everything in a poker game. Phyllis bought a few of these for close friends and family. Most people

312

could not resist lifting the wooden barrel, which then disclosed the naked man inside and much more. The barrel concealed a huge, fully distended penis that snapped straight up and out and was proportionately the size of a baseball bat. These were real crowd pleasers.

Monday, April 8, 1968, Quang Duc

"Dear Phyllis,

It is now about 8:30 A.M. on the 8th. . . . The stock market is reported up about 11 points, isn't that great? . . . . Wish we had a lot more stocks. . . .

One of our guards went home last night feeling sick with bad stomach cramps or pains. This morning we are checking him closely for there were two deaths from bubonic plague that occurred in one of our villages nearby. I hope he doesn't have it. . . . The family plans to sacrifice a few animals to make him well. They do not believe in medicine, only in spirits. It is frightening at times to realize how primitive these people really are.

"Not too much going on these days, the VC are quiet. Had a few visitors, like two generator repairmen who came out from Nha Trang; our power went out the other night. And a chopper load of intelligence boys from Pleiku and Nha Trang were here to look at our Phoenix program. . . . The rains have started. Tonight for about an hour and the same amount two nights ago. Just the right amount after our long dry spell. . . . Since last November we have had less than three inches of rain. . . . *Lost in Space* is on the TV right now. I am listening but not looking at it. Ron, the Chef, and I are going to MACV tonight for dinner and a movie, to see something called *Hurry Sundown* with Robert Stack and Elke Sommers. She is in a lot of movies these days. This one is probably going to be a real bomb. I would rather go to a movie called *Phyllis and her Lover* or *The Lost Weekend in Manila*.

"The assassination of Dr. Martin Luther King is really stirring up the country, isn't it?.... Makes me wonder how it will be this summer in the District of Columbia and in other northern cities?...."

Martin Luther King, Jr., the 39-year-old Baptist minister and prominent black civil rights leader, was killed by a sniper as he stood on the balcony of his motel in Memphis, TN, on April 4, 1968. King had gone to Memphis to support a strike of city sanitation workers when James Earl Ray shot him. Ray pleaded guilty and was sentenced to 99 years in prison. King, a proponent of nonviolence in the struggle for racial and economic justice for black people, opposed involvement in the Vietnam War. He had aroused the wrath of official Washington as well as opposition from members of the black community. A Poor People's March on Washington in the spring of 1968 was cut short by his death.

LEAVING QUANG DUC

Two weeks before I left Quang Duc, our group shared a farewell dinner at our compound. Tien, our paymaster and general supervisor of the office staff, acted as master of ceremonies. He gave me a service tray with four tiny cups and a beautifully lathe-turned crop made of the distinctive tan and blond wood from the mountains. The employees prepared some snack foods and soft drinks, which went well with the cheese and crackers that Ron and I contributed. I do not remember making much of a speech but I am sure that I said some nice words, for I had become rather fond of them all. I recall being impressed with Tien, who offered toasts with Cognac and soda served over ice in wine glasses. It was an excellent, strangely dark mixture with a Scotch flavor.

I did not make an official farewell to my Montagnard chief because I was a coward. Last Tet I had given him a bottle of Beefeaters Gin, which he prized so highly that he invited me to his house for a drink from his private stock. His private stock was a vat of rice wine that was quietly fermenting and getting stronger with each passing day. Rice wine ferments best when flavored by tea leaves, which settle to the

314

bottom of the vat. He indicated that I was to sip through a long communal bamboo reed that reached down to the bottom of the vat among the tea leaves. I took a modest mouthful, hoping that the moment would pass quickly. To my distinct relief, it did not taste too badly but was very powerful. I took some intestinal bug remedy when I got home and survived without much distress.

My last few days were quiet yet busy enough. I attended briefings for visiting firemen and even had some overnight guests from Nha Trang who I suspected were assessing the need for more personnel changes. I was in a blissful state of mind contemplating the future. Ron and I prepared our last supper together of nice thick pork chops with a healthy portion of fragrant fried onions. I peeled the potatoes, set the table, whipped up a green salad, and made the coffee. We always enjoyed freshly baked French bread from a little bakery on the road to the airport. On some levels, I was going to miss this place.

Saying good-bye to Ron, my office staff, and the cadre people took most of the morning following the usual 8 A.M. military briefing. I told them that Ron De Costa would be handling any business until my replacement arrived. Never one to make speeches, I must say I rather enjoyed making that one. I planned to take the courier flight from Quang Duc a week before I was due in Saigon. Regulations required that all personnel departing on permanent change of station spend the last five days of their tour in Saigon in case there was some last-minute business. Experience had proven that once a man left Saigon it was very hard to get him back.

My bags were so fully packed that I was glad to be scheduled on a military flight to Clark Field. Military flights did not weigh baggage as strictly as did commercial aircraft. My extra load included a sleeping bag issued to Special Forces people, Montagnard artifacts, several hunting jackets, and a modified German Mauser infantry rifle given to me by an Air America pilot. This 7 millimeter rifle was the mainstay of the German soldier in World War II and fired a 5-round ammo clip using a turning bolt action. It made a fine deer rifle now and required a special permit for me to export it from Saigon. I also took along a Company-issued .25 calibre handgun. Checking out of Nha Trang was routine: in one day and out the next. My financial records, which were most important, balanced out to the penny. I

315

turned in my gear, said good-bye to everyone, and met a few of the newcomers at Ba Da Loc compound before boarding the courier.

I stayed at the Air Branch house in Saigon that Manny and I had first shared. Nguyen and her brood of five children were still on the premises and glad to see me. The little girls clung to my legs, and her teenage son gave me a nice handshake. I always gave Nguyen a few hundred piasters when I was in town, and this visit was no exception. Manny and I kept in touch and years later would serve together in the Washington area. I discovered that Willy had gone home and that Moe was either at home or in Beirut, Lebanon. I would meet Willy later in Thailand but never saw Moe again.

Saigon was still familiar but cleaner and brighter than I recalled. Some of the main streets were newly paved, and there was fresh paint in evidence. Our personnel office and financial people were pleasant and helpful in getting me processed and ready for travel to Manila.

I had a few easy days to spend in town and catch my breath. I lunched at the Caravelle Hotel across from the Rex Officers billet and walked to the rooftop where one overcast evening more than a year ago I watched C-47 gunships circle Ton Son Nhut Airport and drop yellow flares to show aerial gunners where to spray red and yellow fiery streams of .50 calibre bullets. The targets had been VC guerrillas slithering toward the field, hiding in the tall grass and rice paddies, and dragging B-40 rocket launchers that could explode allied aircraft.

I revisited the bar and open veranda at the Continental Hotel where a drink on the open porch was still fashionable. I walked toward the National Assembly Building and glanced up at a second-floor restaurant where Willy, Chuck, and I had lunch one day shortly after I arrived. The French restaurant served hot, garlic-seasoned escargot with fragrant hot rolls and a marvelous French onion soup.

I was saddened at the sight of a very young red-headed GI sitting on the front steps of the Caravelle Hotel wearing boots thick with laterite dust and still holding his M-16 rifle. The bar girls were smiling and waving as always and scantily clad in snug-fitting short skirts or wearing the high slit Au Dai dress. Their youthful faces were made up, lips painted red, and calling out, "Hey You, Hey Joe, You Come, You Come. Me number one...." The PX in downtown Saigon had its shelves heavily stocked with ladies' perfumes and thousands of cans of hair spray. These items were not being shipped home to wives and sweethearts but were bought and then lavished on local lasses in return for certain favors.

I remembered the 7 A.M. wake-up call of the Saigon Radio disc jockey who became famous for shouting "Goooooooood Morning, Vietnam!" I also remembered the long hot evenings in Saigon; it was too humid and stifling for sleeping indoors, so all the little kids were running and playing in the cool night air. I also recall how helpless I felt seeing a young mother with her toddler waiting in line at the sidewalk clinic hoping that the medic would do something about a lumpy, suppurating swelling on her child's head. The young mother had no bandages, nothing with which to treat the abscess, nothing to reduce the swelling or stop her child from crying. When she used a dried leaf to wipe pus from the wound, I had to look the other way and keep on walking. That such conditions existed made a mockery of our sense of values. I had learned quickly that life in South Vietnam was not for the faint of heart. In the days ahead when I would be offered another tour of duty in this impoverished land, I did not hesitate to decline, saying that I was not interested unless there was absolutely no other way for me to make a living.

When it was time for my flight, I was almost the first guy in the processing line. I half expected the VC sympathizer to strike again, but I had double-checked my documents and all went well. With a sigh of relief and only a brief backward look at the receding ground beneath my window, I was off for Clark Field.

Phyllis met me at Clark Field, and we went home to prepare for the next chapter in our grand adventure. The American President liner the *President Wilson* was due to sail for Hong Kong on May 1, 1968, and we would not be late.

THIRTEEN

Phyl Reports from Manila

T his chapter looks back at the 21 months that Phyllis spent in Manila. Our family arrived July 18, 1966, on a Pan Am jet and departed May 1, 1968, on the *President Wilson* ocean liner. Phyllis often wrote to her parents, Ken and Evie Warren, and other family friends about life in the Philippines. Her letters are entertaining and fun to read, as she describes how she and the children adjusted to life in their new world. Phyllis' writings reflect high-spirited boldness, a dash of courage, and a rollicking, pioneering sense of adventure. Perhaps you will glimpse the growth and development of the Swain children as they learned to be members of the community in a country full of brown-skinned people.

Monday, July 18, 1966 Manila

".... You will remember we just arrived at the Manila Airport. Two men from the office were there to meet us and to whisk us through Customs, in spite of the fact that we were last in line because I was trying to help some poor soul through quarantine, when I didn't know what I was doing either, and the usual happened; all the other passengers eased in ahead of our crazy group. . . ."

Tuesday, July 19, 1966, Manila

"Kids got up at 3 A.M. In fact we all did. We were hungry and it was morning time by our mental calendar. This jet set upset is all too true. Did manage to get a few more minutes of sleep but it was up again, down again until about 5 when we all had breakfast. Went to office. Cyndy, Adie and I, to check in and sign various things for ID cards and other papers. Ken went with us but Bill and Tom went to the pool with friend Delores Katsos. I had met her husband at the airport as he was on his way elsewhere with the other guys, like Saigon, and then saw her again yesterday at the commissary. In fact used her membership number as we weren't checked in yet. Everyone is so helpful. Delores has only been here a week, but obviously knows a lot more than we do. They have 4 children; John 3, Marcus 6, Matthew 9, and Kathy 11, so they fit rather well with our family. . . .

Friday, July 22, 1966 Manila

"Kathy Katsos very ill. Appears to have had a cerebral hemorrhage. . . . was found to have had a rare condition from birth which never showed up before. She is to be operated on Monday morning. Still in a coma. I mention this because her family is perfectly satisfied with the treatment she is getting, and with the Drs. in attendance. They flew in a neurologist from Clark Field, but I believe the operation will be performed by a Manila Dr. Her father, who was in Saigon, was contacted immediately and arrangements made to fly him back to Manila. Sorry this emergency arose, but now we know that if there is any trouble in our family we will get the same VIP treatment."

Monday, July 25, 1966 Manila

"Adie left this morning. Temporary duty elsewhere, like Saigon. Ordered curtains throughout the house, not at my expense. Bill has found a new friend, Mike, next door, Eurasian, I believe. Sarah and Dancing [our No 2 maid] are working out just fine. I do nothing as far as the house is concerned except buy food and plan menus. . . . Went to the office for pesos. I can cash checks there and exchange money for a little better rate than at the bank. Checked on the status of our air freight with no luck [still enroute]. Left children at the pool while in town on errands and then joined them for lunch. Cyndy was besieged at pool by group of six or eight boys, while I was swimming with our boys. She didn't think any of them were very exciting but at least she got a little action.

Wednesday, July 27, 1966 Manila

"Appliance guys here again. Worked all day installing 110 fan in 220 outlet. Had to practically rewire the whole house. . . . Had a visitor this A.M. Meg Litton from 18 Arguilla [we are 48]. She came just as we were about to leave by cab for Seafront to get some groceries, so she took us. I accused her of driving like a Filipino which didn't faze her one bit. Said it was the second time today she had been so accused. This means slipping through impossibly small openings, tooting horn at stop signs as no one stops anyway. Didn't stay to swim as Ken had a slight fever and I think a little ear disturbance due to so much swimming. [Ha. Little did we know then it was Mumps!] Came home, rested, took Tom to the Makati shopping center to the drug store which carries chemical supplies for a few test tubes."

Thursday, July 28, 1966 Manila

"Appliance people back again with their Big American Boss. Told them to remove ceiling fan already installed as it made too much noise. Needed a new bearing. This makes the third time they have changed this fan which is about 20 feet from the floor. It is a double-story living room at the point of installation. . . . which means we will have thousands of little Filipinos running around on the fan detail.

"Went bowling this afternoon with the kids. Charming experience. Cyndy and Tom bowled big pins. Ken, Bill bowled duck pins. It was hysterical. Didn't have much time to watch Cyndy and Tom, but the back view of Ken every time his ball went in the gutter was classic, even when the ball was in the gutter after the first few feet, which was the norm, he leaned and twisted with it like a pro. Guess he thought he could charm it out of the gutter. Ken had a glorious score of 6 and Bill came in with a smashing 14. Coranado Lanes, Makati Shopping Center, on Pasay Road, has never seen more gutter balls in such a short time. Guess we won't do that again for a while. Bill, however, when asked how he liked it, said 'It was a gas!' Mother felt like taking same.

"Came home to find drapery man had arrived to install curtains. Mr. Santos and crew of six proceeded to drill, hang rods, make dust, and hang curtains; two girls hemmed them as they hung, while Mr. Santos lounged around talking with me when he could, since I had to chase the boys from the carpenter at the screens and out of the way of the rod hangers. Managed to plan supper with Sarah while generally verged on hysteria. They all left at 5:30. I grabbed a drink, Ken fell asleep, Sarah served dinner, Ken woke up in the middle of same. Finally all quieted down and we retired to our air-conditioned bedrooms. Television in the boys room. I left them there watching *Bonanza* at 7:45 P.M. and now am in my own room where Cyndy will shortly join me since there is no A/C in her room yet."

Friday, July 29, 1966 Manila

"Yep, more fan deal. . . . they stayed all day again. Put up fan, take down fan. Three times for living room fan, twice for the dining room fan. Mr. Santos and crew arrived for more curtain hanging. Really couldn't count all the people coming and going, plus a visitor that came to see Sarah. Stayed in to watch all this going on and wrote invitations for Bill's party on August 1. Delivered same after dinner with Ken and Bill. Rather enjoyed the walking. Had four invitations to deliver, one gal was in bed, but at each other house was invited for a drink and reeled home with two boys about 9 P.M."

Saturday, July 30, 1966 Manila

"All house repairs finished. Thank Goodness. Decided to pretty up a bit so covered tin cans with shelf paper. For greens we have lots of long lasting kinds in our yard and Sarah snitched a lot of trailing variegated philodendron vines from our neighboring walls, which I hung in plastic cups and some Campbell soup cans. Very clever we Filipinos. I am really having a ball.

322

The Time of My Life

Tuesday, August 2, 1966 Manila

"Bill's party came off as planned yesterday, 2 James boys (2 & 4), 3 Watkins (boy 8, girls 10 & 11), 2 Katsos boys (3 & 9), 2 Lytton girls (5 & 7). Served cake made in borrowed pans, with borrowed mixer, ice cream, cokes, and a few favors and just let them race around madly. A few of the moms came in for a drink. Very pleasant and no sweat with my two handmaidens. My Gosh, it is marvy to have help. Next day went to the dispensary at the Embassy where we have privileges of free Doctor, drugs and other medical support. The Embassy grounds are on the bay side of Rojas Boulevard, and Adie's home office is across the street. While Meg (who had driven us in) was busy with the doctor, I decided to walk across Rojas, a feat requiring great skill and courage. (If you think it is tough walking across 41 [the Tamiami Trail] at Siesta Drive you ain't seen nothing.) The natives just go and seem to make it across, but I waited interminably for an opening just to get to the median strip, then I stood close to two Filipino men intending to cross when they did. One went and the other was as chicken as I.... My chief problem was that every taxi driver in Manila seemed to be free at that moment and all thought I was looking for a cab. The result being that each time I saw an opening in traffic, I was so busy waving off cabs that I couldn't make a move.... Made it finally, then home, rested, had dinner, and went out to play my first bridge game in Manila with next door neighbor Maureen Reeves. Met two other gals whose husbands are also engineers with Brown and Root (all three of them are from Houston) whose husbands commute to Vietnam. Their chief engineering office is here in Manila, but all work is performed in Vietnam. Enjoyed them very much.... You can see my life is not empty."

* * *

By the fall of 1966, Phyllis and family were comfortably settled in at 48 Arguilla in San Lorenzo Village. Tom and Bill successfully passed the entrance examinations required by the American School system and were enrolled and hard at work. Tom was in grade 5, Bill in grade 2, and Cyndy and Ken were at home. Cyndy planned to enter the University of the Philippines in December, and Ken would stay home until next year. Visiting the family every six weeks or so was the highlight of my life, as noted earlier. A conference of Asian powers scheduled for mid-October in Manila had the family caught up in the excitement of a presidential visit.

* * *

Monday, October 17, 1966 Manila

"The Asian Conference really has Manila in a complete whirl of cleanup activity. . . . Picture Sarasota's Bayfront Drive thigh high in grass and weeds, trash amidst the weeds, trash along the curbs, axle-breaking potholes in the roadway, fishing shacks on the bayside with bancas (beatup dugouts), nets, baskets and other paraphernalia and you have a general idea of Rojas Boulevard. Now picture thousands of little men with piles of hot asphalt, white paint for curbs, machete wielders, trash collectors, leaf sweepers, really doing a massive cleanup job for the Conference. All the hotels are undergoing a fast cleanup. Some civic-minded women are even doing over suites at their own expense, others doing over their homes and gardens in anticipation of housing the overflow from the hotels. There is feverish activity everywhere.

"As you exit the airport, the route all dignitaries will take crosses a bridge over the Pasig River from which you can see on both sides rows of waterfront shacks, filthy water, and trash beneath the houses built on stilts. I was amused to note that a picket fence is being built along the approaches to this bridge, about 12 feet high. Guess the idea is that which you can't clean, hide!

"I note in the morning paper that a group of ladies took it upon themselves to clean up the Customs Department at the airport, which will be a blessing for all. Hope they prevail upon the various inspectors to keep their ever ready hot little palms in their pockets. I think it would be keen if President Johnson slipped an inspector 20 pesos or so to get cleared in a hurry, in lieu of the usual hour. Also hope someone tells him to have his shot records in order. It seems there is a cholera outbreak in the Philippines, as well as Iraq, India,

Burma, Thailand and South Vietnam, not to mention a little plague. It's not so hard getting into the Philippines if you haven't been to the other places on the above list, but getting out is a different story. For instance, if by some remote chance you wanted to go to Lebanon, you will be subject to five days quarantine, in fact if you have no official reason to go to Lebanon, and who does except maybe Danny Thomas, you will be refused admission altogether.

"We have a very tongue-in-cheek daily columnist here who I read avidly, and he tells me that even the comfort stations in the Congressional Hall are being cleaned, which evidently means a real red letter day. In a way I am surprised they are ever used anyway, for I thought I had seen every man in Manila, at one time or another, taking the well known you know what behind or in front of the nearest tree, bush, fence, wall or nothing at all.

"Another little goodie I have to report is that Gary Lewis and the Playboys are scheduled to be in Manila the same day as LBJ. . . . I haven't decided which show to attend."

LBJ VISITS MANILA

Sunday, October 23, 1966 Manila

"We arrived at Seafront about noon on Sunday for I was afraid if we went any later we couldn't get there as I had read Rojas Blvd was to be closed an hour before the first visitor arrived. We had lunch in the main dining room as it was raining and when it cleared a bit the boys went swimming. About 2 P.M. we walked out to the road to join the group. . . . it wasn't too crowded; there were other club members, the Philippine ROTC, a contingent of the Philippine navy, a band, lots of flags. We were first on the curb. It was hot. It rained a bit and then we steamed, but we did see LBJ. Of course he turned his head the other way as he passed us, but Dean Rusk was on our side and he smiled and waved. Lady Bird was in the middle. They went by pretty fast, but at least we got a glimpse. The next car had [Ambassador] Lodge and [General] Westmoreland, and then a few more cars, but I couldn't or didn't recognize anyone else. The Korean, Vietnam and Thai delegations preceded Johnson who came by about 3:30. It was really quite exciting, particularly for the children who waved paper flags of every nation attending the conferences. So now I know what the Vietnam flag looks like, it was the only one I didn't recognize. Isn't that awful, when you realize we have over 300,000 troops in the country? After Johnson went by the group pretty well broke up not waiting for the Australian and New Zealand Prime Ministers."

October 27, 1966 Manila

"We had a quiet family celebration of Cyndy's birthday, which was almost obscured by a notice we received on the 26th saying President Johnson was going to speak to all government employees and members of the American community at the Embassy at 4 P.M., so I figured I'd better go, but also figured that another hot wait for the kids was not in order, so went by myself. No cars were allowed in the Embassy Compound so we were bused from the Seafront Compound. Mucho people on the front lawn, bayside. The sun was shining brilliantly and it was very hot. I stood with many others quite close to the speakers stand on the terrace. At 3:45 Ambassador Blair, Mrs. Johnson and Mrs. Blair made an appearance. Blair greeted us and informed us that due to prior commitments LBJ wouldn't be there, but Lady Bird would speak to us. Which she did. The only word I remember was "extry" and that really made my afternoon. I suspected that LBJ was in Vietnam and this mornings paper confirmed my suspicion. Glad he made it over there. I do think it was much more important than speaking to us. . . . but not delighted that we were used as a cover-up. I was glad I had not taken the children, because I was feeling a bit guilty about it. It was an interesting experience even if I didn't get to see the President. We were invited to go to the airport this morning to see him off, but I decided to forgo that pleasure. Besides LBJ is not winning any votes here since all leaves to Manila from Vietnam were cancelled for the week before and the week after his visit.

"One other slightly snide observation. There are AID people all over the place. I don't know exactly how many families are in Manila, but there are at least 300. I think they [the Democrats] are trying to get so many people over here that when this year's budget allotment runs out, it will be cheaper for Congress to vote another appropriation rather than transport all these people home. Maybe it is part of the poverty program. Many of them look like they need all the help they can get. I'm probably being unkind, for I guess they are doing a good job. Many are farmer types, and go out in the Barrios [villages]. If you walk off the main road, perhaps I should say leave the main pothole, and walk down any muddy cart path you will find a bunch of houses with a bunch of people and a herd of carabao, and AID folks telling them about fertilizers, plows, tractors, hybrid seeds, rotation of crops, drainage, irrigation, sanitation, and how to get rid of the flies or malaria and H-fever mosquitoes. I imagine they also drop little hints re birth control and the like, or 'we are trying to teach you how to either/or feed this ever-swelling population; increase your herds, and decrease your hordes.' This action is going on in these islands as well as in Vietnam.

"Seriously, though, I really think the Filipinos are great. They have a long way to go but are really trying to help themselves, and they do have the only democratic nation in the far east, which. . . . is quite unique, and quite difficult to manage in view of the many islands, many dialects, many mountains, poor roads and poor communications, as well as many poor people, many lousy crooks, and many illegal-entry Chinese. The Filipinos are friendly, clean of person, kind, humorous and nice looking. They strive for better education, have pride and, except for a corrupt element in government which seems to have fostered a general acceptance of graft and business dishonesty, they do have a good chance of making this a first-rate, self supporting country following. . . . the principles of the United States. We're having a ball."

* * *

Ferdinand Marcos was President of the Philippines from 1965 to 1986 and died an exile in Honolulu in 1989. He first won election as the leader of the Nationalist Party and made good progress in agriculture, industry, and education. He was elected to a second term in 1969, but then his administration began to be troubled by increasing urban guerrilla activities and student unrest. Marcos imposed martial law in 1972 because of Communist and subversive forces and assumed extraordinary powers, including suspending the writ of habeas corpus for the next ten years. As an authoritarian leader in control of the military, he and his wife held the reins of power ruthlessly yet were popular. Imelda, a former beauty queen, was as powerful as her husband and quite a profligate shopper. After they fled the palace in Manila, some 3,000 pairs of shoes belonging to Imelda were found in her closet. The Marcos' led a government that often used strong-arm tactics to thwart or even kill the political competition, while the nation sank into economic stagnation and continued to be plagued by a growing Communist movement in the rural areas. Marcos finally was deposed and fled the country on February 25, 1986, at the urging of the U.S. Government. He and his entourage took up luxurious residences in Honolulu, where he died on September 28, 1989. It was later disclosed that the Marcos family had looted the Philippine economy of billions of dollars through embezzlement and other corrupt practices. The U.S. Government indicted Ferdinand and Imelda on racketeering charges, which in 1991 still remained to be settled.

* * *

During October and November, Phyllis' father was going through a period of depression. Phyllis thought he was suffering from the effect of the drinking man's diet he was following and urged him to drop it. He went to see Drs. Warson and Steele, psychiatrists, and even went into Memorial Hospital for observation, but the doctors could offer no medical remedy. Phyllis knew her father so well that she thought it was all in his head and offered the following advice:

Sunday, November 20, 1966 Manila

"I received the news of Pappy's second stay in the hospital. I sure am sorry and do hope that all is well now and that Pappy is true to his word and keeps smiling. There really isn't much point in doing anything else. One sees and feels an awful lot of misery around here.... believe me, we all have much to be thankful for. Think of all the

328

people who have never known anything in their lives but grubbing around in the muck trying to raise enough rice to live on. I must say that as I travel a bit away from the city the farmers don't seem to have such a bad life. The country is beautiful. Seafood is plentiful, the rice fields look lush, their nipa huts, while crude, are comfortable for the climate, and they seem happy enough. It is the poor people crowded in the cities, like our own cities, that suffer the most. Anyhow, we all have much to be thankful for if we don't live to see another day. . . . we have had all the necessary comforts; love and companionship with those we love and admire, so one who allows depression to take over is just worried about self, which to put it crudely, is just plain selfish. My only suggestion, and you won't like it, is to forget the Steeles and Warsons, as I guess you have, but if you still have trouble seeing the bright side of things, you would be doing me and yourself a huge favor to go to St. Boniface some Sunday to the 11:00 service and listen to Dr. Large. He is the greatest therapist in the world. If you take my advice, don't go on the first Sunday of the month, as that is usually communion and you wouldn't go for that at all. End of sermon."

∗ ∗ ∗

In the fall of 1966, the Republican party in Florida won the governor's seat by electing Claude Kirk. "Hooray for Kirk and the republicans,"wrote Phyllis. "I didn't get to vote as my application for absentee ballot was misdirected to another APO and by the time I got it, it was too late to make all the necessary arrangements. Adie did though, so at least the family was represented."

Sunday, November 20, 1966 Manila

"Billy's books have come! All six at once and he was thrilled. I should have him send you a thank you note, but haven't as yet. It is a bit of a chore with a second grader."

November 29, 1966 Manila

". . . . Am so pleased to get a good report about Pappy's health. Hope the picture continues to be rosy. I think it is great you are going

329

to Summit, NJ, for Christmas [with Shirley and Jack Wade and their family. The visit must have been good therapy for Ken Warren's depression. There were no further reports on this subject. Perhaps Phyllis' advice was good medicine.]

"We had a fine time at our Thanksgiving, which we celebrated a few days earlier because Adie had to go back to Nha Trang.... It is 7:30 A.M. now and I had thought I would get this letter finished before Ken discovered I was up, but the little darling is now at my elbow asking questions. So if my train of thought is more disjointed than ever you will know why.

"Thanksgiving day our Church of the Holy Trinity had joint services with the Union Church and Ambassador Blair read President Johnson's message.... Met the Blairs formally for the first time. They were most cordial and had heard from Janice Palmer and knew who we were. They invited me to dinner on Dec 10th, a dinner preceding the annual Embassy Ball, and though they knew Adie won't be here, they asked anyway. I said I thought not in view of no husband, but Blair said, think it over. They would send me an invitation anyway. Have not received it yet and if I do, am not sure whether to go. Perhaps one does not lightly turn down the Ambassador. I will let you know the outcome, but thought you would be interested in this inconclusive, poorly told story.

"Love and miss you both. Stay healthy and have a wonderful time with Shirlo...."

December 2, 1966 Manila

"I have decided to go to the Ambassador's party. Sort of figured it might be the only time I or we might be asked and decided to take advantage of it. When I called Mrs. Sternburg, head of protocol to whom I was to RSVP, she seemed pleased that I accepted. Said there would be 26 to 30 in the party, and when I mentioned I had hesitated since I would be unescorted, she said not to worry about that at all. In fact, Mrs. Westmoreland is coming down from Clark Field, and of course her husband cannot be with her. I am sure that in the party there will be several unescorted gentlemen.... Wow. I am a little nervous about the whole thing and will have to be very careful about what I drink and say. I do have my long red dress that Christie [Wisner] gave me, you know the one that I wore to Mellie and Jimmy's [McMichael] party. So that is no problem.

"Cyndy is all set at UP. Just has to formally register on the 9th. There is no room available at present at the International House, so she is prepared to commute. Ken is growing up also. Loves Sarah which pleases me a lot. When you realize that none of us have phones, except Delores, so most everyone has to leave their own home to make a call. All these comings and goings, plus visits to the various doctors and delivering the news from house to house in person, is all pretty time consuming, but a really marvelous experience in human relations and in ingenuity. I shall now go and make the rounds of the halt and blind, maimed and unhappy to bring a little of my sunshine into their lives. Oh brother. . . . I'm full of it this morning, maybe I should go back to bed."

THE AMBASSADOR'S PARTY

December 22, 1966 Manila

"Now to the Ambassador's dinner. I looked great, in my long tangerine Dynasty dress. Had shoes dyed to match [done here] and wore a borrowed sari type stole with gold threads in it. My good neighbors, the Reeves, lent me their driver and he deposited me at the doorstep of the Blair's residence not far from the Embassy. A charming old house, beautifully decorated. Time 7:30. Only one other couple had arrived, Mr. and Mrs. [Adele] Simpson, she being the dress designer. I was very pleased to meet her. She is tiny, and sort of cute. We had cocktails in the living room, standing around. The extra man was a Mr. Caulder, minister of economics. Tall, white haired, about 60. His last post was in Jordan and he knew one of our group whose last post had been Jordan. Next to arrive were Admiral and Mrs. Gulickson; he is Commander of Subic Bay, an installation of some 12,000 people. They are a very handsome couple, he looks like [the film star] Michael Rennie. He knows Bill Shawcross and said he had recently reviewed orders for Bill; thinks Bill will soon be at Subic with his own ship. Don't think I am not a little nervous and excited by

331

Adrian Swain

all this brass. Next comes Admiral Kossler and his wife, also most attractive. He is Commander of Sangley Point, a smaller Navy installation where we have commissary privileges. I had just read a book about WW II and the submarine corps, and recognized his name for he was a submariner, now on administrative duty. They knew friends from Arizona, so we had a 'Do you know?' about that part of the world.

"General and Mrs. James Winn arrived next, Major General, that is. He is Commander of JUSMAG [Joint U.S. Military Assistance Group]. He works with the Chief of Staff of the Philippine armed forces, lending them our know-how, I guess. The rest of the guests were less spectacular. Two of note were the Dunns and Aikens, about my age, residing here with the Coppers Company. I sat with Admiral Gulickson, General Winn, Mr. Simpson, Mrs. Aiken and Mrs. Sicip, a Filipino lady of local stature whose husband is an attorney. We had half broiled chicken or perhaps it was something more elegant like Rock Cornish hen, but it was good, preceded by borscht. The Admiral and I both had to look around a bit to figure out which spoon to use. In front of the dinner plate was a large spoon and fork, which turned out to be for dessert. Chinese peas were the only vegetable served. These were young peas in the pod, very green and rather crispy. Dessert was an ice cream dish, with something like cones in it, very crispy and served with a caramel sauce. All very good. Coffee and liqueurs were served in the living room. Then we all went to the ball. I went with Mr. Caulder.

"The ball was outside on the Embassy lawn facing Manila Bay. It was a lovely evening. Lanterns were strung all over. Tables placed around a huge terrazzo dance floor. We did not do too much dancing. I did dance with the Ambassador; however, it was sort of dark and I'm not sure anyone noticed. Darn it. We had two tables adjacent, at ours were the Winns, Kosslers, Dunns, Aikens and Mr. Caulder. It was here that I most enjoyed talking with everyone. Mrs. Westmoreland wasn't at the party. She had some function to attend at Clark, and now that her husband is being mentioned as a possible [presidential] candidate, I am more sorry than ever not to meet her.

"It was a most memorable evening and I felt very flattered to be included, and fairly well equipped to handle the detail. My wealth of acquaintances came in very handy. And of course, the sterling education in the social graces learned from my dear family, kept me on the right track.

"Cyndy started classes on the 14th, after quite a rat race getting registered. There are very few Americans in the school, and she really feels a bit discriminated against. However, I am very proud of her for sticking to it, and I am sure she will be more at home in a week or so. We think there will be a vacancy in the International House by the first of January. Cyndy went to a ball last night at the Manila Polo club. Very ritzy. She looked divine. I made her a dress, red satin bodice and a white satin, long, straight skirt with slit in the side. She was really a knockout. Cyndy's date was an American. A post graduate from the American School from California, named Steve who has a sister that Cyndy likes. And we have applied to the University of South Florida for the fall semester, so we shall see. I took pictures and she took some of me the night I went out, so they will be forthcoming soon."

Monday, January 9, 1967 Manila

"I am an avid reader of *Time, Newsweek, Stars and Stripes, Manila Times* and I am not too pleased with some of the stuff that comes out of the American press. . . . This *New York Times* man in North Vietnam, Harrison Salisbury, is disturbing to us out here in never never land. Will be curious to see what he says after he leaves North Vietnam [which he reports on so favorably]. Am glad that John Steinbeck is in Vietnam. His reports prove interesting. Did not see Bob Hope [who toured the naval base at Subic] but I hear that Barry Goldwater is in Japan and plans to go to Vietnam. If he comes here I will make every effort to see him. [Phyllis knew Barry Goldwater and his family well during her modeling days in Phoenix, during World War II before Barry became the senior senator from Arizona.]"

CORREGIDOR

February 10, 1967 Manila

"Adie and I took a hydrofoil trip across Manila Bay to the island of Corregidor last week. Going over we were on the upper deck, which was more like a pilot's deck with six seats and the pilot. We swayed from side to side; it felt like being on a wildly swaying railroad train. Visibility in the morning hours is usually poor due to ground haze so there was not much to see until we approached the Bataan Peninsula where we stopped to land passengers not going on to Corregidor. The land here was lush, green, and beautiful. . . . except for the mountains the area looked like Boca Grande or Marco Island south of Sarasota. The water was clear and blue.

"We arrived at Corregidor in about an hour and got into Jeepneys, each holding 10 passengers. We were mostly Americans, about 30 in all. We went into the famous Malinta tunnels first. They were not lighted, so couldn't see too much, but to think that there were 13,000 people in these tunnels during the days of the siege is incredible.

"Corregidor was fascinating, slightly eerie, as no one lives on the island today. The jungle has taken over. The silence is complete. The roads are very hilly, mostly gravelly, but vestiges of old curbing and gutters still remain.

"Our guide was very good. Knew his history of the last 27 days of shelling that was so severe it actually changed the topography of the island by eliminating entire hillsides and toppling cliffs. The enlisted mens' barracks were one mile long and could house 8,000 people. The officers' barracks were much the same, but all just ruins now. Most of the damage was done in one day when an estimated 75 tons of bombs were dropped by the Japanese, after that everyone stayed in the tunnels.

"The huge naval gun emplacements guarding the approaches to Manila were impressive, massive, some almost intact, others ruined. It was a very moving experience when you realized the hardships those on the island experienced. They were very brave. It was all the more poignant because of the silence, the lushness of hibiscus gently waving in the tropical breezes and wild flowers growing around the silenced guns. A most memorable trip, and a impressive reminder of the price of freedom and the dearness of it.

Sunday, February 11, 1967 Manila

"8:30 P.M. . . . a typical Swain day. Church in the A.M. for Cyndy and me, beautiful weather before the clouds began to build up and a beautiful view of the harbor this morning. Bataan stood out clearly in the distance and all the ships seemed so close in and brilliant. The harbor is always jammed with ships of all nations, all sizes, hundreds of them.

"There was a huge fire nearby in a new 13-story building. The top two stories were on fire all day. Great flames and smoke, and still not out by five this afternoon. They didn't have hoses long enough, nor ladders long enough to reach, and water pressure was insufficient. Typical. The last time we looked, it had cooled enough so firemen could hose it down from the adjoining building. Much excitement... so much so it must have stirred the fire bug in our small ones. I had taken Ken, Mike, Mark Katsos and Bill to see the fire. At 6:15 I went to get Bill for dinner, believing him to be in the vacant lot near our house. I looked in that direction and saw a raging brush fire. Bill, Gregory, Mark and Mike were all leaving the scene. Bill and Mike were in quest of water but the other two were making tracks. The gardener near the adjacent house had a hose going on it. I quickly put on my tennis shoes, grabbed the fortunately wet floor mop and raced down the road and set to beating it out, which we were able to do but it was dangerously near the foliage of the next property. Thank heaven for the wall. Several of the village guards arrived on the scene, saw that the gardener and I had it under control and left. I believe they will call on me for the next brush fire. . . . I commended the two that stayed with me and did not run. Am not sure who set it, but I figure all are to blame in a case like that.

"Needless to say the whole affair was not one of pervading calm. Ken was running around in the road in his bare feet. Julie [our dog] was loose and also running around, Cyndy and Connie [our new maid] were running around after Ken and Julie, while all the help in the nearby houses were hanging over their respective gates, getting a huge charge out of the whole thing.

"Then we had a few utterances of bad words on the part of Bill and Ken who were sent to the tub and bed. . . . in all of this we did manage to get dinner. Then Tom's friend, Brog, arrived. Mark Katsos arrived to pick up something he had forgotten, accompanied by his mother, sister and brother John, all on bikes. Then Steve arrived to take

Cyndy to the movies, while Sarah strolled in from her day off. And so it goes. . . . never a dull moment."

March 10, 1967 Manila

"Everyone fine. Tom more than ever interested in his chemistry. Has all sorts of equipment and seems to know what he is doing. Our new maid, Connie, is great and takes Ken on outings often. They have been to Cartimer market, which is a huge sprawling place with everything from plants and pets, to shoes, linens, material, and fish. Earlier they went to Luneta Park downtown near the Embassy. They went by bus and Jeepney, which I am not brave enough to do. After the other boys get out of school, I will see that they have similar experiences.

"Ken talks in a very clipped way, such as saying 'lit tle'. I'm not sure why except perhaps in order to be better understood.

"Cyndy is having fun at school now and has a room she shares with two other girls. Goes out to dinner, to movies or to concerts and other activities at school, which she missed before. She is going to the international ball with someone I don't know. The point is, she is doing things even if she doesn't enjoy them 100%. I have a feeling that when she gets back to the States, she will begin to realize how many interesting and fun things she did do while here.

"Incidental information: The Filipinos use 'f' for 'p' and vice versa. I am going to make a list of the odd words that result some day for it is hilarious. Like, "fark your car". . . . Cyndy and I really broke up one day at an elegant fashion show when the M.C. said enthusiastically, while drawing for door prizes, 'The next prize is an excellent sample of Filipino handicraft.' Phonetically it came out 'Filipino handicrap.'. . . A few more good ones: fregnant for pregnant, fink means pink, U.P. comes out U. Fee. . . . Adie wrote that he had heard a Filipino songstress singing with a band in Saigon about the 'Gleen, Gleen Glass of Home'. . . . enough of that.

"I have learned to loaf again and I love it. I don't even have to tell my cook what to serve. In fact I don't tell anyone anything. They all just do what ever needs doing. The house is always spotless. The windows always clean. The car always shining. The dog always clean. Shoes are always shined. The lawn always watered. Even the garbage is collected silently in the dead of night. This garbage detail only applies to ritzy subdivisions such as ours. The rest of the populace just rolls it around until it gets lost, hopefully. The only thing I have to do is wind my watch, brush my teeth, and go to the john. I have even taken to going to the hairdresser. For 5 pesos a throw one cannot afford to spend time washing and setting the head. 5 P's is $1.25. Tips get a little out of hand, as one washes, one sets, one massages the neck, and one combs out, but at 50 centavos a tip it comes to 2 pesos or another 50 cents. Yes, I am really suffering.... The only exciting news to add is that your shy grandson, Tom, has been elected President of his class. Isn't that terrific? He is really quite proud, and so am I, as well as slightly surprised. His report card was quite good. His only A was in science, the rest equally divided between B's and C's, which is ok. Bill came through with all C's which is also ok."

May 8, 1966 Manila

".... We finally got to a beach. Took us two hours by car and 15 minutes by motorized banca to Bamboo Beach. It was lovely. Feeling that salt water and sand underfoot was a great treat. We went with Delores Katsos and her kids. She had a driver for the day, so we followed them. Past the Taal Volcano which is threatening to erupt any day and then down from the 3,000 foot ridge westerly to the China Sea. The scenery was beautiful.... many sheer drops on either side as we descended, but as we drew nearer the coast, the occasional glimpse of the water was spectacular. We reached our destination, a village named Wawa, where we left our cars under guard and boarded two motorized bancas. We had a 15-minute ride along the shore to a cove known as Bamboo Beach. It was quite a sight, clear water and white sand rimmed with coconut trees. Quite tropical with a few private homes nestled in the trees against a high rocky cliff behind them. This was 'break-away' day [like skip day] for the students [15-17 years old] at the Batangas School of Fisheries, so we had quite a bit of company. Filipinos love children and these youngsters were no exception. Soon they began moving in on us, after staring for a while [staring is a disconcerting national pastime]—then playing with our

337

kids, and eyeing Cyndy. Our little boys loved the attention of the Filipinos, made sand castles, were tossed around in the water and generally spoiled. The older boys joined in the water games, while Delores and I were besieged with questions about the U.S. While Batangas is not far from Manila by our standards, it is by theirs. Many never leave their villages and thus see very few foreigners. The fisheries school teaches how to raise food fish in shallow ponds by making dams in the flat land near the sea, as well as making fish pens, weirs, netting, preserving, smoking, canning and the like. Very practical, I must say.

"We stayed at the beach from 10 until 4 so we were all sunburned, happy and exhausted by the time we got home at 7:15 in the dark. The kids are beginning to be good travelers and the trip was well worth the effort.

"May 1st was Philippines Labor Day. I sent the kids to the movies to see *That Darn Cat* with Sarah and Connie. On May 5th, Cyndy, Tom, Matt Katsos and I went out to dinner in honor of Tom's birthday. It was pleasant. We had a good time and I was proud of the group. Next day, Tom and I went on a boat trip on the Pasig River. Ken had a fever, Cyndy didn't care to go, and Bill is a bit fearful of boats at this time. All in all, I was just as pleased not to have the whole gang with me and had a very relaxed time. The trip was arranged by one of the gals, in lieu of our monthly luncheon, so there were 43 in our group including children. We were on the water from 9:20 to 11 when we landed on Celito Lindo Island for lunch before returning to Manila. The temperature keeps pretty well up in the 90's now and if I didn't have an air-conditioned car I probably wouldn't go anywhere.

"Adie and I are now sending tapes back and forth and the kids love it. Hearing me read a letter just bores them, but hearing Dad talk is the greatest. Ken had me play the last one three times in a row, and still wanted more. . . . When we cut a tape for Adie, Ken can't wait till we replay it 'so I can hear that little boy talk to me.'"

Wednesday, June 21, 1967 Manila

"Cyndy, Tom and I went to Clark Field to get some things for Cyndy. Had a nice trip but the roads were much worse than the last time due to recent rains. I have decided the Filipinos repair their roads with flour and water paste plus a few pebbles, for one rain washes out all the potholes as if there was nothing in them."

July 7, 1967 Manila

"Thank you so much for the cute card with the firecrackers and the birthday check, but I can't cash it. You made it out to Phyllis W. Wade. How about them apples? Had a nice birthday. The kids gave me some lovely presents and [cousin] Jane Swanson, bless her heart, brought over a beautiful store cake with *Happy Birthday Aunt Phyl* and *Good Luck Cyndy* on it. We were at their home for dinner the night before my birthday. She had little gifts for both of us and had ordered the cake for that night. When it was not delivered on time, she brought it over the next morning. Very nice of her.

"The boys start to school on Monday. Ken goes to kindergarten at a school here in our village. . . . I don't feel very inspired in the letter department today, but perhaps the next letter will be better." [Poor Phyllis was experiencing the "empty nest syndrome," depressed by the departure of her pal Cyndy, but true to her word she did recover.]

July 13, 1967 Manila

"I am free as a bird in the mornings for the kids are all in school! First time in eleven years we haven't had a baby in the house, and it doesn't make me sad one bit. Ken has taken to school very well. The first day Connie stayed with him, but he has gone alone since then, no sweat. This morning I said, 'Can you go to your room alone?' and he said, 'Oh sure, let me give you a kiss.' And off he went. Feels very grown up. . . ."

August 23, 1967 Manila

"Monday afternoon I went to a tea at Seafront given by Sharon Fink. . . . It was nice as teas go but teas can go you know where as far as I am concerned. I did take Ken and Bill to the pool with Sarah so the afternoon was not a total loss. Tom had homework to do and wanted

339

to launch another one of his rockets. It was abortive, I understand, because new batteries were needed for his launching pad. It was a tad embarrassing because he was in Desmarinas, the new subdivision across the highway from us which has much vacant ground. With the OK of the guard, and with quite a group of Filipinos assembled to witness the launch, it failed to launch. Oh well, you can't win them all.

"Tom had a tennis lesson yesterday afternoon, and guess who had one too. Six pesos per hour and we each took half. I learned a great deal and was not too pooped. A little stiff this morning, but I sure did enjoy it and am looking forward to the next one. The Pro is very good and easy to work with, an older fellow who teaches at the 'Y' part of the time, by the name of Blanco.

"Bill starts Cub Scouts today. Sarah has just returned from a trip to downtown Manila to get his uniform. I sent her, for I knew if I went I'd never get these letters done before I have to ride the school bus at 11:45. That is a real chore."

Friday, September 29, 1967 Manila

"Great Scott.... I can't believe another month is over. The time just seems to fly along. We only have seven months to go, and I will leave with some regret because this has really been great. When I read about the strikes, school problems, riots, and dirty politics, which I do avidly, I'm glad to be removed from it all. Of course, it is difficult to be removed from Cyndy, but I do feel the boys are getting an excellent education, and a better feeling of the world in general. You know, integration problems do not exist here. The government workers are all races, and all mingle freely. The children have met negroes in school for the first time, as well as Japanese, Filipinos, Chinese, English, Dutch, German, and so on. One of our friends is a Puerto Rican negro, married to a white man. She just had her third child and my children can't wait to see what color he is. Her others are light brown, as she is. I saw the baby the other night. He looks white. His hair is straight; however, one of her others has slightly curly hair, and one is almost wooly. It also shows the children that white, negro, brown-skinned and people with yellow skins can be equal socially, given the opportunity. This is good for, certainly in their lifetime, there will be a lot more mingling of the races, and it is just as well they have no built-in prejudices to overcome.

"Not much family news. . . . Tom and I are enjoying our tennis lessons and both doing rather well. Last night went to my second monthly Cub Scout meeting at the American School where all members of the 13 Cub Scout dens meet. Awards are given, there were competitive games, a full program. The kids love it so I will try to be a good sport. Bill is the only scout in our family, and he thinks it is neat stuff.

"A note from Janice Palmer saying she would be on the liner *President Cleveland* which docks at 8 A.M. on October 4th and departs at 10 that same evening. I plan to meet the ship and see if we can get together. Bill Shawcross may be in Subic the weekend of the 7th or 14th. I told Bill to call anytime. He wrote saying he was in the area but was about to go out on a mission. I read recently that his ship, the *Coral Sea*, is participating in air strike sorties over North Vietnam.

"Am reading all about the Republican doings. I think Rockefeller is rather interesting, although I never liked him very much and frowned on his treatment of Barry [Goldwater], but he certainly has experience and the brain resources of his entire family behind him. Certainly his family has far more on the ball and far more integrity than those creepy Kennedys. Will be curious to watch Reagan. I recall the one speech he made for Barry, and how profoundly affected I was by his personality. I can't help thinking if he got on the campaign trail and on television, that his impact might be overwhelming, whether he has experience or not. The U.S. certainly needs someone to bolster its fading image, and to bolster its citizens into some kind of togetherness or patriotism, instead of the apparent trend where everyone thinks what's in it for me, and indulges in mass preoccupation about self.

"Oh well, I certainly am running off at the mouth this morning, the first morning I have been home all week without millions of things to do, which might explain my present mood.

"I have confirmed our return reservations for May 1, 1968. Two adjoining cabins, first class, upperdeck. I believe the tab will be about 4 grand. Couldn't happen to nicer people, say I. We arrive in Honolulu May 15th and, at the moment, plan to fly to the States from there.

K.C., maybe you had better have the fishing tackle ready for the boys when they get there, for that is all they talk about, especially Tom."

Thursday, October 6, 1967 Manila

"I met Janice Palmer's boat when it docked about 8:15 A.M., and managed to bluff my way on board by asking if the Ambassador had arrived yet, and that I was supposed to be with him. Actually, I knew he would be there, and knew he knew I would be there. I meant to watch for him, but was in an out-of-the-way spot on the docks with a bunch of dockworkers. Anyhow, I did get on and he was there. He talked to Janice on the phone and believe it or not she was not up yet. Bill Blair and I had both expected her to be hanging over the rail waving to us. The Ambassador left the ship and I went to her stateroom. It was much fun to see a familiar face. . . . the first since I had left Sarasota. Spent the whole day with her, shopping, then lunch with the Blairs. . . . to my house to see the children and to do a little sightseeing around our area. The Blairs had invited me to dinner, but believe it or not, I turned them down. Actually, I figured I would be exhausted, and had promised the boys to take them aboard ship to see off some other friends who were leaving that evening with Janice. So, around 5 P.M. we went aboard, looked over the ship with Janice and then bid her good-bye so she could dress for dinner with the Blairs. We stayed on the ship until about 8:30 with a gang of other friends saying good-bye to the Goethe family and then went home and tumbled into bed. . . . Janice was most appreciative and so were the Blairs who didn't have a lot of free time to spend with her. The Blairs are leaving on the 24th of the month for home. He has been a good and effective ambassador. I am not sure who his replacement is to be. [William McCormack Blair, Jr., served as Ambassador in Manila from August 5, 1964, to October 23, 1967.]

"Bill Shawcross arrived in town the day after Janice sailed and stayed at the Army Navy club. He came over for dinner and a nice visit with the family. His ship is at Subic Bay. I would love to take the boys to see it, but it is a horrible 5-hour drive, no other way to get there for us. Everything else is fine. Adie in a new spot and new activity [at Quang Duc] and very pleased with the situation."

342

The Time of My Life

October 8, 1967 Manila

"Dear Cyndy, we received your tape and enjoyed it so much, as well as the two letters we received the same day. . . . I love your letters. They are most expressive. Also like the little notes on the envelope. Very Cyndy to me. I am very excited about your sorority. Ebby wrote that Phil [Toale] had mentioned you had joined a sorority which I think is rather cool. . . . it is flattering that you were sought after by so many.

"Have made note of the items you would like to have maybe for Xmas and will do what I can. Haven't been to Sangley for several weeks, but will go next week and see if they have any jewelry goodies. . . . I have ordered a jewelry box for your birthday (great surprise) but it will be a month or two before you get it, because they are out of stock.

"Re Christmas and wanting to see Manila. Oh Cyndy, we would love it but we just can't afford it. As I tried to explain to you once, we were thousands in debt when we came over, and have been paying back like mad, but are still about 4 grand in the hole. Your dad and I have to figure that we aren't getting any younger, and Pop is worried if anything happens to him, how we will get along, or see that the boys get to college, so we can't say, come on and see us, much as we would love to. Love you and miss you greatly, am proud of you, and think you are the greatest. . . ."

October 21, 1967 Manila

"Dear Mother and Dad. . . . sorry about the delay between letters, but as you know it always takes me a little time to settle down into my routine after a visit from Adie. He arrived at Clark Field on the 10th and departed on the 16th. I had planned to drive up alone on the 10th but Sarah, Jan, and a few others were nervous about my making the trip alone during election time, so Jan went with me. The trip through Huk country was uneventful, and while I know of no incidents in the past year involving Americans, they are always shooting up somebody and during the current campaign guns are even more in evidence. Now that paid trips to Manila have been stopped, this is much the best way for Adie to get here. The round trip costs about $45 as opposed to $165 on Pan Am.

"Had a nice note from Kay Brown. Glad she is going to Paris to visit [her son] Fred and Pat Painton [who are with *U.S. News and World Report* magazine]. Give her my love.

"I was so thrilled to get your letter saying you had passports in the works! I am delighted you plan to stop in Honolulu and in Hong Kong. Hope the shots don't get you down. Any time in November is perfect. When I told Sarah and Connie last night they were all excited and are busy making great plans for Thanksgiving. Adie plans to be here on the 17th, so we are hoping this coincides with your plans."

* * *

After the welcome Warren visit, the days and weeks seemed to zip along. I managed to get home for a Christmas visit. The busy and exciting Christmas and New Year's holidays passed, climaxing a very busy 1967. On the war front, there was an unexpected flareup in activity triggered by the Tet offensive in South Vietnam. The *Tet Surprise,* as it was called, created havoc for about six weeks and caused me to wonder if we had been wise to extend beyond January. Before long, Phyllis' letters began to flow again.

February 29, 1968 Manila

"Hi All: I'm happy to report that Adrian did get his leave in February. Things have been pretty hairy in Vietnam since the first of February, and we gals holding the Manila fort have been a bit nervous. However, all husbands are accounted. Adie and four other guys came in on the 18th via Air France, the first flight Air France made out of Saigon since the shooting started. They were to return on the 24th, but Air France decided to overfly Saigon. The same held true for Pan Am, so he had to remain here for an extra week. Hurray.

"They departed this morning at 6:30 and are pretty sure to be in Saigon by noon. A much better time to arrive than the previous schedule of 6:30 P.M., which is only a half hour before the 7 P.M. curfew.

"While Adie was in Manila, his village was mortared by the VC, and his province chief and the chief American advisor were killed in a helicopter crash.... so I figured it was a good time for him to be with us. By now the situation in the Gia Nghia is somewhat under control. He says it is nothing to worry about. So I am trying not to....

"The next few weeks will go quickly for me for I have a million details to take care of and nothing is done easily here. I expect the car will be sold about April 1st, so must get my outside running around done pronto. Next will be the packing out of surface shipment goods about the 3rd week in April. Then the final packing of air freight and all the suitcases. Most exciting. Adie will return about April 26th, which means he has about six more weeks in Province, then to Nha Trang and Saigon for processing out procedures, while I handle all the details at this end.

"We made flight reservations while he was here and expect to leave Honolulu on May 15th, arriving Sarasota at 6:40 A.M. the next day. Wow. Can hardly believe it is that close. As you can imagine I am counting the minutes and hours and days, not so much that we are anxious to leave the P.I., but I am anxious to have Adie leave Vietnam and we can't wait to see you all again.

"As it looks now, we will spend about a month in Sarasota, then on to Washington to find a place to live. Then we can tour around and see all you guys not in the Sarasota area, so be prepared for an influx of Swains."

Monday, March 11, 1968 Manila

".... signed an agreement to sell the Mustang for $3,140 US, so that is done and I am pleased with the price.

"Mom, you mentioned a welcome home party which I think is a terrific idea to have at Jane Gore's house, if she agrees. But, don't knock yourself out."

Wednesday, March 27, 1968 Manila

"Received your letters with the news of the availability of Andy

345

Field's cottages [next door to the old Jungle Lodges]. That sounds fine. Now, the latest on Adie's plans is that he will have to go to Washington on the 20th of May for at least 5 days TDY. This will be a critical period for we understand DC is full of turmoil and the ten percent cutback is taking a toll on availability of jobs, so we must not rule out the possibility that our definite assignment may not be too definite after all. I mention this so that if we do change our plans it won't come as a huge shock. I'll let you know for I don't want KC to run into any trouble if he has to change our reservations with Andy Field.

"I did the pearl [shopping] bit this morning on A. Mabini, Mom. Wasn't such a hot bargainer today. I got four strings of pearls for 28 pesos or 7 pesos per string, which isn't too bad.

"I have one favor to ask. Sarah and Connie both need glasses and they seem expensive here. I wonder if you or KC could pick out some dime store medium magnification glasses. It seems to me that they are a couple of bucks, and I think that is all they need. I sure would appreciate it if you could do that and send them airmail.... That's all I can think of now. I am so excited I can hardly do anything. All is well. ..." [Sarah and Connie both received new dime store glasses within two weeks and they worked out just fine.]

April 5, 1968 Manila

"Time is getting short and I seem to be doing nothing, just looking around at the mess, but I think I know what I have to do with everything. Latest word is that future assignments won't be definite until we return to Washington, and while Adie is optimistic about the company he is putting out feelers in other directions. He has met people in Vietnam who have referred him to other government agencies; he has written to Congressman Jim Haley and to the Civil Service Commission, and to some of his former supervisors over here who are back in DC, seeking advice. So, because of this, we have definitely decided to proceed directly to DC and come to Sarasota when job negotiations are completed.

"I have a strong hunch that something good will turn up in the present employ. I can't help feeling that in another month the timing will be good, the war news will be more optimistic, the stock market better, the heat will be off the government due to Johnson's decision not to run, and I believe the federal agencies will be more relaxed. Let's hope so."

* * *

The last few weeks in Manila passed in a blur of activity. I arrived home from Saigon on April 26 and found that Phyllis had taken care of everything. We used cabs a lot the last days of our tour, now that our faithful Mustang had been sold. The children's school exams were finished, with Tom completing the sixth grade and Bill the third. Phyllis alerted our family and other correspondents not to send mail past mid-month. Among the last mail to arrive was a nice letter from Congressman Jim Haley who did not promise much but invited me to drop in for a visit, which was encouraging. Nick Combitchie wrote too, inviting us to visit him in Greece if we ever got to Athens. Phyllis made arrangements with our friend Libby (at the Warren-Swain office) to take care of Julie, our poodle, who would fly directly to Sarasota and stay there until we arrived. Connie and Sarah, who promised to find a good home for our two cats, went with us to the docks the evening we departed. We all lounged around the docks chatting and looking up at the sides of the mammoth *President Wilson* liner towering above before saying a tearful goodbye to two wonderful and faithful friends.

It was like a dream come true as we sailed on the evening tide aboard a handsome vessel in first-class berths. Our family of five required two adjoining cabins which were only available in first class. It was a tough break, but we could handle it. Our friends Jan and Stan, already back at Langley, surprised us by arranging to have a bon voyage bottle of sparkling wine delivered to our quarters. Our visitors helped to celebrate our departure as they came to say good-bye and toast us good luck. Our tour of duty in Southeast Asia ended when I saw those heavy hawser lines being cast off. Tom, Bill, Ken, Phyl, and I happily tossed confetti from the railing while watching the gap between the dock and gray sides of the *President Wilson* slowly widen as we eased into Manila Bay. Our next stop was Hong Kong.

FOURTEEN

From Manila to Laos

O ur two-week trip to Honolulu aboard the *SS President Wilson* was a time for rest, relaxation, and family togetherness. Our quarters were superb and had porthole views of the sea far below. The boys' room, contained two regular bunks and one very desirable upper bunk in which Tom, Bill, and Ken took turns sleeping. We were assigned a table in the dining room where we had all our meals, including the one celebrating Tom's 12th birthday.

One evening after supper, Bill and his buddy were horsing around at the swimming pool when the other lad accidently fell into the deep end. He could not swim so Bill jumped in and pulled him out. As they went sloshing back to their quarters for dry clothes, one of the stewards took them to task for the watery mess they were making on the corridor carpeting. Naturally, our Bill was outraged that the steward had the nerve to criticize him after the heroics he had just performed. Phyllis and I were sympathetic, glad that he and his friend were safe, and praised him for his courageous work.

Our days were filled with pleasures that our first-class status enhanced. We dined well, slept late, and walked the decks with vigor in a determined but losing effort to burn off those extra calories that were accumulating around our waistlines. We played shuffleboard on the deck, watching the wooden discs slide in often unpredictable ways according to the slant and tilt of the deck. We browsed in the library reading or writing letters and cards home. There were matinee movies for the youngsters and films after dinner, plus dancing or bridge for the adults. Tom beat me at chess, as usual, so I decided not to play him again until I had more practice.

As we sailed northwest toward the British Crown Colony of Hong Kong, about 600 miles away, the weather began to get cooler and less tropical. It was too cool for me to swim, but the boys liked it. Phyllis and I preferred sunbathing in lounge chairs. I also enjoyed watching the long roil of green-white water from our churning ship's propeller as it etched a line on the deeper blue of the sea off to the horizon.

On the morning that we arrived at Kowloon Peninsula off the China mainland, we hurried through breakfast eager to get ashore because we were sailing for Tokyo that night. We would have plenty of time to enjoy the day in Hong Kong and could come back anytime we wanted or stay ashore until the last minute. Our gang of five walked down the gangplank with a crush of fellow passengers and found ourselves in the middle of what had to be one of the world's largest shopping complexes. Called the Ocean Terminal, it has several levels of airconditioned shops with each level connected by escalators. Hordes of people were going everywhere; many were employees who worked there, but most were passengers from vessels docked at numerous piers nearby.

I knew a little about Hong Kong from what I had read at the library and through my mail-order dealings with several outlets when I was stationed on Okinawa in 1949. Under terms of the 100-year lease given to the British, this densely populated jewel of a city-state (with Victoria its capital) would revert to China upon expiration of the lease on July 1, 1997. The colony consists of 234 small islands, including Hong Kong, Stonecutters, and Lantau, plus the Kowloon Peninsula also called the New Territories. It totals about 412 square miles of land on which almost 6 million people live, mostly Chinese. Hong Kong serves as one of the leading trading centers in the world, thriving on international finance, trade, and light industry.

Making money clearly was the name of the game. Manufacturing accounted for about one-fifth of local income; textiles dominated its export business along with electronics, plastic products, watches, clocks, jewelry, and toys of all kinds. It was the free port environment in which very few taxes were levied, however, that created the brisk import-export business that drove Hong Kong's exuberant economy.

The Swains were entranced by the variety of shops. We looked at glazed celedon vases; marveled at intricately carved teak furniture and fine oriental rugs; were dazzled by low prices at dozens of toy stores; and browsed through apparel shops, book stores, and jewelry and gem displays, all duty-free to transit passengers like us. Since it was getting cooler and we might need to ward off any chill when we got to Tokyo, Phyllis bought us all lightweight cashmere sweaters.

Naturally the boys got hungry, so we stopped in a busy little cafe and ordered elaborately powdered sugar rolls and wafers, soft drinks, and hot coffee. We enjoyed this oriental version of junk food called gork by the boys. Exhausted by the hard work of the morning, we all agreed to return to our ship for lunch and a rest.

That afternoon, we strolled down the gangplank past the enticing Ocean Terminal to the Star Ferry Building just beyond our pier and boarded a large, double-deck ferryboat in which passengers could sit on the main floor or the open top deck and cars were driven to the lower hold. The fare per person was about the equivalent of five cents for a one-way, ten minute trip across the harbor to Hong Kong, an exciting trip at a bargain price. Naturally, we all climbed topside where we could feel the wind and look about. We saw several junks with gaily colored slatted sails that could be hoisted only by hand using ropes and pulleys and caught an occasional glimpse of people on board those junks. I told the boys that many Chinese families spent their entire lives on such vessels. I remember one *mamasan* squatting by a glowing charcoal burner over which rice was being steamed for the family's noon meal. The waters were not very clean, with garbage, flotsam and jetsam, blue-gray oil slicks, and ubiquitous plastic bags much in evidence. There were boats of all sizes and shapes, including power boats, customs and harbor police cruisers, rusty old freighters, and the occasional gray, spick-and-span British or U.S. destroyer at anchor; it was fascinating.

Once ashore, we joined the horde of people released from the ferry and now rushing along the corridor from the dock out to the streets of Hong Kong. We emerged safely and then strolled along the sidewalks of Peddar Street taking in the sights. I had Billy and Ken firmly in hand, while Phyl and Tom were paired up for safety. I pointed out a red double-deck bus to Bill, telling him that people ride

351

those in England, which he gazed at with some reservation. Ken was just happy to be in action again and was hopping around like a yo-yo attached to my hand.

All the streets were clean and tidy, as opposed to the disarray in Manila. The throngs about us were civilized, courteous, and disciplined, but we kept close together so no one would get lost. The natives lined up politely to board the red buses or cross the streets at the corners; their behavior was no doubt inspired by traffic police, handsome men wearing white pith helmets, khaki shorts, pistols in white holsters, and silver whistles around their necks. This place was very proper, and we loved it. Bicycle-powered rickshaws were coming and going with the operators also wearing shorts. Their legs were heavily muscled, sinewy, and ropy as a result of hard, daylong workouts. Many appeared middle-aged, but I wondered if they were really young men who had aged prematurely. At least they had a job, which reminded me that I had none. I quickly dismissed that thought, telling myself just to enjoy the day.

After window shopping and strolling about for a couple of hours, including another stop for gork, we took the Star Ferry back to our home aboard the *President Wilson*. In the midst of all this activity, Billy lost his sweater, but Phyllis told him that we would find a new one when we got to Japan in a few days.

Tom wrote to his grandparents:

"Dear Ebby and K.C. . . . We will be in Japan tomorrow. We'll be back in Sarasota about May 20. The date is May 6. Thomas Swain." Tom's terse postcard was mailed from the sprawling port of Yokahama in Tokyo Bay, where we docked on May 7. The 1,400 miles we had sailed since Hong Kong refreshed us and made us eager to go ashore and see the sights. It was cold, gray, and overcast during most of our guided tour in Tokyo. The bus picked us up at the pier and was quite cozy and comfortable, even though the outside temperature was in the mid-50's.

Our female guide spoke English quite well and narrated as we toured the usual sights. We looked at the Emperor's palace, surrounded by its wide, deep moat, and then toured the grounds of the recently held winter Olympic games. There were ultramodern buildings used for ice skating, gymnastics and basketball, and other sports.

Quarters for the visiting athletes now looked forlorn and abandoned, but the Japanese would find some use for them. We stopped for lunch at a rather handsome inn along the roadway. I remember most that the motor traffic was horrendous compared with my recollection of earlier Korean War days when Japan was just getting back on its feet. Those were the days before Japan became a leading producer of automobiles, millions of which now seemed to be in Tokyo crowding around our bus. The going was slow, but the pace orderly. The gloomy weather was depressing me, but the kids and Phyllis seemed to be enjoying themselves. We returned to the ship that afternoon and agreed to stay aboard until we departed for Honolulu the next day.

*　*　*

We docked midmorning on May 15 in the bright, warm sunlight of Honolulu near the handsome Aloha tower. The last week or so had recharged our batteries, and we were eager to go ashore. There was plenty of time to relax before our noon flight to San Francisco, from where we would fly to Dulles Airport around midnight. We arrived in San Francisco in the afternoon and booked into the Holiday Inn near the airport. Everyone thought it a good idea to watch a little television and get some rest before departing. Time passed, and it seemed just a wink of an eye before Phyllis awakened us with a start. She cried out that it was late and we had to get to the airport right away. Luckily, the terminal was close, only a five-minute ride by the Holiday Inn courtesy bus. The Swain sleepyheads barely made it— Murphy's Law and the effects of jet lag had almost done us in.

At dawn, we were sipping orange juice and coffee and finishing our breakfast rolls and scrambled eggs. We were still sleepy yet filled with anticipation as we peered out the windows of our Pan Am 707 and eased quietly toward Dulles. We were soon in the almost deserted, newly opened terminal. No skycaps were around, so we grabbed our luggage from the carousel and lugged it outside. We then hired the biggest cab we could find and drove through the lush Virginia countryside to the Presidential Gardens, a sprawling, red brick apartment complex in Arlington where Company friends had recommended we stay. By midmorning, the family was comfortably settled into a furnished two-bedroom apartment. I kissed Phyllis good-bye and walked to the corner to catch a bus to Langley. Everything was coming down to a crunch for me. It was time to hunt for a job.

JOB HUNTING AT LANGLEY

There was an extra dampness under my arms as I started the in-processing paperwork, which began with a trip to the security office to obtain a temporary employee's badge so I could move about the building. I then had a checklist of things to do as a returning employee. I felt welcome and comfortable wherever I went, and the people were friendly and accommodating. Between appointments, I strolled along the wide, polished terrazzo halls on the main floor that formed a rectangle around a pleasant oasis of green grass, pathways, and small shade trees covered with the freshly minted leaves of May. I walked to the employees' cafeteria beyond semipublic areas such as the insurance office and employees' exchange. Now I knew how Ernie must have felt when he walked these same halls before he ran into the friend who helped him get his assignment to Tokyo.

I finally had an appointment with the job placement advisor. We met in a little interviewing cubicle off the main personnel office and had a friendly conversation but nothing was promised in the way of an assignment. All he could offer me was another tour in Vietnam, which I told him I wanted to think about. I think he knew I planned to shop around for a billet elsewhere. He said to let him know in a day or two what I wanted to do.

I had a nice visit with Evelyn, my friend and confidant who worked in the department that processed personnel going overseas. She had handled our family's overseas travel to Vietnam and Manila. Because of the 10-percent cutback on new employees, her workload had lessened. She seemed delighted to see me, and it was great chatting with her. We talked of current policy changes and other matters including her social life. I learned that our mutual friend, old bunkie John, had taken the assignment to Europe and Jack, one of my Blue U classmates, was now in Laos. Evelyn buoyed up my flagging spirits, urging patience and saying she was sure something good would turn up. Maybe she knew something, but I was not so sure.

The second day passed in much the same way, with me walking the halls, getting my records in order, doing routine administrative chores, and worrying. On the third day, I visited the Air Branch Operations center to talk with Willy hoping that maybe they had something there, even though they had withdrawn their offer last fall. Will said there were no openings and that when I became a Province Officer last year, I had blown my chances of returning to air operations; I knew he was right. It was nice visiting with Willy, but that did not put bread on the table.

While sipping coffee in the cafeteria, I figured I could always take another tour in Vietnam if something did not come up soon. It was a dreadful thought and would mean a separated tour—six months on the job and one month at home. I resumed walking the corridors, pretending to look as though I had an important appointment elsewhere, when a couple of familiar looking guys approached. It was Andy and Big Bob, both former Vietnam field operations officers who I had put on many a flight out of Nha Trang. They greeted me jovially, asking how I was doing. I said I was just fine and was here with the family looking for a job. They looked at each other and then grabbed me by the arms, one on each side, and hustled me toward the elevators. I laughed and asked them where they were taking me. Andy said they wanted me to see Mr. Mustache, the chief of the TBL Desk (Thailand, Burma, Laos), who might have some slots open.

We took the elevator up several floors and then went down some long gray corridors to the office of Mr. Mustache, whose first name was Stu. After introductions, we sat on a couch in front of his desk, me sandwiched between Andy and Bob, while they talked. They pleaded my case, describing what a reliable, thorough, dependable, and all-around good guy I was, and concluded by saying that I was someone he ought to hire. I sat there listening, saying little, nodding at the right moments, and trying to keep from smiling. This was quite a system. Clearly the desk chief of the Agency's various geographic areas had a great deal of leeway in hiring and assigning people to work for him. The office of personnel helped by sending him nominations of qualified people from their records, but final approval rested with the chief. Walking the halls had been well worthwhile.

Mr. Mustache said he would review my personnel file and if I was half as good as these old friends said I was, he might have an opening in Laos. The job was an interrogation officer's slot in Pakse, south of Vientiane. He said he could arrange for me to attend the interrogation training course that had just begun at the Blue U and that I could figure on going overseas in late July. I told him that it sounded good to me but I wanted to discuss it with Phyllis and would let him know tomorrow. He did not waste any time making decisions, and I was impressed. The whole thing happened so suddenly; one minute I was out of work, and 10 minutes later I had an assignment in Laos. My feet floated on air as I left Mr. Mustache's office. I knew that Phyllis would agree to the assignment. Now we could fly to Sarasota and start our vacation at Andy Field's cottages on Siesta Key. My friend Evelyn was most pleased that I had signed on with her old friend Stu. She said I would have a great time and that she did when she worked in Vientiane.

I told the family what had transpired and brought them some maps and briefing material to review. Laos was a subtropical land located to the north of Thailand across the Mekong River. Both North and South Vietnam as well as a tip of Cambodia lay to the east of Laos, with China to the north and Burma to the west. With a population of about four million, Laos had hills and mountains in the north with rice fields to the south along the Mekong. Quite rural and underdeveloped by Western standards, Laos was nothing like the world we had just left in the Philippines.

Phyllis and I talked it over in some detail. I stressed that living in Laos would be like living way out in the country, with no frills or big city shops and restaurants. A number of other families would be there plus an accredited American School with about 20 students through the eighth grade, and we could take a car along. Ever courageous, daring, and self-confident, as I had expected, Phyllis was ready and willing to chance the unknown. She said the main thing was that we would be together and if I could handle it then they all could.

Before flying to Sarasota that weekend, we visited briefly with Paul and Delores and their kids, who were living near Arlington in Falls Church. We had not seen them since last January and had a joyous reunion. Paul was doing some type of background security work and was as chipper and enthusiastic as ever. He asked me to stay with them when I returned from Sarasota to attend my class. It was nice of Paul and Delores to make such a welcome offer. Their house was only a few miles from the Blue U and I gladly accepted. I realized later that many returnees stayed with old overseas friends. You could save a lot of money that way and renew old friendships at the same time.

The Warrens met us at the airport the next day along with Cyndy, who had driven down from the University of South Florida in Tampa. Before long, we were unpacking in one of Andy Field's white frame beach cottages across from the Jungle Lodges. What a treat it was to run and walk on the beach and splash into clean, sun-warmed salt water just beyond the sand dunes, sand spurs, and sea oats by our cottage door. The kids were in seventh heaven, and we all quickly became sandy, sunburned, and waterlogged from almost constant beaching and swimming. We visited with family and other friends during the evenings, but not before we had reclaimed Julie from Libby, our office secretary; Julie had been babied and pampered ever since Libby picked her up at the airport two weeks earlier. She was so excited that her tail almost wagged itself off, and the children were tickled to see her. She took to the gulf like a duck to a pond.

BACK TO SCHOOL

The next month was busy for me. Greatly relieved that I had found a job and with the family settled and having a great time, I flew back to Washington to join Paul and Delores. They loaned me their aging Lincoln sedan so that I could drive to school for the next two weeks. It was fun staying with them; they fixed me up with a cot in their basement where it was quiet and private. I would eat breakfast with Paul and Delores and then return around dinnertime. I sometimes brought them a bag of groceries to help out.

Our classwork centered on the fundamentals of conducting interrogations. Our group of about 15 guys took turns role playing the part of the subject and then the questioner. Our performances were often taped on a VCR and then replayed for classroom critiques. The course material was interesting and similar to my experience in the

FBI. All our activities were monitored by Zeke, the same instructor for my classes two years ago. We also studied debriefing procedures and spent a lot of time preparing written reports, the grist for every intelligence mill. We studied techniques for getting reluctant witnesses to talk using psychological approaches, such as appeals to greed, pride, loyalty, family, and honor. We also watched and learned from films that demonstrated how to interrogate captured prisoners of war and persuade them to talk. I am happy to add that physical violence or the threat of physical torture was never discussed.

The one concession made to high technology was the use of the polygraph. We were not trained to use the equipment because this was a distinct and highly skilled career field, but we became familiar with its use. We understood that the polygraph and its findings had never been accepted in U.S. courts, but its application in the field had proven very helpful. The results of a polygraph test would show whether or not a subject was telling the truth almost all of the time, unless the subject was a pathological liar. Sensitive variations in blood pressure and respiration, which appeared as peaks and valleys on a graph recorder, would indicate any areas of uncertainty. So effective was the use of the polygraph that sometimes the person being examined would voluntarily admit lying, even before he was put on the box.

In the field, the Box Man, or polygraph operator, could be used to check a staff translator or agent handler to make sure that he or she was not a double agent, taking bribes, or stealing from Uncle Sam. In Vietnam, we had some difficulty working with English-speaking interpreters. They were needed to hire, train, and manage other non-English-speaking people. Because we had so many employees, security problems were bound to arise from the occasional bad apple in our barrel. Although our English-speaking polygraph operator was never sure his questions were being translated correctly from English into the language of the person being tested, overall usage of the box was worthwhile.

Our training included working out of a safe house to debrief defectors from Cuba. We also helped to prepare debriefing reports, simulating work we would be expected to do in the field. Later, we were flown to the Farm, the Company's training center along the

James River near historic Williamsburg, Virginia. Here we worked to improve our field skills under mock operational conditions, again role playing among our class members. Some of us pretended to be prisoners, while others played the role of jailer or questioner. By the time this was all over, I was more than ready for some vacation time in Florida, but not without one final dose of bureaucratic paperwork. The afternoon I was due to fly to Sarasota, I had to take a lengthy, multiple-choice psychological test. There were 800 questions apparently designed to discover whether I hated my mother or was a fruitcake or a combination thereof. I think the test was to determine if my assignment in Laos would create a problem. I evidently passed, for I never heard my results.

Sarasota, Florida, June 27, 1968

"Dear Mom,

Enclosed you will find a check for $150.00 to cover round trip expenses [from Freedom] to Florida. You are most welcome any time after the 4th of July holidays.... We are leaving Sarasota on the 20th of July.... I returned from D.C. yesterday with airplane tickets for the whole family and our passports. We will be traveling via New York City, London [overnight], Frankfurt, Istanbul, Teheran, New Delhi to Bangkok. Isn't that great?.... Please call us when you know when you are coming and I'll meet you at the airport. We are all looking forward to your visit.

All our love, Adie."

My Mother spent a week with us, long enough for her to get reacquainted with the grandchildren and for us to enjoy her company. The kids loved her.

Phyllis and I bought a 1968 Chevrolet with air conditioning, black seats, and white exterior. It was nothing fancy, just a solid, six-cylinder car that would get us around Laos with minimal maintenance. Since we had such good luck with our Mustang in Manila, we figured a sporty little Chevy would sell easily in Laos when we left.

359

Had we known that our drives would be limited to about eight miles in any direction in Pakse, we probably would not have bothered to take one, but Uncle Sam was paying for it. We broke it in driving around Sarasota before sending it to the port at New Orleans for transport to Pakse, Laos.

* * *

Ken Warren was a good grandfather to the boys and often took them fishing, usually Tom and Bill, sometimes with Phyllis, who dearly loved to fish. Ken's *Roaring Bessy* outboard motorboat would leave his bayou at dawn's early light with a bucket of live shrimp and avid young fishermen eager to catch a wily redfish, speckled trout, or perhaps a snook or mangrove snapper, depending on the tides and the fishing hole being explored. There were good catches of trout or redfish off Doogie Wheeler's point on Big Pass, hungry red snapper feeding off Coconut Bayou's mangrove-lined shores, more speckled trout off the grass flats by Bird Key, and fighting snook in the Pass. An incoming high tide just after dawn was a fine time to be out there wetting a line. The anglers would return home, bait bucket empty, usually with a nice string of fish and starving. Evie was up by now and would give them all something warm and nourishing to eat.

After the sun had gone over the yardarm, as Ken defined the beginning of the cocktail hour, we would enjoy cookouts with Ken and Evie. Always memorable were K.C.'s charcoal grilled steaks and Evie's special, crispy-topped, creamed baked onion dish. On occasion, K.C. would tell jokes about his days as a manager with Bamberger's Department Store in New York. One that I recall had to do with the Jewish mother who says to her friend, "My son, the playwright, has a a chauffeur. The chauffeur carries him into the house, out of the house, he carries him to the theater, out of the theater. . . "What's the matter?" asks the friend, "Can't he walk?" "Certainly he can walk," replies the mother, "but thank God, he doesn't have to."

TO LAOS VIA EUROPE

Our travels resumed on July 20 with a midday flight to New York's La Guardia Airport. We had a few hours before our Pan Am clipper departed that evening for London. Alerted beforehand by Phyl, old friends Betty and Zoltan Farkas drove to the airport from their apartment in town to visit with us. We had drinks and talked over old times; rather Phyllis and Betty talked about mutual friends in the Big Apple, where they used to work, and of our newest adventure to the wilds of Southeast Asia. Zoli and I joined in occasionally but mostly we just looked wise. There was much talk of daughters Cyndy and Tina, who were both off to school. It was a treat to see them, and they were good to spend some time with us.

We finally embarked on the first phase of the 30-odd-hour flight that would take us halfway around the world. This time we would be traveling east into the rising sun. When it was over, Phyl and I agreed that it seemed more difficult than flying by way of Hawaii, perhaps because traveling east meant longer stretches of daylight hours and more rapid time zone changes, hence a seemingly longer day.

We arrived at Heathrow Airport on the outskirts of London in early daylight. We had opted to spend our mandatory rest stop at a "veddy" old and venerable hotel on Picadilly Square and see some of the town. After resting, my hopes for an appetizing breakfast the next day were painfully dashed. Our food was beautifully served under covered silver dishes at our table in a stately dining room; however, the fried eggs were stone cold, the bacon overdone, the toast lukewarm and pale, and the canned orange juice metallic tasting. On the brighter side, the marmalades were good and the coffee was hot. The best thing about the experience was the service. Maybe if we had ordered fish and chips, the food would have been better. Phyllis and the boys were polite and rather stoic, perhaps wanting to be good allies; more than likely, they were too groggy to be annoyed.

That morning, we bravely set out for some sightseeing from the top deck of a red double-deck bus. Billy was not too keen on this ride, and even Phyllis rolled her eyes a bit; the bus felt as if it would tip over when turning a corner. To further dampen the day, the weather was moist and the sky overcast—typical of England. We watched the changing of the royal guard at Buckingham Palace and were driven past Number 10 Downing Street, where the Prime Minister resided. We were tired after a few hours and happy to return to our hotel, where Phyllis recovered enough to do some window shopping. The boys and I strolled along with her and enjoyed stretching our legs and breathing the English air, which seemed smog free.

Soon we were soaring in sunlight high above the cloud-dappled English Channel. We looked down on the orderly countryside of tiny Belgium before descending into Frankfurt, Germany. At the bustling airport, we waited to connect with another clipper for Bangkok, Thailand. Our itinerary would be interesting from a historical viewpoint. The next stop was Istanbul, Turkey, formerly Constantinople, the ancient and storied crossroads city that sprawls astride a hill with the Black Sea and Russia to the north and the Bosporus Strait to the south. Istanbul's location made it unique, since it was in both Europe and Asia.

We then went to Teheran, the capital of Iran and site of the historic conference held in late November 1943 during World War II by the "Big Three" (Roosevelt, Churchill, and Stalin). Here they agreed to open a second front in Europe and guaranteed the independence of Iran when the war was over. I remember standing on the upper observation deck at the Teheran airport in hot, dry, bright sunlight, while our thirsty 707 was being refueled. Iran, formerly called Persia, lay on a high plateau rimmed on all sides by mountains with an average elevation of 6,500 feet. The highest peak, 18,386 feet, was in the Elburz mountains to the north. More than half of the land was uninhabitable desert wastelands, but there were enormous oil and natural gas reserves underground on the Persian Gulf near the border of Iran and Iraq. Iran's prosperous economy was based primarily on petroleum and gas production from these fields, which held about one-sixth of the world's oil and gas reserves. The area was so rich that in 1980, the covetous Iraqis, led by Saddam Hussein, invaded Iran and started an eight-year war over their boundaries. Iran had about 25 million people in 1968, mostly of the Moslem faith. The population doubled by 1988 despite heavy losses during the Iraq-Iran war, which incidentally seemed to settle nothing.

We were in the air once more and arrived in New Delhi, capital of India, by late evening. We stumbled off the plane into the yellowed lights of the passenger lounge, where we were confined to a rather limited area with hard, uncomfortable benches. The atmosphere was subdued, and we were all tired. We napped, resting our feet on our bags, and later strolled about trying to keep awake. The humidity of late July was like a damp blanket, and the air-cooling system strained to maintain a degree of coolness inside.

It was late at night, and still there were a lot of people in the airport, many wearing native white robes, some women with red dots pasted or painted on their dark-skinned foreheads. I wondered if they were travelers or had no place to call home. A kind of lethargy that spoke of poverty and malnutrition existed. From what I knew, there were so many people that there was not enough food to feed them all; yet their cattle roamed the streets like royalty, forbidden by religious reasons to be used for food, grazing on the very fields that could be planted with crops to feed the people. It did not make any sense to me at all. I was glad when our flight departed.

We arrived around midnight in Bangkok, the capital city of ancient Siam (made famous by the play *The King and I*). Here we would rest before completing our journey north into Laos, the land of a thousand elephants.

FIFTEEN

Tales from Pakse

E ven at midnight, the warm moistness of subtropical Thailand felt twice as humid as a late July afternoon in Sarasota. The air at Bangkok's Don Muang airport smelled faintly of jet engine exhaust mixed with the sweet incense of burnt joss sticks and the musty scent of decomposing water hyacinths. Hyacinths grew profusely in the klongs (canals) that drained the Chao Phya River delta on which the city sprawled. We boarded a bus and within the hour straggled into the Amarin Hotel, a modestly priced, 10-story hotel often frequented by government people on official orders to Laos. Our kids were happy to be on the ground again and especially pleased to learn that the Amarin provided 24-hour room service. It was 2 A.M. local time but 12 hours earlier by our body clocks. It would take four or five days before we adjusted to the time difference.

Phyllis and I shared a room on the second floor, and the boys were in an adjoining room. Phyllis knew they would be hungry soon and told them to order room service whenever they felt hunger pangs. I think the calls started as soon as we said good night, and an unending flow of hamburgers and chocolate covered ice-cream sundaes began. Phyl and I had a nightcap and took a half-hearted look at a Thai television program before we turned in, quite happy that the long day was over.

In the morning, we called Pan Am about Julie, our poodle. We retrieved her from the airport that afternoon and smuggled her into the hotel. She stayed with the boys most of the time and was happy to be with her family. We felt pretty well rested by Friday morning when we checked out and were driven to the airport to board the Company's

C-47 aircraft. The aging silver plane was waiting to take passengers and priority mail to Vientiane, the capital of Laos, a two-hour flight north across the Mekong River.

As we walked across the runway to the aircraft, I noticed an Air America pilot performing his preflight inspection. Something about him was familiar, and I realized it was Don Marsh, a B-29 pilot I had met at McGuire Field, New Jersey, in 1948-49. We shook hands and chatted about the small world we were in. Don commented that it had been 20 years since we met. After getting out of the service, he joined Air America and had been flying C-47s out of Laos for the past three years. He said the pay was good and there were a lot of old-timers around. Don said that Colonel Dunn, our former commanding officer at McGuire Field, was now chief of air operations for Air America. When I told him we were headed to Pakse, we promised to get together but never did. I also never got a chance to contact Colonel Dunn. Don seemed pleased to see me and happy in his work, but I did not envy his life one bit. Flying a beat-up World War II C-47 was not my idea of a good time, even if he did earn twice as much money as I did.

When we climbed aboard, I realized how posh our recent Boeing 707 flight accommodations had been. We strapped ourselves into worn, slightly shaky metal seats with well-used cushions. These seats could be removed easily to make space for bags of wheat, cases of ammunition, drums of petrol and gasoline, a load of Laos paratroopers, or whatever Air America's pilots were asked to transport. To my surprise, a cute little Lao stewardess appeared, dressed in a colorful, silken wraparound skirt. She smiled at the children and made us feel at home. After we were airborne, she served ham and cheese sandwiches on freshly baked bread, along with a banana and cold cola. It was not fancy but pretty tasty and made a nice picnic lunch. The boys adapted to their new environment and looked out the windows enjoying the flight. Julie was on a leash by our feet and rolling her eyes as if wondering when this would all end.

It was a lazy, quiet Sunday afternoon when we landed at an almost deserted Vientiane airport. We were welcomed by an English-speaking Lao USAID driver, who made the traditional Lao greeting by placing his fingertips in front of his face and bowing.

"Sabaaj dii," he said, which meant hello and how are you. He escorted us through Immigration and Customs, loaded our gear into his van, and drove through quiet streets to the Vientiane Hotel near the Mekong River. This was one of the best hotels in town but not up to the modest standards of the Amarin. The four-story hotel was surrounded by tall flame trees, a poinciana variety that burst into red-orange blossoms during spring and early summer. There were many pink and white bougainvillea on the grounds. We entered the lobby under ceiling fans that stirred the warm air. A vacant dining room off to one side had wooden tables spread with clean, well-worn tablecloths. The hotel resembled a turn-of-the-century, slightly dowdy hostel that one might find in South Carolina or Louisiana, and I kind of liked its rustic look.

I checked into the Embassy the next morning, after a nice breakfast with the family on the veranda. I logged in for duty and met Ted, the Laos Station Chief, who soon would become Station Chief in Saigon. Keen, incisive, and a fine intelligence officer, he gave me a brief rundown on the mission at hand. The Kingdom of Laos, which had won its independence in 1954 from the French, was a tiny landlocked country about twice the size of the state of Pennsylvania. Its geographical location made it a strategic buffer between Red China to the north, Vietnam to the north and east, and its free neighbors to the south. Our role was to help Laos, led by its King Savang Vathana, to resist pressure from the Communist forces of the Pathet Lao. Tomorrow I would report to Pancho, the Chief of Base at my duty post in Pakse.

While I was out, Phyl and the boys checked out the local commissary and placed an order for groceries to be delivered later in the week on the courier flight to Pakse. While in the checkout line, Phyl discovered she was about $20.00 short. A lady standing next to her whom she had never met saw Phyl's plight and loaned her the money. "Such nice people," said Phyl when telling me her story, "can you imagine that happening in Sarasota?"

Since there was no scheduled C-47 flight to Pakse until the end of the week, a Pilatous Porter was arranged for us. I was familiar with the single-engine aircraft from my Vietnam days and looked forward to the ride. We jammed our nine pieces of luggage and Julie's cage behind the Porter's seats and piled in. I sat in front beside the pilot, with Phyllis and Ken behind us, and Julie riding shotgun between Tom and Bill in the last two seats. The Swiss-made Garrett engine turned over and soon began its distinctive, high-pitched whine. We surged down the runway and perhaps 300 feet later popped up into blue skies. The Porter's broad, square-tipped wings shaded our cabin and rocked us gently as we climbed to 2,500 feet and then leveled off, flying above the wide, muddy Mekong toward Pakse some 250 miles away. With each succeeding leg of this journey, I realized that our aircraft accommodations had become smaller and less fancy, but none of us minded. Every day of this trip was exciting and different and a new experience for us. We felt like pioneers exploring the unknown.

We landed light as a feather on the asphalt in Pakse, a sleepy town of perhaps 30,000 residents on the banks of the Sedone River where it joins the Mekong. We turned onto a parking ramp where the air operations officer, a cheerful man named Flynn, met us at the plane. Flynn wore a cowboy hat, blue jeans, a short-sleeved sports shirt, and dusty cowboy boots. He welcomed us to Pakse and was an outgoing, friendly fellow whom I liked immediately. His eyes popped a bit at the sight of the beautiful Phyllis emerging with Julie on her red leash. I bet this was the first time a Park Avenue lady and her poodle had arrived in Pakse. He did not say anything, however and just greeted the boys and then introduced his wife, Dorothy Mae, a slender, blue-eyed blonde with a bright smile. She and Flynn were from Houma, Louisiana.

Meanwhile, Tom, Bill, and Ken were busy inspecting the new territory, with Julie nose down sniffing everything as she tugged at her leash. I noted the well-maintained metal hanger and storage area, plus a few oil-streaked, dusty, and wellworn T-28 single-engine aircraft parked across the runway. Flynn explained that Laos Air Force pilots flew those old four-bladed propeller aircraft in ground support and bombing missions against the Communists. Their target was the VC supply route, the infamous Ho Chi Minh Trail, about 75 miles east of Pakse near the Laos-Vietnam border.

Phyllis and Dorothy Mae were chatting away like old friends about Sarasota. Dorothy Mae's parents lived there and although we had never met them, it helped establish an instant bond of friendship.

Flynn and Dorothy Mae had three children: Skipper, about Tom's age, and two girls, Jena and Janelle. Dorothy Mae said they had been in Laos for two years and were just starting another tour. She thought it was not bad if you did not expect too much and could adapt to country living. She said the little school was pretty decent and had three or four teachers and only twenty students this year, which made for a good teacher-student ratio.

Flynn and I loaded the luggage and we all drove to our temporary quarters, a two-story house in the USAID compound located between the airport and town. Our weathered wooden house was comfortable enough but sparsely furnished. There were two bedrooms, one with three beds for the boys; Phyllis and I shared the other room, which had a double bed with a lumpy mattress so high in the middle that I felt I would roll onto the floor at any moment. There was an air-conditioner in the boys' room, and ours had a ceiling fan. Phyllis was not too happy about that; but two new homes were under construction nearby, and we would get one of them in a couple of weeks. Phyllis was more upset about leaving her favorite soft pillow in Vientiane than she was about the lumpy bed.

Flynn said the local contractors were not well qualified, especially the plumbers. They had been known to install bathroom tubs and commodes without connections to the outside septic tank. I did not know whether to believe him, and although his story seemed plausible I hoped he was kidding. Because I had been a pilot and he was the air operations officer, Flynn and I became good friends and always got along well together.

We were invited to dinner that first night with a smiling, sociable man named Lenny, the deputy chief of base, and his lovely wife, Robin. We met their two sons, John and Keith, who went to the Pakse elementary school. Over a fine dinner of buffalo steak, tossed green salad, potatoes, and freshly baked bread from the local bakery, we added up all the school-age kids. Pancho, our boss, had six children, Len had two, the Swains had three, and Colonel Bill, a retired West Point officer, and his wife Therese, had two teenagers by her first marriage and two pre-schoolers of their own. Flynn had three children, Tim had one, Jack had two, Pete and Lucy had two, and Dutch had two. Altogether, there were twenty-one grade schoolers, several preschoolers, and two or three high-school students, who took correspondence courses. Phyllis and I were delighted that our boys would have plenty of company.

* * *

In the morning, I reported to the boss in the two-story, white stucco Annex Building, inside a chain-link fence. Pancho had a pleasant smile and brisk manner and was energetic. I knew he had graduated from Arizona State College and been on their track team and spoke fluent Spanish. Pancho extended his hand and welcomed me to the group. After some small talk, he said I would be working with Tim and then take over his intelligence network. Tim was going home in two months, so there would be plenty of time to learn the ropes. The field operations guys would work with the troops on the hill. Pancho hinted that he preferred working intelligence operations more than field operations, which was fine with me. I was not looking for field operations work, which meant taking a Porter to work every day.

Pancho pointed to his wall map and some colored pins that identified half a dozen bases and their landing field designators, such as P-1 and P-2. All these bases communicated by side band radios with Pakse and were within fairly close range of the Ho Chi Minh Trail. Most bases were on the Bolovens Plateau. Our local mission was similar to the cadre operations I had performed in Quang Duc: to support operations designed to stem the flow of men and military supplies down the Ho Chi Minh Trail into South Vietnam.

I was a bit surprised when he asked if Phyllis wanted to work but said I thought she would be very interested. A number of wives worked in the office, including Mary, his secretary, whose husband, Don, was assigned to PS-22 on the 3,500-foot-high Bolovens Plateau. Several wives worked in the file room upstairs, while others helped to process reports from our bases and other liaison contacts. Lao secretarial personnel were nonexistent in Pakse. Even if they could speak and write English, none could pass the security clearance required to handle classified materials. The office work might never get done if American wives did not help. Our situation in Pakse was no different from that of other overseas Agency bases.

After leaving Pancho's office, I took a quick tour of the building and met our Operations Chief, the retired West Point colonel. Bill was courteous and soft-spoken and had a habit of stroking his upper lip with his forefinger. I also checked out the communications section where our base radio and cable facilities were in constant contact with our upcountry bases, the USAID director, Earl Diffenderfer, and our headquarters in Vientiane and Washington. I then met Tim, who gave me a rundown on his intelligence operation.

INTELLIGENCE OPERATIONS

Our work began with interrogations of Pathet Lao soldiers who had defected to the Lao side. Tim had talked to a man who was a former Lieutenant Colonel in the Pathet Lao army based in Attopeu, a sizeable town some 75 miles from Pakse. Tim had seen some potential for turning him into an intelligence agent and before long was able to convince him to provide information about the activities, plans, and intentions of the Pathet Lao. Tim learned that the ex-colonel still had contacts with several military friends who also might provide intelligence on the Pathet Lao. It appeared that Souk, the ex-colonel's new *nom de guerre* or operations name, and his friends held no great loyalty to the Communist cause. Being in the Pathet Lao had apparently provided a lot of risk, room and board, and little else. After carefully evaluating Souk's potential, and with the blessing of senior officers up the Agency line, he was recruited. He would maintain his rank as a colonel and work for the Royal Lao Government in return for a monthly salary that was a bit more than his previous pay in the Pathet Lao.

During the next two months of testing and training, Souk molded into a conscientious and responsive intelligence agent, who was bright, alert and energetic; Tim had found a gold mine. Souk was perhaps 35 years of age and had tanned, slightly pockmarked skin and a cool, calculating look in his eye. Souk's training was accomplished at a safehouse, a private home rented by one of our interpreters, a Thai called Ambrose who spoke fluent Lao. Through Ambrose, Souk was briefed and instructed on how to contact his potential recruits and told to assign them "war" names so their true names would never appear in any reports. Should a message be intercepted by the Communists, the agent's identity also would not be given up.

Soon after training, Souk returned to the Attopeu area near the Laos, Vietnam, and Cambodian border and began recruiting former associates. By the time Tim turned Souk over to me, Souk had 20 recruits, many of them junior officers who knew Souk from the old days and were still loyal to him. Some of these officers recruited other friends who unwittingly provided Souk with information. Two of Souk's friends also were recruited as couriers to deliver intelligence reports from the Attopeu area because the regular mail service was censored by the Pathet Lao and was not reliable.

Souk learned that Sam, one of his best recruits, was to be transferred to the North Vietnamese training center in Samneua, not far from Hanoi. If we wanted to keep in touch with Sam, we would have to use the regular mail system and train him in secret writing (SW). Souk first had to learn SW and then train Sam in the technique. Souk practiced writing secret messages between the lines of a page written in normal pen and ink. The normal part of the letter was intended to be read and censured by the VC in Samneua. The secret part was written in a colorless chemical between the normal lines of the letter using a mirror or other piece of glass so the imprint of the pen and secret ink would not show through. The SW message would become legible after submerging the letter in a chemical solution for two minutes. The treated letter would turn dark brown with the secret message appearing in white. The chemicals we used were commonly available in any chemist shop, even in Pakse. Should any message to Souk be intercepted, it would not reflect on the U.S. government. The big risk, however, would fall on the letter writer. None of Sam's letters were intercepted, and several contained useful political news and some intelligence, but nothing that changed the course of the war.

* * *

The Time of My Life

"Dear Family:

This is our first communication from Pakse, since arriving. On the whole the situation is good. Of course, we have found a new way of living here on the frontier, with no TV or 7-11 stores, but our cultural shock is softened by our fine and cooperative group of people. There are many kids for our boys to play with, and a lot of very attractive wives for the men to look at. The gals all pitch in, and several of them work in the office. Phyllis has submitted her personal history questionnaire for the required security clearance. When that comes back and after school starts in September, she will begin working, at least half days. Pay is $2.50 per hour, but it is something to keep her busy and involved. Our compound community is quite convenient with a dozen or so houses, all within easy walking or commuting distance of each other unless it is raining. I can see my office building from our house.

It is simply great to come home to the family every night. For entertainment we get first-run movies flown down from Vientiane, and can check out a projector for overnight use. Right now the boss has first dibs on the movies and keeps the projector at his house. Rank does have its privileges, (and he does have six children), but after school starts we are planning on using the main room downstairs to show movies for everyone on the weekend evenings.

Shopping is no problem. A weekly commissary flight from Vientiane brings in our basic foods. Commissary prices are much better than the local marketplace. When required we can get almost anything we need in town from the two general merchandise stores operated by Vietnamese ladies. These ethnic-Chinese ladies speak English, French, Lao, and several dialects of Chinese-Vietnamese. Their stores are nick-named Macy's and Gimbel's. When shopping in town you must cross the Sedone River via a rickety, vintage 1915 steel-and-wood-planked bridge that accommodates one-way traffic, like the old Stickney Point bridge in Sarasota. A guard at the east end of the bridge turns the red-green traffic light on and off. The Sedone River is fairly wide during the rainy season, a six-month period which ends in October. The water can rise fifteen to twenty feet, or more. The current runs swiftly at flood tide and merges with the much broader Mekong less than a half mile distant. The Mekong is an exceptional body of water, much like our Mississippi, a river that has never been bridged, so I am told. Ferry boats transport people and goods back and forth to the Thailand side. This is how our Chevy sedan will arrive one day.

I bought a fine shortwave radio at Macy's that receives *Voice of America* news and jazz concerts, as well as Saigon's AFRS (Armed Forces Radio Service) and even Radio Hanoi, if you care to listen. Tom and I strung a 75 foot aerial from our second floor to a far tree which really helped reception. (Twenty years later our Macy's radio was still okay but beginning to rust out.) We receive two-day-old newspapers from Bangkok, and can buy weekly English language magazines such as *Time* and *Newsweek* overseas' editions in town. There are two service stations, Esso and Shell, also a busy bike repair shop, plus a couple of barber shops in which the barbers use hand-powered clippers. But the price is right, about a dollar per haircut.

Wild life around here is something straight from Ma and Pa Kettle's farm. Lots of chickens and ducks harried by assorted short-haired Lao dogs whose genetic trait seems to be a long tail with a loop in it that stands straight up but tilting forward like an antenna. There are buffalo and an occasional milk cow that graze in the fields around us. Pigs are penned in at the *abattoir* (slaughter house in English—the French word makes it sound better) where squeals can be heard when they are being slaughtered for the market. Phyllis is not too happy about this activity, but since I am at the office during the daytime I do not mind so much.

Lao money is called Kip. The exchange rate is 500 Kip to one U.S. dollar, five times what it was in 1960. The salary for a maid is $20 to $30 per month. A good male cook, if you can find one, earns $45 to $50, according to the double standard applied here. Phyllis plans to hire two ladies, as she did in Manila. A *number one* for cooking and a *number two* for house work. . . There is some talk of a boy scout troop being formed and with about 20 kids here, I think a troop might easily be gathered, but who will be the scout master? That is not an easy task, so we shall see.

After finishing a tour of duty in SVN, this place has its appeal because the danger of a sudden uprising is not ever present, as it was in South Vietnam. I think that Phyllis and Tom have suffered most from what is known as 'cultural shock.' We are far removed from family and the refinements of Sarasota but have most of the comforts and conveniences, except television. The shock comes from living in a land where most of the people do not read, write or speak a language we understand. Knowing some French is helpful, and the kids are getting lessons in school every day from Therese, one of our wives, and a native of southern France. This has been a long letter, written during those quiet night duty officer hours, but I hope you can tell our life is full and busy. . . Hope you are all well and happy. . . Love to you all, Adie and family."

* * *

Souk and his men were steady producers of intelligence. Souk would go into the field once a month for two or more weeks at a time and make the rounds of his old friends. Perhaps they knew he was collecting intelligence but did not hold it against him. Souk was always careful to keep his sources separated and did not tell the others who else was working for him.

A typical trip would start with Ambrose driving Souk south from Pakse as far as possible and dropping him off in one of the little towns to the west of Attopeu. Souk then would take a bus into the back country, being careful to avoid Pathet Lao patrols and camps. Sometimes he took unusual means to reach his destination. He would submit a monthly statement of his expenses, and Ambrose would translate his accounts from Lao into English for me. One entry was for hiring an elephant for the day. I had to laugh at the notion of Souk riding an elephant through the brush toward Attopeu. This was common practice in certain areas, since Laos was known as the land of the elephants. I never questioned Souk about the elephant and just paid his bill, plus his salary of 60,000 kip per month, about $120.00 U.S. All of Souk's people were paid a decent wage, but half of their earnings were routinely withheld in our office in their account. It just was not good business to risk having some agent in the field flash a wad of kip.

When pressed for time, Souk occasionally would be flown in our twin-engine Baron Beechcraft to the eastern rim of the Bolovens Plateau. The higher elevations of the Bolovens had apple and peach orchards, strawberry fields, and acres of pineapples. There also were tea, coffee, and rubber plantations, planted by French colonialists during the French Indochina period. When the plane landed at our site where we were training and supporting Royal Lao Government troops, Souk would vanish into the brush. He would reappear ten days later as scheduled and be flown back to Pakse.

My work was interesting, rewarding, and time consuming. Phyllis knew none of the details or identities of the people I was working with, except for Ambrose and Pornchai, our two Thai interpreters. She knew not to ask questions. To the outside world, I was a USAID advisor. Within our Company's close family circle, the "need to know" principle was an important part of our lives. If you did not know something, you could not talk about it. For our own protection, we tended to mind our own business and tried not to be curious about the affairs of our neighbors.

* * *

Any reason to throw a party at Pakse was acceptable: a birthday, a local or American holiday, the weekend, a new arrival or a farewell, a promotion, going on leave, returning from leave, an anniversary of any sort, you name it. Phyllis casually mentioned one day at work that August 10 was our wedding anniversary. Pancho heard about it and a party was on. Everyone was invited for drinks and an impromptu finger food buffet with wine toasts. The spontaneity of this kind of entertaining was charming and a lot of fun. Phyllis and I happily acknowledged the toasts that honored our life together and made us feel we were members of Pancho's Pakse family.

Shortly after our arrival, Pancho's office staff and their wives were invited to a Baci given by Prince Boun Oum Na Champassak, who ruled the southern province of Laos and whose request was akin to a command. A Baci was the Lao way of giving special recognition to a person who is being reassigned. When we arrived, I noticed a huge array of shoes indicating that about fifty folks were attending. We removed our shoes and entered a large room with high ceilings and fans turning above glistening wooden floors. Many people were seated on woven grass mats, and we joined Dutch and Fanny, who briefed us on the Baci ceremony involving spirits that guard the human body. The Lao believe there are thirty-five spirits, one for nearly every part of the body, and that a person can become ill if some of his protecting spirits leave the body.

Toward the front of the room, a holy man was chanting in a low, monotonous, sing-song voice while three musicians played atonal music. The musicians were seated cross-legged in a small circle; one stroked a drum on his lap, another used a small hammer on round metal gongs, and the third had a stringed instrument that looked like a violin but was played like a cello. The guest of honor was a USAID officer who was going to the States soon; he was seated with Boun Oum and his wife beside a low table containing flowers, a beautiful bowl of fruit, some sugar cane, pieces of coconut and cakes, and several white cotton strings about ten inches long twisted together. When the chanting stopped, the holy man called all the good spirits down on the honored guest. After the spirits were offered fruit and other sweets, the holy man gently tied the white strings around the wrists of the honored guest and his family. Custom had it that as long as the Baci strings remained on the wrist no harm would befall you. It was a simple, dignified, and rather touching ceremony.

After the Baci, there was dancing to the lamvong, the stately national dance of the Lao people in which partners face each other and slowly move in a circle not touching one another. The lamvong is done with the arms and hands moving up and down in a kind of wave that is graceful and dignified. The ceremony lasted about an hour, and then refreshments were served while we newcomers went into a receiving line to meet the Prince and his family. Boun Oum was tall and weighed over 250 pounds. The heavier you were in Laos the more significant you were in rank. Wealthy, powerful men ate as much as they could to gain poundage and thus demonstrate their high rank.

Prince Boun Oum's wife was also a big woman, about twice the size of Phyllis. The royal couple was very pleasant and welcomed us to Pakse; they smiled a lot, as we did, to make up for our lack of language skills. He wore a white, wraparound cotton shirt with wide sleeves tied by a broad red sash around his waist and a golden medal of rank on his broad chest. His loose, black pantaloons reached just below his knees, and he was barefooted. It was an interesting costume, but as the prince he could dress in whatever fashion he wanted.

* * *

Our air freight arrived bringing cherished items of clothing and furnishings that would help make life more comfortable: lamps, table linens, and blankets, Phyl's sewing machine and patterns, our typewriter, Tom's chemistry lab equipment, Bill and Ken's toys and books, and our four-track tape deck and speakers. Music played an important part in our home life. Everyone in our group had a tape deck and would borrow and then copy tapes from each other. For a reasonable fee, the sergeant in the music store at the PX at Udorn Air Force Base would copy any record album in stock and produce a tape within twenty-four hours.

We picked up our car at the Immigration and Customs office on the Mekong River where the ferry landed. Ambrose had driven it from Vientiane where it had arrived via a military cargo flight. After washing off the road dust and servicing it at the Esso station in Pakse, we were again on wheels. I had been assigned the four-wheel drive Land Rover that Tim used, so now we had two vehicles and nowhere to go.

The Time of My Life

* * *

Three months after we arrived, it was our turn to spend a week in Bangkok. Every family got time away from the station on a regular basis to go shopping, visit the dentist, and boost our morale. The kids were excused from school and looked forward to the plane ride and watching some television at the Amarin Hotel.

We ate several times at a Thai restaurant next door to the Amarin, where the food was quite good and the clientele very interesting. The young ladies who usually were dining there would smile and nod and chat with us. Months later I heard that many of these attractive young women were ladies of the night who were just beginning their day's work.

Shopping in Bangkok was a delight for all of us, especially Phyllis. There were many little shops and large department stores within walking distance, where Phyl was able to complete most of her Christmas shopping. For entertainment, we hired a driver to take us to tourist sights such as the Dusit Zoo and the royal palace. One afternoon we visited Timland, a tourist trap with an imitation Thai village that featured an elephant farm. The huge beasts displayed their log rolling and lifting talents, quite impressive. The day before returning to Pakse we took a bus to Pattaya Beach, which was more than a two-hour ride over good roads. The famed beach resort on the Gulf of Siam was delightful and reminded us of Siesta Beach in Sarasota. At lunchtime, we feasted on sweet pineapple chunks and ham and cheese sandwiches on a shady hotel patio. We swam, sunbathed, and sipped cold beers and colas until it was time to return to Bangkok. This certainly was our kind of beach, and we vowed to return for a longer stay as soon as we could.

* * *

Souk's two couriers were very helpful in assisting him to retrieve intelligence reports. They would be flown to the Bolovens and wait at the rendezvous location for their contact to deliver his report. Sometimes they returned empty-handed because they had to flee from Pathet Lao patrols. Souk's trail watchers had been reporting heavy vehicles and tanks moving along the Ho Chi Minh Trail, suggesting a possible enemy buildup and that an attack might be coming. Our reports section sent these accounts via cable to Vientiane and to Langley. The experts in Washington questioned that tanks or armored vehicles could be moving anywhere along the trail since the Air Force was pounding it daily. Heavy traffic was not supposed to be moving, and Washington asked us to verify these reports.

Souk gave his men some simple, automatic cameras to take pictures of the vehicles that were said to "roar and clank" making the "earth move and shake." At risks beyond imagination, the trail watchers tried to photograph the monsters that moved in the gloom of night, but screened by brush and in poor lighting, it was almost an impossible task. Souk's men managed to take some shots which were brought back and developed in our office photo lab. These photos showed the uniforms and slung rifles of enemy troops walking south along the trail, proof to me at least that Souk's men were on the job and operating under high-risk conditions. Other military intelligence reports later indicated that tanks were being moved south. It turned out that Souk's men had been among the first to verify that Russian-built tanks were moving into Vietnam in significant numbers.

We suffered some losses in this dangerous game. Souk had recruited and trained two friends in the use of ground-to-air, hand-held radios and sent them on their first mission. Should a military target be sighted, they were to call and describe the target and give its location if possible. They pretended to be cattle herdsmen and were cautioned never to have their radios in their possession around the Pathet Lao. Within a week, the two men were challenged by a patrol and either forgot to get rid of their radios or tried to bluff their way through the encounter. When the Pathet Lao searched their duffle bags and found the radios they were shot without further discussion.

Another of Souk's recruits, a junior officer named Si, wrote about a meeting of regional commanders to be held in three weeks that included the Pathet Lao commanding general. This information was relayed through our military channels, and midway through the three-day meeting, T-28 bombers struck the conference site. We waited anxiously in Pakse for word from Si. Finally a letter arrived advising Souk that several high-ranking officers had been killed but the regional commander had escaped unharmed. To my dismay and sorrow, Si had been wounded in the upper leg by a bomb fragment and was now recuperating in a field hospital. Knowing the rude condition of such facilities, I despaired of Si's recovery. Filled with guilt, I blamed myself for not warning Si of his danger. Under optimum conditions, the T-28 bombs would have killed the commanding general and his staff, thereby seriously disrupting the effectiveness of the Pathet Lao actions in the region; but we missed the general and succeeded in harming our own agent. I consoled myself that the mission had followed military logic, which maintains that the individual is expendable and subordinate to the success of the mission. Many good men have been lost this way. Si was a good man and I hope he survived. His letters to Souk soon stopped.

* * *

We moved into a house that had just been built and were flooded out almost at once after several days of monsoon rains. Phyl was downstairs around midnight when she saw a steady flow of brown rainwater flooding our house. The children slept soundly while Phyl swept and mopped inside, and I stumbled groggily into the rain and built an earthen dike to divert the flow past the door. Safe for the moment, we returned to bed.

Anh-Anh, our number one house girl, said that bad Pi's (spirits) in the house caused the problem. A bad Pi was not to be taken lightly, especially when the flood came on the heels of a near electrocution a few days earlier. Phyl heard a terrified scream from the laundry and raced downstairs to find Chi-Chi, our number two girl, quivering in the grip of the electric current. Her bare feet were on the damp floor with her hand locked to the washing machine's On-Off switch. The power line to the washer was not grounded properly, and poor Chi-Chi's bare feet had served to ground the current. Phyl swatted her hand free to break the circuit, and Chi-Chi was rescued. Bad Pi's were definitely lurking in our house.

I reported the flooding to Pancho the following morning and lucked out. George and Bunny were due to leave soon. Pancho offered us their house, one of the nice, older ones in the compound, which had good Pi's and the extra bedroom we needed. We moved into the third house we had lived in since our arrival and loved it. Made of hard wood stained a dark oak color, it sat high on concrete pilings with a large screened area and a kitchen and pantry below; upstairs, an open balcony with railings ran around the front bedrooms and living room area. A handyman installed some clear plastic drop curtains inside the porch screens downstairs to protect our dining space from the rains. Phyl planted castor bean seeds along the sides that grew ten feet high, which blunted the rain and gave us more privacy. She had a green thumb and was always planting shrubs and bushes. Before long, all the other houses were outfitted with drop awnings like ours. One of the nice things about this house was that from our upstairs balcony or windows we could see for miles across rice fields and buffalo pasture toward the low mountain range between us and the towns of Saravane and Savannakhet. When the rainy season ended and the clouds lifted, we could gaze beyond the Mekong to the south at Sleeping Lady Mountain, named for the silhouette that it suggested.

* * *

Tom had assembled his chemistry materials on a workbench in our downstairs laundry and storage room. During the summer vacation, he was preparing rocket propulsion fuel from assorted chemicals he had acquired in town, such as sulphur, charcoal, and perhaps saltpeter. Not entirely sure of what he was doing, yet steeling himself with the admonishment that all scientists took risks, he began to stir this mixture of potentially explosive materials in an open-ended beaker. The new mixture, intended to propel Tom's latest rocket into space, reacted violently to the agitation and blew up, searing about two inches of Tom's chest. Phyl called me home from the office, where I found Tom in the shower with cool water running over his lacerated breast. Anh-Anh and Chi-Chi were wringing their hands and crying "Oi, Oi", while Phyl and I tried to treat Tom, who was in pain but stoic and calm as a cucumber.

The nearest hospital that could treat first-degree burns was at the Air Force base in Ubon, twenty minutes by air across the Mekong

River in Thailand. Flynn scheduled his twin-engine Baron to take Tom and me that afternoon. Air Force medics in Ubon treated Tom's wound with antibiotics and removed most of the implanted explosive particles. They then scheduled him for further treatment by burn specialists at the Fifth Field Hospital in Bangkok, where we flew that evening on a C-130 cargo flight.

An ambulance met us at the airport and whisked us to the hospital, where Tom would be treated by burn specialists first thing in the morning. I stayed in the Amarin hotel for the next two days, visiting Tom twice daily, until he was released. Tom was very good about his ordeal and never complained of discomfort, which had to be severe at times. The medics prescribed daily application of a yellow salve called Ferasin. When we returned to Pakse, he went to the clinic where Pauline Hubig, our USAID nurse, would strip off his bandage every day, remove all dead or contaminated flesh around the wound to make sure it remained clean, and then apply another coating of Ferasin. The wound healed very well but left a reddish welt of scar tissue. Within a few years, all evidence of the combustible explosion was gone, and only the memory remained. Tom quietly decided that chemistry would no longer be on his preferred list of avocations and took up photography. His chemistry lab equipment was dismantled and put into storage.

* * *

Time and events passed in a blur of activity. Christmas was most memorable because of our tree. There were no Kiwanis or church lots filled with Scotch pines and Douglas firs from Michigan or North Carolina this year, so Jack and Don brought a plane load of scrawny junipers that had been felled by their troops on the slopes of the Bolovens. When decorated with Christmas balls and some lights Phyl found at Macy's, our tree was fine. The boys got new bikes made in France, also courtesy of Macy's and Gimbel's, with balloon-tires as good as we would find at Sears or the Schwinn Bike Shop in Sarasota.

Julie was about one and a half years old when Phyl thought it was time to breed her with a poodle who lived with one of our communication families. After the nuptial arrangements were made between consenting owners, a carefully supervised pairing took place. A week or so before Christmas, Julie produced a healthy litter. Although Julie and the sire were miniature poodles, or medium size, all five of Julie's litter were toy poodles. As agreed, the pick of the litter went to the communications family for their stud fee. From the remaining four, we kept an apricot-colored male we named Thateng, after one of the area mountains. The two females were sold for $40 each to Americans from Vientiane. The remaining male, named Bolovens, was purchased by Fred and Pauline Hubig. As soon as he could walk, Bo followed Fred around like a little bloodhound.

Former President Dwight D. Eisenhower passed away about this time. "Ike" was a 1915 graduate of West Point and a father figure to many Americans, as well as to me. He served two terms (1953-1961), both with Richard M. Nixon as his Vice President, and was able to balance the budget three out of his eight years in office, during which the population of the nation rose from 155 million to 179 million people. Our heavy postwar commitments to support other nations were largely responsible for the deficit years. Highlights of his presidency included increasing the minimum wage to $1.00 per hour, broadening the social security system, and establishing the Department of Health, Education, and Welfare. He was broadly conservative and believed in reducing taxes, balancing budgets, decreasing government control over the economy, and returning certain Federal responsibilities to the states. His domestic program became labeled modern Republicanism.

* * *

Phyllis wrote the following letter:

Pakse, Laos, Monday, 16 April 1969

"Hi All: Quite a bit going on this week. It is Pi Mai, the Lao New Year and also the end of the dry season, which makes for many celebrations. Saturday was Pi Mai eve and the dry season ended with a vengeance. We had the first rain in many months and it was a dilly. We actually had hurricane force winds for about 10 minutes and high winds and rain for about an hour. The rain was 100% horizontal sweeping across our porch, bringing with it all the collected dust and dirt of the dry months. We found it quite exciting and didn't suffer too much damage. Most of our houses here are wood structures and with the prolonged dry season the wood naturally shrinks leaving plenty of space for hard driven rain to come in through the walls, the loosely fitting windows, the roof. Wow. Glad it is not our own furniture that got wet. But it was a lovely storm and the air was so fresh and cool after it stopped. We were told it always rains on schedule, and is the official day of the end of the dry season.

"It is amazing to see the green taking over in the yard and in the brown fields. I can't believe that things would start growing so fast.

"Sunday was quite a day, it rained again but not so violently. Part of the celebration of Pi Mai is what they call the "three water" days. The object is to see how much water you can throw on your friends and naturally our children thought it was a neat idea. There were no dry clothes on Pakse small fry for three days. I escaped but many of our other adults got wet. The Lao youngsters would line up outside the office and at the approaches to the one lane bridge (woe unto you if you had to stop for the traffic to change). They would also wait at Henry's (where we get our money changed) with buckets and pans of water and try to get everyone who passed. An open jeep, bicycles, motor scooters, samlors, are all very dangerous. Still, it is a rather fun way to celebrate when you think of what our kids do on Halloween with soap and paint.

"Yesterday, Tuesday, we went to a Baci given by Prince Boun Oum held in a huge house about 4 kilometers out of town. It had 60 rooms or more (an unfinished hospital, I believe). There were over two hundred people there. Many Americans, although not all of us were invited, members of the French community, as well as Lao Military and political dignitaries from all over the country. We arrived at 9 A.M., and were served beer and Scotch before the religious ceremony began at 10 A.M. This was much the largest Baci we had attended. They had six Buddhist priests who chanted in union for about 15 minutes. Very impressive. Then we went downstairs for more drinks and a buffet lunch served on long tables set in a huge hall. They were laden with more or less native fare: chicken, duck, rice, noodles, salads, sauces, most of them hot, and a variety of things that I can't describe. Most of it was quite good, but I was a bit leery of trying some of the dishes. Then the band commenced to play, and there was much dancing of the lamvong. It was fun and we joined in the dancing. If we didn't, General Phasouk made sure we did by pairing up the gals with a Lao and vice versa. We left the party about 1 P.M. with about ten other couples, to go home and take naps. I told the general my father would be proud to see me down a glass of Scotch at 10:30 in the morning in the company of princes and generals... I really have to pinch myself every now and then to believe I am really in this remote place.

"From a fading, fattening, freckling, frizzling, fraying, formerly fantastically fashionable feminine mother of four, your Fifi [Phyllis], who wants to pass on a couple of observations from son Bill, who said recently that he "can speak Japanese, but can't understand what he is saying." Our Bill is more sensitive than some and is prone to consider the vicissitudes of life carefully. A recent example: before we left Manila, he decided that ships could sink, and jets could crash. He suddenly acquired a great love for living in the Philippines and "wondered why we should ever go home."

I wrote the following letter:

Pakse, 8 June 69

"Dear Mom and family: Once more on the night duty shift so I can report that Tom and Bill have finished their school year, both with very good reports. Ken is still working because his first grade did not get started on time, but he is doing fine, like his brothers, he is giving it a strong finish. I am proud of all of them.

"The upstairs sleeping and sewing room is finished and is fine. We can open the boys' rooms and let cool air flow out to air-condition this new space as well as their own. . . The daughter of our USAID coordinator, Earl Diffenderfer, is due out about the same time as Cyndy. He said he would see they had some work to do for extra money and to keep them busy. (I am not so sure that Cyndy will like this idea, but we shall see). . . Hope Diffenderfer will have Tom as her only 8th grade student next year. They are going to tailor a school course to suit him. She can teach him Physics, for instance and perhaps beginning German. Tom passed his French course this year, but says he didn't like it too well. The lower grades study Lao for their language.

"Phyllis stopped smoking about three weeks ago, and it looks as if she will stick it out this time. She says her appetite is growing and she has to fight an increase in weight, but I am so glad she stopped. A lot of the women at the office have quit, three of the gals there got after Phyl and that must be why she stopped. Good, I say.

"The work is going well. Now that the rains have started, there is a general slowdown of enemy activity. This means we can relax and not worry unduly about unexpected moves on their part. They can't move around as much with roads being washed out and without air transport they have to rely on small boats, trucks and strong backs.

Best wishes and love from Adie and the family."

* * *

By the end of August, we returned from a very restful and relaxing leave in Thailand. We spent ten days on the beach at the Nippa Lodge and four days in Bangkok, again at the Amarin Hotel. The Nippa Lodge was built around a pool that was shaded by tall coconut trees. A few Air America pilots and their wives were seen lounging by the pool and displaying huge gold bracelets called the Four Seasons bracelet. Ostensibly these were good luck charms, but they were also valuable bartering items should the pilot be shot down in enemy territory.

We did not swim at the beach because it was not very clean; in fact, the beach was used as a pony track. The boys rode ponies led by a handler, and Phyl and I noticed how all the horse dung was washing into the water, not to mention the runoff from the nearby hotels and street buildings. We took a couple of half-day cruises to a sprinkle of small islands about a mile offshore on a fishing boat that slowly chugged out with us laid back in shaded beach chairs, our cooler tucked between our knees. The clear, clean waters were alternately deep and then shallow as we passed over coral rocks and patches of seaweed that hid spiny sea urchins and little sea horses. We anchored and then swam, snorkeled, and sunbathed until noon when we waded ashore and found a lean-to kitchen where we ate freshly sliced pineapples. There was no fresh water on the island, and only primitive bathroom facilities. The beach was clean and relatively unspoiled because not many round eyes like us had found this spot. As the war in South Vietnam expanded, increasing numbers of GI's began coming here on R and R, joined later by hordes of Germans and the Scandinavians.

We thoroughly enjoyed the hot, near-perfect summer weather. We swam in our Olympic-size pool, sunbathed, and sampled the hot and spicy Thai foods at the dining pavilion and various restaurants along the beach. We rode in little jitneys where the fare was "one man one baht" (about 5 cents per fare) or three-wheeler samlor vehicles along the quarter-mile main street, hopping off to shop and buy trinkets from the tourist stores. I kept trying to like Thai food, but the searing spices must have destroyed my taste buds. Phyllis and the boys did much better, especially Ken and Bill.

* * *

The Time of My Life

Following are some of Phyllis' notes on our vacation:

"14 August: 7 A.M. Beautiful morning, sun brilliant on the Gulf of Siam, and on the pool directly beneath our window. We all arise, Adie gives us 10 minutes to be on the beach and moving toward JUSMAG where they serve breakfast. We just make it, dressed in bathing suits and shirts to cover up, and have a nice breakfast. The young boy who took Ken for a horseback ride yesterday (50 cents for a half hour) was waiting on the beach so off went Ken on the pony, named Howdy; Bill joined him on another pony whose name I don't know.

"That afternoon we planned to take the 1 P.M. boat to the islands so we packed some cokes and beer for our little cooler, rented some snorkels and fins, and waded out to the boat off shore. We had all boarded the boat when Ken announced he had cut his foot (on a piece of glass, we think). Much blood. I took a look and knew we weren't going to make the trip. Then a young man who said he was a medic took a look also, confirming my thoughts, so—we all waded ashore, thankful these were U.S. facilities with a dispensary right at hand. Ken was cleaned and bandaged in short order. They didn't suture the 1″ cut, instead used a new type of adhesive bandage that takes the place of stitches and is supposed to fall off in about ten days. We will try the boat trip in the morning. Ken is not to swim for we don't know how long, which puts a damper on things, but we hope to keep him amused.

"15 August. . . Another beautiful morning with cool clear air. We boarded our twin outboard catamaran which had a roof and a well in the middle, from which a glass bottom viewing box gets lowered when we stop to examine the coral reefs. The reef formations and underwater scenes were beautiful. We went to a cove and anchored off shore. Coconut trees fringing the shoreline, high cliffs beyond. Adie carried Ken to shore where he played happily in the sand. He was a good sport about not being able to swim.

"Sunday was a lazy day. Had breakfast at the outdoor dining patio overlooking the pool. There were two tame monkeys housed in one of the trees that kept us amused. Ken had his daily ride on Howdy and is quite friendly with the young boy who handles the horse. The boy gets on behind Ken and they go racing along the beach.

"Monday, Tom and Cyndy made a date to rent a boat with driver for water skiing after lunch. The younger boys went pony riding on the beach as usual.

"We all watched Tom and Cyndy ski; Ken rode in the boat which was a rather nifty fiberglass job. Both Cyndy and Tom did well on the skis, which were a sled type used for beginners. While they were busy, Bill rented a kayak kind of small boat and paddled around off shore. After skiing and a relaxing lunch we took Ken to the dispensary. OH JOY! They said he could swim this afternoon. So we dashed back to the pool and he has been swimming like mad.

"Next day (Tuesday) we had our first rain, a hard thunder shower, but that was okay. That evening we went to dinner at the Coral Reef, an elegant place right over the water. Would be a real knockout on Siesta Key or Longboat. Just smashing, as was The Outrigger, another place we visited last night. Both places are on the water and are open to the stars; one could see the lights of fishing boats coming and going as well as flashing beacons on the tops of the outer islands. Pattaya Beach is growing rapidly and many new restaurants and bars are opening up. There is no need for air-conditioning in the evenings, but most of these places are now.

"Thursday we returned to Bangkok, and Cyndy, Tom and I spent the morning at J.C., the Jeweler, trying to decide on something nice for Cyndy's 21st birthday. Adie kept the younger kids entertained watching TV at the Amarin. JC sent his car around to the hotel and insisted we use it and his driver for the afternoon. It was a grand help as his car was big enough to hold us and all the groceries and stuff we bought. Regular taxis are rather small and we would have needed two of them. As a rule I don't buy groceries in Bangkok, but this time I did for the Mekong River is rising and threatening again to flood Vientiane. The last time this happened the commissary and airport at Vientiane were flooded and Pakse didn't get any food for several weeks.

"Cyndy and I took the temple tour while Adie took the boys to the Bangkok Zoo. The most memorable thing we saw was a 5 ½ TON solid gold Buddha. It was dazzling.

"Sunday, August 24. Sunning, swimming and bowling before we went to Timland in the afternoon. This is a well-run tourist attraction showing many facets of Thai Culture, such as milling and winnowing of the rice, pottery making, musical instruments, elephants working with monstrous teak logs, Thai classical dancing, Thai boxing, sword fighting, cock fighting, all well done and highly entertaining.

"That evening we packed for a 9 A.M. departure for Pakse. We are all anxious to get home which is a good sign. We loved our vacation and now are ready to get back in the everyday routine of things, anxious to see Julie and Thateng and Taurus (the cat), and all our friends in Pakse."

I wrote the following letter:

Pakse, 12 Sept 69

"Dear Mom and family: Cyndy left us on the 5th, returning to the States by way of Saigon, Manila and on to San Francisco. She is back at school now. We certainly enjoyed her company, she was fun to have around. She has been pretty uncommunicative (must have been the yankee in her coming out) and is inclined to reticence, but I do need her travel receipts so I can clear up her travel account at the office. (The Government paid for her air tickets since she was a full-time student). Anyway, we do love her and she was a bit teary at departure time, says Phyllis. Tom and I were away getting his burn treated in Bangkok.

"I am sorry to hear of Everett Dirkson's death but not at all depressed by Ho Chi Minh's demise. It is too soon to tell what effect that will have on the outcome of the war but I hope his troops will become demoralized and not have the heart to continue. At present our side is doing well but the dry season is coming and then the enemy gets his turn at bat. Will try to keep you posted.

"Phyl says she has gained about five pounds but we all assure her we would rather have a fat Momma than a dead Momma. She plans to quit work at the office November first, so she will have more time to help the boys with their homework and to be a better president of the school board. Take care until next time, love, Adie"

Pancho finished his tour of duty and left on home leave. His next posting was as Chief of Base in Nha Trang, my old stomping rounds in II Corps, South Vietnam. He had been a good boss, and I worked hard for him. He promoted me to a GS-13, which meant about $2,500 more per year. His place was taken by Lenny, our deputy.

* * *

Around this time, Phyllis contracted an odd illness. One day she complained of a terrible headache that caused intense pain right behind her eyeballs, becoming even more painful when she moved her eyes. At first, she thought it was another migraine, but this was far worse. Suddenly, she had a fever, chills, a backache, and pain in her joints and muscles. She took to her bed, hardly able to move, and treated herself with aspirin, lots of water, and some good Scotch whiskey. We all thought it would pass, but it did not let up for almost a week. Phyl did not know what to do, so she simply took it easy and endured, hoping it would not get any worse. Her pain gradually lessened, and within a week her fever went down and the aches in her joints diminished. When she was able, she went into town and talked to Dr. Alex, who told her she had had a classic case of dengue or breakbone fever, so called because you feel as if your bones are breaking. It is a viral disease caused by the bite of the Aedes mosquito, which does not occur in the United States. The only treatment is rest, and there is no preventive vaccine.

Every afternoon during the work week at precisely five o'clock, we were jolted by a booming explosion. The blast occurred about a mile away at our local granite quarry, but we felt the concussion. It took us a long time to get used to this interruption, especially Phyl and the boys who were at home.

Some of the quarry rock was used to build the lane to our house and was spread in our carport and walkway areas. Phyl was wary of these sharp rocks since they could easily cause someone to turn an ankle. On rainy days, the combination of slick mud and loose rocks made it more hazardous. When the sun came out and the rocks dried, little black snakes sometimes lurked there. More than once I heard an "Eeeeeek" from Phyllis as she skipped away from the dreaded but nonpoisonous snake. When Julie saw one she would rush at it barking and yipping until the snake fled.

The rice fields adjacent to our house were unfenced when we moved in. We later installed wire fencing to restrain the neighborhood buffalo from wandering over and eating our castor bean plants and nibbling all our green grass. In the pastures were tall mounds of red clay that looked like sandcastles. Upon closer inspection, they were about three feet tall and filled with thousands of termites. The boys gingerly poked around with sticks, prepared to leap away should we be attacked; but the inhabitants ignored us, and in time we learned to ignore them. I wondered where they went for food since there were no trees nearby for them to infest. I kept a sharp eye on these mounds but never saw a termite trail lead toward our house.

SIXTEEN

Rockets and Rice Bowls

In Laos, the dry months of October through January are filled with delightfully cool nights and bright days. The sun's heat gradually intensifies, first drying and then parching the land. As the waters in the turbulent and bridgeless Mekong begin to recede, the river banks reemerge, and waters that once surged with awesome force gradually become placid and easily navigable. In May or June, cyclical rains reappear in the form of gusty, heavy torrents that drown and thrash and scour the mountains and valleys from China to Vietnam, dissolving trails and turning village roads into quagmires. Streams from countless crests and hills run into the Mekong and turn it a rich coffee-with-cream color. Soon the river banks are covered by a brown tide that seeps far and wide and embraces vast tracts of rice paddy lowlands along its 2,700-mile length. The fertile Mekong curves snakelike through Laos, Thailand, and Cambodia, depositing layers of fresh topsoil along the way, until she finally reaches South Vietnam's broad southern delta and drains into the South China Sea. From August to September, when the river crests, the Mekong can reach depths of 30 to 40 feet and measure more than a mile wide. It is a fascinating river by any standard.

Pakse - 16 October 1969

"Dear Mom and family: A report this morning says a small army outpost on the Sedone River 15 kilometers north of us has been hit by a commando raid which killed and wounded several Lao Government troops and damaged some buildings. I mention this incident to assure you there is no threat to Pakse, but you might get that impression from the television. A TV crew was here the day of the attack. General Phasouk, our regional commander who was hosting the visitors, took the TV crew to the scene via his helicopter. The TV cameras were very busy, but there is no telling if the story will appear on national TV or not. Reporters have been running in and out of Pakse at top speed, all of them spouting questions.

"The *NY Times* continues to run stories on the military situation in Laos and to highlight our involvement in great detail, none of which is helpful to our cause. Slanting the news for political impact is still very popular with the press these days; they are against whomever is in the White House [then Richard M. Nixon who had defeated Hubert Humphrey handily in 1968]. Naturally, those of us posted here feel as if we are being attacked personally and make a conscious effort to avoid talking to any news people; they in turn are proving to be hard-nosed and tenacious, looking for any possibly controversial lead. Obviously, the politically astute PL and NVA who conducted the raid know the value of hit-and-run tactics and are happily capitalizing on the over-hyped news coverage they usually receive.

"Aside from the above situation, life in Pakse is going on rather well. I directed a Lao work party that has painted our school classrooms so now the kids have a pretty decent facility. We are working to air-condition all the rooms, and by November new floor rugs and carpets will be installed. The large classroom downstairs is used on Friday and Saturday nights for family movies. . . .Phyllis is busy with her school board job and soon will stop working at the office so she can devote more time to school activities.

"The rains are gone and the air is clear and cool in the morning. October is a nice month and the kids have planned a Halloween Party at school. . . The latest from the commissary is that we now can order ice cream and Foremost milk from Vientiane. (American troops abound in such numbers in Thailand now it is profitable to produce milk and ice cream locally. Foremost bid for the contract.) More later and with love to all, from Adie and family"

* * *

Despite the reassuring letter to my Mother, the dry season brought a noticeable increase in enemy pressure on Pakse as well as Vientiane. It was particularly heavy at Xieng Khoung airstrip and Phou Nok Kok, an outpost that overlooked the main enemy supply route to the strategic Plain of Jars. The Plain of Jars literally contains jars. Two sites on the plateau are littered with several hundred jars that stand about four feet tall and are carved from solid rock, many with well-fitted lids. Their origin is a mystery, but the most likely explanation is that they are ancient burial urns. NVA attacks against other bases and landing strips, such as our Lima sites on the Bolovens, were intensifying. There had been unprecedented night raids on supply depots only 13 miles from Vientiane.

The previous summer, Premier Souvanna Phouma had visited Paris to appeal to the British and French, and through them to the Russians, for help in curbing Communist China's influence in Laos. We were worried that the Chinese may become increasingly involved in the ground war, a fear rooted in our experience with the fanatic Chinese hordes during the Korean War. There were rumors, but no hard evidence, that Chinese advisors were working with Pathet Lao troops, much like our American advisors were working with the Laotian government, so we really did not want to complain too loudly.

The poor Laos were facing military invasions by North Vietnamese and Pathet Lao troops from the north and military penetrations by the VC troops on the Ho Chi Minh Trail to the southeast. They were in a no-win situation but stoically continued to struggle for independence against long odds. From what I could see, the Laotian government's troops were nearing the bottom of the manpower barrel. Thanks to Uncle Sam's taxpayers, they remained fairly well equipped and had our air support, but after five or six years of constant warfare they were now using 12- and 13-year-old boys in their front lines. Around the Lao homes and camps near the Lima airstrips, which were used to resupply troops and their families, quite a few young men could be seen on crutches, minus a leg or a foot shattered by antipersonnel mines while patrolling jungle trails.

THE DRY SEASON OFFENSIVE

The rains slackened, and the Ho Chi Minh Trail began to dry up. Bomb craters filled with mud and water were repaired, making the roads accessible again. As the tonnage of war material moving south from Russia and China increased, U.S. airpower became more active in response. Souk's men began to report more and more incidents of heavy vehicles rumbling through the darkness toward South Vietnam.

Our sites on the Bolovens came under more frequent night attacks, the traditional time favored by the NVA and Pathet Lao. One early morning while I monitored the upcountry radio, Chuck called in a garbled, ghostly voice saying their perimeter was being probed and taking some light fire. I told him to stand by until I could get Ray, our senior night operations officer. I was grateful I did not work paramilitary operations where I could be threatened by Vietnamese soldiers slithering toward me intent on blowing me to pieces. In this case, the enemy probe was not a serious attack, but if it had been, we might have required some air support.

Fortunately, we could radio *Moonbeam*, the Air Force C-130 command ship, and ask for help. A *Raven* observer aircraft would respond and direct a fighter-bomber or flare ship to our rescue. It was reassuring to know that *Moonbeam* was circling just across the Mekong, known as the Fence. F-4's or F-5's departing from Udorn or Ubon airfields would radio *Moonbeam* and ask if they needed assistance. *Moonbeam* then would assign any targets they might have on the Trail. If one of our Lima sites on the Bolovens was under attack, *Moonbeam* would tell the Raven controller to contact the site for directions. Fortunately, none of our bases had been overrun, but several were hit hard. Usually flares from a C-47 Spooky or a C-130 Spectre gunship were sufficient to discourage the attackers.

We briefly experimented with sending one of our officers to Ubon Air Base at night to verify quickly if Americans were on the ground in the Bolovens when an emergency arose. The Air Force was understandably uncertain of us, since it was hard to believe that Americans would be on the ground in the Bolovens. One of the reasons we Agency people were called spooks was probably because we were often in unbelievable places.

The Royal Thai Air Force Base at Ubon was home to the 8th Tactical Fighter Wing, which was outfitted with 72 F-4 Phantoms built by McDonnell Douglas. Each F-4 and its two-man crew weighed more than a B-17 bomber and its 10-man crew and carried three times as much ordinance. Its two jet engines were seven times more powerful than the four piston engines of the ancient B-17. Such high technology was expensive though; the B-17 cost $276,000 in 1943 dollars, whereas the F-4 cost $2.4 million in 1967 dollars.

I drew the Ubon night duty only once. After a briefing with the operations officer, I was told I could rest on the Commanding Officer's couch. The evening was quiet, and I rested lightly until about 5:30 A.M. when I heard the Commanding Officer walk in. When I rose from the couch beyond his desk, he was quite surprised. Standing stock still and measuring me with his cold blue eyes, he tried to decide whether I was friend or foe. I opened my hands wide and introduced myself, assuring him I was from Pakse and had been assigned by the Operations Officer to his couch for the night. He did not say anything and then left for what I assumed were much bigger fish to fry.

I smelled coffee somewhere and followed my nose to the mess hall where I got some breakfast. Before I left the flight line, I walked through the pilot's ready room with its rows of metal lockers and green survival vests whose pockets were crammed with maps and other useful items. Hanging on hooks alongside hard bubble helmets and black oxygen masks were the familiar dark green flight suits with zippers, lifeless without their owners. I thought of all the fine young pilots out there going about their fearful business and remembered that twenty-five years ago my crew and I dressed for a different war but the same kind of mission. It was twenty-five years, a generation ago, yet the basic business of war had changed very little. The

Colonel may have complained about his office being used by some spook from Pakse, because the whole idea was scrapped shortly thereafter.

THE ROCKET ATTACK

Phyllis wrote the following letter:

Pakse, January 15, 1970

"Dear Family: At risk of scaring you a little bit I am going to attempt to write you about the night we were attacked by rockets and try to relate some of the aftermath.

"At 12:40 A.M., on January 9th we were awakened by the eeriest whistle you ever heard followed by a loud explosion. Adie immediately knew what the whistle meant and we were out of our beds and on the way to get the children when another whistle and a second rocket hit with a horrendous crash. Tom was awake and said he tried to get out of bed, but just couldn't move until I opened his door. Then we all beat it for the downstairs. Ken, Tom, and Adie were on the stairs when we heard the next whistle. I was waiting for Bill at the top of the stairs; he was walking toward me when the whistle came at us and as I watched he just stopped and slowly started walking backward. I grabbed him and we started down the stairs just as a rocket exploded across the street from the Chief's house, which we could see from our stairs which are protected from the outside only by the screen. We huddled against the downstairs cement wall with our backs against it while two more rockets landed. The scream of them is the damnedest thing you ever heard.

"Then we had a lull and a chance to get organized. Adrian quick went back upstairs, got his carbine and some blankets. The kids and I spread some mats and pillows on the floor and pulled the foam rubber mattress (about 6 inches thick) from the maid's

400

bed downstairs and we all got in position against the wall with the mattress placed so we could put it over our heads.

"It was pretty obvious to us our compound was the target for the rockets sure were close. We could hear our neighbors down the street calling back and forth, so we knew they were okay. It was very still and quite dark as the generator was hit by the first few rounds, and voices carried very well in that atmosphere. Adie called down to Dutch that we were all right and the seven families within shouting distance all reported in. The guy across the street from Dutch shouted the order for him to get his family in the ditch by his house. We could hear all this activity but elected to stay put. Lina, who lived between Dutch and us, was alone with her two small kids since her husband, Leon, was up country for the night, so Dutch went and got them and their blankets. Dutch and Fanny and their two children bedded down in the ditch with another couple, two other single gals and the wife of the USAID medic and her son.

"All of this happened within ten minutes if you can believe that. We were very scared, shaking and dry in the mouth but no one panicked or cried or complained. I think we were too frightened. The only other sound we heard for a while was Dutch (who had a bull horn voice) yelling, "Everyone down, here they come again." We dived under our mattress, Julie and Thateng with us, shaken as badly as we were, but it was a false alarm.

"We began to stir around a little bit at that point. Got water from the kitchen, more blankets, a bath robe for me (I was in my new pink nylon nightie). Remarkably enough, we heard no sounds from the ditch, which spoke well for all the children, Lina's are 1 year and 4 years old, and are usually quite noisy. Our dogs didn't make a sound either. We kept our position against the wall for almost an hour and then decided it was all over, that they had just made a quick hit and run foray which is the pattern of the NVA. At about five minutes of 2, we decided to go up-stairs and get some sleep.

"We had no sooner reached our rooms when we heard the now unmistakable sound of a rocket leaving its launcher. You have never seen five people move so fast. We were downstairs and under the mattress before the whistle stopped. That's the hell of it, they come in screaming and then the sound stops and you are sure it is right overhead, then you get as small as possible and wait for the boom. It seems like hours between the whistle and the boom, but it is seconds. I really don't know how long that barrage lasted but it consisted of at least 10 rounds and each one seemed to get a little closer. They landed behind us, below us, near the USAID offices and our school and above us near the four houses where we used to live. We were sure someone up there got hit, but we couldn't see anything. We were certain we had been hit too when some of our windows broke from the concussion, and we found some shrapnel in our yard the next day.

"During the second barrage we improved our position by mov-ing into the maid's room which has cement walls. We took up positions on the floor where we could all manage to stretch out. We put the little boys on the maid's bed with instructions that at the first noise they were to hop on the floor with us under the mattress.

"About this time, the Lao Army came to life and started shoot-ing their mortars to the north, in the general direction from whence the rockets came. Once we realized that these were outgoing rounds, not incoming rockets, we relaxed a little. Also about this time, we heard aircraft overhead and realized that one of the big gun ships called Spooky's was overhead. He started dropping flares and we felt much happier knowing these ships had tremendous firepower and that if the baddies launched any more rockets they would be zapped in a hurry.

"Then word was passed there was a possibility that enemy

ground troops would follow the rocket attack so our new found serenity was shattered. However, Adie was of the opinion that if we had been zapped with mortars, ground action might follow, but he didn't think such would be the case with rockets, and his prediction turned out to be accurate.

"We managed a few winks of sleep between 3 A.M. and 5 A.M., and as the sky started to lighten we felt safe enough. We Swain dependents were very thankful that Adie had experience with this sort of thing in Vietnam, for he knew exactly what to do and in general what to expect.

"Golly, I have gotten myself nervous again just writing this. Think I will take a break and go play some tennis on our new court that was just finished the day of the attack, and was not harmed.

"Friday dawned bright and sunny. Everyone was out early surveying the damage and picking up pieces of razor-sharp shrapnel. [It was determined later the rockets were Russian-made 122 millimeter Katyuska rockets about five feet long with an explosive warhead and a range of 12 to 15 kilometers.] A total of 15 rockets landed around our Compound and in the vicinity of the airport. The airport was probably the main target, but you could have fooled us. Fortunately, no one was hurt, frightened nearly to death, yes, and several of the houses very close to us sustained some damage, the worst one was not occupied at the time—as Delmar [one of our communicators] was in Bangkok. The office building lost all of its windows, many of the houses in the upper compound had broken windows, and one had a piece of shrapnel slash through its roof.

"Everyone was pretty shaky and tired. Some of the gals were badly scared, oh, we all were, men included, but in the light of day it didn't seem too bad to some of us. There was speculation about whether the dependents would be taken out of Pakse. Some said they were going if they had to walk, which was stupid cause in less than half a mile you hit the Mekong and it is too wide to swim. We just went about our normal routine, sort of. I laid out clothes to pack for the boys in the event we were told to leave. The men started making plans in the event of another attack, and finding out why we didn't get air support any earlier. [It was a communications problem, but as soon as the Air Force was alerted they got right over us, but we felt they should have been here sooner.]

"Plans were made right away to provide each house with a sandbag bunker. Then at 2 P.M. a message was passed saying that transportation would be provided for those dependents who wished to fly to Vientiane, the plane would probably be leaving by 4 P.M. This was not an official evacuation, which can only be ordered by the Ambassador and is a major political step, but ours would be on a strictly voluntary basis. Adrian and I decided I should go with the children particularly as our bunker would not be completed by nightfall. We really didn't expect another attack that night, but figured it was a free trip to Vientiane and that the children should be able to get a good night's sleep.

"So I quickly packed and we took off about 5 P.M. on a twin-engine Caribou cargo plane which had bucket seats along each side with cargo space between the rows of seats. Wish I had a picture. The kids (13 of them) all sat in the forward seats with the women (12) we just about filled the plane. The kids thought it was a great treat, most of them, and we had a pleasant two-hour ride, except that it was cold. On this big aircraft they leave the rear loading door open (big enough to drive in vehicles) until an altitude of about 8,000 feet is reached. Then they closed the door until we began to descend for a landing. Very exciting and the view from the open rear space was beautiful.

"We arrived in Vientiane about 7 P.M. and were met by some of our people who took us to the USAID guesthouse in two buses. There we were each assigned an apartment, we had two bedrooms, a kitchen, living room and bath. Very nice. We unloaded our gear and went across the street to the Embassy compound where there is a very nice restaurant. Everyone had a good dinner and was glad to get to bed.

"Next day the kids had a ball, going to the commissary, swimming, saw two movies, and ate all day. I went out to dinner with some old friends.

"Sunday was another day of play and speculating when we would return to Pakse. Monday we were told there was transportation back for those who wished to go, that there had been no further enemy action in Pakse, and there was no objection to our return. So the Swains elected to return with Fanny Snyder and her two children, Bill (12) and Carol (13) both good friends of our children. We quickly packed again and got a C-47 flight to Udorn arriving there about 3 P.M. and transferred to a C-46 cargo flight which arrived at Pakse about 5 P.M.

"Unbeknownst to us, during our absence in Vientiane, our darling Julie gave birth to five puppies. Adie was the mid-wife to their arrival about midnight in our bunker. Julie didn't need much help from Adie, who was groggily aware of what was going on, but pretty tired. The puppies are going to be very cute, but the father was definitely a Lao dog (we had hoped that Thateng had been the one) and we don't know yet whether they will have poodle characteristics or not, but hopefully some of them will. Julie was delighted to have us back and my was she proud, and Thateng was out of his mind with joy to have his family back. Even Tauris the cat seemed relieved and Adie, of course, was glad to see us.

"We rearranged the bunker a bit, put in pillows and water and bug spray, and then hit the sack early upstairs. We had no trouble that night or since, but we do keep on the alert.

"More later, with love to all, Phyllis."

405

Adrian Swain

* * *

Phyllis kept a detailed diary during these uncertain days, which she referred to when writing home. Some of her random notes are more entertaining than the actual events. Selected samples follow:

"Friday, February 6, 1970. . . . Another peaceful night, thank goodness. The Vietnamese New Year starts today and tension is running high for we feel there is to be another attack during the Tet holidays. . . . We have had three practice alerts, two were only "Bunker Alerts" during which we got into our bunkers while ward leaders checked to see everyone was in place. The third alert was a gathering at our HLZ [helicopter landing zone] last Sunday morning. We all walked to the rice paddies nearby. It was a bright sunny day and we all felt a little foolish gathering in the field with all the carabao dung. The children were disappointed that a chopper didn't appear. Sorry no one had a camera. Would have been a good shot to remember Pakse by.

"We thought perhaps they would attack the night before Tet began on the 4th. . . . Lucy, Robin, and I got out the weegee [ouija] board and the message we got was not very reassuring. It said there would be an attack at 12 midnight on the 4th, that there would be 20 rockets, and that 5 of the houses would be hit, including ours. Well, we were in a quandary as to what to do. Should we tell the people involved, or what? Robin, who is a great believer in spiritualism, decided to warn those involved. As a result, most people spent the night in their bunkers, including us.

"Thankfully nothing happened, but we gals got the devil from our husbands for spreading rumors and getting everyone all excited. But, golly, suppose there had been an attack? and our friends were injured? So guess what??? Natch, Robin and I had another go at the board yesterday. We contacted Robin's grandmother Ida, who said we had stopped working the board too

406

soon, and in truth we were in a hurry the afternoon before as it was nearing dinner time. Ida said we had misunderstood the message, that the attack would be in four days, not on the fourth of February, making the day of the attack the early morning of the 9th, which figures because that is the day the cease-fire ends. She spelled out that the Dotys and the Mercers and the Snyders should relocate their bunkers, and that the Swain house would be hit in the area of the parents' bedroom. I am assuming that means the upstairs bedroom but just now realized it might mean the downstairs room where we now sleep. Better check on that today. The board went on to say the rocket attack will last until 2 A.M., the target will be the FAR [Forces Army Royal] headquarters to the north of us, that enemy troops will not enter our compound but would get to within 1 kilometer of us, and the ground attack would last until 5 in the morning, at which time all women and children would be evacuated by helicopter to Udorn. Asked why Udorn and not Ubon (which is much closer) the chilling answer was that Ubon would also be under attack.

"I have not said anything more about our ouija sessions as Adrian asked me not to, but Robin told those involved about redoing their bunkers.

"Tonight Lucy will spend the night with us as Pete has upcountry duty. Tomorrow, Fannie and her children, Bill and Carol, will stay with us while Dutch is upcountry.

"At this point, most people have a bag packed. I have things packed for the boys and keep clothes handy in case we have to leave in a hurry. I have a camouflage jacket with big pockets loaded with my jewelry and other small pertinent things like my makeup and our tooth brushes.

"I don't know what to think as I sit here this morning at my typewriter. Everything is very normal. Chi and An are off for the weekend for this is their new year. I have not done the breakfast dishes as I wanted to write while the spirit moved me (Oh, Oh, the spirit again), and while the children are at school. I mostly think there will be an attack. I'm not sure what the men think because they are all pretty tight-lipped these days (I don't know what they think they are saving us from) but I think they expect it too.... This period of waiting is difficult but there is no panic or hysteria.... On the nights of the 8th and 9th I am going to insist that from 11:45 P.M. on everyone is in the bunker, for you see, I more than half believe the message we got from Ida....

"March 5th.... Well, Adrian and I didn't sleep in the bunker the nights of the 8th and 9th, but I had one foot out of bed but no attack.... the interesting aftermath of the ouija sessions was that the powers that be got busy and rebuilt everyone's bunker, and believe me, some of them were pretty flimsy. Ours was OK because Adrian—the old VN bunker builder—engineered it. Also we did get another attack on the night of 15-16 February, and everyone felt safe in their new bunkers.... Also, Ida had told us to be prepared during the Tet holidays, which ended on the 15th. To be fair, there were intelligence reports to this effect at the office, so we can't give all the credit to Ida."

* * *

An article from the *New York Times*, datelined Pakse, Laos, March 7, 1970, by Henry Kamm, reports the second rocket attack on our area and describes our fair city.

"Pakse is one of the biggest towns in Laos and one of the most secure. After dark, a roundeye—as many a non-Asian calls himself in Asia—can venture about five miles to the east or west, as far as the next town to the south and perhaps 25 miles to the north, with reasonable assurance of survival. The margin of safety is greater for a Laotian.

But on January 9 and again on February 16, Communist forces got close enough with 122-mm rocket launchers to fire at Pakse, 15 rounds the first time, 12 the second. They set some fires the first time and damaged an air force plane and a helicopter at the air base the second. They could do it at any time, and they could inflict more damage.

People who live around the air base have dug holes under their houses, which are set on piles, but even in Pakse war is so much a fact of life that no one shows signs of worry.

Pakse is the capital of the southern region dominated by Prince Boun Oum, the leader of the rightest faction in the three-way division recognized in the Geneva agreement of 1962.

Prince Boun Oum is not now active in domestic politics, but in a country where the central Government in Vientiane controls very little besides Vientiane, the Prince's regional influence in what was once the Champassak kingdom remains dominant.

The eastern reaches of the panhandle are under North Vietnamese domination because the Ho Chi Minh Trail runs through them. Two other provincial capitals in the region—Saravane, 55 miles to the northeast and Attopeu, 70 miles to the east and south—have long been surrounded by the Communists and are linked with the outside only by air.

In Attopeu, no plane has landed in months because the airstrip is within enemy range, and only helicopters make the hazardous flights bearing supplies. The pilots do not shut off their rotors while unloading, and they take right off again.

But Pakse enjoys peace, constantly menaced but living its own life.

Pakse is hot and sleepy. Dust blows freely in the dry season, spreading over all surfaces and penetrating clothing. Chinese shopkeepers sit in their openfront stores and fan the flies off their children as they nap.

Officially 15 Americans* live in Pakse. The real number is considerably higher because Pakse is the seat of the fifth military region and the air base is important.

The American influence has not wiped out the feeling of a French colonial town, largely because the architecture is of the yellow stucco style—looking tropical on the outside but remarkably cool within— that France built throughout her empire.

Most of the signs on public buildings are French, as is the bread. There is still a Rue Coloniale. A former colonialist's home houses the Alliance Francaise, where French is taught and French movies are shown. The practical value of English is on the rise in Laos, but the prestige value of French remains higher.

And the hunchback who runs the 007 James Bond Tailor's shares his shop with a public scribe whose own sign announces, 'Ecrivain Public.' The scribe performs in Laotian and French; no English written here."

THE SECOND ATTACK

The second rocket attack was far more bearable than the first. We endured it more comfortably inside the shelter of our sandbagged bunker. I even had time to place a tape recorder on top of the bunker roof with another recorder inside. The only legible voice was mine plaintively asking, "Where is the flashlight?" Our interoffice radio volume was turned on high in our bedroom, so we heard Flynn tell Lenny he had called *Moonbeam*, which was very reassuring.

The barrage lifted after a few hours, but none of us felt comfortable about sleeping upstairs. Phyl and I permanently transferred our bedding downstairs into the maid's room and arranged the boys' bunks in the storage room next to us. All the downstairs rooms were

---

* My estimate of American residents in Pakse was about fifty, not counting dependents and children: overt USAID members totaled perhaps fifteen; military attaches for the Army and Air Force numbered about five, including some TDY Raven pilots detached from Vientiane; there were a few Air American pilots also out of Vientiane; and the balance were civilians like me assigned under USAID.

now air-conditioned, so we spent the rest of the night feeling snug and secure.

Pakse, 9 April 1970

"Dear Mom: All is well here. I am on the night duty watch again catching up on my letters.

"There seems to be little threat from the north these days but there is a lot of political action going on, and something is going on in Cambodia to the south of us. I'm trying to keep up with it all, but it is not easy. Many rumors in the air about a negotiated peace, but rumors are not very dependable.

"We are still not sure where our next assignment will be, so we don't know which way we'll be returning. I kind of favor the west coast, maybe a stop to see Jack Stickel and let the kids spend a day or so at Disneyland. On the other hand we might go via Europe and stop in Paris to see Phyl's cousin [Jane Swanson] whose husband is with Mobil Oil and whom we met in Manila.

"Life is interesting and very busy. The boys are doing well in school, and looking forward to their return to the states. I think all they really want is to go to the beach and swim. The two dogs are great and so is the Siamese cat, although he is bad, not house broken yet and a problem. Do not plan on bringing that one home at all. The parakeet we have is also expendable. So there. Nature lovers, animal lovers, sue me if you will.

"All my love and best wishes to the clan. Say hello to Esther and the neighbors. Hope you had a nice Easter. Love, Adie"

* * *

During the early months of 1970, fighting continued throughout most of South Vietnam as it had during 1969, but not as heavily as in 1968. In March, a military coup d'etat deposed Prince Norodom

411

Sihanouk of Cambodia while he was out of the country. His successor, General Lon Nol, appealed to the United States for arms. In May, President Nixon sent an expeditionary force of U.S. and South Vietnamese troops across the Cambodian border on search and destroy missions looking for secret staging areas and stock piles that the NVA had established in Cambodia.

Lenny called me into the office in early April to show me a personnel cable offering me a tour in Vietnam at a place called Parrot's Beak on the border between South Vietnam and Cambodia in Tay Ninh Province. With a sinking feeling in my gut, I looked at the map and saw at a glance that this area was pretty hot. A lot of NVA troops and war supplies were hidden along the Cambodian border not far from Tay Ninh Province. I had bad vibes about this one and without even talking to Phyllis resolved that there was no way I was going to put my tender butt anywhere near that province. It looked like I was in for another cliff hanger deciding where the Swains would go next. I assured Phyllis I would return to Vietnam only as a last resort.

LAO NOW NEWS

The Swain family had a lot of varied and interesting experiences in Pakse, some of which were recorded and saved. The monthly publication of the American School in Pakse called *LAO NOW* was filled with journalistic gems like the following:

THE FLOOD (Vol. 1, No. 1, September 1, 1969)

About a week ago there was a monsoon, which is a wind, accompanied by rain in most cases. A hurricane also veered off Pakse. For several days and nights it rained very hard.

In Attopeu, some distance from Pakse, 4,000 were left short of food because of the flood.

The Sedone River overflowed its banks, rising many feet. In all, it rained for about 72 hours. There is a bridge that spans the Sedone. The water from the torrential rains was very close to it.

Most of the people came and went from their houses by boat, since the water was very deep.

The monsoon season is still not over, but the rains and winds have quieted down. Many of this country's rice paddies overflowed. —by Thomas W. Swain

AS I WILL REMEMBER IT

The first day at Pakse School was vague. There were neither chairs, desks, nor books. Workmen were still working on the building.

Today, the second day, we do have chairs, tables, books and desks. I am in grade 7, and think that it's not too bad at all.

The building is being painted and there is going to be a refrigerator put in to keep lunches cold. School starts at 8 A.M. and ends at 1 P.M. Fans and lighting have not been put in yet.

The school here in Pakse, which is in Laos, is different from anything I've ever been to, since it is small, but it is comfortable. It has two stories, and I am on the second floor, with a window beside me. As I sit here I can see many things, but they are not in the school grounds.

There is barbed wire around the school, a water tower in back of us. The drive to the building is a little bumpy, but that is what I think of Laos. —Thomas Swain

"What did the mother sardine say when her baby saw a submarine?" "Don't be afraid. It's only a can of people."

FRENCH LESSONS

Nous sommes vraiment heureux.

Though our school is small, we have an unusual opportunity. We are learning French. Mrs. [Therese] Dodds comes to the classroom each day at 10 o'clock to give us our lessons.

413

As we look back over the past week, we have really learned a lot. We have learned a few phrases. She gives us directions in French, and we seem to understand. We learned the colors, days of the week, and the months. Also some foods and items of clothing were in the vocabulary. —Janelle Perry.

VACATIONS

My family and I went to Pattaya. We stayed two weeks and then we came home in time to go to Penang. We stayed two weeks. Now we are back and going to Bangkok. We like Pakse. —Kenny Swain

ACTIVE PTA STRIVES TO KEEP PAKSE A PROGRESSIVE SCHOOL

The PTA meeting last Tuesday night was the biggest of the year. It was held at the Lao Officers Club. Three things were going on at the same time, so there was some confusion about who was supposed to be doing the lamvong, who was supposed to be eating a Chinese dinner and who was supposed to be at the PTA. But everyone got sorted out.

There was some confusion when the President called the meeting to order by striking a gavel on the table. The gavel broke and struck the secretary on the head. The secretary passed out and the minutes of the last meeting were dispensed with.

Since there was no money in the treasury, the treasurer's report was dispensed with. An irate parent demanded to know what happened to the money. The treasurer then departed and was last seen running toward Cambodia.

The meeting was adjourned.

Most people went home. Some were lulled into doing the lamvong, and one parent was strangled by a Chinese noodle. [Author unknown, but it contains Tom Swain's dark humor.]

The Time of My Life

* * *

As president of the Pakse PTA, Phyllis was obligated to head a group of Pakse wives in welcoming Congressman John Rhodes, a member of the Congressional Oversight Committee for Intelligence. He was traveling throughout Vietnam, Laos, and Thailand to look into the war effort with particular emphasis on our intelligence collection activities. Mr. Rhodes was a Republican from Arizona and a close friend of Senator Barry Goldwater. Rhodes and Phyllis got along famously, especially when he learned that Phyl was an old acquaintance of the Goldwater family from her World War II modeling days in Phoenix. After lunching with the PTA, the congressman visited our refurbished school building. Mr. Rhodes was pleased with the school and promised to send a flag that had been flown over the capitol building, which was a nice touch. Sure enough, the flag arrived two weeks after he returned to Washington and was ceremoniously hoisted over Pakse Prep. I was out of the office the day of his visit and did not meet the congressman or any members of his staff. Lenny and his operations chief were much better at this sort of thing and made it quite clear that only essential employees should be seen around the office during the visit.

On Sundays when the weather was fair, our family occasionally would pile into the Land Rover, dressed in shorts and tennis shoes with a cooler of soft drinks and snacks, and drive to the Lao Army rifle range. The range was out in the almost deserted country about five miles north of Pakse. We parked our vehicle, walked down a slope to a shallow stream, and waded across to the firing range.

I would borrow an AK-47 Russian-made infantry weapon and take along my M-1 carbine and a .9 mm handgun with ammunition obtained from Flynn or Dutch. I showed each of the boys in turn, except Kenny, how to load and fire the guns. We took turns firing our weapons, while Kenny watched with much interest as did Phyllis, who already knew how to fire a rifle. Bill, Tom, and I blasted away at paper bull's-eye targets we stapled to posts set against dirt bunkers about 150 yards away; the handgun targets were set much closer for pistol practice.

In my opinion, the AK-47 was a fine weapon. It was used widely by the NVA as well as our guerilla troops in Vietnam and Laos. The weapon could fire a whole clip of 25 rounds rapidly and accurately up to 300 yards. Our friend, Bill, whose family lived near us in Manila, was assigned upcountry north of Vientiane and could testify to that. Bill was in an Air America Porter over enemy sites north of Vientiane when a AK-47 round smashed through his shin bone as he sat beside the pilot. The pilot immediately poured on power and headed toward the air base at Udorn. Bill was on the ground and in the hospital within 30 minutes, his leg saved by the pilot's quick action, some fine doctors, and six months of bone graft procedures.

* * *

Phyllis wrote the following:

Pakse, May 1, 1970

"Dear All: I have an overwhelming desire to say "Ho Hum"—another rocket attack last night. When it gets to the point where you can say "last night wasn't as bad as the first time but worse than the second time" I believe one might say we are becoming old veterans of the now not-so-secret war in Laos.

"The day before the attack we were sobered by the news that Attopeu, to the southeast of us, had fallen to the enemy who are maintaining pressure on all fronts. We were all in our sacks, but had been alerted that an attack was imminent. We were rudely awakened at the magic hour of 1:45 A.M. by the all too familiar sound of a rocket. We all made it into our bunker before the 2nd one hit, and were remarkably blase about the whole deal. We didn't hear the whistle, only the *boom* of the first one, so we knew it was not very close.

"The 7th one, with whistle, pushed our panic button a trifle, but it proved to be the last. Shortly thereafter, we heard and saw our friendly flare ship and correctly figured the worst was over. The time was 2:15. The sky was cloudy and some of the flares dropped behind the clouds and made a beautiful sight as they lit up the sky almost as daylight, then we went back to our beds and slept until 7:15.

"Pakse Prep got a late start in the morning, but school kept as usual. That afternoon, the name of the game was "shrapnel collecting" as the boys came home with a goodly number of souvenirs. . . . and a Happy May Day to you. Sorry you missed the fireworks."

Pakse, Laos, Monday, May 25, 1970

"Dear Mom and Dad: Let's see. We left Pakse on the 11th in quite a rush. We had been on alert for more rockets for several days, and then over the weekend of the 10th it was reported that two battalions of NVA troops were within 20 kilometers of Pakse. If they wanted to walk into Pakse they could, so Lenny arranged for cargo planes to take women with children to Vientiane. I had been packing like mad for a few days, had packed all our paintings and other valuables, most of them anyway, and was trying to organize things so that if we didn't get back the packers could take care of the rest without too much confusion. It was a real rush job and we were exhausted when we climbed aboard a C-47 with 4 women and ten children, 2 cats and 2 dogs plus many suitcases and footlockers. We were met with a truck and a bus and taken to the USAID guest house where we settled down and had a good night's sleep. The kids had fun as usual.

"Tuesday another gal arrived with 2 more children and all the other goods we had left behind. My shipping weight was 800 pounds not counting the 7 suitcases and 4 footlockers I had brought the day before. Wednesday, more people arrived and the Vientiane people are going crazy. At this point only the gals with no children remain in Pakse. Adie has moved in with his friend Flynn for the duration. [Dorothy Mae and her three children were also in Vientiane.]

417

"The Pakse kids are all going to school here and it is really a nice break for them. It is quite a change from a student body of 14 to one of 400. Ken was a little unhappy his first day since he has never been to a real school, but now is loving it and has lots of friends. The other guys are adjusting well and having a good time.

"We are living in a house at Kilometer 6, a large housing development, like a stateside subdivision. The school is within walking distance as are friends Fannie and Robin from Pakse. . . We are in a large house with sparse furniture, but it is comfortable and we can manage. We will have to move again on the 6th of June as the tenants of this house are on home leave and will be returning.

"Adrian came up Saturday the 16th and brought the car! How marvelous. The Chevy was driven inside the cargo bay of an empty C-123 plane. The boys' bikes came too so they have wheels. Adie stayed until the following Saturday and we had a nice much-needed vacation. We were to have gone on leave to Pattaya, but under the circumstances decided to postpone that trip. The car is wonderful for we are about 5 miles out of town, and it does come in handy. Tomorrow, they are going to pack us out in Pakse. I am now trying to get organized. We have belongings all over the place. I have to arrange for some furniture we ordered in Udorn to be shipped to Vientiane. Then I have to mentally pack our air freight and suitcases for home leave, get the packers to this house, repack what we have here, and then get everything from all three places together and ready for sea shipment. Great Scott, then I will probably have to move to another house. Since being in Pakse this is the 5th house we have lived in.

"Regarding our future plans, everything seems subject to change. Adie has been offered an assignment in Vietnam, which we had anticipated, but hoped against. He will accept it to stay on the payroll and will hope to better his position when we get back to the states. If he does indeed go back to Vietnam, the children and I will plan to stay in Sarasota for a school year at least, which I know will make you all very happy as far as the kids and I are concerned, but with the financial situation in the States (depressed as it is) and with a federal pay raise (in the offing) plus other monetary considerations involved, it will be a difficult assignment to turn down. So, that's how the situation stands at present, we'll just have to play it by ear.

"So, we'll see you guys in Sarasota. I thought I asked you to go ahead and try to rent an apartment at Gulf View for a month starting the 10th of August? We would like some time at the beach. . . . Love to all, Phyllis"

* * *

In early July, I told Ambrose to pass the word that our little Chevy was on the market. Ambrose and Pornchai flew to Vientiane and drove the car back to Pakse without incident. The two-year-old car had less than 3,000 miles on it, mostly from being driven to and from shipping ports in the States and from Thailand to Laos. The price was set at $2,500, about what we paid for it.

Pakse's Chief of Police, Colonel Heng, had seen the car down at the flight line and decided such a vehicle would improve his image. When Ambrose brought him around for a close look at it, the Chief tested the airconditioner (which blasted him with cold air), lifted the hood to examine the clean engine block, and decided to buy. The closing date was set for Friday afternoon at 2:00 P.M. at the Chief's residence in town.

At the appointed hour, Ambrose and I arrived at the Chief's house. The Chief was perhaps in his early 40's, had a pleasant round face and slightly oriental eyes, and was dressed in a brown uniform with no obvious trappings of rank. As is customary, he offered strong coffee with syrupy sweet Carnation milk and cold, canned Bing cherries in their own sweet juice. The Chief then abruptly excused himself, and I wondered if something had gone wrong with the deal. The Chief returned shortly and told Ambrose in Lao that

419

there was an unavoidable delay. The Chief had said we must wait for the 3 P.M. Royal Air Lao flight from Saigon because his money was on that plane.

It was almost 4 P.M. when a junior police aide arrived and handed the chief a small satchel. The Chief opened the bag and began to count out greenbacks. The old U.S. greenbacks looked good to me, but an odd smell like rotten cabbage arose from the money on the table. Soon there were 125 twenty dollar bills in a neat stack. With cash in hand, I no longer worried about the smell but wondered why it was there. Perhaps the bills had been buried in some dank cellar in Saigon. We signed the necessary title papers, and the Chief drove the car into his garage. I went home to Flynn's house and after a celebratory drink of Scotch decided to spread out the money to air in my upstairs bedroom. When the odor diminished, I took the bills to Ralph, our finance officer, who exchanged the bundle of twenties into Lao kip to be used for household and moving expenses. I was lucky to have sold the darn car, and the Chief probably made a fortune when he decided to sell, so it was a win-win situation.

* * *

Jim, my replacement, arrived in mid-June with his wife and moved into our old house. He looked as if he had just graduated from college and was so intent on studying the Lao language that I did not see much of him. He was a cocky young fellow who felt that he knew all there was to know about the intelligence game. This worried me because I knew there were a lot of pitfalls involved when dealing with Asians. Still, I guess it was natural—when you are young you are so sure of yourself that no one can tell you much. Ambrose, Jim, and I continued working with Souk to keep his network properly directed and to collect battle data on the enemy, despite the fall of Attopeu. When Souk submitted his monthly accounting statements during his regular debriefings, Jim would sit in to get acquainted. I kept good files and charts on all of Souk's nets, so there was something for Jim to study and review after I was gone.

* * *

420

Every house was assigned a guard after the January and February rocket attacks. A strapping young teenager stayed around our grounds during the day when I was at work. He was paid by the office but did not carry a gun. To keep busy, he cut the grass every day. Soon our Pakse lawn was as neat as that of our old home in Sarasota, even though our guard had no lawnmower; instead, he used a three-foot-long piece of sharpened bamboo. I watched in amazement as he squatted on his haunches swiping at the grass, cutting it as neatly and evenly as would a mower. He was darn good, and I was quite proud of him for such industry. One day earlier in May when I came home for lunch and a siesta, Phyllis told me that our guard had a badly infected leg. I took him to Dr. Alex who said that the wound was caused by a mosquito or other insect bite. It was now a red and yellow mess and looked as though it might soon become gangrenous. Dr. Alex provided his proven treatment: an injection of penicillin and a shot of vitamins in the fanny, followed by a thorough cleansing of the wound and a generous coating of ointment. The infection cleared up within days.

* * *

I stopped in the station chief's office in Vientiane one day while visiting the family and personally appealed for an assignment in Vientiane. I hoped mightily that there might be an intelligence slot available, but the boss did not give me any encouragement. He reviewed my personnel file and said he could use me as a reports officer, no doubt intrigued by the fact I had a degree in journalism from Penn State, but for the life of me I could not see myself writing reports all day. Perhaps it was a mistake that I turned it down, because such an assignment meant that our family could live in Vientiane. I felt strongly then, as I do today, that it is very important to feel good about yourself and your work. There was nothing demeaning about writing reports, but I felt the work would be difficult and confining, and that would drive me nuts. I wanted to be active in intelligence collection work, so I told Phyllis we would just have to go back to Washington and take our chances walking the halls at Langley. It worked before, and we could do it again. Phyl agreed, bless her heart.

Phyllis, ever the shopper, had acquired a modest taste for gold. There was a well-known shop in Vientiane on the Embassy's list of reputable dealers called Villay Phone's. The owner was of Chinese ancestry, as were the ladies who operated Macy's and Gimbel's. Villay did a lot of business selling Four Seasons bracelets to Air America pilots and other kinds of jewelry to families assigned to the Embassies in town. Gold was pegged at $36 per ounce by government regulation, and gold charm bracelets were very much in fashion those days. Phyl and Cyndy had launched a program of buying charms for their bracelets; their goal was to obtain a charm or two from every area they visited. So far they had charms from Hawaii, Manila, Hong Kong, Bangkok, Penang, and now Vientiane. By now, their arms surely were getting heavy. Who knew where it would end? I sometimes called Phyllis "Goldie," and she would smile.

Just before Christmas in 1969, I asked one of my Lao contacts in Pakse, a minor prince named Chao Sith, to help me buy a gold bracelet for Phyllis. He knew just the right place, a small jewelry shop in town that displayed its wares in an open window. Robbery was never much of a threat to shops in Pakse for some reason. I bought a simple bracelet of soft, yellow 24 karat gold for $70 that measured about five inches long and a quarter inch in diameter. The gold contained a hint of redness, supposedly common to gold mined in South Africa. Because it was so pure, the metal could be bent and wrapped around one's wrist and needed no clasp. Its simple design resembled a plain twist of rope, and Phyl loved it. I wish I had bought more, because three or four years later the United States went off the gold standard, and the price of gold climbed to $425 an ounce. Phyllis loved that bracelet, and her friends exclaimed about the softness of the metal that was so pure and heavy and elegant.

Phyl also bought yards of fine Lao skirt and sash material from which she fashioned her own silken skirts and gay sashes for appearances at social functions. General Phasouk, his operations chief Colonel Souchay, and other Lao staff officers were often at the cocktail and buffet gatherings with their wives. I noticed that the Lao women were usually quiet and subdued and would sit in chairs around the dance floor talking among themselves while the men talked shop with each other over their whiskey or Singha beer.

During the cocktail hour, *hors d'oeuvres* included tasty strips of steak dipped in a tangy sauce and then seared at the mongolian barbecue pit. Phyl let the Lao officers show her how to take pieces of raw buffalo steak with her chopsticks and place them on the hot, corrugated metal surface of an inverted bowl over a hot bed of charcoal. It was not bad tasting either. Lao social functions were quite pleasant, and I always made a point of dancing with as many ladies as possible, anything to get them off those chairs. The only time Lao ladies became involved was when the lamvong was played. Phyl and I tried hard to join in the spirit of these outings so that the Lao would not think all Americans were party poopers, but it was not easy given the language barrier.

The highlight of one affair was when General Phasouk awarded Phyl and me the grand prize for being the best dancers on the floor, a bottle of Dewars White Label Scotch, which was my favorite drink and much appreciated. General Phasouk Somly spoke English well, but seldom in public because he was fearful of mispronouncing a word. He spoke French, the language in which he was educated at the French Air Force Academy and the Sorbonne. A native of Saravane, with no royal family connections, he was well liked and admired by both his troops and his American contacts. He always seemed to have a quiet, knowing smile on his face, and reminded me of Souk. I wondered if they were related, but would never know for that was not a subject one brought up at a cocktail party.

Our Lao hosts liked the Chinese custom of drinking rounds of Scotch in shot glasses, while standing in a circle giving toasts to the guest of honor. After each toast, the guest of honor had to respond by drinking his glass to shouts of "Gom Bei," meaning bottoms up or good luck. Lenny was the guest of honor at a reception after a Lao Army Day celebration in which the troops marched past the reviewing stand where General Phasouk and our Chief of Base stood. At a long lunch afterward, Lenny accepted far too many Gom Beis and was put to bed where he remained for the next two days. Lenny was not much of a drinker and obviously did not handle it well. The trick was to take only a tiny sip of Scotch each time a toast was made. The Lao officers' unspoken agenda was simple—get the guest of honor drunk. The honoree's goal was to stay sober; Lenny failed, and we Americans lost some face.

Adrian Swain

DEPARTURE TIME MEMORIES

As our departure time approached, the days seemed to fly. Phyllis and I were more than happy to be moving but were saddened to leave fine friends and the scene of some unusual and memorable times. The boys would certainly remember their Pakse schoolhouse where on Friday nights we would watch movies brought in on the commissary plane from Vientiane. I was sure they also would remember the ever present bottle of Kaopectate. We used about a bottle per month, because someone was always coming down with diarrhea. I was sure I always got mine from the drinks at Lao parties in which the ice was chipped from blocks kept outside in some dirty icehouse. Water was never boiled in Lao houses, as it was in ours, so we could count on coming down with you know what every time.

We would all carry memories of these times, small keepsakes serving to remind us of the time we spent in this very different world. We would also remember the friendships we forged and the special times we shared as a family. My friend Flynn got me a ceremonial sword that I still treasure. The sword measures two-and-a-half feet from sword point to ivory handle and is a work of art skillfully crafted by Meo silversmiths. It cost $70.00, and I would not sell it for ten times that amount. It is a beautiful memento of Laos, the lovely, lonely, and unsophisticated land of the elephants.

* * *

I turned over my intelligence operations to Jim and hoped he would survive until he learned the ropes. He had only to ask Ambrose for guidance in handling Souk. I will never know what happened, because in the intelligence world we operated on a strict need-to-know basis. I only received a hint about what occurred after I left Pakse. The reports officers at Langley who reviewed and analyzed information from Souk and his nets mentioned that they thought Souk might have become greedy and perhaps falsified reports, but nothing happened on my watch. If things were going sour, perhaps the box man could straighten it out. I was satisfied that I had done a credible job during my two-year tour in Laos and and was ready to rejoin Phyllis and the boys.

424

In mid-July, I returned to Vientiane, which meant sandalwood city in English, and rejoined the family. My orders said we were to depart on or about the 20th of July for Headquarters in Washington with home leave in Sarasota. No mention was made of a new assignment; instead, the orders said I was to be processed for discharge. This was the bureaucratic way of saying they did not know what to do with me.

As we prepared to leave Laos, I thought of those who had distinguished themselves during the long Laotian battle for freedom (which was lost to the Pathet Lao Communist forces in 1975), people who were true champions of the Lao cause. Edgar "Pop" Buell, a retired farmer from Hamilton, Indiana, came to Laos in 1960 as a $60-a-month volunteer with the International Volunteer Service (USAID). He stayed until the early 1970's doing what he could to help house, clothe, feed, and care for the Meo tribes in the northeastern region on the Plain of Jars.

The outstanding and heroic leader of the Meo tribesmen was Major General Van Pao, the feisty, charismatic leader of the nomadic group who migrated out of China by way of Vietnam to settle in northeastern Laos and later in northern Thailand. Himself a Meo, Vang Pao operated from his headquarters at Long Tieng, a 20-minute plane ride north of Vientiane, where he lived with his soldiers in huts about the airstrip known as 20 Alternate. I spent a few hours there at the Company's intelligence center getting some data one afternoon and was greatly impressed with the activity.

The asphalt runway was capable of handling heavy cargo loads as well as T-28s, FAC flights, and helicopters. The strip was memorable for the towering karst at the far end known to pilots as Titty Karst. The formation looked like two chicken croquettes stuck in the ground and was a definite hazard to any aircraft landing long. Empty oil drums were stacked at that end of the runway to help snare any aircraft that might be out of control. All around the area were hundreds of neat, little tin-roof huts, some built on the slopes of the ridges that protected the valley, with the runway right down the middle of it all. The dusty streets were filled with women, children, and off-duty soldiers, plus a lot of stalls filled with colorful yard goods, silver and wood products, and seasonal fruits and vegetables. Vang Pao lived here, and these were his troops. Meo soldiers traveled with their families in nomadic fashion and were supported by arms, food, and other necessities delivered by Air America planes under contract to USAID. Whenever the troops had time, they and their families planted poppies to produce opium gum, their best cash crop.

* * *

Infamous in their own way were a couple of institutions in Vientiane called Lulu's and The White Rose, described in the novel *The Laotian Fragments*. Being a married man, I never visited these places, whose reputations had spread over Southeast Asia. Both Lulu's and The White Rose were private homes that catered to lonely men seeking companionship.

Lulu's was an old teak house built around 1920 that was set back under the trees and surrounded by high privacy walls. Lulu, the owner, was a dumpy little lady of indeterminate age who had blonde hair and resembled a miniature Mae West. She reportedly had owned brothels in Paris, Madrid, Beirut, Saigon, and Bangkok. Lulu's stable of girls were known for a variety of love-making techniques.

The White Rose, Lulu's only serious competitor, was a more modern stucco house with a larger dance floor and bar area surrounded by darkened booths. Music was provided by an American-style juke box. The main attraction at The White Rose, other than the usual variety, was a naked girl who strutted about the dance floor with several cigarettes (reports say as many as six) sticking out from between her legs. She could make the cigarettes glow, which is quite an astonishing feat, and many witnesses swear it is true. I report this story only because it is unique to Southeast Asia. No story about Laos would be complete without it.

SEVENTEEN

Joining the War on Drugs

The highlight of our trip from Laos to Sarasota was traveling in a
Pan Am 747, Boeing's latest, long-range jumbo jetliner. We
arrived in Tokyo from Bangkok around midnight in late July muggi-
ness and spent the night in an older hotel on the Ginza. We took the
airport limousine to Haneda Airport the next morning, where we
cleared customs and then boarded the fabulous 747. We could not
believe the size of that monster. It easily seated more than 300
passengers, none of whom were crowded into their seats, in sharp
contrast to our Boeing 707 economy class seats that made me sit up
straight and carefully calculate each move I made. There were several
movie screens to choose from, several restrooms, and a sky lounge.
This bubble-like affair atop the fuselage was reached by climbing a
circular stairway behind the pilots' compartment, accommodated
about 20 people, and provided a marvelous view of the Pacific far
below. We soared nonstop to San Francisco in what seemed only a
few hours, arriving there midmorning in brassy July sunlight. After
we landed, it took almost as long to disembark and shuffle in long
lines through Immigration and Customs checkpoints. Our fatigue
was eased by the pleasure of speaking English to American customs
officials after years of speaking pigeon-English in Southeast Asian
airports. The customs people were especially kind and considerate,
welcoming us back as though we were relatives they had not seen for
a long time, which made us feel pretty good.

We arrived on the red-eye flight at our Sarasota-Bradenton Airport, armed with gift loaves of sourdough bread from the San
Francisco airport, and were met by an enthusiastic Cyndy, KC, and

427

Evelyn Warren. Ken and Ev had been able to get us a two-bedroom apartment with a kitchenette at the Gulf View Inn on the beach. Anything would have satisfied as long as we could get into the warm waters of the Gulf of Mexico within minutes. Since I was not due at Headquarters until the first week in September, I put all thoughts of work aside and simply enjoyed being home. Cyndy was doing well with her courses in education at USF. She had joined the Phi Gamma Delta sorority and was seeing Phil Toale regularly; it looked as though she had found a comfortable niche.

In life, there is always good news and bad news. The bad news was that I would be job hunting again. The good news was that we were now renting a two-story, Spanish stucco home (nicknamed the Fort and built in the 1920's by former Mayor Edwards) overlooking Sarasota Bay. We just loved it; there was plenty of room, and the kids had a television upstairs in the huge front sunroom where we often watched *Batman* in the afternoon. The view was magnificent, and we would pretend to be on the prow of a big ocean liner moving down the bay.

BACK TO SCHOOL

By early September, Sarasota's schools reopened and Phyl popped our boys back into class: Tom to 9th grade, Bill to 6th grade, and Ken to 3rd grade. I also was back in school attending training classes at the Blue U for assignments in South Vietnam—déjà vu. I was able to skip some of the classwork and use this time to search for other employment. The CIA personnel officers were very cooperative and took a personal interest in how things were going with me. Their compassion was all the more welcome when it appeared that my efforts to find a position in other than Tay Ninh Province were coming up empty.

An administrative guy I had known in Vietnam was teaching one of our classes, and we chatted during a break. He commented that I really should not be in this class after having been in Southeast Asia for four years. I took his remark to heart. I should not even be thinking of going to Saigon; it would not be fair to the family. His comment made me even more determined to work harder at job hunting. Armed with my resume and the Civil Service letter, which said I was eligible for employment in the Federal Government at the GS-13 level, I began calling in earnest at a number of agencies who could possibly use my services.

The Law Enforcement Assistance Agency (LEAA), which dealt with state and local police departments, said they had no openings. I contacted Earl Diffenderfer at USAID, but again the personnel freeze was still in effect. The Department of Agriculture needed an investigator in their office of inspection, but after an interview it appeared they were looking for a great deal more expertise in the agricultural field than I possessed. I even looked into managing a Wackenhut Agency security office and had an interview with the area manager, but the welcome mat was not out for me.

The big problem was that I could not talk about what I had been doing for the past four years. My record only showed that I had been employed by USAID, and there were too many ex-USAID people looking for work. I kept Phyllis informed on my progress, or lack thereof. She suggested that she might come to Washington so we could visit her old Arizona friends on Capitol Hill—Senator Barry Goldwater and Congressman John Rhodes. I thought that was a great idea. I had not given that possibility a thought and realized again how brilliant this wife of mine really was.

Phyllis arrived at National Airport on a lovely fall evening. She looked tan and fit and was smiling; life on the beach was agreeing with her. We took a cab to Arlington where we had a pleasant dinner at a neighborhood Italian restaurant within walking distance of the Clarendon Motel. Candlelight, a red-checked table cloth, a bottle of Chianti, and an update on all the family activities went well together. We then walked home to make love in the fold-down bed in our cozy efficiency apartment. Tomorrow promised to be a brighter day.

In the morning, I felt fit and ready for anything. Phyl called Senator Goldwater's office, but Barry was tied up with Senate committee meetings all day. Her call to Congressman Rhodes went better. Mr. Rhodes' secretary asked us to come to the Congressman's office in the House of Representatives Building that afternoon.

John Rhodes was pleased and delighted to see Phyllis, whom he readily recalled from his visit to Pakse. He was very cordial and interested in hearing how things were in Laos. He became more receptive and friendly when he and Phyllis talked about the Goldwater family. More important, he was interested in our future. Phyl pointed out that we had just finished serving four years in Southeast Asia. With one child in college and the other three back in public schools, we really did not want another tour in Vietnam. I asked if he knew of any other job opportunities in Washington. Congressman Rhodes looked at me and said he would talk to the Attorney General. I gulped; clearly, this man had contacts in the right places.

He asked if I was interested in a political or career appointment. Without hesitation, I told him career, knowing full well that political appointments were often of short duration. I gave him my updated resume, which he pocketed without looking at, and he told me to call his secretary the following afternoon. After thanking the Congressman for his time and assistance, we said good-bye and departed on a cushion of air. It was then that I first felt guilty about being a registered Democrat, but Phyl was a registered Republican, which somehow made our visit more proper. Privately, I vowed to become a member of the Grand Old Party at my first opportunity, which I did a few years later in Sarasota. Phyl could only stay another day, but her work was done.

Two days later I received a message from the office of Richard Kleindienst, Assistant Attorney General, telling me to contact John W. Parker at the Bureau of Narcotics and Dangerous Drugs (BNDD) in downtown Washington. The word was that BNDD was expanding their intelligence collection capability and looking for an expert on Southeast Asia.

John Parker was a laid-back Georgian whose country drawl did not hide his keen mind. He was a courteous man with considerable charm, and I liked him immediately. He looked over my Civil Service Form 171, a detailed dossier of my history, and discussed my recent past. He seemed quite interested that I was a former FBI Agent and suggested I would qualify as an investigative agent without any additional training. We talked about my experience in Southeast Asia, and he told me that my old stomping grounds, known as the Golden Triangle (Thailand, Burma, and Laos), was becoming a very troublesome drug source area. Pure heroin and potent marijuana produced there were being consumed in horrendous quantities by GI's in Vietnam. Parker also said that the BNDD was expanding its intelligence collection capability overseas and was quite interested in my background. Without being told any more, I knew that BNDD could use someone like me. I was not surprised when John said he wanted me to work for him. He said I could start as soon as the transfer details were worked out between the CIA and the BNDD.

John Parker made his verbal commitment in early October, but it would take almost four months for the paperwork to be shuffled back and forth between the Civil Service, the CIA, and BNDD. The transfer would be a lateral move in my current grade, without a break in service. The Civil Service would have to update and verify my past four years of employment, but could do so only after receiving a statement from the CIA that there were no security objections. I also would need an updated background security check. It made me shudder to imagine Civil Service investigators going to South Vietnam and Laos doing neighborhood checks to verify my employment in Quang Duc or Pakse.

In an effort to help, I went to the CIA security office and spent an afternoon writing a succinct statement for the file that described in nonsensitive terms what I had been doing for the past four years. With a half-page draft in hand, I walked from one office to another until finally my draft was initialed and stamped with the magic words NO SECURITY OBJECTIONS. This statement unblocked my file and allowed it to be released to the Civil Service and the BNDD. The transfer process began.

Following is the resume I wrote concerning my four years of intelligence and air operations work:

Mr. Adrian Swain
Central Intelligence Agency
Summary Employment Statement
1966-1970

During the period of employment served two consecutive tours in different countries of Southeast Asia. In the first tour, I served as an advisor to local authorities at a provincial level. Also served as an operations officer at regional level and as a staff officer at higher headquarters. Duties involved liaison with both local and high level US staff officers on matters of budget, logistics, policy implementation and future planning. Frequently field trips were made. Supervised up to 10 people.

During the second tour I served as an intelligence and operations officer. Duties were administrative in general involving frequent field trips, close association with the people on all levels and included supervision and direction of a variety of developmental projects. Also supervised a four-man staff of officers, and was responsible for monitoring project budgeting, reporting thereon, and making staff presentations and recommendations to my superiors.

(stamped)   NO SECURITY OBJECTIONS

(SCRAWLED ILLEGIBLE SIGNATURE)

OJ/EAB

9 Oct 70

By mid-November I was beginning to despair of official approval, but John assured me that all was on track. I told the Agency's finance office to take me off per diem and that I would be at home in Sarasota until the transfer date was set. Just before Thanksgiving, I packed my bags, told John Parker where I was going, and returned to Florida to spend the holidays with the family.

In early December, notice came that our household goods would soon arrive in the Port of Baltimore. They would be warehoused at Cameron Station, near Washington, for 60 days awaiting delivery. That was good news, but it meant that we needed to find a home soon. We resolved to make a house buying trip after the first of the year.

* * *

Phyl called our friends Stan and Jan, who invited us to stay at their house near Fairfax. There we met Ed Albert, a former Agency employee and neighborhood Realtor who had helped them find their house. Ed knew all about the difficulties that Agency employees usually encountered when trying to qualify for new mortgages. Spooks coming in from the cold often needed extra help getting their overseas employment verified without delay. Ed was competent, friendly, and reassuring and got right to work with Phyllis on our needs, while I went to the office.

Within two days, they narrowed the search down to a tidy, split-level, brick and aluminum-siding house with three bedrooms, two and a half baths, and a den off the downstairs family room. It had a red-brick fireplace, a one-car garage, and a utility room/workshop and was on a nicely landscaped corner lot. The community was called Lake Vale Estates. There was a clubhouse with a swimming pool, two tennis courts, and a small pond at the bottom of the hill, which promised fishing and small boating in summer and ice skating in winter. The schools were good, and my commute downtown would be a little more than an hour each way, which I did not mind. Phyl and Ed had done a nice job.

A Western Union Telegram arrived on January 29, 1971. Strips of teletyped words were pasted on two pages of yellow paper, just like the War Department telegram my Mother received during World War II when I was missing in action in France. This news was considerably better. It read:

WE ARE PLEASED TO OFFER YOU AN APPOINTMENT TO THE POSITION OF CRIMINAL INVESTIGATOR, GS-1811 13/4, AT AN ANNUAL SALARY OF $19,537. YOU WILL BE ASSIGNED TO THE OFFICE OF ENFORCE-MENT, INTELLIGENCE DIVISION, IN WASHINGTON, D.C. YOUR APPOINTMENT WILL BE CAREER-CONDITIONAL. THE FIRST YEAR WILL BE A PROBATIONARY PERIOD. A CAREER-CONDITIONAL APPOINTMENT BECOMES A CAREER APPOINTMENT WHEN YOU HAVE COMPLETED THREE YEARS OF SUBSTANTIALLY CONTINUOUS SERVICE.

ARRANGEMENTS HAVE BEEN MADE WITH YOUR PERSONNEL OFFICE TO RELEASE YOU AT CLOSE OF BUSINESS FEBRUARY 15, 1971. YOU SHOULD REPORT FOR DUTY TO 1405 I STREET, N.W. WASHINGTON, D.C. AT 9:00 AM ON FEBRUARY 16, 1971. IF YOU HAVE ANY QUESTIONS REGARDING YOUR APPOINTMENT, PLEASE CONTACT MRS. ELLISON OF THIS OFFICE ON 202-382-4823. WE ARE LOOKING FORWARD TO YOUR JOINING OUR AGENCY.

N E BENTSON ADMP BNDD HQS.

I immediately called Ed and told him to close the deal on our house. He called the next day to say that the paperwork was finished and we could move in next week. That's what I call action.

We would be driving the 1968 Oldsmobile Vista Cruiser station wagon that we bought the previous summer. A small trailer was rented and filled with luggage, our television, and clothes. Saying good-bye to the Warrens, we loaded the three boys and two dogs in the wagon and headed north. We stopped to have lunch and visit with Cyndy on the beautiful, sprawling USF campus in Tampa. Before we left, we suffered a mild rear-ender when a construction truck did not stop in time at a traffic light. Ben S. Brown, my friend the ex-Air Force pilot and now Sarasota insurance agent, said he would take care of it and I should call him when we got to Washington. We spent the night in Bushnell with Nancy and Dave Davis and their son, Matthew, who was a year younger than our Ken. It was fun sitting around the fireplace after a nice supper, sipping a drink and talking about our changing world.

The spacious back deck of the wagon was used for naps, and Phyl, who had lapsed again into her nicotine habit, occasionally would climb back there to smoke a cigarette. After two days of steady driving through damp, drizzly weather on Interstate 95, we coasted into the Holiday Inn off Route 123 in Fairfax. They were always nice about allowing the dogs to stay in our rooms, despite motel regulations. We remained there until the house utilities were turned on in time to receive the moving vans, which arrived in the rain two days later. Julie and Thateng were glad to be out of bondage and were released in their new backyard complete with juniper shrubs and other bushes surrounded by a chain fence.

Phyl and I took the master bedroom, Tom and Ken shared the larger second bedroom upstairs, and the den off the family room downstairs became Bill's bedroom. The third bedroom became a combination sewing room and bedroom for Cyndy when she could be with us. Our new house was comfortable and snug and had a spacious kitchen with a bay window facing east overlooking the backyard.

Sometime during our move-in day, Bill and Ken decided to explore the pond below the community clubhouse, which we could see from our front window. They set out for the pond and later wandered into the nearby meadow. Two hours later they reappeared in a deputy sheriff's squad car after having become totally disoriented. A concerned neighbor a few blocks away talked to our boys and realized they were lost. She called the deputy sheriff, who picked up the boys and then cruised around until Bill finally recognized our house. Bill allowed he was not lost but admitted it seemed to be a long way home. Ken was not fazed and rather enjoyed the adventure. Tom was appalled that they would do something so stupid, and Phyl and I were just relieved they had made it home.

The boys soon were going to school on the bus, while I planned to take the Express Metro bus from Tyson's Corner into town. Phyl drove me to the bus stop on Route 123 where I caught the 7:30 A.M. ride, which took an hour and 10 minutes and dropped me off only one short block from my office. Eventually, I would join a carpool.

* * *

The New Federal Building at the corner of 14th and I Streets was quite a change from the stately, palatial CIA headquarters secluded in the manicured woods of Langley. In contrast, BNDD was housed in the midst of the District's pornography and neon-lit discotheque area. An old gymnasium next to the office building was used by BNDD agents for firearms and physical training. I hoped that the roughness of the neighborhood would not be indicative of my new employment, but after Pakse and Quang Duc, this place looked pretty good to me.

While waiting in the lobby for an elevator to the 5th floor, I noticed there were no security guards monitoring the traffic. Anybody could walk in and go right upstairs. From the look of some of the street people outside, I felt a little uneasy. Several men lounging at the elevator doors definitely looked like hippies, with scraggly beards, long hair, and mustaches. They crowded into the elevator with me, and I soon realized from their conversation that some were BNDD trainees. The more suspicious looking ones were American Civil Liberties Union (ACLU) attorneys or staff going to their offices. ACLU people have always been worrisome to me and disturbing to BNDD as well. Many ACLU people smoked marijuana and sturdily defended those who argued that marijuana should be declared legal. Many were antiwar advocates and far too liberal for me. Happily, the ACLU moved out of the BNDD building a year later.

The Director of BNDD, John E. Ingersoll, a former Chief of Police in Charlotte, North Carolina, was appointed by President Nixon August 1, 1968, when BNDD was formed. A ruggedly strong man in his early 40's, Jack Ingersoll was a conservative, determined leader. Ingersoll's new Bureau combined the Federal Bureau of Narcotics, which had functioned under the Department of the Treasury, and the Bureau of Drug Control, which had been part of the Food and Drug Administration. J. Edgar Hoover, Director of the FBI, had been asked to take over the new drug law enforcement agency but refused. I think Hoover knew what a troublesome thing drug enforcement could be and did not want to sully his carefully polished image.

Within a few days, I was assigned as a senior analyst in the Office of Strategic Intelligence (SIO). The Chief of the SIO was John Warner, a solid, German-speaking narcotics expert who John Ingersoll had recruited from the California State Bureau of Narcotics. John W. Parker, who hired me, was deputy of the SIO and my immediate supervisor.

Since the SIO was a relatively new and expanding office, I knew my experience in Southeast Asia could contribute to the fledgling intelligence collection effort. I went to work with enthusiasm to learn my new trade and for the next two months attended new agent training classes. I learned about drug identification, how the BNDD was organized and structured, and how BNDD special agents conducted undercover operations. In short, I learned how a BNDD drug enforcement agent lived and worked in a world inhabited by drug abusers and drug traffickers. I was introduced to the systems concept, the brainchild of Enforcement Chief George Belk, by which BNDD was targeting loosely knit drug conglomerates instead of individual drug violators. BNDD was organized into 20 regional territories, each with its own Regional Director (RD) and support staff. There were satellite district offices within each region as well as narcotics attache offices in Europe, Mexico, South America, and in the Far East.

Director Ingersoll was expanding his overseas offices to prevent illicit drugs from entering our country and to work with police agencies in areas where the drugs were being produced to nip drug shipments in the bud. Because many diverse government agency employees were working in BNDD, I was not surprised at the less-than-enthusiastic reception I received. For every enforcement agent who was willing to work with intelligence analysts there seemed to be 10 who were politely wary. These agents, supervisors, and street agents seemed to view ex-FBI and ex-CIA people with suspicion and distrust. Perhaps with reason, these people believed that a good narcotics enforcement agent needed help from no one and preferred to be their own intelligence agent. I suspected that my life in BNDD was not going to be easy.

Luckily for me, Ingersoll decided to hire additional intelligence analysts and collection agents to support increased enforcement operations at home and overseas. In spite of foot-dragging by some of the old guard, he meant to stop the flow of drugs at home and at the source. BNDD was not going to wait for drug shipments to be unloaded on the streets of New York, Miami, Chicago, or San Francisco and was going to stop the shipments from overseas.

My office was to provide intelligence to expose overseas routes, help identify the organizations and individuals involved in drug

Adrian Swain

GENEALOGY OF DRUG ENFORCEMENT ADMINISTRATION

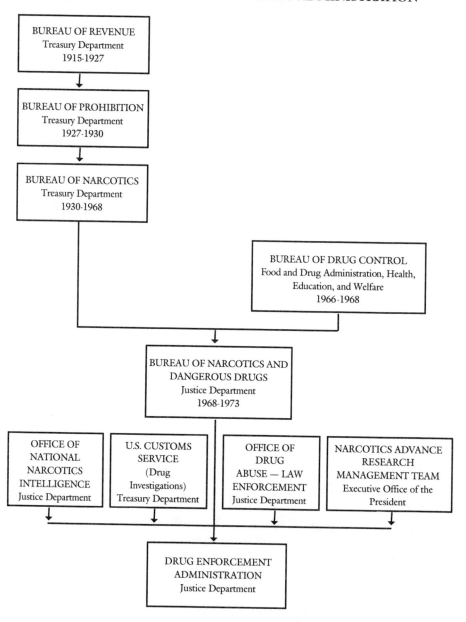

trafficking, and develop operational intelligence that would lead to arrests. Ingersoll's strategy was sound and almost immediately began to pay dividends. In early 1971, to my knowledge, there were no BNDD intelligence analysts assigned overseas. The handful of intelligence analysts and agents were primarily in Washington, D.C., with one or two in New York. Our ranks were thin, but I did not care. I was happy at almost fifty years of age to have a challenging job that offered security, advancement, and a potential overseas assignment.

* * *

Our family enjoyed our first cold winter in 1971. Our children had never seen snow falling, slipped on a frozen pond trying to ice skate, or had a sled ride. While northern Virginia's climate was not frigid, it was cold enough for our thin blood. We bought several hooded parkas from an army-navy store and wore them while gathering firewood. There were scads of fallen branches and dead trees in the woods beyond our pond, which we hauled home in our big station wagon. We stacked a double layer of wood against the wall of our garage and covered it with a tarp against rain and snow. The boys and I loved to keep the fireplace blazing in the family room.

Julie and Tango also were learning about wintertime. A light snow had fallen in late January and they frolicked in the backyard with Ken and Bill until it got too cold. During the night, the surface of the snow turned into an icy glaze. When Julie dashed out the back door the next morning, she hit the glaze and with her paws scratching in vain began a helpless slide until she came to rest against the chain link fence. Her face expressed complete bewilderment. When we stopped laughing, Phyl crunched through the icy snow to rescue her. After that episode, I took care to shovel a circular dog run through any new snowfall.

THE INGERSOLL TRIP

In the spring of 1971, the South Vietnamese had launched a damaging drive into southeastern Laos and Cambodia to cut the Ho Chi Minh supply route. The drive was to prevent Laos and Cambodia from serving as Communist sanctuaries in the future. American war-planes and ground troops continued to strike North Vietnamese military targets, despite mounting antiwar sentiment in the States. Heroin and marijuana abuse by our soldiers in South Vietnam increasingly concerned our military leaders and the BNDD, and Ingersoll decided to visit Southeast Asia to assess the situation.

Since I was the only one available in BNDD Headquarters with recent experience in Southeast Asia, I was tapped to accompany the Director as his aide. The State Department also assigned a narcotics liaison representative, a scholarly gentleman named Harvey Wellman, to coordinate visits to U.S. Embassies during our two-week trip. Wellman was probably told to watch Ingersoll so he would not do or say anything contrary to State Department policy. It was my feeling that while the State Department was very helpful and necessary to BNDD's overseas efforts, their policy planners moved too slowly and carefully. Ingersoll moved rapidly and decisively, traits that the striped-pants set found somewhat unnerving but that I applauded.

During March and most of April, I prepared the Director's briefing book which included State Department background papers on each area we would visit, maps from the CIA, economic studies, climate reports, assessments of drug-abuse patterns and local production capabilities, and photographs and sketches of key people Ingersoll might contact. I also checked with our travel section, which was updating our visas, passports, and shot records. I sent teletypes to our men in Tokyo, Hong Kong, Saigon, Bangkok, Rangoon, Singapore, and Canberra and to BNDD in Honolulu advising them of the Director's schedule. Fully appreciating the honor and responsibility I had traveling with the Director, I wanted to perform my tasks competently. I was confident that I knew Southeast Asia fairly well, at least geographically, but had precious little experience in the protocol of visiting dignitaries of foreign governments and so began to get edgy as our departure day neared.

On Saturday afternoon, I said good-bye to the boys and headed to Dulles Airport. Phyl dropped me off with a hug and a kiss at the check-in counter where Ingersoll and Wellman were just unloading their bags. I introduced Phyl, who said a quick hello and good-bye before we went inside. We soon were buckled in our soft seats and soaring aloft, following the setting sun northwest across Alberta and British Colombia. We were about halfway to Japan when we stopped in Anchorage, Alaska to refuel. I had forgotten that in the land of the midnight sun daylight never seemed to end. Our pilot then began the long arc that lifted us swiftly over the Bering Sea, above the Aleutian and Kuril Islands, to a featherlight landing at Tokyo on Honshu Island.

It was early Friday morning when Russ Arslan, our Japanese-speaking narcotics attache, whisked us through Customs and Immigration without examination and drove us to the Okura hotel downtown for a few hours rest. Russ was marvelous that afternoon, leading us on an obligatory round of meetings with inscrutable and scrupulously polite Japanese police and narcotics experts and with our own less inscrutable Embassy people. Ingersoll had little assistance to offer the Japanese, since they had no significant drug abuse problem. Drug abusers in Japan were treated harshly by our standards. Any citizen caught dealing or abusing drugs was publicly condemned and given mandatory cold-turkey treatment in rather bleak prison conditions. Addicts were cured quickly and seldom relapsed.

While in Tokyo, Ingersoll was contacted by the commanding general of American ground forces on Okinawa and asked to stop and see him on his way to Hong Kong. Drug abuse was becoming such a problem that the general wanted Ingersoll to assign some BNDD agents to Okinawa full time. Russ Arslan was making monthly visits from Tokyo, but the general said that was not enough and wanted more assistance. By the time we landed at Kadena airfield on Okinawa, it had already been a long day. John Ingersoll spent an hour and a half, almost until midnight, discussing the pros and cons of assigning a full-time BNDD agent to Okinawa. My head kept dropping sideways as I struggled to keep from falling asleep. The general was persuasive, and Ingersoll promised to find an agent. Charley Casey, a veteran agent who had been in Korea and served earlier in Bangkok, was sent to Okinawa later in the year.

It felt good to return to Hong Kong, where a group of BNDD agents assigned to Region 16 were gathered for their annual three-day conference, the highlight of which was to meet and talk with

441

John Ingersoll. Ingersoll made a courtesy visit to our Consul General, as well as other narcotics chiefs and key officers in the British Police and Customs agencies, but most of his time was spent with the BNDD group. My role was to take notes and draft periodic status reports for the Director to review and cable to Washington. Telephones were readily available and were used despite the 12-hour time difference. I observed the BNDD agents' penchant for using the telephone instead of the written word. They disliked putting anything in writing, operating on the premise that spoken words were less incriminating than written records. I was beginning to learn how the criminal investigator's mind worked.

In the warm evenings of that lovely spring, we often dined in grand fashion. In particular, I remember our dinner afloat. We met all of our BNDD guys and boarded a small motorized launch in which we were ferried across the busy harbor to a huge, lantern-lit, triple-deck floating restaurant anchored among dozens of small fishing junks. We were on the waters inhabited by the boat people of Aberdeen. Well-iced gin and tonic drinks with a slice of lime plus cold Singha beers appeared instantly. After another round of drinks, we were served spicy and delectable dishes, mostly sea food, chicken, and sweet and sour pork, accompanied by platters of wonderfully fluffy rice and stir-fried vegetables. It was a mouth-watering array of one superb dish after another borne on the arms of white-jacketed waiters who moved with the grace and timing of Tai-Kwan-Do experts.

Equal to this almost endless round of great food were the sights, sounds and smells surrounding us. Throngs of people seated on three levels of dining rooms created a steady chorus of sing-song voices that rose and fell in muted melody. Hundreds of satisfied diners murmured softly above the clicking of chop sticks against rice platters and the clatter of empty serving plates being gathered. As we were leaving, I noticed a steady stream of launches crammed with more hungry people coming our way. It looked like a small invasion fleet. I half-feared the restaurant might sink, for as I glanced back at the huge floating structure, outlined in red lantern lights against the black water, the boat was definitely listing slightly to port.

Our BNDD office was located in the Peak Tram Building, so it was very convenient for us to climb aboard the world-famous tram and scale the steep mountain to Victoria Peak high above Hong Kong Island. We gazed down on Victoria Harbor beyond the skyscrapers that jostled for space between the Central District and Causeway Bay. The domed City Hall building far below was dwarfed and half hidden by shiny glass buildings, like a tidy lettuce patch surrounded by a field of tall corn. I could see the Star Ferry pier where we docked after crossing from Kowloon's Kai Tak airport. Above us were the great houses on Victoria Peak, impressive and serene in the cooler heights.

Hong Kong was a city of glitter, dash, and energy. New buildings protruded from every tiny bit of land or man-made turf created by dumping rocks and fill dirt along the harbor's shoreline. The demand for office space was voracious. BNDD's tidy, four-room office was located in the heart of Hong Kong and leased on an annual basis. The landlord would negotiate a new lease with BNDD for only one year at a time, and every year the cost went up, as did the cost of living in Hong Kong. Many of the buildings in Hong Kong were on land that had a 100-year lease, even the new high-rise buildings. The philosophy was that they did not care because after a hundred years, they would not be around. The land was owned by the Chinese, and they were tough negotiators.

As I took snapshots from Victoria Peak, I looked over at Kowloon in the distance and watched the aircraft arriving and departing from Kai Tak airport. Beyond were the blue mountains of the New Territories, which separated us from the sprawling mass of China. One afternoon we took a drive to this border. We got out at a little British police station at Man Kam To and gazed across empty fields; there were no signs of life, nothing, a sobering sight after the jostling Hong Kong scene. I browsed in a gift shop and noticed Chairman Mao Tse-tung's little red book *Quotations from Chairman Mao Tse-tung*, acclaimed as the bible for all Chinese Communists. The foreword proclaimed: "Comrade Mao Tse-tung is the greatest Marxist-Leninist of our era. He has inherited, defended and developed Marxism-Leninism with genius, creativity and comprehensively (sic) and has brought it to a higher and completely new stage.

"Mao Tse-tung's thought is Marxism-Leninism of the era in which imperialism is heading for total collapse and socialism is advancing to world-wide victory. It is a powerful ideological weapon for opposing imperialism and for opposing revisionism and dogmatism. Mao Tse-tung's thought is the guiding principle for all the work of the Party, the army and the country. . . .

"Once Mao Tse-tung's thought is grasped by the broad masses, it becomes an inexhaustible source of strength and a spiritual atom bomb of infinite power. . . ."

The book exhorted its readers to "Study Chairman Mao's writings, follow his teachings and act according to his instructions." I studied this book in days to come, trying to find something inspirational within its striking red cover, but concluded it was at best boring. Perhaps something had been lost in the translation. When I got home, Bill Swain was intrigued enough to take it to class for a show-and-tell project.

We soon departed Hong Kong for Saigon where Ingersoll had meetings with Prime Minister Nguyen Van Thieu of South Vietnam; Ambassador Ellsworth Bunker and the deputy to the Ambassador, who was largely responsible for narcotics affairs; and General Creighton Abrams, Commanding General of our armed forces in South Vietnam. Saigon appeared hyperactive and jammed with traffic, even more so than it had been in 1966. With dismay, I noticed that all the stately trees that had graced the main boulevard had been removed to accommodate more asphalt and twice as much traffic. Our sedan delivered us to the faded Caravelle Hotel at Le Loi, across from the Rex and Continental Hotels. Fred T. Dick, our Narcotics Attache, briefed Ingersoll on current affairs in his office in the new Embassy Building on Thong Nhut.

We had a brief appointment with the CIA Chief of Station, Ted, who I remembered from a meeting three years ago when he was Chief of Station in Vientiane. After Ingersoll was introduced, we spoke for a moment. Ted said with a smile that I certainly had come up a long way in this world. Apparently he was impressed that I was now the aide to the Director of the Bureau of Narcotics and Dangerous Drugs. I recalled that my old boss Pancho, now in Nha Trang, had asked Ted to assign me to him when and if I reappeared in the pipeline of replacements. I had resurfaced all right. I smiled back and asked him to give Pancho my very best. Ted then briefed Ingersoll on the personalities, politics, background, strengths, and weaknesses of a half dozen South Vietnamese officers and civilian chiefs with whom Ingersoll was scheduled to meet. I understood why he was the Chief of Station. Ted had almost total recall and encyclopedic knowledge of the people and convoluted forces opposing each other in South Vietnam and particularly in that Pearl of the Orient known as Saigon.

That night we dined at Ambassador Bunker's residence. I sat to the right of the Ambassador, a fatherly, white-haired, courtly man in his 70's, and Ingersoll and Wellman sat to his left. I wondered why I was accorded such an honor, until much later when I noticed that my credentials (specially issued for this trip) declared that I held the grade of GS-17, only a few notches below the rank of the Ambassador himself! This reminded me why Keith and Russ wanted promotions; the higher the rank, the greater the respect afforded, especially in the diplomatic service.

The next day we were driven to the sprawling military base at Bien Hoa, about 15 miles north of Saigon. This was a simple orientation trip to show Ingersoll some of our military activity. We mostly saw helicopters landing and taking off and then attended another briefing before going to lunch in the Officer's Club. On the walls of the Club's dining room were oil paintings by local artists that were for sale. I picked one that I liked and had it rolled up in wax paper so it would not get crushed. Phyllis and I had wanted to buy a painting from every country we visited, and I suspected this might be my last chance to get one in Vietnam. The painting was a colorful scene of fishing sampans on the shore with their sails furled during a slashing, slanting downpour. The feel of the heavy monsoon rain appealed to me. Perhaps even more appealing to my Scottish instinct was the feeling that the memories that went with the painting would be worth a lot more than the $5.00 purchase price.

We left Saigon on a short flight to Don Muang Airport in Bangkok. After the usual harrowing ride, we checked into the sedate Erawan Hotel. Across the street sprawled the sun-bleached buildings of the Thai police station and its adjacent hospital. Just around the corner was the Amarin Hotel, our family standby. Bangkok was bustling as usual, hot, grimy, filled with traffic, and gray with clouds of diesel fumes that choked the streets and throngs of people. This land was quite different from the sophisticated, energetic, and crowded chaos of Hong Kong but far better than dreary, war-torn, Communist-tainted South Vietnam.

Since we had already met with most of our regional BNDD people in Hong Kong, Ingersoll was scheduled to fly to Chiang Mai in northern Thailand in the morning. Chiang Mai was the gateway to narcotics production in the Golden Triangle, that hilly, remote, forested land through which squiggled the boundary lines between Burma, Thailand, and Laos. The region was called golden for the money being minted by narcotics trafficking.

Harvey Wellman had made the unhappy mistake of swallowing some tap water while in Saigon. He came down with the trots and asked to be excused from the outing to Chiang Mai. Ingersoll said he was sorry Harvey did not feel well but was just as pleased to leave our State Department watchdog behind. Regional Director Bill Wanzeck joined Ingersoll and me at the front desk. We drove in light traffic past the towering statue known as the Victory Monument to the airport where we boarded a small Thai Airways propjet plane for Chiang Mai.

Jim Pettit met us at Chiang Mai, dressed in his khaki two-piece safari suit, and showed us to our hotel. That afternoon our helicopter flew over the rugged border hills where poppy crops were grown. We could not see the purple, red, and white blooms of the poppy from the air because we had to fly high enough to avoid possible ground fire. Pettit advised that the Thai narcotics police and military forces could not control the countryside, and neither could the Burmese or Laos Governments. The Golden Triangle had been controlled for generations by insurgent groups who operated in northern Burma and engaged in the narcotics trade for their livelihood. Chief among these opium warlords was Chang Chi-Fu, also known as Khun Sa, who reportedly commanded a private army of 4,000 to 10,000 soldiers.

Our helicopter landed in a green pasture near a Thai village. Coffee plants, beans and apple trees were being grown in hopes that such crops would provide cash to replace the money now made from harvesting opium gum. USAID funds were used to support this project, which was a worthy endeavor and had the blessing of Thailand's King Bumiphol. After briefings by USAID specialists on crop substitution programs, we returned to our hotel.

Our Thai police hosts treated us with kid gloves. At an official reception at our hotel, I was amused when the senior Thai officer got carried away introducing our Director. The official was waiting at the entrance to the reception area for Jack Ingersoll to appear. "Ladies and Gentlemen," he called out in a booming voice that carried to the sidewalk, "May I present the Director of the Bureau of Narcotics and Dangerous Drugs, MR. JOHN INGERSOLL." Everyone froze in midair and turned to stare. Ingersoll stopped in his tracks, startled and a trifle embarrassed. If there were any drug traffickers in the hotel they now knew that Ingersoll was in town. Ingersoll gamely recovered and began to shake hands and mingle with the guests. He was fuming, smoke almost visibly coming out his ears; it was a sight to behold. Jim Pettit told me later that this touristy hotel was used by out-of-town narcotics kingpins to negotiate deals. I would not have been surprised to learn that a certain Thai official was a party to some of the drug business.

A STEP BACK IN TIME

Our next stop was Rangoon, Burma, only a few hundred miles west of Bangkok, but a quantum leap backward to the late 1940's when the British still ruled. The passage of time had not been kind to the Burmese, who languished under the depressing, paranoid control of General Ne Win. He had led the military coup that seized control of the country in 1962 from a shaky parliamentary government led by Prime Minister U Nu. Ne Win closed the borders, kicked out those who would provide foreign aid, and imposed a rigidly closed system that he dubbed "the Burmese Way to Socialism." He attempted to create a self-sufficient state free of both capitalist and communist taint, but his idealistic attempt was not working.

Even though I had prepared the briefing book about this land of some 38 million people and knew of its valuable natural resources,* I was stunned by the overwhelming sense of stagnation I felt upon

---

* Burma had silver, copper, lead, zinc, teak forests, and vast rice fields in the Irrawaddy River Valley. There was fine fishing in the Bay of Bengal and high-quality jade from the mountains to the north.

447

arriving in Rangoon. Ragged baggage porters, both young and old, swarmed at us to carry our luggage. The airport itself was spartan and cheerless, the arrival/departure board noting only a few flights in and out of a facility that had not been modernized in years.

I probably should have had a better idea of what to expect when I learned that our visit had been reviewed a second time by the Burmese government after we arrived in Thailand, despite our 7-day travel visas that had been issued in Washington. I found out that very few seven-day tourist visas were permitted, and then for only specifically designated, restricted stops to such areas as Rangoon, Mandalay, or Pagan. The well-established economic principle that tourist trade generates positive cash flow apparently made little impression in Burma. Ne Win simply did not want strangers poking around and examining the economic disarray in his poor, beggared land. He probably could not admit that things were not going too well. Perhaps because Ne Win lacked charisma, confidence, or enough political talent to lead the people, he seemed to have isolated and surrounded himself with yes men, hoping that somehow all would get better. By the early 1980's, after Ne Win had been in power 20 years, Burma was ranked among the 10 poorest countries in the world with a per capita income of $200 per year.

Because Ne Win was so paranoid, I think that our State Department worriers followed his lead. We were booked into an old and formerly grand British hotel downtown in full view of all concerned. I felt sure that the hotel desk personnel kept the Burmese internal security officials advised of our comings and goings and watched for any Burmese people who might try to contact the visiting Americans. Perhaps I was getting paranoid too; this place had me looking over my shoulder all the time.

We attended several meetings with U.S. Ambassador Hummel, who would soon be replaced by Edwin W. Martin. After a pleasant lunch on the veranda, he proudly displayed a small tame bear in a cage in his backyard. Ingersoll had been urging the Ambassador to approve a BNDD agent being permanently assigned to his Embassy staff. The Ambassador seemed in favor provided that the Burmese could be persuaded that a narcotics agent would not be a threat. The ever-cautious Burmese worried that if they admitted another American to the country, they also would have to admit additional Russian, Chinese, British, or French representatives. Ne Win was concerned about maintaining his neutrality and he could not or would not make any decision that appeared to favor one nation over another. He was so concerned that he neutralized Burma into a state of near abject poverty.

In making his pitch, Ingersoll dealt with Colonel Tin Oo, Chief of Intelligence for the National Intelligence Bureau of the Socialist Republic of the Union of Burma. Tin Oo, a charming, well-spoken officer who might have served in the British Army as a youth, appeared receptive to the idea and said he would present the proposal to his superiors. He seemed to be a reasonable man, and I was encouraged with our visit. When we left his office, he presented each guest with a beautiful lacquer piece in the shape of a miniature pagoda. Each pagoda was six inches at the base and twelve inches tall and a glistening black with intriguing gilt borders. The pagoda came apart in sections, which made packing and mailing easy. They were made near Mandalay, 200 miles north of Rangoon, that famous city "Where dawn comes up like thunder..." on (Rudyard Kipling's) road to Mandalay. Today, my little pagoda rests on the family piano with Colonel Tin Oo's calling card inside.

As we traveled between our hotel and the Embassy to meetings with Burmese officials, it seemed that not one building had been painted since the demise of the British. The few civilian automobiles on the roads were 1940's or 1950's models; the newer vehicles bore diplomatic plates. Military trucks were unmistakably ancient British lorries. I was told that import taxes on private cars, except for the diplomatic corps, exceeded the total value of the car itself. Exorbitantly high taxes were levied on everything brought into Burma. It was no wonder that there was virtually nothing in the shop windows or on the streets of Rangoon. Burma's military leaders were simply bad economists.

Rangoon's existence depended on its extremely active, widespread, and thriving black market. Our embassy driver took us to a crowded, darkened, barn-like row of buildings where Hindu shopkeepers were selling rice, fruits of all sorts, a variety of fish, freshly butchered chicken and pork, and a bewildering array of unidentified food that smelled of curry. We joined the throng of shoppers who were dressed rather shabbily in aged but clean clothes. We were offered trinkets, jewelry, gem stones, cigarettes, tobacco, and small lacquered tables that could be folded up for mailing. There were religious bells and chimes, wickedly-curved Gurkha knives and other cutlery, antiques, magazines, bolts of cloth, priceless artwork, cheap watches and plastic toys, face powder, and soap, most of which was being backpacked into the country over the mountains and rivers from Thailand. This was an international black market of the first order. It was almost like being in Hong Kong, except that here I felt as if it were 1948 and the British were still in control.

Since 1948, about 38 million Burmese barely existed in the timeless vacuum between two of the largest countries in the world, China and India. After more than twenty years of Ne Win's neutralist, socialistic government, nothing had changed; in fact, the country appeared worse off than ever. For example, our Embassy driver had a degree in engineering, and others with equally fine college degrees were without suitable employment in a land that offered few decent jobs. Aware of these deficiencies, Ne Win remained committed to keeping Burma a nonaligned country, refused to adjust to reality, and avoided links favoring either Russia or the United States. The United States chose to be patient, to offer help, and to wait for the forces of free-market economics to show Burma a way out of its dilemma. By 1975, after farmers began hoarding their rice, food riots broke out in the streets of Rangoon. Burma's leader had to turn to the outside world for aid, and cracks began appearing in the wall of Ne Win's isolation. Within five years, Ingersoll's work paid off, and a narcotics professional with intelligence training was assigned to our Embassy in Rangoon.

Before we left Burma, I was pleasantly surprised to meet an old friend in our Rangoon Embassy, Terry Baldwin. When last seen, he was living near us in San Lorenzo Village in Manila. Still with the Company, Terry had been assigned to Burma after his tour in South Vietnam. He wanted to be introduced to Ingersoll which I arranged, at one of our Embassy functions. I was not surprised to hear that Terry wanted to join BNDD and find work that offered long-term career potential. Six months later, Ingersoll remembered Terry when his application for agent training came across his desk and approved it. Terry completed his training and a year of domestic field experience in the Baltimore office and was dispatched to Chiang Mai to work with Jim Pettit. Terry's wife Nita and their two children accompanied him to Chiang Mai where Phyllis and I and the family would meet them later.

* * *

The pages of my notebook overflowed as we made courtesy appearances in Singapore and in Sidney and Canberra, Australia. After this final leg of our trip, we were dropped in Honolulu for a rest at Fort DeRussy on Waikiki Beach. I borrowed a typewriter and spent a day working on a trip report.

Harvey Wellman and I talked about our last couple of stops, and I asked him what he remembered best about our stay in Singapore. He said it was probably the cleanest city he had ever seen, and I had to agree. If you tossed a cigarette butt or chewing gum wrapper out a taxicab window, the driver would have apoplexy. If he were caught in such a violation, he would be banned from driving in the city and heavily fined. The island city's anticommunist government under its most notable and first Prime Minister, Lee Kuan Yew, ran a tight and tidy ship.

Singapore, known for its famous Raffles Hotel and Tiger Balm Gardens, was less well known for being tough on drug users, even tougher than the Japanese. Addicts were summarily sent to a small island off Singapore where they remained until completion of cold-turkey treatment; if found guilty, drug dealers were executed. Another important control that was strictly enforced was a maximum of two children per family as the acceptable norm; more than that, and the parents paid a heavy tax. Singapore was the only nation I knew that had a tax on children, and it seemed to work. The predominantly Chinese population spoke English and Mandarin. Singapore was one of the top 10 port cities in the world and rivaled, if not equaled, fabulous Hong Kong as a shopping mecca.

The sights in Australia stick in my mind. A nation that alone constitutes a whole continent, it is vast, sprawling, sparsely populated, largely arid and nearly the same size as the United States.

Australia is a frontier land, intriguing and attractive to the adventure-some, self-reliant, and tough people who have settled there. It took our plane three-and-a-half hours to span seemingly endless miles of open, desolate range and brown pasture before it dropped us at Sidney on the east coast.

Statistically, an average of five people per square mile lived in Australia, with most on the 10 percent of arable ground lying along the coastline. The people were warm, open, and friendly and reminded me of our Westerners and Canadian cousins. They spoke English in what is called *Strine*, in which *bloke* was a man and *sheila* was woman. *Bonzer* meant great or terrific, *dinkum* or *fair-dinkum* meant honest or genuine, *dinki-di* meant the real thing, a *jumbuck* was a sheep, an *ocker* was a basic, down-to-earth Aussie, a *pom* was an English person, to *shout* was to buy a round of drinks, *tucker* meant food, *swag* was a bedroll and blankets, a *ute* was a utility or pickup truck, a *barbie* was the barbecue grill, *station* was a sheep or cattle ranch, and to *waltz matilda* was to carry swag.

While I enjoyed visiting beautiful and proper Canberra, a nicely planned capital city of some 270,000 residents, it was the lusty port city of Sydney with over 3 million people that caught my fancy. I remember visiting the jewelry shops that displayed bushels of polished and sparkling red, blue, green, yellow, and purple opals, so-called gems of the desert, which bring in millions of dollars in trade each year. I did not bring any home, being fearful of customs checks and also short of cash.

Our group was given a police power launch ride around Sydney Harbor one fine Saturday afternoon in autumn air. It was the fall of the year in this land down under, just the reverse of our seasons at home where spring was in the air. Thankfully, Phyllis had packed my London Fog raincoat so I could ward off the chill. We cruised by the famous white scalloped Opera House in Sydney Harbor, whose striking design reminded me of Sarasota's garishly purple-pink Van Wezel auditorium on the bay. I felt particularly close to the Aussies because they sent troops to fight alongside us in South Vietnam as members of SEATO (South East Asia Treaty Organization).

Our final meeting was in Honolulu with Admiral McCain in his CINCPAC (Commander-in-Chief, Pacific Area Command) offices on the hill near Tripler General Hospital. From the front entrance we gazed down on Pearl Harbor. I could almost see where the sunken remains of the battleship Arizona rested on the muddy bottom of its last anchorage and felt a melancholy tug on my heartstrings.

Admiral McCain listened intently as Ingersoll gave him a firsthand report on the status of our military's drug abuse in Vietnam. Ingersoll outlined the steps he had in mind for sending additional BNDD agents to Southeast Asia, starting with Okinawa, South Vietnam, and Thailand. Even though it was like closing the barn door after the horse was gone, Ingersoll was determined to rein in the runaway and repair the barn door as well.

As we talked with the Admiral, my thoughts drifted from Ingersoll's briefing to the Admiral's son John, a downed Navy carrier pilot who was being held prisoner in the Hanoi Hilton jail in North Vietnam. I could not bear to imagine the hellish conditions he had been enduring and felt guilty somehow because I was so well off and healthy here in Honolulu. I thought that the Admiral must spend many sleepless nights wishing Johnson would discard his no-win strategy and order the capture of Hanoi lock, stock, and barrel. After six and a half years, John was returned to his home and family. He eventually entered politics and became a Republican U.S. Senator from the State of Arizona.

While I had enjoyed traveling with the Director and was sorry that the trip was ending, I felt that I had been away a long while and needed to return to my family waiting at home. I had a hunch that someday I would be coming this way again.

EIGHTEEN

D.C. to Thailand

P hyllis and I often thought of Southeast Asia wistfully as we reluctantly adjusted to the more demanding realities of life during our first year with BNDD. Phyllis was busy reactivating her real estate license, which on top of her housekeeping chores, kept her pretty busy. She sorely missed having Chi-Chi and Anh-Anh around to help out. My long bus rides to town plus a reduced income (down 25 percent with no overseas pay differential or paid housing) made life a bit spartan. No wonder we looked back at those past four years in Southeast Asia with a certain longing.

In July, John Ingersoll asked me to escort a group of Congressmen to Southeast Asia. The Congressional Delegation (known as a CODEL) was led by Paul Rogers, Chairman of the Subcommittee on Public Health and Environment, and comprised three other Congressmen. This group was only one of several CODELs planning to vacate the halls of Congress for summer junkets around the globe. Officially, such trips provided Congressmen firsthand information about their areas of interest; unofficially, it meant they had first-class paid vacations courtesy of the U.S. taxpayer. Ingersoll hoped that I might help Mr. Roger's committee better appreciate the military's drug abuse problem in Southeast Asia and thus be more inclined to support BNDD's request for more money and people in the fall budget hearings.

The junket ran August 5 - 22, 1971, according to my notebook, which I managed to fill with a jumble of information and impressions and from which I prepared my final report. The CODEL comprised Democratic Congressmen Paul V. Rogers from Florida, Richardson

455

Preyer from North Carolina, Peter Kyros from Maine, and David E. Satterfield from Virginia, and Stephen Lawton, a law student and staff assistant who worked for Rogers.

The day before we departed, Ingersoll confided that he had some misgivings. He said that he would not have sent me if he had known they were all Democrats. I wondered what that meant but did not ask. He asked me to be alert to any criticism of the Administration's drug programs and to send him a cable if I heard anything critical. I was to note whether Nixon's programs were presented in a positive fashion and to keep BNDD's role in the drug enforcement business in the background.

I assured the boss that I would do my best but was a bit concerned that I was getting in over my head. After the trip, I remember how carefully I reviewed my notes and impressions, telling Ingersoll that Rogers' CODEL had not made a single remark or comment that was critical of the Administration; Ingersoll was very pleased. My service may not have had any bearing on the CODEL's attitude toward the Administration, but it certainly did not do any harm.

I told Phyl that being with a group of Congressmen was a lot different from traveling with Ingersoll. When we got to Hong Kong in mid-August, the place was jumping with CODELs. We kept bumping into Americans who were traveling with House Speaker Carl Albert, who had filled a whole plane with Congressmen, their wives, and assorted staffers. Albert's group had been touring Korea, Taipei, Hong Kong, and Tokyo. It seemed as though half of the Congress had rooms in the Mandarin Hotel in Hong Kong. Phyllis was incredulous when I told her that Speaker Albert had chartered his own military aircraft, which meant that customs checks would be meaningless and they could bring in a plane load of goods practically duty-free. She asked me what was interesting about the trip, so I gave her a rundown, which included stops in Honolulu, Bangkok, Chiang Mai, Saigon, Hong Kong, and Tokyo.

After boarding at Dulles, we were told that our plane would be delayed. I noticed that all the CODEL had first-class seats and I took my usual economy seat feeling like a second-class citizen. Paul Rogers told me to telephone John Warner and get my seat upgraded so I could be with the rest of them. Warner agreed and I used my Travel

Request coupons to authorize myself a firstclass seat; this Rogers guy was not all that bad, I thought. Two hours later, we departed for San Francisco and then took Pan Am to Honolulu for our rest stop at the posh Kahala Hilton. Honolulu was gorgeous, as usual.

The next afternoon we attended a military briefing conducted by our old friend and navy four-striper, Admiral John S. McCain. It seemed like three years rather than three months since Ingersoll and I had been in his office. The Admiral said there were four priorities in Southeast Asia: first was curing drug abuse; second was our military assistance program to the South Vietnamese; third was the outcome of the battle now being waged; and fourth was freeing our prisoners in Hanoi. You could have heard a pin drop when he mentioned the prisoner priority, for most of us knew his son was still in the Hanoi Hilton prison. He said that drug testing centers had been established in South Vietnam at Long Binh, Cam Ranh Bay, and Nha Be. All servicemen needing treatment would be tended to in military hospitals while in the service and in Veterans Administration hospitals when discharged.

McCain concluded by recommending that an office or bureau be established in the Bangkok area to coordinate drug treatment, training, and enforcement activities. Ingersoll would be pleased to hear about this turn of events. I thought this could be right down BNDD's alley, but given the military's penchant for building empires, no doubt McCain meant the new office to be controlled by the military.

We flew to Bangkok where we booked into the elegant Erawan Hotel before more briefings the next day by our State Department people. Leonard Unger, our Ambassador to Thailand, was there, as were BNDD director Bill Wanzeck, Paul Brown, and a few others. The briefing officer, Special Assistant for Drug Control George S. Newman, said that the Thai narcotics priorities were more pressing than those of the U.S. Government, considering that the security and control of the hill tribal regions, where the opium poppy is cultivated, was still in doubt. The people there were struggling for economic and national survival.

The next day we boarded a Thai Airways plane for a quick trip to Chiang Mai for more briefings followed by a rather perfunctory flight in an Air America Porter over the rugged hills where the poppies grew. We then returned to the refinements of Bangkok where on Sunday I took the group to see the wonders of the Bangkok floating market. The guys seemed to enjoy the boat ride along the klongs.

I had almost forgotten to tell Phyl that immediately after the Bangkok briefings, I noticed that my CODEL people all trooped into the Embassy finance office where each one was handed $50 for each day they were to be in Thailand. I was astounded to learn that visiting Congressmen received cash gifts from our Embassy. There was no accountability; all they had to do was sign for it. My eyes popped when I saw them pocketing the cash. I found out later that I was not qualified for the same treatment because I was a government employee, not an elected representative of the people.

Phyllis and I discussed this matter with curiosity and decided that elected officials on official travel abroad were authorized such largess, which was probably yet another self-serving law Congress had enacted to benefit their membership. It also could have been a form of per diem similar to the allowance I was paid while on official travel status. Still, my feelings toward Congressman Rogers cooled somewhat because of it. I did not mention this to Ingersoll, but perhaps I should have.

The next two days in Saigon were interesting yet depressing. We had more lengthy briefings, during which I was struck by how dependent our military briefers were on the use of charts, graphs, and overhead slide projections. They probably had a dozen graphic art specialists tucked away in a special room cranking out nothing but briefing aids.

That afternoon our group split into teams to inspect the area detoxification centers. Rich Preyer and I flew to Cam Ranh Bay to look at the air force center, Paul Rogers and Lawton went to Long Binh to see the army center, and Kyros and Satterfield looked in on the navy installation at Nha Be. Detoxification was the first step for any G.I. returning to the States for reassignment or discharge. If any drugs were detected in his mandatory urinalysis test, he went to a detoxification center. Because of Nixon's accelerated reduction of troops in Vietnam, the flow of troops homeward was getting pretty heavy and varied from 300 to 700 a day during August. It was estimated that 10 to 12 percent of our troops showed some sign of drug abuse.

I described the men detained at Cam Ranh Bay to Phyllis as being young and scrawny, most of them just out of high school. Depending on the extent of their drug addiction, these men would be sent for 30 days of further treatment in a military hospital; more serious addiction cases would go to the States for treatment at Veteran's Administration hospitals before discharge.

One of the prime concerns of our Bureau was that returning servicemen would bring their heroin and marijuana addictions home to infect other Americans. Fortunately, the plague of drug abuse that swept the battlefields of Vietnam did not become the blight on the country that BNDD feared. Most of the young men who used drugs did so out of boredom, loneliness, and peer pressure and dropped their drug abuse habits as soon as they returned home to families, jobs, and girlfriends. Besides being back to normal living conditions, returning G.I.s found heroin and potent marijuana very expensive, a definite damper on casual usage. Fred T. Dick, BNDD's Narcotics Attache, had been assigned to the Embassy in Saigon for the past year and knew what was going on in the area. He was a streetwise veteran from the Federal Bureau of Narcotics (FBN). When Ingersoll asked for a volunteer for the new Saigon post in 1970, Fred had just completed his master's degree at the War College at Fort McNair in Washington and signed on for the job. In time, Fred and I became friends. He was a charming man but could be curt when dealing with subordinates. Luckily he had a good sense of humor to blunt his sharp edges. Possessing an alert, quick mind and a liking for thoroughness and precision, Fred knew the narcotics traffickers' trade inside and out and had well-honed instincts for what made people tick.

Fred briefed Congressman Rogers in his office after Rogers had completed a private session with Ted, the Company's Station Chief. Fred said he supported the concept of a drug czar in Bangkok who could coordinate all government agencies involved in narcotics affairs. He was not above name dropping and mentioned that he had recently talked with Bud Krogh, a high-ranking Nixon staffer, on this very subject; but Rogers was noncommittal. Fred said that the primary need was for action against the sources of the drugs, with due consideration for the political aspects involved. He knew that most of the drugs affecting our troops in South Vietnam came from heroin refineries in the remote hills of the Golden Triangle—Thailand, Burma, and Laos. Getting those governments to take aggressive action against these drug traffickers was nearly impossible, given the security problems, amount of money involved, and endemic graft and corruption.

If an office was set up in Bangkok, Fred wanted to be in on it. He said he knew the military mind and thought he could manage them. I thought this was saying quite a bit, but admired Fred's confidence.

HONG KONG AGAIN

My spirits uplifted as we left Saigon for Hong Kong. We were greeted at the airport by Keith Shostrom, Hong Kong's Senior Agent, and taken to the Mandarin Hotel. That night at dinner, we noticed Keith across the room engrossed in conversation with Congressman Edwards from California. Since our group was scheduled to meet with Keith in the morning, I thought nothing of it; but my dinner companions became agitated and upset. They were seething with jealousy because Shostrom was dining with another Congressman and not with them. Somehow they blamed me for Shostrom's dinner date, which floored me completely. I tried to placate them, astounded that they viewed Shostrom's meeting with another member of Congress as an affront to them. They kept asking me to explain, but I had no excuses. I reassured them the Edwards dinner with Shostrom meant nothing. In the morning, Keith explained that the dinner date had been made several days in advance and that no slight was intended. I was so upset, I thought of sending a cable to Ingersoll but decided the incident was not worth the Director's time. From that moment on, though, I was more alert to the sensitive feelings of my prima donnas.

Our first official duty was to attend a briefing in the offices of the Consul General of Hong Kong. The Congen, a tall distinguished man named Osborne, had been busy briefing one CODEL group after another. By some State Department measurement, Hong Kong does not rate ambassadorial status but is headed by a Consul General. Hong Kong is a plum in the diplomatic fruit bowl of assignments, however and many an Ambassador would gladly take a demotion to Consul General if the assignment was to Hong Kong.

Congen Osborne kept his briefing informal and filled with comments about the weather, shopping conditions, and routine political matters. He added in an offhand manner that the Chinese and Russians would continue to support the North Vietnamese and other insurgencies in the future. He also said that U.S. trade relations continued to hold an unstable and unsatisfactory position, with exports of $3 billion and imports of $8 billion. The relative state of affairs is about the same twenty years later; apparently, we are satisfied with how things are going or simply unable to do anything about it.

Keith Shostrom's briefing provided interesting glimpses into narcotics trafficking in this crowded city of four million Chinese. My cryptic notes identified the Golden Triangle as the source of most of the opium and heroin coming into Hong Kong. During January through March, four tons of opium gum were seized by British Customs and harbor patrol boats in Hong Kong waters, mostly from shipments concealed in Thai fishing trawlers. Ten to twelve fishing boats from Thailand arrived every day and were quickly absorbed in the 10,000 or more fishing junks in the area, while harbor police boarded and searched 200 or 300 boats a day. Smoking opium is the black, tarlike substance extracted from dried, raw opium gum; little balls of this black gum are smoked by older Chinese in special long-stemmed opium pipes. Morphine base, a hard substance refined from opium gum, the intermediate product in the process of making pure heroin, was intercepted in lesser amounts.

The British estimated that 15 illicit factories in the area were converting morphine base into smoking heroin (Keith put this figure closer to 50), with each factory capable of producing 5 to 10 kilograms of heroin per day. The British blamed Thailand for their problem and planned to appeal to Interpol (the international police organization) in Ottawa, asking them to lean on the Thai's to stop their involvement in trafficking. There were no signs that the

461

Communists were involved in drug trafficking, as the Chinese merchants from nearby Canton were behind the drug business in Hong Kong. Firearms were being imported and gold was being shipped out, while corruption was a continuing problem among police officers at the street or constable levels. Keith thought we were running out of time and had to work harder to intercept the current opium poppy crop by whatever means possible, both overt and covert. Hong Kong's addict population was about 120,000, with one-third addicted to smoking opium and the rest smoking #3 heroin (not as pure as #4). Singapore did not ship narcotics to Hong Kong, since local prices were the same and there was no profit to be made. Laos was a minor narcotics producer.

Since most of the illicit heroin refineries were known, perhaps some of our own mercenaries could be hired to destroy them. Rogers, very hawkish, thought we could mount counteractions against refinery operators. Others said we had to consider preclusive purchases of last year's opium production, which could have been used for legitimate narcotics purposes in hospitals in the United States. The United Nations had a role as well, perhaps considering a blockade of the Gulf of Siam by the U.S. Seventh Fleet to stop the trawler traffic. Favoring this approach, the British considered trying the United Nations as a pressure group. It was suggested that we pay our informants on a graduated scale; for example, pay $10,000 U.S. for 40 kilograms of morphine if seized before trial and only $4,000 for the same amount if seized afterwards.

Methods of smuggling included small packets of pure #4 heroin carried in by couriers who concealed the heroin on their bodies and took commercial air flights into Hong Kong. Crew members from fishing boats also smuggled packets of opium and morphine when they went ashore. The penalty for simple possession was three years and up to life for trafficking offenses of five or more packets of heroin. The defendant had to prove his innocence, just the opposite of our American brand of justice. First offenders got only nine months. Hong Kong police had broad powers of presumptive arrest, with simple suspicion of a crime sufficient for an arrest. On addict treatment, the British had a pilot methadone program, but the results were not clear. My head was spinning at the end of

Keith's briefing. Rogers and the others were impressed as well.

Hong Kong went on a typhoon alert, and for the next two days the hatches were battened down. From my room, I looked down on Victoria Harbor and watched small boats and gray war ships of visiting nations slowly move through the mist and rain from the inner harbor to safer anchorage in deeper water. There they could swing at anchor, face the storm, and ride it out. The sturdy Star ferryboats plowed their way back and forth in the slanting rain until dusk, allowing office workers to get home to the Kowloon side. At midnight, accompanied by howling, ripping winds, the eye of the typhoon passed us to the east flinging sheets of water sideways into the window casements and structural joints of our building. I drew the heavy, inner window curtain to catch any flying glass that might come into my room during the night. I said my prayers carefully and then went to sleep, listening to the rise and fall of the moaning wind and wishing Phyllis were here to keep me company. The next morning, water was dripping down the elevator shafts and debris filled the streets, but no real harm was done.

Before we left Hong Kong for Tokyo, I talked to Russ Arslan by telephone and asked him to meet our plane and have dinner with us our first night in town; I thought Rogers would like that. I also asked Russ to set up meetings with the Japanese Ministry for Public Health so the CODEL could visit hospitals where addicts were being treated. I mentioned that Rogers was interested in the extent of Japanese abuse of amphetamines and anything to do with treatment.

Russ met us when we got to Tokyo and escorted us to the Okura Hotel, where we dined together and had a relaxing evening. The next day, after more obligatory briefings at the Embassy, Rogers' CODEL met with the Minister of Public Health, Mr. Hitihashi, who made a lengthy speech that was doubly long since it had to be translated in our two languages. My notes said that local addicts were admitted to hospitals where they remained for an average of 50 days undergoing withdrawal treatment aided by tranquilizers; they did not use methadone. It was pretty dry stuff but perhaps worth reporting. My cup was running over with briefings on drug abuse, so after two days I took leave of Rogers' CODEL and left them with Russ, who would see that they got on their way back to the States. I left for

Bangkok and was soon in my room at the now very familiar Amarin Hotel. My final assignment was to review and report on the expansion of BNDD's intelligence office. The next few days were spent talking with DEA agents, U.S. Customs people, and others in the Embassy working on narcotics. Regional Director Bill Wanzeck was hosting Phil Smith and Howard Safer, who were visiting from BNDD Headquarters.

On a lighter note, I enjoyed an unexpected lunch with some old Agency friends who were staying in Bangkok. Dave from Quang Duc was now assigned to the Embassy in Bangkok and had learned to speak Thai very well. He invited me to join him and some of the gang for lunch. Sure enough, there were four of the old Pakse group plus two others I remembered from Saigon. We all ate steamed crabs, nicely seasoned and dipped in drawn butter, and drank cold Singha beer at a big round table at the restaurant atop the Chok Chai Building. The view from the 20th floor was fine. At midday, the sun was bright and white hot, and the air outside was beginning to get steamy, but inside it was cool and hospitable. In the course of our long lunch, I realized how much I missed these old friends, who seemed so different from my new BNDD associates.

* * *

A few days later, I returned to Washington and BNDD's grubby headquarters and to the confusing yet stimulating life inside the beltway in the heart of our nation's capital. I was curious about how the concept of expanding BNDD's intelligence capability was progressing. I knew it was not being eagerly accepted by the FBN veterans in BNDD, who were from the old school and understandably reluctant to accept changes suggested by Ingersoll and his new organization. The reason was that for more than thirty years, the worth of a narcotics agent was measured by the amount of drugs he seized and the number of cases he made. The agents were trained to make undercover buys from a drug pusher or dealer using informants who set up the deal. After the deal went down and the arrest was made, a trial followed, during which the identity of the informant was made public. The usefulness of that informant in future cases ended. The agent then had to develop a new informant and start the cycle all over again.

Now there was a newer approach, one that would add a layer of narcotics intelligence agents and analysts to recruit informants who not only had access to drug trafficking groups or organizations but also would not be expected to appear in court. Hopefully, they would provide drug-related intelligence on important drug members and their plans, intentions, and operations. Out of this association would flow investigative leads that would be passed to enforcement agents in such a way that the informant would not be exposed. Obviously, these sources were not expendable. It was no wonder that some of the old FBN group felt their turf was being usurped.

In spite of the solid logic of the intelligence approach, the old guard was slow to give ground. One important factor that tipped the balance in favor of intelligence was the law itself. No matter how you tried to work around it, BNDD agents had no legal arrest authority when overseas. They were restricted to training and conducting liaison with police counterparts and were authorized to participate in drug operations as observers, but they could not function as arresting officers. In the years to come, resistance to the concept of sending intelligence-trained BNDD agents and analysts overseas dwindled and finally ended.

The CIA was the acknowledged lead agency in intelligence-collection activities overseas. It had access to a number of people capable of providing narcotics intelligence, but there was a problem. The CIA's sources of information sometimes were involved in narcotics trafficking, and the CIA did not want to identify them.

This problem in Bangkok was forced into the open by increasing pressure from the White House, which did not care who did the reporting as long as narcotics intelligence was obtained and the hemorrhage of drugs stopped. All of the agencies' chiefs and their staffers, led by the Embassy DCM (deputy head of the country team) met in the bubble to discuss this issue. The bubble was a Plexiglas conference chamber enclosed within a room on the third floor of the Embassy Building. The bubble sat on an elevated platform covered on all sides by two inches of Plexiglas. Inside the clear plastic was a wooden table with seating for approximately 15 people. All conversations within the soundproof bubble were secure, and the door to the bubble room was locked and guarded when in use.

The CIA cautiously admitted that it could provide the needed narcotics intelligence but some ground rules were needed when there was a conflict of interest. For example, the CIA narcotics officer asked how they were to handle a highly placed agent who had been providing intelligence on the plans and intentions of the Shan United Army (3,000 or more men led by Chang Chi-Fu in northern Burma) when this same agent was involved in pack mule shipments of opium to heroin refineries in northern Thailand. If they intercepted the pack mules, they would probably lose their intelligence agent. He wanted to know what was more important: the life of a good, well-placed agent or a shipment of opium.

The answer to this kind of dilemma, and others like it, was worked out in Washington by top-level policy managers. A compromise was reached, and BNDD's Strategic Intelligence Office soon began to receive sanitized reports from the CIA's man with the SUA relating to some narcotics activities. However, CIA sources of information were not to be exposed without express permission. This was a classic example of half a loaf being better than no bread at all.

After my trip to Southeast Asia with Director Ingersoll, my friend Tom Tripodi and I drafted a memo for John Warner detailing the need for an expanded role of our Strategic Intelligence Office. We pointed out that BNDD's systems approach had not proven to be as successful as originally hoped in impacting the availability of narcotics and dangerous drugs in the country, the primary reason being a lack of sufficiently comprehensive and timely intelligence on narcotics traffickers' plans, intentions, and activities.

The memo read:

"At present, enforcement officers rely heavily on tactical intelligence furnished by informants, who are often *burned* or exposed when normal enforcement procedures are employed. . . . to improve BNDD's approach and to upgrade its effect on trafficking, better and more timely intelligence operations are needed, domestically and abroad—particularly abroad.

"BNDD needs to add a special operations or strategic operations staff as a compartmented part of its enforcement responsibilities. The special operations staff can function as BNDD's own CIA using a backdoor approach to gather intelligence in support of operations, and to give the Director intelligence for policy planning. Liaison and close joint operations with the CIA and BNDD in the field of foreign activities is required.

"The difference between classic BNDD informant-oriented enforcement procedures and proposed strategic operations intelligence collection is not one of competition; it is rather one of complementation. . . . Special operations will be able to funnel additional intelligence into enforcement operational efforts from separate sources, by using longer range, deep penetration, clandestine assets, who remain undercover, do not appear during the course of any trial and are recruited and directed by Special Operations agents on a covert basis. . . . headquarters approval will be required for all recruitments."

This special operations concept was never fully implemented. George Belk made an effort to form a cadre of former CIA officers in the Strategic Intelligence Office, but there were too many bureaucratic hurdles to overcome. The special operations concept never bore much fruit, but Tom and I had been in there pitching.

* * *

House of Representatives
Washington, D.C.

September 24, 1971

Dear Adrian:

Many thanks for the courtesies that you rendered during our recent subcommittee mission. I believe that our findings will have significant impact on legislation which the Committee

467

intends to report to the Congress in the near future, and we are grateful for your assistance.

My kind regards and best wishes.

Paul V. Rogers

This note from Paul Rogers was a pleasant surprise. I appreciated his message but do not recall seeing any legislation that he mentioned.

ASSIGNMENT TO BANGKOK

During the fall, Phyllis and I decided that it would be nice if we were assigned to Bangkok. There was a lot of work for me to do there, and we felt the timing was right. Shortly before Thanksgiving, I casually mentioned to John Parker that I would be willing to go to Bangkok to work on regional intelligence operations. I reminded him that my former Agency background would provide some credibility with the intelligence agencies in Thailand, which in turn would help improve BNDD's position. Within two weeks, John Warner announced in a Friday afternoon staff meeting that Director Ingersoll had approved my assignment to Bangkok.

One condition for my assignment was that I be transferred as an investigative officer, not as an intelligence analyst. As an investigative officer, I would qualify for the extra pay differential for uncontrolled overtime work that enforcement agents receive. I knew it would take months before a reporting date would be mentioned. I hoped it would not be until school was out but could always go before the family on temporary assignment.

At home around the supper table, I asked the boys if they would like to go to Thailand. Tom said that would be fine, and Bill said that Japanese bubble gum was as good as any around here. I had not thought of equating Southeast Asia with the quality of its bubble gum. Ken said it was okay, meaning he would go wherever the family went. Cyndy had received her Bachelor of Arts in the School of Education last summer and thought it would be neat to go with us to

Bangkok. She was working at a nearby Marriott Hotel and was not quite ready to teach full-time.

The Nixon Administration regarded the narcotics problem seriously and created various federal narcotics committees to deal with this deadly epidemic. For the next several months, I represented BNDD at weekly meetings at the Department of State, which included representatives from USAID, Customs, Immigration, the Department of Defense, and the CIA. The U.S. Postal Service also sent a representative because our ingenious G.I.s were sending dope home through the mail.

Each agency was willing to discuss the drug problem in general terms but was very reluctant to concede an inch of jurisdictional turf to another agency regarding corrective actions. As a non-bureaucrat, I did not care who did the work as long as the job was done; but I soon realized that this viewpoint was not shared by many others. I should not have been surprised, because even BNDD disputed among itself whether to expand its intelligence capability overseas.

My notes of one meeting of the Southeast Asian Working Group held February 8, 1972, with guest speaker Hawthorne Mills, the State Department's narcotics coordinator on leave from Saigon, provide a flavor of that time:

"1,800 MACV military personnel are engaged in narcotics programs in South Vietnam, dealing with drug rehabilitation.

"'Tan Turtle' is the code name for the military's new computerized program... designed to develop a fast retrieval system on drug-related information. Success of the program is still undetermined, but progress is satisfactory so far. [Computers were becoming very popular in all government branches, including BNDD. Because of the volume of narcotics violations occurring in the armed forces, we needed computers to help track the activity.]

"The Vietnamese Air Force remains a problem with respect to the smuggling of narcotics by air. . . . Vietnamese Air Force officials are cooperative, but with over 300 airfields in South Vietnam, air inspection is difficult [i.e., impossible.]

"Korean and Thai troops [serving in South Vietnam] do not do well in policing their own troops. Vietnamese officials press them to do better, but are wary because the Thais and South Koreans might just pull out completely.

"A three-man survey team, led by State Department's own Fred Flott, is now in Hawaii writing up its trip report on the movement of narcotics by air and sea and how to control it. [This trip was viewed by others in the working group as another State Department boondoggle. The military had surveyed the problem already, but the State Department was unwilling to take the military's word without a double check. Another example of the NIH syndrome [not invented here]—any solution derived by an outside agency is automatically suspect because they might be following their own hidden agenda].

"The Vietnamese Customs chief is an effective man but has difficulty with his subordinates who continually sabotage efforts to stop smuggling. Pressure to motivate SVN officials must come from the top, but has not been forthcoming, despite Ambassador Bunker's strong appeals to President Thieu.

"During the meeting, Bill Wanzeck, on home leave from Bangkok, spoke to the group. He said the Royal Thai Government (RTG) had just signed an order activating the Special Northern Operation (SNO), an anti-narcotics program against drug smugglers in the northern border area, to be run from Chiang Mai, under Jim Pettit. . . . Wanzeck said that getting anything done in Thailand requires a total commitment from the RTG which we are a long way from getting. Speaking of corruption, Wanzeck added, 'there is no conflict-of-interest law in Thailand, therefore corruption and taking bribes is normal and accepted. Bribe money flows upward, not downward; connecting bribe money to seats of power is not easy.' [Sounds like our own Political Action Committees (PACs) that seek to influence our officials at the national level by making contributions. It appears our system is not that much different from the Thai's.]

"Wanzeck continued, 'On the other hand, in local enforcement operations, the Thai police removed 80 pounds of heroin from the Bangkok area market, a significant achievement compared to their effort of the last year.' [A classic example of the left hand never knowing what the right hand is doing.]

"Phil Vandivier, Working Group Chairman, reported that the APO mail system overseas was being used to smuggle drugs into the United States. He said, 'A special inspection machine has been ordered; it is an X-Ray machine that will screen luggage and hand-carried goods. It can detect suspect items inside a suitcase, a box, or an envelope. Made by *Phillips*, fourteen machines costing about $9,000 each will help screen the stacks of mail being processed at APO's. This machine is capable of detecting a test vial of sugar tucked in the toe of a shoe, well wrapped in clothing inside a suitcase. . . . it can also display a hollowed-out cane, or show the blank spaces inside a hollowed-out alarm clock hidden inside a box and surrounded by other hardware.'

"In Laos, General Khamhou, [the national narcotics chief of the Special Enforcement Group] is doing a good job of getting his new program underway. His effectiveness is limited by his inability to penetrate the military regions which remain the fiefdoms of regional commanding generals. [Apparently nothing has changed since I left Laos, but, at least, an anti-narcotics toe-hold has been established.]

Bill Wanzeck did not mention to the group that BNDD had just authorized our Ambassador in Thailand to proceed with a $1 million purchase of about 20 tons of opium from Chinese Irregular Force Generals Li Wen-huan and Tuan Hsi-wen operating near the border of Thailand and Burma. This transaction would be coordinated by the Thai government's General Kriangsak. The purchase had two purposes: the first was to dry up drug trafficking in Thailand; the second was to resettle the Chinese hill people who grew and collected opium and have them cultivate opium-substitute crops provided by the Thai Government. The purchase was made, and an impressive mound of opium was ceremoniously burned by Thai officials in Chiang Mai, witnessed by assorted BNDD and State Department leaders and press reporters. Despite much fanfare, this first preemptive buy did little to halt the flow of narcotics. There were even rumors that most of the burned opium was of poor quality and the good stuff eventually would be sold on the blackmarket. Sure as the sunrise, opium caravans soon were winding south from the Burmese and China border area. The drug trafficking had only slowed, not stopped. The United States never gave serious thought to future proposals for preemptive opium purchases.

In late February, the State Department received Congressional inquiries about a Jack Anderson column* in *The Washington Post* in which Congressman Lester Wolff accused high-level Thai officials of involvement in narcotics trafficking. Always sensitive to the press, the State Department cabled its posts in Bangkok, Manila, and Hong Kong for their views and was told there was no hard evidence. The Department then prepared a position paper that was sympathetic to the Congressional inquiry yet not offensive to the Thai government. The effect was to show Congressional members, especially those on budget approval committees, that their charges were being taken seriously.

Embassy reports from abroad continued to bear worsening news.

---

* Twenty years later, on April 12, 1992, Jack Anderson was still ripping the State Department in his nationally syndicated column "Merry-Go-Round": "Uncle Sam sometimes likes to be the piano player in the brothel. He knows what is going on upstairs, but keeps on tickling the ivories.... State Department officials now privately denounce the US approach to Thailand, which has amounted to stroking corrupt government officals with direct links to major heroin-trafficking organizations that move hundreds of tons of heroin every year.... Our sources say that it finally dawned on the diplomats that the Thai government that took power in 1989 is even less interested in the drug war than its predecessor, that drug traffic is on the rise in neighboring Burma and that heroin continues to flow into the United States in increasing tonnage every year."

The Philippines reported, "Marijuana use is epidemic. . . the use of heroin among U.S. personnel is increasing. Heroin at Clark Field is 70 to 80 percent pure. . . there is increasing need for more rehabilitation and equipment, as well as law enforcement training and advisors."

Thailand said, ". . . the climate of the U.S. Mission here is one of frustration and some bitterness. Too many visitors from Headquarters, and some lack of support on Mission recommendations. . . . U.S. Customs needs to do more in the Bangkok Harbor area and along the shorelines. . . . The only significant progress being made is the BNDD effort in northern Thailand."

Laos reported, "There is lack of funding to support paying for informant leads to the police. BNDD has made some arrangements, but a funding mechanism is needed to keep up the morale and momentum of local police. . . . The work of General Khamhou, head of the GSI, [Group Special Investigations] and the Laos Intelligence Service, continues to be coordinated with Tony Morelli, BNDD's Attache in Vientiane."

In Saigon, "The military is still cumbersome and difficult to work around. Public Safety, BNDD and the local narcotics police are doing Okay. . . . The general feeling is that when our troops withdraw the narcotics problem will resolve itself, or at least become a secondary problem." This State Department view was not shared by BNDD or military officials, who were concerned we might have a domestic epidemic on our hands when the war ended in Vietnam.

* * *

By mid-March, BNDD's personnel office had completed most of the paperwork for sending the Swain family to Bangkok. Ingersoll and Warner were anxious for me to get started, while I continued dragging my heels. I finally told John Warner that I was willing to go to Bangkok on temporary duty for 60 days if I could return in early June when school was out, take some leave, and then return to Thailand with the family later that month.

By the end of March, I was in Bangkok at the fabulously ritzy Dusit Thani Hotel not far from the Embassy. The Dusit Thani had thick, red carpets, rich panels of wood in the lobby, and a baby elephant tethered by the elevated, curving driveway at the entrance to the hotel. The elephant was only about six feet tall and covered with a bright red and yellow blanket. A young Thai mahout, dressed in a similarly bright outfit, stood on guard by the bewildered beast. This attraction did not last long, as it was too messy an operation.

Bill Wanzeck was glad to see me, and I soon was assigned a desk to begin work. A few days later, my Saigon and Quang Duc friend Dave and I were having lunch in the Embassy cafeteria, when he invited me to stay with him until my family arrived. Of course I accepted and soon was riding to work with Dave in the mornings. Jim, another old partner from Quang Duc, had also just arrived in town and was living a few blocks away. It was almost like old times in the evenings.

Aside from assessing the needs and limitations of establishing a new narcotics intelligence unit, I needed to get to know all the Embassy staff as well as our regional people. Another priority was to locate suitable housing for our Swain gang. I finally selected a two-story stucco house behind a high wall with a swinging metal gate painted rusty red, which was opened by the gardener who lived there. The house was owned by a Thai general and was located around the corner from the 5th Field Hospital. Rent was $375 a month, $50.00 a month over my State Department allowance, but the house was very spacious and adequately furnished and had a manicured, tree-shaded lawn. There was one other house inside the wall which was occupied by a Thai woman and her husband, an alcoholic American retiree. The house had four bedrooms, a lovely front portico, and a separate garage building with a basketball hoop. There was a decent bedroom and storage space above the garage for overflow guests.

This extra space would come in handy when Bunny, one of Phyllis' Pakse buddies, became pregnant. She and George were living in Phnom Penh, Cambodia, where maternity medical facilities were rather primitive. When Bunny was several months pregnant with her first child, Bunny stayed in that apartment while her husband went home for his father's funeral. Phyl had been especially glad to have her company. Bunny also brought her beautiful Irish setter named Sam to keep her company, much to Julie's delight. One afternoon that big dog sprang from the second-floor window onto the concrete driveway below, without injury, because he was so anxious to see Julie and explore the grounds. Tango of course was barking like mad, trying to defend his turf. The boys and I often played impromptu basketball on the driveway court. It was a happy time for us all.

* * *

By mid-May my efforts to plan and launch our Regional Intelligence Unit were coming along nicely. I wrote a summary memorandum for Bill Wanzeck that outlined the mission of the Regional Intelligence Unit (RIU) to collate, collect, and assess narcotics intelligence from all regional sources. RIU recommendations for enforcement actions would be prepared and forwarded through mission coordination channels. I noted that the RIU would be under the direct guidance of the Regional Director and headed by me on a full-time basis. Special Agent Brown would be assigned to this unit if possible, along with a BNDD clerk typist, a CIA reports officer on loan, and an experienced secretary. The occasional services of Customs or Department of Defense representatives would be called for as needed, but no permanent desk space for these people was to be provided.

By late summer, Tom Becker (an analyst) and Lois Schaffner (a reports officer) were assigned from the CIA. Eventually, a secretary with top-secret clearance who lived in Bangkok was hired. She was the Chinese-American wife of the resident FBI agent. Harry Fullett was the first BNDD agent to be assigned to the intelligence unit. Counting myself, six of us were assigned to the RIU by the end of the first year.

OPIUM TONNAGE UP

Since I left Thailand in 1976, the flow of Asian white #4 heroin from the Golden Triangle has increased dramatically. By 1990, DEA analysts estimated raw opium cultivated in Burma at about 2,600 metric tons, with an additional 350 tons from Laos and another 50 tons from Thailand. These estimates are about four times the estimated tonnage I recall of 20 years ago.

During the 1980's, cocaine was the drug of prime concern. By the early 1990's, increasingly heavy amounts of #4 heroin began appearing on the streets of New York and Los Angeles, with purity levels up from 8 percent to as high as 40 percent.

Enforcement efforts were significant but still the tide of heroin was rising. In one significant strike, Thai Border Patrol Police raided a heroin refinery in Burma, exchanged gunfire with the traffickers, seized a large, well-equipped laboratory, and confiscated more than 400 pounds of morphine and heroin. Recently in San Francisco, DEA officials announced a seizure of over 1,000 pounds of Asian white heroin. This largest seizure in U.S. history was the work of the Federal Organized Crime Drug Enforcement Task Force and involved agents from New York to California. The heroin was concealed in boxes of commercial products from Taiwan and had a street value of $1 billion.

Despite notable efforts like these, and despite escalating state and federal budgets to combat drug crime, old drug abuse patterns continue and newer ones emerge. Does the increased availability of heroin mean a lessening in the abuse of crack cocaine? Or will newer addicts take up the old technique of "speed balling," combining heroin and crack cocaine? Would addicts turn to "chasing the dragon," a technique dating back to the 1920's whereby heroin is sprinkled on a piece of tinfoil, a match is held under it, and the fumes are inhaled through a rolled up bill. At least this technique would avoid the spread of the AIDS virus through contaminated needles.

One thing is clear: the level of drug abuse continues to rise. The constant demand for drugs in our cities and towns is fueled by a variety of social and economical reasons, including poverty, permissiveness, unemployment, peer pressures, and lack of direction in life. The bottom line is that our addicts, most of whom are willing participants, provide huge profits to drug dealers and traffickers, at home and abroad, for which they keep the supply lines open. The game remains the same, only the players change.

* * *

As it drizzled, I took a cab to catch the midnight Pan Am flight home. The 707 was delayed several hours by engine problems, but I napped on the soft seats in the passenger lounge listening to mosquitoes until it was time to go. I was so used to flying in and out of Don Muang airport that I slept a good deal on our route home. I caught the New York shuttle to Washington where Phyllis picked me up for a happy reunion in Vienna with the family and KC and Evie Warren, who were up from Sarasota to visit. My Mother and Joan and Chuck Carson drove over from Freedom. We vacationed with everyone for a week before packing air and sea freight boxes, readying our trusty station wagon for shipment, and working with our real estate expert, who was charged with renting our house during our absence. It was the end of June when we left Virginia for our third family trip to Southeast Asia in six years.

It took Phyllis a few weeks to readjust to the reality of returning to Asia. She resumed writing long, entertaining letters to the family, but with a touch less enthusiasm than before.

July 10, 1972   US Embassy, Thailand
                                   APO San Francisco, 96346

"Dear Family, We had a grand trip out here. We spent our overnight stay in the Los Angeles area with Paul and Delores Katsos and their children (who were great pals of ours four years ago in Manila). It was marvelous because we had a chance to see Disneyland, which was only about 20 miles from their house. The only thing that marred our trip southward from the airport to their house was when the muffler on Paul's car began to drag on the ground at 60 miles per hour. We managed to get to a gas station where the offending muffler was wired up so we could drive on. Our boys enjoyed visiting with their old pals Matthew and John who are now young giants. Paul drove us to the airport in the morning, dropping us off as he went to work at his security office nearby. (He never said exactly where he worked. I knew better than to ask.)

"On to Hawaii where we spent two glorious days. Our rooms

were on the 17th floor overlooking Waikiki, a sight for tired eyes. When we departed, the plane was not too crowded so they booked 9 seats for us, so each two of us had three seats which made it ever so comfortable, despite being served dinner three times on the long flight out.... The boys were all in great shape, all old enough to entertain themselves which made for a very pleasant and relaxed flight for Adie and me and Cyndy.

"We met two very interesting people on the plane. The first a Thai student of about 24 who has been studying at MIT for five years and was making his first trip home. (Imagine being away from home five years!) He will return for a final year and a masters degree in engineering. The other was a gal, a former correspondent and now author of several books on Southeast Asia. Jane Hamilton Merritt, who is presently in a Wat [Buddhist temple], a rare calling for a woman, where she is studying meditation with the monks. She plans to write of her experiences. She was very worried about her husband since he was in the Newport to Bermuda race during the current hurricane threat and she did not know of his whereabouts.

"We arrived at Don Muang, were met by an Embassy limousine and whisked to the plush Siam Intercontinental Hotel. We found flowers, booze, snacks and soft drinks in our rooms with a nice note from our friends the Lyttons, old buddies from Manila. We went to their house that Saturday night, but folded early.

"A few days later, after checking in at the Embassy and getting our paperwork started, we met the Pan Am freight flight with Julie and Tango aboard. When they brought the dogs out of Customs clearance, Julie was fine but the dog in Thateng's cage was a complete stranger. He was bigger than Tango, white and very friendly, a kind of wire-haired mongrel. We took the stranger back to the hotel and started back-tracking Tango through the freight office. Sure enough, he was still in Virginia due to some stupid mistake made at the kennel club, but Pan

Am said to send the strange dog back and they would send Tango to us. Poor Tang, he arrived about three days later, with a touch of pneumonia and a voice that was barely a whisper. He was a pitiful sight. [He slept between Phyllis and me for the next few nights]. . . . The owners of the other dog were probably more horrified than we for I suspect Alfie [as we named him] was left at the kennel for a weekend but instead got a trip around the world."

LIFE AT SOI 44/1

"The house is great, every bit as big as Adie said it was. It will be much more attractive when our sea shipment gets here, but as long as our air freight is at hand, we are in pretty good shape. Soontorn, the gardener who came with the property, has a cute wife named Souli who is an experienced maid. We promptly hired her and her aunt and all three will live happily in the servants quarters in the rear. . . . The yard is huge; we have been playing badminton and hope to find a croquet set. The kids haven't made any friends yet, but they seem to be happy enough. It is a bit hard to get around without a car, but cabs are plentiful. Adie has a car for his use at present, so we try to do things on the weekends.

"Will try to write more often, but at the moment I am swept up in the lethargy of the Far East and don't seem to be getting much accomplished. . . . Thinking of you with love, Phyl"

August 22, 1972

"Dear Thook, Thook Kohn (meaning everyone), I am learning more Thai each day and Souli, my #1 maid, knows enough English so that we communicate fairly well. Our friend Sompote, the Thai lad we met on the plane, got back in town a few days before his return to school at MIT. He took us to the Sunday market which is quite a sight to see. It fills a huge parade ground and is surrounded by many shade trees. There, local merchants put up stalls on the weekend. They sell everything imaginable, fruits and vegetables (some are varieties I've never seen before), fish, pets, fabrics, cooking utensils, surplus uniforms (mostly U.S.), all kinds of trinkets, jewels and handicrafts, and there is a great nursery plant section. We didn't buy much, but spent about 3 hours looking around. I did get four bougainvillea plants for 20 cents each. The big excitement of the day was the purchase of two ducks for Bill and Ken. They are very cute and are surviving but Charlie (Ken's duck) has a bad leg and I fear is not too long for this world. Freddie (Bill's duck) is doing very well. Thateng and Julie are very curious as you can imagine.

"Sompote came for dinner that night as we were having the Hills and Lyttons with their kids for a spaghetti supper, sort of a farewell for the Hills who are leaving next week after four years here. Sompote took some of the kids to see the lights downtown which are beautiful, I understand, in honor of the Queen's birthday. All the business buildings are decorated lavishly.

"Wednesday the 16th, we again went to Pattaya, this time for three days. Adie was able to arrange a business trip to Sattahip, the US-Thai Air Force base south of the Beach area [where the B-52's are based]. He had some liaison duties to carry out while we stayed at the JUSMAG cottages which are comfortable but not air-conditioned. The cost is $10.50 per night for a three-bedroom two story house near tennis courts, pool, movie, and cafeteria. This was a very inexpensive mini-vacation with much swimming and tennis. We also hired a native fishing boat for the day which chugged along slowly, through the waves, for again it was very rough. We were really rolling. . . . too rough for fishing, which we had planned, so we anchored in a quiet cove and waded to the beach where Adie and I had fresh-caught crabs for lunch. The kids decided to eat sandwiches we brought from the cafeteria. I had hurt my left hand in a fall on the tennis court (not serious, just sprained) so was unable to break up the crabs. Our nice boatman sat beside me cracking and peeling crabs for me, quite a scene. Down the beach from us we could see a row of little thatched stalls in which *mamasans* were offering a variety of foods. When we were here last, about three years ago, there was only one stall which offered coral and fresh pineapples. Now Pattaya is famous, our little island is going commercial, but still quaint. (Still no toilet facilities, I might add.)

"We were back in Bangkok by Saturday afternoon with much too much sunburn. Tom really really got it and is still a bit miserable, but will survive. [Tom stayed aboard the boat while the rest of us went ashore for lunch. He failed to don his T-shirt, badly misjudging the intensity of the noon rays in the southern latitudes of Thailand which are about 12 degrees north of the equator.]

"The boys registered for school which begins on 28 August... Adie is working hard, but happily, and it's nice he can get away every now and then, not like in Pakse where it was almost a seven-day-a-week job. . . . Love to all, Phyl"

By mid-September, Phyl had better news to report:

"The Vienna house has been rented to a foreign service family named Brady who have three boys. They have been in South America for five or six years. The same day we got that news, we learned our car was on a ship due the 15th. Our sea shipment of household goods arrived over the Labor Day weekend, so we had a grand time unloading. Now the house is in pretty good shape with all our junk around. Our paintings and other artifacts are fine, but the big living room couch arrived with four legs broken off. I hope to replace most of this furniture before we leave since the Thais do a pretty good job of woodworking. [In fact, Phyl had already scouted a rattan furniture store on the corner nearby and ordered some round chairs and porch tables. Our home was really shaping up very well.]

"The boys are all in school, and seem to be getting along well, even enjoying it. Their classes are definitely smaller than those in the states. . . . We had quite a storm last week, tropical storm Elsie, it rained for about three days, on the second day Adie made it to the Embassy by wading. Then his boss called in saying he could not get out of his Soi, then the boys got home with the news there would be no school on Friday. Our house is high and dry but the drainage klongs all overflowed and much of Bangkok flooded; traffic was impossible in many areas. Adie allowed it was a pretty tough way to make a living.

"I have a maternity report as regards Thateng, the great stud of our compound. The ragged little mutt next door was in heat a few weeks ago much to Thateng's joy. He was quite exhausted. But he hardly had a chance to recover when Julie came in heat. Heretofore she would have nothing to do with Thateng at such times, but comes he with his newly acquired expertise and we begin to suspect he caught her off guard. There seems to be a suspicious swelling in the tummy of our Julie, and there have absolutely not been any other dogs around. Tango looks a bit smug these days, and I wonder if he is really aware that soon this compound may be overflowing with his offspring? [Julie did indeed produce a litter of five small pups, one still-born; homes were found for three and one we had to keep, but this last one sickened and finally died after three short weeks. This litter was to be Julie's last.]

"This next news is that Cyndy has decided she will go back to the States, and we rather agree that would be in her best interests much as we hate to see her go. It really isn't very exciting here for her and she really should have the experience of being on her own. Her plan is to leave on the 6th of October, go to Vienna, Austria, to see the Jeffers [old Manila friends], and then on to Sarasota. She will probably go to the DC area where she has friends and get a job. She really likes the DC area which is an exciting place for a young gal to be. More on this later. Love to all, Phyl"

482

"October 31.... The big news is that we finally got the car a week ago. Joy! I have been doing quite a bit of driving and find it is no problem to drive on the wrong side of the road. Of course I am drafting this letter sitting in a garage, Shell Station, no less, on Petchburi Road waiting while someone finds a water hose to replace the one that blew as I was driving Bill home from the orthodontist. Ho Hum.... the boys' teeth are all coming along just fine. Making rapid progress. The guy here trained in the States and seems to work just like our dentist in Virginia.

"Other boys' news is that Ken has joined a bowling league which meets on Saturday mornings. He seems to enjoy it and is improving.... I got conned into bowling in the Ladies League. I am perfectly terrible and rather embarrassed about the whole thing, but will keep plugging away. Bill started bowling but was completely demoralized by a five-year-old boy who was the best on his team.... and Tom is busy with a science club, working on a ham radio, and he also tried out for a play his school will put on in December, and got a part. Would you believe he had to sing during his audition? I told him I couldn't remember ever hearing him sing. We are proud of his perseverance, determination and motivation. Love, Phyl"

* * *

Bill Wanzeck and his family returned to Headquarters after completing a two-year tour, and none other than Fred T. Dick, our Attache from Saigon, replaced him. A new Ambassador named Charles Whitehouse arrived from Laos where he had been Ambassador. I remembered Fred from Saigon and was pleased at his assignment to Bangkok. Fred was courting a lovely South Vietnamese lady named Thanh in Saigon, whom he later would marry.

BUILDING THE RIU

As Fred was organizing his office, we were discussing the role of the intelligence unit when he pleasantly remarked, "Who needs you,

Swain?" There was nothing personal in the question, since he was referring to the fledgling Regional Intelligence Unit, but the query did not bode well for the RIU. Fred was implying that he did not intend to support or assist the RIU more than required; the RIU existed, but he did not have to like it. I was astounded and dumbstruck by the situation. We both worked for BNDD, and he was my boss. I did not get upset and realized the only way to convince Fred that the RIU was worthwhile was to do a good job for BNDD. After some sober reflection, I understood that I could expect nothing from Fred because he probably was one of the hard-core FBN veterans who had been against the idea of expanding BNDD's intelligence effort ever since its organization in 1968. This difference of opinion never became an issue between us and was not discussed further. I did my best to earn his confidence and build a professional working relationship over the next two years of Fred's stewardship in the region.

* * *

Our social life became more active as our circle of new friends and business associates expanded. Tom Becker, the senior analyst on loan from the CIA, was urbane, witty, pleasant, and self-disciplined. He also had a way with words, having worked on a newspaper in Nebraska right after college. Tom had a strong background knowledge of Southeast Asia and was hardworking, serious, and a fine addition to the RIU. After a year, he transferred to BNDD as a permanent analyst in the RIU. His wife, Mary, was a feisty free spirit who roamed the city without fear and with intense curiosity. The Beckers had adopted a Thai girl and boy soon after their arrival in Bangkok, a very brave thing to do under these conditions.

Lois Schaffner was a single lady who came from the CIA to work as our reports officer. Serious and determined to make a contribution, she was a steady and dependable worker. She and Tom helped train Harry Fullett, our first BNDD agent, a streetwise sports enthusiast who had no idea what intelligence was all about but was amiable and smart. He borrowed my book on *Tradecraft* and never returned it. Harry worked in the RIU for six months before going to Vientiane to help Tony Morelli and Vietnam veteran Charley Vopat.

484

We started from scratch by opening files on major traffickers, organizing maps and reference material, and reviewing reports from our District Offices in Singapore, Hong Kong, Tokyo, Manila, Kuala Lumpur, and Chiang Mai. BND-6s were field agents' Reports of Investigation and the source of all raw intelligence on traffickers and their organizations and methods of operation. From these reports we hoped to glean and refine leads that might develop into future enforcement actions. All of this required a lot of typing and filing, which we did ourselves until Fred finally agreed to let me hire our first secretary. As we neared the end of the year in Krungtep (Thai name for Bangkok), the fledgling RIU was beginning to function fairly well.

Tom Swain sent some terse, year-end news to Grandmother Swain and the Carsons in Pennsylvania:

"Dear Grandmother: The calendar you gave me is fine and thanks to Uncle Carson, Aunt Jo and yourself for the diary and pen. . . . Here's how I crunched my foot. A twenty-five yard long rope has been suspended on an incline between two palm trees in our yard. It has been up since Christmas but my hands haven't gotten tough enough to climb it. So the day before yesterday, I found that having comfortably made it up the rope to the high end, I couldn't make it down again. Therefore, I voluntarily ejected from a height of twelve feet, and hit the ground hard with my 160 pounds. Anyways, the foot is recovering. . . . Another strange incident occurred last night, which was the Thai New Year. Our walled compound contains two houses, our and *theirs*. *Theirs* had this Thai combo group blasting away until twelve, and there must have been two hundred people massed everywhere. Incredible. (Bill Swain has just gotten out of bed now at 12:15 P.M. as I write this!)To continue, tonight at our place there's going to be another celebration which will leave me only Monday to recover. This ordinarily would be ample time to regain lost sleep, but semester examinations around the sixteenth tend to require a gross amount of time for preparation.

"Enclosed is a program from the musical I was in several weeks ago; I played the part of Caesar Rodney, identifiable in the picture by the scarf around his head and almost black stockings. . . . I wish a profitable New Year to all. Thomas W. Swain"

NINETEEN

Tales from Bangkok

B NDD was organized 1968 with 1,361 Special Agents and a budget of $14.5 million. By the time I arrived in Bangkok four years later, the budget was $64.3 million and there were almost 2,000* agents. While BNDD was striving mightily to stop the flow of drugs at home and abroad, many people were urging the federal government to do more about drug-related crime in the streets.

To satisfy these appeals, Nixon authorized a new federal agency, the Office of Drug Abuse Law Enforcement (ODALE), which immediately opened nine regional offices in the United States to thwart street pushers through special grand juries and to pool intelligence with federal, state, and local law enforcement agencies. There was so much drug intelligence being obtained by all these new agencies that some confusion and general lack of communication resulted. Nixon, who took pride in being a tough, decisive law-and-order President, authorized yet another office within the Justice Department, the Office of National Narcotics Intelligence (ONNI), to be the focal point for collecting, analyzing, and distributing drug intelligence.

ONNI immediately ran into a big roadblock because it had no data base of its own. It looked to the other agencies for data but found them reluctant, if not openly hostile, to provide their hard-won drug intelligence to an upstart newcomer. These agencies questioned who these new guys were, whether they could be trusted, what they would

---

* By 1991, DEA agent strength was 3,500; by 1995, this total was projected to reach 5,000, with a budget of more than $700 million.

do with dope information if they got it, and what experience these new people had. ONNI's potential for success was rather shaky and never did gain nationwide acceptance. BNDD had the same reluctance. The street agents felt that ONNI should do their own work if they wanted intelligence and were reluctant to give up their information. The net result was predictable. The FBI and BNDD dragged their feet, while the U.S. Customs, Immigration and Naturalization Service, armed forces and Coast Guard, and reclusive CIA draped invisible screens over their narcotics intelligence files and kept ONNI outside to twist slowly in the wind.

* * *

Meanwhile, things were not getting better on the city streets and in the outlying neighborhoods of the United States. Local police and sheriffs' departments were being overwhelmed by the blossoming drug scene, which was now in full flower after years of being cultivated by a mix of college students called peaceniks (protesters against the war in Vietnam), Yuppies, and flower children whose lifestyles centered around communes, casual sex, and doing as much dope as they could buy, barter, beg, make, or grow. One had only to read *High Times* to find the latest prices and brands of marijuana, learn how to grow it, or order "bongs" for smoking it; BNDD was one of the magazine's subscribers. The demand for illicit drugs had spread from inner-city ghettos (where for years it had been treated with benign neglect) to the suburbs and small towns of predominantly white, middle-class America. As the demand for drugs increased, entrepreneurial drug syndicates in Mexico, Europe, the Middle East, and Southeast Asia expanded to supply the demand.

Nixon shook his jowls over all of this and created a new agency to coordinate all the antidrug agencies under a single, unified command. The Drug Enforcement Administration (DEA) was unveiled July 1, 1973, with Nixon saying, "This administration has declared an all-out global war on the drug menace."

DEA combined BNDD, ODALE, ONNI, and a large group of Customs agents to produce a force of some 2,000 men under the overall guidance of the Attorney General. The first DEA Administrator was John R. Bartels, Jr., an attorney from the ODALE organization, replacing John E. Ingersoll, who waited in vain for the call that never came from the White House. It was sad to lose Ingersoll, who had served with distinction for five years; but he soon was selected as chief of security for IBM overseas through his contact with former Ambassador to France, Thomas J. Watson, whose family started the IBM empire.

For most of us in the field, the change to working for the new DEA did not make a great difference. It was a positive move at least administratively because the fight against drugs had been raised to a higher level. The shuffling and internal jostling for power within the upper levels of the new agency, like all the others before, did little to improve the immediate effectiveness of the war on drugs. As with every merger, some momentum was lost as many former BNDD workers leaned on their shovels waiting to see what the new boss would be like. Only a sense of professional pride and a desire to produce a day's work for a dollar's pay kept most of us going. Meanwhile, the drug syndicates, with less bureaucratic turf to defend and millions in profits to be made, moved ahead efficiently and ruthlessly, with speed and daring, imagination, and cunning, to seek out and exploit the gaps in DEA's new armor.

* * *

The windows of my small office on the second floor of the Embassy were crisscrossed with strips of masking tape so the glass would not shatter from shifts in the foundation that trembled as a pile driver outside thumped monstrous columns of reinforced concrete pilings into the muckland of the river delta on which our building rested. The new expansion would be finished within the year, we hoped.

One afternoon, John Doyle, our Deputy Director, advised me that a visitor was being escorted my way. The visitor was David Cornwell, better known as John le Carré, the British author of many spy novels featuring a middle-aged hero named George Smiley. He had a quiet demeanor and was quite proper and courteous. After brief introductory comments were exchanged, I learned that Cornwell was staying at the Oriental Hotel on the Chao Phya River (where another famous

British author, Somerset Maugham, had stayed) to gather some research on Southeast Asia and the drug business for his next book.

As we talked, I had the feeling that Cornwell could have blended in with a crowd of people anywhere and not been noticed, but his mind was keen and his manner was alert and precise. When he got down to business, asking questions about the ways and means of drug trafficking in Bangkok, I was impressed with his orderly grasp of information. We talked some about the regular movement of Thai fishing trawlers that steadily smuggled narcotics, including bales of smoking opium, to Hong Kong. I was careful to avoid mentioning that this kind of activity was the subject of one of our more active intelligence collection efforts. I found out later that Cornwell made five trips to Southeast Asia visiting Hong Kong, Cambodia, northeast Thailand, and Laos while accompanying David Greenway of the *Washington Post*. Along the way, he habitually noted information on little file cards. Perhaps this explains why his writing is full of facts. This attention to detail, along with his ability to portray characters who have recognizable human frailties, has made Cornwell a most believable storyteller.

I was not able to provide Cornwell with much information, given such short notice, but we talked for about an hour while I traced trafficker routes, mentioned some of the concealment methods we were encountering, and agreed with his observation that there was a constant intertwining of ethnic Chinese at certain levels of the drug business, particularly financial. I gave him as much information as I could within the limits of the need-to-know principle, which was ingrained in me and which Cornwell, having been in the British Intelligence service, would certainly understand.

I had almost forgotten Cornwell's Bangkok visit when *The Honourable Schoolboy* was published in 1977. A copy of his book arrived from England in July 1977 with a note from the publisher that read, "With the author's compliments;" it was a pleasant surprise to be so remembered. The book was well plotted, tautly written, and quite credible, another excellent piece of work. Cornwell earned a handsome income, even after eighty percent of his gross was siphoned off in taxes by the British government.

* * *

The Time of My Life

In a letter to Shirley Wade written in mid-May 1973, Phyllis wrote of the shockingly abrupt death of her Aunt Helie, a longtime buyer at Macy's in New York. Helie died of a heart attack on the sidewalk on her way home from work one day early in May. Shirley went to New York to sort out Helie's belongings, which filled every spare inch in her small apartment.

"Regarding the disposition of Helie's things, you know that anything you decide is OK with me. Just sorry you have to be the one to do it. I am glad you planned to have everything sent to your house to sort out later. I really don't remember all that Helie had, so, as you suggested, will rely on your best judgment to see that each child gets a small token as a remembrance. . . . Bill Swain has requested, if not too late, any of Helie's art supplies you think he might use. Helie always encouraged Bill in his art endeavors. . . . [Bill never got the art supplies.]

"A possibly amusing digression to all the foregoing. . . . I was so tickled on Tom's 17th birthday in May. He is a very straight guy with short hair, (I had to talk him out of getting a crew cut). I gave him a pair of trousers, flares, they are called, which he has resisted wearing. I didn't realize why until I got home from the PX and noticed that not only were they flares, but had a button fly and were hip huggers to boot, sort of the kind Elvis Presley wears. Tom, after trying them on, said 'I think you are trying to make me into a sex symbol.' Not very funny when I read it over, but if you can visualize 6′ 2″ Tom, with the same reserve and dry humor of his Dad, you'll get the picture. . . . We will miss dear Helie. Love, Phyl."

* * *

Before the Embassy expansion work was completed, our DEA office was relocated to the old finance building near the rear wall of the Embassy compound. A big poinciana tree shaded our new office, and we had plenty of room for our expanding DEA group. After some cleanup and modifications, the former bank's money vault became the storage room for our DEA funds and classified files. I moved into my own private office, and there was room outside my door for Charlsie, our pretty blonde secretary, a military wife who hailed from Tennessee and replaced Marge. There were desks for our analysts and agents in a large neighboring room. Double glass doors separated intelligence operations from the rest of the building, which housed the enforcement agents, administrative section, and Regional Director's office and his staff. Once more, the days, weeks, and months began to run together as we settled into our routines.

We took family trips out of town in our venerable station wagon, which sported a clear plastic curtain between the front passenger seats and the luggage compartment. The zippered curtain conserved our air conditioning and was another one of Phyllis' better ideas, which cost only a few dollars and was easily fabricated at a neighborhood awning installation shop. Phyl and I quickly learned to drive on the opposite side of the road and found that the average little Toyota taxicabs and other smaller cars and scooters respected the sheer size of our larger wagon. They knew they would come off second best should a collision occur, particularly when Phyl was at the wheel. For some reason, we seemed to get a wider berth than when I was driving. Our air conditioning reduced the intake of smog from thousands of exhaust pipes that belched black diesel smoke until Bangkok's streets seemed under a gray cloud. Many traffic cops at busy intersections wore white masks over their noses.

We drove to Hua Hin once, a quiet little town across the Gulf of Thailand from Pattaya on the Thai Railways route to Malaysia. The Hua Hin Hotel was owned and operated by the Thai Railways system and was one of a government chain of hotels throughout the country. I stayed at a similar railway hotel at Chiang Mai once, which was also quite nice. These hotels provided decent overnight accommodations to the general public and to railway passengers who needed a good night's sleep or just wanted to take a break from their travels.

Our hotel was within view of the quiet, little railway station and sat back on spacious, landscaped grounds with well-kept walkways, a quiet garden, and clean but rather spartan accommodations. Our rooms were not air conditioned but had tall wooden shutters that deflected the glaring sunlight yet admitted the breezes. We left our unscreened windows wide open, allowing fresh air to sweep freely over old-fashioned beds equipped with mosquito nets. The porous, white gauze netting could be lowered at night to protect the sleeper from malaria-carrying mosquitoes. We strolled past a little-used golf course on our way to the gulf beaches. We were hoping to find another Pattaya, but the water was shallow and filled with jellyfish, and the rocky bottom was strewn with yellowing grass. We were disappointed but felt very welcome at the hotel, even though there were only a few farangs (foreigners) staying there. This gave Phyl a chance to practice her skill in the Thai language. Not surprisingly, we found the Thai people to be gentle, pleasant, eager to please, and happy. It is no wonder that Thailand is called the Land of Smiles.

WATERGATE

A young man named John Dean, President Nixon's personal attorney, and his wife, Maureen, visited the Bangkok Embassy en route to Hong Kong. His arrival was heralded by a flurry of cables that created anxiety on the part of the Ambassador, who owed allegiance to the White House. Dean was an unknown to most of us in DEA, but this soon changed when the United States was racked by the greatest political and historical scandal in American history, an event known as Watergate. John Dean gained nationwide notoriety when he blew the whistle on Richard Nixon in June 1973 by testifying before a Senate Select Committee chaired by Democratic Senator Sam Erwin.

The tip of the Watergate iceberg had emerged a year earlier when five rubber-gloved men were arrested with wiretap gear while breaking into the Democratic National Committee Headquarters in the Watergate apartment complex in Washington. Those arrested included an ex-CIA employee, James W. McCord, Jr., who was now chief of security for the Committee to Reelect the President (CRP). Others arrested in the scandal included E. Howard Hunt, another former CIA agent, and G. Gordon Liddy, a former FBI man serving as counsel to the CRP. The group of arrestees were called the Watergate 7. The finger of suspicion was soon pointing at President Nixon, for these men were all members of his reelection team. To no

Adrian Swain

one's surprise, Nixon denied any knowledge of the Watergate burglary. Some of Nixon's closest associates were implicated: Attorney General John N. Mitchell, who later went to jail, Jeb Stuart Magruder, Nixon's deputy campaign director, and John W. Dean III, who elected to testify against Nixon in exchange for immunity.

Through the months that followed, the scandal reached a fever pitch, which was aided and abetted by daily reports from antiadministration *Washington Post* reporters Woodward and Bernstein and television bloodhounds hot on the trail. Their quarry was soon at bay in the big house on Pennsylvania Avenue. Dean sang like a bird, testifying that the White House had an enemies list of 256 persons in the media, business, entertainment, politics, and academic world. He said that the White House plan was to use available federal machinery to screw its political enemies through such government actions as tax audits. Dean also told of efforts to have the CIA block a full FBI investigation of Watergate and said he had secretly delivered $250,000 in cash to the seven Watergate defendants.

President Nixon continued to deny knowing anything until the existence of some sixty-four reels of tape recordings, all made in the oval office during the Watergate period, were made public. Nixon protested, claiming executive immunity, to no avail. The tapes were subpoenaed and finally admitted into evidence. Nixon was doomed, for the tapes clearly showed he had direct knowledge of the whole affair. The mystery is why Nixon ever let himself be taped, and then when he knew the tapes were going to cause trouble, why he did not simply destroy them and claim he did so in the interests of national security.

On August 9, 1974, Nixon went on television to resign his office as President of the United States. It was the first time that a President of the United States had resigned rather than be impeached. Vice President Gerald R. Ford was sworn in as President, and Nelson Rockefeller, former Governor of New York State, became Vice President.

* * *

Among our trips were jaunts to Penang, Kuala Lumpur, Singapore, and the cool and delightful Cameron Highlands, a fine resort

494

area developed by the British in west central Malaysia. We hired a car and driver from the Kuala Lumpur airport and traveled for about an hour northward, climbing winding roads to a plateau almost 4,500 feet high where we found our European-style lodgings. The temperatures were bracing and averaged about 65 degrees. Along the way we saw many Chinese gardens and roadside stands displaying big red strawberries, crisp cabbages, vine-ripened tomatoes, and lettuce. Tea plantations covered the hillsides. This was the setting in which Jim Thompson vanished. Famous for starting the Thai silk industry in Thailand after World War II, Jim Thompson went for a walk one afternoon beyond the hilly golf course fairways near his quarters and disappeared. Perhaps he became lost in some rugged, wooded ravine while looking for butterflies, which in these parts, have wingspans wider than a baseball. His body was never found. Thompson's disappearance is unsolved to this day, but rumor has it that he was devoured by a hungry tiger.

While staying overnight in Penang, we walked into a local supermarket near our hotel to buy some snack foods for our room. The Swain definition of a vacation stated that it never started until there was a complete stock of junk food on hand. The store we entered was reasonably well stocked and not too crowded. All the customers, mostly Chinese women, were well dressed. We stocked up on some C's: cheese, crackers, cookies, candy, and a carton of Coke, all necessary to the survival of the family for whom three meals per day was just the beginning. Phyllis alone was self-disciplined and weight conscious enough to forego snacking, although occasionally, even her steel will could be bent. Passing the checkout cashier, I mentioned to Phyllis that there was a guard at the door. She took a second look and her eyes popped slightly. There stood a grim-faced, middle-aged man in a light blue uniform holding a double-barreled shotgun across his chest. In a quiet, peaceful, well-mannered vacation spot like Penang, where the rich soil provides several crops per year and bananas and coconuts drop off the trees, I could not believe it was necessary to have an armed guard at the grocery store in the middle of the afternoon.

* * *

Adrian Swain

Henry "Hank" Aaron, playing with the Atlanta Braves in his 21st season (including 12 years with the Braves in Milwaukee), hit his 715th home run Monday night, April 8th, 1974, before a television audience of 35 million and a home stadium crowd of 53,000. We watched the rerun of his famous home run on our television in Bangkok. Aaron's homer broke Babe Ruth's lifetime record of 714. By the end of the season at 40 years of age, "Hammerin Henry" had stroked 733 homers. He retired in 1976 having hit 755 home runs, an unbelievable record.

* * *

On one of our long-weekend getaways, we took the Thai Railway's night train to Chiang Mai, some 450 kilometers north of Bangkok. I booked three, first-class roomettes well in advance. Each compartment had two tiny bunks, similar to U.S. trains, but in Thailand everything was smaller, even the width of the railroad tracks. Souli traveled with us so she could visit her parents in Chiang Mai. Food was available from vendors who crowded the station platforms at each stop and thrust trays of their offerings up to the open train windows. There were soft drinks in plastic bags sealed with rubber bands and straws to suck from, sticky rice wrapped in banana leaves served with cooked or smoked fish, oranges, tiny bananas, and slices of sweet pineapple, as well as cigarettes, hard candy, and other sweets.

The next morning, about an hour after sunrise, we were at Chiang Mai, having chugged through stations named Phra Nakon, Lop Buri, Ta Khli, Nakon Sawan, Phitsanulok, Uttaradit, Den Chai, Lampang, and Lamphun, all of which were pronounced as they were spelled. The trip had taken 12 hours; by air it took about an hour and a half, but the time was well spent. A trip like this happened once in a lifetime. Ken, Bill, Tom, and I took turns sitting in the observation car in a remarkable chair that rotated from side to side and reclined like an old-fashioned barber chair. We gazed on misty valleys below the ancient steel bridge trusses we were crossing as our train slowly snaked its way through the hills. When we got to the Rincone Hotel, we immediately headed for the coffee shop to satisfy ravenous appetites.

We visited with Terry Baldwin, my ex-paratrooper friend who had transferred to BNDD from the Agency and was now assigned to Chiang Mai with his wife, Nita, and two sons. We rode in Terry's Land Rover up the Doi Saket road to cruise by the spacious summer palace where MIT-educated King Bhumibol Adulyadej and Queen Sirikit occasionally took refuge from hot and steamy Bangkok. By noontime, the morning clouds that clung to the higher peaks were burned off by a sun so bright and intense it soon put a glow on the tips of our noses.

I remember the tiny, family-operated silversmith shop where Phyllis bought ornamental silver bowls for me and the boys, each engraved with intricate, ornate designs of either elephants, tigers, or unicorns. We watched a barefoot woodcarver seated cross-legged on the dirt delicately tapping his wooden mallet on a woodcarving awl to create the ornamental curlicues that adorned the legs and edges of a handsome coffee table. Phyl ordered a large table with the top made from one slab of solid teak. The legs could be carved, but she wanted the top to be plain and smooth and show only the flowing grain of the wood. Phyl wanted her table to darken with age, and not to resemble the ornately black, highly glossed, varnished look favored by the Thai.

Teak logs were dragged from forests in the north by elephants and then trucked to furniture shops like this one in Chiang Mai and to other towns such as Lampang and Phayao. Teak has an ivory color much like newly cut North American white oak and a beautiful grain. Phyllis assured me that in another year or so, after regular applications of Old English polish and exposure to air and light, the teak would gradually darken and take on a pleasingly warm color, and she was right. Phyl paid $60 for her table and another $15 to have it delivered to Bangkok. Before we left Thailand, we ordered more teak furniture: a dining room table with eight chairs, a matching buffet table, a queen-size bed with lamp tables, a tall bureau with drawers, two dressers with matching wall mirrors, a chair and secretary desk for Phyl's office, and a three-door cabinet with a lift top to house our assorted tape decks, records, receivers, and speakers. This handsome teak furniture replaced our aging Danish pieces bought years ago. Garage sales were popular in Bangkok, and

497

and before we left, we sold everything we did not want to ship home.

Phyllis wrote the following letter to my sister:

October 8, 1973

"Dear Nan, Our life here is very pleasant. With two and some-times three servants I have no complaints. Adie works hard but gets some pleasure and satisfaction out of it, and it seems a bit easier on him here than in Washington. The boys are doing well and have more opportunities for activities now than in the States, such as scuba diving lessons, mini vacations and trips, dinners out and that sort of thing because we can afford it over here.

"Nan, I was so grateful to you for taking Cyndy to Vermont with you this summer. She wrote on several occasions about the wonderful time she was having, so my sweet, I'm sure some of your good sense rubbed off on her.

"The boys are all so handsome. Tom gets better looking all the time, Bill is almost six feet tall and a doll, Ken is his usual feisty, darling self. We still fight over his school work all the time, but he just got his report card and it was very good. He is interested in soccer and plays often at school and with the Thai boys down the street. Bill is doing well in basketball. He is really cute. I am so proud of all my children.

"We had a big party last Saturday, about 45 people all mostly DEA agents and their wives with some neighbors. Ken and Bill helped Soontorn bartend. Tom was rehearsing for a part in his senior class play, Thornton Wilder's classic, *Our Town*. Love, Phyl"

The play opened on a scene in which Tom juggled three white batons, a skill he had picked up with the Sailor Circus in Sarasota, while the narrator sat on a stool and described what it was like living in *Our Town*. Tom also appeared later in his role as the town drunk. Toward the end of the show, Tom moved off the stage and popped up in the theater aisle down front; he looked around and then went staggering and reeling up one aisle and down the other, as though he were looking for an exit and not able to find one. He created quite a stir as he lurched and weaved through the audience looking like a rudderless ship three sheets to the wind. It was all part of the show, which I found fascinating. I was filled with pride at Tom's performance and wondered from whence came his urge to act. Who knew, maybe we had a theatrical genius in our midst. Phyllis had been a model and had tried out for a theater group in Sarasota years ago, so perhaps it was her theatrical gene at work in our son Thomas.

* * *

May 9, 1974 [Tom's 18th birthday]

"Dear KC and Ebie:

"Somewhat in haste as I have a million things to do in preparation for the big move coming up this Saturday [from Soi 44/1 to a smaller three-bedroom house on Soi 47, a mile closer to the Embassy]. Happily, Souli and Soontorn and Mou will move along with us. Adrian is in Pattaya attending a DEA Regional Conference the next three days, but he'll be back in time for the move. Our gang had a grand weekend there just last week staying until Monday night as the kids had Monday and Tuesday off. Not too much sunburning, but much swimming and snorkeling over beautiful coral beds. Never have I seen so many varieties of fish.

"The good news is that Tom has been accepted at both the University of Florida and the University of South Florida, and he is getting quite excited about it. We are sending the first payment today.... Cyndy writes that there IS GOING TO BE A WEDDING and since DJ and Ebby Brown have offered us the

499

use of their house on Turtle Beach during our leave [July and August] that will work out fine. As you know DJ and Ebbie Brown spend the summer near Asheville, North Carolina.

"Cyndy's wedding (tentatively set for mid-August) may not be the best planned operation in the world but I am sure we will work things out and it will be wonderful, for with such wonderful people involved, how can we miss. . . . besides, I find I can manage to get things done regardless of circumstances, so no sweat. . . . Feeling very confident this morning, aren't I?

"Guess that will be it, must get ready to make my mercy mission run to the hospital to see Souli's little boy, Mou, who had a fever and convulsions from being dehydrated. . . . His father, Soontorn, caused a bit of a stir at the hospital. He fainted while watching the medics put the IV in Mou. Jolly fun. Then I have to check on Monat, Tom and Mary Becker's 3-year-old boy who had been bitten by their Alaskan Akita house dog, while the Becker's were vacationing in Nepal. [He had to be hospitalized and Phyl volunteered to act as substitute mother for Monat during the Beckers' absence.] Then to the new house for final check, then to embassy to get money, then to PX to order delivery of refrigerator for new house and then, and then, and then. . . . with love, Phyl"

* * *

At our DEA conference in May at the JUSMAG military compound at Pattaya Beach, DEA's new Geographical Drug Enforcement Program (G-DEP), was introduced which would classify and assign priorities to drug violators and drug cases according to amounts and types of drugs involved. G-DEP was the brainchild of Allan R. Pringle* and replaced the old systems concept instituted

---

* This was the first time I heard of Al Pringle, father of the new G-DEP system. Both are still going strong twenty years later. Al Pringle retired in 1983 and started a drug education consultant and publishing business, the Institute for Substance Abuse Research, in Vero Beach, Florida.

by George Belk five years previously. We gathered in the base theater with Bill Wanzeck at the podium. Paul Brown was there as staff assistant to Wanzeck; other agents present included Fred T. Dick from Saigon, Bill Cunningham from Kuala Lumpur, Arthur Wilson from Chiang Mai, Tony Morelli from Vientiane, Keith Shostrom from Hong Kong, and all our Bangkok agents. Walter Yates led a visiting team from Headquarters, and spent hours briefing us on the new G-Dep program.

A BORDER INCIDENT

One evening Fred Dick called and asked me to come to the office and help him find some maps of northern Thailand. I was there in 10 minutes and quickly located a detailed map and took it to Fred's office where he and John Doyle spread it out on the desk. Fred explained that Ed Rosenthal and his chopper pilot were in jail in Rangoon after being shot down over Burma somewhere north of Chiang Rai. He checked the coordinates on the map and discovered they had been flying at least 10 klicks over the border.

We learned later that the chopper had been hit in the engine or suffered a damaged rotor from ground fire. The American helicopter, flown by USAID pilot Rudy Hall, spun down to a partially controlled crash landing. Eddie Rosenthal, the American Embassy narcotics liaison officer to DEA, was the only passenger. Both men suffered minor bruises and were now in a Rangoon jail charged with unauthorized flight over Burmese territory, which was a serious offense. Given the paranoia of the Burmese Government, this easily could escalate into an international incident. Ed and Rudy protested their innocence, claiming that bad weather was responsible for a simple error in navigation. Whether Ed and Rudy had in fact drifted off course in cloudy weather or were looking for illicit narcotics refineries in Burma, it made no difference to the trigger-happy Burmese. They thought the intruder was a Thai police chopper and fair game for their weapons.

Rosenthal and Hall stuck to their story that the flight had gone off course on their approach to Chiang Rai near the Thai-Burmese border. Because of his diplomatic immunity, Rosenthal was released after a day or two. Rudy Hall was not so fortunate and stayed in the Burmese jail for about 60 days undergoing daily questioning until he was released. Even though neither Fred nor John had authorized the flight, Fred was very concerned over the incident. If DEA was found to have been involved with an unauthorized flight over Burma, that would put a very big monkey wrench in DEA's efforts to persuade Ne Win's government to accept a full-time DEA agent in Rangoon.

Not long after the chopper incident, I got another call from Fred at night saying he needed me and my official car at the Thai Police operations room. I arrived there and joined a small group of Thai policemen being briefed by Major Viraj Jutimitta, chief of the Special Narcotics Unit. Jutimitta was a good cop, smart and aggressive and spoke English well. Another DEA agent, Bud Shoaf, was there and said I was needed to help with a narcotics intercept mission planned for the next morning north of Chiang Mai. Major Jutimitta's car was not working, and mine was the only DEA car available. I was not very flattered to be chosen for a job on the basis of having a car that could be loaned to the Thai police. I swallowed my pride, remembering that our job was to support the Thai police.

One of Major Jutimitta's informants from Chiang Mai had sent word that a load of heroin would be aboard the first bus from Fang (on the Thai-Burma border) arriving at Chiang Mai at 8 A.M. The major's plan was to intercept the bus before it entered the Chiang Mai terminal. Bud Shoaf would take three men with him in his car; Major Jutimitta, another sergeant, and I would go in mine. To assure secrecy, none of the police from Chiang Mai were notified of the planned raid. We had about 10 hours to cover the 400 or more miles between Bangkok and the intercept point. I had time to go home and grab a toothbrush and fresh shirt. I told Phyllis where I would be for the next day or so, looked in on the boys who were fast asleep, and was back at the operations center in 30 minutes.

The major drove while I relaxed in the back seat half asleep but keeping an eye on the empty highway that unwound before us like a white ribbon in our headlights. An occasional car would loom before us, flash by, and then disappear leaving us alone in the darkness again. The flat, rice paddy land drained by wide deep ditches on both sides of the road hurried past. By two A.M., we were approaching the town of

Tak, when I saw two headlights far ahead but growing larger and brighter and coming from our side of the road. The major flicked his high beams at the other vehicle but got no response. The oncoming lights were aimed straight for us. He wrenched the wheel sharply toward the open side of the road a split second before the huge hulk of a truck roared by with a blast of turbulent air. We were flung toward the ditch on the far side while the major wrestled to control our swaying, skidding machine. Luckily, a driveway that curved across the ditch appeared; we raced over it with dirt flying, wheels skidding, and the underside of our car scraping the ground as it spun around and finally thumped to a halt. The major had done a magnificent job. The only damage was a flat tire and some jangled nerves. Bud Shoaf pulled in behind us, having seen the near miss, and confirmed that a truck loaded with logs had almost done us in. Most likely the driver had dozed off at the wheel. While we changed the tire, Bud and his people went on ahead to the Chiang Mai rendezvous, where we would catch up as soon as we could.

By 8 A.M., we rejoined the others by the side of the road north of Chiang Mai. We were tired, hungry, and anxious to catch some drug smugglers. Our target was an ancient, dust-streaked, pale green bus with luggage and crates of vegetables lashed to wooden racks on top and crammed with villagers and workmen going to town. The major's policemen stopped the bus, carbines at the ready. For the next hour or more the men searched and probed, looking in vain for narcotics. Bud and I remained in our cars at a distance observing the scene, waiting and hoping that something would be discovered, but nothing was found. The policemen gloomily returned to their cars, and we headed toward Bangkok without talking, each of us tired and suddenly very hungry.

Over breakfast at Lampang, the major relaxed a bit. We talked about the near accident last night, and I thanked him for his skillful driving. He smiled and said with a nod that Buddha had protected us, and it was not our time. I think he was right, but I also thanked God for the driveway that appeared just as we headed for the drainage ditch. Those driveways only appeared every mile or so. Buddha and the Good Lord both had been on our side that night.

The major was an intense man in his mid-to-late-thirties who had a flair for police work, a dedicated policeman cut from a different cloth than most Thai officers. He had a master's degree from Berkeley and had spent two years with American narcotics and vice police officers in San Jose and San Francisco before returning to Bangkok where he headed the elite police narcotics squad. In his book *The Underground Empire* published in 1987, author and DEA buff John Mills, whom I met in Bangkok, wrote words of praise concerning Viraj Jutimitta and his unorthodox, unrelenting, and honest work against Thai narcotics syndicates.

Because he was an honest cop, a man who wanted to restore good to the Thai police, he was passed over for promotion and considered an outsider. He refused to accept bribes, accepted low pay for dangerous work, and lived in a house surrounded by barbed wire with several guard dogs trained to protect his wife and children. His men loved and respected him. Of the disappointing raid, he mused that several things could have happened. The traffickers may have guessed that a search was going to be made or simply changed their minds; the couriers may have overslept and missed their bus or also changed their minds. With a rueful smile, the major said there could be lots of reasons. He was sorry the trip was a waste of time and said it happens that way many times.

* * *

There was a lot going on during the summer months before we flew to Sarasota to launch Cyndy into matrimonial waters and prepare Tom for his swan dive into the waters of higher education at the University of Florida. Tom and Bill protested loudly but finally yielded to fatherly insistence and attended confirmation classes at the old Episcopal Church in Bangkok. I was worried that they would never be confirmed if we did not do it this year. The rector, an elderly Englishman about to retire from service, was kindly, world weary, and now past the prime of his original zeal but willing to fit our lads into his small confirmation group. Soon after Easter, Tom and Bill became members of the Episcopal Church and were sworn in by the visiting Bishop for Southeast Asia who came from Singapore. Kenny would have joined the group but was too young to grapple with confirmation.

The boys and I had wedding suits tailored at Somsumai's neighborhood shop, the same place where the boys obtained their school uniforms that looked like Safari suits. Phyllis made a full-length, shocking-pink, Thai silk gown that was simply stunning.

Going to movies in Bangkok was like going to the Van Wezel Theatre in Sarasota. I would reserve first-class loge seats days in advance for a weekend showing. Afterward, we would order ice-cream sundaes in the plush lobby coffee shop. I remember seeing *The Godfather, Part II*, with Al Pacino; *Chaka*, starring Charles Bronson; and *Little Big Man* with Dustin Hoffman. The sound tracks were in English, and sometimes Thai subtitles appeared across the bottom of the screen. Roger Moore, who played 007 in the James Bond spy movies, made a film called *The Man with the Golden Gun* during the summer of 1974. The city scenes were shot around Bangkok and in the Chok Chai building near our house. Some beautiful rural shots were filmed in the little fishing village of Phukhet off the Strait of Malacca about 400 kilometers south of Bangkok.

Phyllis' birthday celebration coincided with the 4th of July fireworks display at the Embassy, to which all Americans were invited. The pinwheels and shooting stars sputtered uncertainly, almost winking out, dampened by the moist, muggy air. These fireworks proved a poor substitute for the powerful display of rockets we used to watch arching high over Sarasota Bay.

Bill and Tom spent a week at the Green Beret camp at Nong Takoo, a training site in the mountains 100 miles northeast of Bangkok. There they slept in tents, learned to cook over an open fire, rappelled down steep slopes, and studied map and compass reading. The boys learned to identify snakes, edible plants, and game animals and how to trap. The 10-man squads were led by Special Forces personnel and were rained on, took 10-mile hikes, did push-ups, played volleyball, had a track meet, did some shooting, and ate snake meat.

RIU REPORTS

During its first two years, our RIU had filled its support role assigned by uncertain DEA leadership at Headquarters who continued arguing over the merits of having an intelligence unit in the first place. Easygoing Bill Wanzeck, the first Regional Director to have an intelligence unit, was willing to have us on board. Fred T. Dick, who replaced Bill, saw minimal need for analysts or intelligence agents, feeling that a good narcotics agent was capable of doing his own intelligence work. Fred functioned as his own intelligence unit, kept his own council, and kept the RIU at arms length, preferring to rely on his own judgment. Tom Becker and I stayed busy slogging through the flow of field agent investigative reports, from which we began the laborious process of building intelligence base files on known or suspected traffickers and their activities. We occasionally would be asked to provide a summary on certain significant developments or prepare an in-depth strategic study, the kind that often was fated to be read and filed. While Tom did most of the analysis, I made weekly liaison visits to army intelligence and narcotics people at JUSMAG, the air force's OSI, U.S. Customs, and the CIA's narcotics specialist.

One study by Tom Becker, *The Anatomy of a Network*, dealt with the Southeast Asian narcotic situation and proved helpful to newly assigned enforcement agents and analysts. It provided information necessary to understand the traditional and predominant role of the ethnic Chinese in Southeast Asia, a role that was tacitly acknowledged and accepted by the local population. The following excerpts from the study describe the trafficking structure:

"These Chinese traffickers service a broad-based demand for narcotics, primarily for smoking opium which is consumed by the ton throughout the region, made from the poppy grown in the tri-border areas of Burma, Thailand and Laos. Morphine base and #4 heroin are also furnished in considerable quantities. The ethnic Chinese trafficker also seeks to export his product to more lucrative markets, including the United States, with mixed results.

"Narcotics trafficking in Southeast Asia is conducted almost exclusively by local Chinese operating from within a number of independent trafficking networks. These networks, while dominated by tightly knit "core-groups," nevertheless tend to be relatively loosely-organized and divided hierarchically into roughly three levels, based on function and remuneration.

"First, the core group or nucleus of any network, then the second or middle level group which consists of managers, middlemen, financiers and heroin chemists. At both the core group and middle levels, mutual needs, shared backgrounds and business integrity, are the rule, more often than not, since the identities and activities of most of these participants are known to each other.

"Couriers, local wholesalers, street sellers, and flunkies make up the third or lowest level of the narcotics network. At this level, connections to core group or middle level management are remote, if at all. Generally, the profits at this level are much lower, while the risks are much greater. Few at these lowest levels are even Chinese, demographic testimony of its unworthy state.

"While the core group may deal with different buyers, producers and couriers, use various methods of completing a transaction, and see that the goods are moved to their destination one way or another, the core group's integrity remains inviolate, its membership static and its internal security absolute. The core group, then, represents the driving force within the network, and its members are hard to pin down as to their culpability for they are careful to insulate themselves from the work-a-day aspects of trafficking.

"Middle level managers are not unlike managers of western corporations since both are responsible for running a smooth operation and reaping maximum profits for the core group. As the middleman plays an important role in many phases of life in the Orient, so they often play a similar role in the opium business.

"Financiers provide backing for the core group and in return receive a proportionate share of the resulting profits. Their risk is fiduciary only; sometimes they engage in narcotics trafficking, but it is more customary for them just to monitor the business and await the profits.

"While refining #4 heroin—the purest quality heroin usually injected by needle—is not a science, it is an art. As such, there are no authorized textbooks or technical schools to aid the novice. He must learn how much of what chemical to use [*acetic anhydride, for example, is a critical ingredient], or when to apply a certain degree of heat at the proper time, from a skilled and practicing "chemist." The chemist is well paid for his labors, sometimes receiving a percentage of the sale of the heroin, or even being allowed to personally merchandise some of his product. Generally, the #4 chemist is independent and contracts his skills to large producers or networks, such as the Khakweyei leaders who own and operate a number of refineries at Tachilek, Burma. Successful chemists are well-known in the business where a good reputation means steady work and where a good product means greater profit.

"Within the upper levels, it is not uncommon for the identities

---

* Acetic anhydride is a sour, colorless vinegar-like chemical compound commonly used by commercial photo labs to develop film; there are a few other legitimate manufacturing usages. (As you can imagine, the diversion of legally obtained acetic anhydride from legitimate outlets in Bangkok occurs regularly.) I did a study of commercial records available from the attache in our embassy and found that the main source of this chemical was in West Germany; a minor supplier was a firm in England. Large quantities of acetic anhydride were shipped regularly in 50-gallon drums by freighter to Bangkok. I suspected the volume being shipped was more than legitimate needs would require; however, there were little data available to show the final destination of these drums once off-loaded at Thai Customs on the Chao Phya River. I suggested that the Thai government could monitor the distribution of this chemical more easily, if they wanted to do so. I also suggested that the U.S. Government could appeal through diplomatic channels and request German manufacturers to report when and to whom unusually high volumes of acetic anhydride sales were made. Realistically speaking, I did not have much hope. It was like asking the R.J. Reynolds tobacco company to stop shipping cigarettes just because cigarettes can cause cancer.

and roles of the membership to be well-known. Specifics regarding sales, purchases, associations, contacts and sometimes even financial arrangements often become common knowledge within the trade. In short, there are few secrets within the Chinese trafficking business community. The members of the community do, in fact, consider themselves as businessmen whose duty it is to turn a profit. They do not suffer from guilt feelings, as they have no sense that their activities are stigmatized by immorality in any way. While they know that their activities are illegal, Chinese traffickers are seldom part of an organized or identifiable "underworld", nor do they generally consort with criminals. Often they own legitimate business concerns—gold shops or other small commercial firms seem to be favored—and are active in Chinese association activities. Among the Chinese so engaged, narcotics trafficking is a way of life and of earning a good living.

"Shifting alliances and relationships within the trafficking fraternity are common and, by and large, amicable in nature. Desire for profit and similarity in background are their shared characteristics. Traffickers in the tri-border area are, almost without exception, Chinese, many from or with antecedents in China's Yunan Province, and a number are of the Muslim faith. Family relationships are also an important consideration, witness the Hu brothers in Vientiane and the Ma clan in Northern Thailand.

"The principal core group in Vientiane was the Wui Tat Company, comprised of Hu T'ien-hsing—the leader—plus his brothers Fa and Fu, and including Liu T'ien-shun, who served as the company's manager and the core group's general factotum who oversaw heroin production at the Ban Houi Tap refinery. This refinery operated for at least four years and was at its peak just prior to General Rathikoun's retirement and the promulgation of the Laotian drug law. The refinery was disbanding during the latter half of 1971. Its chief money maker was heroin which was distributed overland and by air through

Laos and Cambodia to the GI's in Saigon; to Bangkok for onward boat shipment to Hong Kong, even via air drop to Singapore. Additionally, Liu T'ien-shun had shares in the Mekong Wine Company, an associated core group with the Hu T'ien-hsing network, an example of the flexibility found within Chinese trafficking networks.

"Outside of, but essential to the success of the networks, are the cooperating, indigenous local police and military officials who—for a price—provide information, protection, authorization, means of transportation, and other forms of assistance to the Chinese traffickers. Generally, the officials are not part of the networks themselves, but do receive payment—either regularly or on an *ad hoc* basis—for their service. Occasionally, a local official will not actively assist in drug trafficking, but will receive payment for closing his eyes to such activity.

"Perhaps the most famous example of official collusion involved General Ouan Rathikoun, the Lao Army Chief of Staff who assisted Hu T'ien Hsing. In return for a share of the profits, General Rathikoun provided regular Lao troops as protection for Hu's refinery operation at Ban Houei Tap. He also made military vehicles available for transporting opium and narcotics to and from the refinery site, as well as arranging clearance for passage through government checkpoints. Other Lao military elements provided air transportation for Hu. Similar instances of collusion between the trafficking networks and local officials have been reported elsewhere (but never proven) in Southeast Asia, principally in Thailand and in Burma."

* * *

Estimates of the illicit opium produced in the Golden Triangle have varied over the years; however, the total tonnage has remained consistently high, despite the harsh, labor-intensive work involved, restrictive growth limitations (higher elevations and cooler weather are required), and the harassment of a variety of antinarcotic police efforts. Our 1971 study, based on a number of reliable sources, concluded that a total of 750 tons was produced. Of this, 450 tons was consumed by the local hill tribes who eat opium to cure diarrhea or smoke it to ease their aches and pains. Another 200 tons was spirited abroad by truck, plane, ship, and couriers to established Chinese opium markets: 30 tons to Hong Kong, 29 tons to Vietnam, 20 tons to Malaysia and Singapore, 10 tons to the Philippines, 10 tons to Macao, and 1 ton to Cambodia. The networks retained the remaining 100 tons in Bangkok, Vientiane, and Hong Kong to be refined into heroin for sale to U.S. troops in South Vietnam, the Philippines, Thailand, and Okinawa and to meet the growing and highly profitable demand for heroin in the United States.

FLEEING THE SCENE

Like Thai bus drivers who have been involved in an accident and quickly disappear into the crowd, our family slipped out of Don Muang airport at the end of June. We surfaced in New York, after making a rather abortive rest stop in Madrid where the service at our downtown hotel was only grudgingly polite. I had never encountered such rude and haughty hotel people before. Our visit was made unpleasant because the front desk clerk did not want to provide a small bed for Ken, even though our reservation said we were a family of five.

While in Madrid, we toured the famous Prado Art Museum with a group guide. Even there misfortune dogged me, when I was caught innocently taking a picture of Phyllis in the sunny central foyer by a huge, uniformed guard who loomed about seven feet high and wore a peculiar black hat. He waved a finger at me indignantly and then led me like a truant student to the office, with the family following. We trooped downstairs to the front desk where the offending camera was stored and then rejoined our tour. The museum itself was magnificent, especially the extensive collections of such famous masters as El Greco, Valazquez, Francisco de Goya, Raphael, Peter Paul Rubens, Rembrandt, Van Dyck, Claude Lorrain, and Antoine Watteau. There was also a fine collection of Greco-Roman statuary.

We strolled the wide streets of Madrid, did some window shopping, and rested. The boys swam in the tiny outdoor pool atop our hotel twelve floors up while Phyllis and I watched carefully, wondering what would happen if the pool should spring a leak. To my dismay, dinnertime in Spain started around 9 P.M., but we managed to get into the dining room earlier. By the time dessert was served, the room was filling up and we were entertained by a handsome Spaniard in skintight trousers and a silver-braided caballero jacket who strummed his guitar and played classical music to the accompaniment of clicking castanets and energetic boot stamping by a beautiful, flashing, swirling, black-skirted female partner. "Ole!" shouted the audience with delight when the show was over.

We jetted into muggy New York where Jack Wade met us at the airport in a big sedan. It was good to be in Allenhurst and celebrate the 4th of July at a fine cocktail party hosted by Shirley and Jack. We gathered with some friends and neighbors of the Wades on the grounds of their stately home known as The Bluff. The rooms assigned to us were high in the air and open to the warm, salt air breezes. We adjusted our body clocks for two delightful days while visiting with the Wade family. I took nice walks on the coarse yellow sand of the Atlantic early in the morning with Jack and later took some snapshots of the boys modeling Thai wraparound fishing pants for their admiring cousins.

The next morning we loaded our rented station wagon and were soon in sleepy Princeton, quiet now during the summer months. My brother, Chuck, and his wife, Agnes, met us at the Peacock Inn. We stayed at their big home, which was close by the famous inn, the 1776 home of Jonathan Deare. Feeling ready for anything, we said goodbye and cruised along the scenic Pennsylvania Turnpike to the Perrysville exit where we turned onto a narrow road that led to Freedom.

The kids remembered the thrill of riding that stomach-churning road that climbed and fell like a roller coaster. We traveled through farm and orchard country passing an occasional trailer home, where a TV antenna reaching skyward was the only sign of life within, and then began easing down the winding asphalt road. I glanced nervously at the restrainer cables strung on two-foot-high, whitewashed posts buried deep in the cinder shoulders of the road to prevent you from sliding off the shoulder into somebody's house down below in case you lost control. Just after the road straightened out, we turned onto a yellow brick avenue and in a minute stopped at the Carson's snug, two-story house. Chuck, Joan, and Momma were on hand to greet us. My Mom was getting frail and shrinking in size but chipper and beaming as we approached. The Carsons welcomed us warmly and always seemed to have a bottle of red wine on hand for the occasion. After being plied with food and drink, the ageless way in which company is greeted in Pennsylvania, we all sat around and talked. Chuck, Phyl, and I sipped something stronger than the iced tea offered to take the aches and pains from our stiffening bodies, while Phyl gave out some jewelry she had bought from a Bangkok jeweler.

There was little to do or see in Freedom, so we drove to the Three Rivers Stadium to watch the Pittsburgh Pirates lose to the Cincinnati Reds. If I remember correctly, the Reds had Hall of Famer-to-be Johnny Bench behind the plate catching "Tom Terrific" Seaver. Our seats were in the center field bleachers facing the afternoon sun, but it was a nice outing. I took the boys to the banks of the placid Ohio River, hoping to see some riverboat traffic. Across the calm, green water was the town of Aliquippa, where the Jones and Laughlin steel mill used to operate three shifts a day. All the mills along the river were slowly cutting back. It was incredible that our steel industry, once a world leader, would be content to operate ancient mills and foundries that dated to the turn of the century and not update or replace equipment to keep abreast of the market. The economic results were as clear as the smokeless skies over Aliquippa. The message was also clear: America was losing the economic war. On the plus side, we were doing well with fast-food franchises like McDonalds, Kentucky Fried Chicken, Burger King, and a raft of pizza parlor chains. While these endeavors are laudable, they do not impact our economy in the same way as our magnificent steel industry. Not even our successes in the computer field can offset this.

We turned in our rental car at the Greater Pittsburgh Airport and flew to Sarasota, eager to see Cyndy and the Warrens. After exchanging hugs and greetings, we borrowed Evie's car and drove to the Brown's spacious home on Turtle Beach. We were in bathing suits and submersed in the salty gulf waters within minutes.

* * *

On August 16, a few weeks after our arrival, Cyndy and Phillip Toale were married at St. Boniface Church. The simple affair conducted by Assistant Rector Joe Drawdy took place on a bright Saturday afternoon. It did not seem possible that twenty years earlier, almost to the day, Phyllis and I were married in the Warren's house on Hanson Bayou. Cyndy's ceremony was more formal and stately than ours had been. The reception at the beach house was attended by an assortment of friends and neighbors. Champagne was flowing, the hors d'oeuvres were tasteful and plentiful, and there were two cocktail bars. Bill Swain managed to spirit a bottle of bubbly to the pine-shaded lot next door where he shared it with some pals, including his young, innocent brother. The result was Ken's first hangover. Cyndy tossed her bridal bouquet from the stairs to one of her bridesmaids and had a multitude of photos taken. The traditional rice showered the newlyweds before they fled to a honeymoon spot on Longboat Key.

* * *

We celebrated the birthdays of Bill and Ken with steak cookouts on the beach. Our last and final mission of the month was to get Thomas established as a freshman at the University of Florida in Gainesville. We checked in at a Holiday Inn near the campus and spent the weekend helping him settle into the freshman dormitory, opening a checking account, and getting acquainted with the town.

Leaving for school marks a big step into adulthood. It was tough on all of us to be separated, but Cyndy had done it, and now it was Tom's turn. We knew that Tom was a self-starter with confidence and inner strength. He had obtained his Florida driver's license the past month and was now driving a secondhand Ford Pinto. He would be able to drive to Aunt Nancy's in Bushnell and to Sarasota to visit Cyndy and Phil Toale, as well as his grandparents on the bayou. It was not as if he were being left all alone in the world. We parted with 18-year-old Tom trusting that his sense of values would prevail and that with the company of others in the same boat he would make it until next summer, when he would fly out and join us in Bangkok for his summer break. Tom promised to write, and did he ever. A few of his lively accounts of college life are included in the next chapter.

TWENTY

Bangkok Revisited

The Swain family arrived in Bangkok after a long yet curiously pleasant nonstop flight from Los Angeles to Hong Kong. The flight gave us time to adjust to the realization that we were again en route to Southeast Asia after an all too brief sojourn in America, the land of the "Big PX."

By late September, Tom Swain was beginning to adapt to university life in Gainesville, which was bewildering and raucous, challenging and boring, and exciting and discouraging all at the same time. Writing from his desk in Rawlings Hall dormitory, shoehorned into a two-man room that had been expanded to accommodate a third student due to heavy enrollment, Tom wrote of his travails with wry humor. Some highlights of these epistles, the chief means that Tom used to vent his frustrations and report his successes, are reported here.

"The first week of classes has concluded; however, I'm reasonably certain many more will follow. I've had no problems with any of the courses other than the required, mandatory Physical Education (P.E.) which is boring (exception: the first day of classes I and six others were computer-directed to attend a girls' class, which made things quite lively), my math class is at 5:45 P.M., which tends to interfere with most evening activities and meetings, and the computer class has about 140 students.

"The Sunday morning sun comes burning in here about 8:00 A.M., and sears the grass outside at 11:00 A.M. with temperatures

515

regularly hitting the 90's. Now, but for the ever-playing stereos, all is quiet. Yesterday, however, there was a football game. Needless to say, everybody came and every available parking space was taken. I could hear the roar of the crowd easily, when there was a particularly good play, though the stadium is a half-mile away.

"Several times this week, I've found that frequently the place that cashes checks is also out of money. As a result, last night I had two oranges for dinner. That fruit, by the way, may have been the only nourishing thing here as the cafeteria serves little more than sandwich and grill items, such delicacies as the Gator-burger, Gator-Cheese burger, fish burgers, plain burgers. . . . Bleah! Essentially, therefore, I've been on liquid sustenance, drinking ice tea, orange juice, wasser, milk, and eating grilled cheese sandwiches and ice cream. This morning upon awakening at seven o'clock I remembered I had run out of money the night before (again because the cashiers had run out of money too); my roommates too had run out. My problem was soon solved when the cafeteria secretly disclosed that they would cash checks after all.

"I actually managed to initialize and execute the printed formated washing statements on both the washing and drying devices found on our floor, and the product from each contained no errors.

"Speaking of computers, this place is fantastic. Indeed, everyone using the computer facilities is given a code number and a password, and an account. The code number identifies your course and which class you are in, plus exactly which student. The password is an eight-digit private number designed to prevent anyone from using your allotted funds. The Science department gives everyone ten dollars, placed in a computer account, though the money is indeed real, about $1,400 dollars for our class alone. The fees are $2/per hour for simply sitting at a remote terminal, $2/minute for card-batch jobs. . . . Anyhow, I've got a great start.

"I've yet to grow fond of the campus' physical size and organization. My car parking decal requests me to go a quarter mile away while there is ample space one hundred yards away. . . . Club organizations meet randomly, with respect to time and place, for instance, there is a Thai Club here, with about thirty Thais, who meet semi-annually and speak in Thai. I caught the tail end of one such meeting and only understood they had just elected a new president. They were pleased I had come, I was one of two farangs there. Actually, I feel like a farang [foreigner] in the whole of America.

Post Scriptus

"Now at midnight, I expect to be up for some time. . . . I finally got to eat after cruising around in the Pinto which was functioning properly. After being turned down at Arby's and a Mini-Market store (for cashing checks), I settled upon a restaurant in a big hotel for dinner. London broil, it was, with refills on tea, orange juice, a good salad, with lots of bread rolls. . . . It was great. The price was less than five dollars. However, simply getting off campus and driving around was enlightening. I had forgotten I could do such things. Anyway, I saw a Sears and a J.C. Penneys and even a Woolworth. I didn't know they had any around here. All in all this was a pretty good evening. After supper I went to the computer place and successfully ran our class assignment and some other stuff. I now plan to finish this writing, finish some social science reading and probably drop. . . . Tom".

Sunday, October 6

"Greetings: I have fled the scene and taken refuge fifty-five miles away from the campus [in Bushnell with Aunt Nancy and Uncle Dave]. Time and gas permitting, I'd have fled the country. The thought of leaving the whole mess occurred to me late Friday afternoon, an unconscious solution to the ever-present noise, parties and football games. Our residence hall, for instance, was supposed to launch an offensive on the fourth floor of a neighboring building using such weapons as shaving creme and toilet paper. Yesterday was the day of the big game. I knew very well I wouldn't be able to survive; the cafeteria lines swell to umpteen thousands, people get "bombed" and the noise level threatens to level the buildings. Within the hour, then, I was on my way. I hated to miss out on throwing toilet paper, one of my specialties, but I had to think of my general welfare. . . . What's really strange, to my way of thinking, is why so many people go from the country to the campus to attend these rather vile football matches. Really crazy people, it's good there aren't too many of them around.

"My timing was perfect in choosing the correct hour to leave thereby avoiding civil war. The golfer from Pittsburgh and the watermelon picker from Clewiston (my roommates) are daily at each other's throats; I sit back like a nuclear physicist to make sure things don't go 'critical', providing the services of a go-between. Of course, I also get things started by taking sides with the golfer and then chastising the Southerner for his twang. The watermelon boy is very physical in his response and consequently pummels the Northerner; I escape his wrath since, after all, I am a rebel. But it has no significance for me otherwise. After that, I balance things out by siding with the Southerner and criticizing the Northerner for his helter-skelter unplanned schedule which causes him to miss class, forestall assignments, curse and scream; we rub it in. His invariable reaction is the heavy use of expletives, some indirectly directed to the Catholic Church, of which he is a member (being one of 12 children). . . . I'm having a great time.

"In conclusion, I have just about completed adjusting to life here in all its strangeness. Though I am thinking of getting some earplugs to shut out the stereos and am looking for a way to get a place off campus, due to the excessive crowding (28,000 students this year). The administration is permitting first-year students to seek shelter elsewhere.

Thomas W. Swain"

The Time of My Life

* * *

Meanwhile back in Bangkok, the monsoon season arrived with more than customary rainfall. Our porch was blanketed with white and pink bougainvillea petals that had fluttered down, sodden and limp, from the latticed bower above onto the wicker chairs where we often sat to review the events of the day. Phyllis chose this spot from which to write:

Wednesday, October 9th. . . .

"The rain started early this morning and has not let up much. Right now it is six o'clock and I am waiting for Adie to get home. The sky is dark and leaden, and water from the Soi is beginning to flow backwards into our driveway. It must be a foot deep outside our gates, if not more. I am watching cars go by, throwing great bow waves, the kind that would upset KC if someone did it in his bayou on Flamingo Avenue. I mean there is really a lake out there. Here come some lights. Not Adie. . . . Yes, Adie."

Thursday morning, the second day. . . .

"Last night it continued to rain. The kids and servants were all out in the Soi enjoying the water. There was a man fishing with a cast net and catching FISH. Where they came from I'm not sure. Probably from the klongs which are all overflowing, and the Chao Phya River is supposed to have high tides today which will back up the flooded klongs even more. . . .

"Thursday afternoon our Soi was the scene of a water holiday. Thai kids, American kids, gardeners, maids, all splashing about watching cars stall out, fishing, riding bikes and playing a sort of aerial soccer in which Ken and a neighbor participated with their Thai friends. The game degenerated into more or less water polo, with not a dry head in sight. Yuuch. That water is far from clean. . . ."

Friday, the third day. . . .

"Last night it started to rain hard about 10 P.M. I had a device for measuring the rainfall and discovered this morning three more inches had fallen. Bill and Ken and Adie all made it to work, but Mou's bus couldn't make it. There is no high water danger to our house as the floor level is three feet above ground level. The servants' quarters are considerably closer to ground level but the service area between house and their quarters was under about two inches of water. Two more inches will mean our servant's rooms and the storage rooms will flood. More rain is predicted for today. Souli and Soontorn are busy building wooden dikes across their doorway thresholds.

"By 6 P.M. the rain is letting up but I hear more thunder. LO AND BEHOLD! The garbage truck cometh. First time in three days. Great. The servants on the Soi (not ours) continued putting garbage on the curb the past two days, and as there is no curb, it is beginning to be a problem. One basket tipped over today, and fittingly enough it drifted right back into the neighbor's yard to whom it belonged. Justice."

Saturday morning, the fourth day. . . .

"Two and a half more inches of rain last night. If it rains much more today we may have problems. Soontorn is once again building his dike."

Sunday, the fifth day. . . .

"Fortunately just had a little rain yesterday. Today is bright and sunny. The Soi is still flooded, but we must try and get out to the PX for our food supplies are running low. Yesterday I noted that most of the stores on Sukhumvit were flooded. We walked-waded up to observe. It was quite a scene as buses raced by making tremendous waves. I pity the shopkeepers. They all had batter boards up of some sort, but the water displaced by racing buses and trucks continued to dislodge the boards. Everyone was in a holiday spirit however. Much laughter and good fellowship. I took many pictures for the family scrapbook."

Monday, the sixth day

"Everything seems to be drying out. So we made a successful trip to the PX and commissary. The larder is again full and all is well. From soggy Bangkok, love, Phyl."

* * *

Tom continued his periodic visits to Aunt Nancy's house to escape the chaos he found on campus and for some home cooking. He wrote on October 15th:

"Last Friday I again went to Bushnell and as it happened Aunt Joanne was there from Pennsylvania and Cyndy came up from Sarasota. I went swimming in Nancy's pool although it was cold. I hit some golf balls with Matt, then we went out to the junk pile and fired the shotgun, twenty-two rifle and a .22 semi-automatic pistol. The pistol was surprisingly accurate, and my marksmanship superb, even amazing.

"While Matt went horseback riding with some friends, Nancy, Cyndy, Joanne and I went to see this lady (named Gladys, I think) who raises cats. It was hard to believe; she had two full-grown leopards (in a glass room within a cage) and some babies. . . . one Siberian lynx twice the size of Julie who was very docile but he could easily kill (their jaws lock on to the victim in some fashion), one black jaguar is allowed to roam loose in the house, worth about $7,000, and one puma. These last three "babies" are fairly hefty, weighing about thirty pounds. Then there were two tiny one-month-old babies—one a fantastically rare white leopard and a black something-or-other. Far out.

521

Adrian Swain

"When Gladys let the black jaguar loose, it would run around and leap up on one's leg (it had half-inch long claws but didn't use them, fortunately) and start to nibble. It was necessary to "whack" it off your leg. It seemed to enjoy attacking Cyndy. Then the beast would tear into the master bedroom and start racing around on the bed, flinging pillows everywhere and jumping on the curtains. It was very similar to the antics of Julie and Thateng. In fact, the jaguar had a cat's body but a very large head with huge eyes and an even larger mouth somewhat like a dog's. Most entertaining. . . .

"When it was time for me to return, Nancy gave me another bundle of food which included bread, fudge, fruit, a pecan roll, and cheddar cheese and crackers. I'm halfway civilized as I sit here eating cheese and crackers.

"Aha! A knock on the door brought tidings of possible great joy. A note from the Administration saying that some triple-occupant rooms will revert to two-man rooms, and asking whether or not I prefer our room to remain as a triple (at triple room rates) or convert back to a double room (at lesser room rates). They need to ask? Good Grief. The reason I want to change rooming conditions is due to my mounting frustration. Last Monday, when I returned from Bushnell, the roommate from Pittsburgh revealed a large quantity of marijuana in a plastic bag. My inexperienced estimate would be there was enough for at least one-hundred joints. I told him to remove it from the room. He avoided the issue and wondered why I was getting upset. My response was that I didn't wish to risk getting busted, which made no change in his thinking. I told him to remove the marijuana as soon as possible.

"The next evening, my door was locked and the lights were out in the room. I entered and found the Pittsburgh boy and a golfing friend dividing the grass into equal shares. I suggested using the post office scales in a self-service carousel some distance away and left immediately.

522

"I have been considering ways to solve the problem, specifically police action (which I consider a bit harsh), but have not found a reasonable solution. When I told Nancy of this problem, we finally decided she would make arrangements to talk to B. Brown, Dean of University College, who had written me a congratulatory letter. Nancy, as a "nosey" relative, plans to request a better place for a studious student (which I am) to live.

"A couple of days ago some Peace Corps people were on campus. I asked about their program in Thailand. It seems they provide assistance to countries who request help. Thailand has a need for many English teachers in their universities, as well as agricultural people and a television engineer. Basically, you have to have a degree, and be willing to work for nothing other than living expenses. Sounds like it would be a great experience. It was interesting.

"October 16th. . . . I've just showered after my first class of the day, Physical Education. They keep giving us tests. First they had us climb stairs, then checked heart rate. Today we had strength and coordination tests, such as standing on your toes with your eyes closed, touching your toes and other feats of agility. Each test, there were eighteen, got progressively harder. I failed four of them: jumping up in the air five times with your legs straight out in front of you and touching said toes, spreading legs on ground and placing head practically on the ground without using your hands, jumping to your feet from a weird sitting position, and finally, running in place for two minutes, stopping, sitting down, and now hold your breath for thirty seconds. Impossible! Like I say, they want supermen. Anyhow, I ranked above average in spite of all. Next week more strength tests. Bleeaaaaah!

". . . . Ah, Dad asks if anything can be sent upon my request. Yes, I'd like another pair of Chinese plastic-rubber flip-flops, thongs, or clogs. Usually what I wear each day are good ol' Samsumai (the tailor on Sukhumvit) pants and shirt, and flip-flops.

"Other sartorial notes: I have conquered the technique of using the washer and dryer, and my hair hasn't been cut since you left; it is shoulder length, but I now comb it over the ears. By the way, Ken, Kung Fu has a pony tail now. I no longer care or worry about my hair—I've no plans to give it much attention for the next year. . . . Love to all, Tom"

* * *

Tom wrote of the depression that settles upon all students from time to time, especially when they consider the depths of their lack of knowledge, and was able to unload some of his frustration in some self-analysis, which seemed to help him and his distant family:

"The reason for my present depression is that while I have the time, the ability, and the desire to learn, I'm very limited in actually doing something about it. There are two ways of learning: one by attending classes, the other by listening to people outside of class. The latter is what I am talking about. . . . I think I'd like to be an "apprentice" under some professor or learned person, because what I expect from learning isn't all necessarily academic. . . . It is truly wasteful to go through many years of intermediate and often 'slow' work when a higher degree of learning and satisfaction could be had by jumping directly into the work without all the intermediate steps. I think the core of my problem is that I really expected to enter into an atmosphere of learning in all things.

"I almost exploded today because I could not be alone, or even quiet. When my roommates come in, they evidently feel obligated to start a conversation. So, they talk and I occasionally grunt. Do not get the impression that I'm becoming totally isolationist—only once or twice a day. To continue, I came back to my room after class and wanted to do some calculus studying. Impossible—#$&*%$—stereos! Desk a mess!! Roommate barges in, passes oral flatus of completely trifling nature!!! I got my hands on a frisbee and flung it viciously down the halls, narrowly missing decapitating heroic fools curious as to the bonkings on their doors. My arm grew tired and the throng in the hall picked up where I stopped. I still remain frustrated. . . .

"I think I would like to be a student under the tutelage of some professor or mentor as it was several hundred years ago. Today, however, no one is that well rounded, sadly, instead all are specialized.

"My calculus teacher is most interesting. He rarely makes mistakes of unforgiveability, goes through things quickly but explains slowly and clearly if asked, and with quite a sense of humor. The entire class resembles an episode of "Laugh-In", [the popular TV show starring comedians Dan Rowan and Dick Martin]. He too is a computer freak; several times we have done problems lasting three hours after class was over. Far out computer problems too. . . . In a subsequent walk and talk with said teacher, I learned he is single and is starting to freeze in the trailer he lives in, now that the weather is starting to get colder. He is from Minnesota, and says he is used to it. We also talked about the relative pay scales graduate assistants like himself are stuck with, I learned that mathematicians don't get as much as physicists.

"I purchased a basic music notation manual which I hope to convert to computer language and then begin total analysis. Have also checked out half a dozen books, some dealing with music and others with electronics and computers. My intention is to educate myself in my spare time.

"Speaking of spare time, during one of my evening walks, I found a secret room where professors and above have access to TV screen terminals any hour of the day. To use them it is necessary for one to nonchalantly walk in and pretend to belong. My technique is to walk into an area with the greatest of familiarity, though the place is of course completely new to me, look around, manipulate the dials on some equipment, make

525

some notations. . . . thus I pass for some undergraduate brain-child on a junior level. Last evening I walked forthrightly into this bizarre room filled with analog computers, wires were everywhere in complete confusion to me, but they obviously made sense to the dudes operating these machines which were like telephone terminals, completely different from the digital computers I work with. I went up to a table, picked up and started reading some technical manual with limited compre-hension. Then I started staring at the guy fooling around with this switchboard. He eventually became flustered with whatever it was he was doing, though my knowledgeable stare might have given him something bordering on an inferiority feeling, and so he said, 'Do you want to use this?' I replied with a straightfor-ward negative response and resumed reading with interest. He immediately departed.

"In my wanderings I have also discovered the electronics work-shop, electronic music room, radio astronomy and chemistry labs, and even the electronics printed circuit board darkroom which also had two remote computer terminals, which is great because 99% of the people in my class are aware of only one building which has fourteen terminals available for all of us. I go to this other building and have the place to myself. . . . I may get into trouble, but no one seems to object.

"For entertainment of the student body last weekend, they showed the movie *Jesus Christ Superstar*; this weekend the offer-ing is Hitchcock's *Frenzy* plus some Spanish guitarist and also auditions for a play requiring acrobats. . . . I think I will slip away to Bushnell. . . . Tom Swain"

* * *

Phyllis was feeling a bit of the same depression that Tom expressed in his letters, which was quite understandable. She had to part with two of her children: Cyndy given away at the altar, so to speak, and then Tom lost in the halls of academia. She wrote Tom, trying to cheer him up, October 23:

"Sweetie, once again let me say how much we enjoy your letters, and appreciate the time it takes to keep us informed of your activities. Golly, when Dad came home tonight with TWO, his announcement was 'The mail cometh' and I couldn't wait to hear the latest developments. I was glad to hear your week seemed to pass quickly, for that is a good sign.

"I must admit time has been heavy on my hands. I am now, I think, pulling out of a slightly depressive situation. Can't exactly explain why it occurred, but since we have been back (and I wanted to come back) I have been in a state of limbo. Couldn't seem to make myself go out and do anything. Part of me was missing, you and Cyndy. I sort of got "down" on everyone here, didn't want to see anyone, didn't want to entertain or be entertained, didn't want to go anywhere, didn't want to drive—all very negative and I was probably very difficult to get along with as far as the rest of the family were concerned. So—I read a lot, slept a lot, ate a lot, again all negative, just sort of retreated. NOT GOOD. SELFISH I said to myself. Perhaps I had to have a let down, after the hectic summer and regroup myself. Anyway, I am happy to say, I think I am out of it. Am exercising daily, started bowling again (which I am not mad for but realize I have to make a commitment to get out and see people), and will get into tennis next week if the rains truly stop. I guess my purpose in saying all of this is to make me face up to my own problems, a confession of weakness of sorts, and to let you know all of us have problems in just day-to-day living, and yet the basic joy and desire for life and for the continuity of life persists. . . . With love from us all, Mom"

* * *

About this time, Tom wrote a paper for his English class explaining calculus, which his parents found enlightening, having never taken calculus. Tom made the difficult subject seem easy, the hallmark of all good writing [see Appendix]. After graduation, Tom would become a technical writer for Piper Aircraft in Lakeland and then work at United Technologies' jet engine plant in West Palm Beach. He later came back to Sarasota to work for the Loral Corporation as a computer engineer.

There were highs and lows in Tom's life. He discussed the evolution of his relationship with the Clewiston watermelon picker:

"I shouldn't delay describing what occurred not long ago. I was sitting on the golfer's bed reading a paper late in the afternoon when this simian from Clewiston comes in. He annoys both the golfer and me by his habit of picking, hitting, pinching and otherwise physically abusing us for fun. I think he does it unconsciously. He picks on the golfer mostly. The golfer gets mad and screams at him which the watermelon picker enjoys. He rarely does it to me, but I don't react when he does, because I thought it didn't bother me. I learned rather shockingly that it does bother me. As I was sitting on the bed, the Watermelon boy comes in with half a broomstick and ruffles the paper I was reading. It set me off. I loosed a choked oath and tore the broomstick handle from his hands, and, still cursing, stalked down the hall and hid the stick in a ventilating groove. Let me tell you, this oaf from Clewiston is less sensitive than a rock. I had dropped my pen as I stalked off, and he seized the pen, declaring he would break it unless I returned his broomstick. I ignored him.

"Anyway, I went off to class and thought about it; when I returned we had another confrontation. He wanted to know why I had gotten so mad. I said I didn't know, although it probably was an unconscious build up that finally exploded. Well, he went on the defensive again. He always does. When we have conversations and he feels inadequate for some reason, he starts shouting and cursing at people and becomes very nasty, crude and immature.

"So after he says, 'Gosh, I was only hitting the paper,' with a totally surprised expression on his face and in his voice, I said a temporary solution I could see was simply for him not to disturb me. I had barely said this when he threw himself on the defensive again. I swear, he has only two reactions, surprise and defense. He cut me off before I could further explain that I didn't like being picked on (and believe me, the golfer room-mate has made this point perfectly clear many times), he said, 'Listen, Tom, you just don't disturb me.'

"There is one major thing I have learned from all of this. Now I know why Bill got so mad after I'd been playing around with him, 'playing' being synonymous to the activities of the water-melon picker. . . . Bleeaah, let's just say now I know what it's like to be picked on and I can't stand it. And I had been picking on both Bill and Ken for years. . . . I ask you for your eternal forgiveness." [Bill and Ken got a big bang out of reading Tom's description of his encounters with the watermelon picker, and were very appreciative of Tom's apology.]

Fired with interest in his basic computer class, Tom wrote:

"I plan to continue in computers for I find the field most enjoyable. . . . I have been promised an assistantship in the computer lab, which has the possibility of pay and I thought it was a volunteer job. . . . But right now, for gross entertainment, the Clewiston wizard is making fun of the Pittsburgher's laugh, which is, I admit, strange, but nevertheless no reason to abuse one's fellow-man. Now I must conclude this sordid saga of life in room 346, amidst such artistic phrases as calling someone a 'caw' (meaning a rejected watermelon), or '. . . . in the brain,' 'Glory be' and other sarcastic derision unparalleled in the mouths of man.

"Before I go, may I make a comment on reviewing Bill's report card, sent in some recent mail from Bangkok? It's unbelievable! For one who hides in the depthless shadows of a sunless room for much of the day, such a positive achievement is totally unwarranted and quite unexpected. Though I was always quite sure Bill had it in him, as of course does Ken. . . . who according to a previous report, did not perform in the mental mannerisms of his predecessors, but instead excelled in the social world. There is not a thing wrong with this for as long as an individual utilizes himself to his full capacity, he is equal in his endeavors to anyone else, regardless of the task. . . . As ever, Tom"

In the spring semester, Tom found time to play a role in Shakespeare's, *The Taming of the Shrew* and wrote:

"My part is relatively minor. I, with three other guys, serve the Lord as huntsmen and servants. The director is the reincarnation of the International School of Bangkok's past wonder, Mr. Wheetly (who is now working in California). The audition (let the story be told) lasted two days. I was called back on the third day. The cast is large, twenty-five, mostly men. I presume I performed reasonably well. My projection was half-way decent, but it seems there are skills I lack, all things considered. As I see it, being at the bottom means there is but one direction to go: skyward, nay heavenward. . . . The play opened on February 10, 1975, and ran for six nights, every seat was sold out. Cyndy, Nancy and Matt wanted to attend, but it was too late for me to get them tickets."

Then came word of the solution to the overcrowded room situation:

"Speaking of great things, I'm in a double room! Yes, Yes, sighs of relief can now be sighed. The Clewiston wonder ejected to a room down the hall and around a corner on the same floor. Still, there is now extra room and even more solitude. The new year promises to be merciful."

* * *

With the war winding down in Southeast Asia, a recession was affecting the economic scene during 1975. Tom reported the following:

"Next year, the University is laying off 100 teachers, while student enrollment will be about the same, if not more. Budgets all around will be cut, and some small courses will be eliminated. The last time this happened was in 1968, but then the enrollment was 20,000. I think the same problem is hitting every college. You remember the much appraised calculus teacher I had first quarter? I ran into him the other day and learned of his absence. He wanted to change from mathematics to physics so he quit his math teaching assistantship and then found he couldn't get back into physics. So, he still lives in his trailer and waits. No money to attend classes even. I know several people who live in trailers, $80 a month for the trailer and $40 for lot rental, plus $60 to $80 for utilities. It can get expensive."

Tom managed to enroll in most of his required courses and then initiated some belt-tightening. This account of his experimentation with vegetarianism is interesting and a foretaste of the future:

"Yesterday, I got on the old bike and pedaled to the Winn-Dixie Store, where for five dollars, (all I had) I purchased a two-quart aluminum pot for $2.50, a pound or so of fresh string beans, two great bunches of celery and two equally massive stalks of carrots (I have something mixed up here, besides my mind). It was quite a load, all for $4.60. I have been living on these for this day in its entirety. I woke up and got a handful of beans, the pot and my knife, went to the lounge where there is an electric stove, washed the beans, then cut and boiled them. I didn't know what I was doing as to timing, but they turned out to be quite edible, but lacking in the old Bangkok bean flavor. Oh, I forgot to mention, I also purchased a 50 cent head of lettuce and I snacked on that throughout the day. I washed it and put it in the freezer for fifteen minutes. Great lettuce. For lunch I boiled some carrots in the equally ignorant manner as the beans and they weren't too hot in taste either. I trust things will improve. Things are cheaper this way and if not wholly supportive at least they can supplement my diet. So be it, Tom"

Tom's cooking improved when Phyllis explained how to season and steam the vegetables in the old Bangkok manner to retain all their vitamins and flavor. He supplemented his vegetables with celery, milk, and orange juice from the cafeteria plus "doughnuts sold by some girls from Broward Hall."

*　*　*

The Pittsburgh golfer joined the Phi Kappa Tau fraternity and invited Tom to visit his house. Tom was properly impressed: "Pat's fraternity is great. It isn't on the campus proper, and is set apart from the relatively staid, competitive row of fraternity houses which are mere meters apart. I had a free dinner, met quite a diversified crew of guys, and on hand were a few of the little sisters from a neighborhood sorority. I had a great time. The rooms were mind-boggling in their comforts and luxury."

A few weeks later, Tom was asked to join the fraternity, which he described as "smaller in size compared to most other fraternity buildings. There are about twenty rooms, with two men to a room." If he joined that spring, he most likely could become a full-fledged brother by the fall term. Phyl and I were pleased to get this news and were not surprised when Tom wrote that he wanted to pledge Phi Kappa Tau, saying it "will involve learning 60 names, helping around the house on weekends, and there is a party tonight, Gads. There are four other pledges like me and if we get all our work done we can be initiated at the end of this quarter. If I am initiated it will mean living for a week at the Fraternity house except for class attendance." On May 2, Tom formally pledged Phi Kappa Tau.

VIETNAM UPDATE

I had to review a number of reports to sort out the complex and rather depressing events occurring in Vietnam. Phyl and I had clippings from newspapers (the Bangkok *Post* and *Nation* and the Hong Kong *Standard,* all printed in English) plus reports from our Embassy sources concerning the gradual withdrawal of American troops from South Vietnam, which began in 1972 and continued through the spring of 1975. The armed forces of South Vietnam were collapsing under the pressure of North Vietnamese troops, who were in constant violation of the 1972 peace agreement signed in Paris by which we agreed to withdraw our troops gradually from South Vietnam. This agreement was made largely because of the secret and drawn-out efforts of Henry Kissinger, who was acting as special envoy for President Richard Nixon. When we began to withdraw, it became apparent that the South Vietnamese (ARVN) troops and most of their leaders had neither the will nor the heart to fight the war against the North Vietnamese without U.S. troops at their sides. As U.S. troop levels decreased, the weakness in the hearts and minds of ARVN soldiers was so obvious that the determined and disciplined NVA became more aggressive.

In January 1975, the VC left their sanctuaries on the Cambodian-Laos-Vietnamese border and pushed into Phuoc Long Province. Without U.S. troops to support them, ARVN troops wilted before the NVA threat and retreated from the province. The VC immediately filled the vacuum and were thus encouraged to launch more widespread attacks. When the ARVN troops again fell back, a fearful and timid President Thieu ordered all of the highlands evacuated, thinking he had better bring his troops closer to Saigon and conserve his forces. A circling of the wagons mentality was settling over Saigon.

Instead of a controlled and orderly evacuation of troops from the highlands, which Thieu envisioned, a panicky rout ensued. Led by terrified ARVN troops, the remaining occupants of the region—men, women and children, and farm animals pulling carts loaded with household goods—began moving from the hills and clogging the roads leading east toward the coast as they fled to safety from the VC. With virtually no opposition, the VC and NVA troops then moved against the cities of Hue and Quang Tri in I Corps far to the north. Again, President Thieu's troops surrendered these key cities. The South Vietnamese military machine had begun to come apart.

By early April, the northern half of South Vietnam was occupied by VC troops. With the handwriting on the wall, President Thieu began packing his bags (some say loaded with gold bullion), while bitterly blaming the United States for not giving him the troops and monetary support he had been promised by former President Nixon, but not approved by Congress. On April 21, Thieu fled to Taiwan and in 1985 was living quietly near London. Thieu was succeeded by Vice President Tran Van Huong, who offered to negotiate with the VC, but they ignored his overtures. Huong then was replaced by neutralist General Duong Van Minh, but the VC ignored him as well, for by now they were planning a final assault on Saigon. NVA troops had begun to form a ring around the "Paris of the Orient."

On orders from President Gerald Ford, all remaining U.S. personnel were evacuated from Saigon on April 29 and 30 by a fleet of 81 helicopters, which flew 1,383 Americans and 5,695 Vietnamese civilians to U.S. ships of the Seventh Fleet cruising off shore near Vung Tau in the South China Sea. In threatening weather, all manner of helicopters—Stallions, Chinooks, and Jolly Green Giants— lumbered back and forth to the tennis courts at Tan Son Nhut airport and the lawn inside the American Embassy compound. Smaller, silver-colored Bell-205 helicopters of the Air America fleet lifted small groups of Americans and Vietnamese employees from hotel rooftops where they had taken refuge. Pete and Lucy, our old Manila buddies who were in Saigon working for the Company, were airlifted to Bangkok a few days earlier and eventually returned to the States. Bill Cunningham, our DEA man in Saigon who had replaced Fred T. Dick, was also evacuated to Bangkok. The next to last military helicopter from Saigon lifted off with a tired and distraught Ambassador Graham Martin, who clambered aboard just before dawn from the tiny chopper pad atop the Embassy building. With him were Tom Polgar, Chief of Station for the CIA and State Department and military aids. Some 140,000 Vietnamese were evacuated by helicopters, planes, boats, and even fishing vessels. About 132,000 refugees were eventually resettled in the United States after being processed in camps hastily set up in Thailand.

Graham Martin replaced Ambassador Ellsworth Bunker, who departed Saigon in May 1973 after Henry Kissinger worked out a cease-fire agreement in Paris on January 23, 1973. The agreement between the United States, South Vietnam, the VC, and the North Vietnamese stated that U.S. troops would withdraw gradually in return for ceasing military action and for other political agreements.

The cease-fire did not last long, and the fighting continued over the next two years until South Vietnam, weakened and disheartened by the withdrawal of American support, was finally defeated. Ellsworth Bunker later said that we had achieved our objective at the end of 1972 by making it possible for the South Vietnamese to defend themselves. When the North Vietnamese continued to violate the cease-fire agreements and Congress decided against providing more money to support the South Vietnamese, the tragic result was inevitable.

By the end of April 1975, what was left of Thieu's government surrendered unconditionally, and Saigon was occupied without a struggle. In July, South Vietnam was officially made part of the Socialist Republic of Vietnam with its capital in Hanoi. Battered and bedraggled but still lovely, Saigon was renamed Ho Chi Minh City to honor the dead leader of the North Vietnamese Government.

These were not good times for American interests in the region. Cambodian President Lon Nol's pro-Western regime collapsed suddenly on April 16. Communist Khmer Rouge troops marched into Phnom Penh and ousted most of its two million people because they could not feed them. Top military and political leaders were killed, and Prime Minister Khieu Samphan appeared to be in charge. Directed by the infamous Pol Pot, Khmer Rouge troops then engaged in a bloodbath throughout the country. Having any semblance of an education or relatives or friends connected to Lon Nol's government meant a shot in the head and a shallow grave; millions of innocent Cambodians died. Completing the disasters that occurred during this spring of sadness, Communist Pathet Lao troops in Laos finally gained the upper hand in a seesaw war of attrition that lasted almost 10 years. When they seized the capital city of Vientiane, the fighting ended and King Savang Vatthana was deposed. By the end of 1975, the Communist Pathet Lao proclaimed the People's Democratic Republic in Laos.

The results of the war were harsh. About 47,000 Americans were killed and another 300,000 were wounded. The Army of the Republic of Vietnam lost about 250,000 men and almost 600,000 were wounded. The North Vietnamese lost about 900,000 troops and another 2,000,000 were wounded. Hundreds of thousands of civilians were killed and wounded, many from U.S. bombing campaigns, which also left the countryside scarred and defoliated. Displaced refugees from hundreds of ruined towns and villages crowded into the cities and coastal towns looking for food and shelter and to escape the VC.

President Johnson called on Americans to help the South Vietnamese government stem the tide of communism in Southeast Asia, when in fact many South Vietnamese did not care one way or another. The initial response of America was to be ready, willing, and able; but as the years dragged by with no end in sight, this attitude became lukewarm and then hostile. The problem was that many saw no clear purpose or goal to justify our involvement in the war. Lyndon Johnson and his council of elders heeded too late the wisdom of President Dwight Eisenhower's earlier admonition to avoid a war on the Asian continent. Once we were committed, our military chafed under Johnson's nitpicking rules of engagement that restricted their effort to win the war. Our men fought with one hand tied behind their backs in a war dominated by political priorities and with limited military objectives, such as Johnson's prohibition against destroying the port city of Hanoi, Ho Chi Minh's source of supplies.

Perhaps more fundamentally, the war was lost because Lyndon Johnson failed to get a consensus from the American people to support the war. Essentially, Johnson was dishonest when he sought to unite people for the cause without telling them the truth. He did not trust the American people and even distrusted his own military experts. As time went on, he was sucked deeper and deeper into the morass in Vietnam, despite efforts to manage the war from his White House desk and despite reassuring body count and kill-ratio reports that his field generals fed him every day. Notwithstanding his highly honed political instincts and the high-tech efficiency of our military weaponry, the barefooted guerilla VC in their spider holes along the Cambodian border kept on winning. Johnson's bullheaded management of the war was so unpopular that he announced he would not run for reelection in 1968 and then retired to his ranch on the banks of the Pedernales River to write his memoirs.

Equipment losses from the unexpected, sudden fall of Saigon were staggering. According to Pentagon estimates, NVA forces captured more than $5 billion worth of U.S. military hardware, including 550 tanks, 73 F-5 jet fighters, 1,300 artillery pieces, 1,600,000 rifles, and enough other material to field an entire army, air force, and navy. While the Pentagon claimed that much of this equipment would become unserviceable without American spare parts, even a fraction that might be resold or given away to support insurgent or terrorist movements in Asia or the Middle East would keep them in business for some time. In Bangkok, some Thais were concerned that weapons and other war goods captured by the Communists would be used to support the smoldering guerilla war that continued to plague the Thai government on their northern borders between Burma and Laos.

FLIGHT FROM SAIGON

Phyllis wrote home on April 3, 1975, while sweltering in 95-degree temperatures:

"Right now we are concerned with the plight of the people in South Vietnam. You are probably getting more news coverage via TV than we get, but we get plenty of news through the papers and from friends who have husbands over there.

"I am of the opinion that we should just get all our nationals out of Saigon as well as Cambodia and try to forget the whole miserable situation.... We had a call last night from Lucy Barb, she and her two children [Paula and James] plan to leave Saigon for Bangkok a week from today. I told her she had just better speed it up, for the feeling here is that things will get pretty grim in that city. I understand that the Americans are not going to be able to move out their household effects. Will just have to leave them behind, for the looters, no doubt. What a mess.... Several of the women I bowl with have husbands in Saigon and they were all pretty worried when I saw them yesterday. One gal had just heard that her husband made it safely out of Nha Trang just before it was overrun yesterday morning. That was where Adie was stationed most of his tour in SVN."

On April 9, she wrote:

"Tomorrow I expect to meet Lucy and her children at the airport. I say hopefully, for when I called China Airlines today, they said, 'Call tomorrow. We don't know whether there will be a plane out of Saigon or not.' Hope so, Lucy has three children, the oldest, Rusty, is in the States going to school, the other two must have got caught in Saigon on spring break.

"Next day, I went to the airport to meet the 12:30 China Air Lines flight. After much confusion and delay the plane arrived at 2:45, following a Pan Am flight, Philippine Air Lines, MAS (Malaysian), then the China A.L., followed by Air Vietnam, all within 15 or 20 minutes of each other. Visualize if you can all these people getting off flights, going through customs and immigration, trying to find baggage, mobs of people meeting all the incoming people. It was a mad house. AND, I couldn't find Lucy and her children. Finally, I asked a harassed looking woman with four children if she had come in from Saigon on CAL. She had. She did know Lucy, and was sure she was NOT on the plane. I had already been at the airport for 3 ½ hours and figured there was nothing to do but go home and wait for word which came the following evening.

"Lucy called from the Chao Phya Hotel, here in town, to say that they had arrived safely via Clark Field in the Philippines, thence by bus to Manila and via Japan Airlines to Bangkok. The reason for the roundabout trip was they had with them the 16-year-old son of an American friend, who did not have the proper visa or orders to get out of Saigon. His father was off somewhere in the boonies and Lucy did not want to leave him. The US Air Force was willing to take them without proper credentials, so off they went in a hurry last Tuesday, a day before planned. At Clark, Lucy was able to find a typewriter and added Phillip's name to her orders as a dependent, got it certified and thus was able to get him into Thailand, all a bit illegal, but it worked. Pete (husband) also got out of Saigon on a military flight to Utapao (the Am-Thai Base south of us near Pattaya Beach). He arrived in Bangkok in the wee hours of Thursday night, so all had a grand reunion on Friday. The whole family including Phil, the erstwhile son, had dinner with us both Friday and Saturday.

"Pete has now left for Clark Field for medical reasons, not serious, but a good excuse not to go back to Saigon. Phil has gone to Singapore to join his father, and Lucy and children have gone to Hong Kong, hoping Pete will be relieved of his job in Saigon and be able to join them in Hong Kong for the trip back to the States.

"This is just one of many stories of displaced families. The Chao Phya Hotel, which is an Officer's billet, was full of evacuees from Cambodia and Saigon. I was surprised to see several familiar faces of friends formerly stationed in Bangkok and Laos. Generally, most of these people are glad to be out of the troubled areas, but are heartsick at the friends they are leaving behind and feel very ashamed of the U.S. government. I can sympathize with them, but frankly, I don't know what more we could have done, without risking more American lives for people who seem to have little will to fight for themselves, and God knows their leaders are quick to turn on the U.S. Today we got the report of Thieu's resignation and speech condemning the U.S., which followed a similar speech by Lon Nol, in Phnom Penh. Never have I seen a word of thanks for the aid, however misguided, we have given in the past. It particularly galls me that the SVN expected us to immediately re-supply them with all the equipment they abandoned in the provinces north of Saigon—equipment completely intact for the NVA to re-supply themselves. Also, the actions of the SVN military at Da Nang and Nha Trang were disgraceful and disgusting. All those troops could think about was saving their own necks, women and children be damned.

"I am also upset that I have not read one item in the newspaper anywhere that in anyway condemns the NVA for breaking the Paris Peace Accords. Our own press, as well as the rest of the world, seem to think it perfectly fine that the NVA invade SVN; fine that China and Russia supply the NVA. Why is it that all the blame is on the Americans? Why are the SVN blameless for their poor judgment and inability to defend their country or protect all the outright gifts to them by the Americans, according to what I read. What does the world expect from us? I am disheartened.

"Last night I read *Newsweek* and was appalled by the tone of the reporting. These are American writers, but I couldn't find anything but criticism of our government, our statesmen, our military; I felt as if the articles were written by an enemy press. An example: the caption under one picture of the evacuation of Phnom Penh reads 'U.S. Abandons Cambodia.' It seems to me that this is very hostile reporting. Why not a caption 'U.S. Pulls Out of Cambodia' or 'U.S. Evacuates Employees'?

"Of course, all these adverse stories are having a profound effect on the Thai people as well as the rest of South East Asia. I could accept such stories if they were written by foreign reporters, but our own people are stirring up more trouble for the U.S. in South East Asia. *Time* and *Newsweek* are probably the most widely read international publications in this part of the world and their reporting, as I read it, is nothing but inflammatory regarding U.S. actions.

"The next few months will give us an idea of how the Thai Government will respond to current events. They, of course, are already calling for the withdrawal of U.S. troops so as not to incur the displeasure of the soon-to-be communist regimes surrounding them, as they have no faith that we can help them protect themselves if insurgency becomes a problem.* Whether this

---

* The Thai government's Prime Minister, Khukrit Pramot, had already formally asked the U.S. to withdraw the forces based in Thailand during the IndoChinese war, including the B-52 bombers from Sattahip and all the fighters from bases at Udorn, Ubon, Korat, and Nakon Phanom, which was being done. The last 23,000 U.S. forces were out of Thailand by march 1976.

desire for the removal of U.S. military will progress to a general feeling of anti-Americanism remains to be seen. However, let me assure you that if anti-Americanism becomes a reality, any harassment will be verbal and there will be no physical danger to any of us. The Thai are basically a peaceful, friendly people and have no desire to endanger their neutrality.

"A bit more on the plight of refugees.... The other day I met the Vietnamese wife of one of the DEA agents stationed in Saigon, who had just arrived from Saigon with her little boy. Tho must be about 23 years old. Very pretty and petite. Tho is a well-educated girl from a well-to-do family. She knew she could get out of Saigon for she had a valid U.S. passport, but she and her husband wanted to bring out her two younger sisters and a brother, who had been living with them. As the children were not legal dependents they were denied exit visas. On the advice of a Vietnamese lawyer, friend of her family, this is what she did. She dressed herself up as a 35-year-old matron (her words), borrowed a dark gray dress, high heels, much makeup, hair styled up high, glasses; had one of her sisters, a 14-year-old, borrow a young school girl's outfit of blue pleated skirt, white blouse, white socks, hair in pigtails.

"Tho then took them all to the court where they issue birth certificates. At the court she gave a rehearsed speech to the effect that these were her three children and she now wanted birth certificates for them. When asked why she never applied before, she said she was uneducated, couldn't read, and just learned how to get the certificates. When asked about the father, she said the children were illegitimate and he had abandoned her. While she told us this story she got nervous all over again at the enormity of what she had done, for had they suspected her she could have been put in jail. Out of desperation she managed to carry off her masquerade, and received the certificates. Now, you see, her American husband was in a position to go to another agency and adopt the 'illegitimate children' of his legal wife. What a story. We were still having coffee at another friend's house when Tho finished her story. Just then her husband phoned to say he had successfully gotten the sisters and brother out of Saigon, and was even now about to go to Guam with them where he could obtain U.S. passports and bring the children to Bangkok to join her and their son. The look of joy and relief on her face was more than enough to make us all misty eyed."

* * *

In the aftermath of America's withdrawal from South Vietnam and North Vietnamese occupation of that country, the United States had to readjust its political and military strategy. Communist forces were dominant now: the Russians supported the Pathet Lao in Laos; the Mainland Chinese propped up the Khmer Rouge government in Cambodia, now called Kampuchea; and the North Vietnamese dominated Vietnam. Despite our reverses, the United States remained the richest nation in the world but with an increasing debt. The cost of our Guns and Butter activities was an estimated $200 billion for the failed venture in South Vietnam and for a host of Great Society programs (many of them worthwhile) that had been bulldozed through Congress by the arm-twisting might of Lyndon Johnson.

In spite of huge deficits, the strength of the American market still meant the difference between economic well-being and stagnation in America and those nations with whom we did business. In short, considerable leverage still remained in the hands of Washington, if used wisely and less wastefully. America was forced to accept that it could not be the policeman for the world and should have stayed out of Vietnam entirely and instead used its tremendous economic leverage to achieve strategic and political goals. The United States did what it should have done earlier and declared an economic embargo on doing business with Vietnam, instructed its citizens to stay out of that country, and treated Vietnam as it had treated Fidel Castro's Cuba since the mid-1950s.

* * *

The Time of My Life

During a muggy, overcast night on the 20th of August, Phyl and I drove to Don Muang to meet the midnight Pan Am flight from Honolulu bearing Jerry and Donna Nunemaker and their three children. Jerry, a retired Air Force military analyst, was very qualified and a most welcome addition to our intelligence staff. Tom Becker was especially delighted to have someone to help him. It was not long before pleasantly helpful and always reliable Jerry Nunemaker was settled in busily helping us analyze and track the activities of our area's nefarious narcotics traffickers.

* * *

Birthdays came around again: Bill's 16th was on August 1, and Ken's big day was on the 22nd, as he officially became a teenager. In a cryptic letter to his grandparents, Bill says it all:

"Dear KC and Ebby, Thank you for the $10 check. I'm trying to save up for something so every little bit helps.

"We registered for school yesterday, something which is never fun. When is Cyndy expecting her baby? [Michael Toale was born August 23, but the word had not arrived in Bangkok from Cyndy.]

"I find summer vacation very boring, being that all my friends are on home leave. Because of that there isn't much to write about. I hope you are feeling well, and I'm thinking of one year from now when we will all be back together again. After living in Thailand three years this place is getting a little boring!! Love, Bill"

* * *

The rains fell all during August and into the fall months, and the klongs and main rivers overflowed their banks. Schools were shut down sporadically all around Bangkok for some weeks because of poor road conditions. The International School of Bangkok students did not mind and got most of their work done. Phyl wrote home in early November:

"On the 8th of November, Adie and I went to the Marine Ball. It was the 200th year anniversary of the U.S. Marine Corps and they had a great party at the Indra Hotel, one of the posh newer ones in town. There were cocktails, dinner and dancing. All great fun. [Phyllis never met a party she didn't like.] I made a dress of gold brocade I had bought in the Philippines. It turned out rather well, at least Adie liked it. He was resplendent in a maroon dinner jacket with all the frou-frou. It was the night of flooded streets and the area around the Indra was one of the worse hit places. We had a ride to the Ball with the Beckers whose driver was brave enough to take us. The Marines provided buses from the Embassy and the Fifth Field Hospital for those who didn't want to drive. It really would have been impossible to make it in your own car, for all the parking spaces were several feet under water.

"There are no new crises to report. There seems to be sporadic shooting on the Mekong River near Vientiane along the Thai border, but I hope it is just some trigger-happy river patrols, and that the Pathet Lao are not really trying to stir up trouble, at least let's hope that if they do want trouble they will wait until we get out of town."

THE YEAR ENDS

Before we knew it, 1975 was drawing to a close. Phyl wrapped it up in her letter of December 29 to her parents:

"Dear Mother and Dad, the box of Xmas candy and slivered almonds was greatly appreciated by all. . . . The new Atlas travel book from the National Geographic is on its way, and the Miles Kimball box arrived. I wrapped the 'Got-A-Minute' word game for Adie and we have all enjoyed it, except I always win so they don't like that too much. I haven't tried the 'Save your Curls' sleep cap yet, but will when I have something worth saving. Bill got the silly can of peanuts, and Ken the woolie spider. It is very cute. Thanks so much.

"We did have a nice Christmas with a mad-huge pile of packages, but the boys' tastes are becoming just too expensive these days. Our house looked lovely, the weather nice and crispy, so much so that Adrian and I played tennis, while the boys went ICE SKATING. Yes. One of the local bowling alleys converted to a rink. Quite marvelous. Bill and Ken have blisters the size of quarters, as they have been skating every day. Today we sent off an order to Sears for ice-skates. It seems so ridiculous to go ice skating in Thailand but we figured if they really like it they better have skates that fit and not the rental kind. Besides we hope to go back to Virginia, and they can skate there.

"Christmas afternoon, we asked in about nine couples, the younger DEA guys who were having their first Christmas overseas. It was a very pleasant and warm party. . . . For New Year's eve we have invited the Addario family here. He is the DEA boss and we'll have a quiet evening here with them. [They have three boys who are pals of our boys.] I think Dan and Joy relax more with us than with anyone else. Cyndy wrote that Tom was having a ball in Pennsylvania [where he had gone to spend the holidays with his friend the Pittsburgh golfer.] I'm so glad he has learned how to have fun. On our re-assignment, Washington seems to be the front runner at the moment. Actually, it is the most logical place for us to go for Adrian's experience here is more valuable in Headquarters.

"As soon as the Christmas tree is put away, I will start cleaning and heaving out in preparation for another great move. Very exciting even if it is six months away. I know how fast the last six months can disappear. So my darlings, that's all for now, and thanks again for everything.

"Oh yes, the red seal on the envelope is my name in Chinese, called a Chop. It was made by a beautiful little marble hand-held stamp with a temple dog on top and a raised seal on the bottom. Adrian has one too. They were Christmas gifts obtained by a Chinese-American friend who lives in Hong Kong who had them made for us. With love and best wishes for the New Year. Phyl"

TWENTY ONE

Intelligence Operations

I n February of our fourth year in Bangkok, a bulletin from Head-quarters announced an intelligence supervisory position opening in El Paso, Texas, the home of DEA's El Paso Intelligence Center (EPIC). Personnel in grades GS-13 or GS-14 with intelligence or criminal investigative experience were invited to apply. I was not particularly interested in going to El Paso, but more important, the announcement meant that my current position had been upgraded to a GS-14. With more than six years as a GS-13, I was more than ready for a promotion.

I asked John Doyle, our Deputy Regional Director, to review my performance as the Bangkok Regional Intelligence Chief over the past three years and consider recommending me for promotion, which he was happy to do. Regional Director Addario also approved the recommendation and sent it to Headquarters for action.

Nothing moved quickly in DEA Headquarters. Memorandums and cables were sent from Bangkok urging action, but nothing happened. With time growing short, our Administrative Officer, Eddie Berkowitz, suggested that I contact the Civil Service's classifi-cation appeals board. According to a seldom-used regulation, the Civil Service had the power to decide the merits of my appeal, and their decision would be binding. With nothing to lose and knowing that I clearly qualified for an upgrade, I filed an appeal with the Civil Service in May. I truly had begun to despair that DEA's personnel office would ever reach a decision. I reminded myself of the agoniz-ing months of delay when I made a simple transfer in 1972 to BNDD from the CIA. Some things never change.

I think a lot of the stalling was because of the influence of old FBNers. Their old boy network zealously guarded against newcomers no matter how qualified or deserving. One of the FBN cliques was called the "purple gang"; its members supported the unwritten code that all enforcement agents with narcotics undercover experience were entitled to one grade higher than intelligence officers, analysts, or compliance investigators who worked in other disciplines. The FBNers seemed to regard former FBI agents and CIA officers as outsiders, which baffled me, for I thought we were all in the service of Uncle Sam. Because of the rapid expansion of the DEA, there were a variety of newcomers from BNDD, the FBI, the CIA, and the Immigration and Customs services intruding into what had been almost exclusively FBN turf. We newcomers had not paid the same dues that most of the hardy FBN breed had paid. Being one of the newcomers was hard to take, but take it I did for the good of the service and for my family.

A new chief of Intelligence for DEA was being selected from a number of outsiders. The leading candidate was William Gordon Fink, a bright, ex-navy officer from the National Security Agency. When it was apparent that Gordon would be selected as the new Chief (a supergrade slot requiring approval of Congress, which was granted), a young, articulate, and bright FBN palace guard reportedly asked whether Gordon was trainable.

* * *

By June, Headquarters sought to bargain my promotion for reassignment orders. Stalling my promotion, Acting Chief of Intelligence, Phil Smith (one of the purple gang), asked if I would transfer to Philadelphia as a GS-14 to run the intelligence unit, a tacit admission that I was entitled to the grade of GS-14. If that was not acceptable, he asked if I would take a senior analyst slot in Headquarters at the GS-13 level with a chance for promotion later.

I thought the idea of working in Philadelphia was not all that bad, but Phyl put her foot down. She pointed out that we had a perfectly good house in Vienna, all our belongings and our friends and neighbors were there, and the boys should go back to school in

Vienna. Phyllis did not think it would be good for us to go to Philadelphia and wondered what "those clowns in Washington were thinking about." Of course, she was right. I cabled Washington and said that while I very much wanted to return to Headquarters, I did not want to confuse the issue of reassignment until the promotion question had been resolved and was prepared to stay in Bangkok until it was addressed.

On July 17, 1975, Phyllis wrote home with the good news that I had received confirmation of my promotion to GS-14 retroactive to February. The gain was made at some cost, however, I finally had been promoted but had offered to revert to my intelligence analyst status, which meant giving up the 25-percent overtime pay that enforcement agents all receive. On the other hand, the possibility of having to retire at age fifty now did not apply. I was already fifty-four years old and worried that as an enforcement officer I could have been asked to retire.

INTELLIGENCE SUMMARY

Our Bangkok unit prepared a summary report of our intelligence activities and sent it to Phillip R. Smith, Acting Chief of Intelligence in Washington, over the signature of Daniel Addario, Regional Director, on April 26, 1976. Originally stamped as confidential, this material was declassified in 1982.

The following portions of this report illustrate the scope of our region's intelligence activity:

"At an East Asia Narcotics Conference held last spring at Kuala Lumpur, William Gallegher, State Department Narcotics Coordinator, and John Kennedy, Special Assistant on Narcotics at CIA Headquarters, expressed interest in the intelligence operations being conducted in Bangkok's Region 16 and expressed concern for the need for greater coordination on operational matters. [This was an understatement, for the DEA still did not put much trust in the State Department's narcotics experts or the CIA people. I hoped by this memorandum to brief DEA more fully as well as show State and the CIA how productive and helpful our fledgling regional intelligence unit had been in support of narcotics enforcement work.]

"DEA intelligence probes, which often employ ethnic Chinese informants who can penetrate the Chinese-dominated narcotics trafficking organization in the Far East, are proving to be effective. Current operations which employ ethnic Chinese informants are Operations LOTUS, NORD, GARNET, CAYENNE and MARJORAM.

"Operation LOTUS began in November 1974 to identify the persons, organizations, routes, and communications techniques used by narcotics networks supplying heroin to Europe and possibly to North America from Southeast Asia. Specifically, the operation was targeted against Tran Van Ninh, a Bangkok-based trafficker, using a Cooperating Individual [CI] from Vientiane, Laos, who was acquainted with Tran Van Ninh. The CI was managed most of the time by a DEA intelligence trained officer working out of Hong Kong and Bangkok.

"Tran Van Ninh was arrested in Paris in July, 1975, while smuggling six kilograms of heroin. He was sentenced to three years in jail. Numerous other members of his organization were also identified including a group of six females who routinely travelled into Paris from Hong Kong by way of Seoul, Korea. They, too, were arrested in Paris.

"Operation LOTUS required continual close cooperation between three DEA Regional offices, [Paris, Bangkok and Manila] and good liaison with the British Hong Kong Narcotics Bureau and the French Central Narcotics Bureau.

"Operation ACORN began in the fall of 1974 to collect intelligence on illegal sea shipments of raw opium and morphine base from Thailand to Southern Malaysia and Hong Kong hidden on Thai fishing trawlers. The delivery of opiates to distant buyers by Thai trawlers had been a traditional method of shipping opium throughout southeast Asia. By 1975, ACORN had helped identify and seize at least two of these trawlers and other seizures in Hong Kong." Our intelligence unit analyzed files back to 1971 and 1972, from which Tom Becker was able to define a number of smuggling personalities, networks, and related modus operandi. This material was forwarded to narcotics police counterparts in Burma, Hong Kong, Singapore, and Malaysia.

"Operation GARNET began in early 1975 to collect intelligence on narcotics being concealed aboard steel-hulled passenger or freight vessels bound for Europe, the Far East and U.S. ports."

Our idea was to seek out and recruit officers or seamen on ships that made regular calls at Bangkok or other regional ports. When recruited and trained, these ships' personnel were given DEA contacts along their route should they want to make a narcotics report. Drug searches then could be made by local harbor police or customs officials, with any dope found seized and our informant's identity protected.

In connection with this program, we also produced a drug identification book with color photographs illustrating the kinds of drugs most often smuggled and indicating some of the places that drugs had been hidden, such as in air-conditioning ducts or behind cabin wall panels. The guidebook, entitled *The Ship Captain's Guide to Drug Smuggling*, was printed in Bangkok. Hundreds of copies were distributed to DEA narcotics liaison contacts for delivery to cooperating ships' personnel. And finally, the report states:

"Operation CAYENNE was a joint program between the DEA and CIA in northern Thailand which provided Ne Win's Burmese military forces with information on heroin laboratories on the Burma side of the Thai-Burma border. Information obtained through this channel was used to help his armed forces destroy heroin factories. Best of all, the general public remained unaware of any American involvement." This is the hallmark of any good intelligence program, since any attribution or publicity would have meant shutting down the operation.

* * *

DEA leaders in Washington and Bangkok were delighted with the destruction of heroin laboratories by the Burmese military, thanks in part to the work of CAYENNE. Our goal was to eliminate heroin laboratories and thereby halt the production of heroin at its source and prevent its flow into international markets. It was a lot easier said than done, but there were some successes.

The Rangoon press reported the following:

"The 88th Light Infantry Division of the Burmese Army made an assault on a heroin refinery at Na Mun village in northern Burma at 11:30 A.M., April 26, 1976. Burmese troops fought fiercely against an armed force defending the factory and finally captured the camp and the laboratory by 6 P.M. the same day. The enemy fled in disorder across the border into Thailand, leaving nine dead behind. Burmese Troops captured 30 pounds of almost pure heroin, 288 pounds of raw opium, 440 gallons of opium still in a heavy solution, over 2,000 pounds of partially burned opium abandoned by the defenders, drums of chemicals sufficient to keep the heroin factory churning out heroin for weeks; and armaments that included 4 recoilless rifles, 5 rocket launchers, several light machine guns, 4 grenade launchers, 24 carbines, 3 revolvers, 1 pistol and many rounds of ammunition for all these weapons."

* * *

On May 17, Dan Addario and I met with the Burmese narcotics people in Rangoon. These liaison trips were used to help persuade the Burmese that a permanent DEA agent assigned to Rangoon would be in their best interest. The Burmese were being cautious, fearful that adding another American to the Embassy would obligate them to permit Russia and China the same courtesy. We were making progress, however.

Staying at an attractive hotel beside Lake Inya near town, I learned that the hotel had been funded and constructed through the Russian equivalent of our American USAID program. It was spacious and fairly modern in appearance. I was particularly impressed by the size of the Russian-made bathroom fixtures, especially the commode. It was commanding and regal in size, truly thronelike, and on a little dais several inches off the floor. The seat was so wide that you were in danger of falling through. I wondered how the tiny Burmese people, who were about one-third the size of an average Russian, could possibly use these facilities without getting wet. Perhaps the Russians were trying to impress the Burmese by the physical size of their people.

This visit to Rangoon included talks with newly assigned Ambassador David Osborne, whom I had last seen when he was Consul

General in Hong Kong. Addario and I enjoyed a quiet dinner at the Ambassador's residence one evening. In attendance were five Americans and five Burmese. Two of the Burmese men were former high-ranking officials, both of whom had served six-year prison terms when Ne Win overthrew the government in 1962. One scholarly gentlemen explained that when the Japanese occupied Burma during World War II the Thai government was given administrative control over the Shan State area near the northern Thai border. The people in that area considered themselves to be Thai because their language was similar to Thai and they physically resembled the Thai people. Many of them said they were not Burmese in any way. Prior to 1959, when opium production was outlawed by the Thais, opium cultivated in the Shan hills had been the basic cash crop. No satisfactory substitute crop had been fully implemented since then. These insights helped me understand how opium cultivation had become so deeply imbedded in the area and why it remained so difficult to change.

One afternoon, Addario and I were taken by our Embassy guide to a quiet residential neighborhood where we met a black market gem merchant displaying his goods on a gunny sack by an unpaved side road. We glanced around to make sure that no Burmese police were watching before we squatted down to finger through the sparkling jumble of necklaces and rough stones. There were hundreds of beautiful pieces of jadeite, the gem-quality silicate often called imperial jade, in an array of appealing colors: white, emerald green, apple green, pinks, red, yellow, and even black. Our escort explained that jadeite was fairly rare and came from rocks that had been subjected to high pressure deep below the earth's surface and then uplifted nearer the surface where they were exposed by ages of erosion.

Dan and I bought several jade necklaces for Joy (Dan's wife), Phyllis, and Cyndy. I then spied one flat, circular piece of apple-green jade streaked with darker gray-green patches. It was polished on one side, flat on the other, and about an inch in diameter. I bought it for the equivalent of five or six dollars and gave it to Phyl, who had her jeweler in Bangkok mount it with a gold rim to wear as a pendant. It was now transformed into a gorgeous adornment that subtly complimented her beautiful blue-green eyes. Phyl loved wearing her jade pendant because it went so well with the simple, rather austere bracelet of heavy, twisted gold from Laos. When we returned to Virginia, these two pieces often were the subject of conversation when Phyllis, who loved to entertain an audience, would tell the story of where each piece originated. She loved to unwrap the twisted gold bracelet from her arm, drop it into the hand of one of the ladies in the group, and enjoy the gasp of surprise caused by the weight of the gold.

* * *

In the morning, Dan and I gathered in the Embassy conference room with other staff where we learned that the Burmese military were aggressively patrolling their side of the Thai border in the Lao Lo Chai area near the Salween River. This had always been an area of insurgency strife and was the headwaters for opium caravans to the south. The Burmese were continuing to pursue their ancient foe, Chang Chi Fu, the longtime leader of the Shan State insurgents whose opium caravans had been trying to reach the Thai border for the past three weeks. Chang's caravans had been hit three times, but not destroyed. This information was interesting but not surprising, since Chang had always been an illusive and wily foe. His Shan United Army (SUA) constantly was agitating for control of the Shan State and supported their guerilla efforts through the sale of opium produced from the poppy bulb that grew so well in the Shan hills. Chang had been captured last year and imprisoned in Rangoon but wasted no time in returning to his old ways when he was released in exchange for two Russians that the SUA had captured.

Historically, political conditions in the remote, sparsely populated and heavily forested areas of northern Burma had been uneasy since the British colonial period in 1885-1948. About a quarter of Burma's more than 40 million people live in these remote highlands: the Shan people on the Shan Plateau north and east of the Salween River, the Kachin tribal groups in the upper Irrawaddy Valley and the Kumon Range north to the Chinese border, and the Chin tribes in the Chin Hills to the west bordering India. More than 100 indigenous languages are spoken in Burma, but Burmese is the official language. Luckily for Americans, a rudimentary knowledge of English was required in their schools and colleges.

* * *

Southeast Asia remained much in the news as the war in Vietnam wound down, and efforts to control the flow of heroin from the Golden Triangle continued. *Newsweek* magazine printed a prominent article on the cause and effect of opium trafficking in which it named some of the principal players in northeastern Burma during the autumn of 1976. I was asked to brief Conn Daugherty, DEA's public relations chief, and Ed Clark of *Newsweek*. Below are excerpts from a paper I prepared to help them better understand the situation and the key players in the border areas between Burma and Thailand.

THE OPIUM TRAFFICKERS

"General LI Wen-Huan, head of the Chinese Irregular Forces (CIF), and General TUAN Hsi-Wen are former commanders of the old Kuomintang (KMT), the former 93rd Division of the non-Communist Chinese Army which fought with the Allies in Burma during World War II. After the war, these commanders and their troops elected to remain in their old operational area along the Thailand-Burma-Chinese border. They gave up their claim to citizenship in Nationalist China, now confined to the Island of Taiwan, in exchange for permission to live in northern Thailand, a condition which the Thai government granted.

"Many of these ex-Chinese troops intermarried with Thai villagers or hill tribe girls in their areas. The Thai Government was happy enough about all of this for they could use the CIF as a buffer between themselves and their common enemy, Mao Tse-tung's communist China to the north. The Thai government even offered land and citizenship to any of the CIF forces in return for their pledge of loyalty and continued service in the north.

"Both LI and TUAN, along with CHANG Chi-Fu, head of the Shan United Army (SUA), plus other lesser tribal leaders of the

Kokang and Kachin tribes, have been involved to one degree or another in the opium business—the main source of their income. Of these traffickers, General LI is currently rated as being very active. He professes to have quit the business and to have ordered his troops not to touch opium, but old habits are hard to break. Field reports provide overwhelming evidence that he is in fact still very busy. He is reported to be one of the chief suppliers to Lu Hsu-shui, a Bangkok-based distribution chief. LI's activities have been documented in the Thai press, and he has talked with Congressman Lester Wolff, Democrat, N.Y., [who was and still is a very vocal and active anti-narcotics member of Congress who often visited the Far East and loves to twit the noses of the Administration]. LI is very close to the leaders of the Thai Government who need LI's forces as a buffer along the border. LI has a home in Bangkok and tells visitors his troops on the border earn their money by jade mining in the hills. Sometimes he says they make their living as farmers. He has a son away at college in the United States. This man is a survivor.

"General TUAN, who also has a home in Bangkok, appears to live quite simply and states he is not in the business. Our reports tend to substantiate his position, for he is of advanced years and not in good health. Nevertheless, he has long been a key figure in the cooperative effort of the Thai Government and the ex-KMT leaders against the threat of Communist China. [General TUAN died sometime after this briefing was prepared. His troops were taken over by General LI Wen-Huan whose strength was increased.]

"CHANG Chi-Fu, a former prisoner of the Burmese, released last year in exchange for two Russians who had been captured in SUA territory, says he is not now in the business, but his SUA forces are very busy. CHANG is currently rated as the most notorious of all area traffickers, and is apparently making up for all the time he spent in jail in Rangoon.

"The Thai Government obviously has put their highest priority on national survival and are mindful of the threat of insurgency in the border areas. They have been working closely with the Chinese irregular forces for years. This relationship is not likely to change because both share a common interest in keeping communist China beyond their borders. Officially, and with obvious good intentions, the King of Thailand has issued orders against any involvement in narcotics trafficking, but orders from the top often have a way of not being completely enforced at the working level where it is a reality of life that opium trafficking is the one sure means by which Chinese irregular forces can acquire guns and ammunition, food and shelter, and other basic necessities.

"The opium business shows no sign of going away despite constant narcotics suppression efforts of the Thai government and the Drug Enforcement Administration. We must continue to support crop substitution programs as well as rehabilitation and educational efforts designed to reduce demand for drugs among the Thai young people. . . ."

On March 14, 1988, U.S. Attorney General Dick Thornburgh held a press conference at the Justice Department in Washington to announce the indictment of Khun Sa (another name for Chang Chi-Fu) for trafficking heroin in New York. The odds of his capture on the charges filed in Brooklyn, NY, were desperately long, but at least he had been put on official notice for his international trafficking. DEA's investigations over the previous years had documented that the notorious warlord had transformed production of heroin into the chief commodity of his massive criminal kingdom. He had loyal troops to protect him (approximately 4,000), farmers to work for him, and Western addicts eager for the white powder he refined at some 12 crude laboratories scattered along the Thai-Burmese border. Even more disheartening was that opium production in Burma, estimated to be 600 tons in the early 1980s, was expected to reach nearly 2,500 tons within the next ten years. DEA agents estimated that Chang Chi-Fu supplied 60 percent of the Asian heroin reaching the United States.

In February 1989, workers on Bangkok's rainy Klong Toey dock saw some milky goo seeping from bundles of raw strips of rubber piled on the pier. Upon examining the 200 bundles, 2,389 pounds of heroin worth $1 billion were discovered, the world's largest heroin seizure. Chang's shipment was consigned to Amarin Imports, Inc., in Queens, where it was to be distributed from parking lots of local fast-food chains.

* * *

While in Rangoon that May, Addario and I learned that the laboratories identified in the April 26 raid were no longer working, thanks largely to the DEA's precise and timely advice. The Burmese were gracious enough to thank the DEA unofficially and personally for lending assistance. There was a slight yet definite improvement in diplomatic relations with Colonel Aung Htay, the Director of Defense Services Intelligence, Ministry of Defense; things were starting to look up.

In a follow-up meeting, which no Burmese attended, I described some other areas where refinery activity was being watched, specifically an area with five refineries on the Burmese side of the border. As before, the DEA intended to pass current intelligence through our Rangoon channels to the Burmese narcotics people. One big problem was that the monsoon rains were just beginning in the north. The first sprinkles of what would amount to 200 inches (15 feet) of rain between now and October were starting to fall. All military operations soon would be reduced to bare minimums until November. This was poor timing for us, as the Burmese just were beginning to accept and respond to the intelligence leads we could provide. I consoled myself that now we had more time to get our act together. My time was running out, however, and someone else would have to pick up the ball and run with it.

* * *

The following State Department report in the travel section of the *Sarasota Herald Tribune* on Sunday, August 23, 1992, indicated that little had changed in Burma:

"U.S. citizens traveling to Burma should defer all travel to the highland areas [such as Mandalay or Pagan] and exercise extreme caution in the rest of the country. Occasional political unrest and insurgent activity in the highland regions continue, while unrest in the delta area [near the capitol of Rangoon] has abated. Air travel within Burma is not safe, and U.S. citizens are urged to avoid all

travel on Myanmar Airways. All tourist travel must be approved by the Burmese government, but this can be arranged through private travel agencies."

Reading this article reminded me of being at the airport in Rangoon where older men and young teenage boys fought with their fists, snarling like dogs over a bone, to carry our luggage from customs to the passenger lounge because of a shortage of jobs. I still can see the raggedly dressed teenage mother with a child slung on hip in a crowded market pinching me on the fanny to get my attention. Dan Addario said that all the beggars would be after me if I gave her any money. I could neither resist those imploring eyes, nor ignore the hard pinch that stung with reality and slipped her a kyat note. Sure enough, the word spread like gossip at a cocktail party, and I was beseiged by a horde of beggars. I took Dan's advice and turned my back, ignoring my feelings of pity and guilt, and took a few more sharp pinches without flinching before the crowd fell away.

* * *

There have been a few changes since my last visit to Burma in 1976. On the plus side, DEA has had an agent assigned to Rangoon since the late 1970s. More important, Ne Win abdicated in 1987, following waves of anti-government demonstrations. On the down side, the country was led briefly by two civilians until a military junta lead by General Saw Maung, an old associate of Ne Win, seized power in September 1988. The new military dictator ordered his troops to shoot or imprison hundreds of peaceful demonstrators. A new wave of protest in the summer of 1989 resulted in the jailing of more high-ranking opposition leaders, including my old friend from the John Ingersoll visit, U Tin Oo, former Chief of Intelligence.

As a sop to quiet smoldering resistance, Burma's name was changed to Myanmar in 1989. The new name, The Union of Myanmar, was chosen to show that the country is made up of various ethnic groups, not just the ethnic Burmese who reside around Rangoon and in the lower Irrawaddy River basin. Even the name Rangoon was changed to Yangon. Despite this window dressing, insurgency forces led by the

Adrian Swain

Shan State people, one of the largest of about twelve ethnic groups, continue to struggle for autonomy in the Shan hills to the north.*

AGENT RECRUITMENT

During this time, DEA and the CIA agreed to join forces and recruit an agent. Our prospect was an ethnic Chinese-Thai citizen who had been spotted and assessed by Terry Baldwin as a possible candidate for recruitment. He was the younger brother of a man who worked for Lu Hsu-shui, one of the more active traffickers in the Chiang Mai area. Our new man seemed extremely well positioned to elicit intelligence on Lu's narcotics business and the movement of troops and other insurgency personnel in the area. The CIA and DEA were equally interested in recruiting this new man and willing to share the intelligence take: DEA would get all narcotics leads, and the CIA would get all insurgency information. Since I was a former CIA officer, the CIA agreed to work with the DEA in making the recruitment approach.

None of our DEA agents spoke Chinese very well, so the CIA agreed to provide a Chinese-speaking officer to travel with me and make the recruitment pitch. If all went well, the new agent then would be introduced to me and advised that henceforth all debriefings would be with me in Bangkok. If the recruitment failed, no harm would be done because the recruiting officer was a stranger from out of town and would never surface in Chiang Mai.

On the day set for the attempt, George (the CIA officer) and I flew to Chiang Mai and took separate rooms in the quiet but clean Thai Railways Hotel to hole up until nightfall. For the job at hand,

---

* The origin of political anarchy goes back to the Colonial era when the minority peoples of Burma were persuaded by the British in 1948 to join the independent union of Burma on the condition that they could leave the union within 10 years if they wished. The Rangoon government, dominated by a majority of Burmese people, backed out of the agreement. Ne Win then seized power in 1962 and tore up the constitution. He also locked up the leaders of the Shan State, who were in Rangoon negotiating a political compromise. Ne Win and his military successors have never been able to extend their power completely over the minorities, who continue to remain in rebellion. (H.D.S. Greenway, *Hong Kong Standard*, Sunday, May 23, 1976.)

George wore a false mustache and a wig that made him look ten years older. I was my usual worried-looking self. It was quite dark when Terry Baldwin picked us up outside the hotel. We climbed into his dusty Ford Bronco, a common vehicle in the area, and took a round-about way along darkened streets to a quiet, residential part of town. Our prospective informant was expecting us in his modest bungalow barely visible from the driveway. Terry pulled in and parked, and he and George went to the door and were admitted. I waited for about fifteen minutes, when Terry came out and told me to come in and that everything was fine.

We christened our new agent Leong. He was a stolid, well-fed man about forty years old and was smoking with quick, nervous drags that made his cigarette constantly glow red. He and George were chatting in Chinese. Terry introduced us and said that Leong would meet me in Bangkok in a few weeks to deliver written answers to some questions that would be passed to him through a letter drop in Chiang Mai. Leong would report on the plans, intentions, and activities of Lu Hsu-shui, a high-ranking heroin trafficker whose dealings had been under investigation since 1971.

Terry said that Leong's brother was a member of Lu's organiza-tion but Leong himself was not involved in the trafficking. Leong thought he could obtain the information we needed from this older brother. Terry failed to mention that Leong and his elder brother were not on particularly good terms. When Terry said that Leong was something of a playboy with a suspected heroin habit, a warning bell went off in my head. As I considered all of this, I wondered what was going to happen. Heroin had a way of making people do strange things, and I resolved to be very careful with Leong.

A month later, a cable came from Chiang Mai saying that Leong was due in Bangkok next Thursday and would be in room 315 at the Montien Hotel. This was a decent hotel patronized by many tourists as well as servicemen on leave from Vietnam. It was an easy walk to Patpong, the famous block-long street of girlie shows, bars, night-clubs, restaurants, and gift shops, where many ladies of the night plied their trade. I would not be noticeable in the hotel lobby and expected no problems in finding Leong's room, paying his salary, and obtaining his intelligence report.

On the appointed evening, I had my usual two drinks of Scotch with Phyllis before supper. I told her that I had to meet a man on business at the Montien and would be back around 9:30 P.M. I parked my car in the hotel lot, took an empty elevator to the third floor, and knocked on Leong's door, making sure that the hallway was empty. Leong opened the door, and we greeted each other with polite bows and hands together as if in prayer, the courteous form of greeting common throughout Thailand. Our first meeting went well, and Leong was alert and cooperative as we chatted briefly. He handed me a two-page report, I paid him, he signed the receipt, I thanked him for his work, and that was it.

Our next two meetings were repetitions of the first. He would hand over sheets of answers penned in Chinese calligraphy on notebook paper, which were then delivered to George for translation; I also made a copy for Peter Wang to translate later. We asked Leong a few test questions, to which we already knew the answers, to make sure he had a definite pipeline to Lu Hsu-shui. Leong passed this part of his training, which gave us a gauge to assess the accuracy of his future reporting.

Leong's reporting soon began to get spotty and sometimes provided no new information at all. He hinted that his older brother did not seem to trust him or want him around. Leong provided just enough new information to lead us to believe that he might develop into a solid source of intelligence. We continued because we had plenty of money to spend for intelligence that might help destroy Lu's refinery operations or at least help the military intercept one of Lu's shipments.

As in all intelligence collection efforts, the tricky part was to use the information obtained in a manner that it would not blow up in our faces, or specifically in Leong's face, and thus disclose our involvement. We would have to wait and see if Leong could regain the confidence of his brother.

A few meetings later, Leong had his ten-year-old son with him, who had come along to Bangkok to see an eye doctor. Leong seemed embarrassed at this breach of conduct and was jeopardizing himself and disclosing my presence as well. His speech seemed a bit slurred, his movements were lethargic, and he was almost in a daze. He probably had been smoking heroin sprinkled on the end of his cigarette before lighting up. There were no needle marks that way, and the heroin was inhaled directly into his lungs and his bloodstream. I tried to make the best of the situation and remained friendly and polite. Leong finally produced a scrawled report containing only a few paragraphs that he probably dashed off in the hotel room while waiting for me. I obviously could not question him with his son there, so I paid Leong, got his signed receipt, and got out of there. I turned in a contact report of the dismal meeting expressing my opinion that Leong had been smoking heroin and had brought his son along as a cover for his trip to Bangkok and maybe as an excuse for his poor reporting.

Ten days later, a cable from Chiang Mai tersely advised that Leong had been slain by an unidentified assailant who greeted Leong at his door with a single bullet to the head. Terry later surmised that Leong's perfidy had been discovered, probably by his older brother. Leong paid the ultimate price for becoming an informant. We would never know for certain, but for Lu Hsu-shui it was but a casual snap of the fingers to authorize the execution. Assassins were a dime a dozen for this kind of work. The sad truth is that Leong was an addict who willingly took the high risk of informing on his brother to satisfy his heroin needs. I felt sorry for Leong's wife and young son.

Mary Greenly, a Far East analyst in DEA headquarters, summarized Lu Hsu-shui's activities in a Centac Briefing as reported in James Mills' fine book *The Underground Empire:*

"Lu Hsu-shui was first reported [to BNDD] in 1971 when a close associate [of Lu's] told an informant that a 2,000 kilos of opium seized in Kowloon was Lu's. Less than one year after the 1971 report, 2,700 kilos of opium, morphine base and heroin found in a house in Mai Sai. . . .

"On Christmas Eve, in 1973, Thai police arrested Lu's brother-in-law after seizing 13 kilos of heroin in his Chiang Mai home. A few months later, Lu talked to an informant about shipping heroin to the United States [concealed] in spirit houses, which are miniature shrine-like structures."

This was the famous *Pedestal Case* which was handled by a group of New York DEA agents, led by John Coleman. Some 16 pounds of 92 percent pure heroin were found hidden in the base of a five foot tall spirit house in New York. DEA agents, tipped by an informant, traced the spirit house shipment to a customs warehouse, opened it and removed the heroin. Then they waited and watched until the spirit house was claimed from the customs warehouse at the World Trade Center by a Thai named Prasorn. Prasorn paid the duty charges and then asked that the pedestal shrine be delivered to an apartment house at West 110th Street in Manhattan. Upon delivery by DEA agents disguised as delivery personnel in a rental Hertz van, Prasorn was arrested. Prasorn was willing to talk, but he was only a pawn in the deal. He said he was to receive $10,000 upon his return to Bangkok when the spirit house was safely delivered. Of course, Prasorn had never met Lu, and knew nothing incriminating about him.

By 1976, Lu had so much extra cash on hand he bought the Shaw Hotel in San Francisco for one and a half million dollars, while other family members bought several expensive homes in and around San Francisco. Lu was so well connected with the Thai Government that he received the Order of the White Elephant, first class. Additionally, according to CIA sources, he was involved in sensitive international deals—which affected national security concerns—including weapons sales to Taiwan. Such were his legitimate political connections in Bangkok (where as a front he operated the Lang Hong gold shop), that the major source of his huge wealth—narcotics—was never officially tried in criminal courts. Lu Hsu-shui has been able to keep himself isolated from direct criminal actions and thus has kept himself beyond the reach of prosecution for narcotics trafficking. This is the kind of case that frustrates narcotics law enforcement agents overseas.

Another less extreme cause of frustration was the activities of a well-established and disciplined group of former black American servicemen who operated in and out of Bangkok for years. Our files showed that heroin smuggling had been conducted by active duty and retired black servicemen since 1967, coincidental with the build-up of American forces in South Vietnam. One of the focal points for this ring of activity was a soul food restaurant around the corner from our house. The owner was named Robert (not a true name), a retiree married to a Thai woman. DEA investigators decided to monitor all telephone calls into Robert's restaurant through a wiretap that the Thai police authorized for a 30-day period. Paul Brown asked me to help review the tapes. For the next four weeks, I took home countless reels of tape to keep curious office ears from hearing anything and to assure that the chain of evidence would remain untainted should the tapes yield anything incriminating.

Many nights after supper, I would retire to our cool bedroom to listen to tapes and take notes on casual talk about the weather in North Carolina, comments about restaurant supplies, and calls regarding deliveries or inspections by Thai officials. Robert took most of the calls, which were occasionally brief calls from Willie or John or Albert each saying that "he would be coming in on the Wednesday night flight," or "he had arrived okay," or that the "thing" had been delivered, there "were no problems," or "everything is cool at this end." Full names were not mentioned, but after a while I recognized the voices of some regular callers. Although there was no mention of illicit activity in what I transcribed, I reported the highlights in notes to Paul Brown. It was not surprising that we found nothing incriminating because Robert often cautioned callers not to talk too long on the telephone saying "it was not private." Robert knew better than to connect his business with narcotics trafficking, because it could get him kicked out of the country at the very least or, more than likely, result in a brutal sentence in a Thai jail.

As far as I know, Robert never was accused of smuggling, although his restaurant was a perfect cover for running such an operation, located in the middle of the supply stream of heroin from the north, and had ready access to both military and commercial air transportation from nearby bustling Don Muang airport. Although Robert never may have been found guilty of smuggling narcotics from Bangkok, other former servicemen from the North Carolina area were arrested for heroin smuggling aboard military evacuation flights from Saigon to Washington, DC, flights that landed at Andrews Field just off the beltway in Washington. This loosely knit group of black servicemen smuggled more than 1,000 pounds of heroin into the United States in baggage being shipped by returning servicemen from Vietnam, in household shipments, or in packages mailed via the U.S. postal system.

Some heroin deliveries were bizarre if not outright ghoulish. Caskets sometimes contained packages of pure heroin concealed inside body cavities of cadavers that were recovered in the States by members of the smuggling ring at the receiving post. It was a pretty sick way to make a living and proved once again that some people will do anything to make money. By the end of 1975, as the war in South Vietnam dragged to a halt, the heavy volume of military flights, many with caches of narcotics secreted aboard, slowed to a trickle and finally stopped. Thank the Lord and President Nixon.

The technique of smuggling dope in body cavities reminds me of an equally bizarre smuggling technique that U.S. Customs inspectors encountered some years later at the Miami International Airport. Young to middle-aged men and women from cocaine-producing countries in South America were recruited as couriers to smuggle cocaine into the United States. These couriers were paid a few thousand dollars, provided a round-trip ticket to Miami, and given the name of a contact in Miami who would meet them at the airport. These poor, uneducated, and extremely gullible souls were prepared to do most anything for cash, including filling their stomachs with condoms that contained an ounce or two of pure cocaine. Reassured that the condoms were safe and that Customs inspectors at Miami would never detain them, great numbers of these swallowers, as they soon were named, began to arrive in Miami aboard a variety of commercial flights. Once safely past Customs, the swallowers were taken to a nearby hotel to wait until the cocaine was recovered, apparently none the worse for the wear and tear of travel through the labyrinth of various intestinal tracts. It was soon ready for distribution to an unsuspecting but eager clientele of cocaine sniffers throughout Miami and points beyond. Their work finished, the swallowers returned home. This scheme seemed to be foolproof until Miami hospital emergency rooms began reporting a rash of deaths caused by cocaine poisoning. Subsequent autopsy reports showed that the condoms had ruptured inside the victims' stomachs and intestines. It was not uncommon to find 25 or 30 condoms inside victims. Death by an overdose of cocaine in the blood stream is swift and unpleasant.

Alerted by these gruesome findings, U.S. Customs and DEA agents began to x-ray people they detained who fit the profile of the swallower. Although the x-ray procedure has deterred swallowers, the practice has not stopped completely. There also are new variations that demonstrate the fertility of the smuggler's mind. A press release from Bogota, Colombia, in October 1992, noted the arrest of a woman attempting to fly to Miami, who was detained because of her unusual profile. Upon examination, it was found that her disproportionately large buttocks had been surgically implanted with eight bags containing one pound of heroin. A graphic report on Colombian television showed parts of the operation in which the heroin was removed. This is a world in which truth is often stranger than fiction.

* * *

Some of my memories about our four years in Bangkok relate to our family and the care and attention that Phyllis provided us. Our home, for example, always was made comfortable, inviting, and attractive and the house on Soi 47 was particularly memorable for the bougainvillea that formed a glorious umbrella of white and pink blooms above the porch. I remember the cool, gray terrazzo floor partially covered with straw-colored squares of sisal sewn together. Ceiling fans in each room kept a breeze stirring. Souli and Soontorn were always helpful, smiling, and pleasant. Their quarters were just outside our kitchen door, and Ken would often eat there with his second family and little friend Mou. That is where Ken learned to love Thai food, even the red-hot peppers that cause your eyes to tear and beads of sweat to pop from your forehead.

After supper on Sunday evenings, we would read or enjoy the random presentations of Thai television programs, some of which were good and others quite bad. Ken loved to watch the Thai kickboxing matches, which were similar to boxing matches in the States except that Thai fighters bound their bare feet with layers of adhesive tape, leaving the toes free and bare to grip the ring mat. Thus prepared, their feet firm and rock-hard, the fighters were ready to strike slashing kicks at their opponent's torso or head. Thai boxers seemed to concentrate on trying to crack rib cages with sweeping kicks or knock the wind out of their opponent with a knee or toe to the stomach. Failing these kicks, they would try to trip the other guy by knocking his feet out from under him. Blows with the gloved hands were secondary; it was the kick that counted. Now and then, one of the fighters would whirl around with a sweeping backward swipe of his heel at the head of his opponent. These were mostly razzle-dazzle kicks to show off and seldom landed on target.

I preferred listening to a British or Irish vocalist named Val Dooni-gan, who had a mellow voice that was sort of a cross between Bing Crosby and Roger Whittaker, the Australian-born balladeer. Phyllis and I also liked to watch the Dean Martin show on Sunday nights to see Dean sitting on his baby grand piano, played by his friend Ken, and singing old favorites like "Everybody loves somebody some-time." Dean had an unfortunate habit of holding a cigarette while singing, which distressed me, but then Frank Sinatra, Sammy Davis Jr., and other members of the Hollywood rat pack did the same; poor Sammy Davis eventually died of throat cancer.

During our last year in Bangkok, I was afflicted with an ailment that originated in a harmless tennis game at Pattaya. When Tom slammed a crosscourt shot to my left side, I lunged with my backhand and felt a tug from my right shoulder. It was not painful, so I paid little attention to it. As the weeks and months went by, I knew that something was not quite right. The range of motion in my arm became limited to brushing my teeth and using the typewriter at work. I could not lift my right arm over my head and could barely reach into my rear right pocket for a handkerchief. When I could swim only by using a side stroke or tried to dive and my right arm stayed by my side, I knew it was time to go to a doctor.

A medical officer at 5th Field hospital tested my arm and then sent me to a Thai physical therapist whose office was just behind our Embassy. The therapist seated me in a chair and stretched my arm upward with a pulley attached to the ceiling. In a series of simple exercises, which soon became more difficult and painful, the therapist stretched and pulled my stiff arm and shoulder joint outward and up, up, up, slowly breaking loose adhesions that had formed through long disuse of the shoulder joint. I had a classic, aptly named, frozen shoulder.

I worked out daily with the therapist for about two weeks and then continued the exercises at home. Every morning for months, I stretched as high as my stiff shoulder would permit by using a pulley rope attached to our front porch. Every day or so I gained a fraction of an inch until full range of motion finally was restored after almost six months. Now I knew what football players go through when they have knee, arm, or shoulder operations and endure the same kind of adhesion removal workouts. My frozen shoulder taught me the merit of keeping my aging body functioning by regular exercise.

* * *

Our last summer in Bangkok was almost at an end. Tom arrived from Gainesville and worked at the air force reception center at the airport for several weeks. Ken got in a few more soccer games with his Thai pals, including Ouan, the chubby son of the neighborhood deli owner at whose restaurant we got wonderful, purple sticky rice that graced the marketplace only at Easter time. This special rice was an extra treat when laced with sweet coconut milk and eaten with your fingers from its little plastic bag.

This summer was filled with presidential politics. Gerald Ford, who had finished out Nixon's term, was running on the Republican ticket. An obscure peanut farmer and former Governor of Georgia, James Earl Carter, came out of a pack of better-known Democratic candidates to win 20 of 30 primary elections and the party nomination. Some of his opponents included Governor Jerry Brown, Governor George Wallace, Representative Morris Udall, and Senator Frank Church. Carter's appeal was so simple that it was working, which distressed Phyllis, who thought that Jimmy Carter was "for the birds." Carter, who was much like the straight-talking Ross Perot (the Texas billionaire who was to run and lose as an Independent in 1992), said that the nation needed a more efficient government, one that was as good and full of love as the American people. Carter said that he would not lie to the people and would reorganize the federal government and make citizens proud of their government again. Phyllis, a die-hard Republican, scoffed at his naivete and stuck up for Gerald Ford. There was an anti-Washington mood in the air that year, however, and the election was going to be close. Jimmy Carter and Fritz Mondale won with 50.08 percent of the popular vote and 297 electoral college votes to 240 for Gerald Ford and his running mate, Senator Robert Dole. Years later, in the election of 1992, I would recall the Carter years and hope that our people had learned there is little to be gained by electing well-intentioned zealots who make promises they cannot keep.

* * *

The Embassy movers came on July 20 to pack up our household belongings. I remember the hustle and bustle and happy confusion of the next three days and Phyllis orchestrating the packing activity with Souli as her interpreter. Luckily, or shall we say as usual, I had to go to the office and thus missed most of it. Ken, ever sociable and curious, started talking to the crew one morning in Thai. In some astonishment, the English-speaking foreman of the crew turned to Phyllis and said, "That not American boy, that Thai boy!"

With our household goods packed and gone, we booked into the Siam Intercontinental Hotel where all the Pan Am flight crews used to stay. This modern pagoda-like structure was set back from the crush of heavy traffic on several acres of tropically planted grounds owned by the King of Thailand. The Siam Intercontinental was situated on a slope of land perfectly graded to provide just the precise setting to display its distinctiveness. The lower-level rooms were always cool and slightly musty smelling yet faintly perfumed because the smiling Thai maids, who turned down the beds at night, left fragrant baby orchid offerings on the pillow.

Phyllis and I marveled at the lobby where vaulted wooden ceilings soared from the wide overhanging eaves in an arc. The roof was made of layered steps of red stucco that gently graduated upward to a square top. Points at the corners of overhanging eaves suggested an uplifting of hands in the polite Thai greeting. Tall panels of tinted glass filtered soft daylight inside and allowed guests to view the stars at night. We enjoyed walking the wide terrazzo-covered terrace and the splashes of color of frangipani trees on the manicured grounds. There were expensive and elegant fashion shops to entice visitors, two outdoor swimming pools, several bars and a coffee shop, a gourmet dining room, and a grassy tract of land behind the hotel where I jogged in the cool morning air. We also were assigned especially nice rooms because the Senior Assistant Manager at the front desk was on the DEA payroll.

HOMEWARD BOUND

Our trip home from Bangkok was bittersweet but more sweet than bitter, since our departure for the land of the big PX was far more joyous than the sadness of separation from close friends. We enjoyed a farewell party with our intelligence group and were given a handsome bronze tea service with an engraved platter. We had a brief layover at the Miramar Hotel in Hong Kong, where Phyllis managed to get in some last-ditch present buying, before proceeding to Honolulu. Phyllis and I strolled along Waikiki Beach, relaxing and enjoying a glimpse of the majestic and unforgettable silhouette of Diamond Head. Today was our 22nd wedding anniversary, celebrating another good year.

As our Pan Am jet lifted off the runway the next day and curved gently toward Los Angeles, Bill sat quietly in the seat next to me. I turned to speak and saw that his eyes were closed and a tear was trickling down his cheek. I had not realized that the happiness of our trip home could be the occasion for such sadness. Bill's feelings have always been a tad more sensitive than those of our other children, or so it seemed to me. Bill was barely seventeen years old and a fine, sensitive young man whose separation from good friends was clearly more difficult for him than for oldsters like me, who sometimes tend to overlook the sensitive emotions of younger people still struggling to learn the lessons of life.

It takes years to accept the truism that when everything is going smoothly, something or someone is apt to come along to change it,

571

despite all your plans and good intentions. When changes occur, it means starting over again, making new friends, proving yourself, trying new ideas, becoming more flexible in your outlook. It is not easy for anyone, and it was even tougher for Bill. I should have told Bill that while growing up is never easy, it is those very uncertainties that can make life more interesting. Optimists, like me, feel that when one part of life is over, the next part will be better. With the passage of time, I have found that all my past experiences have been valuable in ways I never suspected. Nothing is lost and nothing is wasted; there is a purpose and a usefulness in life for all who have the courage and faith to reach out. Not wanting to embarrass Bill, I looked out the window for a long time and said nothing. I have thought about that poignant moment and wish I had put my arm around him and told him how very much I loved him and that I understood his pain and would have done anything to ease his grief.

We landed after a flight of four and a half hours and checked in at the Hacienda Hotel near the airport, where we were joined for dinner by Betty and Zoltan Farkas and former Pakse pals Chuck and Carol Gutensohn and passed the evening pleasantly in good company. The mid-morning sun was bright in another cloudless day in Los Angeles as we piled into our rental car and headed east. We traveled across the southern part of the sprawling Mojave Desert and stopped for a break at Pisgah Crater in the middle of nowhere to inspect a mammoth, saucerlike depression about half a mile wide and 200 or 300 feet deep, blasted there by a streaking meteor ages ago.

Our goal for the night was Flagstaff, Arizona, where we found a Holiday Inn with adjoining rooms on the ground floor. After freshening up and a good supper, Phyllis and I were relaxing in our room while the boys explored outside the motel. Bill suddenly burst in to tell us how cold it was, particularly the ground. He said the sky was so clear that the stars were almost at his fingertips. Bill had gone out without his shoes, an old Bangkok habit. I advised him to put shoes on because there might be some rattlesnakes out there, and he laughed. Ken then came in to say that they had seen a train go by at a road crossing up the street. Tom just smiled benignly and said nothing. Phyllis and I were delighted that our boys were experiencing the rapid changes in temperature that can occur after sundown in the west. It could go from 100 degrees at noon to near freezing at night because of the lack of moisture in the air, something that would never occur in Bangkok. I was also glad to see that Bill's spirits had rebounded; the wonders of Arizona's climate were healing his blues. Phyllis and I smiled—life was good.

On the way to visit friends in Albuquerque, New Mexico, we paused to marvel at the ancient fossilized trees that lay on the ground in the Petrified Forest National Park. By mid-afternoon the following day, we passed the town of Truth or Consequences and farther on saw signs with arrows pointing to White Sands Missile Range, Holloman Air Force Base, and Alamogordo. These names awakened memories of top secret atom bomb tests made during World War II. I wanted to see these places that had made such an historic and momentous impact on our world, but time was pressing and El Paso was calling.

Of El Paso, Phyllis would later state that she was glad we had stopped for a visit but would not have wanted to live there. She said the air was so dry that her face would have cracked in a thousand pieces and she would have looked twenty years older within a month. I had to agree that the city left much to be desired. It was a sun-baked place that sprawled between mile-high mountain peaks in the middle of nothing and was just the opposite of Florida, with no greenery to speak of. El Paso (meaning the pass) and its sister city in Mexico, Juarez, lay along the dusty valley through which the shallow Rio Grande wandered. Rocks and sand were washed in white sunlight that seemed to glare all day long from the cloudless sky on a combined population of over one million people. Given its desert locale, which many citizens doubtless found attractive, El Paso was prosperous looking with its neat, wide asphalt streets lined with modern buildings. When I looked beyond the river into Mexico, I was shocked to see unpaved dirt streets and rows of ramshackle homes. The economy of the two sides of the River sharply contrasted. Because the U.S. dollar was so strong and the Mexican peso so weak, and since the Rio Grande was invitingly shallow, you might see illegal immigrants wading over the border in the mornings to clean houses for wealthy gringo ladies, who did not make social security deductions or keep records on their employees. Oil refineries lined the river and emitted a distinctive scent that was as distracting as the aroma of the cattle stockyards in Dallas.

We spent a comfortable night at yet another Holiday Inn near the entrance to Fort Bliss. In the morning, I visited the El Paso Intelligence Center (EPIC) where I met Dick Brand, the operations officer on duty, Jim Wilkins, watch commander, and Jim Baker, senior analyst. They each gave me a briefing and a walk-through of their operation, which was impressive. Only a few years in existence, EPIC was housed in a handsome, tightly guarded building. By the fall of 1988, an expanded and more secure EPIC headquarters would be erected within the confines of Fort Bliss. EPIC was manned around the clock by agents and analysts from various federal agencies that pooled their resources and knowledge to fight smugglers bringing drugs into the United States. Jim Brand showed me how EPIC's automated data systems could receive, collate, compare, and prepare reports for federal, state, and local law enforcement customers to help them find and arrest smugglers in the air, at sea, at ports of entry, and within the United States. When I left the building, I felt proud of the DEA and what it was doing and was glad we had made the trip to El Paso. I still thought that EPIC would be a good place to work, should Phyllis ever change her mind about moving to El Paso.

Later that morning, we returned our rental car at the small, glass-enclosed airport and boarded our flight to Sarasota. By the end of the day, we had a happy reunion with KC, Evie, Cyndy, Julie, and Tango. We especially enjoyed visiting with Cyndy and her new son Michael, who was now a year old. We stayed in a little cottage on Hanson Bayou for the remainder of August, relaxing and resting before our return to Vienna, Virginia.

We departed Sarasota on August 28 for a festive visit with Nancy and Dave Davis at their house near Lake Panasofkee. The boys enjoyed swimming in the screened pool with cousin Matthew while Uncle Dave grilled steaks on the poolside barbecue. The boys were mightily interested in Uncle Dave's Cessna four-seater aircraft, which was tied down near the house just off the grass strip that stretched down the middle of his cow pasture. Dave often used his plane to commute to Tampa on court business.

By high noon we hit the road again, Tom still with us since his classes in Gainesville would not begin for a few more weeks. We made it as far as Bamberg, Georgia, and stayed at another reliable Holiday Inn. They usually were handy when we needed them and were always willing to board our poodles. We left early the next morning and ground out the mileage to Vienna, where we stayed at yet another Holiday Inn.

Ed Albert met us the next morning to let us in our house on Oak Valley Drive. It looked a little overgrown with summer foliage but was freshly painted inside per Phyl's earlier instructions. Julie and Tango raced into their fenced backyard with yips of recognition, while Phyllis and I walked around, glad to be home after a four-year hiatus in Southeast Asia. Bill commented that the house seemed smaller than he remembered. He was now a six-foot-tall teenager, a lot bigger than he had been four years ago. For the rest of the family, it was much the same as before. As soon as we picked up our air freight at Dulles in the morning, we would be back in business and citizens once more in our native land.

Phyllis said it was good to be home, as she poured us a cup of freshly perked coffee while we sat in our familiar kitchen. Through the bay window we could see Julie and Tango strolling around their yard. I agreed, saying we should stay put for a while and not move until it was time for me to retire.

AFTERWORD

We spent the next four years in Vienna, Virginia, grateful for neighbors and friends who spoke our native language and for the blessed changes of the seasons. Our time on Oak Valley Drive passed quickly but with none of the exotic flavor of living abroad. Phyllis kept active in the real estate business working with DEA families returning from overseas.

Kenneth Carleton Warren was 85 years old when he died from lung cancer in Sarasota's Memorial Hospital on September 29, 1977. KC tried to quit smoking more than once but was hooked on nicotine and could not break the habit. Born in Fall River, Massachusetts, Ken came to Sarasota in 1948 after retiring from R.H. Macy and Company where he was a senior management executive. Ken served with the First New York Cavalry National Guard on the Mexican Border in 1916 and then transferred to the Army Air Corps during World War I. He went to England as a night bomber pilot, but the war ended before he could fly bombing missions. Evelyn Warren lived alone in Sarasota until she died at age 91 in 1985.

Tom Swain continued studying at the University of Florida in Gainesville to become a computer specialist. He came home for the holidays in Virginia and joined the family whenever we were in Sarasota during our summer and winter breaks. In 1979, we vacationed in Jane Gore's cottage on the Bayou, where Phyllis and I celebrated our 25th wedding anniversary. Bill graduated from Madison High School in 1977 and finished two years at nearby George Mason Community College. Ken graduated from Madison High in May 1980 and took courses at the community college in Opalocka when we moved to Miami Lakes. Cyndy was not idle during these years and gave birth, after Michael Joseph in August 1975, to William Patrick in September 1977; Richard Hawley in April 1979; and last but far from least, a lovely rose amid the thorns, Sarah Kingsley in March 1983.

During the cool fall and damp winter nights in Virginia, we kept a warm fire burning in our den and television room. We became staunch fans of the heroic Redskins football team, coached by

577

George Allen with his inspired "over the hill gang" of aging, over-weight, but still dauntless linemen. Skins quarterbacks were Sonny Jurgeson and his backups Billy "Whiskey" Kilmer and former Notre Dame star Joe Theissman. These were great football years for George Allen and his teams. Oddly enough, we Swains never went to a game at the Redskins stadium and preferred to watch in comfort by the fireside. Enthused by the spirit of football, we males would occasionally don parkas and sweaters at halftime to dash outside and play touch football in our backyard. Ken and I usually teamed up against Bill and Tom. There were no winners or losers in these games because it was usually too cold to play very long or I would laugh so hard I had to quit and go inside.

During this time, I was chief of the Dangerous Drugs Section for three years and Staff Assistant to DEA's new Chief of Intelligence, W. Gordon Fink, a likeable and charming man. Peter B. Bensinger, DEA's Administrator (1976-1981), was an energetic and charismatic leader who strove to sharpen public and political focus on the drug problem. He was widely admired and respected for his dedication, professional skill, and personal interest in the welfare of his agents and their families.

Washington's Metro subway system opened, and I could zip from the underground station across the street from DEA Headquarters to National Airport in quiet comfort in less than 30 minutes. I enjoyed riding in the modern, graffiti-free, air-conditioned cars, which glided smoothly on electric-powered rails past the George Washington University exit, under the Potomac River to surface near Arlington, and then past the great eight-sided Pentagon and Crystal City to an elevated terminal near the airport. The Metro beat taking a nerve-wracking cab ride that cost five times more and took twice as long.

In the spring of 1980, I applied for the position of regional intelligence supervisor in the Miami office. Although I could foresee no snags in my way, it was an anxious six weeks before I was selected for the assignment. An extra bonus was the reinstatement of my enforcement agent classification, which meant I would receive automatic overtime pay that would bump up my income and retirement pay. The family was pleased to be returning to Florida, where Phyllis and I planned to retire in the next two years.

I worked with some fine officers in Miami, including Jonathan Stockstill, Kenny Goodman, John Arnst, Mortimer Benjamin, and Irwin Weinstein. I also met Allan R. Pringle, (originator of DEA's G-DEP program) now Agent-in-Charge of the Miami District Office, who soon would be tapped as the first director of Vice President Bush's newly formed South Florida Task Force. This task force combined members of the U.S. Customs Service, U.S. Coast Guard, Border Patrol, U.S. Marshalls Office, and U.S. military forces and was in daily liaison with State, County, and local drug enforcement agencies. The task force was directed to concentrate all available resources against the flow of narcotics into South Florida. I was assigned to supervise the task force's intelligence effort, which had a staff of four to six analysts on temporary duty in Miami from all over the country and Puerto Rico.

* * *

For many men, retirement is probably the single most important event in adult life, ranking right up there with getting married. With great anticipation and some relief, I reached this goal on my 60th birthday, September 18, 1982, after 24 years of federal government service. It was with a sense of gratitude that I attended a farewell luncheon with a crowd of my office cronies, at which I received a fine leather attache case, had my picture taken, and spoke a few words of appreciation. I even donned a baseball cap that had a green marijuana leaf on it with the words BUSH LEAGUE emblazoned across it. It was now time to let that wonderful civil service pension start.

Phyllis and I moved to a cozy Siesta Key house in Sarasota. It was a flat-roofed, two-bedroom cypress house built in 1951. Phyllis made a deal with Fred Painton, who had inherited the house after his mother died. Fred was working for *U.S. News and World Report* in Paris and was happy to have us live there and fix it up after years of neglect. From this base of operation, Phyllis and I planned to reenter the world of real estate and do lots of fishing off the grassy flats in nearby Coconut Bayou. I also planned to do some consulting work for Sheriff Jim Hardcastle and was thinking of beginning the memoirs that all former CIA and federal agents feel compelled to produce.

Phyllis seemed to settle into this new lifestyle as effortlessly as an autumn leaf drifting to the ground, while I clung to the branch and felt the need to keep working. I had trouble relaxing, and the boys would eye me curiously as I persistently typed and then retyped memoir rough drafts at our dining room table. "Come on, Dad, take it easy. It's Saturday afternoon. The sun is out. Let's go fishing," said Ken. More often than not, I regret to say, I would resist and keep typing away ignoring the logic of Ken's request. It would take another year or more before I finally outgrew the feeling of guilt caused by my lack of productivity. I tempered my workaholic tendencies by remembering the old saying, "Things are never as bad as they might be, and never as good as you expect".

* * *

The boys all graduated from college—Tom from the University of Florida in Gainesville as a computer specialist and Bill and Ken from the University of South Florida in Tampa—and began finding their way in the business world. Then there occurred one of those changes in life that usually happen when least expected.

One day in March 1985, Phyllis brought home her annual physical reports and x-ray film and asked, "Are you ready for this?" She showed me an x-ray chart and pointed to a little abnormality that would turn out to be a small tumor in her chest near the heart on the left side. Dr. Jim Fergeson, an old friend and fine surgeon, tried to cut it out, but the tumor was too close to the aorta. Two lengthy series of radiology treatments did what they could to destroy the dreadful lung cancer that eventually claimed Phyllis' life two and a half years later on October 20, 1987.*

Phyllis left behind a legacy filled to the brim with memories that evoke smiles and laughter whenever we remember the pleasures of her company. Beneath her beautiful countenance and her gentle yet vivacious personality was a strength and eagerness for life that not many can claim. William D. McLean II, Rector at St. Boniface, spoke of her

---

* As though to underscore our numbing loss and deep sorrow, the day before her death was Black Monday, the day the stock market plunged 520 points.

580

from the pulpit saying, "She was a bold woman." I had not thought of Phyl as being bold: it is such a masculine word. Phyllis, or "FiFi" as the grandchildren called her, was anything but masculine. Yet she was bold in her courage, strength of spirit, and confident nature.

Her remains rest at St. Boniface, beside Ken and Evie Warren, which our family visits often. I frequently think of Phyllis and of the 33 years, 10 months, and 10 days we were together and find comfort in the lines of the following poem:

Tho I have had to leave you, whom I love,
To go along the silent way,
Grieve not, nor speak of me with tears;
But laugh and talk of me, as if I were beside you.
For who knows but I shall be oft times!
I'd come, I'd come could I but find the way.
And would not tears and griefs be barriers?
So, when you hear a word I used to say,
Or touch a thing I loved, let not your
Thoughts of me be sad, for I am loving you just as I always have.

Anonymous

* * *

In the months that followed, many family friends and acquaintances provided solace, friendship, and companionship to us all. Gradually, the regular rhythm of life renewed. For me, some brightness appeared in the presence of Anne O. Luria, a longtime friend of Phyllis', whose husband Saul had died of leukemia a few years earlier. She and her family attended St. Boniface Church and lived not far away. Anno and I found that we had much in common and became close friends. Our shared experiences of being aging single parents and grandparents, plus being regular members at St. Boniface, led to unexpected results.

The following news release appeared in the *Sarasota Herald-Tribune*.

Adrian Swain

Swain-Luria

Anne O. Luria of Siesta Key and Adrian Swain of Siesta Key were married at 4:30 P.M., Saturday, Nov. 5, 1988, at St. Boniface Church on Siesta Key.

The bride is the daughter of Mr. and Mrs. L. Allen Osborne of Siesta Key.

The bridegroom is the son of the late Mr. and Mrs. Charles F. Swain.

Matron of honor was Patricia O. Smith of Pittsburgh. Bridesmaids were children of the bride and bridegroom: Susan E. Atyeo, of Gainesville and Cynthia K. Toale, Katherine A. Hayes and Nicole L. Evans, all of Sarasota.

Best man was Winthrop Whipple of Sarasota. Groomsmen were the sons of the bride and bridegroom: Thomas W. Swain, William A. Swain, Kenneth C. Swain and David A. Luria, all of Sarasota.

* * *

Today, I enjoy each day as it comes, avoid living life according to the clock, and have simple goals in mind. I try to do something for myself each day and leave the rest of the day for whatever Anno and our expanded family wants or needs, which is another book in itself.

A country boy at heart, I find myself rising early, often before dawn, and heading for the kitchen to make coffee and let Molly and Kitser, our cats, in for breakfast. While the coffee perks, I stroll out to get the morning paper. Sometimes I catch a glimpse of the moon or a bright star through the boughs of banyan and pepper trees that overgird the driveway. The air is moist, fresh, and cool, the paper's plastic cover damp with morning dew. Now and again a hoot owl asks, "Who, Who, Who?"

No single moment during the day is more satisfying, more promising, or more rewarding than when I open the newspaper and pour steaming coffee into my mug on which is inscribed these words of advice: "When in doubt, Mumble—When in charge, Ponder—When in trouble, Delegate." I settle into the familiar chair by the sturdy oak table in the kitchen and crank open the awning window to admit the

582

fresh gulf breezes that have begun to stir the branches of the banyan tree. Dawn approaches and I cannot wait to see what is going on in the world today. If anyone should ask me at that moment, "How are you doing?" I would say, "I'm having the time of my life."

APPENDIX

INTEGRAL CALCULUS

Integral calculus studies the amount of change in continuously varying functions. A function is defined as a quantity so related to another quantity that any change in one produces a corresponding change in the other. For example, in the formula

Distance = (Time x Rate)

the quantity *Distance* is immediately affected by any change in either *Time* or *Rate*. *Distance*, in this example, is said to be a function of the product of *Time* and *Rate*. Functions may also describe geometric figures or falling, spinning bodies. Frequently, the math used in integral calculus becomes laborious as the functions become complex, but the concepts on which it is based are fairly simple.

Finding the volume of a sphere will illustrate the concepts used in integral calculus. Suppose that the sphere is filled with marbles of known volume. By totaling the individual volumes presented by each marble, the volume of the sphere is approximated. If this process is repeated, using sand grains of uniform volume, a more accurate approximation of the sphere's volume will be obtained. However, just as in using marbles, there still will be air spaces between the grains.

The obvious solution is to fill the sphere with water. By removing the air spaces, the sum of the volumes of the water molecules

---

* A paper that Tom swain wrote for an English class at the University of Florida, as mentioned on page 527 in Chapter 20.

would no doubt give the sphere's true volume. Yet there are spaces between molecules, between atoms, and even between subatomic particles. Something is needed that is very, very small. It must be smaller than atomic particles and therefore will not exist physically.

This something is found in integral calculus and exists mentally. It is the concept of continuing the progression from large to small, of going from marble to atom and from atom to the imaginary world of the infinitely small. In so doing, it is necessary to abandon marbles, sand, and atoms in favor of broad slices.

Instead of filling the sphere with objects, suppose that the sphere is sliced. If a perfectly rectangular bread loaf is similarly sliced, it will yield other rectangles. A sliced cylinder will yield cylinders of a sort. They would not be perfect because a sphere is curved. The slices would have one end slightly larger than the other. Critical thinking reveals that if the slices were extremely thin, one end would still be larger than the other. The difference between ends would be very small, however, and the slice would be almost a perfect cylinder.

Integral calculus slices the sphere an infinite number of times, thereby making the slices exactly cylindrical, finds the volume of each cylinder, and simultaneously adds the volume together. The slices are one-dimensional, without thickness, and there are an indefinite number of slices. This may strain the imagination, but both are necessary and quite valid applications of mathematics.

This concept of approaching zero is also applicable in differential calculus. This second branch of calculus is concerned mostly with bodies in motion, while integral forms deal with areas bounded by lines. Both combined make up the body of calculus and provide accurate answers to a wide range of problems related not only to mathematics, but also to physics, oceanography, psychology, and astronomy.

BIBLIOGRAPHY

The Bay of Pigs, Peter Wyden. Simon and Schuster, 1230 Avenue of the Americas, N.Y., N.Y. 10020. 1980.

A Bright Shining Lie, Neil Sheehan. Random House, Inc., N.Y. and simultaneously in Canada by Random House of Canada Limited. 1988.

The CIA and the Cult of Intelligence, Victor Marchetti and John D. Marks. Dell Publishing Co., 1 Dag Hammarskjold Place, N.Y., N.Y. 10017. 1974.

Counsel to the President, Clark Clifford. Random House, Inc., N.Y. and in Canada by Random House of Canada Limited, Toronto. 1991.

Decent Interval, Frank Snepp. Random House, Inc., N.Y. and in Canada by Random House of Canada Limited, Toronto. 1977.

The Fighting 463rd, Harold Rubin.

Honorable Men: My life in the CIA, William Colby. Simon and Schuster, Rockefeller Center, 1230 Avenue of the Americas, N.Y., N.Y. 10020. 1978.

The Illustrated History of the Vietnam War—Gadget Warfare, F. Clinton Perry, Jr., Bantam Books, 666 Fifth Avenue, N.Y., N.Y. 10103. 1988.

The Laotian Fragments, John Clark Pratt. The Viking Press, Inc., 625 Madison Avenue, N.Y., N.Y. 10022, published simultaneously in Canada by the Macmillan Company of Canada Limited. 1974.

My Secret War, Richard S. Drury. Aero Publishers, Inc., 329 West Aviation Road, Fallbrook, CA, 92028. 1979.

Saigon, Anthony Grey. Dell Publishing Co., 1 Dag Hammarskjold Place, N.Y., N.Y. 10017. 1983.

The Underground Empire: Where Crime and Governments Embrace, James Mills. Dell Publishing Co., Inc., 1 Dag Hammarskjold Place, N.Y., N.Y. 10017. 1986.

Valley of the Mekong, Matt J. Menger, O.M.I. Catholic Missionary, Vientiane, Laos. Etienne Loosdregt, O.M.I., Vicar Apostolic, of Vientiane, Laos. 1969.

INDEX